WALTONS OF OLD VIRGINIA

AND
SKETCHES OF FAMILIES IN
CENTRAL VIRGINIA

Booker, Christian, Coleman, Davis, Fields, Guthrie, Harris, Harrison, Harvey, Hunter, Jones, Shepherd, Stratton, Vawter, Walker, Williamson, and Word

Wilmer L. Kerns, Ph.D.

HERITAGE BOOKS
2009

HERITAGE BOOKS
AN IMPRINT OF HERITAGE BOOKS, INC.

Books, CDs, and more—Worldwide

For our listing of thousands of titles see our website
at
www.HeritageBooks.com

Published 2009 by
HERITAGE BOOKS, INC.
Publishing Division
100 Railroad Ave. #104
Westminster, Maryland 21157

Copyright © 2005 Wilmer L. Kerns, Ph.D.

Other books by the author:
Historical Records of Old Frederick and Hampshire Counties, Virginia (Revised)

All rights reserved. No part of this book may be reproduced or transmitted in any form or by any means, electronic or mechanical, including photocopying, recording or by any information storage and retrieval system without written permission from the author, except for the inclusion of brief quotations in a review.

International Standard Book Numbers
Paperbound: 978-0-7884-3513-3
Clothbound: 978-0-7884-3362-7

Acknowledgements

Lloyd G. Walton and Ruby (Davis) Walton at the 2004 Walton reunion

Many people participated in making this book a reality. Not all can be mentioned in this short section. Perhaps the most knowledgeable and helpful person throughout the four decades of this research journey was Ruby (Davis) Walton, of Buckingham County. Aunt Ruby will be 96 years old on June 27. Her keen librarian-mind not only gave information, but she led me to people and sources that could not have been found without her help. We trudged to tick-laden cemeteries that had almost been forgotten.

A major person who contributed time and talent in collecting information on the Eugene A. Walton branch was Mary Evelyn (Payne) Strickland of Nelson County. She helped faithfully with the annual Walton reunions and promoted the development of the book in word and deed.

Next in line is our reunion president, Lloyd G. Walton, of Appomattox County, who kept me on track regarding the Cove Farm and the Bent Creek Waltons. He also took me to several important cemeteries. His wife Shirley is an excellent contributor who works behind the scenes. Lloyd and Shirley have been a wonderful source of encouragement throughout this process and have promoted the book.

Dr. Peter McDearmon Witt of Duke University contributed information and edited an earlier version of the manuscript. Carole Ruff of Leesburg, Virginia has been a strong supporter for almost a decade. She contributed information generously on the allied families of Christian and Scruggs. Betsy (Drake) Chatlin of Salt Lake City, Utah became a best friend through this research. Thanks to all who contributed information.

Walton Crest by Britain W. Walton, Edenton, North Carolina

Table of Contents

Acknowledgements...iii
Walton Family Crest...iv
Table of Contents..v
Foreword..vi
Introduction...1
Generation 1..9
Generation 2..11
Generation 3..21
Generation 4..53
Generation 5..105
Generation 6..169
Generation 7..211
Generation 8..235
Generation 9..259
Generation 10..281
Notes on the Settlement of Central Virginia....................................285
Booker Family of Amelia and Cumberland Counties.......................289
Christian Family of Amherst and Nelson Counties..........................321
Coleman Family of Buckingham County..337
Davis Family of Buckingham County..341
Fields Family of Campbell County..357
Guthrie Family of Cumberland County...361
Harris Family of Nelson County...375
Harrison Family of Cumberland County..381
Harvey Family of Charlotte County...387
Hunter Family of Campbell and Appomattox.................................391
Jones Family of Campbell County..399
Shepherd Family of Buckingham County......................................413
Stratton Family of Buckingham County...419
Vawters of Lynchburg..421
Walker Family of Buckingham County..429
Williamson Family of Charlotte County...435
Word Family of Buckingham County..439
Appendix A—Samuel L. Walton of Alabama..................................455
Appendix B—Edward Walton of Hanover County..........................457
Appendix C—George Walton of Brunswick County.......................461
Index..465

Foreword

To research, organize, compile, edit and publish a genealogy requires exceptional talent, self-discipline, patience, time and sacrifice. Dr. Wilmer Lee Kerns has exemplified these qualities as he worked tirelessly over the past eight plus years to gather information on the Waltons and Allied Families. This publication is more than a compilation of names, dates, places and family lineage; it is a volume of interesting events, family successes and hardships, and contributions of members to society. Woven into the fabric of this genealogy, the author skillfully revealed personalities, values and ambitions of a proud and patriotic Virginia family that spans more than two centuries.

Although this genealogy will interest many in the general public, members of the Walton and Allied Families will consider it a special treasure. For those families who are anticipating a genealogical study, it will serve as an inspiration and guide. For the Walton family and others, the book will have a special place in each home as a quick reference to family connections, dates, births, deaths, places, and occupations. More importantly this book is our legacy upon which future generations of Waltons and others will read with pride and appreciation. It is a living masterpiece of the past, as well as the present and future. To capture this breadth and depth of a family's history in one volume speaks of the author's devotion to family, exceptional knowledge and skills, and desire to provide a lasting legacy for those who follow.

Related to the Walton family through marriage to Shirley Mitchell Walton, Dr. Kerns has written a comprehensive genealogy not only of the Waltons but also of allied families, which include Booker, Christian, Coleman, Davis, Fields, Guthrie, Harris, Harvey, Hunter, Jones, Palmore, Shepherd, Vawter, Word, and Walker. This outstanding publication is a work of love, for only one who is committed to quality research and the preservation of a family's history would give the time and resources to bring such a project to fruition.

You are our family's hero, Bill. We thank you for sharing your knowledge and skills through this genealogy.

                                        Lloyd Gray Walton, Superintendent
                                        Appomattox County, Virginia Public Schools
                                        July 1, 1973-October 1, 1991

Introduction

A family tradition says the ancestral Walton immigrant was named John. The implication is that one immigrant ancestor was the progenitor for all the Waltons in Virginia. This is rarely the case, except for unusual surnames with a small population. A search in the records of Colonial Virginia reveals the names of at least eight different John Waltons who came to the Colony between 1621 and 1666. Which John was our ancestor, assuming that the tradition is correct? We do not know, because a generation-by-generation process needs to be completed before that question can be answered. Genealogy commences with oneself and traces backwards in time.

Waltons were among the earliest settlers in the New World. In 1618, The Virginia Company passed a law that any person who settled in Virginia or paid the transportation expenses for another person to settle in the Colony, was given fifty acres for each occurrence. This gift was known as a headright. The free land was given as an incentive to populate the New World. It was through these land records that we learned the names of the earliest Walton immigrants to Virginia.

The Walton surname appeared in records as early as the 1620s. In 1621, one John Walton, aged twenty-eight years, came to Virginia on the ship *Elizabeth*. Source of this information is from a "census" or compilation of persons living in Virginia in 1624-1625. The same John Walton was named in the Muster of Alexander Mountney.[1] There is no evidence that this John Walton left descendants, nor the seven other Johns who were imported to Virginia before the year 1666, none of whom have been connected to living descendants.[2]

In addition to the eight known Johns, who were mentioned twenty times in early land records, there were George and Robert Waltons who came to the Colony of Virginia during the early seventeenth century. Sometime between 1618 and 1620, a George Walton was one of three servants transported from England to

---

[1] John Frederick Dorman, Virginia M. Myer, *Adventures of Purse and Person VIRGINIA, 1607-1624-5*, revised, (Richmond, Virginia: The Dietz Press, Inc.), 1987, p. 51.

Virginia by John and Jane Cooke for "personal adventure." Cooke died and his widow Jane married second Alexander Stonar, who was awarded the land patent on June 22, 1635.[3] Nothing more is known about this George Walton, whether he married or had children or not. About the same time, William Beard paid the transportation costs for seven servants to migrate to Virginia, one of whom was Margaret Walton. A land patent for 450 acres "within the Corporation of James City" was granted to Beard on June 19, 1635.[4]

Robert Walton and three other persons were transported to Virginia by John Laydon of Warwick River County according to a court order dated Feb. 29, 1631.[5] On Nov. 24, 1637, John Broche received 300 acres in Charles River County for transporting six persons to the Colony who were: John Walton, Thomas Sewell, Nicholas Bates, William Savary, Mary Osborne, and Francis Perris.[6]

On April 9, 1648, John Landman received 300 acres of land in Nansemond County for transporting six persons from England to Virginia, including John Walton, Matthew Wallace, Thomas Brewer, Dorothy Cole, Edward Spencer, and Richard Jones. On March 13, 1649, Thomas Dale, son of Nicholas Dale, deceased, received 800 acres on the south side of the Rappahannock River for transporting these same persons, apparently a duplicate claim.[7]

Henry Lee and William Clapham transported one John Walton to the Colony on Aug. 20, 1650.[8] Henry Soanes of New Kent County received a land patent on March 10, 1653 for bringing a John Walton to Virginia. Another John Walton was among 40 persons transported to the Colony of Virginia by John Drayton of

---

[3] Nell Marion Nugent, *Cavaliers and Pioneers*, (Baltimore, Maryland: Genealogical Publishing Company), Vol. 1, 1979, pp. 28-29.

[4] *Ibid*, pp. 28-29. The land patent was dated June 22, 1635.

[5] *Ibid*, pp. 38-39. The land patent was dated May 6, 1636.

[6] *Ibid*, p. 76.

[7] *Ibid*, p. 190

[8] *Ibid*, p.196.

Westmoreland County, June 10, 1654.[9] William Moseley and John Hull imported John Walton, Robert Walton, and Richard Walton to the Colony on Feb. 20, 1662. The sponsors received land in Farnham Parish, Rappahannock County.[10]

The earliest record of land ownership of a Walton in Virginia was that of one John Walton who was granted 200 acres in Accomack County on March 24, 1638, for paying transportation costs across the Atlantic Ocean for four persons.[11] This or another John Walton received 300 acres "in Northumberland County alias Westmoreland County, on South side of Hallowes Creek toward the head thereof," on Sept. 15, 1641. Major John Washington purchased this property on June 1, 1664.[12] More than likely this was the same John Walton who lived in Westmoreland County during the 1650s and was referenced in the records as a cooper.[13]

The New Kent County Waltons— Our Branch

We cannot make a connection between our Waltons of the late seventeenth century with those listed above. Our lineage is traced and proven back to Edward Walton Jr., 1672-1720, of New Kent County, Virginia. Hence, we call this branch of the family "The New Kent County Waltons." The County is located in the east central part of Virginia, bounded today by Henrico, Hanover, King William, King and Queen, James City, and Charles City Counties. It is just off Interstate 64 between Richmond and Williamsburg.

The Waltons worshipped at St. Peters Church,[14] which is still an active congregation in a rural area about four miles north of the New Kent courthouse. It was an official Church of England until after the

---

[9] *Ibid*, p. 301.

[10] *Ibid*, p.468.

[11] *Ibid*, p. 106.

[12] *Ibid*, p. 468.

[13] *Ibid*, pp. 331 and 447.

[14] Address of the church is St. Peter's Church, 8400 St. Peter's Lane, New Kent, Virginia 23124-9633. The parish records have been preserved and published.

Revolutionary War when the Episcopal Church USA was formed. In 1759, George Washington married Martha (Dandridge) Custis in and of this parish. The General Assembly later designated St. Peter's Church "The First Church of the First First-Lady." The historical church has been named a National Landmark by the United States Government. The church cemetery contains numerous burials, although not as many as expected for a church that is over 300 years old. St. Peters is listed as the second oldest parish church in the Episcopal Diocese of Virginia, and the fourth oldest parish church in the Commonwealth of Virginia.[15]

St. Peter's Episcopal Church, New Kent County, Virginia

Our Walton branch moved westward when land became available in new frontiers. On June 26, 1731, Thomas Walton, 1703-1772, received a land patent for 400 acres in Goochland County.[16] That land is now in Cumberland County, near Cartersville. It bordered Muddy Creek which separates Cumberland from present Powhatan County. Thomas' brother, William Walton,

---

[15] Don W. Massey, *The Episcopal Churches in the Diocese of Virginia*, (Keswick, Virginia: Diocese Church Histories), 1989, p. 174.

[16] The Library of Virginia, Land Office Patents No. 14, 1728-1732 (pt.1 & 2), p. 174 (Reel 11).

received a patent for 400 acres in the same vicinity of present Cumberland County, in September 1731. William's children migrated, but Thomas Sr. has descendants who still live on or near this ancestral site. His son, Thomas Walton Jr., 1742-1815, moved further west in 1803 to establish business operations at Bent Creek, which was then in Buckingham County. Through this lineage came the Appomattox Waltons. The focus of this book is geared toward the descendants of Thomas Walton, Jr., an ancestor of the compiler's wife Shirley (Walton) Kerns. Not only are there many errors about our Waltons in the literature, but this branch has been neglected. Information on ten generations is presented. No genealogy is complete nor free from errors, including this one. Hopefully, descendants and researchers will fill in the information gaps to make this a more complete account.

Waltons of Virginia Not in Our Ancestral Line

The compiler encountered numerous Walton branches that do not connect with the New Kent Waltons. It is worthwhile to identify and sketch these branches for the benefit of those who are searching for their roots. See Appendix A and B for more genealogical detail on The Brunswick and Albemarle County Waltons. Both of these branches produced a very large number of offspring and descendants.

The Brunswick County Waltons

One George Walton, 1680-1766, settled in Brunswick County, Virginia to become the progenitor of "The Brunswick Waltons.". This George may have come to Virginia via Barbados. He was not the same George Walton who married Sarah Roper in New Kent County, Virginia about 1710. According to the Ledbetter family history, George settled in Brunswick County, Virginia, where he had a distinguished record.[17] He was elected High Sheriff on May 7, 1734, and was elected Judge of Chancery Court on June 5, 1746. George died on Oct. 31, 1766 in St. Andrews Parish in Brunswick County. His will was dated July 7, 1764 and it was probated on Jan.

---

[17] Roy C. Ledbetter, William R. Ledbetter, Justus R. Moll, and James D. Tillman Jr., *Ledbetters From Virginia*, (Dallas, Texas: Wilkinson Printing Company), 1964, pp. 45-50.

26, 1767.[18] Elizabeth, widow of George Walton, filed her will in Brunswick County on Feb. 12, 1771. She named the same children as her husband in his will. A Harris history says that Elizabeth's maiden name was Scott.[19] Others say that her maiden name was Rowe. It is interesting to note that George Walton's immediate descendants lived in Brunswick County, and we find no evidence of intermarriage with other branches of the Waltons in Virginia.

The Hanover or Albemarle County Waltons

Edward Walton (ca 1720-1791) of Hanover County, Virginia is classified as miscellaneous, although there is a strong possibility that his branch belongs to the Waltons of New Kent County from which Hanover was formed. One hypothesis is that he was a son of Edward Jr. and Elizabeth Walton. There is a parallel between Edward of Hanover and John Walton, 1709-1772, of the same County. Both were associated with the Baker and Sims families.[20] Edward was a witness to the will of John Walton who married Mary Sims, which indicates a possible relationship. However, the naming pattern does not lend support of the hypothesis, because there were no Edward, Robert, nor George Waltons in the early generations. The name of Edward's wife is not known but her maiden name may have been Thompson. Edward's branch is often referred to as "The Albemarle Waltons." See Appendix B for more information.

The Byberry Waltons

The Byberry Waltons were so named after four Walton brothers who emigrated from England to William Penn's Colony in 1683.[21] The four brothers, Nathaniel, Thomas, Daniel and William Walton, settled in the Byberry Township of Philadelphia. Moses Walton,

---

[18] Brunswick County Virginia *Will Book 3, 1751-1769*, pp. 462-463.

[19] *Ledbetters From Virginia*, p. 45.

[20] ____ Davis, *Hanover County Deeds, 1783-1792*, ( ), p. 396. This citation is from Julia Crosswell's website (see footnote No. 2 on p. 457).

[21] Norman W. Swayne, *Byberry Waltons, an Account of Four English Brothers, Nathaniel & Thomas & Daniel & William, Who Settled About 1683 in Byberry Township, Philadelphia*, (Philadelphia, Pennsylvania: Quintin Publications), 1958.

1703-1764, who was a grandson of immigrant Daniel Walton, came to Old Frederick County, Virginia in the Shenandoah Valley during the early 1740s. He left a legacy of prominent descendants in Shenandoah County, which was formed from Frederick in 1772.

There is no known connection between the Byberry Waltons, who were Quakers, and those in Old Virginia, who were affiliated with The Church of England. Old Virginia is usually defined as the territory east of the Blue Ridge Mountains, which is known as the Piedmont, and east of that is the Atlantic Coastal Plain. New Virginia is defined as the frontier land on the west side of the Blue Ridge.[22] It appears that the Byberry Walton descendants remained on the west side of the Blue Ridge in the Shenandoah Valley. The Byberry Waltons were important people, but are beyond the scope of this book. One common error is that some researchers claim that George Walton, Signer of the Declaration of Independence, was born in the Shenandoah Valley near Winchester. This mistake is discussed and resolved elsewhere in the book.

The Waltons Television Program

What are the roots of the Walton family who appeared in the TV series *The Waltons*? Was the program based on a real-life family of Waltons? The popular show was broadcast by CBS from 1972 to 1981. It was based on a book, *The Homecoming*, which was filmed as a movie, written by Earl Hamner Jr.[23] Earl also wrote and narrated the TV show. The Waltons were portrayed as a poor-but-happy family during the Great Depression of the 1930s. The theme of the program was that family bonds and personal relationships are more important than money and material possessions[24]. It is well-known that the TV Waltons were a Virginia family who lived in the Blue Ridge Mountains. The setting for the program was Earl's hometown in Schuyler in Nelson County, Virginia, just south of Charlottesville on U. S. Route 29. Ironically, the compiler's wife's

---

[22] Warren R. Hofstra, *The Planting of New Virginia: Settlement and Landscape in the Shenandoah Valley*, (Baltimore, Maryland: The Johns Hopkins Press), 2004.

[23] Earl Hamner Jr. was born at Schuyler, Virginia on July 10, 1923.

[24] http://www.delsjourney.com/close-ups/us/waltons/waltons_home.htm

family holds its annual reunions in Nelson County. It was essential to track down these Waltons for inclusion in this book.

The compiler searched in vain for a Walton's Mountain in Nelson County. Furthermore, the name Walton was not found in census records. The truth is that the Waltons were a fictitious family based on the real life of the Hamner family.[25] The family was originally called Spencer in Hamner's books. The Walton name may have been an arbitrary selection for the TV series.

Wal-Mart

Here is a question that many people have asked the compiler: Who was Samuel Moore "Sam" Walton, 1918-1992, the founder of the giant retail store Wal-Mart? Is he one of our Virginia Waltons? Yes, his Walton ancestors came out of Virginia. Sam was born in Oklahoma; earned a degree in economics at the University of Missouri in 1940; and started his career with a management internship at a J. C. Penny Company Store in Iowa. We know that Sam was a son of Thomas Gibson Walton and his wife Nancy Lee Lawrence, 1899-1950, of Cooper County, Missouri. It is reported and supported by the U. S. census that Sam's grandfather was Sam W. Walton, 1848-1894[26] and his wife was Laura H., who lived in Cooper and Webster Counties, Missouri. The 1860 and 1870 censuses for Cooper County shows Sam's great-grandparents as William P. and Louisa J. Walton. William was born in Virginia between 1815 and 1820, as reported by the census records. It appears that William P. Walton went to Missouri about 1840, where he married and established himself as a farmer. In 1860 and 1870, he was living in Cooper County, where he presumably died. There was another William P. Walton in Lafayette County, Missouri during the 1830s and onward, but he has been traced back to Tennessee, the son of James, 1786-1861, and Jane (Parr) Walton. We have not yet determined to which branch of Virginia Waltons the Wal-Mart people belong.

---

[25] Email from William Atkins <william.atkins@verizon.net> on Oct. 6, 2002.

[26] See the 1860 and 1880 U. S. Censuses for Cooper County, Missouri, Familiy Nos. 1186 and 231 respectively.

Chapter 1

First Generation

Edward Walton Jr. (1)

The earliest proven ancestor in our direct Walton lineage is Edward Walton Jr. (ca 1672-1720) of New Kent County, Virginia.[1] Edward's wife was named Elizabeth[2] but could not have been a daughter of Lemuel and Ann (Seawell) Mason, as often accepted by Walton researchers. Depending on who is estimating the dates, Elizabeth Mason would have been almost a generation older than Edward Walton Jr., and would have commenced bearing children in her 40s. A marriage year of 1671 is given, which cites Edward Walton paying 5,000 pounds of tobacco to marry Elizabeth.[3] If so, she was childless for twenty-three years before her first child was born in 1694. It doesn't fit. Also, the Masons and Waltons lived in different cultural and geographic bands of Virginia, that is, the James River versus the York River water basins. In Colonial Virginia, intermarriage usually occurred within the same geo-cultural band. New Kent was a long distance from Norfolk. We conclude that Elizabeth's maiden name was not Mason. There is no direct evidence, and the circumstantial evidence is not sufficient to build a case. We concur that Elizabeth Mason of Lemuel married a Walton, but his given name is not in the records.

On March 7, 1701/02, Edward Jr. was commissioned an ensign in the New Kent County Militia.[4]

---

[1] One Edward Walton Sr. allegedly died in 1688, but the compiler has not seen the documentation. It is possible that Edward Walton Jr. was not a son of an Edward Sr. During early times, Jr. was given to the younger of two persons with the same name, regardless of relationship.

[2] *The Register of St. Peter's Parish*, New Kent County, Virginia, says that "Elizabeth, wife of Edwd Walton, Departed this Life April 5th, 1717."

[3] Margaret Bickel Adams, *Old Burke County (NC) Relatives*, (Privately Printed), Margaret Bickel Adams, 301 Broad Street, Marion, NC 28752-4515, 2000

[4] Lloyd DeWitt Bockstruct, *Virginia's Colonial Soldier's*, (Baltimore, Maryland: Genealogical Publishing Company, Inc.), p. 217.

The father of Edward Walton Jr. may or may not have been named Edward Sr. In seventeenth and eighteenth century Virginia, the titles junior and senior were given to show relationships between ages of persons, and not necessarily to show a father-son relationship or other kinship. For example, Virginia County land and tax records sometimes designated a person as "John Doe of John" or "John Doe of Edward." The designation John Doe Jr. meant something different; that this John Doe was younger than the other John Doe who lived in the same political jurisdiction.

Children of Edward Jr. and Elizabeth Walton:

1. Robert Walton was born circa 1694, probably in New Kent County, and died after 1734. Robert married Frances Sherwood, 1697-1780. (2)

2. Mary Walton was baptized in St. Peter's Parish, Dec. 4, 1698. Nothing more is known about her. (3)

3. William Walton was baptized on Dec. 25, 1700 in St. Peter's Parish, New Kent County, and died in Cumberland County, Virginia in 1747. He married Susannah Cobb. (4)

4. Thomas Walton Sr. was baptized Feb. 20, 1703/1704 in St. Peter's Parish, New Kent County, and died in 1772 in Cumberland County, Virginia.[5] In 1734, Thomas married Martha Cox, daughter of George and Martha Cox of Henrico County, Virginia. (5)

5. Elizabeth Walton was baptized at St. Peter's on Feb. 4, 1707; she may have married Peter Rowlett, son of William and Frances (Worsham) Rowlett, although this is unproven. Peter Rowlett died in Lunenburg County, Virginia in 1754. His widow Elizabeth was given a letter of administration, which a George Walton (presumably her nephew) was the security for the administration bond.[6] (6)

6. John Walton Sr. was born in St. Peter's Parish, New Kent County, on Aug. 7, 1709, and died in Henrico County in 1772. John married Mary Sims, and settled on land in Henrico County that is now in Louisa County. (7)

---

[5] Cumberland County, Virginia *Will Book 2*, pp. 54-55.

[6] Lunenburg County, Virginia Will *Book 1*, p. 131.

Chapter 2
Second Generation
Robert Walton (2)

Robert Walton Sr., probable son of Edward Jr. and Elizabeth Walton, was born circa 1694 and died after 1734. He is listed as Robert Walton "Jr." in the St. Peter's Parish records of New Kent County, where he served as Clerk of the Vestry from 1723 to 1734. The designation "Jr." does not necessarily mean that his father was named Robert, but that a Robert Walton older than he was living in the same locality. It is believed that Robert "Jr." lived and died in New Kent County, where he, as eldest son, would have inherited his father's estate in 1720. William and Thomas Walton, alleged younger brothers of Robert "Jr.," resettled in an area of Goochland County that became, in 1747, Cumberland County. Two children of Robert— George and Robert Jr.— settled in the same vicinity of Goochland and/or Cumberland County, as evidenced by land records and other courthouse documents. Robert married Frances Sherwood who was born on Jan. 17, 1697 and died on March 10, 1780.[1] One of Robert's great-grandsons, George Walton Jr., 1786-1859, son of George the Signer, reportedly told Josiah Nichols Walton, 1805-1884, that he possessed a tree of the Walton family, and that they were of the same blood. Josiah N. was a great-grandson of Thomas Walton who married Martha Cox, which would define the two men as second-cousins.[2] This kind of information is valuable, coming from that time period.

Children of Robert Sr. and Frances (Sherwood) Walton:

1. Robert Walton Jr. was born on Jan. 7, 1717/1718 in New Kent County, Virginia and died circa 1750, in Cumberland County, Virginia. Robert Jr. married Mary Hughes, daughter of Robert and Martha (Morton) Hughes. (8)

---

[1] George Edward Pankey, *John Pankey of Manakin Town, Virginia and His Descendants*, (Kingsport, Tennessee: Kingsport Press, Inc.), 1961, p 122.

[2] *The Richmond Standard*, "Notes and Queries," Saturday, Sept. 19, 1879, Vol. 11, No. 2, col. 5. The genealogical information in the column was submitted by Nathan Womack Walton, 1803-1880, a resident of Richmond, Virginia, who communicated with his first-cousin, Josiah N. Walton in Mississippi. Thanks to Bob F. Thompson, Esq. of Nashville, Tennessee.

Second Generation

2. Rebecca Walton was born April 20th, 1720, according to parish records at St. Peter's Church. She married Charles Pearson. (9)

3. Joseph Walton, born Feb. 10, 1722, married a woman named Mary.[3] A Joseph Walton bought 400 acres in on both sides of Brimmer Creek (*sic*) in Goochland County, July 10, 1745. On Sept. 5, 1749, Joseph bought 192 acres along Bremore Creek of the Fluvanna River. A son named William Walton married Sara Grinage on Dec. 20, 1792. They had one child Jesse Sims Walton, 1801-1866, who married Palatia Ellis Jones. (10)

4. George Walton was born Feb. 17, 1724/25[4] and died July 7, 1797 in Prince Edward County, Virginia. He married Martha Hughes on Aug. 14, 1749 in Cumberland County. (11)

5. Frances Walton was born Jan. 14, 1726-27, and allegedly died about 1766 in Bedford County, Virginia. Frances married Col. Richard Callaway. (12)

6. Sherwood Walton was born on July 10, 1728 in New Kent County and died by 1816 in Amelia County, Virginia. His wife was Susanna Jouett. (13)

William Walton Sr. (4)

William Walton Sr., son of Edward Jr. and Elizabeth Walton, was baptized on Dec. 25, 1700 in St. Peter's Parish, New Kent County, and died in Cumberland County, Virginia in 1747. William bought numerous lands that were originally a part of Albemarle County, but later became Amherst and Buckingham Counties. Also, he owned land along Muddy Creek in Cumberland County, where he may have died.[5]

---

[3] *St. Peter's Parish Record*, New Kent County, Virginia

[4] George Edward Pankey, *John Pankey of Manakin Town, Virginia and His Descendants*, (Kingsport, Tennessee: Kingsport Press, Inc.), 1961, p 122.

[5] Albemarle County was formed from Goochland County in 1744 and Cumberland from Goochland in 1747. Buckingham and Amherst Counties were formed from Albemarle in 1761. Powhatan County was formed from Cumberland County in 1777.

On Aug. 19, 1740, William Walton was commissioned an ensign in the Goochland County Militia.[6] Hezekiah Mosby was sworn in as an ensign on the same day.

William married Susannah Cobb, daughter of John and Susannah (Hughes) Cobb. Susannah was born circa 1712 and died about 1765. After the death of her husband, Susannah married second Clayborn Rice, son of Edward Rice of Amherst County, on Jan. 2, 1749.[7] One child, Clayborn Rice Jr., was born to this union.

William bought 400 acres in Goochland County on Jan. 1, 1731. He paid 50 pounds to Thomas and Leonard Ballow for the land in St. James Parish.[8] William and his brother Thomas Walton owned land in the same area of Cumberland County,[9] and some of their descendants intermarried. One of William's 400-acre farms was located on both sides of the north branch of Walton's Creek of the Slate River, which would be in the northwestern section of present-day Buckingham County. Walton's Fork of Slate River to this day is the designation of this watercourse, and is shown on the General Highway Map of Buckingham County.[10]

Children of William Sr. and Susannah (Cobb) Walton:[11]

---

[6] Lloyd DeWitt Bockstruct, *Virginia's Colonial Soldiers*, (Baltimore, Maryland: Genealogical Publishing Co., Inc.), p. 17.

[7] Goochland County, Virginia *Deed Book 8*, p. 477, says that "Clayborn Rice and his wife Susanna, widow of William Walton..." This proves that Susannah (Cobb) Walton married second Clayborn Rice.

[8] Benjamin B. Weisiger III, compiler, *Goochland County, Virginia Wills and Deeds, 1728-1736*, (Athens, Georgia: Iberian Publishing Company), reprinted 1995, p. 27.

[9] See *Patent Book 14*, p.174, June 26, 1731; and *Patent Book 15*, p. 17, June 20, 1733 showing that William and Thomas Walton lived on adjoining land on the south side of James River along Muddy Creek.

[10] Prepared by the Virginia Department of Transportation, 1401 East Broad Street, Richmond, Virginia 23219, © 1989.

[11] Information is from *Heritage of Burke County 1981*, published by the Burke County Historical Society, information submitted by Joseph Moore Walton, pp.

Second Generation

1. Susannah Walton, "eldest daughter" in her father's will, was born on June 14, 1732, and her funeral was held on June 14, 1760, with a biblical text from Job 3:17, in Goochland County. Susannah married James Hilton, son of George and Hester Hilton, on Jan. 18, 1749 in Goochland County. After her death, James Hilton married second Mary Hall, on July 28, 1763. Susannah's fathers will gave her 400 acres in Albemarle County on the south side of the James River, and on North Fork of Slate River. This land is in Buckingham County today. James Hilton died in 1786 in Bedford County.[12] (14)

2. Louisa Walton was born circa 1734. She married Jeremiah Terrill and they were living in Elbert County, Georgia in 1798. (15)

3. William Walton Jr. was born Dec. 2, 1735/36, and died Jan. 31, 1806 in Burke County, North Carolina. He married Elizabeth Tilman, Dec. 1, 1758. Elizabeth was born May 29, 1744, and died Sept. 8, 1787. William Jr. married second Mildred Lavender, May 16, 1792. (16)

4. Mary Ann Walton, born circa 1737, married Absalom Jordon[13] about 1758. Her father left her 220 acres on the Southside of the James River in the Fork of Slate River adjoining her brother Jesse Walton. (17)

5. Anne Walton[14] was born circa 1738. She married Capt. Charles Cobb of Campbell County, Virginia. Some of the descendant families lived in Charlotte County, Virginia. (18)

6. Frances Walton was born circa 1739. She married Henry Mullins on Dec. 9, 1762.[15] Henry died before April 1789, when an administrator was appointed for his estate.[16] (19)

452-453. William Walton's will is cited in the *Virginia Magazine of History and Biography*, p. 318. Seven children are named and the executor was his cousin George Walton who married Martha Hughes. See, also, Goochland County *Deed Book 4*, pp. 418-420, a deed dated Dec. 14, 1798 between the heirs of John Mullins.

[12] Bedford County, Virginia Will *Book I*, pp.12-13.

[13] Bedford County, Virginia Will *Book 6*, p. 312, Will of Absalom Jordon, written Jan. 23, 1824. His wife, Mary Ann, was alive when the will was written.

[14] Gayle M. Fitzsimmons, 5508 California Avenue, Santa Cruz, California 95060, provided information on this family unit.

7. Jesse Walton, "youngest son" in will, was born in Goochland County, Virginia in 1740 and was killed by Cherokee Indians, July 1789 in Franklin County, Georgia. He was a frontiersman, and is credited with founding Jonesboro, Tennessee. He served in the Revolutionary War, and received 200 acres of land in Wilkes County, Georgia for his service.[17] Jesse filed his will in Franklin County on June 13, 1789, and it was probated on Aug. 10, 1790.[18] He married Mary Walker, who died in Franklin County in 1801.[19] Their descendants lived in Georgia, Tennessee, and Mississippi. (20)

Thomas Walton Sr. (5)

Thomas Walton Sr., son of Edward Jr. and Elizabeth Walton, was baptized Feb. 20, 1703/1704 in St. Peter's Parish, New Kent County, Virginia, and died in 1772 in Cumberland County, Virginia.[20] In 1734, Thomas married Martha Cox, daughter of George and Martha Cox of Henrico County, Virginia.[21] Martha (Cox) Walton's will was dated June 6, 1798 and probated on Aug. 27, 1798.[22] The father of Martha (Cox) Walton was George Cox, son of Bartholomew and Rebecca Cox.[23] There were two contemporary George Coxes who married

---

[15] W. Mac. Jones, editor, *The Douglas Register*, (Baltimore, Maryland: Genealogical Publishing Company), 1972, p. 92.

[16] Goochland County, Virginia *Order Book 21*, Court of April 1789.

[17] *Revolutionary Records of Georgia*, Vol. 2, 1908, p. 713.

[18] Franklin County, Georgia *Will Book, 1786-1812*, pp. 3-4.

[19] Her will was written on Nov. 8, 1800 and probated on Oct. 6, 1801 in Franklin County, Georgia

[20] *Cumberland County, Virginia Will Book 2*, pp. 54-55.

[21] *Hopkins of Virginia and Related Families*, pp. 114-117.

[22] *Cumberland County, Virginia Will Book 3*, p. 122.

[23] Virginia M. Meyer and John Frederick Dorman, *Adventurers of Purse and Person*, (Order of the First Families of Virginia), 3rd edition, 1987, pp. 211-215.

women named Martha.[24] This George Cox's wife was Martha (maiden name not known but not nee Stratton), and he left a will and died in 1728. After his death, his widow Martha married second Isaac Hughes.[25]

Researchers have sometimes confused this Thomas Walton with Thomas Walton, 1736-1789, who was a son of John and Rebecca (Person) Walton of Brunswick County.[26] Our Thomas Walton did not serve in the Brunswick County Militia

Thomas Walton was a large landowner. On June 26, 1731, he purchased 400 acres on Muddy Creek, on the south side of the James River, in what was then Goochland County.[27] It is believed that this land was located in what is now Cumberland and Powhatan Counties. This parcel of land was adjacent to Ashford Hughes and to his brother William Walton. Sept. 15, 1741, Thomas Walton Sr. of St. James' Parish, bought 200 acres from Joseph Ballenger, who was from a Quaker family up north. This land was located along the south side of the Fluvanna River in Goochland County.[28] March 16, 1741, Thomas

---

[24] Elaine W. Gordon, 3719 Hunters Circle, San Antonio, Texas 78230-2816, in a letter to the compiler, dated May 25, 1997, flagged an error passed down by Walton researchers. The George Cox, who married Martha Stratton, died in 1728. See *Henrico County, Virginia Miscellaneous Court Records I*, p. 183. This George Cox of Henrico County was an uncle of Martha Cox who married Thomas Walton. The will of Martha (Stratton) Cox was written on Oct. 17, 1729, and probated in June 1734. See *Henrico County, Virginia Wills and Deeds, 1725-1737*, p. 443.

[25] Proven by the will of Martha Hughes, Cumberland County, Virginia *Will Book 2*, p. 7, dated Sept. 8, 1769. She named three children: (a) George Cox (b) Henry Cox, and (c) Martha (Cox) Walton.

[26] John Frederick Dorman, *Adventurers of Purse and Person: VIRGINIA, 1607-1624/5*, (Baltimore Maryland: Genealogical Publishing Company), 2004, Vol 1, pp. 743-744. Dorman's error may be attributed to his source: William and Mary College Quarterly Historical Magazine, 2nd series, Vol VI, p. 345.

[27] Virginia *Land Patent Book 14*, Library of Virginia, p. 174.

[28] Goochland County *Wills and Deeds, 1736-1742, Deed Book 3*, p. 472. Robert Walton, who was probably William's older brother, witnessed the deed.

Sr. purchased 675 acres from John Alexander, also located on Muddy Creek along the south side of the James River, Goochland County.[29]

Some of these lands were sold within a couple of years, to wit: on Nov. 16, 1742, 200 acres located along Deep Run of Muddy Creek was sold to John Creasley and William Palmer.[30] On Oct. 18, 1743, Thomas and Martha Walton sold 475 acres to John Alexander.[31] These two tracts were the totality of the 675 acres mentioned above.

Thomas and Martha then sold, June 19, 1744, the 200-acre Ballenger tract to Mrs. Judith Ware.[32] That Goochland County land later fell into Buckingham County, described as being "opposite the seven islands" on the Fluvanna River. Judith (Scott) Ware was born on Dec. 4, 1728 in New Kent County (Parish Register), and died in Buckingham County in October 1785. She married second Samuel Jordan in 1744,[33] who was born in 1715 and died in 1789.[34]

On Sept. 23, 1765, in Cumberland County, Thomas Sr. made a "deed of gift" to his son Thomas Walton Jr.[35] of 250 acres on both sides of Deep Run of Muddy Creek, "beginning at Carter's Ferry along Harrison's line."

Children of Thomas Sr. and Martha (Cox) Walton:[36]

---

[29] *Ibid.* p. 517.

[30] Goochland County, Virginia *Deed Book 4*, p. 89.

[31] *Ibid.* p. 335.

[32] *Ibid.* p. 404.

[33] *William and Mary College Quarterly Historical Magazine*, Vol. 7, No. 2. (Oct., 1898), p. 98

[34] Mary B. Warren (compiler), *Virginia's District Courts, 1789-1809: Records of the Prince Edward District: Buckingham, Charlotte, Cumberland, Halifax, and Prince Edward Counties*, (Danielsville, Georgia: Heritage Papers), 1991, p. 31

[35] Cumberland County, Virginia *Deed Book 4*, pp. 47-48. This land was part of 500 acres that Thomas Walton purchased of William Elliott on May 25, 1762.

[36] The ordinal list of children is from his will, her will, and from *Historical Genealogy of the Woodsons*, Memphis, Tennessee, 1915, p. 308: the latter alone

Second Generation

1. Elizabeth Walton, born circa 1737, married Jesse Miller on March 1, 1758 in Cumberland County. His will was filed in Powhatan County on Feb. 23, 1804. (21)

2. Martha "Patty" Walton was born circa 1738, and died in 1794. She married Edward Mosby in May of 1755.[37] On April 24, 1758, Thomas Walton Sr. made a "deed of gift to Patty Mosby, wife of Edward Mosby." Their children: Hezekiah Mosby, Elizabeth Mosby married John B. Carter, Martha "Patty" Mosby married John B. Bradley, Thomas Mosby, and Agnes Mosby married her first cousin, Thomas G. Walton. Edward Mosby died by 1769,[38] and Martha married second John Peter Bondurant.[39] (22)

3. George Walton was born circa 1740 and died intestate in Cumberland County circa 1817.[40] He married Margaret Tabb in Buckingham County on Nov. 22, 1759. (23)

4. Thomas Walton Jr. was born circa 1742 and died at Bent Creek, Buckingham County, on Nov. 21, 1815. Thomas Jr. married first Phoebe Murray, daughter of Anthony and Mary (James) Murray. He married second Nancy Armistead, and married third Martha, whose maiden name has not been proven. (24)

5. Josiah Walton Sr. was born circa 1744, probably in Goochland County, and died in Cumberland County, about 1776. He married Jane Flippen, daughter of Ralph and Martha (Scott) Flippen. (25)

---

mentions a Thesius Walton. Dr. Peter McDearmon Witt of Richmond, Virginia suggests that "Thesius" Walton was a scribal error for Thos=Thomas.

[37] Cumberland County, Virginia *Order Book*, date of marriage proven by court depositions taken on April 24, 1758. The essence of the deposition was to determine the ownership of slaves given by Thomas Walton Sr. to the Mosby's.

[38] Cumberland County, Virginia *Will Book 2*, p. 3, contains an inventory and appraisal of Edward Mosby's estate, Oct. 23, 1769.

[39] Cumberland County, Virginia *Will Book 21*, Aug. 28, 1775, p. 187.

[40] Appraisal of estate of George Walton is found in Cumberland County *Will Book 6*, p. 105. The sheriff was appointed administrator of the estate, according to Cumberland County, Virginia *Order Book 1815-1818*, p. 195.

6. Edward Walton was born circa 1747, and died in Cumberland County on Oct. 2, 1807. He married Nancy Murray. (26)

7. Robert Walton was born Sept. 25, 1749 and died July 24, 1837, in Powhatan County. Robert married Mary Hobson Nov. 20, 1769. (27)

John Walton Sr. (7)

John Walton, probable son of Edward Jr. and Elizabeth Walton, was born in St. Peter's Parish, New Kent County, on Aug. 7, 1709. This may be the same John Walton who married Mary Sims. If so, they settled in nearby Henrico County, Virginia where he died in 1772.[41] Circumstantial evidence suggests a relationship between John and the New Kent County Waltons, although direct proof is still being sought.[42] The will of John Walton of Henrico made provisions for twelve children, and his wife. John owned two plantations, including "New Design," in Louisa County. He owned many slaves and became wealthy from his land. Tradition says that he was a botanical herb doctor, a pharmacist who created prescriptions from certain plants.

Children of John Sr. and Mary (Sims) Walton:[43]

1. George Walton was born circa 1736 in Hanover County, Virginia and died about 1806 in Wilkes County, Georgia. He married Elizabeth Jennings on June 20, 1758. She was born circa 1733 and died on July 11, 1799 in Lincoln County, Georgia. They moved to Georgia before the Revolutionary War. (28)

---

[41] According to the New Kent Parish records, one John Walton died on Jan. 23rd, 1721-1722.

[42] There are numerous inconsistencies among stories told by descendants. One story says that John Walton walked 60 miles from his home in Henrico County to visit his father in New Kent County. This cannot be a true if John Walton was born in 1709 and his father died in 1720. Why was an 11-year old boy living 60 miles from his father? What was John doing in Henrico County during his pre-teen years?

[43] The writer is indebted to Ann Lynn Crass Bailey of 638 South Magnolia, Palestine, Texas 75801-3536. She shared generously her records and documentation on the family of John and Mary (Sims) Walton. She also furnished a printed copy of Tennessee State Library and Archives, *"Walton Family Papers, 1710-1879,"* Microfilm Accession No. 916.

Second Generation

2. John Walton Jr. was born on April 1, 1738 in Hanover County and died Sept. 23, 1793 in Louisa County, Virginia. He married Mary Baker. (29)

3. Jesse Walton, son of John and Mary (Sims) Walton, was born on Nov. 10, 1739 in Hanover County and died April 30, 1822 in Pittsylvania County, Virginia. He married Ann Pleasant. (30)

4. Simeon Walton was born Sept. 3, 1741 and died March 23, 1798 at Germantown, Bracken County, Kentucky. He married Agnes Hester. (31)

5. Edward Walton was born in 1743 and died in 1823 in Hanover County. He married first Ann Murray, and married second Barbara Hester, daughter of Robert and Mary (Cook) Hester. (32)

6. Mary Walton was born circa 1745 and died about 1800. She married William Baker, who was born in 1735 and died on Dec. 16, 1811. (33)

7. Elizabeth Walton, born circa 1750, married Isham Watkins. (34)

8. Robert Walton was born in 1752 in Hanover County and died on May 2, 1836 in Warren County, Georgia. He married first Keziah Overton, and married second Elizabeth Walton, and married third Sarah Rees. (35)

9. Frances Walton was born about 1755. She married first John Brooks and married second John Mason on Sept. 26, 1794. (36)

10. William Walton was born in 1757 in Hanover County, and died in 1811 in Goochland County, Virginia. He married Agnes Sims. (37)

11. Mizapina Walton was born in 1760 and died in September in Louisa County. She married Robert Harris. (38)

12. Newell Walton was born Dec. 13, 1763 in Hanover County and died in 1834 in Abbeville District, South Carolina. He married Agnes Woolfolk on Jan. 21, 1782. He served as a private in the Revolutionary War. In 1795, Newell moved his family to Lincoln County, Georgia, and then back to South Carolina in 1821. (39)

Chapter 3
Third Generation
Robert Walton Jr. (8)

Robert Walton Jr., son of Robert Sr. and Frances (Sherwood) Walton, was born on Jan. 7, 1717/1718 and died circa 1750, in Cumberland County, Virginia. Robert Jr. bought land along the James River in Goochland County, which later became part of Cumberland County. Robert was an extensive land owner, including thousands of acres as far away as possibly Ohio.[1] He wrote his will in Cumberland County in 1749 and he was deceased by June 25, 1750.[2] Settlement of his vast estate was still being processed in 1756. Witnesses to his will were Anthony Hughes, Samuel Cocker, and Eliza Hughes. His codicil, dated Sept. 5, 1749, was witnessed by his brother Sherwood Walton.[3] Robert Jr. married Mary Hughes, daughter of Robert and Martha (Morton) Hughes. Mary was born March 11, 1724 and died Dec. 18, 1821. Mary married second John Winfrey, 1728-1821, on April 27, 1752 in Cumberland County.[4] A study of the extensive court records and accounts suggests that Robert's family was very affluent. It reveals that Patrick Henry served as an attorney for the family. The accounts also show that the children received many benefits and privileges that were not customary in Colonial Virginia. There is a record of Robert Jr. selling land in New Kent County, and payment for surveying 4,012 acres.[5] George Walton, his brother, was executor of the estate and guardian for the four children named below.[6] Annual accounts were filed in court through the year 1763.[7]

Children of Robert Jr. and Mary (Hughes) Walton:

---

[1] Cumberland County, Virginia *Will Book I*, p. 276-277.

[2] *Ibid.* p. 16.

[3] *Ibid.* pp. 15-17.

[4] William and Mary College Quarterly Historical Magazine, Vol. 20, No. 1.(July., 1911), pp. 21-30

[5] Cumberland County, Virginia *Will Book I*, p. 168.

[6] Cumberland County, Virginia *Will Book I,* pp. 174-175.

[7] *Ibid.* p. 278.

Third Generation

1. John Walton was born circa 1743, probably in Goochland County. John's father willed him 150 acres of land. His guardian, Tucker Woodson, filed an account in 1760 in the Cumberland County Court, showing that John boarded with Robert Hughes in 1759.[8] In the August 1763 court, his Uncle George Walton filed an account for renting orphan John Walton's James River plantations for seven and fourteen pounds respectively.[9] John moved to Georgia where he married Elizabeth Claiborne in 1769. Her father, Leonard Claiborne Jr. had moved his family from Virginia to Georgia. John became a planter near Augusta, Georgia. Feb. 26, 1778, he was elected to the Continental Congress, and signed the Articles of Confederation for Georgia on July 24, 1778. He served also as surveyor for Richmond County, Georgia. John filed a will in St. John's Parish on June 11, 1778, and he was deceased by Aug. 1, 1783 when his estate was appraised in Richmond County. His brother George Walton was one of the executors for his estate. John left descendants. The widow Elizabeth (Claiborne) Walton married second David Douglas, who was dead by 1791.[10] (40)

2. Sally Walton was born Oct. 8, 1745/46 and died Nov. 20, 1805, in Hopkinsville, Kentucky.[11] Sally received slaves from her father's estate. She married Thomas Watkins Jr. of Powhatan County, Virginia on Feb. 8, 1762. Thomas Jr. was killed during the Revolutionary War. After his death she married second the Rev. Joshua Morris, a well-known Baptist minister. (41)

3. Robert Walton III was born circa 1748, probably in Goochland County, and died in Savannah, Georgia. He married Frances Carter, daughter of John Carter of Henrico County, Virginia. (42)

4. George Walton was born in December 1749 in Cumberland County, Virginia and died Feb. 2, 1804 in Georgia. He married Dorothy Camber in 1775. Dorothy died in Tallahassee, Florida on Sept. 12, 1832. (43)

---

[8] *Ibid.* p. 400.

[9] *Ibid.* pp. 408, 416-417.

[10] John Frederick Dorman, *Claiborne of Virginia*, (Baltimore, Maryland: Gateway Press, Inc.), 1995, pp. 298-301.

[11] George Edward Pankey, *John Pankey of Manakin Town, Virginia and His Descendants*, (Kingsport, Tennessee: Kingsport Press, Inc.), 1961, p 213.

Joseph Walton (10)

Joseph Walton, son of Robert Sr. and Frances (Sherwood) Walton, was born Feb. 10, 1722 in New Kent County, Virginia and died by 1768. He married a woman named Mary.[12] Joseph bought 400 acres in on both sides of Brimmer Creek (*sic*) in Goochland County on July 10, 1745. On Sept. 5, 1749, he bought 192 acres along Bremore Creek of the Fluvanna River. A descendant of Joseph says that he died in Richmond County, Georgia. That is not consistent with a court record in Lunenburg County, Virginia, dated Oct. 3, 1768, where his orphan son, Jesse Walton, was bound to Isaac Hill. Allegedly, another child was born to Joseph and Mary, that was William Walton, born on Feb. 11, 1754, and died Oct. 8, 1819 in Columbia County, GA.[13] This William Walton married Sara Grinage on Dec. 20, 1792. William and Sarah had a child named Jesse Sims Walton, 1801-1866, who married Palatia Ellis Jones.

Children of Joseph and Mary Walton:

1. William Walton[14] was born on Feb. 11, 1754 in Virginia and died on Oct. 8, 1819 in Columbiana County, Georgia. He married Sarah Grinage on Dec. 20, 1792. (44)

2. Jesse Walton, an orphan of Joseph Walton was bound to Isaac Hill in Lunenburg County, Virginia on Oct. 3, 1768. (45)

George Walton (11)

George Walton, son of Robert Sr. and Frances (Sherwood) Walton, was born Feb. 17, 1724/25[15] and died July 7, 1797 in Prince Edward

---

[12] *St. Peter's Parish Record*, New Kent County, Virginia

[13] Information was furnished via letter to the compiler on Feb. 5, 1999 by W. Lindsey Walton, PO Box 7493, Hilton Head, South Carolina 29938. Sources of information were not provided. See The National Genealogical Quarterly, "Some Waltons of Georgia" by William H. Dumont, vol. 57, p. 17.

[14] Information was furnished via letter to the compiler on Feb. 5, 1999 by W. Lindsey Walton, PO Box 7493, Hilton Head, South Carolina 29938. Sources of information were not provided. See The National Genealogical Quarterly, "Some Waltons of Georgia" by William H. Dumont, vol. 57, p. 17.

County, Virginia. He married Martha Hughes, daughter of Robert and Martha (Morton) Hughes, on Aug. 14, 1749 in Cumberland County, Virginia. Martha was born on Nov. 25, 1734, and died in Prince Edward County on Sept. 18, 1813. George held a high office, as proven in the estate records of his brother Robert Walton III. It says that Robert Walton paid Clement Reed "for swearing my brother to his commission."[16] A courier was paid to hand-deliver the document to Williamsburg. George was appointed guardian for Sally and George Walton, children of his brother Robert.[17] The orphan George Walton lived with his Uncle George until 1769, when he moved to Georgia to practice law. Of course, we know that George was later one of the Signers of the Declaration of Independence. The Pankey history provides extensive information on these Waltons.[18]

Children of George and Martha (Hughes) Walton:[19]

1. Jesse Hughes Walton was born on Sept. 17, 1750, and died Feb. 2, 1791, unmarried. He lived and died in Prince Edward County. (46)

2. Frances Walton, born on April 26, 1752, married a Mr. Scott. (47)

c. Robert Walton was born on Feb. 4, 1754, and died in 1801 in Richmond County, Georgia. He served as an ensign in the Prince Edward County Militia. Robert married Blanche Glasscock in 1775.[20] (48)

3. Molly Walton was born on Feb. 7, 1756 and believed to have died before 1781. She married Francis DeGraffendreidt on Nov. 18, 1771, in

---

[15] George Edward Pankey, *John Pankey of Manakin Town, Virginia and His Descendants*, (Kingsport, Tennessee: Kingsport Press, Inc.), 1961, p 122.

[16] *Ibid.* p. 174.

[17] Cumberland County, Virginia *Order Book* I, p. 469, dated May 23, 1759.

[18] See George Edward Pankey, *John Pankey of Manakin Town, Virginia and His Descendants*, (Ruston, Louisiana), 1969, pp. 120-124.

[19] Marriage records of the children of George and Martha Walton may be found in the Prince Edward County courthouse in Farmville, Virginia.

[20] Britton Walton's Chart

Prince Edward County. He was born on Feb. 24, 1746/47 and died in 1815 in Lunenburg County. (49)

4. George Walton Jr. was born on Oct. 5, 1758, and allegedly died in the Revolutionary War. He was not mentioned in his mother's will. (50)

5. Nancy Hughes Walton was born in April 1760. She married Thomas Moore on March 22, 1774 in Prince Edward County. It is believed that they moved to Georgia. (51)

6. Patty Walton was born on June 8, 1762 in Prince Edward County, and died on Nov. 9, 1824 in Lunenburg County, Virginia. She married Woodson Knight, son of John and Elizabeth (Woodson) Knight, on June 18, 1781, in Prince Edward County. He was born in 1752 and died on July 10, 1831 in Lunenburg County. (52)

7. Doshia Walton was born on March 4, 1764, and died in 1787. She married John Walton, son of Sherwood and Susanna (Jouett) Walton, on Jan. 22, 1784, in Prince Edward County. (53)

8. "Suckey" Susannah Walton was born on May 22, 1766. She married William Morton on April 24, 1784, in Prince Edward County. (54)

9. Temperance Walton was born March 5, 1769 and died in 1804. She married Joseph Yarbrough in Prince Edward County, Virginia. The marriage bond was dated Dec. 19, 1785 and the marriage occurred on Jan. 12, 1786. Joseph was born on Nov. 6, 1758 and died on May 10, 1827 in Lunenburg County, Virginia. (55)

10. John B. Walton was born Nov. 30, 1770. He married Mrs. Nancy Bagnois on Oct. 4, 1796.[21] He was buried in a family cemetery near Ft. Lewis in Roanoke County, Virginia.[22] (56)

11. Sarah "Sally" Walton was born about 1772 in Prince Edward County, and died March 5, 1857 in Roanoke County, Virginia. She married Elisha Betts on June 27, 1787, in Prince Edward County. He preceded her in death. Apparently they had no children, because her

---

[21] *Virginia Gazette*, Oct. 8, 1796, p. 3, c. 3.

[22] Patricia Law Hatcher, *Abstracts of Graves of Revolutionary Patriots*, (Pioneer Heritage Press), Vol 4.

estate in the Roanoke County Court was divided among her nieces and nephews. (57)

12. Thomas Walton was born on Feb. 13, 1775 and died in Prince Edward County in 1817. He married Elizabeth Pankey on Oct. 6, 1796. She was born in 1777 in Chesterfield County and died in Prince Edward County on Jan. 13, 1815.[23] They had seven children, and were owners of twenty-four slaves. Nathaniel Jackson, brother-in-law, was administrator for the estate of Thomas Walton.[24] (58)

Frances (Walton) Callaway (12)

Frances Walton, daughter of Robert Jr. and Frances (Sherwood) Walton,[25] was born Jan. 14, 1726-27, and allegedly died about 1766 in Bedford County, Virginia.[26] Frances married Col. Richard Callaway, son of Joseph Jr. and Elizabeth (Jones) Callaway. Richard was born June 17, 1717 in Caroline County, Virginia. He fathered twelve children with Frances and had three more children from his second marriage to Elizabeth Jones. Richard was a rugged frontiersman who went to Boonsboro, Kentucky[27] with Daniel Boone and was killed there by Indians on March 8, 1780.

Children of Richard and Frances (Walton) Callaway:[28]

---

[23] *Virginia Argus*, p. 3, c. 5, issue of Jan. 28, 1815.

[24] Prince Edward County, Virginia Will *Book 5*, pp. 346-347.

[25] Mary Denham Ackerly and Lula Eastman Jeter Parker, *Our Kin*, (Harrisonburg, Virginia: C. J. Carrier), 1976, p. 316. The authors cite the Draper MSS that says she was a sister of Sherwood Walton.

[26] For more information on the Callaway family, see Mary Denham Ackerly and Lula Eastman Jeter Parker, *Our Kin*, (Harrisonburg, Virginia: C. J. Carrier Company), 1976, pp. 313-326.

[27] From *Walton Chart* by Britain W. Walton, Edenton, North Carolina.

[28] Major source of information for the Callaway family was from adgedge@burgoyne.com and web-page http://www.burgoyne.com/pages/adgedge/ CALLAWAY.htm

a. Sarah Callaway was born May 7, 1746 in Bedford County, Virginia and died Jan. 22, 1826 in Amherst County, Virginia. She married Gabriel Penn on Sept. 24, 1761 in Amherst County. (59)

b. George Callaway was born on Jan. 12, 1748 in Bedford County, and may have died about 1773 in the same county. He married Amelia "Milly" Callaway, daughter of William and Elizabeth (Crawford) Callaway, May 8, 1770. Amelia was born on June 5, 1759 in Bedford County and died April 7, 1773. (60)

c. Zachariah Callaway was born Sept. 4, 1750 in Bedford County, Virginia, and died circa 1781 in the same county. He married, on Dec. 18, 1774, Susanna Miller. (61)

d. Mary "Molly" Callaway was born circa 1752 in Bedford County. She married Charles Gwatkin. (62)

e. Anna "Nancy" Callaway was born circa 1754 in Bedford County, and died in Amherst County. (63)

f. Mildred Callaway was born about 1756 in Bedford County. She married Thomas A. Noel, son of Cornelius and Anne (Fogg) Noel of Essex County, Virginia. (64)

g. Isham Callaway was born in September 1758 in Bedford County and died before 1790. (65)

h. Elizabeth Callaway was born Aug. 14, 1760 in Bedford County, and died in Winchester, Franklin County, Tennessee. She married Samuel Henderson on Aug. 7, 1776 in Boonesboro, Madison County, Kentucky. (66)

i. Caleb Callaway was born Aug. 9, 1762 in Bedford County, and died Sept. 8, 1829, in Bowling Green, Warren County, Kentucky. Caleb married Elizabeth Callaway, daughter of John and Tabitha (Tate) Callaway, Oct. 19, 1784 in Campbell County, Virginia. She was born on April 20, 1763 in Campbell County, and died on Jan. 4, 1804. (67)

j. Frances Callaway was born on June 16, 1763 in Bedford County and died about 1803 in Kentucky. She first married Capt. John Holder on Dec. 13, 1802 in Clark County, Kentucky, and married second John McGuire. (68)

k. Lydia Callaway was born Oct. 14, 1764 in Bedford County. She married first Christopher Irvine and married second Richard Hickman on Oct. 29, 1789 in Clark County, Kentucky. (69)

l. Theodosia "Doshea" Callaway was born on Aug. 8, 1766 in Bedford County, and died June 13, 1822 in Campbell County, Virginia. She married William Callaway. son of John and Agatha (Ward) Callaway, Jan. 7, 1796 in Campbell County. William was born on Oct. 11, 1769 and died Feb. 28, 1808. (70)

Sherwood Walton (13)

Sherwood Walton, son of Robert Jr. and Frances (Sherwood) Walton, was born in New Kent County, Virginia on July 10th and baptized on Aug. 11th, 1728.[29] He died before 1816 when his will was probated in Amelia County, Virginia. Sherwood was a professional surveyor, with a commission from the College of William and Mary,[30] which required him to pay one-sixth of his fees to the endowment of the College. Surveyors in Colonial Virginia were in a powerful position, as they helped to allocate land, to lay out new towns, to establish boundary lines, and to accumulate land for themselves. In 1761, Sherwood was asked the lay out a proposed town in Halifax County for James Roberts Jr., owner of the land. The proposed town was to be called Peytonsburg, but it failed because the surveyor crammed 208 lots into 100 acres with only two streets that crossed in the center of town. Most of the lots had no access to a street or road.[31] Sherwood's wife was Susanna Jouett, born ca 1732, daughter of Matthew and Susanna (Moore) Jouett.[32] Six children have been identified.

---

[29] New Kent County Virginia, *St Peter's Parish Register.*

[30] Sarah S. Hughes, *Surveyors and Statesmen: Land Measuring in Colonial Virginia*, copyright © by The Virginia Surveyors Foundation, Ltd., and The Virginia Association of Surveyors, Inc., Richmond, Virginia, 1979, p. 97.

[31] *Ibid.* pp. 135-136.

[32] The marriage is based on circumstantial evidence, especially the naming patterns of Matthew Jouetts descendants and Sherwood Walton's children. Matthew had children named Mary, John, Henretta, Frances, Matthew and Charlotte Jouett,

Children of Sherwood and Susanna (Jouett) Walton:

1. Matthew Walton was born circa 1754 in Virginia, and died in Springfield, Kentucky on Jan. 18, 1819.[33] Interment was in the Springfield Cemetery. He married Frances Watkins on Jan. 25, 1791 in Prince Edward County, Virginia.[34] Matthew attended the College of William and Mary to receive his surveyor's certificate, and went to Kentucky in 1776 as a surveyor. He was one of the wealthiest landowners in Kentucky, receiving 67,698 acres in 48 grants throughout Kentucky during the period 1783-1813.[35] Prior to that, he received a number of "Virginia Grants" in Kentucky. He settled near Springfield and his 1784-historic house is still standing. In 1792, he helped found Washington County, which was formed just before Kentucky became a State. Matthew was elected in Kentucky as a Republican to the 8th and 9th U.S. Congresses, serving from March 4, 1803 to March 3, 1807. They left no known descendants. (71)

2. Frances Walton was born circa 1756 in Virginia and died circa 1786, probably in Amelia County, Virginia. She married Joshua

---

whereas Sherwood had children named Matthew, Frances, John, Susanna and Charlotte Walton. Both families were at St. Peters Parish in New Kent County, Virginia at the same time. Matthew was not a common name for Waltons in Colonial Virginia. A good example was the naming pattern of twelve children of a granddaughter of Matthew Jouett: Frances H. Williams (1780-1851), who married John Knight. Among their twelve children were: Matthew Jouett Knight, Sherwood Walton Knight, Hughes Walton Knight, and John Woodson Knight. I might add that Jouett researchers are confused over the genealogy of Matthew Jouett's daughter Mary Jouett who married John Moore; some referring to her as Mary Susan, with a birth year ranging between 1706 and 1732.

[33] Washington County, Kentucky, *Will Book C*, p. 172. His will was probated on Feb. 7, 1819. His personal estate sale yielded only $557.95. Apparently he lost much of his fortune.

[34] Catherine L. Knorr, *Marriages of Prince Edward County, Virginia, 1754-1810*, privately published, 1950, p. 81.

[35] Willard Rouse Jillson, Sc.D., *The Kentucky Land Grants*, (Baltimore, Maryland: Genealogical Publishing Company), 1971, p. 248.

Atkinson on Aug. 5, 1777 in Amelia County.[36] Joshua was born in 1755 in Amelia County and died circa 1837 in Adair County, Kentucky. (72)

3. John Walton was born circa 1760 and died in 1809 in Columbia County, Georgia. He married his cousin, Doshia Walton, daughter of George and Martha (Hughes) Walton, on Jan. 22, 1784, in Prince Edward County, Virginia.[37] Younger[38] believed that this John Walton married second Mary Jenkins on July 16, 1786 in Amelia County, Virginia. Matthew and Sherwood Walton witnessed James Jenkins' giving consent for his daughter's marriage. However, Doshia's father, George Walton, remembered his daughter Doshia in his 1796-will, "moved to Georgia." Younger's papers contain a list of eight children who were fathered by John Walton. They were: (a) James S. Walton (b) Ann P. Walton (c) Frances J. Walton (d) Matthew Walton (e) John W. Walton (f) Sherwood Walton (g) Susanna Walton and (h) Rebecca Walton. This may have been the same John Walton who received land grants in Nelson and Mason Counties, Kentucky.[39] (73)

4. Jesse Walton, not a proven son, was listed in 1800 on the personal property tax list for Amelia County.[40] He may have been a son of Josiah Walton of Cumberland County. (74)

5. Susanna Walton, born circa 1762, apparently did not marry. She was mentioned in the will of her brother Matthew Walton to receive "one good horse and saddle, worth thirty pounds."[41] (75)

---

[36] Marriage record was found in an account book of Thomas Atkinson, father of Joshua Atkinson. Information provided by Rhoda Fone RhodaFone@aol.com on March 26, 2002.

[37] Catherine L. Knorr, compiler, *Marriages of Prince Edward County, Virginia, 1754-1810*, (Privately Published), 1950, p. 80.

[38] Ida Bowman Younger (1903-1993), "Genealogy Papers (Walton), MS2098" Jones Memorial Library, Lynchburg, Virginia.

[39] Willard Rouse Jillson, Sc.D., *The Kentucky Land Grants*, (Baltimore, Maryland: Genealogical Publishing Company), 1971, p. 248

[40] 1800 Personal Property Tax List, Amelia County, Virginia, Library of Virginia

6. Charlotte Walton was born circa 1764 in Amelia County, Virginia and died in Kentucky. She married Anthony Hundley Jr., son of Anthony and Ann (Dupuy) Hundley, on Sept. 28, 1785 in Amelia County.[42] Anthony Jr. died circa 1817 in Washington County, Kentucky.[43] (76)

William Walton Jr. (16)

William Walton Jr., son of William Sr. and Susannah (Cobb) Walton, was born on Dec. 2, 1735/36 in Albemarle County (now Amherst), and died on Jan. 31, 1806 in Burke County, North Carolina. Burial was in the First Presbyterian Church Cemetery at Morganton, North Carolina. He married Elizabeth Tilman, daughter of Thomas and Lucy (Hix) Tilman, Dec. 1, 1758, in Goochland County. Elizabeth was born May 29, 1744 in Goochland County, and died Sept. 8, 1787, probably in Amherst County, but descendants claim she died in Morganton, Burke County, North Carolina. William Jr. married second Mildred Lavender, May 16, 1792, in Amherst County. William Jr. enlisted in the Revolutionary War on Nov. 26, 1776 in Amherst County, Virginia. He participated in the battles at Brandywine, Germantown, and Monmouth. William Jr. and his son Tilman were with General Horatio Gates at his defeat in Camden, South Carolina in 1780 and later at King's Mountain in North Carolina, and still later at Yorktown.

---

[41] Washington County, Kentucky, *Will Book C*, p. 172.

[42] Oscar K. Lyle, *The Lyle Family—Ancestry, Posterity of Matthew, John, Daniel, & Samuel- Pioneer Settlers in Virginia*, published circa 1902. Information was sent to compiler by Mary Lou Franklin, 54 Golf Links, Kincardine, Ontario N2Z 1K4

[43] This Anthony Jr. did not die in 1811. Anthony Jr. was alive in 1813 when Charlotte and his son-in-law, Stephen Ray (married Nov. 30, 1809 to Susannah M. Hundley) bought land from Anthony Jr., per Washington County, Kentucky *Deed Book D*, p. 173, July 3, 1813. Thanks to Mary Lou Franklin smlfranklin@bmts.com

Third Generation

Children of William Jr. and Elizabeth (Tilman) Walton:[44]

1. Tilman Walton was born on Jan. 9, 1760, probably in Albemarle County (now Amherst), and died Feb. 3, 1831, in Burke County, North Carolina. He married Judith Walton, daughter of Edward and Nancy (Murray) Walton, on April 12, 1787, in Cumberland County. (77)

2. Thomas Walton was born April 15, 1764 and died Aug. 11, 1766. (78)

3. Jesse Walton was born on March 15, 1766 and died Sept. 23, 1766. (79)

4. William Walton III was born in Amherst County on Jan. 12, 1767, and died May 18, 1844, at Strawberry Hill in Green County, Alabama. He married Jennie McEntire, daughter of James and Nancy (Young) McEntire. (80)

5. Elizabeth Walton was born Sept. 13, 1769. She married Samuel Eliot Goodrich, son of James Goodrich, Dec. 25, 1789 in Amherst County, Virginia.[45] (81)

6. Lucy Walton was born on March 25, 1770 and died Aug. 20, 1771. (82)

7. George Walton was born on Nov. 8, 1773 and died Aug. 9, 1835. He married Nancy McEntire. (83)

8. Robert Walton was born on April 15, 1786, and died Aug. 9, 1835. (84)

9. John Walton was born on June 24, 1788 and died Sept. 17, 1817. (85)

10. Pauline Walton was born on Nov. 5, 1779. (86)

11. Thomas Walton was born on Aug. 1, 1782 and died July 27, 1859. He married Martha Matilda McEntire. (87)

---

[44] Information on the children of William and Elizabeth (Tilman) Walton Jr. was provided by Patricia Morrow, 6506 Prairie Dunes, Houston, TX 77069.

[45] William Montgomery Sweeney, compiler, *Marriage Bonds and Other Marriage Records of Amherst County, Virginia*, 1763-1800, (Baltimore, Maryland: Genealogical Publishing Company), Reprinted in 1973, p. 33.

12. Nancy Walton was born on May 24, 1784, and died in 1825. She married Amos Davis. (88)

13. Edward Walton was born on July 15, 1786 and died Sept. 14, 1807. (89)

Anne (Walton) Cobb (18)

Anne Walton, daughter of William and Susannah (Cobb) Walton Sr., was born circa 1738, in Goochland County, Virginia, and died after 1800 in Campbell County, Virginia. On Jan. 17, 1758, in Goochland County, she married Capt. Charles Cobb of Old Albemarle County. It is believed that Charles' father was Thomas Cobbs whose will was probated in Albemarle County in 1761.[46] Executors for the estate were Thomas Jr. and Charles Cobbs, sons of Thomas Sr. Charles and Anne settled in Campbell County, Virginia where he was listed as a Presbyterian minister in County records, and later became a Baptist. His will was dated March 3, 1798, and was recorded in Campbell County on Jan. 13, 1800.[47] Some of the descendant families lived in Charlotte County, Virginia. The name was sometimes spelled Cobb.

Children of Charles and Anne (Walton) Cobb:[48]

1. Jesse Cobb, born circa 1758, married Elizabeth McCoy on July 24, 1780 in Bedford County, Virginia. (90)

2. John Cobb was born on Oct. 12, 1759 in Bedford County, Virginia and died in Campbell County on April 6, 1847. He may be the John Cobb who married Jane Dixon on Oct. 8, 1810, but not proven. (91)

3. Charles R. Cobb married Martha Bailey on Dec. 4, 1783 in Campbell County, Virginia. (92)

4. Caleb Cobb married Mina Ann Wills, daughter of Euclid Wills, July 6, 1792 in Campbell County. (93)

---

[46] See Albemarle County, Virginia *Deed Book 2*, dated Aug. 11, 1760, *and Deed Book 2*, p. 272, which conveys land from William Walton to Charles Cobbs.

[47] Campbell County, Virginia *Will Book 1*, pp. 409-411.

[48] Information on this family unit was provided by Gayle M. Fitzsimmons, 508 California Avenue, Santa Cruz, California 95060.

5. William Walton Cobb was born April 16, 1777 in Campbell or Charlotte County, and died Sept. 14, 1839 in Green County, Kentucky. He married Nancy Newton Brent, Oct. 6, 1797, in Charlotte County. She was born June 14, 1780 in Charlotte County, and died in Green County on April 4, 1824. They had seven children, after which William W. married second Mary and had one more child. (94)

6. Frances Catherine Cobb married Nathaniel Rogers in August 1783, in Campbell County. (95)

7. Samuel D. Cobb married Ann Noell, daughter of Cornelius and Sally (Miller) Noel, on Aug. 27, 1787 in Bedford County, on Aug. 27, 1787. (96)

8. Thomas Cobb married Betty Wills on Dec. 3, 1788 in Bedford County, Virginia. (97)

Elizabeth (Walton) Miller (21)

Elizabeth Walton, daughter of Thomas Sr. and Martha (Cox) Walton, was born circa 1737, in present Cumberland County, Virginia. She married Jesse Miller on March 1, 1758 in Cumberland County. His will was filed in Powhatan County on Feb. 23, 1804. Thomas Walton Sr. made a "deed of gift" to Jessie and Elizabeth (Walton) Miller.[49] Residence: Cumberland County, Virginia.

Children of Jesse and Elizabeth (Walton) Miller:[50]

1. Jesse Miller Jr. was born circa 1760. One Jesse Miller married Polly Isbell on Feb. 16, 1803. (98)

2. Thomas Miller, born circa 1761, and may be the same person whose obit appeared in The Inquirer (Richmond, Virginia) May 7, 1819. He married Joanna Armistead, daughter of William and Frances (Anderson) Armistead, on Nov. 22, 1784 in Cumberland County. They moved to Franklin County, Virginia. (99)

3. William Miller married Martha Street. (100)

---

[49] Cumberland County, Virginia *Order Book,* dated on March 27, 1758.

[50] Information on Jesse's children is found on a handwritten old page, source not determined. The list of children is is not proven, but given as possible clues for further research.

4. John Miller married Hannah Armistead, born circa 1763, daughter of William and Frances (Anderson) Armistead, on June 27, 1785 in Cumberland County. (101)

5. Martha "Patty" Miller married Dudley Street of Cartersville, Virginia. (102)

6. Nannie Miller, born circa 1770, married James Armistead, 1767-1827, son of William and Frances (Anderson) Armistead, on April 16, 1789 in Cumberland County, Virginia. (103)

7. Judith Miller married a Mr. Richardson. (104)

George Walton (23)

George Walton, son of Thomas Sr. and Martha (Cox) Walton, was born circa 1740 in Goochland County, and died intestate in Cumberland County circa 1817.[51] He married Margaret Tabb, daughter of Thomas and Lockey (Langhorne) Tabb, of Buckingham County, on Nov. 22, 1759.[52] Margaret was born on April 4, 1744, probably in Charles Parish, York County. George Walton may have served in the Revolutionary War. George and his sister Patty (Walton) Mosby were scheduled to receive one-half of the remaining estate of their stepfather, Isaac Hughes.[53]

Children of George and Margaret (Tabb) Walton:

1. Langhorn Tabb Walton was born in Cumberland County circa 1763, and died in June 1821 in Williamson County, Tennessee.[54] Langhorn signed a Buckingham County petition in 1785 for submission to the Virginia Assembly regarding Church and State. He married Elizabeth George on July 24, 1786 in Cumberland County. They had moved from Cumberland to Buckingham County by 1789, as shown by the

---

[51] Appraisal of estate of George Walton is found in *Cumberland County Will Book 6*, p. 105. Apparently, the sheriff was appointed administrator of the estate, according to *Cumberland County Order Book 1815-1818*, p. 195.

[52] Cumberland County, Virginia marriage bond dated June 25, 1759.

[53] Cumberland County, Virginia *Will Book I*, p. 145, dated Jan. 22, 1758.

[54] Williamson County, Tennessee *Will Book 3*, p. 246.

personal property tax list. About 1816, he moved his family from Buckingham County to Williamson County, Tennessee. Their children were: Jesse Walton, Ivey Walton, Thomas Walton, William Walton, Peggy Walton, and Milley Walton. (105)

2. Jesse Walton was a proven son.[55] (106)

3. Thomas G. Walton was born circa 1765 in Cumberland County, and died in 1825 in Smith County, Tennessee, where he had migrated during the late 1790s.[56] Thomas G. married Agnes Mosby, daughter of Edward and Martha "Patty" (Walton) Mosby, his first cousin. (107)

4. Maurice H. Tabb Walton married Elizabeth __. Maurice's father appointed him to serve as his attorney to sell 200 acres of land in South Carolina.[57] (108)

5. Lockey Walton was named in her grandmother Martha (Cox) Walton's will. (109)

6. Elizabeth H(atcher) Walton was born circa 1775 and died in 1854. She married John T. Merryman on Sept. 4, 1800. John served in the War of 1812, and died on Sept. 4, 1814 of a disease contracted in the War.[58] (110)

7. Minjum H. Walton, born circa 1779 and died circa 1839 in Cumberland County. He married Sally F. Mann, daughter of William F. and Elizabeth Booth (Woodson) Mann, on Feb. 5, 1806 in Cumberland County. (111)

---

[55] Cumberland County, Virginia *Will Book I*, p. 122, and Cumberland County, Virginia *Deed Book 10*, p. 269, recorded on Sept. 22, 1806.

[56] Information provided to compiler by Sharlee Winn (MSWINN@aol.com) via e-mail on Feb. 21, 2000.

[57] Cumberland County, Virginia *Deed Book 10*, p. 73, dated Oct. 29, 1805.

[58] Virginia Genealogical Society Quarterly, Vol. XVI, No. 3, "Abstracts From the John K. Martin Papers," July 1, 1978, p. 84. Elizabeth is not a proven daughter of George; she could be the oldest daughter of Robert Walton who married Mary Hobson.

Thomas Walton Jr. (24)

Thomas Walton Jr., son of Thomas Sr. and Martha (Cox) Walton, was born circa 1742 in Goochland County (present Cumberland County), and died on Nov. 21, 1815, at Bent Creek, Buckingham County, Virginia.[59] His early life was spent in Cumberland County, which was formed from Goochland County in 1749. In 1765, he received a gift from his father for 250 acres on both sides of Muddy Creek near Carter's Ferry.[60] He was executor for both his father (died in 1772) and his mother (died in 1798) in Cumberland County. In 1803, he purchased 1254 ½ acres on Bent Creek in Buckingham County and made that locale his seat until his death in 1815.[61] The property was known as "The Cove Farm." In 1841, his son William Walton sold the farm to Archibald Bolling Megginson, 1798-1851, who then sold it to Silas P. Vawter in 1850. Vawter gave it to his daughter Mary Jane whose husband was John W. Walton, 1821-1889. The property was deeded to his daughter because of John W. Walton's bankruptcy in 1858. The Cove Farm eventually came back to the Walton name after Mary J. (Vawter) Walton's death in 1888, when her son Eugene A. Walton, 1850-1921, gained possession at the close of the nineteenth century. The Cove Farm was passed down to Eugene's son, Dallas Eugene Walton, 1887-1968, who died without descendants. The farm was passed down to his "adopted" nephew, Calvin Walker Harris, 1928-present, who lived on the farm until 2004 when it was sold. Lloyd G. Walton and his sister Elizabeth own 150 acres of the former William Walton estate.

Thomas was married three times: (a) Phoebe Murray,[62] daughter of Anthony and Mary (James) Murray.[63] (b) Nancy "Nannie" Ann

---

[59] Proven by the family Bible record of his son, William Walton, which is reproduced on page 40.

[60] Cumberland County, Virginia Deed *Book 4*, pp.47-48.

[61] Library of Virginia, "Scruggs Walton Childers" papers, No. __, includes indenture between John Elgin of Buckingham County for Thomas Walton of Cumberland County, Oct. 20, 1803, 1245 ½ for 1090.

[62] Phoebe Murry (sic) is named by her daughter Martha Walton in her pension application for her husband Walter Christian (1760-1829).

Armistead, daughter of William and Frances (Anderson) Armistead[64] of Cumberland County. Nancy died at Bent Creek on Nov. 22, 1810.[65] Thomas Jr. married third to a woman named Martha, who was born circa 1760 [66] and died circa 1840 on the "Cove Farm" at Bent Creek. Martha's name appears on the Buckingham County personal property tax books beginning in 1817. She was head of her household on the 1820 census for Buckingham County. In 1830, it appears that she could have been in the household of her stepson William Walton. Martha's name is found in a Bent Creek account book, "Walton and Phelps Merchandise," March 20, 1829, "Col. Chick for rent of my plantation for the year 1828, $140."[67] She was alternately referred to as "old Mrs.

---

[63] Anthony Murray was deceased by May 25, 1762, when Mary Murray was listed as a widow. See Cumberland County, Virginia *Order Book I*, p. 503.

[64] Parents of William Armistead were John Armistead, 1718/9-1769, and his wife Hannah Harrison, daughter of William and Elizabeth Harrison of Westmoreland County. William Armistead filed a will in 1816 and it was probated in 1823 in Cumberland County. See *Will Book 8*, pp. 304-307, 825-826, 886-887, and *Will Book 9*, pp. 42-45. Frances (Anderson) Armistead was born in 1744 and died in 1832. The Jan. 28, 1832 issue of *The Richmond Whig* said, "Died at her residence in the County of Cumberland, on the 20th instant (1832), Mrs. Frances Armistead in the 88th year of her age. She was a woman of a strong mind and industry." Children of William and Frances (Anderson) Armistead: (a) John Armistead married Mary A. Spencer, (b) James A. Armistead married Nannie Miller, (c) Hannah Armistead married John Miller, (d) Theodocia Armistead married the Rev. Jacob Levy Abraham, (e) Nancy Armistead married Thomas Walton Jr., (f) Mildred Armistead married Robert Walton, (g) Elizabeth Armistead married Charles Perrow, and (h) Frances Armistead married Pleasant Tucker who died in Noxubee County, Mississippi on April 22, 1854. See also Magazine of Virginia Genealogy, "Abraham, Anderson, Cary, Dabney, and Jennings," John C. Bell, Vol. 23, November 1985, pp. 28-41. Please note the error in that article; Nancy Armistead married Thomas Walton Jr., not William Walton.

[65] Proven by the Bible record of William Walton, her son. The record states her name simply as Nancy Walton. The person who possesses the Walton Bible does not want to be identified in this publication.

[66] The 1810 and 1820 censuses for Buckingham County list her as over 45 years old. The 1830 census shows a birth year range between 1760 and 1770.

[67] Library of Virginia, *Business Records*, Miscellaneous Reel 253, Dr. David C. Jones, and *Account Book 1827-1830*, "Walton & Phelps," p. 35.

Walton" and Martha in that book. According to land tax records for Appomattox County for the year 1850, 177 acres of the estate (widow's dower) of Thomas Walton had not been settled. Dr. David Crawford Jones' medical account book shows this entry for July 14, 1833, "To visit Jane's child at old Mrs. Waltons." Mrs. Martha Walton may have been the widow of Capt. Henry Christian who died about 1805 in Amherst County.[68] She appears to be the Martha Christian listed on the 1810 U. S. Census for Buckingham County. If so, Martha is believed to have been a daughter of Jonathan and Elizabeth (Christian) Patteson of New Kent and Lunenburg Counties, Virginia. However, *The Richmond Enquirer*, issue of Sept. 8, 1820, page 3, states that a Martha Christian died in Buckingham County on July 27, 1820 in her 72nd year. This could have been the Martha Patteson who married Henry Christian; hence, she would not have been the third wife of Thomas Walton Jr. More research needs to be done to identify Martha, the third wife of Thomas Walton Jr.

William Armistead, father-in-law of Thomas Walton Jr., disinherited the children of his daughter Nancy, for whatever reason. He wrote his will 1816 in Cumberland County; it was probated in 1823; and finalized in the 1824 term of court. Differences between the families may have played a role in Thomas Walton Jr. moving to Bent Creek in 1803. Armistead was a wealthy man with plenty of assets to divide among his descendants. In 1816, William Walton wrote a letter, below, to his grandfather Armistead about the inheritance and their relationship:[69]

Buckingham, Virginia
July 1, 1816
Dear Sir,

---

[68] From family group sheet and research notes provided to the compiler by Carole Ruff of Leesburg, Virginia. She cites Amherst County, Virginia *Will Book 4*, p. 174.

[69] Letter was copied by Kent Gregory (1872-1950), and preserved in her "Genealogy Papers (Walton/Bransford), MS1288," Jones Memorial Library, Lynchburg, Virginia. Apparently the original letter was among the court papers on the settlement of William Armistead's estate.

I have been Maturely thinking of the conversation that took place between you and myself the night I got to your place which you no doubt recollect— I have been led to believe that the cause of your telling me that you did not intend giving my deceased mother's children any part of your Estate, was, that I had visited you as you supposed with Expectations of you giving me something, & that I had no such Expectations. I thought it a duty that I owed to you as well as to myself, knowing our relative situations to visit you whenever an opportunity would offer. I am rejoiced that I can anticipate a lively hope that your three discarded surviving grandchildren, the offspring of your deceased daughter, in all probability will do as well, and be as much respected as the balance of your grandchildren whom you patronize and give your estate to.

I am Dr Sir Yrs respectfully,

(signed) William Walton

The children of Nancy (Armistead) Walton received only "$1 and no more." They filed an unsuccessful court suit in Cumberland County. It appears that William Armistead favored those grandchildren who were given the name Armistead, either their first or second name, and those who remained in Cumberland County.

Children of Thomas Jr. and Phoebe (Murray) Walton:

1. Martha Walton, born Dec. 2, 1766 in Cumberland County and died on Aug. 8, 1847 in Davie County, North Carolina. She married Walter Christian, son of Charles and Mary (Leake) Christian, July 1, 1783. Walter was born on Sept. 23, 1760 and died in August 1829. (112)

2. Anthony Walton Sr. was born circa 1769 in Cumberland County and died in 1819 in Buckingham. Anthony married Rebecca Johnson, daughter of Daniel Johnson. (113)

3. Robert Walton was born circa 1772 in Cumberland County and died in 1823 in Amherst County, Virginia. Robert married Mildred A. Armistead, daughter of William and Frances (Anderson) Armistead, Nov. 28, 1795. Mildred died before 1815, and Robert married second Elizabeth Wilson. (114)

4. Elizabeth Walton was born circa 1775 and died on Aug. 28, 1837 in Cumberland County. It is believed that she married first William Walton on March 24, 1794 in Cumberland County. Thomas Walton

gave consent for his daughter Elizabeth. She married second Robert Frayser of Cumberland County. (115)

5. Nancy Ann Murray Walton [70] was born circa 1777. She married William Isbell, son of Lewis and Hannah (Anderson) Isbell, on Nov. 2, 1795 in Cumberland County. William was born on June 1, 1777 in Goochland County and died in 1853 in Buckingham County. (116)

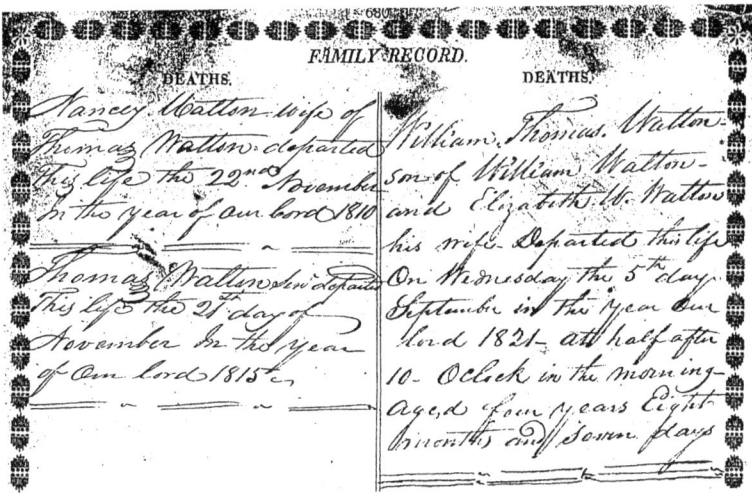

The document above was reproduced from the family Bible of William Walton. The death records say, "Nancy Walton wife of Thomas Walton departed this life the 22nd November in the year of our Lord 1810. Thomas Walton Sen. Departed this life the 21st day of November in the year of our Lord 1815."

Children of Thomas Jr. and Nancy (Armistead) Walton:

6. Phoebe Walton was born on Nov. 7, 1779 in Cumberland County and died on Dec. 19, 1852, in Lynchburg. She married Samuel Bransford. (117)

---

[70] Nancy's given name on the 1850 Census for Buckingham County was Ann. Information on Nancy M. (Walton) Isbell was contributed by Debra Tucker.

Third Generation

7. Mary Walton was born circa 1780 and died about 1814.[71] She married John Harris Jr., son of John Sr. and Mary (Duiguid) Harris.[72] They lived near Bent Creek, Buckingham County, Virginia. (118)

Children of John Jr. and Mary (Walton) Harris:

    a. John A. Harris was born on July 9, 1813 at Bent Creek. He married Ann Maria Jordan, daughter of William C. and Mary A. (Franklin) Jordan.[73]

    b. Other children were indicated in the will of Mary's maternal grandmother (Armistead) in Cumberland County, Virginia.

8. Capt. William Walton was born on Sept. 18, 1782 in Cumberland County and died on Dec. 18, 1851 at Bent Creek. He married Elizabeth White Chick, daughter of Col. William and Elizabeth Chick of Bent Creek. (119)

9. Frances Walton, born circa 1786 in Cumberland County, and died during the 1870s in Appomattox County. Frances married John Scruggs. (120)

Josiah Walton Sr. (25)

Josiah Walton Sr., son of Thomas Sr. and Martha (Cox) Walton, was born circa 1744 in Goochland County, and probably died in Cumberland County in late 1776. Josiah inherited one-half of the home plantation of his father Thomas Walton Sr.[74] An inventory of

---

[71] See *The Virginia Genealogist*, Vol. 15, p. 293. See also Library of Virginia, *Cumberland County Superior Court Judgments, 1823-1828*, Box 33, loose papers. Also, the Cumberland County will of her grandfather, William Armistead indicates that she was deceased in 1816.

[72] Death of John Harris Sr. was reported in *The Lynchburg Virginian*, Dec. 24, 1824, p. 3, col. 4. The death of Mary (Duiguid) Harris was reported in the *Religious Herald*, April 26, 1833. It stated her age as 83, which would give a birth year of 1750. She raised nine children, and was a member of Red Oak Baptist Church, now in Appomattox County. This information was provided by Mrs. Eleanor H. McCrae of Virginia Beach, Virginia.

[73] Henry Morton Woodson, *Historical Genealogy of the Woodsons*, (Memphis, Tennessee), 1915, p. 676.

[74] Thomas Walton's will was written on Aug. 26, 1771 and it was proven on April 27, 1772, as shown in Cumberland County, Virginia *Will Book 2*, p. 52.

Josiah's estate was made on Jan. 27, 1777. He married Jane Flippen, daughter of Ralph and Martha (Scott) Flippen.[75] They lived in Cumberland County, Virginia, where Jane was granted Letters of Administration, for estate, on Aug. 26, 1776. Could it be that Josiah was killed during the Revolutionary War or died from wounds received?[76] After Josiah's death Jane married second David Carter. Several of Josiah's children settled in Charlotte County, and later went south.[77]

Children of Josiah and Jane (Flippen) Walton[78]:

1. William Scott Walton,[79] born Feb. 6, 1771, in Cumberland County, and died July 15, 1845, in Monroe County, Mississippi. William S. married first Sally Womack, and married second Julia Pollard, Dec. 5, 1836, in Cumberland County, Virginia. (121)

2. Mary "Polly" Walton was born June 4, 1772. She married Thomas Mosby, June 28, 1790, in Cumberland County. (122)

---

[75] Ralph Flippen (ca 1714-1770) was a son of Thomas and Elizabeth Flippen of Gloucester County, Virginia. Martha Scott, daughter of Col. John and Judith Scott of New Kent County, Virginia, was born April 28, 1716 and died in 1794 in Cumberland County, Virginia. The website for this information was located at http://www.homestead.com/FlippinFamilies/SecondGen.html.

[76] A private claim for one Josiah Walton was presented to the U. S. House of Representatives, which was approved in 1794. This is probably a different Josiah. See *Alphabetical Claims Which Have Been Presented to the House of Representatives from the First to the Thirty-first Congress*, (Baltimore, Maryland: Genealogical Publishing Company, Inc.), 1970, p. 574.

[77] Floyd Smith, 1553 El Dorado Drive, Thousand Oaks, California 91362-2114, contributed information on Josiah and Jane Walton and their offspring. (psamika@aol.com).

[78] The *Richmond Standard*, Vol. II, No. 2, Sept. 13, 1879, lists only four children of Josiah.

[79] William S. Walton signed a marriage bond for an Isaac Walton, which suggests a relationship, but not a proven brother. Isaac married Mary Nelson, Feb. 22, 1785 (bond), in Cumberland County. Possibly Isaac was raised by Josiah and Jane Walton.

3. Jesse Walton was born July 6, 1773, in Cumberland County, Virginia, and died Nov. 20, 1830 in Monroe County, Mississippi. He married Joanna Lawson Hobson. (123)

4. Josiah S. Walton Jr. was born April 19, 1776, and died on April 22, 1816 in Williamson County, Tennessee. He married Nancy Woodfin. (124)

Edward Walton (26)

Edward Walton, son of Thomas Sr. and Martha (Cox) Walton, was born circa 1747, and died in Cumberland County in October 1807.[80] Edward owned many slaves and land on both sides of the Willis River. He married Nancy Murray, daughter of Richard and Judith (Allen) Murray. Richard died in April 1772 in Buckingham County, Virginia. Nancy was born circa 1748 and died on Feb. 23, 1825.[81] This Walton family lived in the northern section of Cumberland County, near Cartersville.

Children of Edward and Nancy (Murray) Walton:

1. Martha "Patty" Walton was born April 21, 1768, and died Feb. 14, 1811, in Franklin, Madison County, Georgia. She married Dr. George Christian, 1762-1831, on Aug. 27, 1782, in Cumberland County. George served in the Revolutionary War. They had nine children. George died in Wilcox County, Alabama. (125)

2. Judith Walton was born Feb. 19, 1770 and died Aug. 31, 1846. She married Tilman Walton, 1760-1831, son of William and Elizabeth (Tilman) Walton, April 12, 1787. William Walton was born Dec. 12, 1735/36 in Albemarle County (changed to Amherst County), and died Jan. 29, 1806 in Morganton, North Carolina. His wife, Elizabeth Tilman, 1744-1787, was a daughter of Thomas and Lucy (Hix) Tilman.[82] (126)

---

[80] Cumberland County, Virginia *Will Book 3*, pp. 377-378.

[81] See Cumberland County, Virginia *Will Book 8*, p. 86, which contains Nancy Walton's will dated July 14, 1824. She stated that her age was 80 years. The *Richmond Whig* stated her death date as Feb. 23, 1825.

[82] *The Tilman Family*, p. 120.

3. Thomas Murray Walton was born Dec. 14, 1772 and died June 7, 1821 in Cumberland County. Thomas M. married Frances Anne Carrington, daughter of Nathaniel and Phoebe (Harris) Carrington, April 6, 1796. Frances was born April 10, 1779 and died Feb. 16, 1824. (127)

4. Sarah "Sally" Walton,[83] born circa 1774 and died circa 1826 in Livingston County, Tennessee. She married David Johnson, and they had a daughter named Susan Johnson, according to the will of her grandfather. (128)

5. Phoebe Ann Walton was born circa 1776 and died before 1822 in Cumberland County. She married Thomas Hales Steger, son of John Perratt and Sarah Eppes (Harris) Steger. He was born on April 15, 1772 and died in 1839 in Cumberland County. Thomas and Phoebe had seven children. After her death, Thomas married second Nancy Shores, daughter of Thomas Shores, on Dec. 23, 1822. The name of the Steger estate in Northern Cumberland County was called "Bloomfield."[84] (129)

6. Edward Walton Jr. was born circa 1778 and died about 1840.[85] He first married Janette Carson (McLaurine) Swann, April 4, 1809, in Cumberland County. After her death, he married second Martha (Isbell) Wright. (130)

7. Frances "Fannie" Walton, born circa 1780, may have married Benjamin Steger of Cumberland County who was born in 1768 and

---

[83] Cumberland County *Deed Book 7*, p. 121, dated Oct. 23, 1797, shows that Sarah received slaves from her father, Edward Walton.

[84] William E. Steger and William F. Steger, *Descendants of Thomas Hale Steger*, (Privately Published), 1994. This documented, spiral-bound book contains family group sheets on the early Steger family, plus a good account of the descendants of Thomas H. and Phoebe (Walton) Steger. A copy of the book was furnished to the compiler by William F. Steger, 12717 Gores Mill Road, Reisterstown, MD 21136.

[85] Cumberland County, Virginia *Will Book 10*, pp. 209-21.

died before 1825.[86] Her father willed her five slaves: Thornton, Fanny, Wilson, Peter, and Gabriel.[87] (131)

8. Susannah Walton was born circa 1782 and died about 1824. She married William Agee, ca 1782-1826, Oct. 28, 1805, in Cumberland County. Their daughter Mary Agee received six silver tablespoons and six teaspoons provided in the will of her grandmother Nancy (Murray) Walton.[88] (132)

Robert Walton (27)

Robert Walton, son of Thomas Sr. and Martha (Cox) Walton, was born Sept. 25, 1749 in Cumberland County, and died July 24, 1837, at the home of his daughter Nancy Hobson (Walton) Brown in Powhatan County, Virginia.[89] Robert married Mary Hobson, daughter of William and Elizabeth (Merryman) Hobson, Nov. 20, 1769. Mary was born in 1752 and died in 1789. Robert served as an ensign in the Revolutionary War, and then resettled in Cumberland County. Brown said, "I knew him well and often heard him talk about the service in the Army."[90] Robert built Walton's Meeting House on his own land at his own expense, and entertained ministers of all denominations, according to Brown. Bishop Early lived at Robert Walton's house before he became famous. "He (Robert) was a Methodist who was strict in holding family prayers.

---

[86] Phone conversation with William E. Steger of San Diego, California in Aug. 2002. This relationship is probable but not proven.

[87] Cumberland County, Virginia *Will Book 3*, p. 378, Will of Edward Walton.

[88] Cumberland County, Virginia *Will Book 8*, p. 86, dated July 24, 1824.

[89] A 15-page Letter from Robert's grandson, Edward Smith Brown, dated Aug. 15, 1905, Lynchburg, Virginia, was written to his niece Emma Walton Ivy for application for DAR membership. The letter gave information from Robert Walton's family Bible and verbal information by Brown. He stated that he knew his grandfather well because he lived in the Brown home during his later years and died there. Original letter is in Jones Memorial Library, Kent Gregory (1872-1950), "Genealogical Papers (Walton), MS1288."

[90] *Ibid.*

Robert married second a Mrs. Willborne but they had no children."[91]

Children of Robert and Mary (Hobson) Walton:[92]

1. Elizabeth Walton was born Nov. 27, 1770 and died young. (133)

2. Martha Walton was born Sept. 20, 1772 and died young. (134)

3. Thomas Hobson Walton was born Oct. 31 1774, and died on Jan. 20, 1872, in Prairie County, Arkansas. Thomas H. was thrice-married: (a) Mrs. Elizabeth (Hatcher) Richardson, (b) Susannah Woodson Bates, daughter of Thomas F. and Carolyn M. (Woodson) Bates, and (c) Mrs. Anne (Brackett) Harris, March 3, 1809, in Amelia County. (135)

4. William Walton, born Jan. 9, 1777, moved to East Tennessee and Kentucky. He married Rebecca Ellen Murray on Aug. 21, 1794 in Cumberland County, Virginia.[93] (136)

5. Polly Walton, born June 23, 1779, and died Nov. 26, 1863, in Cumberland County. She married Noton Goodman, Aug. 4, 1796. Noton was born circa 1774 and died on July 7, 1829. (137)

6. Fannie Walton was born April 7, 1782 and died Feb. 2, 1855 in Cumberland County. She married Robert Alexander Flippen, son of Francis and Mary (Hudgens) Flippen. Robert died in 1821 in Cumberland County.[94] (138)

7. Agnes Elizabeth Walton, born Oct. 19, 1784, and died about 1850 in Cumberland County. Agnes E. married William Flippen, son of Philip

---

[91] *Ibid.*

[92] One source of information for the vital data on the children of Robert and Mary (Hobson) Walton is from a 1982 publication by Eunie V. Christian Stacy, 942 Loren Avenue, Natchitoches, Louisiana 71457.

[93] Found in a letter written by Edward S. Brown, maintained by the Jones Memorial Library, Lynchburg, Virginia. The marriage record was filed in the Cumberland County, Virginia Courthouse.

[94] Cumberland County, Virginia *Will Book 6*, p. 322.

and Martha (Cox) Flippen, on Oct. 22, 1804.[95] William was born on Aug. 10, 1781 died in 1866 in Cumberland County.[96] (139)

8. Nancy L. Hobson Walton was born on March 24, 1788 and died April 25, 1880. She married Daniel Brown, 1776-1863, son of James and Mary (Spearman) Brown, in Cumberland County on Nov. 7, 1808. They raised a family at their "Somerset" in Powhatan County. (140)

John Walton Jr. (29)

John Walton Jr., son of John Sr. and Mary (Sims) Walton, was born on April 1, 1738 in Hanover County and died Sept. 23, 1793 in Louisa County, Virginia. He married Mary Baker about 1757 in Louisa County. Mary was born on Dec. 5, 1739 and died in December 1812, probably in Robertson County, Tennessee, where she had gone to live with her son Martin Walton. John served in the Revolutionary War in Capt. James Scott's Company of Virginia Troops. They bought and lived at Glen Beau, a 332-acre farm near U.S. Route 33 on the east side of Cub Creek in Louisa County.[97]

Children of John Jr. and Mary (Baker) Walton:[98]

1. Ann Walton was born May 31, 1758 in Hanover County, Virginia and died after 1836 in Robertson County, Tennessee. She married William Edwards, who was born on March 24, 1751/1752 in Louisa County and died on April 13, 1836 in Robertson County. (141)

2. Joel Walton was born Sept. 30, 1759 and died April 13, 1840. He married Sarah Sims. (142)

3. Martin Walton was born Oct. 1, 1761 in Louisa County and died Nov. 15, 1844 in Robertson County, Tennessee. He married first Elizabeth Johnson on April 10, 1788, and married second Chloe Pool. Martin's mother came to live with him, and died there in 1812. (143)

---

[95] From website http://www.homestead.com/FlippinFamilies/ThirdGen3.html

[96] Cumberland County, Virginia Will *Book 13*, p. 446, dated Feb. 20, 1866.

[97] Claudia Anderson Chisolm and Ellen Gray Lillie, *Old Home Places of Louisa County*, Louisa County Historical Society, Louisa, Virginia.

[98] Information was provided by Ann Bailey of Texas.

4. Temperance Walton was born on April 26, 1764 in Louisa County and died Jan. 21, 1834 in Robertson County, Tennessee. She married Richard Nuckols, son of Charles and Keziah (Yancey) Nuckols, on Nov. 1, 1789 in Louisa County. He was born in February 1762 in Louisa County and died on June 20, 1835 in Robertson County. Richard served in the Revolutionary War. They were Baptists. (144)

5. Frederick Walton was born in Louisa County on Jan. 4, 1766. He did not marry. (145)

6. John Walton III was born Nov. 3, 1767 in Louisa County. He married Nancy Smith on Dec. 13, 1792 in Louisa County. (146)

7. Garland Walton was born on Nov. 8, 1769 and died after 1853. He married Nancy O. Sharp. (147)

8. Frances Walton was born Oct. 30, 1771 in Louisa County. She first married Henry Lipscomb on Dec. 13, 1798 in Louisa County. She married second David Smith. (148)

9. Meredith Walton was born on March 28, 1774 and died Sept. 5, 1855 in Robertson County, Tennessee. He first married Sarah Elizabeth Yates, and married second Ann Sharp. (149)

10. Simeon Walton was born on Aug. 11, 1776 and died Nov. 24, 1836 in Bracken County, Kentucky. He married Elizabeth A. Walton about 1810. (150)

11. Mary Walton was born Sept. 19, 1778 in Louisa County. She married Richard Yancey (1770-1861), son of Robert and Philadelphia (Jones) Yancey, on Jan. 1, 1797 in Louisa County. (151)

12. Nelson Walton was born on Nov. 6, 1780 in Louisa County, and died after 1853. (152)

13. William Walton was born on June 27, 1784 in Louisa County, and died Sept. 8, 1862 in Boone County, Kentucky. He married Barbara Walton, daughter of John and Susanna (Anderson) Walton, on June 14, 1805 in Mason County, Kentucky. (153)

Third Generation
Jesse Walton (30)

Jesse Walton,[99] son of John and Mary (Sims) Walton, was born on Nov. 10, 1739 in Hanover County and died April 30, 1822 in Pittsylvania County, Virginia. He married Ann Pleasant, who was born on May 11, 1749 and died on May 3, 1823 in Pittsylvania County. Jesse served as a Lieutenant in the Revolutionary War. The ancestral home of the Waltons was about six miles north of Danville, Virginia, and was called "Pleasant Gap." The present-day Post Office is Dry Fork, Virginia.[100]

Children of Jesse and Ann (Pleasant) Walton:

1. Pleasant Walton was born on Nov. 9, 1766 and died in 1824 in Lincoln County, Georgia. Pleasant married Milly Covington, daughter of William Covington. (154)

2. Mary Walton was born on Dec. 29, 1768 in Amelia County (now in Nottoway County), Virginia. She married Herbert Crowder on Dec. 12, 1785. (155)

3. Martha "Patsy" Walton was born Sept. 15, 1774 (twin). She married Jesse Grigg, who died in Nottoway County in 1811. (156)

4. Nancy M. Walton was born on Sept. 15, 1774 (twin) and died Jan. 11, 1835. She married a Mr. Tanner, and later married Rawley W. Carter on Nov. 28, 1829. (157)

5. William Walton was born Sept. 18, 1776 and died May 20, 1865. He married first Mrs. Sally Tanner on Jan. 24, 1800 in Pittsylvania County and married second Mary Lanier on Sept. 9, 1832. (158)

6. Jesse Walton Jr. was born July 12, 1787 in Pittsylvania County, Virginia. He married Mary Hutchings, daughter of Moses and Lucy (Parks) Hutchings, July 7, 1808 in Pittsylvania County. Mary was born on July 5, 1788. (159)

---

[99] See Ruth Giles Fischer, *Giles, Walton, and Cox Families*, (Bassett, Virginia: The Bassett Printing Corporation), 1957, for detailed information on Jesse Walton and his descendants.

[100] *Ibid.* p. 2.

The Rev. Simeon Walton (31)

The Reverend Simeon Walton, son of John and Mary (Sims) Walton, was born in Hanover County, Virginia on Sept. 3, 1741, and died on March 27, 1798 in Germantown, Bracken County, Kentucky. He married Agnes Hester who was a daughter of Robert Hester, on Feb. 24, 1763 in Amelia County, Virginia. Agnes was born on March 28, 1746 in Louisa County, Virginia, and died on Nov. 10, 1821. Information on Simeon's family unit was gleaned from his family Bible, which was printed in 1769 by Cambridge University. The Bible was passed down to his son Josiah Walton to John B. Walton of Burlington, Kentucky.[101] The Reverend moved his family to Amelia County in 1765. Their home was located just south of Burkeville in present-day Nottoway County. He served as county surveyor as well as pastor of the Nottoway Baptist Church from 1784-1795. In 1795, Simeon and members of his family were part of a migration of Baptists to Kentucky.

Children of the Rev. Simeon and Agnes (Hester) Walton:

   1. Barbara Walton was born on Dec. 20, 1763, and died in October 1792. Barbara died of childbirth with her fourth child. She married Thomas Harvey, 1760-1844, of Butterwood Creek, Charlotte County, Virginia, on May 24, 1779. After her death, Thomas married second Mary Vawter, daughter of Samuel and Agnes (Richardson) Vawter, in Charlotte County. (160)

   2. John Walton was born on July 17, 1765 and died on March 21, 1840 in Mason County, Kentucky. He married Susanna Anderson on May 30, 1787, in Amelia County, Virginia. She was born on Feb. 16, 1768. (161)

   3. Ann Hester Walton was born on Jan. 17, 1767, and died July 14, 1785. She married Milner Bennett on Dec. 23, 1784. (162)

   4. Simeon Walton, Jr. was born Dec. 31, 1768. He married Jemima Wooten on Dec. 22, 1791. (163)

   5. Agnes Walton was born Jan. 31, 1771. She married William Harvey on April 2, 1789. (164)

---

[101] Information provided to the compiler by Karen Wood of Delaware.

Third Generation

6. Tabitha Walton was born Dec. 10, 1772. She married Samuel Wooten on Dec. 20, 1790. (165)

7. Mary "Polly" Walton was born Nov. 21, 1774. She married James McCoy on Dec. 24, 1793. (166)

8. Nancy Walton was born Feb. 27, 1777. She married William Penick of Nottoway County on Feb. 12, 1795. (167)

9. Elizabeth Walton was born on June 22, 1780. She married Edward Robertson on April 13, 1797. (168)

10. Robert Walton was born on June 19, 1782 and died on April 18, 1852 in Boone County, Kentucky. He married Elizabeth Holton on Dec. 24, 1801. (169)

11. Edward Walton was born on June 15, 1785, and died Aug. 19, 1809. He married Elizabeth Black on Aug. 18, 1803. (170)

12. Josiah Walton was born Sept. 26, 1787, and died Sept. 28, 1830. He married Susan Humlong on Sept. 23, 1813. (171)

13. Susanna Walton was born in Nottoway County, Virginia on May 29, 1790, and died in 1807 in Kentucky. She married Withers Conway on March 6, 1806. (172)

Chapter 4

Fourth Generation

Robert Walton III (42)

Robert Walton III, son of Robert Jr. and Mary (Hughes) Walton, was born circa 1748 in Goochland County, Virginia. His father willed him 680-700 acres of land on the "Stanton River" in Virginia. The will also provided for 400 acres in Albemarle County, Virginia. The codicil added 125 acres in Cumberland County on "Chapple Road."[1] Robert III married Frances Carter, daughter of John Carter of Henrico County, Virginia. Some of these lands were in present-day Counties of Charlotte and Prince Edward, Virginia. He sold his Charlotte County land on June 6, 1767 to John Stewart. Robert moved his family to Burke County, Georgia where he received a head-right grant. and died on July 12, 1797 while on a trip to Savannah, Georgia.[2]

Children of Robert III and Frances (Carter) Walton:[3]

    1. John Carter Walton was born circa 1768 in Charlotte County, Virginia and died during the 1830s. He moved his family to Burke County, Georgia where he was a practicing attorney. (173)

    2. Mary Walton was born circa 1770 in Charlotte County, Virginia. (174)

    3. Elizabeth Walton, born circa 1772, married her cousin Robert Watkins, son of Thomas and Sally (Walton) Watkins.[4] (175)

    4. Robert Walton IV was born circa 1775. (176)

    5. William Walton moved to Wilkes County, Georgia. (177)

---

[1] *Ibid.* p. 15

[2] National Genealogy Society Quarterly, "Some Waltons of Georgia," by William H. Dumont, Vol. 57, pp. 13-15.

[3] Ida Bowman Younger (1903-1993), "Genealogy Papers (Walton), MS 2098," Jones Memorial Library, Lynchburg, Virginia.

[4] June Cottrell sent information to the compiler on Oct. 20, 1998. She cited Essie Martin, *Waltons American Patriots*, Bronson, Texas, Copy 28 at the Genealogical Library, Raleigh, North Carolina.

George Walton the Signer (43)

George Walton, son of Robert Jr. and Mary (Hughes) Walton, was born in December 1749 in Cumberland County, Virginia and died on Feb. 2, 1804 in Augusta, Georgia. He was one of the Signers of the Declaration of Independence. Almost every branch of Waltons has tried to claim him as a descendant or relative. More than one genealogical researcher has confused him with George Walton (son of John) of Brunswick County, Virginia, who died in 1804, the same year as the George the Signer. Writers and researchers have given a range of birth years between 1740 and 1749. Had they studied the voluminous records in *Will Book I* in Cumberland County, Virginia,[5] they would not have erred on his date and place of birth. One group claims that George was born in Winchester, Virginia, which would make him a descendant of the "Byberry Waltons," the Quakers who came to William Penn's Colony during the 1680s. This, too, is an error with no documentation.[6] Perhaps Bradshaw[7] presented the best discussion of the fallacies and myths regarding the time and place of birth of George the Signer.

George's father's will in Cumberland County referred to his unborn son as "the child my wife now goes with." The orphan's account shows that George was well-clothed, and had a Bible and books to read as well as private instruction. For example, in 1758, a Mr. Martin was paid one pound of currency for one year of schooling.[8] John Hughes was named as the guardian for George Walton in September 1760. Hughes kept the slaves that were to be equally divided between George and Sally Walton by their father's

---

[5] See p. 21 in this book, which gives references in Cumberland County, Virginia *Will Book 1*.

[6] See John W. Wayland, *A History of Shenandoah County, Virginia*, (Strasburg, Virginia: Shenandoah Publishing House, Inc.), 1969, pp. 570-571 and 657-658.

[7] Herbert Clarence Bradshaw, *History of Prince Edward County, Virginia*, (Richmond, Virginia: The Dietz Press), 1955, pp. 823-824.

[8] *Ibid.* pp. 389-390.

will.⁹ George served an apprenticeship under Christopher Ford, commencing on Aug. 19, 1765.¹⁰ His namesake, Uncle George Walton, oversaw his education and welfare until 1769, when he moved to Georgia to practice law. This George of Robert Walton became a close friend of Patrick Henry, who was also the family's attorney.

George Walton married Dorothy Camber in 1775. Dorothy died in Tallahassee, Florida in the home of her second son, Col. George Walton, Jr., Sept. 12, 1832.¹¹ At the age of thirty, George Walton the elder became the first governor of Georgia, serving in 1779-1780. He also held the distinction of being a Signer of the Declaration of Independence, and the first U. S. Senator elected in Georgia, in 1795. Walton County, Georgia was named for him. There are no living descendants of George and Dorothy, the last one being George Walton Reab, 1872-1925, of Richmond County, Georgia.

Children of George and Dorothy (Camber) Walton:

> 1. Thomas Camber Walton was born in 1776 and died on Oct. 3, 1804. He did not marry. (178)

> 2. George Walton Jr. was born on Aug. 15, 1786 in Augusta, Richmond County, Georgia and died on Dec. 20, 1859, in Petersburg, Virginia. He married Sarah Minge Walker on Jan. 10, 1809 in Richmond County, Georgia. (179)

---

⁹ *Ibid.* pp. 395.

¹⁰ Prince Edward County, Virginia Deed *Book 3, 1765-1771*, pp. 15-16.

¹¹ *Macon Telegraph* (Georgia), Vol. 7, No. 3, Oct. 17, 1832 issue.

Fourth Generation

Frances (Walton) Atkinson (72)

Frances Walton,[12] daughter of Sherwood and Susanna (Jouett) Walton, was born circa 1756 in Virginia and died circa 1786 in Kentucky. She married Joshua Atkinson, son of Thomas Atkinson, on Aug. 5, 1777 in Amelia County, Virginia.[13] Joshua was born in 1755 in Amelia County and died circa 1837 in Adair County, Kentucky. Joshua served in the Revolutionary War under Capt. Edward Booker of Amelia County and others. He filed for a Revolutionary War pension through a deposition made on March 11, 1833 in the Circuit Court of Adair County, Kentucky. After the death of Frances, he married second Frances Haskins on Feb. 22, 1790 in Chesterfield County, Virginia.

Children of Joshua and Frances (Walton) Atkinson:[14]

1. Thomas Walton Atkinson was born circa in 1778 in Amelia County, Virginia and died in 1862 in Montgomery County, Tennessee. He married Elizabeth Hundley who died in 1809. He married second Betsy Carlyle on Nov. 8, 1810 in Green County, Kentucky. Thomas was an attorney and tobacco merchant. (180)

2. Sherwood Walton Atkinson was born circa 1782 in Amelia County and died on Oct. 3, 1857 in Russellville, Logan County, Kentucky.[15] He moved with his father to Adair County, Kentucky, and about 1815, he moved to Logan County. He married first Catherine M. Cates and married second Mrs. Maria L. (Williams) Grant Gatewood, daughter of General Samuel L. Williams, Oct. 26, 1847. Sherwood had no children

---

[12] Green County, Kentucky, *Deed Book 7*, p. 410. This document appointed Peter Rison, a power-of-attorney in Amelia County, Virginia, to sell the Negroes that were mentioned in the will of Sherwood Walton. Information was provided by Rhoda Fone, 999 Bridgeport Way, Rio Vista, CA 94571.

[13] Marriage record was found in an account book of Thomas Atkinson, father of Joshua Atkinson. See Library of Virginia, Archives and Manuscripts, Accession No. 32706.

[14] Information on the Atkinson children was provided by Rhoda Fone RhodaFone@aol.com on March 26, 2002.

[15] His will is located in Logan County, Kentucky, *Will Book 1*, pp. 33-34, dated May 27, 1857 and probated Oct. 26, 1857.

of his own but adopted Kate Woolridge and three children of his second wife. Sherwood was a well-to-do merchant. (181)

3. Elizabeth "Betsy" Ann Atkinson was born on April 24, 1784, probably in Amelia County, and died on March 31, 1853 in Todd County, Kentucky. She married Joseph Watkins about 1809 in Green County, Kentucky. They later settled in Todd County, Kentucky. He was born on March 3, 1773 and died on Dec. 8, 1833. (182)

Tilman Walton (77)

Tilman[16] Walton, son of William Jr. and Elizabeth (Tilman) Walton, was born on Jan. 9, 1760, probably in Albemarle County (now Amherst), Virginia, and died Feb. 3, 1831, in Burke County, North Carolina. He married his first cousin, Judith Walton, daughter of Edward and Nancy (Murray) Walton, on April 12, 1787, in Cumberland County, Virginia. Judith was born in Cumberland County, Virginia on Feb. 19, 1770, and died on Aug. 31, 1846. Tilman served three years, 1776-1779, in the Virginia Continental Line during the Revolutionary War, and was discharged by Nathaniel Gist in Morristown, New Jersey.[17] He later served two more years as a Lieutenant and Captain in the Virginia State Troupes with his brother, William Walton III, and was present when Cornwallis surrendered at Yorktown. He moved to Burke County in 1791[18] with his father and brother, where he received two 100-acre land grants on the north side of the Catawba River. Tilman applied for and received a Revolutionary War pension in 1821. Although

---

[16] The name has been spelled variously as Tilman, Tillman, and Tilghman. For consistency, the name is spelled Tilman.

[17] Lenora Higginbotham Sweeny, *Amherst County, Virginia in the Revolution*, (Baltimore, Maryland: Clearfield Company), reprinted 1998, p. 178.

[18] The 1791 date may be in error, as Tilman Walton was appointed Captain of Light Infantry, 28th Battalion, Amherst County Militia, on April 22, 1794 by Lt. Governor James Wood Jr. See Virginia Historical Society, Richmond, Virginia, Mss4 V8 a 34.

only sixty-one years old, he stated that he was old and infirm and not able to carry on his trades as carpenter and millwright.[19]

Children of Tilman and Judith (Walton) Walton:[20]

1. Nancy Murray Walton was born on Feb. 28, 1788. She married Rev. James T. Askew on March 5, 1803 in Burke County, North Carolina. (183)

2. Elizabeth Tilman Walton was born on Feb. 15, 1790. (184)

3. William Orrell Walton was born on July 28, 1792. He may have been the William Walton, age 54, carpenter, who was living with his brother on the 1850 U. S. Census for McDowell County, North Carolina.[21] (185)

4. Judith Cox Walton was born on June 22, 1795.[22] (186)

5. Edward Marshall Walton was born on March 10, 1798. (187)

6. Thomas Madison Walton was born on Aug. 7, 1800 and died on Sept. 21, 1801. (188)

7. Josias Wesley Walton was born June 2, 1803 and died July 18, 1808. (189)

8. George Sidney Walton was born Dec. 12, 1805 and died on Aug. 19, 1886 in McDowell County, North Carolina. He was on the commission that laid out the lots for the County seat at Marion, and he served as a Magistrate. George's wife was Sarah Higgins (190)

9. Jesse Tilman Walton Sr. was born in 1809 and died circa 1853. He married Elmina H. Spencer on Jan. 25, 1830. The family made their home in McDowell County, North Carolina. Children listed on the 1850 U. S. Census were: Tisdale Walton, Elizabeth T. Walton, Elmina Walton, Jesse T. Walton Jr., Mary L. Walton, Alfred F. Walton, James M. Walton and Henry Walton. (191)

---

[19] U. S. National Archives, Washington, D. C., Pension Papers, Number W4373

[20] Higginbotham, p. 178.

[21] 1850 U. S. Census for McDowell County, North Carolina, p. 302.

[22] One Jane Cox Walton married Roland Duncan in Burke County on Nov. 3, 1813.

William Walton III (80)

William Walton III,[23] son of William Jr. and Elizabeth (Tilman) Walton, was born in Amherst County, Virginia on Jan. 12, 1767 and died on May 18, 1844 in Greene County, Alabama.[24] He married first Jennie McEntire and married second Justine Louisa (Smith) Gennerick on Feb. 3, 1807. She was born in 1790 and died in 1868.[25] Before he was old enough to serve as a soldier in the Revolutionary War, he carried grain to the mill for flour to be used by the army. In May 1780, he went with his father into the military service under the command of General Gates and was at the battle of Camden. They both participated in the Battle of King's Mountain on Oct. 7, 1780. In March 1781, he volunteered in Captain Cabell's Company of Virginia Troops, and returned home in 1782.[26] He lived in Charleston, South Carolina from 1800 to 1815 where he engaged in trading slaves. He moved to Mississippi Territory in 1815, and later to Greene County, Alabama, where he died.[27] He was at one time a member of the Legislature of Alabama Territory.[28]

Children of William and Justine Louisa (Smith) Gennerick Walton III:[29]

1. Amelia Tilman Walton was born circa 1807 and died in 1855. She married Williamson Allen Glover. (192)

---

[23] See Lenora Higginbotham Sweeny, *Amherst County, Virginia in the Revolution*, (Baltimore, Maryland: Clearfield Company), reprinted 1998, pp. 178-179, for an account of his military experiences.

[24] Emmett R. White, *Revolutionary War Soldiers of Western North Carolina: Burke County*, pp 302-303.

[25] *Ibid.* p. 302.

[26] *Ibid.* p. 301.

[27] *Ibid.* p. 302

[28] The National Archives, Pension Papers, Number 17184

[29] *Ibid.* p. 302

2. Louisa W. Walton was born in 1823 and died in 1879. She married Samuel L. Creswell. (193)

Thomas Walton (87)

Thomas Walton,[30] son of William and Elizabeth (Tilman) Walton Jr, was born on Aug. 1, 1782 in Amherst County, Virginia and died on July 27, 1850 in Burke County, North Carolina. Burial was in the First Presbyterian Church Cemetery in Morganton. He married Martha Matilda McEntire, daughter of James and Nancy (Young) McEntire, circa 1803. She was born circa 1783 in Tyrone County, Ireland and died on Sept. 23, 1868 at Morganton. Thomas moved with his family to Charleston, South Carolina before 1790 and then to Morganton, North Carolina in 1795, where he opened a store with his brother William III. He served as a justice of the Burke County Court of Pleas and Quarter Sessions in 1809. In short, he was a postmaster, merchant, civic leader and plantation owner.

Children of Thomas and Martha M. (McEntire) Walton:

1. James Willie Young Walton was born on Sept. 22, 1805 and died on July 26, 1842. (194)

2. John Alfred Walton was born in 1807 and died on Aug. 25, 1830. (195)

3. Jane Clarissa Walton was born in 1809 and died in May 1837. She married James W. Patton of Asheville, North Carolina on Jan. 24, 1828. Thomas Walton was the bondsman. (196)

4. Louisa Ann Walton was born in 1811 and died on Oct. 28, 1844. She married Thomas T. Patton of Buncombe County, North Carolina. (197)

5. Martha Matilda Walton was born on Oct. 13, 1814 and died on May 12, 1850. She married William Crawford Erwin, 1809-1876, of Burke County. (198)

---

[30] Information on Thomas Walton's family unit was gleaned from *The Heritage of Burke County 1981*, published by The Burke County Historical Society, P.O. Box 151, Morganton, North Caroline 28655. Credit is given to Joseph Moore Walton, whose name appears on the articles on the Walton family. Thanks to Patricia P. Morrow of Houston, Texas for supplying these sources.

6. Thomas George Walton was born on Oct. 5, 1815 and died on June 15, 1905 at Morganton, Burke County, North Carolina. He married Margaret Eliza Avery Murphy on Dec. 28, 1837. (199)

7. William McEntire Walton was born on Dec. 3, 1819 and died March 3, 1900. He married Harriet Louisa Murphy on Dec. 31, 1845. He was a planter and a one-time manager of the Walton Hotel. Their children were raised on the Brookfield Plantation in Burke County. (200)

8. Elizabeth Tilghman Walton was born on Jan. 3, 1823 and died on Oct. 15, 1882. He married Clark Moulton Avery of Burke County, June 23, 1841. Clark was born on Oct. 23, 1819 and died on June 18, 1864. (201)

Thomas George Walton (107)

Thomas George Walton, son of George and Margaret (Tabb) Walton, was born circa 1765 in Cumberland County, Virginia and died in 1825 in Smith County, Tennessee, where he had migrated during the late 1790s.[31] Thomas G. married Agnes Mosby, daughter of Edward and Martha "Patty" (Walton) Mosby, his first cousin. One of their children was named Lockey Walton, named for her great-grandmother Lockey (Langhorne) Tabb.

Children of Thomas G. and Agnes (Mosby) Walton:

1. Edward Mosby Walton, born circa 1790, married Agnes Turner. (202)

2. Phoebe C. Walton, born circa 1793, married William H. Armistead. He was born circa 1781 in Cumberland County, Virginia and died about 1860 in Franklin County, Missouri. (203)

3. Mary "Polly" Walton, born circa 1794, married Edward Glover. He was the administrator for the estate of his father-in-law. (204)

---

[31] Information provided to compiler by Sharlee Winn (MSWINN@aol.com) via e-mail on Feb. 21, 2000.

4. Martha M. Walton was born circa 1796 and died in 1849. She married Seth Burton, 1787-1860.[32] (205)

5. Nancy F. Walton, born circa 1798, married William N. Nichols. They settled in Marion County, Illinois. (206)

6. Lockey Walton, born circa 1800, married Edward Bradley. (207)

7. George H. Walton was born on Jan. 20, 1801 in Virginia and died July 26, 1852 in Marion County, Illinois. He married Mary Ann Terry.[33] George was a farmer. (208)

8. Narcissus Walton, born circa 1802, married Francis Binnion, son of Martin Binnion, in Smith County, Tennessee, in 1823. She died in 1847.[34] (209)

Minjum H. Walton Sr. (111)

Minjum H. Walton,[35] son of George and Margaret (Tabb) Walton, was born circa 1779 in Cumberland County, Virginia and died circa 1839 in Cumberland County.[36] Minjum married Sally F. Mann, daughter of William Ford and Elizabeth Booth (Woodson) Mann, on Feb. 5, 1806 in Cumberland County. The Manns were next door neighbors in Cumberland County. The name Minjum may have been a variation of Benjamin, but was written unmistakably as Minjum in public records. On April 4, 1827, he bought 72 and ¼ acres from Jesse Parker.[37] In 1831, he sold 85 acres of land to his oldest son, Jesse W. Walton.[38]

---

[32] Information from John Mueller (Mueller@ucalgary.ca) on March 3, 2004.

[33] http://www.williamshomes.net/tree/familytree/tree/d278.htm

[34] http://www.rootsweb.com/~tnsmith/tngen/smith97-2.htm

[35] See Ancestral File Number 14PX-CLX at the LDS Library in Salt Lake City.

[36] Death date was estimated from the Library of Virginia, "Personal Property Tax Lists for Cumberland County, Virginia, 1817-1844," Microfilm Rolls 74 and 75.

[37] Cumberland County, Virginia *Deed Book 18*, p. 387.

[38] Cumberland County, Virginia *Deed Book 20*, p. 199.

Children of Minjum H. and Sally F. (Mann) Walton:

1. Jesse W. Walton was born in 1807 in Cumberland County and died on Jan. 25, 1890 in Goochland County, Virginia. He married Elizabeth Emeline Cheatham, daughter of Isham and Hannah (Spears) Cheatham, on Dec. 15, 1834 in Goochland County. She was born on Oct. 4, 1812 and died in Goochland County on April 12, 1848. (210)

2. William Mann Walton was born in 1809 in Cumberland County and died on Feb. 8, 1883. He married first Margaret Ann Gills on Dec. 1, 1853 in Henrico County, Virginia. He married second Margaret Ann Seay, daughter of Matthew and Eliza (Layne) Seay, on Dec. 24, 1860 in Goochland County, Virginia. (211)

3. John T. Walton was born on March 28, 1811 in Cumberland County, Virginia and died on July 21, 1892 at Greensboro, Alabama. He married first Jane D. Hudgins on March 23, 1840 in Cumberland County, Virginia. He married second Sarah Frances Gills, daughter of Pleasant and Nancy (Fowlkes) Gills of Amelia County, Virginia. (212)

4. Elizabeth Walton was born circa 1812 in Cumberland County and died circa 1847. She married Jesse Daniel Parker, son of Jesse and Sarah (Guthrey) Parker, on March 8, 1840. He was born in Cumberland County in 1809 and died on April 26, 1877. After Elizabeth's death, Jesse married second Mary Jane Gills, daughter of Pleasant and Nancy (Fowlkes) Gills. (213)

5. Joseph M. Walton was born on Feb. 5, 1814 in Cumberland County and died on Oct. 19, 1888 at Greensboro, Hale County, Alabama. He married Lucy Gills, daughter of Pleasant and Nancy (Fowlkes) Gills. Lucy was born on May 1, 1818 in Virginia and died on Sept. 12, 1882 in Hale County. (214)

6. Minjum H. Walton Jr. was born circa 1821 in Cumberland County and died after 1880, probably in Powhatan County. He married Judith Palmore, daughter of Robert and Elizabeth (Bagby) Palmore, on April 13, 1848 in Buckingham County, Virginia. Judith was born in 1823.[39] (215)

---

[39] 1880 U. S. Census for Powhatan County, Virginia, Macon District, p. 181A, Family 194.

Martha (Walton) Christian (112)

Martha Walton, daughter of Thomas Jr. and Phoebe (Murray) Walton, was born on Dec. 2, 1766 in Cumberland County, and died on Aug. 8, 1847 in Davie County, North Carolina.[40] She married Walter Christian Sr., son of Charles and Mary (Leake) Christian, on July 31, 1783 in Cumberland County, Virginia. Walter was born on Sept. 23, 1760 in Goochland County, and died in August 1829 in Amherst County, Virginia. Martha drew a widow's pension based on her husband's service as a sergeant in the Virginia Continental Army during the Revolutionary War. Walter made a bond as a Methodist minister on July 17, 1797, with bondsmen John Christian and William Breedlove. This gave him the legal authority to officiate marriages. He officiated the marriage of his brother-in-law, Robert Walton who married Elizabeth Wilson on April 23, 1816 in Amherst County. Residence: Amherst, Virginia.

Children of Walter Sr. and Martha (Walton) Christian:[41]

1. Martha Christian was born ca 1784 and died after 1834. She married William Dempsey. They are listed on the 1820 U. S. Census for Amherst County, on page twenty-four. (216)

2. Robert W. Christian was born ca 1788 and died ca 1828 in Amherst County.[42] He married Courtney Landrum on Nov. 4, 1822 in Amherst County. (217)

3. Wesley E. Christian was born ca 1790 and died on Jan. 28, 1851 in Saline County, Illinois. He served in the War of 1812. Wesley married first Lucy Pendleton, daughter of Richard Pendleton, on July 30, 1821 in Amherst County. Lucy died in 1832. Wesley married second Evelina

---

[40] Alycon Trubey-Pierce (abstractor), *Selected Final Pension Payment Vouchers, 1818-1864*, (Athens, Georgia: Iberian Publishing Company), Vol. 1, pp. 106-107. Joel Lyon was named the administrator of her estate. See also Amherst County, Virginia, *Will Book 12*, p. 285, Administrator's account from April 1849 to Sept. 17, 1849.

[41] Information on this family unit was obtained from Eunie V. Christian Stacy, *Christian of Charles City*, (Shreveport, Louisiana: Insty-Prints), 1982, pp. 130-132.

[42] Amherst County, Virginia *Will Book 7*, p. 152. See *Will Book 9*, p. 62 for guardian's bond.

Christian, daughter of Elijah L. and Sally H. (Martin) Christian, on Sept. 12, 1836 in Amherst County. Wesley married third Mahala Gibson, widow of William B. Gibson, on April 12, 1847 at Nashville, Washington County, Illinois. (218)

4. Sarah Christian was born ca 1792, probably in Amherst County. She married James Potterwith on May 20, 1817 in Amherst County. (219)

5. William Lafayette Christian was born ca 1797 and died after 1850. He was living in Davies County, Kentucky in 1830; Knox County, Tennessee in 1840; and Perry County, Illinois in 1850. (220)

6. Walter Leake Christian Jr. was born ca 1806 and died after 1850. (221)

7. Thomas C. Christian was born ca 1808 and died after 1850. He married Mary Ann Thaxton on Jan. 27, 1831 in Bedford County, Virginia. They were living in Montgomery County, Virginia when the 1850 U.S. Census was taken. (222)

8. Emily M. Christian was born ca 1810 and died after 1850. She married James Grisham Christian, son of John Christian, on March 18, 1830 in Amherst County. (223)

9. Elizabeth Ann Murray Christian was born in 1812 in Amherst County and died after 1850. She married Nicholas P. Taylor on Dec. 21, 1829 in Amherst County. (224)

Anthony Walton Sr. (113)

Anthony Walton Sr., son of Thomas Jr. and Phoebe (Murray) Walton, was born circa 1769 in Cumberland County, Virginia, and died at Bent Creek, Buckingham County, now Appomattox County, circa 1819.[43] He was the first member of his immediate family to settle at Bent Creek, purchasing 360 acres in 1796. Anthony married Rebecca Johnson, daughter of Daniel and Hannah (Edwards) Johnson.[44] Anthony sold his share of his father's estate to his half-

---

[43] Evidence is found in land tax records of Buckingham County, Virginia housed in the Library of Virginia. Also, the personal property tax records show "Anthony Walton estate," which indicates a death year of 1819.

[44] See Cumberland County, Virginia *Will Book 3*, p. 72.

Fourth Generation

brother, William Walton. The 1810 census for Buckingham County, Virginia shows four male and four female children in the household of Anthony Walton. We have no private record of these children's names. The land tax records for Buckingham County in 1825-1827 show five sons and two daughters involved in the distribution of land. In 1825, the real estate of Anthony Walton Sr. was divided among Anthony Walton Jr., Edward Walton, Robert Walton, William Thornhill, and Henry Trent. By 1829 most of this land had been sold to William Walton, 1782-1851, half-brother of Anthony Walton Sr., indicating that those children had left the County.

Children of Anthony Sr. and Rebecca (Johnson) Walton:[45]

1. Phoebe Walton was born circa 1789. She married Henry Trent, 1784-1845, son of Thomas and Elizabeth (Edwards) Trent.[46] Henry bought 125 acres in 1816 from his father and sold it to his brother Thomas in 1819. That land was located along the Appomattox River in Buckingham County. In 1825, Henry bought 118½ acres from his father in Bent Creek, Buckingham County and sold that land the following year to his brother-in-law, Robert Walton.[47] Henry and Phoebe Trent moved to Chariton County, Missouri. (225)

---

[45] Names of children were constructed from public records, such as Buckingham County, Virginia land tax, personal property tax, census, and other. The list may not be in chronological order.

[46] Information from James Quinn via e-mail <rsajq@erols.com> on May 21, 2001. Thomas Trent, a disabled Revolutionary War veteran, was born on Feb. 6, 1757 and died at Bent Creek, Virginia on June 28, 1820. He married Elizabeth Edwards on Oct. 3, 1783 in Chesterfield County, Virginia. Elizabeth was born on Feb. 18, 1757 in Chesterfield County and died on Aug. 18, 1830 in Buckingham County, Virginia. Their children were: Henry Trent married Phoebe Walton; Thomas Trent Jr. married Martha D. Holland; Mary Elizabeth Trent married Elliott R. Thomas; William Trent married Elizabeth Webb; Elizabeth Trent married a Mr. Webb; Alexander Trent (1797-1851) married Mary Hicks; and Nancy Patteson Trent married Thomas Cook Walton.

[47] Roger G. Ward, compiler, *Buckingham County, Virginia: Land Tax Summaries & Implied Deeds, 1815-1840*, (Athens, Georgia: Iberian Publishing Company), vol 2, p. 363.

2. Edward Walton married Nancy Hansford on April 22, 1819 in Amherst County, Virginia by the Rev. Pleasant Thurman. Edward owned 289 ½ acres on Bent Creek from Anthony Sr.'s estate. He sold this land in 1828 to his half-uncle, William Walton, possibly to pay off debts. Edward was a frequent purchaser of whiskey from the Walton & Phelps Mercantile store at Bent Creek. He bought a gallon of whiskey on Feb. 3, 1828; ten pints of whiskey on March 28; and three quarts of whiskey in September; and borrowed $3.50 on Sept. 9 "to pay Mrs. Johnson."[48] In 1829, he and Anthony Walton sold all their interest in their grandfather Thomas Walton's—died in 1815— estate to William Walton. (226)

3. Robert J. Walton was born circa 1794, probably in Buckingham County, Virginia, and died after 1860. He married Elizabeth ___ of Campbell County, Virginia. (227)

4. Thomas Cook Walton was born on Nov. 18, 1795, and died on March 20, 1842 in Chariton County, Missouri. He married. Nancy Patteson Trent, daughter of Thomas and Elizabeth (Edwards) Trent, on Dec. 13, 1817 in Buckingham County, Virginia. Thomas appeared on the personal property tax list for Buckingham County in 1818 (228)

5. Lucy Walton married William Thornhill, son of Jesse and Elizabeth (Stevens) Thornhill,[49] on June 8, 1820[50] as his first wife. William was born on Apr. 4, 1796 and died on May 12, 1857. Lucy's lot from Anthony Walton's estate was 237 acres, which was sold in two parcels to her brother Robert Walton in 1825 and 1826. After Lucy's death, William Thornhill married Jeanette Steger, 1812-1900, daughter of William Steger. (229)

6. Henry Walton, in 1825, bought 118 ½ acres from the Bent Creek estate of Anthony Walton Sr. He resold the land in 1826 to Robert

---

[48] Library of Virginia, Buckingham County Records, Walton & Phelps Account Book, 1828, pp. 7-8.

[49] Nathaniel Ragland Featherstone, *The History of Appomattox, Virginia*, (Marceline, Missouri: Walsworth Brothers, Printers), 1948, p. 269

[50] *Lynchburg Press and Public Advertiser*, June 13, 1820, p. 3, c. 5.

Walton. Henry disappeared from local records and may have emigrated. (230)

7. Anthony Walton Jr. was born circa 1800 and died after 1850 in Appomattox County. He married Martha A. Daniel of Powhatan County, Virginia. (231)

Robert Walton (114)

Robert Walton, son of Thomas Jr. and Phoebe (Murray) Walton, was born circa 1772 in Cumberland County and died circa 1822 in Amherst County, Virginia.[51] Burial was in the Wilson family cemetery, formerly known as the "Wilmer Place," now owned by R. L. Bowler. Robert's tombstone states his age at "about 50 years," and his father's name as Thomas Walton.[52] Robert first married Mildred "Millie" Armistead, daughter of William and Frances (Anderson) Armistead, Nov. 28, 1795, in Cumberland County, Virginia. The date and place of death for Mildred is not known, but she was alive in November 1804 when she and Robert sold a tract of land in Cumberland County to William Armistead. She was deceased before 1822,[53] and before 1816 when Robert remarried. Mildred's children received an inheritance from their grandfather, William A. Armistead of Cumberland County, while the children of her sister, Nancy (Armistead) Walton were disinherited by receiving each "$1 and no more." After Mildred's death, Robert married second Elizabeth Wilson, daughter of Robert Wilson,[54] on June 29, 1816 in Amherst County, Virginia.[55] Elizabeth

---

[51] *Gravestone Inscriptions in Amherst County, Virginia*, compiled by Amherst County Museum and Historical Society, 1999, pp. 296-297 give a death year as 1823. See also Amherst County *Will Book A*, p. 56, where his brother-in-law, Walter Christian, gave bond on April 21, 1822 as administrator for Robert Walton.

[52] *Ibid.* p. 296-297. Buried in the same graveyard is Robert B. Walton, born Feb. 7, 1820 in Amherst County, and died March 29, 1859 in St. Louis, Missouri.

[53] The Virginia Genealogist, Vol. 12, No. 3, July-September, 1968.

[54] Some of Elizabeth Wilson's siblings were: sister Catherine married John W. Tyler, brother Reuben Walker Wilson, and brother Capt. John P. Wilson (died in 1865) who represented Campbell County in the Virginia Assembly in 1824-1825.

[55] See Amherst County, Virginia marriage records in the courthouse

was born on Jan. 9, 1792 and died in Amherst County at the home of her brother-in-law, John Tyler, on June 16, 1845.[56]

Children of Robert and Mildred (Armistead) Walton:[57]

    1. William Walton was given one Negro slave named Absolem. William signed the probate for his grandfather, William Armistead.[58] Further research has not been able to locate this William. (232)

    2. Thomas Walton was given a Negro slave named Randolph. (233)

    3. John Anderson Walton was born circa 1798 in Cumberland County and died in 1849 in Obion County, Tennessee.[59] He married first Ann Crank, daughter of Lipscomb and Polly (Parish) Crank. After her death in 1835, he married second Martha (Scott) Talley, widow of Joshua Talley, circa 1838.[60] (234)

    4. Phoebe Walton, born circa 1799, married John Shrader in Amherst County on Jan. 28, 1824. Phoebe received only $1 from the estate of her grandfather, William Armistead. She was the only child who was cut from his will.[61] John Shrader was listed on the 1840 U. S. Census for Amherst County, showing one male between the ages of 30-40 and a female between the ages of 40-50, along with six young children.[62] The 1870 U. S. Census for Amherst County shows one John Shrader,

---

[56] *The Lynchburg Virginian*, June 23, 1845, p. 3, column 3, printed this obit: "Died in the County of Amherst at the residence of John Tyler on the 16th instant after an illness of four weeks, Mrs. Elizabeth Walton aged 53 years, 5 months, 10 days. Mrs. Walton has left behind two sons to mourn her loss."

[57] Children are named in the order that they appeared in the will of William Armistead.

[58] Cumberland County, Virginia *Will Book 7*, p. 234.

[59] Contributed by Gene Talley GTa1056569@aol.com of Bartlett, Tennessee, in an email to the compiler dated Aug. 5, 2002.

[60] http://genforum.genealogy.com/cgi-bin/pageload.cgi?Obion::scott::9836.html

[61] Cumberland County, Virginia *Will Book 7*, pp. 230-234

[62] 1840 U. S. Census for Amherst County, Virginia

age sixty seven, a miller, with a housekeeper Catherine Coleman, aged forty two years. (235)

5. Anthony Anderson Walton was born circa 1804, and died on Sept. 1, 1866 in Buckingham County. He married first Mary Austin on April 18, 1829, in Cumberland County. Anthony A. was a merchant in Cumberland at that time.[63] He married second Sarah J. McDaniel, daughter of Abraham Daniel, in Cumberland County on Oct. 15, 1840. Sarah died Feb. 26, 1847 in her 37th year.[64] Anthony A. married third Margaret (Nixon) Hobart, daughter of William and Wilmuth (Danrig) Nixon, in Buckingham County, on Jan. 29, 1850.[65] Margaret's first husband was a mining engineer from a northern state. They moved to St. Louis where he died. Margaret returned to Buckingham County where she married Anthony A. Walton.[66] (236)

6. Frances Walton was born circa 1806. She married Fleming Palmore Jr. in Cumberland County on Aug. 25, 1824. (237)

7. Mildred "Millie" Ann Walton was born circa 1812. She married William D. Austin in 1834.[67] Children living in her household on the 1850 census were: (a) Virginia Austin, born in 1835, (b).Willie Anne Austin, born in 1837, (c) William C. Austin, born in 1839, (d) Mildred Austin, born in 1842, and (e) Robert Austin, born in 1845. Mildred was living in Cumberland County when the 1870 census was taken, and believed to have been living in Lynchburg as late as 1879 when she was mentioned in the will of a nephew, Robert W. Walton. (238)

Children of Robert and Elizabeth (Wilson) Walton:

---

[63] Cumberland County, Virginia *Circuit Court Orders*, 1831-1851, p. 38.

[64] *Richmond Whig*, March 26, 1847, p.2, c. 6.

[65] *Richmond Whig and Public Advertiser*, Jan. 29, 1850, p.2, c. 2.

[66] Stuart Nixon, owner of the Hearthstone Bookshop in Alexandria, Virginia, believes that Margaret and Anthony met each other through her brother, George Washington Nixon through their common membership in the same Masonic Lodge in Buckingham County, Virginia. Stuart provided much of the information on the Walton-Nixon relationships.

[67] Email from Charlotte Art, cnt@mtco.com, on Feb. 20, 2005 stated that William D. Austin died in 1848 in Cumberland County, Virginia..

8. Richard Walker Walton was born circa 1818[67] and died unmarried in December 1891[68] at his farm in Amherst County. His will was written in Amherst County in August 1879[69] and probated in July 1892. Richard's obit stated that he retired from his business in Lynchburg about ten years ago to run his farm and mill in Amherst County. He moved to Lynchburg in early life to work as a salesman and later became a very prominent dry goods merchant in the city. The U. S. Census for Lynchburg and Campbell County stated that his inventory was worth $15,000. Richard, known by his initials R. W., left no descendants. (239)

9. Robert B. Walton was born in Amherst County on Feb. 7, 1820 and died on March 3, 1859 in St. Louis, Missouri.[70] His body was brought back to Amherst County where he was buried in the Wilson Cemetery. (240)

Elizabeth (Walton) Frayser (114)

Elizabeth Walton, daughter of Thomas Jr. and Phoebe (Murray) Walton, was born circa 1775 in Cumberland County, Virginia and died on Aug. 28, 1837 in Cumberland County.[71] She married first William Walton on March 24, 1794. Her father, Thomas Walton Jr., gave his consent. Nothing more is known about this marriage. Elizabeth married second Robert Frayser of Cumberland County.[72] Robert died in 1828 in Cumberland County.[73]

---

[67] 1870 U.S. Census for Campbell County, Virginia lists his age as fifty-two years. He was living with his uncle Reuben Walker Wilson.

[68] *The Lynchburg Virginian*, Dec. 22, 1891, p. 1. c. 2.

[69] See Amherst County *Will Book 22*, p. 68.

[70] Tombstone inscriptions in the Wilson Cemetery in Amherst County, Virginia. *The Richmond Whig and Public Advertiser*, April 6, 1858, p. 1, c.5, gives a death date of March 29, 1858.

[71] *Richmond Whig and Public Advertiser*, Sept. 12, 1837, p. 4, c.6.

[72] Letter dated Oct. 18, 1911, from a niece, Marietta Virginia (Steger) Scruggs, resident in a nursing home on Grove Avenue in Richmond, maintained by the Jones

Fourth Generation

Children of Robert and Elizabeth (Walton) Frayser:

1. Nancy Murray Frayser was born circa 1800. She married Reuben F. Sims, son of Maj. Bernard and Nancy (Walton) Sims, on Feb. 17, 1817 in Cumberland County. (241)

2. Elizabeth Walton Frayser was born circa 1802. She married Jeduthan Holman Davis on Dec. 28, 1832[74] in Cumberland County. (242)

3. Robert Bentley Frayser was born on Aug. 4, 1804 and died in 1876. He married first Maria V. Spears, 1810-1855, daughter of John and Margaret Maria (Bates) Spears, in 1829 in Missouri. He married second Martha Agnes Wilson. Robert B. Frayser was a judge in Missouri. (243)

4. Julia Ann Frayser was born circa 1808 in Cumberland County. She married Thomas F. Womack on June 9, 1830[75] in Cumberland County. They had six children. (244)

5. Melissa M. Frayser married James M. Austin on Oct. 4, 1832[76] in Cumberland County, Virginia. (245)

6. William J. Frayser died in 1842. (246)

7. John Randolph Frayser was in Cumberland County during the 1830s but later moved to Memphis, Tennessee. (247)

8. Albert R. Frayser was born about 1816 in Powhatan County, Virginia and died on Nov. 24, 1872. He married Martha M. Hobson, daughter of Benjamin and Sallie Woodson (Hatcher) Hobson, on Sept. 5, 1842 in Powhatan County, Virginia. They had seven children. (248)

Memorial Library in Lynchburg, Virginia, Kent Gregory (1872-1950), "Genealogical Papers (Walton/Bransford), MS1288."

[73] See Cumberland County, *Virginia Will Book 8*, pp. 493-496. Thanks to Ruby Talley Smith of Wheaton, Maryland for sharing her research on the Frayser family.

[74] Marriage was recorded in the Cumberland County, Virginia Courthouse.

[75] Marriage was recorded in the Cumberland County Courthouse.

[76] Marriage was recorded in the Cumberland County Courthouse.

9. Dr. Benjamin Franklin Frayser was born on Oct. 2, 1819 and died on Jan. 10, 1852 in Cumberland County. He married Elizabeth Deane Irving, 1828-1873, daughter of Robert and Elizabeth Hughes (Deane) Irving on April 12, 1837 in Cumberland County.[77] (249)

Nancy Ann Murray (Walton) Isbell (115)

Nancy Ann Murray Walton,[78] daughter of Thomas Jr. and Nancy (Murray) Walton, was born circa 1777 in Cumberland County and died after 1850 in Buckingham County. She married William Isbell, son of Lewis and Hannah (Anderson) Isbell, on Nov. 2, 1795 in Cumberland County. William was born on June 1, 1777 in Goochland County and died in Buckingham County in 1853. They raised a large family at Rose Hill, Buckingham County, Virginia. He was basically a farmer, although he was listed as a minister in 1829-1830.[79]

Children of William and Nancy Ann M. (Walton) Isbell:[80]

1. Thomas Walton Isbell, born in 1799, was living in Buckingham County in 1840, Cumberland County in 1850 as an overseer, 1860 in Buckingham County, and 1870 in Lynchburg. He married Martha Branch, daughter of Archibald and Elizabeth (Moseley) Branch, who died before 1850. His grave in Lynchburg has no dates inscribed. (250)

2. Phoebe Ann Isbell was born in 1802 and died on April 1, 1884 in Buckingham County. She married Albert Gallatin Steger, 1805-1883, of Cumberland County. They lived in Alabama in the 1840s, and came back to Buckingham County where they are found on both the 1860 and 1870 censuses.[81] (251)

---

[77] Marriage was recorded in the Cumberland County Courthouse.

[78] Nancy's given name on the 1850 Census for Buckingham County was Ann. Information on Nancy M. (Walton) Isbell was contributed by Debra Tucker.

[79] Roger G. Ward, compiler, *Land Tax Summaries & Implied Deeds, 1815-1840*, (Athens, Georgia: Iberian Publishing Company), vol. 2, 1994, p.183

[80] Names of William Isbell's children and their birth years were compiled by Marietta Virginia Steger, his granddaughter, and preserved by the Virginia Historical Society, Richmond, Virginia, Mss6: 1 Is13:1.

[81] 1870 U. S. Census for Buckingham County, Virginia, pp. 40-41

3. Eliza Anderson Isbell was born in 1804 at Rose Hill, Buckingham County, and died about 1849 in Maury County, Tennessee. Eliza married John Archibald Branch, son of Archibald and Elizabeth (Moseley) Branch. He was born in 1804 in Buckingham County and died circa 1869 in Huntsville, Texas.[82] (252)

4. James T. Isbell, born in 1806, married Harriet Branch, daughter of Archibald and Elizabeth (Moseley) Branch. (253)

5. William Purcell Isbell was born in 1807 and died on April 13, 1883 in Madison County, Alabama. He married first Elmina H. Steger, daughter of Thomas H. and Phoebe (Walton) Steger, on Nov. 24, 1831 in Cumberland County, Virginia. He married second Ann Mariah Elam after 1850.[83] (254)

6. Martha Jane Isbell was born about 1811 in Buckingham County. She married Hamilton Breeze, son of William and Sarah (Brand) Breeze of Augusta County, Virginia. Hamilton's family unit was living in Chillicothe, Missouri in 1840 when the census was taken for Livingston County. It is believed that Hamilton obtained a divorce in Missouri and moved to San Diego, California, where he is found living alone as a prosperous farmer on the census of 1860.[84] By 1870 Hamilton had lost most of his assets, and was working as a trader, living alone. Hamilton was born in 1806 in Virginia and died circa 1875 in San Diego. He was buried in the Julian Pioneer Cemetery in San Diego County—no dates given. Perhaps he was attracted to the area to mine for gold. In 1850, Martha was living in the household of her brother Thomas Walton Isbell in Buckingham County. Her age was given as forty-four years. She had a child named Nancy Walton Breeze, age sixteen years and a daughter named Sarah Elizabeth Breeze, age ten years, and possibly William T. Breeze who later served in the 21st Virginia Infantry Regiment, C.S.A. (255)

7. Mary Susan Isbell was born on March 8, 1814 in Buckingham County, and died on Jan. 9, 1893. She married Archibald William

---

[82] See the 1860 U. S. Census for Walker County, Texas, Huntsville P. O., p. 68, Family No. 430.

[83] E-mail from Sarah H. Coon, on May 10, 2001, sscctx@mindspring.com.

[84] 1860 U. S. Census for San Diego Township, San Diego, California, p. 6, Family No. 45.

Carter, son of Theodorick and Martha (Austin) Carter. Archibald was born on April 1, 1812 in Henrico County, Virginia and died on Feb. 2, 1893.[85] Both were buried in the Presbyterian Cemetery in Lynchburg. (256)

8. Mariah E. Isbell was born in 1816. She married the Rev. Samuel Rose Irvine, son of Samuel and Anne Fitzhugh (Rose) Irvine. Samuel was a Methodist clergyman who was born in Lynchburg, Campbell County, Virginia. The marriage date was July 11, 1839 in Buckingham County.[86] Their children were Bettie (married a Robertson), Jennie, James and Hugh Irvine.[87] (257)

9. Lewis Daniel Isbell was born circa 1817 in Buckingham County, and died in 1889.[88] He was working as an attorney in Appomattox County when the 1850 U. S. Census was taken, living in a hotel. Lewis served as Commonwealth Attorney for Appomattox County,[89] and later as a Delegate to the Virginia secession convention in 1861. "Judge Daniel Isbell" allegedly later moved to Missouri.[90] (258)

10. Caroline Matilda Isbell, born on March 5, 1820 in Buckingham County and died on March 19, 1893. She married Tazewell Jones,[91]

---

[85] Kent Gregory (1872-1950), "Genealogical Papers, MS1288," Jones Memorial Library, Lynchburg, Virginia. A death record for the City of Lynchburg gives a date of death of Feb. 2, 1889.

[86] *Lynchburg Virginian*, Aug. 19, 1839, p. 3, c. 3.

[87] Library of Virginia, "Lyons family Bible record, 1779-1849," Accession No. 35616.

[88] http://politicalgraveyard.com/bio/isaac-izlar.html

[89] William Marvel, *A Place Called Appomattox*, (Chapel Hill, North Carolina: The University of North Carolina Press), 2000, pp. 73-74.

[90] Letter from Edward Smith Brown to Mrs. Emma Walton Ivy of Lynchburg, Virginia, dated Aug. 15, 1905, now in Jones Memorial Library, Lynchburg, Miss Kent Gregory (1872-1950), "Genealogical Papers (Walton), MS1288." He was in Buckingham County in 1843 as proven in *The Papers of Col. Richard H. Gilliam of Buckingham County, Virginia*, edited by Carl C. Rosen, (Westminster, Maryland: Family Line Publications), 1992, p. 51.

[91] Birth and death dates come from LDS, no source given. See Campbell County, Virginia *Deed Book 28*, Dec. 20, 1850, p. 400.

son of Dr. James and Nancy (Jones) Jones, on Dec. 21, 1842. Tazewell was born in June 22, 1822 in Buckingham County and died on July 2, 1896. His occupation was listed as a farmer when the 1870 Census was taken for Buckingham County.[92] (259)

11. Amanda Murray Isbell was born in 1822. She married the Rev. Robert A. Gregory,[93] born circa 1821, who was a minister in the Methodist Episcopal Church. They were living in the Brookville District of Campbell County when the U. S. Census was taken in 1870. Unfortunately, Robert was committed to the "Western Lunatic Asylum" in Staunton, where he was listed on the U. S. Census for 1880. He reportedly died in 1884 at the hospital. (160)

12. Virginia Isbell was born in 1824 and died in 1835. (261)

Phoebe (Walton) Bransford (117)

Phoebe Walton,[94] daughter of Thomas Jr. and Nancy (Armistead) Walton, was born on Nov. 7, 1779 in Cumberland County, Virginia and died on Dec. 19, 1852, in Lynchburg. She married Samuel Bransford, son of John and Judith (Amonet) Bransford. He was born on Aug. 4, 1778 and died on Nov. 3, 1837. Both are buried in the Presbyterian Cemetery in Lynchburg. Samuel served as postmaster at Cartersville, Cumberland County from January 1801 to October 1802.[95] He bought land in 1813 on both

---

[92] Jeanne Stinson, compiler, *Buckingham County, Virginia 1870 U. S. Census*, (Athens, Georgia: Iberian Publishing Company), 1998, p. 179.

[93] Richard Mundy informed the compiler that Rev. Robert A. Gregory married Amanda Marie Moore, not Amanda M. Isbell. His email in 2004 was ramundyVA@aol.com. If Mr. Mundy is correct, then Amanda M. Isbell married a Mr. Gregory, given name not known.

[94] Information on Phoebe's family unit was gleaned from two sources: "Genealogical Papers (Bransford), MS1288" of Kent Gregory (1872-1950), and "Genealogical Papers (Walton), MS2098," of Ida Bowman Younger (1903-1993), both in the Jones Memorial Library in Lynchburg, Virginia.

[95] Edith F. Axelson, *Virginia Postmasters and Post Offices, 1789-1832*, (Athens, Georgia: Iberian Publishing Company), p. 50.

sides of Bent Creek in Old Buckingham County,[96] where he lived until he moved to Lynchburg in 1816. Samuel established *The Lynchburg Press*. He sold the 330-acre family farm at Bent Creek in 1820 to William W. Hendrick.[97]

Children of Samuel and Phoebe (Walton) Bransford:[98]

    1. Thomas Alfred Bransford was born in 1809 and died on Sept. 25, 1847. He did not marry. (262)

    2. Phoebe Ann Bransford was born on Feb. 5, 1812, and died on May 18, 1876. She married John Henley Tyree on Oct. 14, 1828. He was born on Sept. 15, 1806 and died on Feb. 9, 1876. His occupation was a tobacconist. Both were buried in the Presbyterian Cemetery in Lynchburg. (263)

    3. Judith Walton Bransford was born in 1813 and died in 1849 in New York City. She married Charles C. Hudson in September 1832 in Lynchburg.[99] (264)

    4. Samuel Jennings Bransford was born in Lynchburg in 1814 and died on Nov. 3, 1840 at West Point, New York. He graduated with honors from West Point, and was an assistant professor of Mathematics. He was killed by a horse while teaching horsemanship to cadets on the parade grounds. He was not married. (265)

    5. Capt. John William Bransford, born in 1826, and died in September 1902. He married Kate L. Biars in 1849. They lived in Richmond, Virginia where he owned a hardware business, Johnson and Bransford. He later moved his family to Lynchburg where he was elected

---

[96] Roger G. Ward, compiler, *Buckingham County, Virginia: Land Tax Summaries & Implied Deeds*, (Athens, Georgia: Iberian Publishing Company), vol. 1, 1782-1814, p. 44.

[97] Roger G. Ward, compiler, *Buckingham County, Virginia: Land Tax Summaries & Implied Deeds*, (Athens, Georgia: Iberian Publishing Company), vol. 2, 1815-1840, pp. 44-45.

[98] Information on the children of Samuel Bransford was gleaned from the files of Kent Gregory (1872-1950), "Genealogical Papers, MS1288," in Jones Memorial Library, Lynchburg, Virginia.

[99] *The Lynchburg Virginian*, Sept. 27, 1832, p. 3, c. 4.

Treasurer of the City in 1880.[100] Four children were born to their marriage. (266)

William Walton (118)

William Walton, son of Thomas Jr. and Nancy (Armistead) Walton, was born in Cumberland County, Virginia on Sept. 18, 1782, and died on Dec. 18, 1851 at Bent Creek, Appomattox County, Virginia. William married Elizabeth White[101] Chick, daughter of Col. William and Elizabeth Chick, June 24, 1807.[102] Elizabeth W. Chick was born on Sept. 30, 1790, and died on June 5, 1844, at 12 o'clock midnight. The family Bible states that she was ill with a protracted disease for twelve months. Her death came one year before Appomattox County was formed from Buckingham County.

William Chick's wife Elizabeth was possibly nee White. Dr. David C. Jones, son-in-law of William Walton, recorded in his medical account book a visit on Nov. 11, 1834 with Mrs. Andrew White of Bent Creek. Furthermore, Dr. Jones sat up with her for several nights in January 1835, which suggests a severe illness or impending death. Further research showed no relationship with this branch of Whites.

Elizabeth's father, Col. William Chick, allegedly served in the Revolutionary War from Henrico County, Virginia and settled at Bent Creek during the War of 1812. However, he owned land at Bent Creek

---

[100] Library of Virginia, Archives and Manuscripts, Accession No. 22379.

[101] We hypothesized that the maiden name of Elizabeth White Chick's mother was White, but found no evidence in the Buckingham area. Andrew White, who lived at Bent Creek, was born on March 13, 1789 at Dunse, Berwick County, Scotland, and died in 1870 at Bent Creek. He married Margaret Ferguson. There appears to have been no connection between these two White families.

[102] Vital records of William Walton and his family are found in his Bible, now in possession of a descendant at Bent Creek, Appomattox County, Virginia, and a copy of which is in the hands of the compiler. The Bible record identifies Elizabeth White Chick as the daughter of William and Elizabeth Chick.

as early as 1792. In 1820, he was an enumerator for the U.S. Census for Buckingham County.[104]

William Walton served in the Buckingham County militia, attaining the rank of Colonel. Over the next forty-four years, William Walton succeeded his father-in-law as Bent Creek's largest land owner and chief entrepreneur. In addition, he came to hold the County's highest offices. In 1808, he was appointed to the County Court, an office he held continuously until 1845, when as senior in service he became the presiding justice of the new court of Appomattox County. He was one of the first postmasters at Bent Creek. Samuel Perkins established the post office in November 1800. Col. William Chick was the next postmaster, serving from July 1801 to July 1810. William Walton followed Col. Chick as postmaster until April 1811.[105] According to information in the Library of Virginia, William insured his house on Main Street in Duiguidsville for $1,500.[106]

William was one of the petitioners to the Virginia General Assembly to establish a private school in Buckingham County. He served a term as sheriff for Buckingham County. In this capacity he certified an election at Goodwin's Church precinct, April 23, 1840.

William was a successful businessman, owning a broad range of enterprises. During the 1827-1830 era, an account book[107] shows that he was in partnership with several persons: "Clark & Walton," "Walton & Phelps,"[108] and "Walton & Lane." Earlier he was a partner of "Chick & Walton." On Oct. 4, 1828, Owans C. Fowler was reimbursed $9.64

---

[104] One tradition says that Col. William Chick married Jean Ragland; another that he married Elizabeth White. No direct proof has been found to date, except that the William Walton Bible shows that William Chick's wife was named Elizabeth.

[105] Edith F. Axelson, *Virginia Postmasters and Post Offices, 1789-1832*, Athens, Georgia: Iberian Publishing Company), 1991, p. 29.

[106] Library of Virginia, Reel 3, Vol. 32, No. 32.

[107] Buckingham County account book in Library of Virginia.

[108] Probably this partner was Capt. Jonathan B. Phelps or Capt. Charles Phelps, and the other was William Lane (or Layne). The man called Chick was probably Col. William Chick or his son Richard Chick.

for attending a meeting at the Charlotte County Courthouse for a hearing on the "Walton & Chick vs. Anthony W. Woodson."

Photograph courtesy of the Library of Virginia
William Walton built this house from forest pine on one of his lands, about 1811. This is where his children were born and raised. It is located six miles north of Appomattox on Route 26, about 300 yards off the highway, on land that was later owned by his great-grandsons, William Jones Walton Sr. and Walker Scott Walton, during the 1930s when the WPA took this photograph. The last member of the Walton family born in the house was Winston D. Walton in 1931. Stephen McCoy (born in 1863) and his family were the last tenants to live in the house, circa 1940s. The building is no longer standing.

The firms "Clark & Walton" and "Walton and Phelps" were mercantile businesses at Bent Creek during the 1820s and 1830s. Another business was called a plant (possibly lime), which implies manufacturing or processing of some type. According to an account book, their products were shipped to several markets, including New Orleans. William Harris was paid $30 to make a trip to New Orleans. Bent Creek is located on the James River near its intersection with U.S. Route 60. Land tax lists show he and a partner owned a tobacco warehouse; that he was co-owner of the Buckingham Gold Mine.

In 1840, William Walton owned forty-three slaves. In 1845, when Appomattox County was formed from Buckingham County, William was the only resident in the new county who was called Esquire on the personal property tax rolls. He owned 2,022 acres, consisting of two former estates of Walton and Chick. Sometime before 1850, William divided most of his land among his seven children. Finally, William Walton was elected Justice of the Peace for Appomattox County, an office that he held until the year of his death.

Children of Captain William and Elizabeth W. (Chick) Walton: [108]

1. Eliza Ann Walton was born on Tuesday, Aug. 28, 1810. On Jan. 10, 1827, she married Dr. David Crawford Jones. (267)

2. Martha Ann Armistead Walton was born on Sunday, Aug. 9, 1812 at two o'clock in the morning, and died Nov. 23, 1888. She married Maj. Samuel Jennings Walker, son of John Meriwether and Susan (Christian) Walker,[109] on Tuesday, June 8, 1830. Samuel was born Jan. 23, 1809 and died Aug. 21, 1866 in Appomattox County. (268)

3. Mary Frances Philadelphia Walton was born on Friday, May 13, 1814, and died on April 9, 1884. She married Col. Samuel Daniel McDearmon, 1815-1871, son of the Rev. James and Mary (Daniel) McDearmon, June 10, 1835. (269)

4. William Thomas Walton was born on Dec. 28, 1816 at 2:30 a.m., and died Wednesday, Sept. 5, 1821, aged four years eight months, and seven days. His given names were a combination of his grandfather Chick and grandfather Walton. (270)

5. James Chick Walton was born Aug. 23, 1819 at Bent Creek, and died May 10, 1886, in Campbell County. He first married Mary Elizabeth White, daughter of Andrew and Margaret (Ferguson) White, and married second, in December 1855, Virginia Caroline Greenlee. (271)

---

[108] Names and dates were copied from the William Walton family Bible, purchased in 1807. The owner does not want to be identified.

[109] Information on this family was published in an undated issue of the *Farmville Herald*, contributed by Stuart McDearmon Farrar. See also, Nathaniel Ragland Featherstone, *The History of Appomattox, Virginia*, (Walsworth Brothers: Marceline, Missouri), 1948, pp. 277-278.

6. John William Walton, son of William and Elizabeth W. (Chick) Walton, was born on May 30, 1821, and died on July 3, 1889. He married Mary Jane Vawter, daughter of Silas P. and Elizabeth Farrar (Christian) Vawter. Mary Jane was born in Nelson County on Oct. 29, 1827 and died at Bent Creek, Appomattox County on June 26, 1888. (272)

7. Virginia Cornelia Walton was born on Tuesday, July 26, 1825, at 11 o'clock in the evening. She married James Nowlin, a physician in Appomattox County. James owned nine slaves. We are unable to trace their descendants. (273)

8. Mariah Louisa Ellenorah Walton was born at 3 o'clock in the evening of May 21, 1829, and died on Jan. 5, 1837 at 10 o'clock at night. She was ill for two and one-half days, according to a notation in the family Bible. The medical book of Dr. David C. Jones has an entry dated July 14, 1833, under the account of William Walton Esq., "to visit a daughter Elenora, bleeding her." Bleeding or draining blood from the body was one of the techniques used by the medical profession during the eighteenth and nineteenth centuries. The assumption was that bad blood would be eliminated and the body would regenerate new blood. (274)

9. Margaret Walker Walton, daughter of William and Elizabeth W. (Chick) Walton, was born on July 8, 1834, at 3 o'clock in the evening. She married John H. McKinney, his second wife, and raised a family of 10 children. (275)

10. Charles Yancey Walton was listed in the William Walton Bible as the youngest child of William and Elizabeth W. (Chick) Walton, but no date was entered. It is believed, but not proven, that he died young. (276)

Frances (Walton) Scruggs (119)

Frances Walton, daughter of Thomas Jr. and Nancy (Armistead) Walton, was born circa 1786 in Cumberland County, Virginia, and died in April 1879 in Appomattox County, Virginia.[110] Frances married

---

[110] Appomattox County, Virginia Circuit Court Case, "Scruggs vs. Scruggs," 1881.

John Scruggs who was born circa 1785 and died circa 1827.[111] John was an extensive landowner in the Bent Creek area of Buckingham County (now in Appomattox County).[112] He received $2,300.25 as a legatee of his father-in-law Thomas Walton Jr.[113]

Children of John and Frances (Walton) Scruggs:[114]

    1. Thomas Walton Scruggs was born on Nov. 19, 1807 and died May 29, 1873 in Appomattox County. He married Elizabeth P. North on April 29, 1858.[115] (277)

    2. John A. Scruggs was born circa 1808 and was still alive in 1880. He married Amanda D. Christian, daughter of James and Cordelia (Watts) Christian, on March 9, 1836 in Nelson County, Virginia. Amanda was born circa 1816 in Nelson County and died before 1870. (278)

    3. Nancy "Anne" Scruggs was born in 1809. She was living with her mother when the 1870 census was taken for Appomattox County. (279)

    4. James Littleton Scruggs was born in 1812 and died on Aug. 22, 1882 in Appomattox County. He married Mary Frances Woodson on Jan. 30, 1843. (280)

---

[111] The land tax records for Buckingham County stated that John Scruggs was deceased by 1831. See Roger G. Ward, *Land Tax Summaries & Implied Deeds, 1815-1840*, (Iberian Publishing Company: Athens, Georgia), vol 2, 1994, p. 319. An entry in the account book of Walton and Phelps Merchandise, 1828-1830, Miscellaneous Reel 253, Library of Virginia, in the account of Thomas W. Scruggs, pp. 18-19, July 19, 1828, it mentions a debt of $89.73 owed by John Scruggs, deceased. Another record in the Library of Virginia, "Scruggs Family Papers, 1803-1896," Accession No. 24643, states that he was deceased in 1827.

[112] *Ibid.* p. 319.

[113] From "Scruggs Walton Childers" file in the Library of Virginia, which settled the Scruggs-Walton affairs after the death of Martha Walton (third wife of Thomas Walton Jr.). William Walton and Samuel D. McDearmon were involved in the administration of the dower estate.

[114] Thanks to Carole Ruff, 40905 Belforest Court, Leesburg, Virginia 20175, who shared her research.

[115] Vital records (birth and marriage) for Thomas W. were found in the Appomattox County court records maintained in the Library of Virginia.

5. Martha Scruggs was born about 1813 and died circa 1896, unmarried, in Appomattox County.[116] She and her sister Nancy were living with their mother when the 1870 census was taken for Appomattox County. (281)

6. William Armistead Scruggs was born in 1815 and still alive in 1886.[117] He married Mary Jane ___, and their residence was in Campbell County, Virginia. (282)

7. Isaac B. Scruggs was listed as a child and heir in the Scruggs Family Papers. (283)

8. Samuel A. Scruggs was born circa 1826 and was still living in 1886.[118] According to Featherstone,[119] Samuel A. Scruggs, 1824-1910, married Adaline Hamersly, 1849-1926. Five children are listed. (284)

William Scott Walton (121)

William Scott Walton, son of Josiah and Jane (Flippen) Walton, was born on Feb. 6, 1771, in Cumberland County, Virginia, and died July 15, 1845, at the home of his son, Charles W. Walton in Aberdeen, Mississippi.[120] One tradition says that he was buried in the Odd Fellows Cemetery in Aberdeen, Mississippi. William S. married first Sally Womack, daughter of Nathan and Anna (McGehee) Womack.[121] After her death on Aug. 5, 1822,[122] he continued to farm in Cumberland County. On Dec. 5, 1836, he married second Julia Pollard in

---

[116] Appomattox County, Virginia *Will Book I*, pp. 42-45. The will was written on June 11, 1886 and probated on May 7, 1896. It mentioned her brothers Samuel A. and William A. Scruggs.

[117] Mentioned in the will of her sister Martha Scruggs in 1886.

[118] *Ibid.*

[119] Nathaniel Ragland Featherstonn, *The History of Appomattox, Virginia*, (Marceline, Missouri: Walsworth Brothers, Printers), reprint, 1995, p. 254.

[120] *Richmond Whig*, Aug. 19, 1845, p. 2, c. 3.

[121] Website http://www.homestead.com/FlippinFamilies/FourthGen9.html

[122] Information was contributed by Dr. Louis Koenig, 26890 Sherwood Forest, San Antonio, Texas 78258 to the compiler. Dr. Koenig died on May 7, 2003.

Cumberland County. On the same day as his marriage, he conveyed 362 acres of land to his children.[123] On March 29, 1845, an additional 240 acres were sold at a public auction to satisfy the debts of William S. Walton.[124] According to Dr. Louis Koenig, one oral tradition says that he moved to Monroe County, Mississippi before 1822, but that may be incorrect, in that he paid land and personal property taxes in Cumberland County and is found on both the 1830 and 1840 censuses for Cumberland County.[125] His move to Mississippi undoubtedly occurred sometime after 1840. The land tax records reveal that this branch of the family lived in the southern part of Cumberland County, near Prince Edward County, whereas the other Waltons lived in the far northern section of the County, in the Muddy Creek, lower Willis Creek and the Cartersville areas.

Children of William S. and Sally (Womack) Walton:[126]

1. Nathan Womack Walton was born on May 10, 1803, and died on Oct. 6, 1880. He married first Sarah Smith Tiernan, daughter of Dr. James Tiernan of Powhatan County, Nov. 18, 1841,[127] and married second Anne E. (Vaughan) Paine, daughter of Joseph and Henrietta Vaughan, June 4, 1867, in Cumberland County.[128] Anne E. was born in 1817. A third marriage was to Pauline Jane (Rock) Saunders. (285)

2. Mary Scott Walton was born on April 23, 1805 and died March 25, 1891. She married Branch Henry Ellington on Jan. 27, 1823 in Cumberland County. (286)

3. Sarah Walton married Isham Seay on May 17, 1834. It is believed that they remained in Cumberland County, or a nearby county, because

---

[123] Cumberland County, Virginia *Chancery Book I, 1831-1851*, p. 194.

[124] *Ibid*, p. 298.

[125] 1830 U. S. Census for Cumberland County, Virginia, p. 210, and 1840 U.S. Census for Cumberland County, p. 295.

[126] See Earl and May (Miller) Frost, *Dejarnette and Allied Families in America, 1699-1954*, (San Bernardino, California: Privately Published), 1954, p.282.

[127] *Richmond Whig*, Dec. 10, 1841, p.2, c. 6.

[128] Cumberland County, Virginia *Marriage Book I*, p. 9, line 7.

both were mentioned in numerous court records in Cumberland. For example, Isham Seay was the bondsman for the second marriage of his father-in-law. (287)

4. Charles William Walton was born on Feb. 20, 1810 and died June 13, 1866, in Monroe County, Mississippi. He married first Arvazena S. Dyche on June 2, 1835, and married second Katherine Stockton Anderson on June 8, 1864. Charles W. was living in Monroe County in 1845, where he died.[129] (288)

5. Elizabeth Ann Walton married Richard G. Hall on Dec. 23, 1836, in Monroe County, Mississippi.[130] They were living in the Republic of Texas when her father died in 1845. Elizabeth sold her share of her father's estate to Charles W. Walton for $756.[131] (289)

6. Edwin D. Walton was the youngest child. He was born in 1814 and died in the 1890s. His guardian in 1834 was Charles Womack.[132] He is listed on the Cumberland County, Virginia tax list in 1835. On Dec. 29, 1834, Edwin received slaves named Nancy, Amanda and George.[133] Edwin moved to Monroe County, Mississippi according to court records in Cumberland County. Edwin D. married Elvira R. Hutchison on Aug. 2, 1840.[134] The 1850 census for Monroe County lists these children: William Walton, age nine; Dan A. Walton, age seven; Sarah D. Walton, age four; and Edwin T. Walton, age three months. (290)

---

[129] Cumberland County, Virginia *Deed Book 26*, p. 291, Dec. 15, 1845.

[130] Monroe County, Mississippi, *Marriage Book 2*, p. 105.

[131] Cumberland County, Virginia *Deed Book 26*.

[132] Cumberland County, Virginia *Deed Book 24*, p. 393, and Cumberland County, Virginia *Guardian Accounts 1832-1860*, p. 2.

[133] Cumberland County, Virginia *Will Book 9*, p. 210.

[134] Information provided by Linda Taylor, 3225 Pioneer Circle, Waco, TX 76712 to compiler on Jan. 22, 1999.

Jesse Walton (123)

Jesse Walton, son of Josiah and Jane (Flippen) Walton, was born July 6, 1773,[135] in Cumberland County, Virginia and died Nov. 20, 1830 in Monroe County, Mississippi.[136] He married Joanna Lawson Hobson, daughter of William, 1748-1835, and Nancy (Brackett) Hobson. Joanna was born on Oct. 9, 1779 in Cumberland County, and died on Nov. 22, 1852 in Pontotoc County, Mississippi.[137] The family moved to Amelia County, Virginia in 1799[138] and then to Maury County, Tennessee circa 1815.[139] About 1821, they settled at Cotton Port Gin, Monroe County, Mississippi. Jesse was an Indian trader and carpenter. After Jesse's death in 1830, Joanna ran a boarding house until the 1840s, when she moved to Pontotoc County to be with her daughter Sarah (Walton) Daggett.

---

[135] In an article in "The Richmond Standard," Saturday, Sept. 19, 1879, vol. 11, No. 2, col. 5, "Notes and Queries" refers to a memorandum from Nathan Womack Walton of Richmond to the paper, which gave a birthdate for Jesse Walton as July 6, 1774. The source for the 1773 birth year is a copy of a family Bible record in Evans Memorial Library in Aberdeen, Mississippi, sent by H. C. Ruffin of Chester, Virginia ("Jesse Walton Bible record"), which contains the birthdates for Jesse, Joanna and their children. In addition, Jesse's birth date is shown as July 6, 1773 and his death date as Nov. 20, 1830 in the handwritten notes of George Miller captioned "Mem of Births Marriages & Deaths, Walton Family," From S. Daggett Feby. 1875 ("Miller Notes" in possession of Bob F. Thompson Esq., 4430 Sheppard Place, Nashville, Tennessee 37205, who provided this information to the compiler).

[136] See Jesse Walton's will in Monroe County, Mississippi, *Will Book 1*, p. 128. Information on the family unit of Jesse Walton was initially provided by Mrs. Jessie Hunter of Springfield, Virginia and later supplemented by Bob F. Thompson Esq., reflecting earlier research conducted by his mother as well as his own research. Mr. Thompson's mother did extensive research on the Waltons of Cumberland County, Virginia, Monroe County, Mississippi, and Tennessee.

[137] See Monroe County, Mississippi *Will Book 1*, p. 28.

[138] Amelia County, Virginia *Deed Book 21*, p. 42, dated Nov. 7, 1799 (per Bob F. Thompson).

[139] Jesse was still living in Amelia County in 1814, per *Deed Book 24*, p. 67, recorded on Feb. 23, 1815 by Walton appearance.

Fourth Generation

1. Nancy Brackett Walton was born on Jan. 18, 1797, and died prior to 1850. She married first John T. Moore and married second Thomas Miller. (291)

2. William Hobson Walton was born on Sept. 2, 1799, and died on Jan. 11, 1830 in Giles County, Tennessee. He married Ellen W. Porter. (292)

3. Jane Scott Walton was born on Nov. 28, 1801 was born in Amelia County, Virginia, and died on June 23, 1819 in Maury County, Tennessee. Jane married Andrew Jackson Edmondson on March 19, 1818 in Maury County. (293)

4. Polly L. Walton was born on Feb. 14, 1803 and died May 4, 1805. (294)

5. Josiah Nichols Walton was born on Oct. 18, 1805 in Cumberland County, Virginia and died April 26, 1884 in Monroe County, Mississippi. He married first Mary J. Prewitt, and. married second Katherine Stockton Anderson. (295)

6. Thomas Madison Walton was born on July 11, 1808 in Cumberland County, Virginia, and died in 1845. He married Priscilla Ann Rutledge. (296)

7. Sarah Hobson Walton,[141] born on July 2, 1811 in Cumberland County, Virginia and died May 18, 1889 in Pontotoc County, Mississippi. She married Stephen Daggett. (297)

8. Mary Elizabeth Walton was born on March 14, 1813 and died Feb. 22, 1869, in Monroe County, Mississippi. She married Robert Gordon. (298)

9. Lucy Catherine Walton was born on Jan. 27, 1816 and died on Jan. 5, 1862. She married William Oscar Cook on May 20, 1834 in Cotton Gin Port, Mississippi. (299)

10. Jesse Ludwell Walton was born on July 16, 1818, and was living in Monroe County, Mississippi when the 1850 U.S. Census was taken. An

---

[141] Information on this family came from Bob F. Thompson Esq. in 2000, who credits Pete Daggett <padagge@netport.com>

1848 tax list shows that he owned land in Cotton Gin and Aberdeen.[141] He was a property owner in Old Aberdeen, Mississippi in 1850.[142] Jesse was an attorney. Apparently he did not marry. He died on Feb. 9, 1857.[143] (300)

11. Susan Grey Walton was born on April 21, 1821 and died on Jan. 10, 1864. She married Hugh Reid Miller, son of Ebenezer E. and Margery (Reid) Miller, on May 9, 1839 in Monroe County, Mississippi. Hugh was born on May 14, 1812 in South Carolina, and died on July 12, 1863. (301)

Thomas Murray Walton (127)

Thomas M. Walton, son of Edward and Nancy (Murray) Walton, was born Dec. 14, 1772 and died June 7, 1821 in Cumberland County.[144] Thomas M. married Frances Anne Carrington, daughter of Nathaniel and Phoebe (Harris) Carrington,[145] on April 6, 1796.[146] Frances Anne was born April 10, 1779 and died Feb. 16, 1824.[147] Executors of her estate were "my friends Edward Walton, Samuel Wilson, and George C. Walton." Thomas M. and Frances owned and operated the Walton Mill which had formerly belonged to her father Nathaniel Carrington.

---

[141] *Ibid.* p. 20

[142] Betty Shaw Rollins, *A Brief History of Aberdeen and Monroe County, Mississippi, 1821-1900*, (Privately Printed), April 1957, p. 62.

[143] His death was graphically described in the *Diary of Robert Gordon* in the Mississippi Department of Archives and History, per Bob F. Thompson.

[144] Cumberland County, Virginia *Will Book 6*, p. 324, dated May 7, 1821, and *Will Book 7*, p. 220, May 17, 1823, recorded on March 22, 1824.

[145] See Cumberland County, Virginia *Deed Book 20*, pp. 58-59, and *Will Book 3*, p. 238, the will of Nathaniel Carrington dated Feb. 10, 1803.

[146] *Richmond Standard*, v. 3, No. 27, contributed by Dr. Peter Witt of Richmond, Virginia.

[147] *Richmond Standard*, v. 3, No. 26, contributed by Dr. Peter Witt of Richmond, Virginia.

Fourth Generation

Children of Thomas M. and Frances A. (Carrington) Walton:[148]

1. George Carrington Walton Sr. was born on Jan. 20, 1798 and died Oct. 12, 1840. He married Eliza Miller, March 2, 1824. Eliza died of childbirth on Jan. 31, 1825. George Jr. married Mary Ann Stark Smith[149] on Nov. 27, 1848. (302)

2. Maria Murray Walton was born Nov. 13, 1799 and died in May 1838. She married John Wilkinson on Jan. 18, 1820. (303)

3. Thomas M. Walton Jr. was born Dec. 11, 1801 and died in April 1823. (304)

4. Phoebe A. Walton was born Nov. 16, 1803 and died May 16, 1827. (305)

5. Ellen Sidney Walton was born on June 22, 1806 and died in November 1830. (306)

6. Nathaniel Walton was born on May 25, 1808 and died on May 30, 1866. He married Evelyn Burton Payne on March 5, 1828. Evelyn was born on Aug. 29, 1808 and died April 12, 1891. (307)

7. Edward Cox Walton was born on Feb. 28, 1811, and died on Sept. 10, 1811. (308)

8. Henry Walton was born on Nov. 24, 1814 and died on Jan. 31, 1852.[150] He married Elizabeth Birch on Sept. 2, 1851. Apparently he was in a joint business with his brother Nathaniel Walton. When his estate was settled, his wife Mary E. received one-third and the rest was divided between John L. McLaurine and his wife, George C. Walton and Nathaniel Walton. Henry and Elizabeth had no children. (309)

9. Sarah Gilbert Walton was born in March 1815 and died in 1822. (310)

---

[148] Library of Virginia, Peyton Carrington Collection, Accession No. 24284, "Letter from Evelyn B. (Payne) Walton to Peyton Carrington," dated May 8, 1868.

[149] Robert Smith, age 72, brother-in-law of George Walton was living in the household when the 1910 Census was taken for Buckingham County.

[150] Cumberland County, Virginia *Will Book 12*, pp. 34, 57.

10. Martha Wilson Walton was born on Nov. 7, 1817, and died in 1821. (311)

11. Benjamin Harris Walton was born on Feb. 23, 1820 and died in May 1849, of "consumption."[151] He was a merchant. Benjamin married Louisa Booker, daughter of Thomas Booker, Dec. 16, 1841, in Cumberland County. Benjamin H. wrote his will on Feb. 7, 1846 and it was proven on June 24, 1850.[152] They had no children. After his death, "Mrs. Louisa Walton" of Cumberland married Rowland Stone on March 27, 1856.[153] (312)

Phoebe Ann (Walton) Steger (129)

Phoebe Ann Walton, daughter of Edward and Nancy (Murray) Walton, was born ca 1776 in Cumberland County, Virginia and died before 1822 in the same County. She married Thomas Hales Steger, son of John Parrott and Sarah Eppes (Harris) Steger. He was born on April 15, 1772 in Powhatan County, Virginia and died in Cumberland County in 1839. Thomas H. married second Nancy Shores of Fluvanna County. The name of their home in Cumberland County was called "Bloomfield."

Children of Thomas H. and Phoebe A. (Walton) Steger:[154]

1. Edward Walton Steger was born ca 1800 at "Bloomfield" in Cumberland County and died in February 1866 in Cumberland County. He married Louise A. Goodman, daughter of Thomas and Elizabeth (Street)[155] Goodman. Louise was born in Cumberland County in 1804 and died in Cumberland County on Aug. 5, 1862 of typhoid fever. (313)

---

[151] 1850 Mortality Schedule for the U. S. Census, Cumberland County, Virginia.

[152] Cumberland County, Virginia *Will Book 11*, p. 507.

[153] *The Lynchburg Daily Virginian*, April, 12, 1856, p. 3, c. 1.

[154] Information for this family unit was provided by William E. Steger of San Diego, California.

[155] Information was secured from David Goodman of Baltimore, Maryland on his website http://www.bcpl.net/~dmg/ben.htm

2. Elizabeth E. Steger was born circa 1801 in Cumberland County. She married Chastain Shores on Aug. 3, 1822. They lived in Fluvanna County, Virginia. (314)

3. Albert Gallatin Steger was born in 1805 in Cumberland County and died on July 14, 1883 in Buckingham County. He married Phoebe Ann Isbell, daughter of William and Nancy Ann (Murray) Walton. (315)

4. Francis E. H. Steger was born on Dec. 25, 1807 in Cumberland County. He married Narcissa W. Taylor on March 20, 1838 in Cumberland County. She was born on Dec. 16, 1819 and died on May 3, 1862. (316)

5. Mary Francis Steger was born in 1808 in Cumberland County and died on Jan. 6, 1883 in Cumberland County. She married John Todd Wood on March 9, 1830 in Cumberland County. John died on Dec. 10, 1865. (317)

6. Elmina H. Steger was born circa 1812 and died in Buckingham County in 1834. She married William Purcell Isbell on Nov. 7, 1831 in Cumberland County. (318)

7. Phoebe Ann Steger was born on June 4, 1817 in Cumberland County and died on Jan. 8, 1899 at "Spring Garden," Fluvanna County. Phoebe married Henry Washington Wood, who was born March 27, 1805 and died March 25, 1893. (319)

Edward Walton Jr. (130)

Edward Walton Jr., son of Edward Sr. and Nancy (Murray) Walton, was born circa 1778 and died about 1840.[156] He first married Janette Carson (McLaurine) Swann, eldest daughter of William McLaurine,[157] on April 4, 1809, in Cumberland County. Janette was born in Powhatan County on April 25, 1787 and died in Cumberland County on March 3, 1818.[158] She first married George T. Swann on Nov. 21, 1806 in Powhatan County. George T. died in 1807. Edward Walton Jr. married second Martha (Isbell) Wright, Nov. 25, 1820 in Cumberland County.

---

[156] Cumberland County, Virginia *Will Book 10*, pp. 209-211.

[157] Powhatan County, Virginia *Will Book 12*, pp. 402-403, "Will of William McLaurine."

[158] *Richmond Inquirer*, March 17, 1818, p.4, c. 3.

She was first married to Dr. Archibald D. Wright, whose will is filed in Prince Edward County, Virginia.[159] Martha died in 1854.[160] Edward was a wealthy plantation owner. He was co-partner of the firm Walton and Powers, which included a lumber house and blacksmith shop. His 600-acre plantation was named "Belfield" and was described as "lying on the Willis River" on the Cartersville Road. It appears that Edward Jr. was the father of a very large family. The following tentative reconstruction is drawn from court records until more information becomes available from private sources. Dr. Robert Henderson and Samuel Hatcher were the executors for Edward's estate.

Children of Edward Jr. and Janette C. (McLaurine) Swann Walton:

1. Edward G. Walton was born circa 1812 in Cumberland County and died in 1866 in Yalobusha County, Mississippi. Edward married Elizabeth Agee of Buckingham County, Virginia. (320)

2. Jane Wingfield Scott Walton was born circa 1821 in Cumberland County. She married Col. Thomas H. Hewlitt, son of Edwin and Nancy (McLaurine) Hulett, on July 27, 1839 in Cumberland County. She received a legacy from Sally Swann. Allegedly, they moved to Madison County, Alabama. Her father's will gave her one of the children of a slave named Mariah. (321)

3. Josephine Walton was mentioned in the estate account, but is not a proven child. (322)

Children of Edward Jr. and Martha (Isbell) Wright Walton,:

4. James C. Walton was not yet twenty-one years old when his father wrote his will in 1840. James C. was to receive two-thirds of the estate. In 1855, he was living in Marshall County, Mississippi.[161] Probably he is the same person who married Martha Lomie McGehee on Sept. 23,

---

[159] Virginia Genealogical Society Quarterly, Vol. XXIX, No. 2 (May 1, 1991), p. 88-90.

[160] See Cumberland County, *Virginia Circuit Court Chancery Orders, 1852-1872*; Aug. term in 1855, pp. 190-192, and Cumberland County, Virginia *Will Book 12*, pp. 167-168, dated June 29, 1853 and probated on March 24, 1854

[161] Cumberland County, Virginia *Deed Book 28*, p. 273.

Fourth Generation

1851 in DeSota County, Mississippi. She was born on Dec. 24, 1832 and died on Jan. 23, 1859.[162] (323)

5. Lewis Isbell Walton was born in 1828 in Cumberland County and died on April 28, 1899 at Blossburg, Jefferson County, Alabama. He married first Margaret E. Boston and married second Elmina Adelaide Taylor Steger,[163] on Feb. 1, 1865 in Cumberland County. She was born on Jan. 30, 1847 and died Nov. 27, 1936 in Alabama. (324)

6. Mary W. Walton was named as a legatee in her father's will. (325)

7. Martha S. Walton was born circa 1833. She married Christopher Kesee, a merchant from Henrico County, March 31, 1857.[164] She was living in Jefferson County, Alabama when her brother Lewis died in 1899. (326)

8. Thomas D. Walton wrote his will on Nov. 22, 1852 and it was proven on Jan. 24, 1853. He willed to his brother Lewis I. Walton a horse, buggy and harness, and the remainder of his estate went to his mother. Total value of his estate was $1,161.49.[165] (327)

9. Cornelia J. Walton, born on Dec. 27, 1837, was called an "infant" when Edward Jr. wrote his will in 1840. She received one-half of her mother's estate plus $200 to complete her education.[166] James D. Isbell became her guardian until she reached the age of 21 years.[167] (328)

---

[162] Dates are from a tombstone inscription in the McGehee Cemetery in Marshall County, Mississippi.

[163] The names of Elizabeth Boston's parents were secured from Kyle A. Tutwiler, 3335 Kendall Dr., Fayetteville, AR 72704. See also the Bible record of Francis E. W. Steger, Library of Virginia, Accession No. 33398. The Bible was printed in 1851.

[164] Martha received one-half of her mother's estate: Cumberland County, Virginia *Will Book 12*, p. 167.

[165] Cumberland County, Virginia *Will Book 12*, p. 38.

[166] Cumberland County, Virginia *Will Book 12*, p. 167.

[167] Cumberland County, Virginia *Guardian Accounts, 1832-1860*, pp 373-374.

Thomas Hobson Walton (135)

Thomas Hobson Walton, son of Robert and Mary (Hobson) Walton, was born Oct. 31, 1774, in Cumberland County, and died Jan. 20, 1872 in DeValls, Prairie County, Arkansas. He was buried in the DeValls town cemetery. Thomas H. Walton became a 32nd degree Mason in 1796 in St. John's Lodge in Richmond, Virginia. He served as Master of the Cartersville Lodge for fourteen years.[168] He owned Walton's Mill at Trice's Lake, and his family lived on a plantation estate called Pleasant Grove near Cartersville, Cumberland County. The plantation was situated in a valley along the Willis River. One year, about 1840, a flood destroyed most of his crops and fields. In 1843, he sold his estate in Cumberland County in preparation for a migration to Marshall County, Mississippi.[169] Thomas H. was thrice-married: (a) Mrs. Elizabeth (Hatcher) Richardson, on March 18, 1800, in Goochland County, Virginia, (b) Susannah Woodson Bates, daughter of Thomas Fleming and Carolyn Matilda (Woodson) Bates, who was killed by lightning while peeling cucumbers in 1806, and (c) Mrs. Ann (Brackett) Harris daughter of Ludwell and Ann Elizabeth (Cox) Brackett, March 3, 1809, in Amelia County. Ann was born in Virginia on June 22, 1786, and died on July 20, 1846 in Marshall County, Mississippi. Burial was in the Castleberry Cemetery in that County. Two of Susannah W. Bates' brothers, James and Frederick Bates, were successive governors of the State of Missouri. A third brother, Edward Bates, was a prominent attorney who served as Abraham Lincoln's attorney general during the Civil War, 1861-1864. Bates County, Missouri was named for him.[170] "Thomas H.

---

[168] Lavinia A. (Wheat) Bryan, *Genealogy of the Wheat Family*, (Benton, Arkansas: Privately Published), 1984. The obituary of Thomas H. Walton provides a thumbnail sketch of his life.

[169] Cumberland County, Virginia *Chancery Book I*, pp. 489-490. A deed dated July 24, 1843 conveyed a dower and slaves to his wife Anne Hatcher Walton.

[170] Letter from Edward Smith Brown (born in April, 1818) of Lynchburg to Mrs. Emma Walton Ivy, dated Aug. 15, 1905, who knew the family very well, and contributed information to the Woodson book. The 15-page letter is in Jones

Walton was a thrifty merchant in Cartersville and afterwards quite an extensive farmer. He owned Walton's Mill."[171] By 1844, Thomas H. Walton had moved his wife and daughter Caroline to Marshall County, Mississippi. Ann H. Walton wrote her will[172] on Feb. 8, 1844 in Marshall County. She named these children in her will: Augustus T. Walton, Richard P. Walton, Louise E. Walton, Lavinia A. Walton, Caroline M. Walton, and Anna S. Woodson. Also, she named Ann E. and Mary W. Watkins as her grandchildren. She named twenty-seven slaves in the will, apparently the ones inherited from her husband in Virginia. Thomas H. was enumerated on the 1850 census for Marshall County.[173] In 1855, Thomas H. moved to Germantown, Tennessee with John M. Woodson's family. When the Civil War broke out, Thomas H. Walton moved back to Marshall County, Mississippi to live with his daughter Caroline and her husband, Anthony T. Scruggs. Caroline died in 1867, and he moved to DeValls, Arkansas to live with his daughter, Lavinia Ann (Walton) Wheat, where he died in his 98th year. His obituary stated that he was Old School Presbyterian.[174]

Child of Thomas H. and Elizabeth (Hatcher) Walton:[175]

1. Mary H. Walton was born circa 1801 in Cumberland County. She married Robert R. Watkins of Goochland County on March 13, 1828,

---

Memorial Library, Lynchburg, Virginia, Kent Gregory (1872-1950), "Genealogical Papers (Walton), MS1288."

[171] *Ibid.*

[172] Marshall County, Mississippi *Probate Court Records, 1842-1846*, dated Feb. 8, 1844. Her will was probated on Oct. 26, 1846.

[173] 1850 U. S. Census for Marshall County, Mississippi, p. 363.

[174] Henry Morton Woodson, *Historical Genealogy of the Woodsons and Their Connections*, (Published by Henry Morton Woodson: Memphis, Tennessee, 1915), pp. 310-312.

[175] See Cumberland County, Virginia *Chancery Book I*, March 29, 1849, pp. 458-459. None of the children listed below were residents of Virginia, except for Richard P. Walton.

with the Rev. Jesse Armistead officiating.[176] They had two children: Nannie Watkins and Mollie Watkins. Both parents died relatively young, and their two children went to Marshall County, Mississippi to live with relatives.[177] (329)

Child of Thomas H. and Susannah (Bates) Walton:

2. Robert Alfred Walton was born Aug. 27, 1804 at Cartersville, Cumberland County, and died Nov. 20, 1867 in St. Charles, Missouri. He married his first cousin, Emily Carolyn Bates, daughter of Frederick and Nancie Opie (Ball) Bates, Aug. 9, 1838.[178] (330)

Children of Thomas H. and Anne (Brackett) Harris Walton:

3. Ann Harris Walton was born Dec. 29, 1814 in Cumberland County, Virginia and died June 22, 1871 in Texas. She married Stephen Greer Jr. in Marshall County, Mississippi on Dec. 10, 1847. They lived briefly in Arkansas and were in Louisiana in 1850.[179] They were living in Boonville, Texas when the 1860 census was taken.[180] Stephen was a prosperous farmer. They had no children. (331)

4. Philip Ludwell Walton was mentioned as a son in *Historical Genealogy of the Woodsons and Their Connections*, by Henry Morton Woodson. This compiler was unable to locate him in public records. (332)

5. Augustus Thomas Walton was born on Aug. 13, 1817 in Cumberland County, and died May 26, 1884. He married Mary Elizabeth Davenport, daughter of William Bentley and Sarah Jane (Goodman)

---

[176] *Richmond Whig*, March 28, 1828, p. 3, c. 6.

[177] See will of Ann H. (Brackett) Walton, Marshall County, Mississippi *Probate Court Records, 1842-1846*, dated Feb. 8, 1844.

[178] 1850 U. S. Census for St. Louis County, Missouri, p. 524, and 1860 U. S. Census for St. Charles, Missouri, p. 770. See also the 1860 Slave Schedule, p. 298.

[179] 1850 U. S. Census for Bienville Parish, Louisiana, p. 270.

[180] 1850 U. S. Census for Brazos County, Texas, p. 81.

Davenport, on July 23, 1843, per marriage bond.[181] Mary Elizabeth was born on May 15, 1824, in Cumberland County.[182] (333)

6. Richard Peyton Walton was born on March 31, 1819 in Cumberland County and died Oct. 17, 1892 in Norfolk, Virginia. He married Mary Jemima Woodson, daughter of Charles Lewis and Linton (Grayson) Woodson, on May 5, 1842. (334)

7. Louisa Eppes Walton was born in 1821 in Cumberland County, Virginia, and died in 1870 in Memphis, Tennessee. She married John Harris in Marshall County, Mississippi on July 26, 1846.[183] (335)

8. Elizabeth Cornelia Walton was born on April 16, 1823, and died July 24, 1865. Burial was in the Castleberry Cemetery in Marshall County, Mississippi. She married John Morton Woodson on April 6, 1842.[184] They lived in Red Banks, Marshall County.[185] His father-in-law, Thomas H. Walton, was living in the same household when the 1850 U. S. Census was taken; see page 363, Family No. 1164. (336)

9. Lavinia Ann Walton was born on March 10, 1825, and died March 6, 1872 in Prairie County, Arkansas. She married Patrick Henry Wheat on Sept. 12, 1845, in Marshall County, Mississippi. After the death of Lavinia in 1872, Patrick married second Martha A. Legate Reynolds in 1873 and married third Louisa Miller Boone on March 11, 1889. (337)

10. Caroline Matilda Walton was less than twenty-one years old on Aug. 19, 1849. She was born circa 1830 in Cumberland County and died in 1867.[186] Caroline moved to Marshall County, Mississippi, and

---

[181] See also Cumberland County, Virginia *Deed Book 25*, pp. 551-552. The *Richmond Whig*, issue of July 21, 1843, states they were married on July 12th.

[182] Information from the Goodman-Walton Family Bible provided by David Goodman of Baltimore, Maryland.

[183] *Marshall County Marriages, 1836-1865*, (Old Time Press), 1986, p. 116.

[184] *Richmond Whig*, April 26, 1842, p. 1, c. 3.

[185] 1850 U. S. Census for Marshall County, Mississippi, p. 363.

[186] From a paper sent to me by Carole Ruff on July 27, 2001.

married the Rev. Anthony T. Scruggs on July 21, 1852.[187] Anthony was an elder in the Methodist Episcopal Church. Caroline was his third wife. The 1850 Census for Marshall County, indicates that Anthony was a physician, born in 1815 in Tennessee. Another record states that Anthony was born on July 18, 1815 in Williamson County, Tennessee, and died on July 23, 1880. He was a son of Finch and Nancy (Thomas) Scruggs. (338)

Polly (Walton) Goodman (137)

Polly Walton, daughter of Robert and Mary (Hobson) Walton, was born June 23, 1779, and died Nov. 26, 1863, in Cumberland County. She married Noton Goodman, Aug. 4, 1796. Norton was born circa 1774 and died on July 7, 1829, in Cumberland County.[188]

Children of Noton and Polly (Walton) Goodman:

1. Nancy Goodman was born on Feb. 6, 1798 in Cumberland County and died in 1806 in Cumberland County. (339)

2. Elizabeth H. Goodman was born Feb. 1, 1800 and died on Feb. 5, 1823 in Cumberland County. She married James Mason on Nov. 11, 1816 in Cumberland County. (340)

3. Meriwether Goodman was born on March 12, 1803, and died after 1870. He married Marie Ann French. Nov. 15, 1824, in Powhatan County. (341)

4. Sally J. Goodman was born on Sept. 4, 1805 and died on Sept. 10, 1889. She first married William Bentley Davenport, son of Jesse and Elizabeth (Hobson) Davenport, April 4, 1823, and married second Sterling Withers on Dec. 6, 1848, in Mississippi.[189] Sterling was born on Aug. 14, 1785 and died on July 1, 1862.[190] William B. Davenport

---

[187] *Ibid.*

[188] Will is on file in the Cumberland County courthouse, dated June 13, 1829.

[189] Sterling Withers was living in Marshall County, Mississippi when the 1850 and 1860 censuses were taken.

[190] Goodman/Walton Bible record that was published by the St. Louis Genealogical Society and transmitted to the compiler from David Goodman on April 23, 2000. (E-mail: dmg@bcpl.net).

became ill with either tuberculosis or cancer during the winter of 1823-1824. In January of 1824, he set sail from Richmond to Norfolk to Charleston, South Carolina to St. Augustine, Florida where he sought a cure. These letters reveal the pain of Mr. Davenport and his attempt to find a cure for his illness.[191] One child was born to William B. and Sally J. (Goodman) Davenport. Mary Elizabeth Goodman was born on May 15, 1824, in Cumberland County. She married Augustus T. Walton, son of Thomas H. and Anne (Brackett) Walton, on July 12, 1843. (342)

6. Robert Joseph Goodman was born on Aug. 22, 1808 and died on March 26, 1896. He married Frances W. Dunkum on March 29, 1838.[192] Frances was born on July 30, 1818, and died on May 12, 1908. Both are buried in "The Old Garrett Cemetery" in Cumberland County.[193] (343)

6. Thomas A. Goodman was born on Aug. 22, 1810 and died Nov. 22, 1857. He first married Jane G. Bransford on Dec. 13, 1832, and married second Lucy Frances Coleman on Dec. 17, 1856, in Cumberland County. His first wife died on Sept. 5, 1856, and his second wife died in 1859. Nine children were born to the first marriage and none from the second union. (344)

7. Mary Agnes Goodman was born on Sept 4, 1812, and died Jan. 22, 1903. She married Daniel B. Flippen on Dec. 18, 1832. (345)

8. Jane Frances Goodman was born on March 20, 1818, and died Dec. 10, 1864. She married the Rev. Henry David Wood on Dec. 11, 1838 in Bedford County. Henry, who was a Methodist minister, died on Nov. 1, 1863. (346)

---

[191] Copies of letters written to his father-in-law, Noton Goodman, and to his wife, are in the hands of Susan Dauro of Mississippi. The old letters were digitized by David Goodman of Baltimore, Maryland, who transmitted copies to the compiler on June 10, 1999.

[192] Goodman/Walton Bible record that was published by the St. Louis Genealogical Society and transmitted to the compiler from David Goodman on April 23, 2000. (E-mail: dmg@bcpl.net).

[193] Annie Pocahontas (Goodman) Aden of Cary, Mississippi, provided the information in a letter to the compiler.

9. Martha J. Goodman was born on March 23, 1822 and died on Aug. 5, 1854. She married Thomas Compton Brown on Dec. 21, 1837. (347)

William Walton (158)

William Walton, son of Jesse and Ann (Pleasant) Walton, was born Sept. 18, 1776 and died May 20, 1865, in Pittsylvania County, Virginia. He married first Mrs. Sally Tanner on Jan. 24, 1800 in Pittsylvania County. Sally was born on June 10, 1775 and died on June 12, 1831. William married second Mary Lanier on Sept. 9, 1832. He served in the General Assembly from 1808-1815 and 1821-1830, representing Pittsylvania County.[194]

Children of William and Sally (Tanner) Walton:[195]

1. Louisa Ann Walton was born on Nov. 4, 1800 and died on Sept. 19, 1876. She married Cornelius Payne, a Primitive Baptist minister, on Aug. 30, 1817. Cornelius was born on Jan. 19, 1787 in Goochland County, Virginia. They first moved to Maury County, Tennessee and then to Hopkins County, Kentucky, where both died. (348)

2. Robert N. Walton, born circa 1802, married Frances ___ of Pittsylvania County. (349)

3. Thomas Wingfield Walton was born on Jan. 4, 1806 and died on Nov. 18, 1879. He first married Nancy Washington Shelton on Oct. 10, 1828. Nancy was born on Oct. 9, 1806 and died on Oct. 20, 1867. He married second Rebecca Hughes on March 5, 1836. (350)

4. Jesse Simeon Walton was born Oct. 24, 1807 in Pittsylvania County, and died in 1890 in Somervell County, Texas. He married first Eliza Jane Lanier, daughter of John and Mary (Robertson) Lanier, on Sept. 27, 1827 in Pittsylvania County. She was born in 1810 in Pittsylvania

---

[194] Cynthia Miller Leonard, compiler, *The General Assembly of Virginia: a Bicentennial Register of Members, 1619-1978*, (Library of Virginia: Richmond, Virginia, 1978), pp. 253, 262, 271, 275, 279, 310, 315, 336, 340, 345, and 350.

[195] Information on William Walton's family unit was gleaned from Ruth Giles Fischer, *Giles and Cox Families*, (The Bassett Printing Corporation: Bassett, Virginia), 1957, pp. 3-5. Obviously, the information is incomplete.

and died in 1842 in Fayetteville, Arkansas, leaving nine children. Giles believed that Jesse Walton was the same person who wrote to relatives back in Virginia bragging that he had twenty-four children by four wives. (351)

5. Pleasant William Walton was born on Jan. 11, 1816 and died on Dec. 8, 1891. He married Martha Ann Washington Robertson on July 7, 1836. She was born on Oct. 10, 1821 and died on March 13, 1883. (352)

6. Thomas Lanier Walton, of whom nothing further is known. (353)

John Walton (161)

John Walton,[196] son of Simeon and Agnes (Hester) Walton, was born on July 17, 1765 in Amelia County, Virginia, and died on March 21, 1840 in Mason County, Kentucky. He married Susanna Anderson, daughter of Charles and Lucy (Stokes) Anderson, on May 30, 1787, in Amelia County, Virginia. Susanna was born on July 17, 1765 in Amelia County, Virginia, and died on March 21, 1840 in Mason County, Kentucky.

Children of John and Susanna (Anderson) Walton:

1. Barbara Walton was born on March 2, 1788 in Amelia County, Virginia, and died on Feb. 9, 1840 in Boone County, Kentucky. She married William Walton on Jan. 14, 1805 in Mason County, Kentucky. He was born on June 27, 1784 in Louisa County, Virginia and died on Sept. 8, 1862 in Boone County. (354)

2. Simeon Walton was born on Nov. 26, 1789 and died after 1844 in Mason County, Kentucky. He married Lucy M. Anderson on March 22, 1813 in Mason County. (355)

3. Elizabeth A. Walton was born on April 17, 1791 and died after 1840 in Mason County. She married Simeon Walton. (356)

---

[196] John Bennett Boddie, *Historical Southern Families*, (Genealogical Publishing Company, Baltimore, Maryland), vol. II, 1970, p. 217. Information on this family unit came from Patrick Joseph Anderson, 9654 Baltimore Avenue, Laurel, Maryland 20723. He stated that credit should also be given to William H. Black of Tennessee.

4. Tabitha Walton was born on June 9, 1792 in Nottoway County, Virginia and died after 1840 in Mason County. She married Charles I. Gooch on Aug. 24, 1810 in Mason County, Kentucky. They moved to Missouri in 1839. (357)

5. Anna Walton was born on Feb. 2, 1795 in Nottoway County, Virginia and died before 1835 in Mason County. She married Samuel G. Pepper on Oct. 8, 1813 in Mason County. (358)

6. Watkins Walton was born on Jan. 31, 1798. He married Lathana Wood on Aug. 10, 1839 in Mason County. (359)

7. Lucy Walton was born on Dec. 10, 1799, and died after 1840. She married William H. Pepper on Dec. 4, 1818 in Mason County. (360)

8. Matthew Walton was born on June 12, 1801 and died after 1840. He married Mary B. Holton. (361)

9. John H. Walton was born on Dec. 9, 1802 and died after 1840. He married Martha A. Osborne on Aug. 26, 1826 in Mason County. (362)

10. Susanna Walton was born on March 17, 1804 and died in 1870. She married John C. Holton on Nov. 24, 1821 in Mason County. (363)

11. Malvina A. Walton was born on Feb. 6, 1810. She married Charles Osborne. (364)

Records of Bent Creek, Buckingham County, Virginia

Ledgers, account books and diaries are an excellent source for genealogists and historians. Two account books in the Library of Virginia, under Buckingham County Records, provide us with a view of some of the people in this community and their business dealings. Bent Creek was originally called Duiguidsville, a town established by the Virginia Assembly on the south side of the James River where present U. S. Route 60 crosses the river. In 1845, Bent Creek was included in newly-formed Appomattox County. One account book covers 1827-1830, which was kept by Dr. David Crawford Jones, a local physician. He recorded his home visits and told about the sick people. Another was Walton & Phelps Mercantile, which started in 1828. This was William Walton, son of Thomas Jr., and Jonathan P. Phelps. Here are some excerpts:

Fourth Generation

1. George W. Kyle was sheriff in 1828. He bought whiskey, brandy, pickles, pork, bacon, tobacco, hardware, molasses, wool, meal, corn and salt. Other items in the store inventory were sugar, all kinds of material to make clothing, gun powder, necklaces, coffee, brown sugar, etc.

2. Edward Walton bought mostly whiskey. Col. William Chick bought whiskey by the barrel at $10.50 per. Thomas Nowlin bought gallons of whiskey. Other customers during that time were James P. Rogers, Anthony McCoy, George Bell, Thomas Spencer, Col. Samuel P. Christian, John T. Bocock, Reins Johnson, Ambrose Plunkett, Owen C. Fowler, Lavender O. Fowler, David H. Ferguson, Thomas Starkes, John Patteson, Alexander Phelps, Capt. Charles Phelps, Nicholas Tyree, Obadiah Gordon, Major John M. Harris, Capt. Richard G. Morris, Robert Moore, Maj. William K. Perrin, Joseph Crews, Benjamin P. Walker, Catherine Williams, Robert Harris, Thomas Russell, Henry Linthicum, Jesse Hood, Robert Beasley, James Phelps, George Williams, William Dillard, Samuel Goen, Samuel Coleman, William Thornhill, Edward Sears, Thomas W. Scruggs, William A. Harris, Charles L. Christian, William M. Lewis, et al.

3. Joel W. Flood inspected 12, 926 pounds of tobacco on May 18, 1828. The tobacco was stored in a Walton or Horsley warehouse.

4. Services were also recorded in the account book. Silas P. Vawter made a vest for $1.50 and a coat for $4.00 in 1829. George Bell was a shoemaker.

5. William Chick sold eleven hogs weighing 1,668 pounds, for $58.38. Capt. James A. Chick also raised hogs.

6. John Dunkum was a hired hand of William Beverley on March 4, 1830. John Wright had a brother named Robert Wright and a son named James Wright. Maj. John M. Harris was guardian for Alexander Moseley in 1829-1830. Silas P. Vawter was a Constable in 1831. Old Mrs. Martha Walton bought leather for shoes for the slaves. Col. Chick rented out his plantation in the year 1828.

7. Merewether Lewis hired a Negro man in the town of Wingfield on Jan. 1, 1828. Richard Chick bought cloth material for old Mrs. Walton in 1829.

Chapter 5
Fifth Generation

George Walton Jr. (179)

George Walton Jr., son of George Sr. and Dorothy (Camber) Walton, was born on Aug. 15, 1786 in Augusta, Richmond County, Georgia and, according to his obituary, died on Dec. 20, 1859, in Petersburg, Virginia. George Jr. graduated from Princeton University and later served as a Delegate to the Georgia State Legislature. He served as Secretary of East-West Florida Territory in 1822-1826 under Governor Andrew Jackson. He was well connected politically. George Jr. married Sarah Minge Walker, daughter of George and Eliza (Talbot) Walker, on Jan. 10, 1809 in Richmond County, Georgia. Sarah was born on July 19, 1792 at Washington, Georgia and died on Jan. 14, 1861 at Mobile, Alabama. In 1839, George Jr. was elected mayor of Mobile. He separated from his wife Sally late in life and moved to Washington, D. C. where he lived with a companion named Andrew.

Children of George Jr. and Sarah M. (Walker) Walton:

    1. Robert Watkins Walton[1] was born in August 1819 in Augusta, Georgia, and died on March 22, 1849 in Mobile, Alabama of encephalitis. He was educated at the University of Virginia. In 1836, he served as a Major in the Creek War. Robert did not marry; he was buried in Magnolia Cemetery with military honors. (365)

    2. Octavia Celeste Walton was born on Aug. 11, 1811 and died on March 12, 1877. She married Dr. Henry S. LeVert. (366)

Nancy Murray (Walton) Askew[2] (183)

Nancy Murray (Walton) Askew, daughter of Tilman and Judith (Walton) Walton, was born on Feb. 28, 1788 in Amherst County,

---

[1] See Frances Gibson Satterfield, *Madame LeVert: A Biography of Octavia Walton LeVert*, (Edisto Island, South Carolina: Edisto Press), 1987, pp. 75-79.

[2] Information on family unit of James T. Askew's family unit was provided by Patricia Morrow, 6506 Prairie Dunes, Houston, TX 77069. She has done extensive research on her ancestors, including the Waltons. She requested that credit be given to Myrtle Moore, Madeline Shepherd, and Alice Mae Morrow, her mother.

Virginia. She married the Rev. James Tilmon Askew, son of Josiah and Priscilla (Lee) Askew, on March 5, 1803 in Nebo, Burke County, North Carolina. James was a Methodist minister. He was born about 1778 in North Carolina and died circa 1852 in Madison County, North Carolina.

Children of James T. and Nancy M. (Walton) Askew:

    1. George Christian Askew was born on Jan. 28, 1809 and died on May 19, 1884. He married Sarah Harrison Lusk in Madison County, North Carolina on Oct. 18, 1831. (367)

    2. Eliza Askew was born in 1810^3 and died after 1870. She married Thomas Burnett on Nov. 27, 1827 in Burke County. They moved to Jasper, Marion County, Tennessee. Eliza married second Dr. W.W. Morris on June 22, 1851. (368)

    3. Judith Askew was born circa 1812 and died on March 12, 1890 in Madison County, North Carolina. She married James Henry Gillespie on Jan. 24, 1831 in Burke County. He died circa 1865. (369)

    4. James T. Askew was born in 1806 and died about 1870. He was listed on the 1850 census as being insane. That label was not defined as well as our understanding today. Sometimes a person was labeled an idiot if he was "deaf and dumb," or hearing impaired in today's nomenclature. (370)

    5. Josiah Askew, born in 1819, married Mary Polly Smart. (371)

    6. Thomas William Askew was born on April 23, 1827 in McDowell County, North Carolina, and died on June 1, 1863. He married Martha W. Bailey, 1830-1916, in 1855. Five children we born to this marriage. After Thomas' death, Martha married second James Michael Case and they had one child. (372)

Thomas George Walton (199)

Thomas George Walton, son of Thomas and Martha M. (McEntire) Walton, was born on Oct. 5, 1815 at Morganton, Burke County, North Carolina and died on June 15, 1905 at Morganton.

---

[3] There is not agreement on her birth year. One source suggests 1804, per Patricia Morrow.

He married Margaret Eliza Avery Murphy on Dec. 28, 1837. She was born on Dec. 20, 1820 and died on Feb. 3, 1886. According to Adams,[4] Thomas George grew up in the business environment of his father's "Walton Store." He became president of the Bank of Morganton, earning $500.00 per year in 1859. He represented Burke County as a Whig in the General Assembly in 1850 and as a Republican after Reconstruction. He served on the Board of the Western North Carolina Railroad, and the insane asylum in Raleigh. During the Civil War, he was a Colonel of the 8th Regiment North Carolina Home Guards. Thomas was an active member of Grace Episcopal Church in Morganton, serving as Lay Reader, Vestryman, and co-chairman of fund raising to build a new stone church in 1893-1894. His death occurred at Creekside, which was his plantation home by Silver Creek in Burke County. This family unit is one of the finest in this volume. The Thomas George Walton Papers are housed and maintained in the Manuscripts Department, Library of the University of North Carolina, as part of the Southern Historical Collection No. 748.

Children of Thomas G. and Margaret E. (Murphy) Walton:[5]

1. Ella Walton was born on Feb. 14, 1839 and died on Oct. 2, 1839. (373)

2. Edward Stanley Walton was born in July 1840 and died on April 10, 1898. He lived at Mountain View, a house overlooking Morganton and built by Samuel Greenlee in 1815. He married Kate Blackwell. (374)

3. John Murphy Walton was born on Oct. 19, 1844 in Burke County and died on Dec. 2, 1872. He attended two military schools, which prepared him for extensive service in the Civil War. He kept a diary, which is a very important first-hand account of the War. He died of tuberculosis at Creekside, his father's home. (375)

4. Margaret Tilghman Walton was born on Oct. 26, 1846 and died on April 15, 1928. Margaret was an Episcopalian, as was her family. She

---

[4] Margaret Bickel Adams, *Old Burke County Relatives*, (Privately Printed), Margaret Bickel Adams, 301 Broad Street, Marion, NC 28752-4515, 2000.

[5] Information is from Margaret Bickel Adams' book *Old Burke County Relatives*.

married Charles Finley McKesson, 1839-1918. An obituary described him as a "Statesman, Scholar, Patriot, and Southern Gentleman, orator of marked ability...highly educated and having a remarkable memory. Margaret's obituary described her as "...the purest type (of) Southern womanhood and motherhood." (376)

5. George Walton was born on Jan. 22, 1849 and died on Nov. 8, 1904. He attended Davidson College for undergraduate studies and finished a medical degree from New York University. He practiced medicine in Christian County, Illinois until 1902, when he started a practice in St. Louis. His wife died on April 16, 1915, name not given. (377)

6. Lucy Walton was born on Jan. 10, 1851 and died on Nov. 17, 1922. She married the Rev. Neilson Falls, 1842-1916, Rector of Grace Episcopal Church in Morganton, on July 19, 1870. He later served as Rector of St. Alban's Church in Washington, D. C. (378)

7. Martha Matilda Walton was born on Nov. 7, 1852 and died on May 19, 1936. She married Charles Stuart Smith, 1847-1915, a building contractor in Morganton. They raised a family, which was very devoted to Grace Episcopal Church. (379)

8. Florence Louise Walton was born on Aug. 24, 1855 and died on March 18, 1930. She married John Henry Pearson (1852-1954), a successful Morganton businessperson. State legislator, and twenty-fourth Sheriff of Burke County. (380)

9. Hugh Collett Walton was born on Sept. 11, 1858 and died on Dec. 16, 1867, from a fall from a horse at Creekside. (381)

10. Hubert Huske Walton was born on Aug. 25, 1860 and died on March 12, 1949. He inherited from his father and lived all his life at Creekside. Hubert married Lola Kirkland, 1861-1891, on Feb. 12, 1889. He was very active at Grace Episcopal Church, serving as Lay Reader, Senior Warden and other positions. (382)

Phoebe C. (Walton) Armistead (203)

Phoebe C. Walton, daughter of Thomas G. and Agnes (Mosby) Walton, was born circa 1793 in Cumberland County, Virginia and died after 1850 at Union, Franklin County, Missouri. She married William H. Armistead, probably in Smith County, Tennessee. He was born circa 1781 in Cumberland County, and died about 1860 in Franklin County, Missouri.

Children of William H. and Phoebe C. (Walton) Armistead:[6]

1. Robert B. Armistead was born on June 12, 1809 in Smith County, Tennessee and died on Nov. 22, 1862 at Stanton, Franklin County, Missouri. He married Agnes Mosby Walton, daughter of George and Mary (Terry) Walton. She was born on Sept. 18, 1821 in Smith County, Tennessee and died on March 7, 1903 in Franklin County. Twelve children were born to this union. (383)

2. Mary B. Armistead was born circa 1814 in Smith County. She married William Blackwell on Aug. 13, 1837 in Franklin County. (384)

3. Agnes Armistead was born in Tennessee and allegedly died at age twenty-three. (385)

4. Thomas Jefferson Armistead was born circa 1819 and died during the 1880s at Union, Franklin County, Missouri. He married first Emily Ann Grooms (1827-1853) on May 20, 1841 in Franklin County and married second Elizabeth Parks, daughter of William and Mary (Stites) Parks, on May 15, 1854. Six children were born to the first union. (386)

5. Nancy A. J. Armistead was born circa 1821. She married David Hogan on Jan. 4, 1855 at Union, Franklin County. (387)

6. Hannah Armistead was born circa 1823 in Tennessee. She married first Joseph Hearst on June 15, 1848 at Union, Franklin County and married second Ebenezer Parks on Aug. 10, 1857 in Franklin County. (388)

7. Phebe Walton Armistead was born on Aug. 5, 1824 in Tennessee and died on Oct. 8, 1910 at Union, Franklin County. She married William Wilburn Hendrix on March 12, 1844. He was born on June 10, 1819 in Tennessee and died on Dec. 11, 1869 in Missouri. Eleven children were born to this union. (389)

8. Fannie Armistead was born in Tennessee, and died at the age of six weeks. (390)

9. Lockey Jane Armistead was born on March 27, 1827 in Tennessee and died on March 11, 1914 at Sullivan, Franklin County, Missouri. She married first Richard Sullens on July 22, 1849 in Franklin County,

---

[6] Information on this family unit was provided by Karen Walker of St. Louis, Missouri,

and married second James Higgens on Aug. 17, 1886 in Franklin County, and married third George Washington Bandy on Oct. 16, 1889 in Franklin County. (391)

10. Elizabeth Priscilla Armistead was born in 1830 in Tennessee and died after 1890. She married first William Edward Gilcrease on April 12, 1855 in Franklin County, Missouri and married second John Sauer on Sept. 16, 1881 in Franklin County. Eight children were born to this union. (392)

11. William T. Armistead was born on May 6, 1832 in Tennessee and died on Oct. 16, 1902 at Stanton, Franklin County. (393)

12. George E. Armistead was born on Sept. 24, 1835 at Union, Franklin County, Tennessee and died on Oct. 28, 1911 at Stanton, Franklin County. He married first Rebecca Greenstreet, daughter of William and Elizabeth (Anderson) Greenstreet, on May 23, 1861. He married second Susan Anderson on April 20, 1874 in Franklin County. Two children were born to the first union. (394)

Jesse W. Walton (210)

Jesse W. Walton, son of Minjum H. and Sally F. (Mann) Walton, was born in 1807 in Cumberland County, Virginia and died on Jan. 25, 1890 in Goochland County, Virginia. He married Elizabeth Emeline Cheatham, daughter of Isham and Hannah (Spears) Cheatham, on Dec. 15, 1834 in Goochland County. She was born on Oct. 4, 1812 and died in Goochland County on April 12, 1848.[7] Both were buried in the Dover Church Cemetery in Goochland County. In 1831, he bought 85 acres from his father.[8] He held this land until 1848 when his wife died and he was no longer able to pay the taxes. John P. Woodson bought the property for back taxes.[9] Jesse was a farmer.

---

[7] *Richmond Whig and Public Advertiser*, p. 4, c. 7, issue of May 12, 1848.

[8] Cumberland County, Virginia *Deed Book 20*, p. 199.

[9] Cumberland County, Virginia *Deed Book 26*, pp. 610-611.

Children of Jesse W. and Elizabeth E. (Cheatham) Walton:[10]

1. Phebe Walton was born circa 1835. (395)

2. Sarah E. Walton was born circa 1838. She may have married William Sinclair, but not proven. (396)

3. Isham Cheatham Walton was born in 1840 and died on June 19, 1895. He was buried in the Dover Church Cemetery in Goochland County. He married Elizabeth Woodson, daughter of Leander and Sarah (Woodson) Woodson, in 1861 in Goochland County.[11] They had children[12] named Blanche Walton, born in 1862; Edward Walton, born in 1865; and Charles Walton, born in 1869. (397)

4. Mary E. Walton was born circa 1841. She was listed as a schoolteacher when the 1860 Census was taken for Goochland County. In 1870, she was listed on the census as a housekeeper for her father. (398)

5. Susan Alice Walton was born in 1843 and died on Oct. 23, 1865. She was buried in Dover Church Cemetery. (399)

William Mann Walton (211)

William Mann Walton,[13] son of Minjum H. and Sally F. (Mann) Walton, was born in 1809 in Cumberland County, Virginia and died on Feb. 8, 1883 in Henrico County, Virginia. He married first Margaret Ann Gills on Dec. 1, 1853 in Henrico County, Virginia. He married second Margaret Ann Seay, daughter of Matthew and Eliza (Layne) Seay, on Dec. 24, 1860 in Goochland County,

---

[10] Names and birth years were obtained from the 1850 US Census for Goochland County, Virginia and the 1860 Census.

[11] Henry Morton Woodson, *Historical and Genealogy of the Woodsons and Their Connections*, 1915, p. 421.

[12] U. S. Census for Goochland County, Virginia, Dover District, Aug. 11, 1870.

[13] Information on William's family unit was researched and contributed by Elizabeth W. (Drake) Chatlin, Zion Summit, 241 North Vine 807-E, Salt Lake City, UT 84103. She cites a Walton family Bible in possession of Alfred Walton, 7333 Osborne Turnpike, Richmond, VA 23231 (copy provided to the compiler).

Virginia. Margaret was born on June 14, 1845 in Goochland County and died on May 17, 1937.[14] According to the 1880 U. S. Census for Henrico County, William was engaged as a "farm manager."[15] Apparently, his lifetime work was farming, in that he stated this occupation on his marriage license. It is believed that William moved across the James River into Goochland County to be near his brother Jesse W. Walton. He was living in the household of his brother Jesse W. when the 1860 U. S. Census for Dover District, Goochland County was taken.

Children of William M. and Margaret A. (Seay) Walton:

1. John Thomas Walton was born on Nov. 28, 1861 and died on Oct. 2, 1950. He married Sallie F. ____. (400)

2. Elizabeth "Lizzie" M. Walton was born on Sept. 3, 1864 and died on Dec. 31, 1903. She married Jacob Alley. (401)

3. Minjum H. Walton was born on Feb. 4, 1868 and died on June 27, 1944. He married Jennie Campbell. (402)

4. Eliza Ann Walton was born on Feb. 14, 1869 and died on May 18, 1916. She married Chastain DeGrasse Proffitt. (403)

5. Joseph M. Walton was born on Aug. 30, 1870 and died on Feb. 10, 1905. He married Mary Elizabeth Denton. (404)

6. Jesse William Walton was born on July 1, 1875 and died on June 27, 1957. He married Julia Pleasants. (405)

John T. Walton (212)

John T. Walton, son of Minjum H. and Sally F. (Mann) Walton Sr., was born on March 28, 1811 in Cumberland County, Virginia and died at Greensboro, Hale County, Alabama on July 21, 1892. The compiler identified John T. Walton through the personal property tax lists for 1843-1844 in Cumberland County and then

---

[14] Commonwealth of Virginia, Department of Health, Bureau of Vital Statistics, Certificate No. 12098, provided by Elizabeth W. (Drake) Chatlin.

[15] 1880 U. S. Census, Tuckahoe District, Henrico County, Virginia, Vol. 16, Ed. 68, Sheet 16, Line 4, enumerated on June 9, 1880.

made a national search on the 1850 census records. John married first Jane D. Hudgins on March 23, 1840 in Cumberland County, Virginia.[16] The surety was Jess D. Parker, who became his brother-in-law. John married second Sarah Frances Gills on April 3, 1847 in Greene County, Alabama. She was born in July 1828 in Virginia and died on July 13, 1908. Sarah was a daughter of Pleasant and Nancy (Fowlkes) Gills of Amelia County, Virginia. About 1845-1846, John T. moved his family to Greene County, Alabama, where his family was enumerated on the 1850 Census. The Gills moved to Alabama before 1850, and were found on the same census page as John T. Walton. In 1860, John T. and his family were living at Morgan Springs, Perry County, Alabama. In 1880, he was living at Greensboro, Hale County, Alabama where he died. Sarah Frances was living with her son Joseph P. Walton when the 1900 census was taken for Hale County. The census record states that she had given birth to six children, with only three living in 1900. This confirms John's prior marriage in Virginia. He was a very successful farmer who accumulated more wealth than his siblings did. Greene and Perry Counties are located in the west-central part of Alabama.

Children of John T. and Jane D. (Hudgins) Walton:

> 1. Sarah Walton was born circa 1841 in Virginia. It is believed that she married Jacob Murff Jr. on July 15, 1858 in Perry County, Alabama. It has been said that Murff lost his life in the Civil War. (406)

> 2. Lucy Catherine Walton was born on Aug. 11, 1843 in Virginia and died on Jan. 20, 1914. She married Alpheus B. Drake on Nov. 15, 1864 in Perry County, Alabama. After his death, she married second James R. Ricard on Sept. 29, 1876. (407)

> 3. Elizabeth "Betty" Walton was born circa 1846 in Alabama. (408)

Children of John T. and Sarah F. (Gills) Walton:

> 4. Fannie E. Walton was born in 1848 in Alabama. She married Wesley (or William) M. Lovell on Feb. 11, 1879. They were living at Benton,

---

[16] The Cumberland County *Marriage Book I* appears to give John's middle initial as a J. See also Cumberland County *Deed Book 24*, pp. 427-428, dated Aug. 18, 1841.

Faulkner County, Arkansas when the U. S. Census was taken in 1880 that place. Wesley was a house carpenter. (409)

5. William H. Walton was born in 1848 in Alabama. He lived with his sister Lucy's family. William died from injuries received from a kicking horse. He did not marry. (410)

6. John Julian Walton was born on Jan. 19, 1850 in Alabama, and died on May 1, 1912 in Hale County, Alabama. He married Mary Alice "Minnie" Roberts on Dec. 9, 1874.[17] (411)

7. Alice Walton was born on Oct. 27, 1853 in Alabama and died in 1927. She married Joseph A. Walker on Nov. 13, 1875 in Perry County, Alabama. Possibly, she is the Julia A. Walton on the U. S. Census. (412)

8. Joseph Pleasant Walton was born on June 4, 1857 in Alabama, and died on June 8, 1929. He married Chellie Lou Nixon, born on Jan. 20, 1859 and died on May 10, 1940. (413)

Note: See page 456 for family photographs

Elizabeth (Walton) Parker (213)

Elizabeth Walton, daughter of Minjum H. and Sally F. (Mann) Walton, was born circa 1812 in Cumberland County and died circa 1847 in Cumberland County. She married Jesse Daniel Parker, son of Jesse and Sarah (Guthrey) Parker, on March 8, 1840.[18] He was born in Cumberland County in 1809 and died on April 26, 1877. After Elizabeth's death, Jesse married second Mary Jane Gills, daughter of Pleasant and Nancy (Fowlkes) Gills. She was born circa 1824. Jesse was a farmer in the Hamilton District of Cumberland County, Virginia.

Children of Jesse D. and Elizabeth (Walton) Parker:[19]

---

[17] Information was supplied by Eleanor C. Drake, P. O. Box 310, Uniontown, Alabama

[18] The Cumberland County Historical Society, Inc., *Cumberland County, Virginia and Its People*, (Walsworth Publishing Co.: Marceline, Missouri), 1983, p. 168.

[19] Their children were identified by the 1850 U. S. Census for Cumberland County.

1. Isham T. Parker was born circa 1840. He married Louisa ____. (414)

2. Sarah Frances Parker was born circa 1842. (415)

3. John Jesse Parker[20] was born in 1847, and died in 1892 in Cumberland County. He married Virginia Alice Robertson on Oct. 18, 1865 in Cumberland County. He was a veteran of the Civil War. John J. was a farmer in Cumberland County. (416)

4. Ella Parker was born in 1849. (417)

5. Mary A. Parker was born circa 1851. She may have been a daughter of his second marriage. (418)

6. Willa Parker was born in 1855. (419)

7. Ida Parker was born in 1858. (420)

Joseph M. Walton (214)

Joseph M. Walton, son of Minjum H. and Sally F. (Mann) Walton, was born on Feb. 5, 1814 in Cumberland County, Virginia and died on Oct. 19, 1888 at Greensboro, Hale County, Alabama. He married Lucy T. Gills, daughter of Pleasant and Nancy (Fowlkes) Gills, on Nov. 17, 1838 in Amelia County, Virginia. Lucy was born in Amelia County on May 1, 1818 and died in Hale County on Sept. 12, 1882. Members of this family were buried in the Greensboro City Cemetery at Greensboro, Alabama.[21] The elder Gills migrated to Alabama during the mid-1840s and were close neighbors of the Walton brothers during the 1850s and 1860s. Joseph M. was identified from the personal tax lists of Cumberland County, Virginia and tracked to Alabama through a national search of the U. S. Census records. He was a well-to-do farmer.

Children of Joseph M. and Lucy (Gills) Walton:[22]

---

[20] *Loc cit.* p. 168.

[21] Kathleen Paul Jones and Pauline Jones Gandrud, compilers, *Alabama Records*, Vol. 69, "Greene County, Alabama," March 1941, pp. 42-44.

[22] Information was collected and transmitted by Eleanor C. Drake, P. O. Box 310, Uniontown, AL 36786.

Fifth Generation

1. Sarah E. Walton was born Nov 25, 1840 and died on Sept. 27, 1937. She married William Alexander Avery. (421)

2. William P. Walton was born circa 1842 in Virginia.[23] He married Mollie Brand on April 14, 1869 in Perry County, Alabama.[24] (422a)

3. Mary Agnes Walton was born in August 1844 in Cumberland County, Virginia and died on Oct. 9, 1900 In Hale County, Alabama. On Feb. 16, 1871, she married Dr. William T. Downey. His dates are Aug. 6, 1848 and July 22, 1919. Both were buried in the Greensboro City Cemetery. (422b)

4. Thomas Howard Walton was born on Aug. 28, 1846 in Virginia, and died Jan. 18, 1908 in Hale County. He married Susan Brand on May 10, 1870 in Perry County, Alabama. She was born on July 5, 1849 and died on Oct. 24, 1910. (423)

5. Josephine Walton was born Dec. 27, 1849 in Alabama, and died on June 17, 1918 in Hale County, Alabama.[25] She married Thomas Jerre Yancey, 1838-1909, on Dec. 21, 1870 in Perry County. (424)

6. Jasper Walton was born in 1850 in Alabama, per 1860 U. S. Census. (425)

7. Samuel L. Walton was born on Jan. 5, 1854 in Alabama, and died on March 10, 1913. He married Sallie E. Melton on Jan. 20, 1875. She was born on Sept. 27, 1853 and died Nov. 6, 1936. Burial was in the Greensboro City Cemetery in Hale County, Alabama. The 1900 census gives the name of ten children. See Appendix C for information that was gathered after this chapter was completed. (426)

8. Robert Walton was born circa 1858 in Alabama and died on Oct. 23, 1918 in Hale County.[26] (427)

9. Ellen Walton was born circa 1859 in Alabama. (428)

---

[23] 1860 U. S. Census for Morgan Springs, Perry County, Alabama, p. 546.

[24] Ancestry.com, Alabama Marriages, 1800-1920

[25] Ancestry.com,"Alabama Deaths 1908- 1959."

[26] Hale County Deaths 1908-1959, Vol. 23, p. 352.

10. Emma Walton was born circa 1860 in Alabama and died in 1942. She married John Richard Beck in Alabama, 1856-1922. (429)

11. Ida Walton was born circa 1863 in Alabama. She married W. J. Giesler on Jan. 14, 1892. (430)

Minjum H. Walton, Jr. (215)

Minjum H. Walton Jr., son of Minjum H. and Sally F. (Mann) Walton Sr., was born circa 1821 in Cumberland County and died after 1880. He married Judith C. Palmore, daughter of Robert and Elizabeth (Bagby) Palmore, on April 13, 1848 in Buckingham County, Virginia. Judith was born in 1823.[27] Minjum raised his family in Powhatan County. The only deed on record for Minjum was a Homestead Deed that he received on Dec. 6, 1870.[28] He showed the court that he possessed farm animals and crops worth more than $900.00 to qualify for the deed.

Children of Minjum H. and Judith (Palmore) Walton:[29]

1. Sarah Elizabeth "Betty" Walton was born circa 1848, per 1850 and 1870 U. S. Censuses for Powhatan County. (431)

2. Thomas Mann Walton was born in September 1849 and died after 1900. According to the 1900 U. S. Census for the Macon District of Powhatan County, Virginia, his wife was named Isibia, and three children were listed: (a) George C. Walton was born in October 1882. (b) Blanche C. Walton was born in July 1885, and (c) Joseph M. Walton Jr. was born on June 24, 1886 and died on June 4, 1902.[30] (432)

3. Anna M. Walton was born in 1852. She married George E. Scott. (433)

---

[27] 1880 U. S. Census for Powhatan County, Virginia, Macon District, p. 181A, Family 194.

[28] Powhatan County, Virginia *Deed Book 21*, p. 452.

[29] Information on the children was secured from U. S. Census records and "Powhatan County, Virginia Births, 1853-1896," in the Library of Virginia.

[30] Dates are from inscriptions in the Hollywood Cemetery in Richmond, Virginia.

4. Infant was born and died in August 1855. (434)

5. Emma Jane Walton was born circa 1858. (435)

6. Joseph M. Walton was born in July 1860. He was living with his brother-in-law George E. Scott when the 1920 Census was taken in Brookland District, Henrico County, Virginia. They were farmers. (436)

Robert J. Walton (227)

Robert J. Walton, son of Anthony Sr. and Rebecca (Johnson) Walton, was born circa 1794, probably in Buckingham County, Virginia, and died after 1860, probably in Texas. His middle initial J, found on the 1830 census for Campbell County, Virginia, may have stood for Johnson, after his mother's maiden name.[31] Robert received from his father's estate 289½ acres at Bent Creek, Buckingham County, and now in Appomattox County. He sold this acreage to his half-brother, William Walton, in 1825. The same year, he bought part of his sister Lucy Thornhill's lot that contained 118 and one-half acres. In 1826 he bought another 118 ½ acres. Robert allegedly married Elizabeth Wilson of Campbell County, Virginia on June 29, 1816.[32] This is possibly a mistaken identity here, in that his Uncle Robert Walton also married an Elizabeth Wilson in 1816 in the same area. If Robert J. married in 1816, it seems unusual that he waited fourteen years before the first child was born. More research is needed to unravel these mysteries. The 1830 census for Campbell County lists one male under five years, one unknown male between five and ten years old, one female under five years, and two females between five and ten years. About 1835, they moved to Kentucky.[33] They were living in Boone County, Kentucky when the 1840 census was taken.[34] In 1850 and 1860,

---

[31] 1830 U. S. Census for Campbell County, Virginia, Roll 194, p. 394.

[32] Jean Boyce

[33] The 1860 U. S. Census for Leon County, Texas, family no. 578, states that their son James Walton was born in Virginia circa 1834 and their son William was born in Kentucky circa 1836.

[34] !840 U. S. Census for Boone County, Kentucky, p. 263a.

they were on the U. S. Censuses for Leon County, Texas.[35] Robert's occupation was a farmer.

Children of Robert J. and Elizabeth (Wilson?) Walton:[36]

1. Murry Thomas Walton was born on March 30, 1830 in Campbell County, Virginia and died on Oct. 2, 1907 in Lehigh, Oklahoma. He married Nancy Elizabeth Taylor. (437)

2. Rebecca Ann Walton was born on April 6, 1832 in Virginia and died on Nov. 4, 1870. (438)

3. Amanda Catherine Walton was born in Campbell County, Virginia in November 1834. She married James John Garland. (439)

4. James W. Walton was born circa 1835 in Virginia. He was living in the household of his parents in 1860. In 1870, he was the head of his household at Waco, McLennan County, Texas. James' wife Martha was born circa 1838 in Mississippi. Living in the household was their daughter Frances Walton who was born in 1867 in Texas. In 1880, in the same County, James was listed as a widower. His daughter Frances, age twelve, was living in the household. James was a farmer. (440)

5. William Walton was born circa 1836, probably in Boone County, Kentucky. In 1860, he was living in the household of his parents. No further information was located. (441)

Thomas Cook Walton (228)

Thomas Cook Walton, son of Anthony Sr. and Rebecca (Johnson) Walton, was born at Bent Creek, Buckingham County, Virginia on Nov. 18, 1795 and died on March 20, 1842 after catching a cold in a rainstorm in Chariton County, Missouri. He was a farmer. Thomas C. married Nancy Patteson Trent, daughter of Thomas and Elizabeth (Edwards) Trent, on Dec. 13, 1817 in Buckingham County. She died on March 26, 1860, aged sixty-four

---

[35] 1850 U. S. Census for Centerville, Leon County, Texas, Roll M653_1299, p. 278.

[36] Information was provided by Jean Boyce, kboyce@junct.com, on Aug. 29, 2004. Other sources included an analysis of U. S. Census records. Names of three children born before 1830 are not known.

years, nine months, and nine days, according to a tombstone inscription in the family cemetery. The 1860 U. S. Mortality Schedule for Chariton County, Missouri says that Nancy died of typhoid fever.

Children of Thomas C. and Nancy P. (Trent) Walton: [37]

    1. Anthony Walton was born circa 1822 and died in 1865 at Red River, Texas. He married Mary Elizabeth Winn, daughter of James and Rebecca (Parks) Winn, in 1843, in Salisbury, Missouri. Allegedly, he served in the CSA and was killed while going down on the USS Kentucky on the Red River in Texas in 1865. (442)

    2. Meriwether Lewis Walton was born circa 1824 at Bent Creek, Virginia. He was living in his mother's household when the 1850 U. S. Census was taken for Prairie Township, Chariton County. In 1900, he was living in the household of his brother, Thomas H. Walton, in Salisbury Township. (443)

    3. Elizabeth Trent Walton was born on Dec. 13, 1826 in Buckingham County, Virginia. She married Ethelrod H. Parkes on Nov. 15, 1843 in Chariton County. (444)

    4. Thomas Henry Walton was born in Buckingham County on Dec. 13, 1826, and died on July 17, 1910 at Salisbury, Missouri. He married Louise Price, daughter of John W. Price of Chariton County, Missouri, on Dec. 25, 1868. (445)

    5. Martina Virginia Walton was born on Jan. 4, 1830. She married Benjamin Franklin Ashby on Sept. 18, 1844 in Chariton County, Missouri. (446)

    6. William A. Walton was born circa 1832 and died on Nov. 26, 1879 in Chariton, Missouri. He was living in his mother's household in 1850. (447)

---

[37] Information on Thomas C. Walton and his descendants was provided in part by Michael Amer of New Zealand via e-mails dated April 16, 1998 and May 18, 2001. The compiler was unable to locate quality information on this family unit. More research is necessary to fill the information gaps.

Anthony Walton Jr. (231)

Anthony Walton Jr., son of Anthony Sr. and Rebecca (Johnson) Walton, was born at Bent Creek, Buckingham County, Virginia about 1800 and died before 1860 in Appomattox County. His wife was Martha A. Daniel, daughter of Henry and Judith Daniel of Powhatan County, Virginia. She was born circa 1801 and died in July 1861, of pneumonia, in Appomattox County, Virginia.[38] Anthony was listed as a carpenter on the 1850 census for Appomattox County. In 1825, he purchased 201 acres from his father's estate at Bent Creek, and inherited an undetermined amount of land. He advertised in a Lynchburg newspaper dated Aug. 20, 1826, for sale 56 acres on Bent Creek in Buckingham County adjoining Robert Walton, John Flood, Snowden Maddox, and William G. Linthicum, his trustee. Anthony was listed on the 1830 U.S. Census for Campbell County (Lynchburg), with a wife and two unnamed male children under the ages of five years. They owned and lived at an estate called "Rose Grove" located on the stage road between Richmond to Lynchburg, about five miles northwest of the old Appomattox courthouse.[39]

Children of Anthony Jr. and Martha (Daniel) Walton:

> 1. Thomas E. Walton was born about 1829 and died in 1882. He married Martha E. Woodson, daughter of Drury Woodson. (448)

John Anderson Walton (234)

John Anderson Walton, son of Robert and Mildred (Armistead) Walton, was born circa 1798 in Cumberland County, Virginia and died in 1849 in Obion County, Tennessee.[40] In 1830, John A. was

---

[38] Library of Virginia, *Appomattox County, Virginia Death Records, 1853-1896*, death record for Martha A. Walton was reported to the Clerk of Court by her son, Thomas E. Walton.

[39] See Appomattox County, Virginia *Land Tax Books, 1860-1865*, located in the County Courthouse.

[40] Contributed by Gene Talley GTa1056569@aol.com of Bartlett, Tennessee, in an email to the compiler on Aug. 5, 2002.

Fifth Generation

living in Goochland County, Virginia where he met his wife. He was living in Wilson County, Tennessee in 1833.[41] This county is located just east of Nashville, which is in Davidson County. The 1840 census for Wilson County does not include the name of John A. Walton. He married first Ann M. Crank, daughter of Lipscomb and Polly (Parish) Crank, on June 28, 1825 in Goochland County, Virginia. Ann died in Wilson County during the winter of 1835-1836. John A. married second Martha (Scott) Talley, widow of Joshua Talley, circa 1838.[42]. John was favored by his grandfather, William Armistead, who gave him an inheritance of 130 acres in Cumberland County, which was formerly owned by his father, and a gift of a Negro named Alexander.

Children of John A. and Ann (Crank) Walton:

1. Mary Eliza Walton was born ca 1825 in Virginia. (449))

2. Robert James Walton was born ca 1827 in Virginia. (450)

3. William Anderson Walton was born ca 1828 in Virginia. (451)

4. Mildred Ann Walton was born ca 1830 in Virginia. (452)

5. Elizabeth Frances Walton was born ca 1832 in Virginia. (453)

6. John Lipscomb Walton was born in Wilson County, Tennessee on Jan. 2, 1834 and died on March 10, 1908 in Logan County, Arkansas. He married Adeline Cravens on July 22, 1869 in Johnson County, Arkansas. She was born on March 22, 1849 in Johnson County, and died on Nov. 18, 1929 at Paris, Logan County. (454)

7. George Henry Walton was born circa 1836 in Wilson County, Tennessee. He was living in the household of Richard Crank when the 1850 U.S. Census was taken in Smith County, Tennessee. (455)

Child of John A. and Martha (Scott) Talley Walton:

8. Sarah Walton was born circa 1839. (456)

---

[41] Cumberland County, Virginia *Deed Book 21*, p. 225.

[42] http://genforum.genealogy.com/cgi-bin/pageload.cgi?Obion::scott::9836.html

Anthony Anderson Walton Sr. (236)

Anthony Anderson Walton, son of Robert and Mildred (Armistead) Walton, was born circa 1804 in Cumberland County, Virginia, and died on Sept. 1, 1866 in Buckingham County. He first married Mary Austin on April 18, 1829, in Cumberland County. Anthony A. was a merchant in Cumberland at that time.[43] He married second Sarah J. McDaniel, daughter of Abraham Daniel, in Cumberland County on Oct. 15, 1840. Sarah died Feb. 26, 1847 in her 37th year.[44] Anthony A. married third Margaret (Nixon) Hobart, daughter of William and Wilmuth Nixon, in Buckingham County, on Jan. 29, 1850.[45] Margaret's first husband was a mining engineer from a northern state. They moved to St. Louis where he died. Margaret returned to Buckingham County where she married Anthony A. Walton.[46] Anthony A. and Margaret lived at Buckingham Court House. In 1866, there were rumors of Mrs. Walton having an affair with attorney named James Leach. Apparently, the rumors were not true. One evening, Anthony A. Walton Jr. became involved in a discussion with attorney Leach. Someone in town overheard the conversation and erroneously alerted Anthony A. Walton Sr. that an argument was taking place. Both Walton men shot at James Leach, but both missed. Leach returned fire and Anthony Sr. died of a pistol shot on Sept. 1, 1866. His son Anthony Jr., who was a schoolteacher in Buckingham County, died of pistol wounds on Sept. 3, 1866. Why was James Leach carrying a pistol?

Children of Anthony A. Sr. and Mary (Austin) Walton:

---

[43] Cumberland County, Virginia *Circuit Court Orders*, 1831-1851, p. 38.

[44] *Richmond Whig*, March 26, 1847, p.2, c. 6.

[45] *Richmond Whig and Public Advertiser*, Jan. 29, 1850, p.2, c. 2.

[46] Stuart Nixon, owner of the Hearthstone Bookshop in Alexandria, Virginia, believes that Margaret and Anthony met each other through her brother, George Washington Nixon through their common membership in the same Masonic Lodge in Buckingham County, Virginia. Stuart provided much of the information on the Walton-Nixon relationships.

1. Anthony Anderson Walton Jr. was born in Cumberland County in 1835 in Cumberland County and died on Sept. 3, 1866 at Buckingham Court House from a piston shot fired by James Leach.[47] He was a schoolteacher. (457)

2. William Robert Walton was born circa 1838 in Cumberland County.[48] He was also enumerated on the 1850 Buckingham County census, as a student under Elijah Haynes. (458)

Frances (Walton) Palmore (237)

Frances Walton, daughter of Robert and Mildred (Armistead) Walton, married Fleming Palmore Jr. in Cumberland County on Aug. 25, 1824. She was born circa 1806 in Cumberland County, Virginia. James A. Armistead, her uncle, gave consent for the marriage, stating that he had kept her since birth. Not much is known about Fleming Jr. Apparently his father had questions about his ability to manage finances because the inheritance of Fleming Jr. was placed under the care and management of Reuben T. Sims. It is believed that he was a grandson of William Palmore who died in Cumberland County, Virginia in 1786.[49]

Children of Fleming Jr. and Frances (Walton) Palmore:[50]

1. William Fleming Palmore was born on 1828 in Cumberland County and died on Jan. 10, 1892 in Brinkley, Arkansas. He married first Sarah L. of Tennessee, married second Amanda Crosswell on Nov. 3, 1864 in Mississippi, and married third Mrs. M. O. Sturdevant. (459)

2. Sarah Frances Palmore was born on March 7, 1833 in Cumberland County and died on Oct. 29, 1908 in Yalobusha County, Mississippi. She married A. H. Clark on July 29, 1856. (460)

3. Ann Palmore was born in 1836. (461)

---

[47] *Richmond Dispatch*, Richmond, Virginia, issue of Wednesday, Sept. 5, 1866.

[48] 1850 U. S. Census for Cumberland County, Virginia, p. 296.

[49] Cumberland County, Virginia *Will Book 2*, pp. 412-413.

[50] Information on this family unit was provided to the compiler by Dan B. Wallace, DBWallace@aol.com , via email on May 19, 2003.

4. Pubilus C. Palmore was born in 1838 in Cumberland County. He married Catharine T. O. White on Nov. 6, 1860. (462)

5. Newton N. Palmore was born in 1840. (463)

Phoebe Ann (Isbell) Steger (251)

Phoebe Ann Isbell, daughter of William and Nancy Ann (Murray) Isbell, was born circa 1802 in Cumberland County and died on April 1, 1884 in Buckingham County. She married Albert Gallatin Steger, son of Thomas H. and Phoebe A. (Walton) Steger, circa 1832. They moved to Madison County, Alabama about 1836, and returned to Buckingham County about 1846 where they are found on both the 1860 and 1870 censuses.[51]

Children of Albert G. and Phoebe A. (Isbell) Steger:

1. Marietta Virginia Steger was born ca 1833 in Buckingham County and died on Dec. 25, 1920 in the Protestant Episcopal Nursing Home on Grove Avenue in Richmond, Virginia. She married Henry Scruggs on July 9, 1856 in Cumberland County. (464)

2. John Randolph Steger was born on March 28, 1835 in Buckingham County and died on Nov. 9, 1897 at Belton, Bell County, Texas. He married Mary Jane Stewart on May 14, 1857 in Richmond, Virginia. (465)

3. Anna Walton Steger was born on Sept. 4, 1839 in Madison County, Alabama and died on Aug. 4, 1916 in Buckingham County. She married John Branch Gilliam on Nov. 16, 1866. He was born on Aug. 5, 1831 and died on April 21, 1908. (466)

4. Albert Gallatin Steger Jr. was born about 1841 in Madison County, Alabama and died in 1893, probably in Buckingham County. He did not marry. Albert served in Company D., 1st Virginia Infantry and was wounded at the Battle of Second Manassas. (467)

5. William David Steger was born on May 5, 1846 in Buckingham County and died on Sept. 20, 1915 at Huntsville, Madison County, Alabama. He married Margaret Frances Sanford on July 20, 1872 in Huntsville. (468)

---

[51] 1870 U. S. Census for Buckingham County, Virginia, pp. 40-41

Mary Susan (Isbell) Carter (256)

Mary Susan Isbell, daughter of William and Nancy Ann M. (Walton) Isbell, was born on March 8, 1814 in Buckingham County, and died on Jan. 9, 1893 in Lynchburg. She married Archibald William Carter, son of Theodorick and Martha (Austin) Carter.[52] Archibald was born on April 1, 1812 in Henrico County, Virginia and died on Feb. 2, 1893.[53] Both were buried in the Presbyterian Cemetery in Lynchburg. In 1840, they were enumerated on the Buckingham County census. He was appointed Postmaster of Clover Hill in Appomattox County on Sept. 23, 1845 and served until June 30, 1849.[54] In 1850, they were still living in Appomattox County, where Archibald was employed as a tailor.[55] A. W. and Mary S. Carter were received by certificates in the Court Street Methodist Protestant Church in November 1861. In 1870, they are found on the Campbell County census. Residence: Lynchburg, Virginia

Children of Archibald and Mary Susan (Isbell) Carter:

1. John William Carter was born on April 21, 1837 in Buckingham County and died on May 5, 1879. He married Mary Eliza (McGhee) Isbell, widow of Matthew Isbell, in 1857 in Halifax County, North Carolina.[56] (469)

---

[52] Theodorick was a son of Sherwood Carter of the Giles Carter branch, per phone conversation on Aug. 16, 2002 with William E. Steger of San Diego, California.

[53] Kent Gregory (1872-1950), "Genealogical Papers, MS1288," Jones Memorial Library, Lynchburg, Virginia. A death record for the City of Lynchburg gives a date of death of Feb. 2, 1889.

[54] "Record of Appointment of Postmasters (Virginia), 1832-Sept. 30, 1971," Vol. 16 (ca 1844-1856), National Archives and Records Service M-841, Roll 130.

[55] Stuart McDearmon Farrar, compiler, *1850 Census of Appomattox County, Virginia*, (Privately Published: Pamplin, Virginia), 1975, p. 19.

[56] Virginia Historical Society, Mss1 C2468 b 130-131, Record No. 159926.

2. Samuel A. Carter was born in 1838 and died in 1860 of suicide in Baltimore, Maryland.[57] (470)

3. Henry Clay Carter was born in Buckingham County on July 4, 1841 and died in 1931 in Richmond, unmarried. At the age of sixteen, he became a deputy clerk of court in Campbell County. In 1858, he served for six months in the State auditor's office in Richmond. He had a distinguished military career, serving in the 3rd Company of Richmond Howitzers, C.S.A.[58] (471)

4. Susan G. Carter was born on May 31, 1846 in Appomattox County and died on Aug. 28, 1929 in Lynchburg. She married Edward Christian Glass, son of Robert Henry and Elizabeth Augustus (Christian) Glass. (472)

5. Martha A. Carter was born in 1848 in Appomattox County and died unmarried circa 1875. She is buried in an unmarked grave in the Hollywood Cemetery in Richmond, Virginia. (473)

Eliza Ann (Walton) Jones (267)

Eliza Ann Walton, daughter of William and Elizabeth White (Chick) Walton, was born on Tuesday, Aug. 28, 1810 at Bent Creek, Buckingham County, and died in 1893 in Appomattox County.[59] On Jan. 10, 1827, she was married to Dr. David Crawford Jones, by the Rev. Thomas Burger. David was born on Nov. 2, 1802 and died in 1859.[60] David was a son of Rowland, 1780-1816, and

---

[57] Information was provided by William E. Steger of San Diego, California, proven by letters that he inherited from the Carter family. These letters were donated to the Virginia Historical Society in Richmond.

[58] ____, *Confederate Military History*, (Morningside Bookshop: Dayton, Ohio), 1975, Vol III, pp 793-794.

[59] Death date is inscribed on her tombstone in the Jones family graveyard at "The Meadows," which is along State Route 615. The Jones family farm was known as "The Meadows," but the farm is now called "Misty Hills Farm," owned by Rollin and Middy Hayden, Box 246, Route 3, Appomattox, VA 24522.

[60] *Ibid.*

Nancy (Crawford) Jones.[61] David practiced medicine from his home and in an office at Bent Creek.[62] His medical account book is deposited in the Library of Virginia. It provides insight into medical problems and treatment of relatives and residents of the Bent Creek and Oakville communities. His medical book contains detailed notes on ailments, diseases, treatments and cures.[63] The sophistication of his notes suggests that he attended a very good medical school. The Jones-Walton family Bible is preserved in the Library of Virginia. Their farm in Appomattox County was called "The Meadows." David and Eliza were buried in the Jones family graveyard on the farm, located on State Route 615. It has been maintained with a cast-iron fence surrounding the graves. Residence: Appomattox County, Virginia.

Children of Dr. David and Eliza Ann (Walton) Jones:[64]

1. Ann Elizabeth Jones was born on Dec. 2, 1827. She married George Fuqua, an attorney, on May 8, 1849. They were living next door to her father when the 1850 U. S. Census was taken for Appomattox County. (474)

2. Martha Susan Jones was born on July 4, 1829 and died on July 4, 1840. (475)

3. Mary Alice Jones was born on Dec. 31, 1831, and died in 1866.[65] She married John S. Bass on Nov. 28, 1854. (476)

---

[61] Campbell County, Virginia *Will Book 3*, p. 435, dated Aug. 12, 1816, *Will Book 4*, p. 429, where David C. Jones is one of the children listed. References were provided by Tom talqt@aol.com on Dec. 20, 2002.

[62] Library of Virginia, Dr. David C. Jones Account Book, 1827-1830, Buckingham County, Virginia, Miscellaneous Reel 253.

[63] Library of Virginia, Dr. David C. Jones Medical Book, n.d. (29332) Miscellaneous Reel 254.

[64] Names and birth dates and marriages of the Jones children are found in the Jones-Walton family Bible record in the Library of Virginia. Death dates for the family are from the Bible record or the tombstones in the Jones Family graveyard, at Misty Hills Farm, Box 246, Route 3, Appomattox, Virginia 24522. The present owners are Rollin and Middy Hayden.

4. Sally Paul Jones was born on March 5, 1834, and died in 1901. She married James A. Walker, 1835-1914, son of John and Martha Stovall (Penn) Walker, on June 9, 1859. He was the overseer for the Jones farm after Dr. David died. (477)

5. Ellen Virginia Jones was born on July 12, 1836, and died in 1911. She married William Anthony Thornhill Jr., son of William and Lucy (Walton) Thornhill of Appomattox County. (478)

6. William Rowland Jones was born on Jan. 15, 1839. He graduated from the University of Virginia in 1861. He married Drusilla Allen, daughter of Dr. James B. and Frances Allen of Sulphur Springs, Kentucky on Sept. 16, 1869. William was a physician who practiced first in Pamplin, Virginia before moving to Union County, Kentucky in 1866. He then returned to Virginia in 1873 before resettling in Trigg County, Kentucky in 1882. It is believed that he died in Princeton, Kentucky. (479)

7. Charles Yancey Jones was born on May 4, 1831 and died Jan. 4, 1843. (480)

8. Frank Boggs Jones was born on Nov. 11, 1843, and died on July 19, 1915. He married Nancy Alexander Elliott, 1845-1929. He served as a prison guard at Libby Prison in Richmond during the Civil War.[66] (481)

9. Ida Walton Jones was born on March 11, 1846, and died unmarried in 1942. She taught school for many years, and ran the Jones farm until her death. She was buried in the Jones family graveyard at "The Meadows" in Appomattox County. While teaching, she was a correspondent for the *Appomattox and Buckingham Times*. According to a Roanoke newspaper published sometime in 1939, Miss Jones attended the funeral of General Thomas J. (Stonewall) Jackson conducted by a Dr. Ramsey in the First Presbyterian Church in Lynchburg. A Ms. Massey sang "Come Ye Disconsolate." Miss Jones

---

[65] Death date is inscribed on her tombstone in the Jones Family graveyard, at Misty Hills Farm, Box 246, Route 3, Appomattox, Virginia.

[66] His sister, Ida Walton Jones, was quoted circa 1939 in a Roanoke Times newspaper. A copy of the paper was provided to the compiler by Lloyd G. Walton of Appomattox County on July 4, 2001.

said that the hearse was accompanied by a Confederate Honor Guard that was brought by train from Chancellorsville to Lynchburg. From the train to the church it was followed by wagons loaded with flowers. From Lynchburg, the casket was taken by packet boat from Lynchburg to Lexington. Miss Jones bragged to a newspaper reporter in 1939, in Roanoke, that she had attended four World Fairs—Chicago, Philadelphia, St. Louis and Jamestown. She also stated that she had never drunk a coca-cola nor a beer, never chewed gum, never used rouge or lipstick, and never used profanity in her life. (482)

10. Cornelia Chapman Jones was born on Aug. 23, 1848, and died unmarried in 1925. (483)

11. Howard Malcolm Jones was born on March 3, 1851 and died on Feb. 14, 1858. (484)

12. Isabel Buchanan Jones was born on Nov. 15, 1854, and died in 1943. She married Samuel G. Payne whose address was 1382 Rivermont Avenue, Lynchburg, Virginia. (485)

Martha Ann Armistead (Walton) Walker (268)

Martha Ann Armistead Walton, daughter of William and Elizabeth White (Chick) Walton, was born on Sunday, Aug. 9, 1812 at Bent Creek, Buckingham County, Virginia at two o'clock in the morning, and died Nov. 23, 1888. She married Maj. Samuel Jennings Walker,[67] son of John Meriwether and Susan (Christian)[68] Walker, on Tuesday, June 8, 1830. Samuel was born Jan. 23, 1809 and died Aug. 21, 1866 in Appomattox County. Farrar[69] says that their primary residence was called "Oakland." The name of their

---

[67] Certain information on this family was published in an undated issue of the *Farmville Herald*, contributed by Stuart McDearmon Farrar. See also, *Kentucky Ancestors*, genealogical quarterly of the Kentucky Historical Society, Frankfort, Kentucky, Volume 1, No. 1, July 1965, pp. 10-11.

[68] Susan Christian was a daughter of John H. and Joyce Christian and a granddaughter of James and Susannah Christian.

[69] Stuart McDearmon Farrar, *Historical Notes of Appomattox County*, (Privately Published: Pamplin, Virginia), 1989, p. 204.

Appomattox County estate was called "Riverview," because of the view of the James River. Samuel J. inherited "Riverview" from his father, and after his death, the estate went to his daughter Susan Christian Walker who married Henry D. LeGrande, who sold it to a Moore family around 1900.[70] Samuel J. served as commissioner of revenue for Appomattox County during 1861-1865. Samuel J. wrote letters of encouragement to his sons who were drafted into the Confederate States of America. Here are excerpts from a letter dated June 19, 1861:

My. Dear Sons:

I feel more than I can express for the perilous condition that you are all placed in. I feel that it is almost certain you all three will never return to the family and friends that regard you with more interest than all the world beside. Which will be the one, if indeed either of you should ever return home, God only knows! We may never see you more.[71] What a reflection. It has filled my mind with thoughts unutterable. You have not only to encounter an enemy bent upon the destruction of all they kill, but you have the dangers of the Camp to encounter. Disease will kill more than the Yankees will kill. I would, therefore impress upon you all to take all the care of yourselves as possible; expose yourself no more than you are obliged to do. Avoid dissipation of every kind. Live moral lives, be obedient and respectful to all who have command over you, and to your fellow-soldiers be always kind and respectful. Avoid the vicious and dissipated as much as possible, and don't forget to feel your dependence upon that God Who is ever mindful of those who call upon and ever look to Him for protection.

My dear sons, you have pledged yourselves for the defense of your Country. I hope never to hear that either of my sons have acted in any way calculated to bring reproach upon themselves or their family. The Army is one of the best places one could be placed to try a man. If it should be my lot never to see you all again, I hope to hear of a

---

[70] Information was provided in letter to the compiler by Bettie Walker Fricke, 304 N. Englewood Avenue, Dothan, AL 36303-3012, dated Nov. 12, 1998.

[71] Father's intuition was accurate; his fourth child, Harvey C. Walker died three months later at Ft. Scott.

good account of you all as men and as soldiers. I shall go to the office to deliver my books tomorrow morning.[72]

We miss you all very much. Not a day passes that I do not shed tears of grief and sorrow on account of your perilous condition. I dread sickness more than the Yankees, and I dread immorality and the evil communications to which you are exposed more than both the Yankees and disease. God grant you all may have firmness to resist every temptation that you may be exposed to, and that you all may be spared to your home and friends, honored and distinguished men and soldiers.

All I live for is my children, and I am willing to do everything in my power to make your situation as comfortable as possible. Do not be backward to call upon me for anything you all may need. Stand by your Country and defend it, with your last drop of blood.

Your affectionate Father,

Saml. J. Walker[73]

Children of Samuel J. Sr. and Martha A. (Walton) Walker:[74]

1. John William Walker was born March 26, 1831 and died March 21, 1832. (486)

2. Benjamin Walton Walker was born Sept. 23, 1832 in Buckingham County, Virginia and died Apr. 25, 1906 in Huntsville, Texas. He went to Texas in 1852, and married Arianne S. Sims, of Huntsville, Texas, May 25, 1854. Their grandson, Lt. Gen. Walton Harris Walker, 1889-1952, was commander of ground forces in Korea, and was the highest-ranking officer to be killed in combat.[75] (487)

---

[72] These books related to his duties as Commissioner of the Revenue for Appomattox County.

[73] Letter was made available through the courtesy of Mrs. Bettie Walker Fricke of Dothan, Alabama.

[74] Information on the children was obtained from *Kentucky Ancestors*, published by the Genealogical Committee of the Kentucky Historical Society, Vol 1, No. 1, July 1965, pp. 10-11, contributed by Mary Walker of Hopkinsville, Kentucky.

[75] Information was provided by Stuart McDearmon Farrar of Pamplin, Virginia.

3. Isaac Winston Walker was born March 7, 1834 and died Oct. 30, 1884. Isaac married Sarah C. (Doswell) Taliaferro, daughter of Major Thomas Doswell of Hanover County, Feb. 14, 1855. (488)

4. Harvey Christian Walker was born Nov. 30, 1835 and died Dec. 5, 1861, at Camp Scott, while serving in the Confederacy.[76] On Sept. 24, 1861, he wrote a letter from Camp Bartow to his father: "Your highly esteemed letter of the 17th inst. reached me last night, and I hasten to give an account of myself and Company. Edmund has no doubt reached home safely where I hope he will soon recruit his health and spirits. (He then describes widespread illness in the Camp.) We are having a disagreeable time of it now digging entrenchments and cutting down old timber within musket shot of this place. General Lee has divided his forces and has joined Wise and Floyd with five thousand men and will come in the enemy's rear, cutting off their supplies and forcing them out of their fortifications. It is believed that they will attempt to pass this post and escape by Petersburg the way or route that General Garnett retreated. We will be well-fortified by tomorrow night, when we will be glad to have a visit from them. I never saw a more determined set of men than we have here, and should make a desperate attempt to cut through it will be the bloodiest battle recorded in modern times. I believe the men here will stand until not enough is left to tell the tale. An order has just come in from General Loving to move all the sick away, which is an indication of fight. It is thought that the enemy are preparing to advance. At any rate there is fight in the wind and we are ready. Capt. Robertson and Col. Scott wish to be remembered to you and Uncle Ben." (489)

5. Maria Elizabeth Walker was born Sept. 15, 1837 and died Jan. 13, 1903. Maria married William H. Jones, Dec. 16, 1857. (490)

6. William Henry Harrison Walker was born July 23, 1840 and died on Dec. 25, 1903. (491)

7. Edmund Winston Walker was born June 7, 1842 and died May 12, 1916. He married Jane Rebecca Massie, 1851-1929, daughter of William G. and Elizabeth V. (Finch) Massie, June 20, 1871, in

---

[76] Buckingham County, Virginia Death Records, 1853-1890, Library of Virginia.

Hopkinsville, Kentucky. They were buried in Riverside Cemetery in Hopkinsville, Christian County, Kentucky.[77] (492)

8. Susan Christian Walker was born July 10, 1844 and died Oct. 25, 1923. Sue married Henry Douglas LeGrand, 1840-1918. (493)

9. Mary Virginia Walker was born Sept. 24, 1846 and died April 16, 1906. She married Bradley W. Babcock, Dec. 18, 1883. (494)

10. Sarah Frances Walker was born Feb. 3, 1849 and died Dec. 3, 1912. Sarah married Col. Robert W. Withers, of Campbell County, Virginia, June 27, 1888. (495)

11. Samuel Jennings Walker Jr. was born Apr. 14, 1851 and died May 15, 1914, in Christian County, Kentucky. He married Lucy Massie, Oct. 20, 1874. (496)

12. Ann Eliza Walker was born Jan 14, 1854 and died Oct 27, 1906. Ann E. married William R. Elliott, July 22, 1886, and they lived in Christian County, Kentucky. (497)

13. Charlie Mundy Walker was born Apr. 7, 1856 and died of diphtheria on Aug. 24, 1862, in Appomattox County. (498)

Mary Frances Philadelphia (Walton) McDearmon (269)

Mary Frances Philadelphia Walton, daughter of William and Elizabeth White (Chick) Walton, was born on Friday, May 13, 1814 at Bent Creek, Buckingham County, Virginia, at five o'clock in the morning,[78] and died on April 9, 1884 in Appomattox County. Her names probably reflect Elizabeth Chick's maternal grandmother Mary ___, and Frances (Anderson) Armistead, William Walton's maternal grandmother. She married Col. Samuel Daniel McDearmon, son of the Rev. James and Mary (Daniel) McDearmon, June 10, 1835, in a ceremony performed by her father's first-cousin, the Rev. Jesse S. Armistead. Col. Samuel was

---

[77] Mavis Parrott Kelsey, M.D., and Mary Wilson Kelsey, *The Family of John Massie, Revolutionary Patriot of Louisa County, Virginia.* (Houston, Texas: private printer), circa 1978, p. 38.

[78] Birth information was obtained from the William Walton family Bible.

born in 1815 and died in 1871, according to tombstone inscriptions in the Liberty Cemetery in Appomattox, Virginia.[79] He was a wealthy miller and merchant in Appomattox County, owning twenty-eight slaves and $38,000 worth of real estate when the 1850 census was taken. He built the bridge across the Appomattox River at Farmville, which caused cash-flow problems that ended in bankruptcy. Samuel was the central figure in William Marvel's book, *A Place Called Appomattox,* because the new County seat in 1845 was planned and built by McDearmon.[80] Marvel unfairly painted McDearmon as the scapegoat for the failure of the first Appomattox town. Samuel represented Prince Edward County in the Virginia House of Delegates in 1845-1846; Appomattox County in 1846-1847, 1850-1851; Campbell and Appomattox Counties in the Virginia State Senate, 1852-1853 and 1853-1854.[81] According to a Lynchburg newspaper, McDearmon planned to immigrate to Texas after financial failures, but the plans did not materialize. The couple lived and died in Appomattox County and were buried in a special family plot in Liberty Cemetery, which is operated by Liberty Baptist Church. Residence: Appomattox County, Virginia.

Children of Col. Samuel and Mary F. (Walton) McDearmon:

1. Mary Elizabeth McDearmon was born April 26, 1836. She first married, on Oct. 7, 1852,[82] David Ambrose Plunkett (1826— Jan. 16, 1860), Sheriff of Appomattox County. She married second Cornelius P. Hill, and they moved to Lynchburg. (499)

---

[79] A birthdate of Nov. 18, 1815 is given in Ancestry.com. According to William Marvel in his book, *A Place Called Appomattox*, p. 305, Samuel McDearmon died of a stroke on May 15, 1871.

[80] William Marvel, *A Place Called Appomattox*, (Chapel Hill, North Carolina: University of North Carolina Press), 2000.

[81] Cynthia Miller Leonard, compiler, *The General Assembly of Virginia: a Bicentennial Register of Members, 1619-1978*, (Library of Virginia: Richmond, Virginia, 1978), pp. 418, 421, 443, 453 and 458.

[82] Email to the compiler from John Hale of Falls Church, Virginia dated May 2, 2003, JHale97811@aol.com

2. Victoria McDearmon died as an infant. (500)

3. William James McDearmon was born Feb. 10, 1844 and died in June 1925. He married his first cousin, Mary Frances Stickley, 1851-1890, daughter of the Rev. William W. and Margaret Jane (McDearmon) Stickley, on March 28, 1866. They had eight children. (501)

4. Samuel Walton McDearmon was born in July 1845, and married Judith Atwood. They had no children. (502)

5. John Hampden McDearmon was born Sept. 25, 1850 and died April 29, 1885. He married Sarah J. Wright, daughter of Pryor and Lucinda Wright. They had no children. (503)

James Chick Walton (271)

James Chick Walton, son of William and Elizabeth White (Chick) Walton, was born Aug. 23, 1819 at Bent Creek, and died on May 10, 1886, in Campbell County, Virginia. He first married Mary Elizabeth White,[83] probable daughter of Andrew and Margaret (Ferguson) White[84] of Bent Creek. She was born in 1823 and died circa 1853. James C. married second, in December 1855, to Virginia Caroline Greenlee, daughter of David Samuel and Hannah Ingram (Grigsby) Greenlee of Rockbridge County, Virginia. She was born July 19, 1836 at Natural Bridge, Virginia, and died July 25, 1880 in Campbell County. James bought a factory in Lynchburg but lost it during the recession of the 1850s.[85] James and his second wife were

---

[83] Stuart McDearmon Farrar, *Historical Notes of Appomattox County*, Virginia, (Privately Published: Pamplin, Virginia), 1989, pp. 128, 205.

[84] Andrew White was born Mar. 13, 1789 in Dunse, Berwick County, Scotland and died in 1870 in Appomattox County. He came to Bent Creek, Buckingham County in 1802, where he later married Margaret Ferguson on Dec. 18, 1816. They raised a large family at Bent Creek (now in Appomattox County). Margaret died of childbirth on Jan. 19, 1835 at Bent Creek.

[85] *The Lynchburg Virginian,* issue of April 7, 1858, contained an auction announcement that would offer to the highest bidder, not only the factory equipment, but a lot of tobacco, six slaves, mules and horses and wagons, but also "Twenty-two factory hand." The auction was held on the steps of the Campbell County Courthouse.

buried in a family cemetery on the Beasley Farm, Campbell County, near the intersection of HW 501 and HW 660.[86]

Children of James C. and Mary Elizabeth (White) Walton:

1. Sarah E. Walton was born in 1838. She married William R. McKinney on April 3, 1854 in Campbell County, Virginia. (504)

2. Virginia C. Walton was born in 1841 and died in 1903. She married Daniel W. McKinney, 1831-1896, on April 12, 1854 by the Rev. John E. Edwards.[87] They had three children, one of whom was Nannie E. McKinney, born on Dec. 1, 1855. (505)

3. John W. Walton was born in 1845. (506)

4. Robert M. Walton was born in 1848. He was living in the household of his father when the 1870 U. S. Census was taken for Campbell County, Virginia. (507)

Children of James C. and Virginia C. (Greenlee) Walton:[88]

5. Emaline "Emma" Louise Walton was born April 19, 1860, and died July 10, 1946. She married Samuel Richardson Martin, March 15, 1883 and lived at Concord, in either Appomattox or Campbell County. The 1910 U. S. Census for Campbell County lists these children: O. Lewis Martin, age twenty-three; John Martin, age twenty. (508)

6. Scottie L. Walton (female) was born in 1860. She married a Mr. Drinkard and lived at one time in Pulaski, Virginia. (509)

7. Cornelia Belle Walton was born in 1862. (510)

8. Margaret W. Walton was born in 1864. It is believed that she married William Deacon and their residence was at 2027 Popular Street in Lynchburg. (511)

---

[86] Information on the cemetery, and inscriptions, was provided by the late Dr. Joseph W. Evans of Boulder, Colorado.

[87] Library of Virginia, "Tyree family Bible record, 1808-1924," Accession No. MBRC3.

[88] Information on this family unit was provided by Lady Alton Dobbs of Erwin, Tennessee. She descends from Richard Thomas G. Walton

9. Catherine Jennings Walton was born in 1866. She married and moved to Michigan. (512)

10. Richard Thomas Grigsby Walton was born in 1868. He married and lived at Pulaski, Virginia at one time. (513)

John William Walton (272)

John William Walton, son of William and Elizabeth (Chick) Walton was born on Wednesday, the 30th day of May 1821, at 11 o'clock in the morning, and died on July 3, 1889, in Appomattox County. John W. married Mary Jane Vawter, daughter of Silas P. and Elizabeth Farrar (Christian) Vawter, on April 2, 1844, at Bent Creek in Old Buckingham County. Mary Jane was born in Nelson County on Oct. 9, 1827, and died June 26, 1888, at the home of her daughter, Annie Eliza (Walton) Mitchell, at Bent Creek, Appomattox County. Mary Jane attended Hollins College. She was buried next to her father at the Cove farm near Bent Creek.

John W. inherited land and assets from his father in 1851, but by 1858 John W. had lost his personal property, including thirteen slaves, a merchant mill, a country store, a large warehouse, a lumber mill, cooper's shop, and mules, oxen, horses, and wagons. His father-in-law, Silas P. Vawter, bought the Cove Farm and placed it in a trust for his daughter, so that she would have financial security. The farm would stay in the family, but John W. Walton's name would not be on the indentures.

An advertisement in the Lynchburg newspaper announced an auction of personal property from the plantation house, including kitchenwares and utensils. The 1860 census listed John as a tenant farmer. By 1870, most of the family farm had been regained, listed as $8,000 in value. Below are three auction announcements that appeared in the Lynchburg Virginian, March 19, 1858. Silas P. Vawter, James Chick Walton, and Samuel D. McDearmon were business partners of John W. Walton. John W. served as deputy sheriff for Buckingham County in 1840 and in Appomattoc County after it was formed in 1845 from Buckingham.

Children of John W. and Mary Jane (Vawter) Walton:

SALE OF VALUABLE GOODS, &c., at AUCTION.—By virtue of a deed of trust executed to the undersigned by Walton, Vawter & Co., I shall, at their storehouse in Bent Creek, Appomattox county, on the 1st day of April, proceed to sell, at public auction, their large and valuable stock of Goods, Wares and Merchandize, comprising the usual variety contained in a country store. A credit of 90 days will be given on all sums above five dollars.

I also offer at private sale the BENT CREEK MERCHANT MILL, with **228 Acres** of valuable Land attached thereto, which will be sold together, or separately, as may suit purchasers, and a large Storehouse, newly erected, in Bent Creek, and a convenient Lumber House. The Mill is in pretty good repair, and has a good Miller's House, Cooper's Shop and Garden conveniently situated, and at this time has a good custom for grinding Corn. To any person disposed to engage in the milling and mercantile business, this property offers many inducements. SILAS P. VAWTER,
mar 12-cwt1apl   Trustee.

NOTICE.—By virtue of a deed of trust executed to the undersigned by James C. Walton and John W. Walton, of record in the Clerk's office of the county of Appomattox, to secure to Silas P. Vawter certain sums of money therein named, I shall proceed to sell, upon the premises, at public auction, to the highest bidder, for cash, on Saturday, the 10th day of April next, the Tract of Land on which the late Col. William Chick resided, in the county of Appomattox, with any parcel which has been added thereto; and two old Negro Men, four Horses, a four Horse Waggon and Gear, two Oxen, an ox Cart, two Cows, and one Sow and Pigs, together with all the Plantation Tools and Farm Implements of every kind upon the premises, conveyed by the deed aforesaid
mar 12-cwt10apl   HENRY S. BEASLEY, Trustee.

SALE OF VALUABLE SLAVES, STOCK, &c.—By virtue of a deed of trust executed to the undersigned by John W. Walton, and duly recorded in the Clerk's office of Appomattox co., the undersigned will proceed to sell, at public auction, at the residence of the said John W. Walton, on Friday, the 19th day of March, 1858, the following property conveyed in said deed, to-wit:—Peter, Henry, Caroline, Sally, a woman, and Sally, a girl, three yoke of Oxen, 22 head of Cattle, 11 head of Horses and Mules, 15 Sheep, 80 barrels of Corn, all the Plantation Utensils, Household and Kitchen Furniture, &c., &c. Terms cash.   W. M CABELL, Trustee.
mar 8-ct19

Advertisement in the Lynchburg Virginian newspaper, March 19, 1858

1. Bettie Christian Walton was born June 22, 1845, and died Aug. 5, 1916. She married George P. Dallas Abbitt, 1844-1883, son of Benjamin Jr. and Mary S. (Patterson) Abbitt. (514)

2. Annie Eliza Walton was born on Oct. 31, 1847 and died on April 12, 1912.[89] She married Col. George W. Mitchell, Oct. 30, 1883. George W. died on March 27, 1893.[90] She was his second wife. They had no children. They lived at Buffalo Ridge Springs near Gladstone, Nelson County, Virginia. (515)

3. Eugene Adolphus Walton was born on Aug. 16, 1850 and died Dec. 19, 1921. He married Nannie Katherine Jones. (516)

4. Martha Susan Walton was born in April 1857 and died of whooping cough on June 20, 1859, proven by an Appomattox County death record in the Library of Virginia.[91] (517)

Thomas Walton Scruggs (277)

Thomas Walton Scruggs, son of John and Frances (Walton) Scruggs, was born on Nov. 19, 1807 in Buckingham County, Virginia and died May 29, 1873 in Appomattox County. He married Elizabeth P. North on April 29, 1858.[92] Elizabeth, known as Betty,

---

[89] The will of Annie E. (Walton) Mitchell is found in Appomattox County, Virginia *Will Book 1*, p. 169, dated April 14, 1902. The witnesses were Benjamin S. Vawter and E. A. Marks. Eugene A. Walton was appointed executor with a $10,000 bond. The will was probated on April 25, 1912. Land was divided between her sister-in-law, Nannie Katherine (Jones) Walton, and "my niece" Mary Lizzie Abbitt.

[90] Information is from the family Bible record of George W. and Annie Eliza (Walton) Mitchell. The Bible record contains additional information, such as "Mrs. S.A. Mitchell died 26th May, 1880, and Mrs. Judith Mitchell died 5th Aug., 1881." The Bible is now in the hands of Mary Evelyn (Payne) Strickland, of Gladstone, Nelson County, Virginia.

[91] Martha Susan Walton's name is confirmed in private papers titled, "Walton Family Record" in possession of Mrs. Mary Evelyn (Payne) Strickland of Nelson County, Virginia.

[92] Vital records (birth and marriage) for Thomas W. Scruggs were found in the Appomattox County court records maintained in the Library of Virginia.

died on April 12, 1893 in Appomattox County.[93] Thomas was the administrator for his father's estate.

Children of Thomas W. and Elizabeth P. (North) Scruggs:[94]

1. Thomas Edward Walton Scruggs Jr. was born in Appomattox County on Feb. 3, 1859 and died on March 11, 1897 in Tarrant County, Texas. He was a schoolteacher. Thomas Jr. married Sallie E. Blevins. (518)

2. Amine Josephine Scruggs was born on Jan. 14, 1861 and died on Feb. 19, 1954. She married Bennett Wesley Bagby in 1882. (519)

3. Andrew Broadus Scruggs was born in April 1862 and died fifteen years before his wife, per her undated obituary. He married Lelia L. Bell, daughter of Charles and Melissa (Sheffield) Bell, on March 4, 1891. She was born Nov. 8, 1864 in Cumberland County. Andrew was a farmer in the Southside Magisterial District of Appomattox County. Children listed on the 1900 census were Walter L. Scruggs, born in March 1892; Andrew Scruggs, born in June 1894; and Leila Scruggs, born in October 1899. The Scruggs were members of the Pamplin Methodist Church. (520)

4. Nancy Frances Scruggs was born circa 1866 in Appomattox County and died in 1939. She married James H. Hammersley in 1882. They raised a family of seven children in Nelson County, Virginia (521)

John A. Scruggs (278)

John A. Scruggs, son of John and Frances (Walton) Scruggs was born circa 1808, probably at Bent Creek, Buckingham County, Virginia and died after 1880, when he was listed on the U. S. Census for Nelson County, Virginia. He married Amanda Dudley Christian, daughter of James and Cordelia (Watts) Christian, who was born circa 1816 in Nelson County and died between 1865 and 1870, probably in Nelson County.

---

[93] Appomattox County, Virginia Circuit Court loose papers, "Scruggs v Scruggs," 1881.

[94] Appomattox County, Virginia Circuit Court loose papers, "Scruggs v Scruggs," 1881.

Children of John A. and Amanda D. (Christian) Scruggs:[95]

1. Frances C. Scruggs, born circa 1838, married C. McKeen on Jan. 9, 1866 in Nelson County. (522)

2. William E. Scruggs was born circa 1840. He married Elizabeth Frances Lambeth, daughter of Lafayette Washington and Mary Ann (Hill) Lambeth, on Sept. 26, 1866 in Lynchburg. He served in the Confederacy in Co. I, 49th Virginia Infantry, from April 1861 to Jan. 12, 1862, when he was discharged because of a spinal disability. (523)

3. John J. Scruggs was born circa 1842. He married Lizzie D. Meriwether on April 27, 1883 in Bedford County, Virginia. (524)

4. Martha A. Scruggs was born circa 1844 in Nelson County. She married Dr. Marcellus H. Mays, son of James and Rosanna Mays, on Dec. 6, 1865 in Nelson County. (525)

5. Frederick Cabell Scruggs was born in October 1846 and died on Dec. 18, 1913 in Nelson County. He married Martha Jane Emett, daughter of Thomas Truxton and Mary Elizabeth (Pendleton) Emett, on April 29, 1875. (526)

6. Mary Emma Scruggs was born circa 1848. (527)

7. Amanda Elizabeth Scruggs was born circa 1850 and died on Sept. 16, 1862, of scarlet fever in Nelson County.[96] (528)

8. Thomas W. Scruggs was born circa 1852. He married Mary Beverly Clay, daughter of Cyrus Clay, on Oct. 1, 1884 in Bedford County, Virginia. (529)

9. Terisha Dillard Scruggs was born on May 22, 1858 in Nelson County and died on Dec. 8, 1917 in Bedford County. He married Lucy C., a widow who was born in May 1868 in North Carolina. (530)

James Littleton Scruggs (280)

James Littleton Scruggs, son of John and Frances (Walton) Scruggs, was born in 1812 in Appomattox County, Virginia and

---

[95] Information on this family unit was contributed by Carole Ruff, 40905 Belforest Court, Leesburg, Virginia 20175.

[96] The *Lynchburg Daily Virginian*, Dec. 1, 1863, p. 1, c. 3.

died on Aug. 22, 1882 in the same County. He married Mary Frances Woodson on Jan. 30, 1843 in Campbell County, Virginia. She was born on June 26, 1817 and died on Nov. 14, 1887 in Appomattox County. James was a carpenter and farmer in The Stonewall District of Appomattox County.

Children of James L. and Mary F. (Woodson) Scruggs:[97]

1. William M. Scruggs was born in November 1843 in Appomattox County, and died in 1924. He married Cordelia Gannaway, daughter of Warren Gannaway, on Dec. 4, 1867 in Campbell County. After Cordelia's death in 1878, he married second Ella Anderson, who died in 1889. He married third Lillie Anderson, who died in 1933. (531)

2. Sterling A. Scruggs was born circa 1845. (532)

3. Ann Elizabeth Scruggs was born on March 17, 1846 in Appomattox County and died on June 25, 1905. She married Richard A. Green, son of Joseph G. and Amanda Sterling (Allen) Green, on Feb. 17, 1860. He was born circa 1838 (533)

4. Mary Virginia Scruggs was born in September 1847 in Appomattox County and died after 1900 and before 1910. She married Richard T. Moss. (534)

5. Lucy Frances Scruggs was born circa 1850. She married C. Candler. (535)

6. Thomas B. Scruggs, a triplet, was born on Nov. 14, 1852 in Appomattox County and died on Dec. 29, 1925. He was a merchant in the Stonewall District of Appomattox County. Apparently, he left no descendants because his estate was divided among his siblings.[98] (536)

7. John J. Scruggs was born on Nov. 14, 1852 in Appomattox County, and died in 1933. John married Elizabeth Rosa Stone. (537)

9. Palmer R. Scruggs was born on Nov. 14, 1852 and died in 1926. He was one of three triplets. (538)

---

[97] See Nathaniel R. Featherston, *The History of Appomattox, Virginia*, (Marceline, Missouri: Walsworth Brothers, Printers), reprint, 1995, pp.254-255.

[98] Appomattox County, Virginia *Will Book 1*, p. 388.

Nathan Womack Walton (285)

Nathan Womack Walton, son of William Scott and Sally (Womack) Walton, was born on May 10, 1803, and died on Oct. 6, 1880, in Cumberland County, Virginia. He married first Sarah Smith Tiernan, daughter of Dr. James Tiernan of Powhatan County, Nov. 18, 1841.[99] He married second Anne E. (Vaughan) Paine, widow and daughter of Joseph and Henrietta Vaughan, June 4, 1867, in Cumberland County.[100] Sarah was born in 1813, per 1850 U. S. Census for Richmond, Virginia. Anne E. was born in 1817. A third marriage was to Pauline Jane (Rock) Saunders, born in 1846, who was forty-three years younger than he was. Nathan was a carpenter and lumber merchant in Cumberland County, but also lived in Richmond during his later life, where he was employed as a bookkeeper.[101] He was interested in the Walton family history, based on letters and a query published by *The Richmond Standard* in 1879.[102] It appears that Nathan had three children from the first union and two children from the third union.[103]

Children of Nathan W. and Sarah S. (Tiernan) Walton:

1. James Tiernan Walton was born in 1844. (539)

2. Nathan Walton Jr. married Gay F. Walton. (540)

---

[99] *Richmond Whig and Public Advertiser*, Friday Dec. 10, 1841 issue, p. 2, c. 6.

[100] Cumberland County, Virginia *Marriage Book I*, p. 9, line 7.

[101] 1880 U. S. Census for Richmond, Henrico County, Virginia, Roll: T9_1371; Family History Film: 1255371; Page:161B; Enumeration District: 83; Image: 522, per Ancestry.com.

[102] *The Richmond Standard,* Sept. 19, 1879, Vol. 11, No. 2, c. 5.

[103] Walton Papers in public library in Marshall County, Mississippi. The notes were taken from a worksheet of an unknown researcher. The papers were furnished to this compiler by Linda Taylor of Waco, Texas. Validity of the papers is uncertain. It shows three children by Nathan's third marriage making him at least 70 years old when his last children were born.

3. Martha Jane Walton was born in July 1846 and died on Aug. 5, 1848 in Richmond, Virginia.[104] (541)

Children of Nathan W. and Pauline J. (Rock) Walton:

4. Charles Saunders Walton was born in 1878. He was living with Nathan and Pauline when the 1880 census was taken for Richmond, Virginia. The stated relationship was "son." Genealogical notes deposited in the public library in Marshall County, Mississippi say that he had no issue. (542)

5. Julia Womack Walton married Dr. Robert Park Griffith.[105] (543)

Mary Scott (Walton) Ellington (286)

. Mary Scott Walton, daughter of William S. and Sally (Womack) Walton, was born on April 23, 1805 in Cumberland County, Virginia and died March 25, 1891 in Petersburg, Virginia. Mary and her twin-daughters were buried in the Blandford Cemetery in Petersburg. She married Branch Henry Ellington, son of William and Elizabeth (Webber) Ellington Jr., on Jan. 27, 1823 in Cumberland County. He was born on Dec. 25, 1800 in Prince Edward County, Virginia and died on March 25, 1850.[106] The first seven of their thirteen children were born in Cumberland County; the eighth one in Amelia County and the last five children were born in Nottoway County, Virginia.

Children of Branch H. and Mary S. (Walton) Ellington:

1. Sarah Elizabeth Ellington was born on 1825. She married Alfred Webster of Amelia County, Virginia. (544)

---

[104] *Richmond Whig and Public Advertiser*, Aug. 11, 1848 issue, p. 2, c. 3.

[105] Not proven.

[106] Information on the Ellington family unit was provided by Alice Sawyer, 15503 Edenvale Street, Friendswood, TX 77546 to the compiler on Sept. 22, 2002. See also Earl C. and May (Miller) Frost, compilers, *DeJarnette and Allied Families in America (1699-1954)*, (Privately Published: San Bernardino, California), 1954, p. 282.

2. Mary Jane Ellington was born on Feb. 3, 1826. She married Reuben Ruffin, son of John Daniel and Jemima (Wheelhouse) Ruffin.[107] Reuben was born on Dec. 8, 1825 in Dinwiddie County, Virginia and died on Oct. 17, 1895. They had no children. (545)

3. Martha Thomas Ellington was born on Jan. 5, 1828, and died on Oct. 23, 1870 in Raleigh, North Carolina. She married Baylor Richardson Sherwood Jr. on May 13, 1847. (546)

4. Rosalind C. Ellington was born on April 25, 1830 and died on June 24, 1904 in Petersburg. She married a Mr. Willett. (547)

5. Roseanne Camilla Ellington was born on April 25, 1830 and died on Oct. 29, 1897 in Petersburg. Burial was in the Blandford Cemetery with her twin sister and her mother. She married Benjamin Greenhow Gates in 1852. (548)

6. Cornelia Frances Ellington was born in 1836 in Cumberland County. She married first Richard Avery Machen on April 28, 1852, and married second Nathaniel Blick. (549)

7. Nathan Henry Ellington was born in 1837 in Cumberland County. (550)

8. Charles Edward Ellington was born on May 17, 1839 in Amelia County, Virginia and died on Nov. 8, 1877. He married Helen C. Moody on Nov. 14, 1866. (551)

9. Maria L. Ellington was born circa 1842 in Nottoway County, Virginia. (552)

10. Josephine Ellington was born in 1843 in Nottoway County and died on March 24, 1923. She married Rubin Ruffin, who was the widower of her older sister Mary Jane. (553)

11. Winfield Scott Ellington, born about 1845 in Nottoway County, died in infancy. (554)

12. William Henry Ellington was born circa 1847 in Nottoway County. (555)

13. Winfield Scott Ellington, born circa 1849, also died young. (556)

---

[107] Information was given to the compiler on Sept. 23, 2002 via email from RUBYGEM@aol.com.

Charles William Walton (288)

Charles William Walton, son of William Scott and Sally (Womack) Walton, was born on Feb. 10, 1810 in Cumberland County, Virginia and died on June 13, 1866 in Monroe County, Mississippi. He married first Arvazena S. Dyche on June 2, 1835. She was born on April 1, 1819 and died on July 31, 1847. He married second Katherine Stockton Anderson on June 8, 1864.[108] He was the first postmaster at Aberdeen, Mississippi.

Children of Charles W. and Arvazena S. (Dyche) Walton:

1. John B. Walton was born in 1837. (557)

2. William Dyche Walton was born in 1837 and died in 1907. (558)

3. Charles Augustus Walton was born in 1841 and died in 1843. (559)

4. Frances Walton was born in 1843. She was enumerated in the household of Eliza E. Finney, No. 170 on the 1850 U. S. Census for Monroe County, Mississippi. (560)

Child of Charles W. and Katherine S. (Anderson) Walton:

5. Charles William Walton Jr. was born in 1866 and died in 1868. (561)

Nancy Brackett (Walton) Moore Miller (291)

Nancy Brackett Walton,[109] daughter of Jesse and Joanna L. (Hobson) Walton, was born on Jan. 18, 1797 in Virginia, and died prior to 1850. Nancy married first John T. Moore, who was born on March 19, 1787 in Northumberland County, Pennsylvania, and died May 17, 1831 Maury County, Tennessee. They were married on Sept. 4, 1817 in Maury County. John was a carriage-maker and one of the first trustees of The Methodist Church in Columbia, Tennessee. Nancy married second Thomas Miller, who died before 1850.

---

[108] Information was provided by Bob F. Thompson of Nashville, Tennessee.

[109] Information on Nancy's family unit was provided by Bob. F. Thompson Esq., 4430 Sheppard Place, Nashville, Tennessee 37205.

Fifth Generation

Children of John T. and Nancy B. (Walton) Moore:

1. Mary Moore was born circa 1820 and died after 1880. She married John B. Valentine, born on Jan. 13, 1818 in Richmond, Virginia and died on Sept. 23, 1865. The family belonged to the Methodist Church. They lived for a while in New Orleans. (562)

2. Jane Moore was born circa 1821 in Tennessee, and died after 1880. Jane married John L. Tindall, a prominent physician who was born in Kentucky. Their residence in 1880 was on Columbus Street, Aberdeen, Monroe County, Mississippi.[110] (563)

3. Susan "Susannah" Moore was born on March 11, 1823, and died on Aug. 20, 1893 at Jackson, Madison County, Tennessee. She married Joseph Newton "Nute" Gates, son of Charles R. and Rose (Reid) Gates, on May 10, 1849 in Pontotoc County, Mississippi.[111] He was born on Sept. 9, 1822 in Georgia and died before 1910 in Jackson, Tennessee. Susan was not mentioned in her father's will, but Bob. F. Thompson has proven her identity through a cache of old letters and public records. (564)

4. Clement C. Moore was born circa 1827. The 1850 U. S. Census for Monroe County, Mississippi states that he was a merchant. It is believed that later he was an attorney, based on family letters. Clement served as a 1st Lt. in Company A, 43rd Mississippi Regiment. He married Mattie ___, according to the 1860 U. S. Census for Monroe County, Mississippi. (565)

5. John T. Moore Jr. was born circa 1831. John served in the Civil War in several units. He was captured in 1864 by Union forces and spent time at Camp Chase, Ohio. John married H. Angie Morris on Feb. 25, 1852 in Pontotoc County, Mississippi. She died in July 1857, according to a family letter. (566)

Children of Thomas and Nancy B. (Walton) Miller:

---

[110] 1880 U. S. Census for Monroe County, Mississippi, per Bob F. Thompson.

[111] Pontotoc County, Mississippi, *Marriage Book 1849-1856*, p. 27.

6. Stephen Miller was born circa 1838 in Mississippi, based on the 1850 U. S. Census for Monroe County, Mississippi, page 224. This was the household of Mary Valentine. (567)

7. Josiah W. Miller was born in May 1839. He was listed in the household of Dr. John L. Tindall when the 1850 U. S. Census was taken for Monroe County. (568)

William Hobson Walton (292)

William Hobson Walton, son of Jesse and Joanna Lawson (Hobson) Walton, was born on Sept. 2, 1799 in Cumberland County, Virginia and died on Jan. 11, 1830 in Giles County, Tennessee.[112] He married Ellen Porter, who was born on Jan. 16, 1807 in Tennessee and died on Nov. 22, 1866 at Cornersville, Tennessee. He was probably the William Walton who was indicted in Maury County, Tennessee in 1819 for stabbing a man, and eventually the case was dismissed.

Children of William H. and Ellen (Porter) Walton:

1. Willis Rees Walton, born on Jan. 28, 1826 and died on Jan. 28, 1888 at Cornersville. He was a druggist and postmaster. Willis married Mary Peacock, who was born on March 29, 1836 and died on Sept. 23, 1877 at Cornersville. (569)

2. Joanna Jane Walton was born on Oct. 3, 1827 and died on Oct. 24, 1896 at Cornersville. She married William Fowler, who was born on Sept. 5, 1816 and died on Feb. 12, 1879 at Cornersville. (570)

3. Sarah E. Walton was born on May 27, 1829 and died on June 7, 1838.[113] (571)

Jane Scott (Walton) Edmondson (293)

Jane Scott Walton, daughter of Jesse and Joanna Lawson (Hobson) Walton, was born on Nov. 28, 1801 in Cumberland County, Virginia, and died on June 23, 1819 in Maury County,

---

[112] Jesse Walton Family Bible Record.

[113] Cemetery Records of Giles County (Tennessee), pp. 192-193.

Tennessee. Jane married Andrew Jackson Edmondson, son of Robert and Isabella (Buchanan) Edmondson, on March 19, 1818 in Maury County. Andrew J. was born on April 13, 1793 in Davidson County, Tennessee and died April 30, 1872 in Memphis, Tennessee. Andrew served in the War of 1812 with Thomas Williamson's regiment of Tennessee Volunteers. Named for Andrew Jackson, who was a Circuit Court Judge and later President of the United States, he served under the command of Andrew Jackson in the Creek Indian Wars and the Battle of New Orleans in 1814. He served as Chancery Clerk in Holly Springs, Marshall County, Mississippi. In 1860, he moved to Shelby County where he spent the remainder of his life.

Child of Andrew J. and Jane S. (Walton) Edmondson:

1. Robert Walton Edmondson was born on June 3, 1819, and died on April 26, 1876 in Shelby County, Tennessee. He married Amarilla Moore Ragsdale, daughter of William H. and Nancy (Moore) Ragsdale, July 27, 1847 in Monroe County, Mississippi. She was born June 11, 1824 in Marion County, Alabama and died on Dec. 1, 1878 in Memphis. Robert was an attorney who was appointed Clerk of the United States District Court for the Northern District of Mississippi, and continued to serve as Clerk of the Confederate Court for the district.[114] (572)

Josiah Nichols Walton (295)

Josiah Nichols Walton, son of Jesse and Joanna Lawson (Hobson) Walton, was born on Oct. 18, 1805 in Cumberland County, Virginia and died April 26, 1884 in Monroe County, Mississippi. He married first Mary J. Prewitt, daughter of Abner and Nancy (McGee) Prewitt, by whom he had five children. Mary J. was born in 1815 and died on Oct. 3, 1867. Josiah N. married second Katherine Stockton Anderson, widow of Charles W. Walton (288) by whom he had two more children. Josiah N. Walton wrote letters

---

[114] Loretta and William Galbraith, editors, *A Lost Heroine of the Confederacy: The Diaries and Letters of Belle Edmondson*, (University Press of Mississippi), 1980, p. xxxv, 158n14.

describing his experiences with the Chickasaw Indians, which was deposited in the Lyman Draper collection in Madison, Wisconsin. Josiah was listed as a gentleman on the 1850 and 1860 censuses, which suggests that he lived from income as a merchant, planter, and investor rather than a salary for laboring.

Children of Josiah N. and Mary J. (Prewitt) Walton:

1. Sarah Daggett Walton was born on July 31, 1835 and died on Aug. 12, 1836. (573)

2. Ophelia Harrison Walton was born on Feb. 17, 1840 and died Aug. 13, 1914. She married Dr. James M. Greene, 1817-1913, of Aberdeen, who served as President of the Mississippi Medical Association in 1883-1884. His education was received at LaGrange College, the University of Virginia and the Jefferson Medical College. (574)

3. Olivia Walton was born in 1850 and died in 1921 in Chickasaw County, Mississippi. married Dr. John Howard Murfree. (575)

4. William Hobson Walton, born circa 1851, married Carrie Campbell. (576)

5. Ida Walton, born circa 1856, married Oscar John Trice of Mississippi. He was in the mercantile business. (577)

Children of Josiah N. and Katherine (Anderson) Walton:

6. George T. Walton, born in August 1871, married Maude Price. (578)

7. Minta Hoyeah Walton, born in March 1875, married William Richard Todd. They lived in Monroe County, Mississippi. (579)

Thomas Madison Walton (296)

Thomas Madison Walton, son of Jesse and Joanna Lawson (Hobson) Walton, was born on July 11, 1808 in Cumberland County, Virginia, and was living in Monroe County, Mississippi when the 1840 census was taken for that County. He was deceased by 1848 when the tax list was constructed.[115] Bob F. Thompson of

---

[115] Mrs. Lillian Plant Nickles, 1848 *Tax Assessment Roll, Aberdeen, Athens, Carmargo, Cotton Gin Port and Monroe County, Mississippi*, (Privately Published), February 1960, p. 20.

Nashville reported to the compiler that Thomas M. Walton was shot and killed by Johnson Bickerstaff, a tavern owner, in August 1845 at Cotton Gin Port, Monroe County, Mississippi. He married Priscilla Ann Rutledge on June 3, 1834 in Athens, Alabama..

Children of Thomas M. and Priscilla A. (Rutledge) Walton

> 1. Helen Jane Walton was born on March 8, 1840 at Cotton Gin Port, Mississippi and died in 1929. She married the Rev. Robert Gilderoy Porter, a Methodist minister. (580)
>
> 2. F. Gertrude Walton was born circa 1842. She married her stepbrother, William N. Westbrook on Aug. 22, 1861 in Monroe County, Mississippi. (581)
>
> 3. Annette Walton was born circa 1844. (582)
>
> 4. Mary J. Walton was born circa 1846. (583)

Sarah Hobson (Walton) Daggett (297)

Sarah Hobson Walton,[116] daughter of Jesse and Joanna Lawson (Hobson) Walton, was born on July 2, 1811 in Cumberland County, Virginia and died May 18, 1889 in Pontotoc County, Mississippi. She married Stephen Daggett, son of Henry and Anna (Ball) Daggett, on Feb. 28, 1828. He was an Indian trader and land speculator, who became an intimate friend and confidential advisor to the Chief of the Chickasaw Indian Tribe. Born on July 1, 1798 in New Haven, Connecticut, and died on Sept. 15, 1880 at Pontotoc, Stephen was a grandson of the fifth President of Yale College, Napthali Daggett.

Children of Stephen and Sarah H. (Walton) Daggett:

> 1. Grace Anna Daggett was born on Sept. 28, 1842. She married Benjamin Randolph Ellis on Jan. 15, 1888 in Pontotoc. (584)
>
> 2. Harriett Hunt Daggett was born on Aug. 15, 1844 and died Oct. 16, 1876. She married James Martin Carter on Dec. 7, 1869, who became Superintendent of Education in Pontotoc. (585)

---

[116] Information on this family unit came from Bob F. Thompson in 2000, who credits Pete Daggett <padagge@netport.com>

3. Mary Gordon Daggett was born on Aug. 12, 1846 and died on April 8, 1856. She was buried in the Pontotoc Cemetery. (586)

4. Julia Driver Daggett was born on Jan. 30, 1847, married John W. Harris on Aug. 1, 1886 in Algoma, Mississippi. She was a kindergarten teacher. (587)

5. Charles Walton Daggett was born on Oct. 9, 1854 at Pontotoc, Mississippi. He married Evie Jones on Dec. 19, 1882 in Lee County, Mississippi. Charles was a house painter. (588)

Mary Elizabeth (Walton) Gordon (298)

Mary Elizabeth Walton, daughter of Jesse and Joanna Lawson (Hobson) Walton, was born on March 14, 1813 in Amelia County, Virginia and died Feb. 22, 1869, at Lochinvar, Pontotoc County, Mississippi. She married Robert Gordon, who was born in Scotland in 1788 and died on March 31, 1876 at Okalona, Mississippi. Robert, a jeweler by training, saw advantages of selling to the Chickasaw Indians, which led him to become an Indian Trader. Robert owned several plantations in Monroe, Chickasaw, and Pontotoc Counties, Mississippi, with overseers for each. He built the ante-bellum mansion *Lochinvar* at Pontotoc. Robert was one of the wealthiest men in Northern Mississippi.

Children of Robert and Mary E. (Walton) Gordon:

1. Joanna Hobson Gordon was born in 1831 and died in 1835. (589)

2. James Robert Gordon was born on Dec. 6, 1833 at Quincy, Monroe County, Mississippi, and died Nov. 29, 1912. He married first Carolina Virginia Wiley in 1856 and married second Ella Neilson. (590)

Lucy Catherine (Walton) Cook (299)

Lucy Catherine Walton, daughter of Jesse and Joanna Lawson (Hobson) Walton, was born on Jan. 27, 1816 in Maury County, Tennessee, and died on Jan. 5, 1862 in Chickasaw County, Mississippi. She married William Oscar Cook on May 20, 1834 in Cotton Gin Port, Mississippi. He represented Monroe County in the Mississippi Legislature in 1842-1843.

Children of William O. and Lucy C. (Walton) Cook:

1. Ellen Cook was born in 1840 and died in 1908. She married Thomas Joel Denton, 1828-1906. (591)

2. William H. Cook was born in October 1843 and died in 1914 in Chickasaw County, Mississippi. (592)

3. John H. Cook was born circa 1844. (593)

4. Armistead Barton Cook was born in July 1849 and died after 1900. His occupation was salesperson. (594)

5. Mary Gordon Cook was born on Nov. 2, 1850 and died on Oct. 29, 1937 in Lexington, Mississippi. She married Cannon McAllister Carter, 1846-1900, a deputy sheriff in Pontotoc County. (595)

6. Kate Walton Cook was born in February 1852 in Chickasaw County and died in 1934 in the same County. She did not marry. (596)

7. Susan W. Cook was born in 1855 and died before 1870. (597)

Susan Grey (Walton) Miller (301)

Susan Grey Walton, daughter of Jesse and Joanna Lawson (Hobson) Walton, was born on April 21, 1821 at Cotton Gin Port, Mississippi and died on Jan. 10, 1864 in Cumberland County, Virginia. She married Hugh Reid Miller, son of Ebenezer and Margery (Reid) Miller, on May 9, 1839 in Monroe County, Mississippi. Hugh was born on May 14, 1812 in South Carolina, and died on July 19, 1863 because of wounds received on July 3 in the Battle of Gettysburg. He commanded the 42nd Mississippi Regiment in the Civil War.

In 1841, he was elected to the Mississippi House of Representatives as a Whig. He was a circuit court judge and an attorney. Bob F. Thompson Esq. possesses a cache of old letters and documents on the Millers that he plans to publish. Additional information is posted on his website.[117]

Children of Hugh R. and Susan G. (Walton) Miller:

---

[117] http://homepage.mac.com/bfthompson/HRMGettysburg.htm

1. George Miller who was born on July 26, 1840 and died Feb. 1, 1897. He married Elizabeth Catherine Wiley, 1846-1919. (598)

2. Edwin Hugh Miller born in 1842 and died on Jan. 7, 1891 in Charleston, West Virginia. He married Mary Virginia Myers, 1834-1934. Edwin served as a Private in Co. G, 2nd Miss. Regt, and as Commissary Sgt. for 42nd Miss. Regt. They left no descendants. (599)

George Carrington Walton Sr. (302)

George Carrington Walton Sr, son of Thomas M. and Frances A. (Carrington) Walton, was born on Jan. 20, 1798 in Cumberland County and died Oct. 12, 1840. George served as executor of his father's estate. He married Eliza Miller, March 2, 1824. Eliza died of childbirth on Jan. 31, 1825. George Sr. was appointed Commissioner of Revenue for Cumberland County on June 22, 1835.[118]

Child of George C. and Eliza (Miller) Walton was.

1. George Carrington Walton Jr. was born on Jan. 16, 1825 in Cumberland County and died on Feb. 21, 1917 in Buckingham County, Virginia. He married Mary Ann Stark Smith. (600)

Nathaniel Walton (307)

Nathaniel Walton, son of Thomas M. and Frances A. (Carrington) Walton, was born on May 25, 1808 in Cumberland County, Virginia and died on May 30, 1866 near Cartersville. He married Evelyn Burton Payne on March 5, 1828. Evelyn was born on Aug. 29, 1808 and died April 12, 1891. Burial was in the Thomas Chapel United Methodist Church Cemetery at Cartersville, Virginia. They had eleven children, all born in Cumberland County, Virginia.[119] Nathaniel was a carpenter, and several of his sons followed the same occupation. Many of his descendants remained in the immediate area of Northern Cumberland County.

---

[118] Cumberland County, Virginia *Order Book 38, 1835-1839*, p. 7.

[119] See *Cumberland County, Virginia and Its People*, © Cumberland Historical Society, Inc. (Walsworth Publishing Co.: Marceline, Missouri), 1985, pp. 212-213.

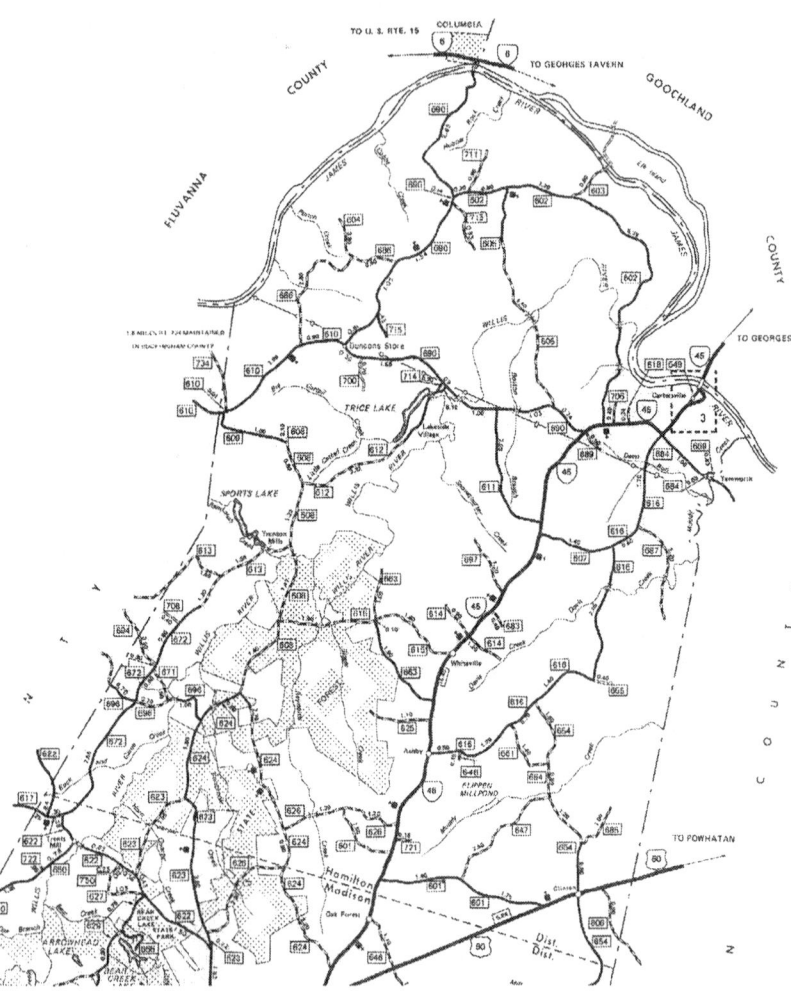

The Waltons first settled in Northern Cumberland County near Cartersville in the upper right section of the map. Descendants of Nathaniel Walton still live in the area, from Columbia in Fluvanna County (top of map) to Cartersville and the Willis River water basin. .As shown on the map above, this part of Cumberland County lies in an elbow of the James River.The map was prepared in 1993 by the Virginia Department of Transportation, 1401 East Broad Street, Richmond, Virginia 23219.

Children of Nathaniel and Evelyn B. (Payne) Walton:

1. Helen Clay Walton was born on May 24, 1825 and died in March 1885. She married Robert Codrington Carrington, son of Codrington and Martha A. (Carrington) Carrington.[120] (601)

2. Elizabeth Frances Walton was born in February 1829 and died March 6, 1915. She married James T. Isbell on Nov. 4, 1850 in Cumberland County, who died on Feb. 5, 1893. They were buried in the Thomas Chapel Cemetery near Cartersville. (602)

3. Thomas Burton Sydney Walton was born on Oct. 27, 1830 and died in February 1905. He married Cornelia Carrington on Dec. 19, 1866.[121] (603)

4. Nathaniel Washington Walton was born on Nov. 24, 1832 and died Sept. 27, 1913. He was buried in the Odd Fellow's Cemetery at Cairo, West Virginia. He married Sarah Jane Allen, who died on Monday morning, Oct. 8, 1866. She was buried in the Hollywood Cemetery in Richmond, Virginia. He married second Mrs. Ann E. (Vaughan) Raines, on June 4, 1867.[122] (604)

5. Mariah Adaline Walton was born on Oct. 31, 1834 and died in October 1907. She married Watkins Riddle. (605)

6. Henry Carrington Walton was born on Oct. 18, 1836 and died Aug. 22, 1909 in Cumberland County. He married Lavinia "Dolly" Allen, daughter of Isaac A. and Susan (Mosby) Allen.[123] She was born on April 7, 1840 in Powhatan County, and died on July 23, 1923 in Richmond, Virginia. (606)

---

[120] Garland Evans Hopkins, *Colonel Carrington of Cumberland*, (Privately issued: Winchester, Virginia), 1942, p. 83.

[121] Cumberland County, *Virginia Marriage Register 1, 1854-1919*, p. 8, line 10.

[122] Library of Virginia, "Walton family Bible Record, 1803-1910," Accession No. 21467.

[123] Library of Virginia, "Accession No. 24732, "Walton family Bible record, 1811-1933).

Fifth Generation

7. Martha Virginia Walton was born on Sept. 14, 1838 and died in May 1904. She married Richard Overton Sclater on Oct. 25, 1865 in Cumberland County.[124] He was born in 1837 and died on Nov. 14, 1923. Burial was in the Thomas Chapel Cemetery near Cartersville, Cumberland County. (607)

8. Louisa Heningham Walton was born on Sept. 19, 1840 and died in 1853. (608)

9. Ellen Hardenia Walton was born March 3, 1843 and died in December 1849 of "rheumatism."[125] (609)

10. Edward Walton was born on June 27, 1847 and died on May 7, 1923. He married Rebecca DePriest on July 18, 1875. (610)

11. Evelyn Wertly Walton was born on Nov. 22, 1849 and died in 1891. She married her widowed brother-in-law, Robert C. Carrington. (611)

Edward G. Walton (320)

Edward G. Walton, son of Edward Jr. and Martha (Isbell) Walton, was born circa 1812 in Cumberland County, Virginia and died in 1866 in Yalobusha, Mississippi. He received land from his father in 1833.[126] Personal property tax records for Cumberland County reveal that he was still living in Cumberland County in 1839. He married Elizabeth Agee. She was born circa 1817 in Buckingham County, Virginia and died in Yalobusha County. Ed. G. Walton was enumerated on the 1850 census for Marshall County, Mississippi.[127] In 1860, they were enumerated in Yalobusha County, Mississippi.

Children of Edward G. and Elizabeth (Agee) Walton:

---

[124] Cumberland County, Virginia *Marriage Book 1 1854-1919*, p. 6.

[125] Death date was found in the 1850 Mortality Schedule for the U.S. Census for Cumberland County, Virginia.

[126] Cumberland County, Virginia *Deed Book 21*, p. 204.

[127] 1850 U. S. Census for Marshall County, Mississippi, Family @ 557, p. 248, Oct. 26, 1850.

1. Edward J. Walton was born in 1837 in Cumberland County and died in 1885 at Water Valley, Mississippi. Ed married Eudora Elizabeth Stockard, daughter of James and Sarah (Neely) Stockard. She was born on Feb. 3, 1844 in Lafayette County, Mississippi and died on April 16, 1924 in Yalobusha County, Mississippi. (612)

2. Victoria Virginia Walton was born in 1840 in Mississippi. She married R. E. Doyle on Oct. 26, 1859 in Yalobusha County. (613)

3. Harris H. Walton was born in 1848 in Mississippi.[128] (614)

Lewis Isbell Walton (324)

Dr. Lewis Isbell Walton, son of Edward Jr. and Martha (Isbell) Wright Walton, was born in 1828 in Cumberland County and died on April 28, 1899 at Birmingham, Jefferson County, Alabama. Burial was in the Oak Hill Cemetery.[129] Lewis was a medical doctor. He married first Margaret Elizabeth Boston, daughter of Fontaine C. and Cynthia B. (Ragland) Boston,[130] on Oct. 1, 1849.[131] Her gravestone epitaph may be found at the "old Jackson's Mill at Sports Lake," in Cumberland County.[132] Lewis married second

---

[128] One H. H. Walton married Lydia Lewis on April 6, 1875 in Lafayette County, Mississiooi.

[129] From obituary provided by Kyle Tutwiler Spicer of Arkansas.

[130] Information provided by Kyle Tutwiler Spicer from an obituary.

[131] Cumberland County, Virginia *Marriage Bonds*.

[132] Information provided by William P. Wood via e-mail (wwood@colpipe.com) on Jan. 22, 2000. The epitaph says: "In memory of MARGARET E.WALTON wife of Louis I. Walton. Born April 28, 1832 died Aug. 21, 1862. Oh, Margaret forever loved forever dear! What fruitless tears hath bathed thy honored bier. What sighs reechoed to thy parting breath. Whilst thou wast struggling in the pangs of death could tears retard the tyrant in his course; could sighs evert his dart's relentless force: Could youth and virtue claim a short delay or beauty charm the specter from his prey thou still hadst lived to bless my aching sight thy partners honor and thy husband's delight if yet thy gentle spirit hover nigh the spot where now thy mouldering ashes lie, here wilt thou read, recorded on my heart, a grief too deep to trust this the sculptor's art what though thy mother lament her failing line, a mother's sorrows can not equal mine! Tho' none perhaps, like thee, her dying hour will cheer, yet, other offspring will soothe her anguish here; but who with me shall

Elmina Adelaide Steger, daughter of Francis Eppes H. and Narcissa W. (Taylor) Steger on Feb. 1, 1865 in Cumberland County.[133] She was born on Jan. 30, 1847 in Cumberland or Powhatan County, Virginia, and died on Nov. 27, 1936. Elmina was born on Jan. 30, 1847[134] in Cumberland or Powhatan County, and died on Nov. 27, 1936. Their final residence was in Jefferson County, near Birmingham, Alabama.[135]

Children of Lewis I. and Margaret E. (Boston) Walton:

1. Edward Francis Walton was born in November 1851. He was a practicing attorney in Huntington, West Virginia in 1899 when his father died.[136] Edward and his wife Fannie were living on Fourth Street in Huntington, Cabell, West Virginia. Fannie was born in 1852 in Kentucky. (615)

2. Haidee Zuleika Walton was born in December 1859 in Cumberland County, Virginia and died on Jan. 7, 1942 in Jefferson County, Alabama. She married Eli Erskine Tutwiler, son of Thomas Harrison and Harriet Magruder (Strange) Tutwiler, on June 15, 1884 in Fluvanna County, Virginia. (616)

Children of Lewis I. and Elmina Adelaide (Steger) Walton:[137]

3. Lewis Walton Jr. was born in 1866 in Virginia. He married Minnie Lawhorn. Frank was a manager of a coal store in Jefferson County,

---

hold thy former place. Thine image what new friendship eface. Ah, none! A mothers tears will cease to flow, time will assuage a younger sister's woe to all, save one, is consolation known while solitary Love here sighs alone."

[133] Library of Virginia, "Steger family Bible record, 1807-1899," Accession No. 33398.

[134] Library of Virginia, "Steger family Bible record, 1807-1899," Accession No. 33398.

[135] William E. Steger, William F. Steger, *Thomas Hales Steger, Son of John Perratt Steger*, (Privately Published), p. 3f.

[136] From the obituary of Lewis I. Walton, 1899, provided by Kyle Tutwiler Spicer. The 1900 Census states that his occupation was plasterer.

[137] Information was provided by Kyle Tutwiler Steger

Alabama. Their children were Lewis Walton III, Frank Arthur Walton, and Jack P. Walton. (617)

4. Arthur Walton was born on Oct. 2, 1868 and died on Feb. 6, 1938. He married Mollie Estelle Shepherd on Oct. 16, 1895. (618)

5. Francis "Frank" Walton was born in 1875 in Alabama. He was attending medical school at the time of his father's death. He was shot and killed circa 1910, by the husband of one of his patients. Frank was on the 1910 U. S. Census for Jefferson County, Alabama. He did not marry. (619)

Robert Alfred Walton (330)

Robert Alfred Walton, son of Thomas H. and Susannah Woodson (Bates) Walton, was born Aug. 27, 1804 at Cartersville, Cumberland County, Virginia and died on Nov. 20, 1867 in St. Charles, Missouri. He married his first cousin, Emily Carolyn Bates, daughter of Frederick and Nancie Opie (Ball) Bates, Aug. 9, 1838.[138] Robert owned a factory that manufactured blankets and woolen goods.

Children of Robert A. and Emily Caroline (Bates) Walton:[139]

1. Frederick Bates Walton was born on June 4, 1839 in St. Charles, Missouri and died on Dec. 24, 1907 at Winter Haven, Florida. He married Louise Conway, daughter of Joseph and Elizabeth Conway. Louise was born on April 24, 1840 and died on June 30, 1895.[140] (620)

2. Lucius Augustus Walton was born on Dec. 24, 1840 in St. Charles, Missouri and died on April 28, 1918 at St. Charles. He married Cynthia A. Barren on May 26, 1864. Cynthia died on Oct. 13, 1918. (621)

3. Mary Peyton Walton was born on June 4, 1843 in St. Charles. She married Charles L. Draper on May 23, 1866. (622)

---

[138] 1850 U. S. Census for St. Louis County, Missouri, p. 524, and 1860 U. S. Census for St. Charles, Missouri, p. 770. See also the 1860 Slave Schedule, p.298.

[139] Information on this family unit was secured from *The Woodsons and Their Connections*, p. 324.

[140] Bible record: http://ftp.rootsweb.com/pub/usgenweb/va/bibles/vabibles-5.txt

4. Nancy Fleming Walton was born on Aug. 26, 1846 in St. Charles and died there on Oct. 6, 1859. (623)

5. Thomas Woodville Walton was born on Nov. 7, 1848 and died on June 22, 1909 in Jacksonville, Illinois. He did not marry. (624)

6. Alfred Walton Jr. was born on Nov. 8, 1850 and died unmarried on Nov. 1, 1879. (625)

7. Susan Woodson Walton was born on Nov. 7, 1853 in St. Charles and died on Nov. 21, 1879, unmarried. (626)

8. Emma Bates Walton was born on Nov. 7, 1853 in St. Charles. She married Robert E. Bland on July 18, 1894. (627)

9. Everett Walton was born on April 28, 1857 and died on Aug. 3, 1858. (628)

10. Charles Woodson Walton was born on Nov. 14, 1862 and died on July 24, 1863. (629)

Augustus Thomas Walton (333)

Augustus Thomas Walton, son of Thomas H. and Anne Harris (Brackett) Walton, was born on Aug. 13, 1817 in Cumberland County, Virginia, and died on May 26, 1884 at 5:30 on the evening.[141] He married Mary Elizabeth Davenport, daughter of William Bentley and Sarah Jane (Goodman) Davenport, on July 23, 1843, per marriage bond.[142] Mary Elizabeth was born on May 15, 1824, in Cumberland County.[143]

---

[141] Mrs. J. R. Donovan, *Goodman-Walton Bible*, (St. Louis Genealogical Society Quarterly, Vol. XXIX, no. 3), sent to the compiler from David Goodman of Baltimore, Maryland.

[142] See also Cumberland County, Virginia *Deed Book 25*, pp. 551-552. The *Richmond Whig*, issue of July 21, 1843, states they were married on July 12th.

[143] Mrs. J. R. Donovan, *Goodman-Walton Bible*, (St. Louis Genealogical Society Quarterly, Vol. XXIX, no. 3)

Children of Augustus T. and Mary E. (Davenport) Walton:[144]

1. Sarah Rosser Walton was born on May 21, 1844 in Cumberland County, Virginia and died about 1907 at North Mount Pleasant, Mississippi. She married J. Robert Johnson on Oct. 9, 1867. (630)

2. Thomas Hobson Walton was born on July 10, 1846 in Marshall County, Mississippi. He married Sally S. Boggan on Dec. 19, 1866. He served in several units of the Confederacy and was captured and imprisoned at Fort Delaware until the end of the War. They lived later in Memphis, Tennessee. No children were born to their union, but they adopted a nephew, Walter Emmet Brown who was born on June 7, 1876 in Memphis. He was a son of William A. and Mary Ann Goodman (Walton) Brown. (631)

3. William Bently Walton was born on June 12, 1848 and died on May 3, 1886 in Marshall County, Mississippi. He married Sarah Ella Crawford of Marshall County on Nov. 19, 1868. (632)

4. Augustus Wilson Walton was born on June 20, 1850 and died on April 27, 1856. (633)

5. Mary Ann Goodman Walton was born on April 14, 1852 in Marshall County and died on May 5, 1878. She married William A. Brown on Sept. 1, 1875. (634)

6. Martha Withers Walton was born on Feb. 27, 1854 in Marshall County and died on Aug. 21, 1856. (635)

7. Ida Eppes Walton was born on June 28, 1856 in Marshall County. She married first Gus W. Hurt of Germantown, Tennessee on Feb. 19, 1879. (636)

8. Richard Alfred Walton was born May 7, 1860 in Marshall County. He married Katie Hodges on Dec. 26, 1883. No children were born to this union. Their residence was Memphis, Tennessee. (637)

9. Robert Lee Walton was born on Sept. 2, 1862 and died on Aug. 7, 1900. (638)

---

[144] Mrs. J. R. Donovan, *Goodman-Walton Bible*, (St. Louis Genealogical Society Quarterly, Vol. XXIX, no. 3). Supplemental information was taken from The Woodsons and Their Connections, pp. 324, 326.

10. Charles Henry Walton was born on Aug. 2, 1865. He married first W. Hammar on May 15, 1889, and married second Maude M. Howard on Feb. 22, 1906 at Memphis, Tennessee. (639)

Richard Peyton Walton (334)

Richard Peyton Walton, son of Thomas H. and Anne Harris (Brackett) Walton, was born on March 31, 1819 in Cumberland County and died Oct. 17, 1892 in Norfolk, Virginia. He married Mary Jemima Woodson, daughter of Charles Lewis and Linton (Grayson) Woodson, on May 5, 1842. Richard graduated from the University of Virginia. He was a surgeon in the 15th Infantry of the Confederate Army and practiced medicine in Cumberland County. He was the first superintendent of schools for Cumberland County.[145] In 1857, Richard built "Morningside"[146] in Cumberland County. There is a difference of opinion as to when Morningside was built it was probably built in 1847. His first residence in Cumberland County was called Pleasant Grove. In later life, Richard P. moved to Norfolk where he practiced medicine and pharmacy at 368 Church Street.

Children of Richard P. and Mary Jemima (Woodson) Walton:[147]

1. Ann Grayson Walton was born on April 3, 1843 at "Morningside," Cartersville, Virginia. She married Dr. Henry Rolfe Dupuy, son of Joel Watkins and Paulina Pocahontas (Eldridge) Dupuy, on May 21, 1867 in Farmville, Virginia. He was born on Nov. 21, 1845. Dr. Dupuy practiced medicine in Cartersville, Virginia for several years before moving to Norfolk where he served as Health Commissioner. (640)

---

[145] Robert and Catherine Barnes, indexers, *Genealogies of Virginia Families* (from the William and Mary College Quarterly Historical Magazine), (Baltimore, Maryland: Genealogical Publishing Company, Inc.), Vol V, 1982, p. 352.

[146] A photograph of this house is located in the Virginia Historical Inventory Photographs, Works Progress Administration Collection, Library of Virginia in Richmond.

[147] Names and dates for these children were found in a paper titled "Walton in America," by Kearney P. Walton II, Burlingame, CA, February 1950.

2. Mary Elizabeth Walton was born on Sept. 15, 1845 and died on July 18, 1848. (641)

3. Charles Cortlandt Walton was born on March 2, 1848 in Cumberland County and died on Dec. 26, 1911. He married Mary Kearney, daughter of Dr. James W. and Almedia (Phillips) Kearney of Dyersburg, Tennessee, on July 31, 1879.[148] (642)

4. Thomas Peyton Walton was born on May 23, 1853. He graduated from Hampden-Sidney College and Union Presbyterian Seminary in Richmond. Thomas married Anne H. Billingsley on May 20, 1884 at Glasgow, Missouri. He served as pastor of several Presbyterian Churches in Missouri, and performed Christian work in Virginia, Alabama and Tennessee. (643)

5. John Morton Walton was born on Sept. 15, 1855 in Cumberland County and died on July 22, 1885 in Norfolk, Virginia. He married Nancy R. McRae on Aug. 19, 1880 in Vicksburg, Mississippi. (644)

6. Robert Augustus Walton was born on June 30, 1857 and died on July 30, 1911. He married Laura B. Richart on April 16, 1891. Robert was a minister of the Gospel. (645)

7. Lavinia Walton was born on May 27, 1859 at Morningside, Cumberland County. She married Charles Albert Fields on Sept. 28, 1893. (646)

8. Richard Lee Walton was born on Feb. 28, 1861 at Morningside, Cumberland County. Richard married first Laura V. deLoney on April 3, 1889, and married second Mary Gibson on Dec. 14, 1904. He was an ordained Presbyterian minister. (647)

9. Louisa Eppes Walton was born on Sept. 19, 1864 and died on Feb. 16, 1894. She married Henry T. Bell on May 2, 1888. (648)

10. Caroline Walton was born on Sept. 9, 1866 and died on March 1, 1891. She married Charles Albert Field on Nov. 14, 1889. After Caroline's death, he married second Lavinia Walton, his sister-in-law. Albert was a direct descendant of Aaron Burr. (649)

---

[148] Robert and Catherine Barnes, indexers, *Genealogies of Virginia Families,* from the William and Mary College Quarterly Historical Magazine, (Baltimore, Maryland: Genealogical Publishing Company, Inc.), Vol V, 1982, p. 352.

11. Alice Walton was born on Feb. 19, 1870 at Morningside and died on July 27, 1870. (650)

Lavinia Ann (Walton) Wheat (337)

Lavinia Ann Walton, daughter of Thomas H. and Anne Harris (Brackett) Walton, was born on March 10, 1825 in Cumberland County, Virginia, and died March 6, 1872 in Prairie County, Arkansas. She married Patrick Henry Wheat on Sept. 12, 1845, in Marshall County, Mississippi. Patrick was born Oct. 24, 1823 in Monroe Co., Mississippi, and died June 15, 1910 in Lanoke, Arkansas. Burial was in the Oaklawn Cemetery in DeValls, Arkansas. Several of their children were buried in the same cemetery. They were still living in Marshall County when the 1850 census was accomplished.[149] Later that year they moved to DeValls Bluff, Arkansas. Patrick H. served as a Captain in Company A of Monroe's Arkansas Cavalry unit of the Confederate States of America. He was a slaveholder according to the U. S. census. After the Civil War, Patrick bought a steamship that transported from Batesville, Arkansas to New Orleans. The ship accidentally burned in 1869.[150] Seven children were born to Patrick and Lavinia, but only one lived to adulthood. After the death of Lavinia in 1872, Patrick married second Martha A. Legate Reynolds in 1873 and married third Louisa Miller Boone on March 11, 1889.[151]

Children of Patrick and Lavinia A. (Walton) Wheat:

1. Thomas Ila Wheat was born on Oct. 5, 1846 in Mississippi and died on Oct. 4, 1855. (651)

---

[149] See 1850 U. S. Census for Marshall County, Mississippi, Slave Schedule, p. 257.

[150] Lavinia A. (Wheat) Bryan, *Genealogy Gems of the Wheat Family, Some of the Descendants of The Basil Wheat Family and Allied Families, Eagle and Walton. Today's and Yesterday's Cousins 1779-1983*, (Privately Published: Benton, Arkansas), 1984.

[151] *Ibid.* p. 22.

2. Robert Searcy Wheat was born on June 26, 1848 in Mississippi and died on Feb. 9, 1853. (652)

3. Richard Henry Wheat was born on Aug. 16, 1850 and died on Aug. 18, 1853. (653)

4. David Greer Wheat was born on July 1, 1854 in Arkansas and died on Feb. 29, 1856. (654)

5. James Elkanah Wheat was born on Aug. 5, 1856 and died on Aug. 7, 1846. (655)

6. Annie Cutler Wheat was born on June 24, 1858 and died on Oct. 4, 1862. (656)

7. Patrick Henry Wheat Jr. was born on July 4, 1861 at Devalls Bluff, Arkansas and died on Jan. 14, 1931. He married Roseanna Charity Eagle on April 16, 1884 in Lanoke County, Arkansas. (657)

Meriwether Goodman (341)

Meriwether Goodman, son of Noton and Polly (Walton) Goodman, was born on March 12, 1803, and died after 1870. He married Marie Ann French on Nov. 15, 1824, in Powhatan County, Virginia.

Children of Meriwether and Marie A. (French) Goodman:[152]

1. William Robert Goodman was born in May 1827 in Virginia and died in 1910-1912. He married Sarah Indiana Farris, who was born in April 1831 in Buckingham County, Virginia. (658)

2. Indiana Goodman was born circa 1834 in Virginia and died after 1870. (659)

3. Hugh French Goodman was born on Aug. 22, 1834 in Cumberland County and died after 1920 in Powhatan County. He married Judith Eugenia Jones on May 6, 1868 in Cumberland County. She was born on Sept. 1, 1847 in Spotsylvania County, Virginia and died on Jan. 21, 1920 in Powhatan County. (660)

4. Laura Goodman was born circa 1838 in Cumberland County. (661)

---

[152] Information on this family unit was provided by David Goodman of Baltimore, Maryland.

5. John H. Goodman was born on Sept. 13, 1847 in Cumberland County and died in 1918 in Powhatan County. He married Alice D. Scott on June 23, 1886 in Cumberland County, and died after 1920. (662)

Martha Jane (Goodman) Brown (347)

Martha Jane Brown, daughter of Noton and Mary (Walton) Goodman, was born in Cumberland County, Virginia on March 23, 1822 and died on Aug. 5, 1854 in Cumberland County. She married Thomas Compton Brown on Dec. 21, 1837 in Cumberland County. He was born on Dec. 27, 1815 in Powhatan County, and died on April 4, 1883.

Children of Thomas C. and Martha J. (Goodman) Brown:[153]

1. Walter Coles Brown was born in 1840 in Powhatan County. (663)

2. Emnella Brown was born circa 1841 in Powhatan County. (664)

3. Bently R. Brown was born in 1843 in Powhatan County. (665)

4. Edmonia T. Brown was born in 1846 in Powhatan County. (666)

---

[153] Information on this family unit was taken from the 1850 Census for Powhatan County, Virginia, and the *Goodman-Walton Bible*, (St. Louis Genealogical Society Quarterly, Vol. XXIX, No. 3)

Chapter 6

Sixth Generation

Octavia Celeste Walker (Walton) LeVert (366)

Octavia Celeste Walker Walton,[1] daughter of George Jr. and Sarah M. (Walker) Walton, was born on Aug. 11, 1811 in Augusta, Georgia and died on March 12, 1877 in Augusta. Her burial place is in the Walker Cemetery near what is now the Augusta State University campus. On Feb. 6, 1836, she married in Mobile, Alabama Dr. Henry Strachey LeVert, who was a physician and scientist.[2] He was born in King William County, Virginia on Dec. 25, 1804 and died in Mobile, Alabama on March 16, 1864. Henry served as mayor of Mobile, but is best known for his service as a physician and founder of a hospital.

Octavia was one of the most cultured, educated, and traveled women of her time. She spoke fluently in English, Spanish, French, and Italian and knew Greek and Latin. She knew sculpture and music. In 1825, she met and translated the French spoken by General Lafayette who came as a guest of her father, Col. George Walton Jr. Octavia met and knew nine U. S. Presidents, Henry Clay, Washington Irving, Henry W. Longfellow, Edgar Allen Poe, Daniel Webster, among others. When she traveled to Europe during the 1850s, she met and visited with Queen Victoria and Prince Albert, Pope Gregory in Rome and many other well-known persons. In 1857, she published a book titled *Souvenirs of Travel*, which was read by most of the literary giants of that time.

In the late 1850s, Octavia was one of the Ladies of the South who helped raise funds to "Save Mount Vernon," the home of George Washington on the Potomac River. She is on almost every list of prominent women of the 19th century.

---

[1] See Frances Gibson Satterfield, *Madame LeVert: A Biography of Octavia Walton LeVert*, (Edisto Island, South Carolina: Edisto Press), 1987. Most of her biography was extracted from this authentic biography.

[2] See Library of the University of North Carolina, Manuscripts Department, "Southern Historical Collection No. 1472, LeVert Family Papers."

The LeVerts wanted a son, but their only male child died at birth in 1844. Octavia had promised Senator Henry Clay to name the son for him. When their fifth child was born, they were hoping for a son. After the baby turned out to be a female, Senator Clay wrote to Octavia to suggest the name Henrietta Caroline LeVert. That name was given, but before the child was six years old, the LeVerts renamed her Cara Netta LeVert.³

After losing a brother and two daughters within two months in 1849, Octavia wrote to Henry W. Longfellow on May 23, 1849, "Oh! My kind friend, no wretchedness was ever so great as mine. I adored my children. They were so perfect, so loving, so beautiful. I cannot be comforted." Some of her letters are in the libraries of Harvard and Columbia Universities.

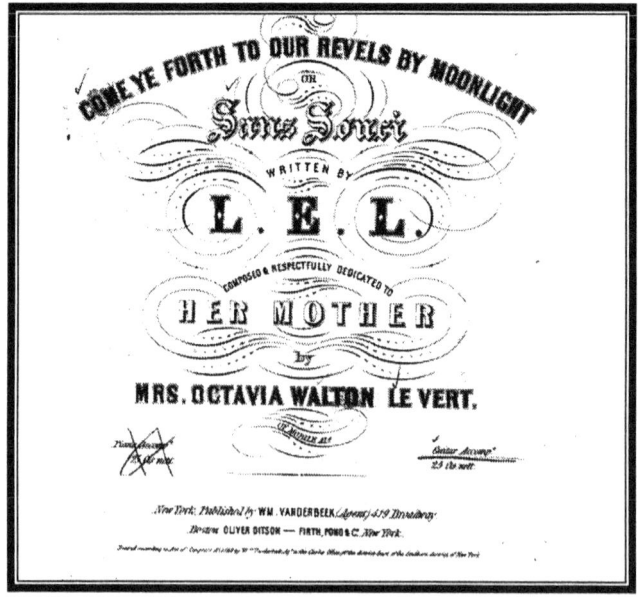

Song "Sans Souci" written by Octavia in 1849, in Library of Congress.

Children of Henry S. and Octavia Celeste (Walton) LeVert:

---

³ Satterfield, pp. 61-62, 112.

1. Octavia Walton LeVert was born on Nov. 20, 1836 in Mobile, Alabama and died on July 4, 1889 at Augusta, Georgia. She did not marry. She was named for and described by her mother as "a brunette with glorious dark eyes, like those of a Circassion Maid, soft brown hair and a radiant intellect." (667)

2. Claudia Anna Eugenia LeVert, born on May 22, 1838 in Mobile, Mobile Co., Alabama; and died on May 3, 1849 in Mobile of scarlet fever. Her mother said, " Claudia Eugenia is a lovely blonde, bright rosy-lipped and sparkling as Hebe." (668)

3. Sally Walker Walton LeVert was born in 1842 and died on May 3, 1849 of scarlet fever. She was described by her mother as "the beauty of the whole South, with golden hair and not one fault on face or form." (669)

3. Henry Clay LeVert, born in 1844, did not live. Octavia wanted a son and had promised Henry Clay to name him for the Senator from Kentucky. (670)

4. Caroline Henrietta LeVert was born on Dec. 6, 1846 in Mobile, Alabama, and died in December 1876. In 1852, her name was changed to Cara Netta by her parents. She married Lawrence Augustus Rigail Reab of Augusta, Georgia, on Dec. 16, 1868. (671)

George Christian Askew (367)

George Christian Askew, son of James T. and Nancy Murray (Walton) Askew, was born on Jan. 28, 1809 in Burke County, North Carolina, and died on May 19, 1884 in Burnet County, Texas. He married Sarah Harrison Lusk in Madison County, North Carolina on Oct. 18, 1831. Her parents were William and Magdaline (Garrett) Lusk. Sarah was born on June 8, 1817[4] at Spring Creek, Buncombe County, North Carolina and died on Oct. 5, 1909 at Koger Ranch, Llano County, Texas. All members of the family moved to Texas in 1871, except for three of their sons. George Christian Askew enlisted in the Confederacy at age fifty-one on July 4, 1861 and served for twelve months. He was a farmer and surveyor in Western

---

[4] From the Lusk family Bible, per Patricia Morrow, 6506 Prairie Dunes, Houston, TX 77069.

Sixth Generation

North Carolina, where he spent most of his adult life in Madison County.

Children of George C. and Sarah H. (Lusk) Askew:[5]

1. William Alfonso Askew was born on Aug. 7, 1832 and died Sept. 6, 1920 at Ashville, Buncombe County, North Carolina. He married Nancy F. Smart on Dec. 22, 1867 in Madison County. (672)

2. James Berry Askew was born on June 20, 1834 and died on April 13, 1909 at Bay City, Matagorda County, Texas. Burial was in the Pleasant Valley Cemetery. He married first E___ before 1864 in Missouri, and married second Isabella "Belle" Utley on Dec. 23, 1876 in Tarrant County, Texas. She was born after 1850 in Virginia. James married third Lithia/Laura ___ about 1910. She was born in 1854 in Indiana. (673)

3. Judith Elmina Askew was born on March 11, 1836 and died on May 13, 1896 in Burnet County, Texas. She married first Joseph N. Duckett on July 31, 1853 in Madison County, North Carolina. He was born on Feb. 20, 1836 and died on July 7, 1863 at Gettysburg, Pennsylvania, from wounds received in the Civil War. Judith married second John Huff Stokely on Oct. 6, 1865 in Cocke County, Tennessee. John was born on Dec. 1, 1810 in Tennessee and died on Dec. 17, 1893. Three children were born to the first marriage and four children to the second union. (674)

4. Joseph Wesley Askew was born circa 1837 and died on July 15, 1863 at Gettysburg, Pennsylvania, fourteen days after he was wounded in the lungs on the first day of battle at Gettysburg. He served for twelve months in Co. H 2nd Battalion NC Infantry; was captured at Roanoke Island on Feb. 8, 1862; and paroled at Elizabeth City on Feb. 20 of that year. His rank was 2nd Lieutenant. (675)

5. George Adolphus Askew was born in March 1840 and died in 1930 at Del Rio, Cocke County, Tennessee. He married first Laura Crowder and married second Sarah Jane Stokely, 1843-1929. (676)

---

[5] Information on the Askew family was contributed by Patricia Morrow. She has done extensive research on this family unit, which is in her direct lineage of ascent. All of these children were born at Spring Creek, Buncombe County, North Carolina.

6. Margaret Louise Askew was born on Feb. 2, 1842 and died on Oct. 4, 1925 at Burnet, Burnet County, Texas. She married Joseph Judson Sarrels, son of Andrew and Sarah (Truelove) Sarrels, on March 28, 1860 in Madison County, Tennessee. He was born on Aug. 8, 1834 in Haywood County, North Carolina, and died on Aug. 20, 1926 in Burnet, Burnet County, Texas. Eleven children were born to their marriage. (677)

7. Thomas Patton Askew was born in 1844 and died on Feb. 4, 1864 at Point Lookout, St. Mary's County, Maryland. He enlisted at age seventeen with his brother Joseph on July 4, 1861 in Co. H 2nd Battalion NC Infantry. Thomas was wounded in his hand in the Battle of Gettysburg; was captured and confined at Ft. Delaware; transferred to Point Lookout on Oct. 18, 1863; and died in Hammond General Hospital of "chronic diarrhorea." (678)

8. Sarah Arene Askew was born on Sept. 3, 1846 and died on Oct. 19, 1939 at Sinton, San Patricio County, Texas. Sarah married Daniel Robert Moore on July 5, 1868 at Spring Creek, Madison County, North Carolina. He was born on April 22, 1845 at Concord, Greene County, Tennessee and died on April 9, 1928 in San Patricio County. Nine children were born to their union. (679)

9. Charles Manley Askew was born on Sept. 18, 1847 and died on June 26, 1928 in Madison County, North Carolina. He married first Sarah Smart, 1849-1887, daughter of Daniel and Sarah (Stokely) Smart. Charles married second Callie Fleming on June 26, 1892. Four months later, on Oct. 27, 1892, Callie gave birth to Willie Lee Askew, who died on Dec. 3, 1974 in Kalamazoo, Michigan. (680)

10. Americus Lafayette Askew was born on Jan. 10, 1851 and died on Dec. 15, 1944 in Pleasant Valley, Burnet County, Texas. He married Mary Caroline Kinser, daughter of Andrew and Mary (Henderson) Kinser, on Feb. 3, 1875. She was born on Jan. 13, 1855 at Midway, Greene County, Tennessee and died on July 29, 1925 at Pleasant Valley. They were parents of eight children. (681)

11. Mary Jane Askew was born on Jan. 23, 1853 and died on Oct. 22, 1932 at Millersville, Concho County, Texas. She married George Pinkney Morrow. (682)

12. Nancy Elizabeth Mackie Askew was born on Oct. 1, 1855 at Spring Creek, Madison County, North Carolina and died on March 30, 1900 at Koger Ranch, Llano County, Texas. Nancy married Henry Harrison

Koger, son of Tillman and Frances (Miller) Koger, on Feb. 25, 1880 in Burnet County, Texas. He was born on Sept. 11, 1845 in Monroe County, Tennessee and died on March 20, 1923 at Temple, Bell County, Texas. (683)

John Thomas Walton (400)

John Thomas Walton, son of William M. and Sally (Mann) Walton, was born on Nov. 28, 1861 in Goochland County, Virginia and died on Oct. 2, 1950. He married Sallie F. ____, who was born in December 1869. They lived in the Tuckahoe District of Henrico County for much of their earlier life, but settled after 1910 at Midlothian, Chesterfield County, where he ran a truck farm.

Children of John T. and Sallie F. Walton:[6]

1. Ada B. Walton was born in May 1891. She married Robert C. Ashworth. He was a truck farmer in partnership with his father-in-law at Midlothian, Chesterfield County, Virginia.[7] They had no children. (684)

2. Eva Nell Walton was born in September 1892. She married Aubrey Lee St. Clair. He was manager of a grocery store in Augusta County, Virginia. In 1930, they lived on Mulberry Street in Waynesboro. They had three children: (a) Aubrey Lee St. Clair Jr. was born in 1920, (b) Eva Nell St. Clair was born in 1922, and (c) Dorothy Bell St. Clair was born in 1925. (685)

3. John "Jack" Thomas Walton was born in January 1894. He married Olivia ____. They lived in Henrico County. No children were born to their union. (686)

4. Ida M. Walton was born in November 1895. She married Marvin Duncan a building contractor in Henrico County. They had five children. (687)

---

[6] Identification of the eleven children of John T. Walton was made by Alfred Walton, 7333 Osborne Turnpike, Richmond, Virginia 23231. This information was confirmed and supplemented through census research by the compiler.

[7] 1930 U. S. Census for Midlothian, Chesterfield County, Virginia.

5. Winnie Davis Walton was born in March 1899. She married James L. Jones, who was an elevator mechanic. Winnie worked at a tobacco factory. They had one child, Lester Earl Jones. In 1930, they were living on Patterson Avenue in Richmond. (688)

6. Rosa Blanche Walton was born circa 1901. She married Burnette Long. The 1930 U. S. Census placed them in the Tuckaho District of Henrico County. (689)

7. Bessie Lee Walton was born circa 1903. She married Floyd Clements. They had one child, Joyce Clements. The family lived in Richmond. (690)

8. Ruby Walton, born circa 1905, married a Mr. Proctor. They had one child, John Proctor. (691)

9. Virginia E. Walton was born circa 1908. She was living with her sister Eva St. Clair in Waynesboro, Virginia when the 1930 Census was taken. She later married a Mr. Burke. (692)

10. William Melton Walton was born in 1910. He married Virginia ____. They had one child, Shirley Walton, who married a Mr. Ferrell. (693)

11. Marion Josephine Walton was born circa 1913. She married Charles H. Snead. (694)

Minjum H. Walton (402)

Minjum H. Walton, son of William M. and Margaret Ann (Seay) Walton, was born on Feb. 4, 1868 and died on June 27, 1944. The 1920 census states that he was a stableman for the City Stable. He married Jennie Campbell, daughter of William and Jennie Campbell, on Oct. 22, 1890. She was born on July 26, 1865 and died on Aug. 13, 1949. Burial was in the Forest Lawn Cemetery in Richmond, Virginia.

Child of Minjum H. and Jennie (Campbell) Walton:

1. Irene Walton was born on Nov. 1, 1893 and died on Feb. 20, 1992. Irene married Raymond A. Pond, who was born on Feb. 12, 1897 and died on July 23, 1958. Both are buried at Forest Lawn Cemetery in Richmond. She died intestate, without children, which caused the Court to conduct a genealogical study to determine her legal heirs. Irene was a stenographer. (695)

2. Julia Pollard was born circa 1907.[8] (696)

Eliza Ann (Walton) Proffitt (403)

Eliza Ann Walton, daughter of William M. and Margaret A. (Seay) Walton, was born on Feb. 14, 1869 at Tuckahoe, Goochland County, Virginia and died on May 18, 1916 in Richmond.[9] She married Chastain DeGrasse Proffitt, son of George R. and Eliza C. (Drumwright) Proffitt, on Feb. 7, 1884 at Tuckahoe. He was born in 1859 at "Sandyhook," Goochland, County, and died on April 5, 1942 in Richmond. Both were buried in Riverview Cemetery in Richmond.

Children of Chastain D. and Eliza Ann (Walton) Proffitt:[10]

1. Shem Walton Proffitt was born on Aug. 20, 1886 in Richmond and died on Dec. 26, 1951 in Richmond. He married Carrie Busser on April 12, 1917. She first married a Mr. Thorpe. Shem was Vice President of Seaton Coal Company. (697)

2. Annie Vivian Proffitt was born on Dec. 8, 1889 in Richmond and died on June 16, 1952 in Richmond. She married John Johnston on Oct. 10, 1910. She was a seamstress, making uniforms for the Defense Department. (698)

3. Chastain DeGrasse Proffitt Jr. was born on Aug. 24, 1890 in Richmond and died on Dec. 15, 1951. He married first Effie Warren Leber on April 12, 1915. He married second Mary Morano. He was a grocer and merchant in Richmond. (699)

---

[8] 1920 U. S. Census for Richmond, Virginia, Clay Ward, Ashland Street, Sheet 7B. Julia Pollard was living in the household of Minjum H. Walton. Her relationship is not known.

[9] All seven children are named in his will in Louisa County, Virginia, *Will Book 25*, p. 114. Information was furnished by Elizabeth Drake Chatlin of Salt Lake City, Utah.

[10] Names and vital dates for this family unit were provided to the compiler by Elizabeth Drake Chatlin, who possesses the Proffitt family Bible.

4. Bessie Wickham Proffitt was born on Dec. 15, 1892 in Richmond and died on May 27, 1985. She married and divorced Charles Cummings. (700)

5. Eliza May Proffitt was born on Dec. 7, 1894 in Richmond and died on Nov. 21, 1976 in Richmond. She married Clarence Woodville Drake Sr. on Sept. 29, 1917 in Richmond. She was a fulltime homemaker. (701)

6. Hugh Mann Proffitt was born on April 19, 1897 in Richmond and died after 1977. He married Mary Elenor "Delsy" Wilburn, who was born Dec. 29, 1901. Hugh served a career in the U. S. Army. (702)

7. Johnathan Atkins Proffitt was born on Aug. 27, 1902 in Richmond and died on Jan. 26, 1971. He was a physician. He married first and divorced Lucille Gilman, and married second Aileen Carter. (703)

Jesse William Walton (405)

Jesse William Walton, son of William M. and Margaret Ann (Seay) Walton, was born on July 1, 1875 in Henrico County, Virginia and died on June 27, 1957 in Richmond, Virginia. He married Julia Pleasants on Dec. 19, 1900.

Children of Jesse W. and Julia (Pleasants) Walton:[11]

1. Raymond H. Walton was born on Oct. 30, 1901 in Richmond and died on Jan. 25, 1975. He married Frances Jones on Nov. 15, 1956. He was a landscaper. Burial was in the Riverview Cemetery in Richmond. (704)

2. Jesse Edward Walton was born on April 24, 1903 in Richmond and died on April 5, 1990. He married Emma Butler Conti on July 12, 1939. They were buried in Riverview Cemetery in Richmond. Jesse worked for the City of Richmond in Parks and Recreation. (705)

3. Herbert L. Walton was born on Jan. 21, 1905 in Richmond and died on March 27, 1992. He married Nellie Barford on Jan. 15, 1937. She was born on Dec. 21, 1939 and died on March 13, 1992. He worked for Nolde's Bakery. They lived in Fredericksburg, Virginia, but were buried in Riverview Cemetery in Richmond. (706)

---

[11] Information on this family unit was provided by Alfred M. Walton,

4. Ruby Walton was born on Aug. 20, 1906. (707)

5. Joseph Lewis Walton was born on Sept. 1, 1907 in Richmond and died on Dec. 30, 1969. He married Alice Hatcher on Feb. 16, 1935. He worked for the City of Richmond Utilities. Both were buried in the Riverview Cemetery in Richmond. (708)

6. Winfrey A. Walton was born in Richmond on March 15, 1909 and died on March 8, 1992. He married Beatrice Fines on July 23, 1938. She was born on Sept. 20, 1910 and died on March 1, 1986. He worked for the City of Richmond. Both were buried in Riverview Cemetery in Richmond. (709)

7. Mary Marian Walton was born on Oct. 30, 1910. She married first Ernest Dowdy, 1913-1948, and married second Johnny Latta. She worked for Thalhimer's Department Store. (710)

8. Julia A. Walton was born on March 4, 1917 in Richmond. She married Joseph T. Williams on April 11, 1936 in Richmond. He was born on July 18, 1917 in Richmond and died on Nov. 27, 1974. They were buried in Riverview Cemetery in Richmond. (711)

9. Alfred Marvin Walton was born on Oct. 31, 1921 in Richmond. He married Barbara Ann Alvis, daughter of James Bryan and Hattie Thompson (Freeman) Alvis, on May 15, 1948. She was born on Feb. 24, 1928 in Henrico County, Virginia. Alfred retired from the Virginia Department of Motor Vehicles. They are members of Laurel Hill Methodist Church in Richmond. (712)

Lucy Catherine (Walton) Drake Ricard (407)

Lucy Catherine Walton, daughter of John T. and Jane D. (Hudgins) Walton, was born on Aug. 11, 1843 in Amelia County, Virginia and died on Jan. 20, 1914 in Hale County, Alabama. She married Alpheus B. Drake on Nov. 15, 1864 in Perry County, Alabama. He was born on Nov. 4, 1841 and died on Feb. 22, 1871. Alpheus served as a Private in Company I of the 20th Regiment of the Alabama Infantry. He received a medical discharge in November 1862. Alpheus owned and operated a landing on the Warrior River from 1868 to 1871 when his brother-in-law purchased it. After his death, she married second James R. Ricard, 1825-1894, on Sept. 29, 1876.

Children of Alpheus B. and Lucy C. (Walton) Drake:

1. William Walton Drake was born on Dec 17, 1868 and died on Sept. 11, 1936. He married Mary Lillian Wilkerson, daughter of Presley Hawley and Eliza Adeline (Allen) Wilkerson, on Dec. 1, 1895. (713)

2. Alpheus Brown Drake was born in July 31, 1871 and died on March 17, 1897, unmarried. (714)

John Julian Walton (411)

John Julian Walton, son of John T. and Sarah F. (Gill) Walton, was born on Jan. 19, 1850 in Alabama, and died on May 1, 1912 in Hale County, Alabama. The 1900 U. S. Census for Hale County gives his wife's name as Minnie A., born in January 1854. She was Mary Alice "Minnie" Roberts, whom he married on Dec. 9, 1874.[12]

Children of John J. and Mary A. (Roberts) Walton were:

1. Lena Walton was born on Dec. 21, 1877 and died on July 27, 1906. She married T. P. Johnston. (715)

2. Jack T. Walton was born on June 25, 1880 and died on Feb. 8, 1945, unmarried. (716)

3. Wyllie Alma Walton was born in 1883. She married Dr. Ernest B. Dunlap on Feb. 20, 1909. They lived for many years in Lawton, Oklahoma. (717)

4. Orah Walton was born on July 31, 1885 and died on Feb. 28, 1975. She married W. O. Turnipseed on Sept. 1, 1915. They were living in Bullock County, Alabama when the 1920 census was taken. W. O. was a farmer. (718)

Alice (Walton) Walker (412)

Alice Walton,[13] daughter of John T. and Sarah F. (Gills) Walton, was born on Oct. 27, 1853 in Alabama and died in 1927. She married Joseph A. Walker on Nov. 13, 1875 in Perry County,

---

[12] Information was supplied by Eleanor Drake of Perry County, Alabama.

[13] Probably she is the Julia A. Walton on the U. S. Census. Information on this family unit is sketchy, but is a good outline for further research.

Alabama. Immediately after their marriage, Joseph and Alice moved to Cherokee County, Texas where all eight of their children were born. The family moved back to Alabama during the late 1890s where the parents died and were buried in the Greensboro City Cemetery. Joseph was a farmer.

Children of Joseph A. and Alice (Walton) Walker:

1. Edna M. Walker was born in Cherokee County, Texas in 1876. (719)

2. Carrie L. Walker was born in Cherokee County in 1878. (720)

3. Bessie Walker was born in 1880. She married Edward Strickland, son of Solomon and Martha A. Strickland, on April 8, 1898. They lived at Pineville in Marengo County, Alabama. (721)

4. Robert Walton Walker was born on Dec. 10, 1883 and died on Dec. 21, 1904, unmarried. He was buried in the Greensboro City Cemetery. (722)

5. Eleanor Walker, born in 1887, married Henry Stockman. (723)

6. Florrie Walker was born in September 1889. She married Cornelius Lowery. (724)

7. Joseph Annette "Josie" Walker was born on Oct. 27, 1891 and died on Feb. 25, 1992, unmarried. She was a schoolteacher. Josie was buried in the Greensboro City Cemetery. (725)

8. Fannie Gladys Walker was born on Dec. 29, 1892 and died on Sept. 9, 1976. She married Henry Robert Martin on Dec. 10, 1911. He was born on Nov. 16, 1887 and died on May 22, 1937. Both are buried in the Greensboro City, Cemetery. (726)

Joseph Pleasant Walton (413)

Joseph Pleasant Walton,[14] son of John T. and Sarah F. (Gills) Walton, was born on June 4, 1857 in Alabama, and died on June 8,

---

[14] Information on this family unit was contributed by Nell Tucker Nelltucker@aol.com of Hale County, Alabama to the compiler, based on a family Bible in her husband's possession.

1929. He married Chellie Lou Nixon,[15] born on Feb. 20, 1859 and died on May 10, 1940. They were buried in the Greensboro City Cemetery in Hale County, Alabama. The 1900 U. S. Census for Hale County named these children: Sarah Walton, born in October 1882; James T. Walton, born in September 1886; Eugenia Walton, born in July 1889; Betty May Walton, born in April 1893; and Mary Alice Walton, born in January 1896. Information from descendants is much more accurate than census data. Joseph was a farmer.

Children of Joseph P. and Chellie M. (Nixon) Walton:

1. Jessie Eleanor Walton was born on Feb. 27, 1881 and died on May 18, 1928. She married Gus Walchup., according to family Bible, but the 1900 and 1910 censuses for Hale County give her married name as Martin. A Jessie E. Walton did marry John T. Martin on Oct. 3, 1899 in Hale County. (727)

2. Sarah Helen Walton was born on Oct. 3, 1882 and died on April 20, 1969. She married David J. Walker. (728)

3. James Thomas Walton was born on Sept. 30, 1886 and died on Oct. 29, 1965. He married Annie Elizabeth Thomas on Oct. 17, 1906. She was born on Nov. 22, 1885 and died on Oct. 6, 1992. Both are buried at the Greensboro City Cemetery. (729)

4. Eugenia Walton was born on July 4, 1889 and died on Sept. 31, 1948. She married N. J. Johnston. (730)

5. Betty Mae Walton was born on April 9, 1893 and died on April 27, 1985. She married Walter Thomas Curb on Dec. 26, 1909. Walter was born on Jan. 29, 1886 and died on Oct. 11, 1973. They are buried in the Greensboro City Cemetery. (731)

6. Mary Alice Walton was born on Jan. 22, 1896 and died on May 29, 1978. She married Thomas Eli Tucker Jr. (732)

Sarah E. (Walton) Avery (421)

Sarah E. Walton, daughter of Joseph M. and Lucy T. (Gills) Walton, was born on Nov. 25, 1839 in Virginia and died in

---

[15] The Bible record gives her dates as Feb. 20, 1859 and May 10, 1940. The Bible gives her middle name as Lou, whereas the census shows M for her middle initial.

Alabama on Sept. 27, 1931.[16] Sarah married William A. Avery, son of William and Lydia (Byrd) Avery. William A. was born on March 1, 1832 and died on March 21, 1910 at Greensboro, Alabama. She was living in the home of her son-in-law, James P. Wilson, in 1930. The 1900 census states that she gave birth to eight children, six of whom were alive. Both parents were buried in the Greensboro City Cemetery in Hale County, Alabama. He was a miller.

Children of William A. and Sarah E. (Walton) Avery:

    1. Edward William Avery was born Oct. 16, 1857 and died Feb. 12, 1870. He is buried in the Greensboro City Cemetery. (733)

    2. Lucy Agnes Avery was born May 25, 1860 and died May 18, 1939. She married Joseph "Joel" Augustus Stephenson on Dec. 23, 1879. He was born on May 5, 1850 and died May 12, 1913. They are buried in the Greensboro City Cemetery. (734)

    3. Anna Beulah Avery was born Dec. 26, 1862. She married Jeff D. Griffin on Dec. 26, 1887. (735)

    4. Wilma Josephine Avery was born March 16, 1866 and died Jan. 19, 1903. She married John Walter Parr, Jr. on July 18, 1893. He was born September of 1862 and died June 17, 1910. Both are buried at the Greensboro City Cemetery. (736)

    5. Ella Gay Avery was born March 3, 1868. She married James S. Jones on Dec. 15, 1894. (737)

    6. Joseph Walton Avery was born Dec. 20, 1871. He married Mozelle Edmondson. (738)

    7. Virginia Emma Avery was born Oct. 20, 1874 and died April 10, 1966. On Dec. 9, 1900, she married James P. Wilson. He was born Feb. 22, 1866 and died Dec. 18, 1934. Both are buried in the Greensboro City Cemetery. (739)

    8. Jerry Yancey Avery was born ca 1877. He was still living during the 1970s in Walnut Grove, California. (740)

---

[16] From tombstone, per Eleanor Drake..

Thomas Howard Walton (423)

Thomas Howard Walton, son of Joseph M. and Lucy T. (Gills) Walton, was born Aug. 28, 1846 and died Jan. 18, 1908. On May 7, 1870, he married Susan Brand. She was born July 5, 1849 and died Oct. 24, 1910. Both are buried in the Greensboro City Cemetery in Hale County, Alabama.

Children of Thomas Howard and Susan (Brand) Walton:

1. Lucy Ella Walton was born Nov. 8, 1873 and died March 3, 1952. She married James Christopher Parr who was born Feb. 16, 1870 and died Nov. 22, 1938. They are buried at the Greensboro City Cemetery. (741)

2. Romulus Foster Walton was born in Hale County on July 6, 1875. After graduating from West Point in 1898, he served in the Spanish American War in Cuba and later served in the Phullipines. He taught at Riverview Military Academy in Poughkeepsie, New York. He was affiliated with the New York National Guard as Inspector Instructor and Adjutant General. Romulus married Marguerite Leverich Ingraham on Oct. 4, 1899. (742)

3. Mary Valentine Walton was born July 18, 1877 and died April 6, 1893. She did not marry and is buried in the Greensboro City Cemetery. (743)

4. Jessie Virginia Walton was born April 4, 1880 and died Oct. 31, 1952. She did not marry and is buried in the Greensboro City Cemetery. (744)

5. Bryan Brand Walton was born Oct. 29, 1881 and died April 23, 1957. On Dec. 18, 1902, he married Della Thomas. She was born March 14, 1883 and died June 3, 1972. They are buried at the Greensboro City Cemetery. (745)

6. Emmett Abbott Walton was born Nov. 15, 1891 and died Feb. 17, 1920. On Aug. 19, 1917, he married Alma Harris. He is buried at the Greensboro City Cemetery. (746)

7. Howard Walton (747)

8. Joseph W. Walton married first Idelle Baker. (748)

9. Lottie Walton married a James. (749)

Murry Thomas Walton (437)

Murry Thomas Walton, son of Robert and Elizabeth (Wilson) Walton, was born on March 30, 1830 in Campbell County, Virginia and died on Oct. 2, 1907 in Lehigh, Oklahoma. Obviously, he was named for his paternal grandparents. Murry is a misspelling of Murray. He married Nancy Elizabeth Taylor, who was born on Aug. 1, 1842 in Mississippi and died on Dec. 21, 1896 at Lehigh, Choctaw Nation, Oklahoma. Their early-married life was spent in Texas and Louisiana. They lived briefly in Arkansas during the 1870s, and finally settled in Indian Territory, Oklahoma.

Children of Murry T. and Nancy E. (Taylor) Walton:[17]

1. Bettie Belle Walton was born on Aug. 4, 1866 in Louisiana and died April 1, 1893 at Lehigh, Oklahoma. She was buried in the Lehigh Cemetery. Bettie married Judge John M. Harrison, son of Zadoc and Elizabeth (Ellis) Harrison.[18] (751)

2. Tommy Walton left home before 1900 to drive a wagon across the country and was never heard from again. (752))

3. Mattie Walton, of whom nothing more is known. (753)

4. Mary "Molly" Walton was born in May 1876[19] in Indian Territory, Oklahoma and died on May 17, 1945 at Coalgate, Oklahoma. She was living in the household of her father on the 1900 Census.. (754)

5. Matilda Walton was born on Aug. 1, 1879 in Indian Territory, Oklahoma and died on Aug. 28, 1917 at Coalgate, Oklahoma. She was living in the household of her father in 1900.[20] (755)

---

[17] Jean Lewis Boyce of Oklahoma kboyce@junct.com was the main source of informatiuon on the children. The compiler did additional research in census records.

[18] http://trees.ancestry.com/owt/person.aspx?pid=52665072

[19] 1900 U. S. Census for Choctaw Nation, Oklahoma, Microfilm Roll 1852, Book 1, p. 164.a.

[20] 1900 U. S. Census for Choctaw Nation, Oklahoma, Microfilm Roll 1852, Book 1, p. 164.a.

6. Amanda Walton was born on June 20, 1874 in Oklahoma and died at Coalgate, Choctaw Nation, Oklahoma on Nov. 11, 1889. (756)

7. Singleton Allen Walton was born on Jan. 10, 1884 at Coalgate, Indian Territory, Oklahoma. In 1910, he was living in Okmulgee County, Oklahoma. Living in his household were his wife Daisy and two children, Hattie W. Walton and Freda L. Walton. He may have served in World War I. Singleton died on Feb. 18, 1945 at a prison in Albuquerque, New Mexico, allegedly killed by a prison warden. (757)

8. Charley Walton was born on April 5, 1888 at Coalgate, Choctaw Nation, Oklahoma and died on Jan. 20, 1889 at the same place. (758)

Thomas Henry Walton (445)

Thomas Henry Walton, son of Thomas C. and Nancy P. (Trent) Walton, was born at Bent Creek, Buckingham County, Virginia on Dec. 13, 1826. About 1832, he moved with his parents to Chariton County, Missouri, where he died on July 17, 1910. Thomas married Louise Price on March 25, 1868. When the Civil War broke out, he was appointed captain of Company B of Elliott's Battalion, and was promoted to major before the end of the war. Louise was born on Sept. 18, 1846. Their residence was Salisbury, Missouri.

Children of Thomas H. and Louise (Price) Walton:

1. John Thomas Walton was born on Feb. 16, 1869. (759)

2. Anna Burch Walton was born on Feb. 16, 1871. (760)

3. Mary Hasking Walton was born on Feb. 11, 1872 and died Oct. 14, 1892. (761)

4. Meriwether Lewis Walton was born on Oct. 26, 1873. (762)

5. Louise Price Walton was born Sept. 28, 1875. (763)

6. William Anthony Walton was born Nov. 11, 1877. (764)

7. Thomas Henry Walton Jr. was born on Feb. 5, 1880. (765)

8. Nancy Trent Walton was born on Dec. 22, 1881. (766)

9. Isabel Price Walton was born July 4, 1886. (767)

Thomas E. Walton (448)

Thomas E. Walton, son of Anthony Jr. and Margaret (Daniel) Walton, was born circa 1829 at Bent Creek, Buckingham County, Virginia and died in 1882 in Appomattox County. He married Martha E. Woodson, daughter of Drury W. and Louisa (Hendrick) Woodson, on Nov. 25, 1855, in Appomattox County.[21] Martha was born in 1832 and died in 1920.[22] Thomas was a farmer, but may have followed his father's footsteps in the carpentry and building trades. He inherited the 123-acre "Rose Grove" estate from his father in 1860. This was located along the stage road leading from Richmond to Lynchburg. The estate was described as being five miles from the original Appomattox Court House.[23] Their final residence was about three miles southwest of Appomattox, Virginia.

Children of Thomas E. and Martha (Woodson) Walton:

1. Thomas Anthony Walton was born on Oct. 12, 1856 and died Oct. 23, 1934.[24] He married Virginia Purdum, daughter of Rufus King and Emily (Brandenburg) Purdum, who came to Appomattox County from Frederick, Maryland. Virginia Purdum was born on July 28, 1862 and died on Jan. 29, 1943. (768)

2. Drury E. Walton was born in 1859, per 1860 census for Appomattox County. (769)

---

[21] Nancy Jamerson Weiland, research assistant at Jones Memorial Library in Lynchburg, provided documentation to the compiler on April 27, 2001. Proof of the marriage was found in the Virginia Department of Health, Bureau of Vital records—Marriage Index—Husbands, Library of Virginia.

[22] Appomattox County, Virginia, *Will Book 1*, p. 240. Martha (Woodson) Walton wrote her will in Appomattox County, Virginia on April 5, 1919 and it was presented to the Court on Jan. 14, 1920.

[23] Appomattox County, Virginia *Land Tax Books, 1860-1865*. The assessed value of "Rose Grove" in 1865 was $774.90.

[24] Appomattox County, Virginia *Will Book 2*, p 18 and p. 46. His will was written on April 2, 1926 and probated on Oct. 26, 1934.

3. Marie E. Walton was born on June 6, 1864 and died April 6, 1954. She married Edward E. Purdum, who was born on June 11, 1860 and died June 13, 1940. Burial was in Liberty Cemetery, Appomattox. (770)

4. George Alexander Walton was born in 1867 and died on Oct. 8, 1938 in Nottoway County, Virginia.[25] He married Emily Purdum. The 1900 and 1910 censuses named these children: Robert P. Walton, born in June 1894; Martha B. Walton, born in February 1896; Emma V. Walton, born in May 1898; Georgie Walton Jr., born in 1902; Ruby Walton, born in 1905. Living also in the household was Martha Walton, age 78, listed as the mother.[26] (771)

5. Annie Walton was born in 1871. She married Robert E. Staples. (772)

6. Ella Amanda Walton was born April 1, 1874 and died on Feb. 8, 1967. She married Roland F. Jamerson on Dec. 7, 1894.[27] He was born on June 6, 1875 and died Feb. 14, 1942. (773)

7. Carrie Walton was born on Jan. 19, 1877 and died May 13, 1958. She married James Drury Moses, son of Charles Thomas and Mary (Woodson) Moses.[28] He was born on April 4, 1871 and died Jan. 19, 1947. The family burial ground is in Liberty Cemetery. (774)

John Lipscomb Walton (454)

John Lipscomb Walton, son of John A. and Ann (Crank) Walton, was born in Wilson County, Tennessee on Jan. 2, 1834 and died on March 10, 1908 in Logan County, Arkansas. He married Adeline Cravens on July 22, 1869 in Johnson County, Arkansas. She was born on March 22, 1849 in Johnson County, and died on Nov. 18,

---

[25] Appomattox County, Virginia *Will Book 2*, p. 345.

[26] 1910 US Census for Appomattox County, Virginia, Enumeration District 0022, Visit 0156.

[27] Appomattox County, Virginia *Marriage Book 1*, p. 7.

[28] Appomattox County, Virginia *Marriage Book 1*, p. 8.

1929 at Paris, Logan County. Burial was in the Oakwood Cemetery in Logan County, Arkansas.

Children of John L. and Adeline (Cravens) Walton:

1. Arkansas A. Walton was born on March 15, 1870 and died on July 29, 1872 at Prairie View, Logan County. (775)

2. John Lipscomb Walton Jr. was born on Jan. 16, 1872 and died on Nov. 10, 1953 in Logan County. He married first Emma Stevens, born on Oct. 1, 1874 and died on Oct. 27, 1904. John married second Teresa Jane Houser, born on Aug. 10, 1884 and died April 10, 1955. All were buried in the McKendree Cemetery in Logan County. (776)

3. Virginia Alice Walton was born on Feb. 2, 1874 and died on Aug. 9, 1877 at Prairie View, Logan County. (777)

4. James Armistead Walton was born on Dec. 17, 1878 in Logan County and died on July 22, 1953 at Poteau, LeFlore County, Oklahoma. He married Anna Mary Morris. (778)

5. William Talton Walton was born on March 28, 1882 and died on Feb. 5, 1917 at Paris, Logan County, Arkansas. He married Lillian M. Callahan. (779)

6. Joseph Cravens Walton was born on March 5, 1885 in Logan County and died on Dec. 2, 1951 in Logan County. Burial was in Oakwood Cemetery. He married Martha E. Kinney, born on Jan. 11, 1896 and died on Oct. 16, 1893. (780)

7. Winnie E. Walton was born in 1890 and died on March 15, 1974 at Ft. Smith, Sebastian County, Arkansas. She married first James B. Stroup and married second Arthur H. Plunkett, son of James Calvin and Mary Ann (Rhyne) Plunkett. (781)

8. Baby boy Walton was born and died on April 2, 1891 at Prairie View, Logan County, Arkansas. (782)

9. Pearl Ethel Walton was born on April 13, 1892 in Logan County and died on Jan. 9, 1982 at Ft. Smith, Sebastian County, Arkansas. Burial was at Forest Lawn Cemetery. She married Lewis Edgar Plunkett, brother of Arthur Plunkett above, and son of James Calvin and Mary Ann (Rhyne) Plunkett. (783)

John William Carter (469)

John William Carter, son of Archibald W. and Mary S. (Isbell) Carter, was born on April 21, 1837 in Buckingham County and died on May 5, 1879. He married Mary Eliza (McGhee) Isbell, widow of Matthew Isbell, on March 12, 1857 in Halifax County, North Carolina.[29]

Children of John W. and Mary E. (McGhee) Isbell Carter:

    1. Patty Austin Carter was born in Lynchburg, Virginia on Aug. 2, 1860 and died on Oct. 6, 1928 in Richmond. She married William Steger in Lynchburg on Nov. 20, 1883. William was born on Nov. 7, 1859 in Richmond and died on March 3, 1945 in Richmond. (784)

    2. Janie Carter died in 1890, unmarried. She is buried in the Carter-Isbell plot in Hollywood Cemetery in Richmond.[30] (785))

Susan Gathright (Carter) Glass (472)

Susan G. (Carter) Glass, daughter of Archibald W. and Mary Susan (Isbell) Carter was born on May 31, 1846 in Buckingham County and died on Aug. 28, 1929 in Lynchburg.[31] She married Edward Christian Glass, son of Robert Henry and Elizabeth Augustus (Christian) Glass. He was born on Sept. 7, 1852[32] and died on Oct. 26, 1931. Burial was in the Presbyterian Cemetery in Lynchburg. E. C. served as Superintendent of Schools for Lynchburg during 1879 to 1931, and as a member of the State Board of Education. In 1920, the E.C. Glass High School in Lynchburg was named for him.

---

[29] Virginia Historical Society, Mss1 C2468 b 130-131, Record No. 159926.

[30] Information was furnished by William E. Steger, 12384 Grandee Road, San Diego, CA 92128, in letter to the compiler dated Sept. 10, 2002.

[31] Obituary of Susan (Carter) Glass in the *Lynchburg News*, Aug. 29, 1929, p. 2, col. 5.

[32] Rosa Faulkner Yancey, *Lynchburg and Its Neighbors*, (Richmond, Virginia: J. W. Ferguson & Sons), 1935, p. 318.

Children of Edward C. and Susan G. (Carter) Glass:[33]

1. Edward Carter Glass Jr. was born ca 1881. He was a civil engineer. (786)

2. Mary Carter Glass was born on May 18, 1883 in Lynchburg and died on July 23, 1973 at Baptist Hospital in Lynchburg. Burial was in the Presbyterian Cemetery in Lynchburg. She eloped to marry Walter Preston Tyree Jr., son of Walter P. and Martha Anne (Anderson) Tyree, on March 2, 1903 in Washington, D. C. Walter was born on Dec. 2, 1876 and died on Jan. 2, 1959. (787)

3. Robert Glass was born ca 1886. He was an editor for the newspaper. (788)

4. Nancy D. Glass was born ca 1889 and died at Wadesboro, North Carolina in October 1976.[34] She married Edward Howard Mayfield. She was a bookkeeper. The 1930 Census for Lynchburg stated that she was a widow. Her obituary stated that she was a lifetime member of Court Street Methodist Church in Lynchburg. (789)

5. Henry B. Glass was born ca 1891. He was an attorney. (790)

6. Elizabeth C. Glass was born in 1894. She was a teacher in the public schools. (791)

7. Susan Sanford Glass was born ca 1901 and died on June 26, 1997 in Lynchburg.[35] She married Richard Henry Lee, son of Henry Bedinger and Lucy Johnston (Marshall) Lee, on Sept. 9, 1926. He was born on Aug. 4, 1897 in Charlottesville, Virginia and died on Dec. 13, 1969 in Lynchburg. They were members of the Episcopal Church. (792)

Frank Boggs Jones (481)

Frank Boggs Jones, son of Dr. David Crawford and Eliza Ann (Walton) Jones, was born on Nov. 11, 1843 in Campbell County,

---

[33] Information on the children came primarily from miscellaneous public records, because the compiler was unable to locate living descendants of E. C. Glass.

[34] *News & Advance*, p. 12, col. 3.

[35] *News & Advance*, Section A, p. 5, col. 3, June 27, 1997.

Virginia, and died on July 19, 1915. He married Nancy Alexander Elliott, 1845-1929, daughter of William Alexander and Margaret Harvey (Hunter) Elliott. Frank served as a prison guard at Libby Prison in Richmond during the Civil War.[36]

Children of Frank B. and Nancy Alexander (Elliott) Jones:

    1. Elliott Rowland Jones was born on Oct. 19, 1874 and died on Sept. 27, 1960. He did not marry. (793)

    2. Marvin Hunter Jones was born on June 17, 1876 and died on Sept. 16, 1932. He married Sally Dickerson. (794)

    3. David Crawford Jones was born on May 20, 1878 and died on May 9, 1880. (795)

    4. Little babes, twins born on Aug. 12, 1879 and died on Sept. 18, 1879. (796)

    5. William Soule Jones was born on Jan. 1, 1881 and died on March 1, 1941. He married Ellen "Nellie" Kingston. (797)

    6. Frank Orman Jones was born on Oct. 10, 1882 and died in 1974. He married his cousin, Macca Virginia Bates. (798)

    7. Annie Eliza Jones was born on Oct. 29, 1884 and died on Jan. 11, 1933. She married William D. Robertson. (799)

    8. Margaret Reva Jones was born on July 12, 1887 and died on July 12, 1887. (800)

    9. Herbert Strother Jones was born on Sept. 14, 1888 and died on Sept. 22, 1917. He married Eunise Ellen Furbush on Sept. 22, 1917. Ellen was born on Oct. 5, 1895 in Campbell County. (801)

Isabel Buchanan (Jones) Payne (485)

Isabel Buchanan Jones, daughter of Dr. David Crawford and Eliza Ann (Walton) Jones, was born on Nov. 15, 1854 in

---

[36] His sister, Ida Walton Jones, was quoted circa 1939 in a Roanoke Times newspaper. A copy of the paper was provided to the compiler by Lloyd G. Walton of Appomattox County on July 4, 2001.

Appomattox County, and died in 1943.[37] She married Samuel Payne of Lynchburg. Isabel outlived all of her brothers and sisters.

Child of Samuel and Isabel B. (Jones) Payne:

    1. Mosby Hale Payne was born on Aug. 24, 1890 and died March 29, 1952. He was a medical doctor in New York. He married Virginia Winter who was born on Sept. 16, 1890 and died on Nov. 29, 1976. They were the last persons who were buried in the Jones family graveyard at "The Meadows." The farm is now called "Misty Hills Farm." Current owners of the former estate of Dr. David C. Jones are Rollin and Middy Hayden of Rt. 3, Appomattox, Virginia. (802)

Edmund Winston Walker (492)

Edmund Winston Walker,[38] son of Samuel Jennings and Martha Ann Armistead (Walton) Walker, was born June 7, 1842 in Buckingham County (now Appomattox), Virginia, and died May 12, 1916. He married Jane Rebecca Massie, daughter of William George and Elizabeth Virginia (Finch) Massie, June 20, 1871, in Hopkinsville, Kentucky. She was born on Feb. 17, 1851 in Todd County, Kentucky and died Aug. 5, 1929 in Hopkinsville. Both were buried in Riverside Cemetery in Hopkinsville, Christian County, Kentucky.[39]

Children of Edmund W. and Jane R. (Massie) Walker:

    1. William Massie Walker was born on July 4, 1873 in Christian County, Kentucky and died Aug. 28, 1959. He married Mary Etta Bowles on Nov. 29, 1898. (803)

---

[37] From tombstone in the Jones family graveyard at "The Meadows" farm in Appomattox County, located east of Oakville.

[38] Information on this family unit was furnished to the compiler by Mrs. Bettie Walker Fricke, 304 North Englewood Avenue, Dotham, Alabama 36303-3012.

[39] Mavis Parrott Kelsey, M.D., and Mary Wilson Kelsey, *The Family of John Massie, Revolutionary Patriot of Louisa County, Virginia.* (Houston, Texas: private printer), circa 1978, p. 38.

2. Martha Winston Walker was born on July 11, 1875 in Christian County and died in Lynchburg, Virginia. She married Irving Powell Whitehead, son of Major Thomas and Martha Henry (Garland) Whitehead, in Hopkinsville, Kentucky on July 3, 1901. He was born on July 6, 1869 in Amherst County, Virginia and died at the same place on Jan. 20, 1938. (804)

3. Mary Virginia Walker was born May 14, 1878 in Christian County, Kentucky and died March 17, 1966. She was buried in Riverside Cemetery in Hopkinsville. (805)

4. Elizabeth Finch Walker was born July 31, 1882 in Christian County and died June 14, 1949 in the same place. She married William Lacy Morrison on June 19, 1907 in Hopkinsville. (806)

5. Nannie Lee Walker was born July 21, 1884 and died Aug. 31, 1912 in Hopkinsville. (807)

Bettie Christian (Walton) Abbitt (514)

Bettie Christian Walton, daughter of John W. and Many J. (Vawter) Walton, was born June 22, 1845 in Appomattox County, and died Aug. 5, 1916. She married George P. Dallas Abbitt, 1844-1883, son of Benjamin Jr. and Mary S. (Patterson) Abbitt. He served in Company H, 2nd Virginia Cavalry under Capt. Joel W. Flood Jr. Known as the Appomattox Rangers, this was the only Cavalry unit from the County.[40] Oral family history says that Mr. Dallas Abbitt served time and died in the State Penitentiary for murdering a man.[41]

Child of George P. Dallas and Bettie C. (Walton) Abbitt:

1. Mary Elizabeth Abbitt was born Dec. 9, 1882, and died July 12, 1955. "Liz" lived with relatives, especially her first cousin, John C.

---

[40] The Appomattox County Museum in the Old County Jail has a history of this military unit that fought at Brandy Station.

[41] Calvin Harris of Appomattox County told this story to the compiler on July 4, 2001. Calvin pointed to the unmarked grave of Dallas Abbitt, located in a cemetery on the former Walton farm known as "The Cove Farm." Harris is the current owner of the 87-acre farm.

Walton of Dillwyn, Virginia. She did not marry. Liz was buried at Red Oak Baptist Church just north of the town of Appomattox. (808)

Eugene Adolphus Walton (516)

Eugene Adolphus Walton,[42] son of John W. and Mary J. (Vawter) Walton, was born on Aug. 16, 1850 at Bent Creek, Appomattox County, Virginia and died Dec. 19, 1921, at Bent Creek. He lived on part of the ancestral homestead that was once owned by his great-grandparents, Thomas Jr. and Nancy Ann (Armistead) Walton. Eugene married Nannie Katherine Jones, daughter of Lamech and Macca Barksdale (Hunter) Jones, Oct. 24, 1884. She was born Jan. 26, 1862, and died Dec. 29, 1931. Eugene farmed and served as a deputy sheriff for Appomattox County, just as his father had been in Buckingham and Appomattox Counties. He was also the owner and operator of a country store at Oakville, known as E.A. Walton & Company. He and his family were active members in the Mt. Comfort Methodist Church at Oakville.

At the turn of the century, numerous descendants of Thomas Walton Jr., who had settled at Bent Creek about 1803, sought information on their Walton ancestors to construct a family tree. None of these curious researchers was successful in compiling their family tree because: (a) Records in both Buckingham and Appomattox Counties were burned. (b) Thomas Walton Jr. was married three times and some of his descendants were reluctant to share information in their hands. (c) William Armistead disinherited all of his grandchildren through his daughter Nancy Armistead, who was the second wife of Thomas Walton Jr., and (d) those who possessed information, such as the William Walton family Bible, held the information in secrecy. Here is a sample reply by E. A.

---

[42] The Bible record of George W. and Annie E. (Walton) Mitchell shows the name as Adolphus Eugene Walton, but he most often used the form of Eugene Adolphus Walton or simply signed his name as E.A. Walton.

Walton to a query by a distant cousin, Miss Kent Gregory, 1872-1950, of Lynchburg:[43]

P. O. Bent Creek, Virginia
Nov. 10, 1911
Dear Miss Kent,
Your letter received several days ago and in reply I fear I cannot give you much knowledge in regard to our Walton ancestors. Our grandfather was William Walton, born and raised in Cumberland County. His sisters married into Carter,[44] Isbell, Harris, and Bransford families. I do not know their given names. Our grandfather William Walton's father was named Thomas, his wife Nannie. I think the Waltons were closely associated with the Armisteads. I have told you all I know.[45]

Sincerely,

E. A. Walton

Children of Eugene A. and Nannie K. (Jones) Walton:

1. William Jones Walton Sr. was born July 19, 1885, and died Dec. 11, 1950. He married Mildred Frances Harvey, daughter of William and Mildred (Walker) Harvey. Mildred "Aunt Frankie" was born on May 20, 1890 and died March 29, 1967. (809)

2. Dallas Eugene Walton was born Feb. 13, 1887 and died April 1, 1968. Burial was in the Mt. Comfort United Methodist Church Cemetery in Appomattox County. He married first Jamie Florence Moss on Oct. 15, 1914.[46] She was born on April 7, 1881 and died Feb.

---

[43] Jones Memorial Library, Lynchburg, Virginia, Kent Gregory (1872-1950), "Genealogical Papers (Walton), MS1288." See also Ida Bowman Younger (1903-1993) "Genealogical Papers (Walton), MS 2098."

[44] Reference to Carter evidently was to Susan Carter (1846-1926), who married Edward Christian Glass of Lynchburg, for whom E.C. Glass High School in Lynchburg was named. If so, Sue was a great-half-niece of William Walton rather than his sister.

[45] He failed to mention that he had in his possession the family Bible of his grandfather William Walton, which would have greatly benefited genealogical researchers.

[46] Appomattox County, Virginia *Marriage Book 1*, p. 52.

2, 1916. After her death, he married second Ruth Harris, on his 42nd birthday. No children were born to either union. (810)

Eugene A. and Nannie C. (Jones) Walton

3. Mary Barksdale Walton was born Feb. 3, 1889 and died on Oct. 19, 1960. She married Carrington A. Bolton. (811)

4. Walker Scott Walton was born on July 25, 1892, and died May 7, 1959, at Spout Spring. He married Nellie Virginia Davis, daughter of Matthew M. and Josephine (Shepherd) Davis, Aug. 2, 1930 by a Baptist preacher in Lynchburg. Her vital dates were Sept. 7, 1907 and Jan. 20, 1973. (812)

5. Lela Mitchell Walton was born April 1, 1894 at Bent Creek and died Dec. 2, 1981. She married Daniel Mosby Harris on Jan. 27, 1915. (813)

6. Bessie Vawter Walton was born on Oct. 16, 1896 and died in 1984. She married Francis Marion Payne, 1885-1958, son of Sterling Claiborne and Sally Ida (Harris) Payne. Known as "Frank," he was born on Aug. 25, 1885 and died on March 24, 1958. (814)

7. Nannie Evelyn Walton was born July 15, 1899 and died June 22, 1941. She married Willis E. Harris. (815)

8. John Christian Walton was born Jan. 7, 1902 and died Jan. 4, 1986. He married Ruby Frances Davis, daughter of Matthew M. and Josephine (Shepherd) Davis. (816)

9. Alexander Wilson Walton was born Aug. 28, 1904, and died on Oct. 28, 1987. He married Mary Cabell Harris, daughter of Walter Mosley and Mary Franklin (Cunningham) Harris. (817)

Thomas Edward Walton Scruggs Jr. (518)

Thomas Edward Walton Scruggs Jr., son of Thomas W. and Elizabeth P. (North) Scruggs, was born on Feb. 3, 1859 in Appomattox County, Virginia and died on March 11, 1897 at Grapevine, Tarrant County, Texas. Thomas Jr. was a schoolteacher. He married Sallie E. Blevins, daughter of William M. and Louisa (Tittle) Blevins. Sallie was born on July 5, 1867 in Dade County, Georgia and died in Tarrant County on April 6, 1945.[47] After the death of her first husband, Sallie married Floyd or Roy E. Rodgers. Sallie and her first husband were buried in White's Chapel Cemetery in Grapevine, Texas.

Children of Thomas E. W. and Sallie E. (Blevins) Scruggs:[48]

1. Betty Lou Scruggs was born in 1889 and died in 1894. She was buried at White's Chapel in Grapevine, Texas. (818)

2. Nannie Lucille Scruggs was born circa 1891 in Tarrant County, Texas and died on June 10, 1980. She married a Mr. Berry. (819)

---

[47] Dates for husband and wife were taken from tombstone inscriptions at White's Chapel in Grapevine, Texas.

[48] Information on this family unit was found in Appomattox County, Virginia Circuit Court papers, "Scruggs vs. Scruggs."

3. Mason Ashby Scruggs was born on Feb. 5, 1892 in Grapevine, Texas and died on Jan. 7, 1968.[49] In 1910, he was living with his grandparents, William M. and Louisa Blevins, in Tarrant County, Texas. (820)

4. William Walton Scruggs was born circa 1895 in Texas. (821)

5. James Andrew Scruggs was born in 1897 in Texas and died on April 20, 1972 in Tarrant County, Texas. He was living with his grandparents, William M. and Louisa Blevins when the 1910 U. S. Census was taken for Tarrant County. In 1920, he was living in the same place with a wife and two children. (822)

Amine Josephine (Scruggs) Bagby (519)

Amine Josephine Scruggs, daughter of Thomas W. and Elizabeth P. (North) Scruggs, was born on Jan. 14, 1861 in Appomattox County, and died on Feb. 19, 1954. She was deaf in infancy from a case of spinal meningitis. Amine attended the School for the Deaf in Staunton, Virginia. She married Bennett Wesley Bagby, son of Bennett M. Bagby, in 1882. He was a circuit rider for the Methodist Church and a schoolteacher in the Stonewall District of Appomattox County. Bennett was educated at both Randolph Macon College and Hampden Sydney College. Bennett was born in Powhatan County, Virginia on Oct. 31, 1838 and died in Appomattox County in 1886.[50] He married first Susan W. Moore. The Bagby family lived in the Stonewall District of Appomattox County during the early years.

Children of Bennett W. and Amine J. (Scruggs) Bagby:

1. Carrie Ethel Bagby was born July 22, 1883 in Appomattox County and died of the flu in September 1918 in Houston, Texas. She married Raymond Shackleford in August 1918. Ethel was adopted by her uncle Richard Bagby and his wife Mollie. (823)

---

[49] Social Security Death Index.

[50] *Appomattox County, Virginia*, 2001, pp. 102-103, Appomattox Heritage Book, P. O. Box 879, Appomattox, VA 24522, submitted by Cary Ann Garrette.

2. Mollie Sue Bagby was born on June 14, 1886 in Appomattox County and died on Jan. 14, 1959. She married Monroe Lumsden Garrette, son of Joseph Henry Wilson and Frances Clementine (Gilbert) Garrett, on June 1, 1907 in Richmond, Virginia. (824)

Frederick Cabell Scruggs (526)

Frederick Cabell Scruggs, son of John A. and Amanda D. (Christian) Scruggs, was born on Feb. 15, 1845 in Nelson County, Virginia,[51] and died on Dec. 18, 1913 "of heart disease" in Nelson County. He served as a Confederate in Co. D, 20 Battalion, VA Heavy Artillery. Frederick married Martha "Mattie" Jane Emett, daughter of Thomas Truxton and Mary Elizabeth (Pendleton) Emett, on April 29, 1875 at Allen's Creek, Nelson County. She was born on July 24, 1851 in Nelson County and died on Aug. 1, 1931. Both were buried on Jim Jordon's farm at Allen's Creek, Nelson County.[52]

Children of Frederick C. and Martha J. (Emmett) Scruggs:

1. Edmund Pendleton Scruggs was born on June 25, 1876 and died on Aug. 4, 1927. He married Nannie Gertrude Wilsher, daughter of George Washington and Laura Mildred (Layne) Wilsher, on Nov. 15, 1908 in Amherst County, Virginia. She was born on June 10, 1883 and died on May 29, 1955 in Lynchburg. (825)

2. Thomas Emett Scruggs was born on May 12, 1878 at Allen's Creek, Nelson County. He did not marry. (826)

3. Samuel Tompkins Scruggs was born on Aug. 8, 1879 at Allen's Creek and died in 1909. He married Lottie Getto. (827)

4. Laura Scruggs was born on Oct. 19, 1882. She married Lavender Eugene Mays on July 4, 1904. He was born on Oct. 17, 1879 in Newport News. (828)

---

[51] Tracy Chernault and Jeffery Weaver, *The Virginia Regimental History Series, 18th and 20th Battalions of Virginia Heavy Artillery*, 1sst edition, per information from Carole Ruff.

[52] Information on this family unit was contributed by Carole Ruff of Leesburg, Virginia.

Sixth Generation

5. John Cabell Scruggs was born on May 28, 1884 and died in 1937. He married Mary Darn. (829)

6. Mary Scruggs was born on Sept. 27, 1886. She married Kenneth McCraw. (830)

7. Martha "Mattie" H. Scruggs was born on Aug. 27, 1889. She married Louis M. Cunningham. (831).

James Robert Gordon (590)

James Robert Gordon, son of Robert and Mary E. (Walton) Gordon, was born on Dec. 6, 1833 at Quincy, Monroe County, Mississippi, and died Nov. 29, 1912 in Mississippi. He married first Carolina Virginia, daughter of Yancey and Eliza Ann (Thompson) Wiley on Feb. 7, 1856 in Lafayette County, Mississippi. Carolina was born on Sept. 13, 1836 in Wythe County, Virginia and died on Feb. 27, 1903 at Okolona. James married second Ella Neilson, 1851-1905.

James attended LaGrange College in Alabama and graduated from the University of Mississippi in 1855. He became a wealthy planter. The 1860 U. S. Census for Chickasaw County, Mississippi reveals that his real estate was valued at $122,700.00 and personal property at $128,725.00. During the Civil War, with rank of colonel, he raised and organized Cavalry units. Jefferson Davis sent him to Europe on a mission to arrange the purchase of a privateer. James was captured and imprisoned on his return to the States. In February 1865, he escaped to Montreal, Canada, where he met John Wilkes Booth. He later successfully defended himself against Government charges of conspiracy to assassinate President Lincoln.[53]

In 1857, 1859, 1876 and 1886 he was elected to and served in the Mississippi House of Representatives. He was a State senator during 1904-1906. James was appointed as a United States Senator to fill out the term of the late Anselm J. McLaurin, which he served in 1909-1910.

---

[53] From *Biographical Directory of the United States Congress.* Bob F. Thompson, Esq. cites James Gordon's biography in *The History of Monroe County.* Many thanks to Bob for digging out this important and interesting information.

Not only was James known for his political and agricultural pursuits, but also he was involved in the literary field, contributing to the leading magazines of the day, including, *Century Magazine, Turf, Field and Farm, American Field,* and *London Field*. He wrote under the pen name of Pious Jeems.

Children of James R. and Carolina V. (Wiley) Gordon:

1. Annie Gordon was born in 1856 in Mississippi and died in 1914 in Memphis, Tennessee. An obit says that she was burned to death from a gas heater explosion in her home. She was well known in Christian Science circles. Annie married John Thomas Barrow of Louisville in 1878 and married second to a Mr. Nehls.[54] (832)

2. Robert James Gordon was born on July 27, 1877 at Lochinvar, Pontotoc, Mississippi and died on July 16, 1920 in Little Rock, Arkansas. He married Susie Kate Cook Carter, daughter of Cannon McAllister and Mary Gordon (Cook) Carter, on Dec. 29, 1909. (833)

George Miller (598)

George Miller,[55] son of Hugh R. and Susan G. (Walton) Miller, was born on July 26, 1840 at Pontotoc, Mississippi and died Feb. 1, 1897 in Oxford, Mississippi. He married Elizabeth Catherine Wiley, daughter of Yancey and Eliza Ann (Thompson) Wiley on May 24, 1866 in Oxford, Mississippi. Known as "Kate," she was born on Sept. 22, 1846 at College Hill, Lafayette County, Mississippi and died on Sept. 21, 1919 in Oxford. She was a sister of Carolina Virginia Wiley, wife of James Gordon (590). Her mother was the sister of Jacob Thompson, United States Representative from Mississippi, 1839-1851, Secretary of Interior under President James Buchanan, 1857-1861, and Confederate Commissioner to Canada, 1864-1865. George was a private in Company G, 2nd Mississippi.

---

[54] The 1910 U. S. Census for Shelby County, Tennessee states that she was a widow (Roll 1521, Part I, p. 14b, line 94).

[55] All information in the Miller and Gordon families was contributed by Bob F. Thompson Esq., of Nashville, Tennessee.

Regt. and Sergeant Major of the 42nd Miss. Regt. The Millers were Presbyterians.

Children of George and Elizabeth C. (Wiley) Miller were:

1. Kate Miller was born on March 18, 1867 and died on April 16, 1959, unmarried. She taught school briefly in early life, and then engaged in farming. (834)

2. Lucy Miller was born on May 16, 1869 and died on July 10, 1941 at Oxford. Apparently, she did not marry. (835)

3. Hugh Reid Miller was born on Aug. 1, 1870 and died on Oct. 22, 1928 at Oxford. He served for thirty years as engineer for the southern division of the I. C. Railroad. (836)

4. George Miller Jr. was born on Aug. 21, 1872 and died on July 6, 1951. He lived his entire life at Cedar Hill, which was the Yancey Wiley home. He married Flora Fernandez on Dec. 31, 1908 at College Hill, Mississippi. (837)

5. Yancey Wiley Miller was born on Sept. 14, 1874 and died on Oct. 20, 1947. Yancey married Lena Paxton Richmond in September 1929 in Cleveland, Mississippi. They had no children. (838)

6. Russell Miller was born on Jan. 17, 1877 and died on July 5, 1947. He was an electrician who moved in 1904 to Armory, Mississippi to oversee the development of electricity for that jurisdiction. He married Minnie Mae Hale on Dec. 12, 1900. She was born on June 16, 1877 and died on April 18, 1970. (839)

7. Virginia Miller was born on Sept. 23, 1879 in Oxford and died on April 4, 1955 at Ruleville, Mississippi. She attended the University of Mississippi, after which she taught in high school. Virginia married Dr. James Andrew Clark on June 5, 1910. He was born on Feb. 16, 1876 at Newton, Mississippi, and died on Sept. 15, 1961 in Memphis. .He graduated from Memphis Hospital College (now the University of Tennessee Medical School). In 1903, he started practice as a physician in Ruleville, which continued for fifty years. (840)

8. Robert Walton Miller was born on Aug. 6, 1881 and died on Aug. 15, 1962. Known as "Uncle Bud," he was a hunting companion and

storyteller to William Faulkner.[56] He married and divorced Elzora Winters. (841)

9. Infant son was born on Aug. 4, 1883 and died on Sept. 21, 1883. (842)

10. Donald Cameron "Dusty" Miller was born on Aug. 23, 1886 and died on Aug. 3, 1950 in Memphis. He spent a career with the City of Memphis, in the engineering and finance areas. In 1937, he became the first comptroller of the municipal government. His degree was in civil engineering in 1908 from the University of Mississippi. He married Marjorie Archer, 1894-1968. He was a Deacon in the Baptist Church and was active in many organizations. (843)

11. Herbert Ashby Miller was born on May 4, 1888 in Oxford, Mississippi and died on June 23, 1955. He was a veteran of World War I and belonged to several organizations, including the Masons, Rotarians and the Presbyterian Church. He was a bookkeeper. Herbert married Madge Elizabeth Anderson on Nov. 20, 1919 in Pontotoc, Mississippi. She was born on Jan. 28, 1895 at Pontotoc and died on Nov. 7, 1957 in Memphis. They had no children. (844)

George Carrington Walton Jr. (600)

George Carrington Walton Jr., son of George Carrington Sr. and Eliza (Miller) Walton, was born on Jan. 16, 1825 in Cumberland County, Virginia, and died Feb. 21, 1917. His mother died in childbirth. George Jr. married Mary Ann Stark Smith,[57] daughter of William Smith, on Nov. 27, 1848 at the residence of Mrs. Mildred A. Austin in Cumberland County.[58] George Jr. and his family were living in Buckingham County, Virginia when the 1860[59] and 1870

---

[56] John B. Cullen, *Old Times in the Faulkner Country*, (Chapel Hill, North Carolina: University of North Carolina Press), 1961, sent to the compiler by Bob F. Thompson, Esq.

[57] Robert Smith, age 72, brother-in-law of George Walton was living in the household when the 1910 Census was taken for Buckingham County.

[58] *Richmond Whig*, Dec. 19, 1848, p. 2, c. 2.

[59] James Randolph Kidd, Jr., *Buckingham County, Virginia: 1860 Federal Census*, (Iberian Publishing Company: Athens, Georgia), p. 15.

censuses were taken.[60] He was on the 1909 Pension List for Buckingham County veterans of the Civil War. George C. Walton was a practicing attorney at Buckingham Courthouse.

Child of George C. Jr. and Mary A.S. (Smith) Walton:[61]

    1. Josephine Walker Walton was born Nov. 3, 1853, and died unmarried, probably in Buckingham County. (845)

Henry Carrington Walton (606)

Henry Carrington Walton, son of Nathaniel and Evelyn B. (Payne) Walton, was born on Oct. 18, 1836 in Cumberland County, and died Aug. 22, 1909 in Cumberland County. On May 13, 1857, he married Lavinia "Dolly" Allen, daughter of Isaac A. and Susan (Mosby) Allen.[62] She was born on April 7, 1840 in Powhatan County, and died on July 23, 1923 in Richmond, Virginia.

Children of Henry C. and Lavinia (Allen) Walton:

    1. Carrington Nathaniel Walton was born on Oct. 8, 1859 and died on Aug.12, 1931. He married Betty Reynolds Brown. They lived on Flippen Mill Road. (846)

    2. Henry D. Walton was born on Sept. 16, 1861. He was living with his mother and sister Annie when the 1910 U. S. Census was taken for Cumberland County. (847)

    3. "The little girl" was born Oct. 9, 1865 and died Oct. 19, 1865. (848)

    4. Ida Elizabeth Walton was born on June 30, 1869 in Nashville, Tennessee. She married Walter Scott Bigger on May 16, 1894. Walter was born circa 1860. Both were living in Cumberland County in 1930. They had a son named Ellsworth Bigger, born in 1904. (849)

---

[60] Jeanne Stinson, *Buckingham County, Virginia 1870 U.S. Census*, (Iberian Publishing Company: Athens, Georgia), 1998, p. 208.

[61] Letter from George C. Walton Jr. of Glenmore, Buckingham County to Peyton Carrington, dated Feb. 10, 1869.

[62] Library of Virginia, "Accession No. 24732, "Walton family Bible record, 1811-1933).

5. Susan Eva Walton (not legible) married Patrick Hay. (850)

6. Floyd Allen Walton was born on June 6, 1873 and died on Nov. 5, 1952. He married Emma Lou Tatum, daughter of William Early and Mary Jenkins (Huddleston) Tatum, on Sept. 25, 1895. In 1900, they were living in Cumberland County with daughters Carrie M. and Shelton Walton. The family was living at Tuckahoe in Henrico County when the 1910 and 1930 U. S. Censuses were taken for that County. (851)

7. Annie Walton was born on Sept. 23, 1875. She was still alive in 1910 when she was living her brother "H. D. Walton."[63] (852)

8. Pocahontas Walton was born on Sept. 23, 1875, per U. S. Census for Henrico County, Virginia, Tuckahoe District. The date in the Bible record is illegible, but it appears that she was a twin. Pocahontas married William P. Stutz who was a merchant in Richmond. (853)

9. Harvey S. Walton was born on Aug. 28, 1878 in Cumberland County and died April 12, 1921 at Cartersville. He married Linda S. Cragwall, daughter of Charles G. and Mary Catherine Cragwall. (854)

Edward Walton (610)

Edward Walton, son of Nathaniel and Evelyn B. (Payne) Walton, was born on June 27, 1847 in Cumberland County, Virginia and died on May 7, 1923 in the same County.[64] His occupation was "mechanic." Edward married Rebecca Jemima DePriest, daughter of John Wells and Elizabeth (Coffman) DePriest, on July 18, 1875. Rebecca was born in 1855 In Augusta County, Virginia, and died in 1899 in Cumberland County. They lived near Cartersville, Virginia, and were members of the Methodist Church.

Children of Edward and Rebecca (DePriest) Walton:[65]

1. Baby Walton was born Aug. 14, 1876 and died Feb. 18, 1877. (855)

---

[63] Information was contributed by Ruby Talley Smith (rubygem@aol.com).

[64] Edward Walton lived in the Hamilton District of Cumberland County when the U. S. Census was taken in 1920, E.D. 85, p. 8B.

[65] Information was contributed by Karen (Crabtree) Adams and Barbara Millner and other noted sources.

Sixth Generation

2. William Frank Walton was born on Oct. 28, 1878 and died on April 14, 1885. (856)

3. Oscar Otway Walton was born on Oct. 2, 1880 and died on Sept. 3, 1885. (857)

4. Roy Kendall Walton was born on June 10, 1883 and died on Nov. 10, 1885. (858)

5. Ruth Elizabeth Walton was born on March 4, 1885 and died on Aug. 24, 1954, unmarried. Ruth lived with her parents until they died, and then lived with her brother Edward C. Walton. She was buried at Thomas Chapel near Cartersville. (859)

6. Luther Lee Walton was born on Jan. 20, 1887 and died on Jan. 5, 1961. He married Myrtle Smith on Dec. 12, 1923. She was born on April 19, 1893 and died on Nov. 4, 1963. (860)

7. Edward Coffman Walton was born on March 6, 1889 and died on Feb. 10, 1980.[66] He married Martha Lavinia Bigger on Feb. 21, 1920. She was born on April 2, 1899 and died on April 9, 1990.[67] (861)

8. Alma Virginia Walton was born on Aug. 22, 1892 in Cumberland County, and died on Jan. 21, 1958 in Lynchburg. She married Ira Green Davis, son of John and Alice (Walker) Davis, on June 15, 1915 in Washington, D. C. (862)

9. Sally Clyde Walton was born on Nov. 17, 1893 and died on Oct. 6, 1925. She married Robert Irving Blanton on June 18, 1918 at Thomas Chapel in Cartersville, Cumberland County.[68] He was born on Jan. 25, 1886[69] and died on Aug. 8, 1944.[70] (863)

---

[66] Social Security Death Index.

[67] Social Security Death Index.

[68] Library of Virginia, "Snoddy family Bible record, 1828-1937," Accession No. 34632.

[69] Library of Virginia, "Blanton Bible record, 1884-1948," accession No. 34631.

[70] *A History of Thomas Chapel United Methodist Church.*

10. Jessie Helen Walton was born May 26, 1896 and died on May 4, 1938 in Bland County, Virginia. She married William Franklin Adams on June 2, 1917, in Cumberland County. (864)

Edward J. Walton (612)

Edward J. Walton, son of Edward G. and Elizabeth (Agee) Walton, was born in 1837 in Cumberland County, Virginia and died in 1885 at Water Valley, Yalobusha County, Mississippi. Burial was in the Camp Ground Cemetery. Ed married Eudora Elizabeth Stockard, daughter of James and Sarah (Neely) Stockard. She was born on Feb. 3, 1844 in Lafayette County, Mississippi and died on April 16, 1924 in Yalobusha County, Mississippi. He enlisted in the Confederate Army on April 26, 1861 at Oxford, Mississippi and was present at the Battle of Seven Pines and the Seven Days Battle.[71] He was a farmer.

Children of Edward J and Eudora E. (Stockard) Walton:[72]

1. Ernest Walton was born circa 1868 in Mississippi. He married Bettie ____ (865).

2. Laurine Elvira Walton was born on March 11, 1869 at Water Valley, Yalobusha, Mississippi, and died on July 11, 1927 at Water Valley. She married Arthur Lee Wood, son of Robert M. and Temperance A. (Stewart) Wood, circa 1890. (866)

3. Annie Walton was born on April 7, 1872 in Yalobusha County, Mississippi and died June 1, 1957. She married Alexander Rushing, who was born on March 1, 1870 and died April 9, 1930. They were buried in Camp Ground Cemetery in Water Valley, Mississippi. (867)

Haidee Zuleika (Walton) Tutwiler (616)

Haidee Zuleika Walton,[73] daughter of Lewis I. and Margaret Elizabeth (Boston) Walton, was born in December 1859 in

---

[71] Walker Coffey, *Confederate Soldiers, Lafayette, Mississippi*, p. 170, source provided by Kenny Wood.

[72] Information on this family unit was contributed by Kenny Wood, 2004 Cheryl, Pearland, TX 77581

Cumberland County, Virginia and died on Jan. 7, 1942 in Jefferson County, Alabama. She married Eli Erskine Tutwiler, son of Thomas Harrison and Harriet Magruder (Strange) Tutwiler, on June 15, 1884 in Fluvanna County, Virginia.

Children of Eli E. and Haidee Z. (Walton) Tutwiler:

1. Erskine W. Tutwiler was born in October 1886 in Alabama. (868)

2. Guy Isbell Tutwiler was born on July 17, 1888 in Adamsville, Alabama and died on Aug. 15, 1930 in Anniston, Calhoun County, Alabama. He married Edna Mae Scruggs on June 13, 1924. (869)

3. Haidee Tutwiler was born on Aug. 3, 1890 at Blossburg, Alabama and died on Feb. 6, 1977 at Athens, Limestone County, Alabama. She married Luther Dillard Glaze on Aug. 12, 1912 in Blossburg, Alabama. He was born on Dec. 4, 1887 and died on Nov. 16, 1960. Their children: Annie Zuleika Glaze, Harriet Tutwiler Glaze, and Haidee LeRuth Glaze. (870)

4. Mary Boston Tutwiler, twin sister to Haidee, was born on Aug. 3, 1890 and died in 1890. (871)

5. Ann Dudley Tutwiler was born in December 1893 in Alabama. She married Joseph Pickens McQueen. Their children: Margaret McQueen, Ann Dudley McQueen, and Florence Temple McQueen. (872)

6. Margaret Chewning Tutwiler was born in 1896 in Alabama. She married Walter Scott Wilson Sr. Their children: Walter Scott Wilson Jr., Margaret Wilson, and Elizabeth Wilson. (873)

7. Harriett Strange Tutwiler was born on Feb. 18, 1900 in Alabama. She married first John J. Nelson, and married second William Warren Malone. Children from the first marriage are John James Nelson and Eli Erskine Nelson. (874)

---

[73] Information on this family unit was provided by Kyle Tutwiler Spicer, 3335 Kendall Drive, Fayetteville, AR 72704.

Arthur Walton (618)

Arthur Walton Sr.,[74] son of Lewis I. and Elmina A. (Steger) Walton, was born on Oct. 2, 1868 and died on Feb. 6, 1938. He married Mollie Estelle Shepherd, daughter of John F. and Lucy H. (Harris) Shepherd, on Oct. 16, 1895. Mollie was born on Sept. 15, 1869 and died on April 28, 1960. The family lived at Columbia, Fluvanna County, Virginia, where Arthur was a merchant. His papers and business ledgers were deposited in the Alderman Library at the University of Virginia.

Children of Arthur Sr. and Mollie E. (Shepherd) Walton:

1. Cora Louise Walton was born on Dec. 23, 1896 and died on Aug. 19, 1954. She married William Flournoy Kayser on July 6, 1927. He was born in 1882 and died in 1941. Burial was in Memorial Cemetery in Columbia, Virginia. Cora attended Westhampton College in Richmond. Their child, Janet Walton Kayser, was born on March 24, 1928. Janet married John Otis Williams on June 24, 1950. (875)

2. Elmina Adelaide Walton was born on Sept. 29, 1898 and died on Nov. 27, 1938. She married Roderick Grymes Cowherd Sr. on Oct. 14, 1919. (876)

3. Maude Wesley Walton was born on Sept. 24, 1901 and died on Feb. 3, 1980. She married Floyd Monroe Basham on June 16, 1921. He died on June 29, 1978. (877)

4. Mary Zuleika Walton was born on Jan. 8, 1904, and died on Oct. 26, 1968. She married William Edward Nelson on Jan. 4, 1965. Burial was in the St. John's Episcopal Church Cemetery at Columbia. (878)

5. Marion Estelle Walton was born on Jan. 7, 1906 and died on June 1, 1918. Her death was caused by blood poisoning in a cut-finger. (879)

6. Arthur Walton Jr. was born on Feb. 21, 1909, and died on June 11, 1977. He married Cora Lee Glass, who was born on April 15, 1914 and died on July 18, 1980. Both were buried in the Columbia Cemetery in Fluvanna County. (880)

---

[74] Information on Arthur's family unit came from the Shepherd-Walton family Bible record in the Library of Virginia (Accession No. 33399), and from cemetery inscriptions in the Memorial Cemetery in Columbia, Virginia.

Sixth Generation

7. Alice Netherland Walton was born Dec. 26, 1910. Unmarried. (881)

Charles Cortlandt Walton (642)

Charles Cortlandt Walton, son of Richard P. and Mary Jemima (Woodson) Walton, was born on March 2, 1848 at Morningside, Cumberland County, Virginia, and died on Dec. 26, 1911. He married Mary Kearney, daughter of Dr. James W. and Almedia (Phillips) Kearney of Dyersburg, Tennessee, on July 31, 1879.[75] He was very interested in the genealogy of the Walton family, but his account of the Walton lineage is not a reliable source. This branch seemed more interested in names and dates than biographical information on what was a very illustrious family.

Children of Charles C. and Mary (Kearney) Walton:

1. Charles Cortlandt Walton II was born on May 30, 1880 at Morningside, Cumberland County, Virginia and died on Sept. 18, 1946. He married Isabel Moniz Santos on March 4, 1902. (882)

2. Kearney Phillips Walton was born on Jan. 8, 1882 at Morningside. He was the last Walton who was born at Morningside. He married Ellen M. Sandy on March 20, 1902. (883)

3. Almedia Walton was born on April 23, 1884 in Norfolk, Virginia. She married Robert M. Bell on June 21, 1911. (884)

4. Mary Walton was born on Oct. 5, 1886 and died on Nov. 1, 1887. (885)

5. William Peyton Walton was born on Feb. 11, 1888 in Memphis, Tennessee. (886)

6. Florence Walton was born on Feb. 14, 1890 in Norfolk, Virginia. She married Samuel R. Dighton on Aug. 24, 1912. (887)

7. Caroline Field Walton was born on Nov. 21, 1891 in Norfolk. (888)

8. Henry Woodson Walton was born April 29, 1893 in Norfolk. (889)

9. John Morton Walton was born on Oct. 1, 1894 in Norfolk. (890)

---

[75] Robert and Catherine Barnes, indexers, *Genealogies of Virginia Families,* from the William and Mary College Quarterly Historical Magazine, (Baltimore, Maryland: Genealogical Publishing Company, Inc.), Vol V, 1982, p. 352.

Chapter 7

Seventh Generation

Caroline Henrietta (LeVert) Reab (671)

Caroline Henrietta LeVert,[1] daughter of Henry S. and Octavia C. (Walton) LeVert, was born on Dec. 6, 1846 in Mobile, Alabama, and died in December 1876 of Bright's disease. In 1852, her name was changed to Cara Netter by her parents. Her birth name was given to her by Senator Henry Clay of Kentucky, who was a close friend. She married Lawrence Augustus Rigail Reab of Augusta, Georgia, on Dec. 16, 1868. He was a Planter at Bellvue at Summerville, Richmond County, Georgia.

Children of Regail and Cara N. (LeVert) Reab:

1. Regail LeVert Reab was born on Aug. 31, 1870 and died on May 7, 1871. (891)

2. George Walton Reab, who was born on June 4, 1872 and died on May 6, 1925, was the last surviving direct descendant of George Walton, a Signer of the Declaration of Independence from Georgia. Rigail Reab married second Maria Ann Jenkins, and fathered several more children. (892)

Mary Jane (Askew) Morrow (682)

Mary Jane Askew, daughter of George C. and Sarah (Lusk) Askew, was born on Jan. 23, 1853 at Spring Creek, Madison County, North Carolina, and died on Oct. 22, 1932 at Millersville, Concho County, Texas. She married George Pinkney Morrow, son of William and Sarah (Doggett) Morrow. George was born on Oct. 12, 1840 at Forest City, Rutherford County, North Carolina and died on July 27, 1885 at Burnet, Burnet County, Texas.

Children of George P. and Mary J. (Askew) Morrow:[2]

---

[1] See Frances Gibson Satterfield, *Madame LeVert: A Biography of Octavia Walton LeVert*, (Edisto Island, South Carolina: Edisto Press), 1987.

[2] Information on this family unit came from Patricia Morrow, 6506 Prairie Dunes, Houston, TX 77069.

Seventh Generation

1. Clarence Taylor Morrow was born on Jan. 22, 1869 at Forest City and died on Oct. 2, 1949 at Odem, San Patricio, Texas. Clarence married first Martha L. Pangle, 1887-1901, on April 18, 1897 at Marble Falls, Texas. He married second Katherine Silvania Hibler Mayfield, 1880-1914 and married third Vergie Hendley on Sept. 23, 1916 in Refugio County, Texas. One child was born to the first union and two children to the second marriage. (893)

2. Ida Estelle Morrow was born on Aug. 11, 1872 at Marble Falls, Burnet County, Texas and died at Pleasant Valley, Burnet County, Texas on Oct. 28, 1873. (894)

3. John Thomas Morrow was born on April 13, 1875 at Marble Falls and died on Nov. 11, 1961 at Gainesville, Cooke County, Texas. He married Helen Leroy Peterman. John was born on May 25, 1885 at Marietta, Indian Territory, Oklahoma, and died on Oct. 27, 1974 at Grandview, Jackson County, Missouri. They had one child. (895)

4. Joseph Harrison Morrow was born on Nov. 16, 1878 at Marble Falls and died on April 27, 1947 at Sinton, San Patricio County, Texas. He married Georgia Ann Landrum. (896)

5. Alden Guy Morrow was born on July 1, 1880 and died on May 3, 1969 at San Angelo, Texas. He married first Nora Lee Lester (1885-1957) on Aug. 9, 1903 in Burnet, Texas, and married second Mary Vinson Bays, 1897-1980. They had one child. (897)

6. Georgia Lusk Morrow was born on May 19, 1884 in Marble Falls, Texas, and died April 15, 1955 at Millersview, Concho County, Texas. She married first Alexander Elmo Jones, 1867-1943, on Dec. 14, 1903 in Marble Falls, Texas, and married second E. C. Cobb circa 1945. (898)

Alfred Marvin Walton (712)

Alfred Marvin Walton, son of Jesse W. and Julia (Pleasants) Walton, was born on Oct. 31, 1921 in Richmond. He married Barbara Ann Alvis, daughter of James Bryan and Hattie Thompson (Freeman) Alvis, on May 15, 1948. She was born on Feb. 24, 1928 in Henrico County, Virginia. Alfred retired from the Virginia Department of Motor Vehicles. They are members of Laurel Hill Methodist Church in Richmond.

Children of Alfred M. and Barbara A. (Alvis) Walton:[3]

1. Carolyn Ann Walton was born on Oct. 31, 1950. (899)

2. James William "Bill" Walton was born on Aug. 29, 1953. He married first Jacqulin Ann Meador on Dec. 26, 1970. She was born on Aug. 23, 1954. He married second Alice Hines Coleman on Dec. 30, 1990. (900)

3. Stuart Bryan Walton was born on July 10, 1958. He married Patricia Wade, daughter of Calvin and Margaret Wade, April 16, 1983. (901)

William Walton Drake (713)

William Walton Drake, son of Alpheus B. and Lucy Catherine (Walton) Drake, was born on Dec 17, 1868 at Greensboro, Alabama and died on Sept. 11, 1936. He married Mary Lillian Wilkerson, daughter of Presley Hawley and Eliza Adeline (Allen) Wilkerson, on Dec. 1, 1895. She was born on Oct. 23, 1873 and died on Oct. 25, 1952. They are buried in the Greensboro Cemetery in Hale County, Alabama. William and his brother Alpheus operated a mercantile business for a while in Greensboro. He farmed most of his life on the land owned by his grandfather, John T. Walton.

Children of William W. and Mary L. (Wilkerson) Drake:

1. Edith Drake was born on Aug. 19, 1897 and died on Nov. 20, 1921. She married Gladwin Swicegood on Dec. 19, 1916. She was buried in the Greensboro City Cemetery. (902)

---

[3] Information on this family unit was contributed by Alfred M. Walton to the compiler in March 2003 at a meeting in Midlothian, Virginia.

2. Bryant Walton Drake was born on May 28, 1900 and died on March 28, 1969. He married Annie Pearl Crawford on Aug. 23, 1924. She was born on June 26, 1901 and died Jan. 13, 1972. They are buried in Mt. Carmel Cemetery in Perry County, Alabama. He farmed and later worked for a gas distributorship. Residence: Greensboro, Alabama. (903)

3. Alpheus Brown Drake was born on Nov. 27, 1902 and died on Aug. 26, 1983. He married Reba Washington Avery on Oct. 18, 1929. She was born on Feb. 22, 1916. He is buried in the Greensboro City Cemetery. He farmed the same land that his father did. (904)

4. Joseph Presley Drake was born July 26, 1904 in Hale County and died Nov. 21, 1958 in Washington, D. C. He married Wilhelmina Saul, who was born on Jan. 26, 1905 and died May 14, 1993. He worked as a security guard at the Pentagon and lived in Silver Spring, Maryland. (905)

5. Lucy Catherine Drake was born on July 7, 1908 and died on Jan. 10, 1965, unmarried. She is buried in the Greensboro City Cemetery. (906)

6. William Wilkerson Drake was born on March 4, 1915 and died on Feb. 9, 1980. He married Myrtle Lorie Fikes on Jan. 31, 1943. She was born on July 14, 1921 and died on May 2, 2000. William worked for the Alabama Department of Transportation. (907)

Fannie Gladys (Walker) Martin (726)

Fannie Gladys Walker, daughter of Joseph Alexander and Alice (Walton) Walker, was born Dec. 29, 1892 and died Sept. 9, 1976. She married Henry Robert Martin on Dec. 10, 1911. He was born Nov. 16, 1887 and died May 22, 1937. They are buried in the Greensboro City Cemetery, Hale County, Alabama.

Children of Joseph A. and Fannie G. (Walker) Martin:

1. Robert Alexander Martin was born Oct. 28, 1912 and died Aug. 20, 1941. He married Oscarlene Hocutt. He is buried in the Greensboro City Cemetery. (908)

2. Ethel Annette Martin was born Oct. 12, 1914. She married Harry Ramey Horn on June 24, 1933. He was born Oct. 8, 1908 and died Aug. 24, 1993. Harry is buried in the Greensboro City Cemetery. (909)

3. Paul Fletcher Martin was born Aug. 28, 1917. He married first Virginia Ruth Pope and married second Mary ___. (910)

4. Henry Edward Martin was born Dec. 15, 1918 and died May 7, 2000. He married Ella Virginia "Tootsie" Martin. He is buried at the Greensboro City Cemetery. (911)

James Thomas Walton (729)

James Thomas Walton, son of Joseph Pleasant and Chellie L. (Nixon) Walton, was born Sept. 30, 1886 and died Oct. 29, 1965 in Hale County, Alabama. He married Annie Elizabeth Thomas on Oct. 17, 1906. She was born Nov. 11, 1885 and died Oct. 6, 1992. They are buried at the Greensboro City Cemetery. He was a mail carrier for the Post Office.

Children of James T. and Annie E. (Thomas) Walton:

1. Robert Aubrey Walton was born Sept. 10, 1907 and died in 1979. He married Pauline Wheat. (912)

2. Una Gayle Walton was born Nov. 3, 1909 and died Nov. 29, 1993. She married William Ross Cox, who was born Oct. 18, 1899 and died June 27, 1959. They are buried in the Greensboro City Cemetery. (913)

3. Eva Louise Walton was born Oct. 13, 1912 and died Aug. 6, 1913. She is buried at the Greensboro City Cemetery. (914)

4. James Lamar Walton was born Sept. 7, 1913 and died Sept. 24, 1979. He married first Elaine ___ and married second Margaret Josephine Argo who was born March 23, 1923 and died April 2, 2000. He and Margaret Josephine Argo are buried at the Greensboro City Cemetery. (915)

5. William Werdner Walton was born in 1915 and died Dec. 6, 1936, unmarried. William is buried at the Greensboro City Cemetery. (916)

6. Mary Elizabeth Walton was born Feb. 5, 1919. She married Melvin C. Harper on April 30, 1939. (917)

7. Dorothy Marie Walton was born Nov. 12, 1921. She married William Henry Jones on May 29, 1941. He was born Nov. 20, 1921. (918)

8. Mabel Reita Walton was born Sept. 16, 1924. She married Francis

Alexander McIlwaine. (919)

9. Mildred Irene Walton was born June 24, 1926 and died Aug. 4, 1999. She married first Johnnie Swafford and married second McEdward M. Nolan. (920)

Bettie Mae (Walton) Curb (731)

Bettie Mae Walton, daughter of Joseph Pleasant and Chellie L. (Nixon) Walton, was born April 9, 1893 and died April 27, 1985. She married Walter Thomas Curb on Dec. 26, 1909. He was born Jan. 29, 1886 and died Oct. 11, 1973. They are buried at the Greensboro City Cemetery.

Children of Walter T. and Bettie M. (Walton) Curb:

1. Mattie Grace Curb was born June 8, 1911 and died May 22, 1981. She married Johnnie T. Stewart who was born Aug. 1, 1908 and died July 4, 1969. They are buried in the Greensboro City Cemetery. (921)

2. Edward Perry Curb was born Oct. 21, 1915 and died Oct. 2, 1977. He married Ruby ___. They had no children. He is buried at the Greensboro City Cemetery. (922)

3. Walter Allen Curb was born Aug. 12, 1919 and died April 25, 1977. He married Bessie Irene Swicegood on Aug. 15, 1985. She was born on June 16, 1919. Walter is buried at the Greensboro City Cemetery. (923)

4. Clarence Walton Curb was born March 26, 1922 and died Jan. 12, 1998. He married Maxie Smith on Oct. 18, 1949. She was born April 1, 1928. He is buried at the Greensboro City Cemetery. (924)

5. Chellie Curb was born Oct. 17, 1924. She married first Leo Edward Kirk on Oct. 31, 1946. He was born on Oct. 29, 1923 and died June 5, 1968. Chellie married second to J. V. Baygents on Feb. 21, 1970. He was born June 21, 1923 and died April 13, 2004. Both husbands are buried at the Greensboro City Cemetery. (925)

6. Mabel Sue Curb was born Nov. 5, 1926. She married Hillard Bonds on April 23, 1946. He was born Feb. 26, 1920. (926)

7. Florence Augusta Curb was born Dec. 29, 1928 and died Oct. 25, 1987. She married Harry Lewis Johnson Jr. who was born May 1, 1926 and died Feb. 22, 2001. They are buried at the Greensboro City

Cemetery. (927)

8. Sarah Alvis Curb was born on June 18, 1934. She married Frank Clark. (928)

9. Mary Virginia Curb was born on Sept. 18, 1936. She married Rocky Cabera. (929)

10. Margaret Irene Curb was born on Nov. 11, 1939. She married Carl Beauman. (930)

Thomas Anthony Walton (768)

Thomas Anthony Walton, son of Thomas E. and Martha (Woodson) Walton, was born on Oct. 12, 1856 in Appomattox County, Virginia and died Oct. 23, 1934.[4] He married Virginia Purdum, daughter of Rufus King and Emily (Brandenburg) Purdum, who came to Appomattox County from Frederick, Maryland. Virginia Purdum was born on July 28, 1862 and died on Jan. 29, 1943.[5] The family burial ground is in Liberty Cemetery in Appomattox. The 1910 census for Appomattox County lists Lonie *sic* Walton, age 18, and William, age 15. It is believed that they later moved to Dinwiddie County, Virginia. He inherited one-third of his mother's land and one-sixth of her money, serving as her executor and security.[6]

Children of Thomas A. and Virginia (Purdum) Walton:

1. Louise May Walton, born in May 1891, married a Mr. Green and was living in Crewe, Virginia in 1943. (931)

---

[4] Appomattox County, Virginia *Will Book 2*, p 18 and p. 46. His will was written on April 2, 1926 and probated on Oct. 26, 1934.

[5] Appomattox County, Virginia *Will Book 2*, p. 234. Her will was filed and admitted to record on Feb. 13, 1943.

[6] Appomattox County, Virginia *Will Book 1*, p. 240. Her will was written on April 5, 1919.

Seventh Generation

2. William Anthony Walton Sr. was born in Appomattox County on May 22, 1894[7] and died on Nov. 25, 1953.[8] He married Hunter Davis Gwaltney. (932)

Ella Amanda (Walton) Jamerson (773)

Ella Amanda Walton, daughter of Thomas E. and Martha E. (Woodson) Walton, was born April 1, 1874 in Appomattox County and died Feb. 8, 1967. She married Roland Ferguson Jamerson, son of Daniel and Mary Jane (Ferguson) Lucado Jamerson, Dec. 8, 1894[9] in Appomattox County. He was born on June 9, 1875 in Buckingham County, Virginia and died Feb. 14, 1942 in Appomattox County. Burial was in Liberty Baptist Cemetery in Appomattox. Ella and her children inherited two-thirds of her mother's land and one-sixth of her money. There were six legatees in the will.[10] Residence: Appomattox, Virginia.

Children of Roland F. and Ella A. (Walton) Jamerson:[11]

1. Louise Hendricks Jamerson, born in September 1897, married Edmund Stuart Meanly on Nov. 24, 1921. (933)

2. Paul Watson Jamerson was born on Feb. 14, 1898 and died Feb. 22, 1914. Burial was in Liberty Cemetery, Appomattox County. (934)

3. Roland Walton Jamerson Sr.[12] was born in 1899 and died in July 1967. He married Frances Smith on June 23, 1926. They had a son

---

[7] E. Griffith Dodson, Clerk of the House, *The General Assembly of the Commonwealth of Virginia, 1940-1960*, (Richmond, Virginia: State Publication), 1960, p. 594.

[8] Dodson, p. 936.

[9] Appomattox *County Marriage Book 1*, p. 7.

[10] Appomattox County, Virginia *Will Book 1*, p. 240. Her will was written on April 5, 1919.

[11] See *Appomattox County, Virginia*, (Summersville, West Virginia: Walsworth Publishing Company), 2001, pp. 124-125

[12] _____, Appomattox County, Virginia, (Walsworth Publishing Company), 2001, p. 125.

named Roland Walton Jamerson Jr., 1927-1965, who died in an automobile accident. The son married Mary Hunt. Roland Sr. and Frances had two daughters: Mary Elizabeth Jamerson, who earned a music degree from James Madison College in Harrisonburg, and Nancy Smith Jamerson earned a music degree from Mary Washington College in Fredericksburg. (935)

4. Henry Jamerson was born in 1900. (936)

5. James Everett Jamerson was born on Oct. 10, 1902 and died on Jan. 5, 1991. He married Lula Grey Smith, daughter of Holmes and Annie (Guill) Smith, on Dec. 23, 1928. (937)

6. William Russell Jamerson was born in 1905 and died in 1975. He married Rebecca Elizabeth Martin on Dec. 28, 1935. (938)

7. Ella Josie Jamerson was born on Oct. 27, 1909. She married Tommy Wiley Ferguson, son of Richard F. and Margaret (Bingham) Ferguson, on Sept. 6, 1930. (939)

8. Mary Elizabeth Jamerson was born on March 10, 1911, and died in 1996. She married Thomas Montigue Harris on Oct. 3, 1942. Burial was in Liberty Cemetery in Appomattox. (940)

9. Carrie Virginia Jamerson was born in 1915 and married Fitz Hugh Martin on June 17, 1938. (941)

10. Raymond Francis Jamerson was born in 1918. He married Beulah L. Farrell on Dec. 28, 1958. (942)

William Massie Walker Sr. (803)

William Massie Walker Sr., son of Edmund Winston and Jane R. (Massie) Walker, was born July 4, 1873 in Christian County, Kentucky, and died Aug. 27, 1959 in Hopkinsville. He married Mary Etta Bowles, daughter of George Washington and Elizabeth (Steele) Bowles, on Nov. 29, 1898. She was born on Nov. 9, 1878 and died on April 28, 1955 in Clarksville, Tennessee. Both were buried in the Riverside Cemetery in Hopkinsville.

Children of William M. Sr. and Mary E. (Bowles) Walker:

1. Edmund Winston Walker was born on Aug. 22, 1899 in Christian County, Kentucky and died Sept. 15, 1968 in Dothan, Alabama. He married Mary Louise Ikerman, daughter of Charles Henry and Rachel

Thomas (Alexander) Ikerman, on Sept. 2, 1926 in Selma, Alabama. (943)

2. William Massie Walker Jr. was born on Sept. 20, 1900 in Christian County and died Jan. 23, 1947 in Knoxville, Tennessee. He married Jackie Sue Roberts, Aug. 15, 1935. They had one child, William Massie Walker III, 1941-1997. (944)

3. Elizabeth Walker was born on April 4, 1902 in Christian County and died Dec. 27, 1984 in Hopkinsville, Kentucky. He did not marry. (945)

4. Anna LeGrande Walker was born on May 1, 1903 in Christian County. She married William Albert Fitzgerald on June 15, 1940. They had no children. She is living in Hopkinsville, where she is still (in 1998) very active with genealogical research. (946)

5. George Bowles Walker was born on March 6, 1906 in Christian County and died July 9, 1996 in Hopkinsville. He married Elizabeth "Pat" Thornber Murphy in Columbia, Tennessee on Dec. 30, 1933. (947)

6. James Elliott Walker was born on April 20, 1908 and died Sept. 18, 1992 in Opelika, Alabama. He married Pertice Tucker on Dec. 26, 1939 at Camp Hill, Alabama. (948)

7. Mary Virginia Walker was born on Oct. 15, 1911 in Christian County, unmarried. (949)

William Jones Walton Sr. (809)

William Jones Walton Sr., son of Eugene A. and Nannie Katherine (Jones) Walton, was born July 19, 1885 in Appomattox County, and died Dec. 11, 1950.[13] He married Mildred Frances Harvey, daughter of William C. and Mildred (Walker) Harvey, on Dec. 21, 1914.[14] Mildred "Aunt Frankie" was born on May 20, 1890 in Appomattox County and died March 29, 1967 in Hampton, Virginia. Burial was in Liberty Cemetery in Appomattox. He was a farmer. Residence: Oakville, Appomattox County, Virginia.

---

[13] Appomattox County, Virginia *Will Book II*, p. 431, filed on Oct. 20, 1937. Wife Mildred was named as executor.

[14] Appomattox County, Virginia *Marriage Book 1*, p. 52.

Front, left-to-right, Louise C. Walton and William Jones Walton Jr.; second row, Katherine and Eugenia Walton; Back row, Mildred Walton, Frankie and William Jones Walton Sr.

Children of William J. Sr. and Mildred F. (Harvey) Walton:

1. Mildred Frances Walton was born on Feb. 18, 1916 at Bent Creek, Appomattox County and died on Dec. 15, 2000. She married Joseph Magri, Aug. 11, 1942. Joe died on Sept. 26, 1979. Both are buried in Spring Hill Cemetery in Lynchburg. They had no children. Residence: Lynchburg, Virginia. (950)

2. Katherine Walker Walton was born on July 25, 1918 at Bent Creek and died on Dec. 5, 2001. She married George Carson, Sept. 26. 1939. (951)

3. Eugenia Vawter Walton was born on June 23, 1922 at Bent Creek, Appomattox County, and died on March 30, 2002. She married Remo Anthony Giaretti Sr. in Lynchburg on July 28, 1946. (952)

4. Louise Clifton Walton was born on May 13, 1927 at Bent Creek. She married Edward Morris in June 1957. (953)

5. William Jones Walton Jr. was born on May 5, 1930 at Bent Creek and died April 20, 1998. He married Shirley Wright in Nov. 1956 in Cheraw, South Carolina. (954)

Mary Barksdale (Walton) Bolton (811)

Mary Barksdale Walton, daughter of Eugene A. and Nannie K. (Jones) Walton, was born Feb. 3, 1889 and died on Oct. 19, 1960. She married Carrington Ammonette Bolton, son of Floyd and Lora (Garland) Bolton. He was born in Nelson County on Oct. 29, 1880 and died in Lynchburg in November 1955. He was a farmer. Their residence was at Gladstone in Nelson County.

Children of Carrington and Mary B. (Walton) Bolton:

1. Harry Walton Bolton[15] was born on Aug. 26, 1923 and died Jan. 22, 1986. He married Ruth Naomi Scruggs, daughter of Clarence Douglas and Virginia Estelle (White) Scruggs, June 8, 1956. Ruth was born on Dec. 28, 1936. (955)

2. Eleanor DuVal Bolton was born Sept. 14, 1925. She married first Sherman Benjamin Hunter and married second William Fletcher Burge Jr. (956)

Walker Scott Walton (812)

Walker Scott Walton, son of Eugene A. and Nannie K. (Jones) Walton, was born on July 25, 1892 at Bent Creek, and died May 7, 1959, at Spout Spring, Appomattox County. He married Nellie Virginia Davis, daughter of Matthew M. and Josephine (Shepherd) Davis, Aug. 2, 1930, by a Baptist preacher in Lynchburg. Her vital dates were Sept. 7, 1907 and Jan. 20, 1973. She graduated from Longwood College, and taught elementary school in Appomattox County. Walker was elected by the voters on Nov. 7, 1939 to serve as Constable for the Stonewall District of Appomattox County.[16] In 1943-1944 during the War years, Judge Joel W. Flood appointed him to serve as a special policeman for Appomattox County, "as provided by Section 479 of the Code."[17] Walker also worked as a

---

[15] Information on Harry W. Bolton and his descendants was provided by his daughter Bonnie K. (Bolton) Bebar at the Walton family reunion at Spout Spring, Appomattox County, Virginia on July 18, 1999.

[16] Appomattox Circuit Court, *Law Order Book 4*, p. 327.

[17] Appomattox County *Law Order Book*, p. 449.

deputy sheriff and as a sales representative for Moses Chevrolet in Appomattox. The Waltons were members of the Methodist Church. Both were buried in the Liberty Baptist Cemetery in Appomattox.

Children of Walker S. and Nellie (Davis) Walton:[18]

1. Winston Davis Walton was born April 20, 1931. He married Glenice Ann Van Cleef. (957)

2. Josephine Walker Walton was born July 24, 1932 at Oakville, Appomattox County. She graduated from Appomattox High School. Her favorite activities are attending high school reunions and eating at McDonald's. Josephine lived with her sister Shirley for twenty-six years in Arlington, Virginia before being placed in an assisted living facility. She now (2005) lives in the Birmingham Green Nursing Home in Manassas. Josephine did not marry. (958)

3. Shirley Mitchell Walton was born Nov. 10, 1934. She married Wilmer Lee Kerns, son of Lee Doil and Madeline (Grim) Kerns, on June 15, 1965. (959)

Lela Mitchell (Walton) Harris (813)

Lela Mitchell Walton, daughter of Eugene A. and Nannie K. (Jones) Walton, was born April 1, 1894 at Bent Creek, and died at Spout Spring on Dec. 2, 1981. She married Daniel Mosby Harris on Jan. 27, 1915. Burial was at Mt. Comfort Methodist Church. Residence: Spout Spring, Virginia.

Children of Daniel M. and Lela M. (Walton) Harris:

1. Richard Mosby Harris was born on June 11, 1916. He married Mary Lorene Gilliam on Dec. 26, 1941. (960)

2. Nannie Franklin Harris was born on Aug. 7, 1918 in Appomattox County and died on June 28, 1989 at the Virginia Baptist Hospital in Lynchburg. She married Elliott Osborn Carson on July 10, 1938. (961)

---

[18] Information was provided by his son Winston D. Walton and daughter Shirley M. (Walton) Kerns.

Bessie Vawter (Walton) Payne (814)

Bessie Vawter Walton, daughter of Eugene A. and Nannie K. (Jones) Walton, was born on Oct. 16, 1896 and died on March 22, 1984. Bessie was active in church and community organizations. She married Francis Marion Payne, son of Sterling Claiborne and Sallie Ida (Harris) Payne, on May 10, 1915 at her home in Appomattox County. Known as "Frank," he was born on Aug. 25, 1885 and died on March 24, 1958. He served as a clerk for the Mineral Springs Baptist Church. Frank was in the lumber business with his father, and later in the mercantile business and a farmer. They lived at Rose Hill, near the James River at Gladstone, Nelson County, where they were buried in the Harris-Payne Cemetery. Residence: Gladstone, Virginia.

Children of Francis M. and Bessie V. (Walton) Payne:

1. Marion Waverly Payne Sr. was born on April 30, 1916 and died on Aug. 9, 1999. He married Lucy Ann West on Sept. 15, 1933. (962)

2. Frederick Eugene Payne was born on March 2, 1919 and died on April 2, 1971 in Roanoke. He married first Juanita Cundiff on June 2, 1950 and married second Alma King on March 7, 1954. (963)

3. John Gordon Payne was born Oct. 10, 1920. He married Clara Louise Glover on Sept. 19, 1942. (964)

4. Sterling Claiborne Payne was born on Jan. 31, 1923. He married Annie B. Wills on July 3, 1950. (965)

5. Sallie Ida Payne was born on July 5, 1925. She first married Gene Marks on March 1, 1945, and married second William L. Watts Jr. on Feb. 10, 1950 (966)

6. Walter Jones Payne was born on Feb. 26, 1928 and died on Sept. 2, 1972 in Lynchburg. Walter married Imogene Alpha Robinson in 1948. She was born in 1932 in Lynchburg. (967)

7. Joseph Dudley Payne was born on Nov. 17, 1930. He married Mary Sue Boaz on Nov. 27, 1954. She was born on May 4, 1934 at Amherst, Virginia. (968)

8. Mary Evelyn Payne was born on July 21, 1933 at Gladstone, Nelson County. She married first Samuel D. Bailey on June 10, 1956. She married second James Strickland Sr. on Dec. 10, 1969. (969)

Nannie Evelyn (Walton) Harris (815)

Nannie Evelyn Walton, daughter of Eugene A. and Nannie K. (Jones) Walton, was born July 15, 1899 and died June 22, 1941. She married Willis E. Harris on Jan. 28, 1921.[19] He was born on Dec. 29, 1898 and died on April 19, 1979. He was a car inspector helper for the C&O Railroad. Residence: Gladstone, Nelson County.

Children of Willis and Nannie E. (Walton) Harris:

1. Willis Lyle Harris was born on June 11, 1926. He lives near Gladstone, unmarried. (970)

2. Calvin Walker Harris was born on May 28, 1928, and did not marry. He and Lyle lived on part of the Walton ancestral home place in Appomattox County. (971)

3. Marshall Walton Harris was born on Oct. 4, 1932. He married Rachel Goin, daughter of DeWitt T. and Alice Goin, on Sept. 5, 1953. (972)

John Christian Walton Sr. (816)

John Christian Walton, son of Eugene A. and Nannie K. (Jones) Walton, was born Jan. 7, 1902 and died Jan. 4, 1986. He married Ruby Frances Davis, daughter of Matthew M. and Josephine (Shepherd) Davis. She was born June 27, 1909. John was a tobacco farmer and trader. Ruby graduated from Longwood College and had a career as an elementary school teacher and school librarian in the Buckingham County Public Schools. They were active members of the Salem United Methodist Church. Residence: Dillwyn, Virginia.

Child of John Christian Sr. and Ruby F. (Davis) Walton:

1. John Christian Walton Jr. was born March 29, 1950 in Buckingham County. He first married Theresa Guthrie and married second Beverly

---

[19] Appomattox County, Virginia *Marriage Book 1*, p. 67.

Diane Nemes, Dec. 23, 1988. Johnny lives near Farmville, Virginia. (973)

Alexander Wilson Walton (817)

Alexander "Zane" Wilson Walton was born Aug. 28, 1904, and died on Oct. 28, 1987 in Appomattox County. He married Mary Cabell Harris, daughter of Walter Mosley and Mary Franklin (Cunningham) Harris. She was born on Nov. 7, 1906 in Buckingham County, and died on Dec. 23, 1996 at the Autumn Care Nursing Home in Alta Vista, Virginia. They lived on a portion of the original Thomas Walton plantation, which he farmed during his lifetime.

Children of Alexander W. and Mary C. (Harris) Walton:

1. Mary Elizabeth Walton was born on Feb. 11, 1930 in Appomattox County. She graduated from Appomattox High School. She married second Clarence Nelson Hancock, son of Carter and Blanche (Spradlin) Hancock, Dec. 14, 1955.[20] Clarence was born on Sept. 10, 1920. He graduated from E.C. Glass High School in Lynchburg. Both worked full careers with Craddock Terry Shoe Corporation. They had no children. Residence: Lynchburg, Virginia. (974)

2. Lloyd Gray Walton was born on Jan. 4, 1936. He married Shirley Elizabeth Williams on June 10, 1960. (975)

Molly Sue (Bagby) Garrette (824)

Mollie Sue Bagby, daughter of Bennett W. and Amine (Scruggs) Bagby, was born June 14, 1886 in Appomattox County, Virginia and died Jan. 14, 1959 in Appomattox. She married Monroe Lumsden Garrette, son of Joseph Henry Wilson and Frances Clementine (Gilbert) Garrette, on June 1, 1907 in Richmond, Virginia. Molly Sue taught in a one-room school in Arvonia.

---

[20] Appomattox County, Virginia *Marriage Book 1*, p. 138.

Children of Monroe L. and Molly Sue (Bagby) Garrette:[21]

1. Frances Christine Garrette was born on March 13, 1909 in Appomattox and died on Dec. 22, 1990 in Lynchburg. She received a B. S. degree from Farmville State Teachers College, now Longwood College). Christine married James Franklin MacKenzie on Aug. 17, 1944. (976)

2. Joseph Monroe Garrette was born May 16, 1911 and died on April 16, 1943 of a heart condition in Appomattox, Virginia. (977)

3. David Bagby Garrett was born in 1913 in Appomattox and died on May 13, 1926 in Appomattox. (978)

4. Lyle North Garrette was born Jan. 27, 1915 in Appomattox and died May 28, 1999 in Lynchburg. He married Alma Burton Carson on May 13, 1939 in Christiansburg, Virginia. (979)

5. Alfra Josephine Garrette was born Aug. 14, 1917 at Appomattox and died March 1, 1998 in Minnesota. She married George Edward Hanson on June 7, 1942 in Staunton, Virginia. She and her husband attended the Virginia School for the Deaf and Blind in Staunton. (980)

6. Marshall Jefferson Garrette was born on March 5, 1920 in Appomattox County. He married Nell Hope Walker on Aug 29, 1947 in Washington, D. C. (981)

7. Alice Elizabeth Garrette was born May 15, 1922 in Appomattox. She married John Thomas Moore on Oct. 6, 1944 at Ashland, Virginia. (982)

8. Garland Burke Garrette was born Sept. 28, 1924 in Appomattox and died Sept. 21, 1987 in Macon, Georgia. He married Frances Marion Barfield Dec, 28, 1952 at St. Pauls Episcopal Church in Macon, Georgia. (983)

Carrington Nathaniel Walton (846)

Carrington Nathaniel Walton, son of Henry C. and Lavinia (Allen) Walton, was born on Oct. 8, 1859 in Cumberland County, Virginia and died on Aug.12, 1931. He married Betty Reynolds

---

[21] Information on this family unit was provided by Cary A. Garrette, 16 Catawba Ridge Court, Lake Wylie, SC 29710-8916.

Brown, who was born in July 1858, according to the 1900 U. S. Census for Cumberland County. The 1910 U. S. Census for Cumberland County lists three children.[22] The 1920 Census lists son James, age 30; daughter Ola, age 25; and daughter Ada B., age 18. Carrington was listed as a farmer.[23] They lived at Cartersville, Cumberland County.

Children of Carrington N. and Betty R. (Brown) Walton:

1. Clarence Walton was born in September 1886 and died after 1900. (984)

2. James Walton was born on Jan. 6, 1889. During World War I, he was a Wagoner in a Field Artillery unit of the U. S. Army.[24] He was living in the household of his father when the 1930 U. S. Census was taken. (985)

3. Ola Walton was born on Jan. 12, 1894, and died in Dec. 1980 at Cartersville, Virginia.[25] She was on the 1930 census in her father's household. She was the administrator for her father's estate. (986)

4. Ada B. Walton was born in Cumberland County on April 1, 1901 and died on Oct. 17, 1993. She was the author of the *History of Thomas Chapel*. She married William Pollard Sanderson on May 3, 1923 at Clifton Forge, Virginia.[26] He was born on Jan. 19, 1895 and died on July 29, 1980.[27] (987)

---

[22] 1910 U. S. Census for Cumberland County, Virginia, ED 078, p. 211.

[23] 1920 U. S. Census for Cumberland County, Virginia, Hamilton District, ED 85, p. 9A.

[24] Library of Virginia, "World War I History Commission Questionnaires," James Walton of Cumberland County, Virginia.

[25] Social Security Death Index.

[26] Cumberland County, *Virginia Marriage Register 2*, p. 9.

[27] Information was provided by Ruby Talley Smith by email rubygem@aol.com on March 4, 2002

Floyd Allen Walton (851)

Floyd Allen Walton, son of Henry C. and Lavinia (Allen) Walton, was born on June 6, 1873 and died on Nov. 5, 1952. He was a farmer during the time he lived in Cumberland County. Floyd married Emma Lou Tatum, daughter of William Early and Mary Jenkins (Huddleston) Tatum, on Sept. 25, 1895. In 1900, they were living in Cumberland County with daughters Carrie M. and Shelton Walton. The family was living at Tuckahoe in Henrico County when the 1910 and 1930 U. S. Censuses were taken for that County.

Children of Floyd A. and Emma L. (Tatum) Walton:[28]

1. Carrie Myrtle Walton was born on Feb. 2, 1897 and died on March 3, 1964. She married William Aubrey Nuckols on June 6, 1917. He was born on Aug. 22, 1889 and died on March 31, 1969. (988)

2. Ruby Thelma Walton was born on Jan. 27, 1900. She married Edward Johnston Waters on Sept. 15, 1920. He was born on May 29, 1894 and died on Oct. 15, 1971. (989)

Edward Coffman Walton Sr. (861)

Edward Coffman Walton Sr., son of Edward and Rebecca (DePriest) Walton, was born in Cumberland County, Virginia on March 6, 1889 and died on Feb. 10, 1980 at Cartersville, Cumberland County. He married Martha Lavinia Bigger, daughter of Walter Scott and Ida Elizabeth (Walton) Bigger, on Feb. 21, 1920 in Washington, D.C. They were Methodists. Their residence was at Cartersville, Virginia.

Children of Edward C. Sr. and Martha L. (Bigger) Walton:

1. Edward Coffman Walton Jr. was born on Nov. 7, 1921 at Cartersville. He married Betty Lee Renn, daughter of the Rev. Edwin Ernest and Irene (Edwards) Renn, on July 1, 1950. Betty was born on Aug. 6, 1927 and went to be with the Lord on Aug. 17, 1998.[29] Burial

---

[28] The Cumberland County Historical Society, Inc., *Cumberland County, Virginia and its People*, (Walsworth Publishing, Co.: Marceline, Missouri), 1983, p. 212.

[29] Social Security Death Index.

was in the Thomas Chapel United Methodist Church Cemetery at Cartersville. Betty worked as a deputy clerk in the Office of the Clerk of Court in Cumberland County. She was highly esteemed by all who knew her. (990)

>   3. Herman Leland Walton Sr., born circa 1923, married Mary Virginia Rowan in 1946. Their two children are named: (a) Herman Leland Walton Jr. and (b) Allen Lane Walton. (991)
>
>   3. Rebecca Elizabeth Walton, born circa 1925, married Ernest Sneed Trice in 1944. (992)

Alma Virginia (Walton) Davis (862)

Alma Virginia Walton, daughter of Edward and Rebecca (DePriest) Walton, was born on Aug. 22, 1892 in Cumberland County, and died on Jan. 21, 1958 in Lynchburg. Alma was murdered by her granddaughter's estranged husband, Sidney McCormick.[30] She married Ira Green Davis, son of John and Alice (Walker) Davis, on June 15, 1915 in Washington, D. C. He was born on Jan. 15, 1883 in Powhatan County, Virginia and died on Sept. 27, 1948 in Lynchburg.

Children of Ira G. and Alma V. (Walton) Davis:

>   1. Alice Rebecca Davis was born on March 1, 1917 at Altavista, Virginia and died on Dec. 21, 1983 in Campbell County, Virginia. She married Beverly Thomas Millner on Oct. 4, 1935. (993)
>
>   2. Alma Virginia Davis was born on July 7, 1924 and died on Dec. 2, 1999 in Lynchburg. She married Baxter Bray Powell. (994)

Jessie Helen (Walton) Adams (864)

Jessie Helen Walton, daughter of Edward and Rebecca (DePriest) Walton, was born on May 26, 1896 in Cumberland County, Virginia and died on May 4, 1938 of heart failure at

---

[30] Information from Barbara Millner, 600 Edgar Street, Lynchburg, VA 24501-3504, Barbwm@hotmail.com, to the compiler on March 23, 2002. Barbara cited *True Detective Magazine, The Lynchburg News*, and Karen L. (Crabtree) Adams famtrees@mounet.com.

Bastian, Bland County, Virginia. Jessie Helen was the second wife of William Franklin Adams, son of William Thomas and Martha Agnes (Apperson) Adams, June 2, 1917 in Cumberland County. He was born on Feb. 24, 1896 and died in November 1974 in Raleigh, North Carolina. He joined the CCC during the depression, and was sent to Camp Wyatt in Bland County. After that service, he worked for a rock quarry at Wytheville and then for Allied Chemical in Pulaski. In 1943, he moved to Raleigh, North Carolina where he worked for Peden Steel Company. He later drove a taxi, and finally he worked for his son William Harvey Adams before retiring. Residence: Cumberland and Bland Counties, Virginia.

Children of William F. and Jessie H. (Walton) Adams: [31]

1. Walton Franklin Adams was born on April 17, 1918 in Cumberland County and died on Jan. 12, 1987 at Norton, Wise County, Virginia. He married Earnie Eileen Colley on July 30, 1938 at Wytheville, Virginia. (995)

2. Martha Leich Adams was born on Feb. 9, 1920, and died on May 4, 1996. She married Morris Clifford Keller, son of Washington and Mary (Adcock) Keller, on Dec. 4, 1937. He was born on Feb. 24, 1915, and died March 4, 1977. (996)

3. John Samuel "Sam" Adams was born on May 26, 1921 and died on Oct. 23, 1999 in Georgia. He married Mary LaVerne Jackson on Jan. 9, 1946. She was born on May 15, 1926. (997)

4. Infant Adams was born and died in 1922. (998)

5. Clyde Ottway Adams was born on Nov. 16, 1923 in Cumberland County. He married Thelma Louise Griffin, daughter of Chilli and Maudie (Atwell) Griffin, on April 9, 1945. She was born on Feb. 7, 1927 in Biloxi, Mississippi. (999)

6. William Harvey Adams was born on Sept. 12, 1927 in Cumberland County. He married Fonue Jones. Their children were Randy Adams, Mark Adams, and Wendy Adams. (1000)

---

[31] Information was provided to the compiler by Karen L. (Crabtree) Adams, P. O. Box 1280, Clintwood, VA 24228; or famtrees@mounet.com

7. Jessie Joyce Adams was born on Sept. 15, 1928 in Cumberland County. She married Edward Kelbough. (1001)

8. Thomas Melvin "Dick" Adams was born on Oct. 27, 1930 in Cumberland County and died on Aug. 27, 1967 in Raleigh, North Carolina. He was buried in the Thomas Chapel in Cartersville, Virginia. (1002)

9. George Chambers "Buster" Adams was born on March 7, 1932 in Cumberland County. He married Suk Cha Kim. (1003)

Guy Isbell Tutwiler Sr. (869)

Guy Isbell Tutwiler Sr., son of Eli Erskine and Haidee Zuleika (Walton) Tutwiler, was born on July 17, 1888 in Adamsville, Alabama, and died by accident on Aug. 30, 1930 in Anniston, Calhoun Co., Alabama. He married Edna Mae Scruggs, daughter of George D. and Bessie (Musgrove) Scruggs, on June 13, 1924 in Birmingham, Jefferson Co., Alabama. She was born on April 17, 1900 in Brilliant, Marion County, Alabama and died on April 10, 1975 in Birmingham. They are both buried at Elmwood Cemetery, Birmingham, Alabama.

Children of Guy Isbell Sr. and Edna Mae (Scruggs) Tutwiler:[32]

1. Guy Isbell Tutwiler Jr. was born on Sept. 24, 1925 in Birmingham, Jefferson Co., Alabama. He married first Jean Ellen Minton, daughter of Fred and Madge Irene (Marsden) Minton on March 12, 1948. They divorced in 1976. He married second Elaine G. Greene in March 1977. (1004)

2. Pickens McQueen Tutwiler was born Sep 2. 1927 in Birmingham, Jefferson Co., Alabama and died on May 17 in San Marino, California. (1005)

Elmina Adelaide (Walton) Cowherd (876)

Elmina Adelaide Walton, daughter of Arthur Sr. and Mollie E. (Shepherd) Walton, was born on Sept. 29, 1898 and died on Nov. 27, 1938. She graduated from high school in 1915 and attended

---

[32] Information on this family unit was contributed by Kyle Tutwiler Spicer, 3335 Kendall Drive, Fayetteville, AR 72704.

Westhampton College in Richmond. She married Roderick Grymes Cowherd Sr. on Oct. 14, 1919.

Children of Robert G. and Elmina A. (Walton) Cowherd:[33]

    1. Roderick G. Cowherd Jr. was born on Aug. 30, 1920, and died soon after birth. (1006)

    2. Marion Louise Cowherd was born on Friday, April 7, 1922. She married Roby B. Janney on June 5, 1943 at Gordonsville Baptist Church. She graduated from Gordonsville High School in 1939 and the University of Virginia School of Nursing in 1943. (1007)

    3. Mary Jane Cowherd was born on April 18, 1925. She married Thomas Humphrey Cook of Louisa, Virginia on July 3, 1954. She graduated from Orange High School, Virginia in 1942, and attended Mary Washington College in Fredericksburg for one year. (1008)

    4. Anne Tyler Cowherd was born on May 31, 1927. She married Wesley Keith Handy of Michigan on March 12, 1960 at the Gordonsville, Virginia Baptist Church. They met in Saudi Arabia where both were employed. She graduated from Orange High School and attended Madison College in Harrisonburg. (1009)

    5. Alice Daniel Cowherd was born on Feb. 17, 1929. She married John Archie Walker on Aug. 25, 1950. She graduated from Orange High School in 1946, and graduated from the University of Virginia School of Nursing in 1950. They lived in Charlottesville for twenty-one years before moving to Cobham, Virginia for their retirement years. (1010)

    6. Walton Rush Cowherd was born on Oct. 31, 1932. He graduated from Orange High School and the McIntyre School of Commerce at the University of Virginia. He worked for IRS in Charlottesville and Birmingham before accepting a partnership position with a CPA firm in Richmond. He married Sara Sherman. (1011)

Maude Wesley (Walton) Basham (877)

Maude Wesley Walton, daughter of Arthur Sr. and Mollie E. (Shepherd) Walton, was born on Sept. 24, 1901 in Fluvanna

---

[33] William E. Steger and William F. Steger, *Descendants of Thomas Hales Steger*, (Privately Printed), 1994, Appendix F.

County, Virginia and died on Feb. 3, 1980. She married Floyd Monroe Basham on June 16, 1921. He died on June 29, 1978.

Children of Floyd M. and Maude W. (Walton) Basham:[34]

    1. Dorothy Walton Basham was born on Wednesday, Jan. 17, 1923. She married William J. McCormick. (1013)

    2. William Monroe Basham was born on June 28, 1943. He married Karen Klingenpeel. (1014)

Arthur Walton Jr. (880)

Arthur Walton Jr., son of Arthur Sr. and Mollie E. (Shepherd) Walton, was born on Feb. 21, 1909, at Columbia, Fluvanna County, Virginia, and died on June 11, 1977. He married Cora Lee Glass, who was born on April 15, 1914 and died on July 18, 1980. Both were buried in the Columbia Cemetery in Fluvanna County, Virginia.

Children of Arthur Jr. and Cora Lee (Glass) Walton:[35]

    1. Ann Carter Walton was born on Oct. 29, 1938. She married Buford Allen Wood on Aug. 30, 1957. (1015)

    2. Linda Lou Walton was born on Feb. 15, 1948. (1016)

    3. Nancy Lee Walton was born on April 24, 1941. She married F. K. Pace on Dec. 26, 1957. (1017)

---

[34] *Ibid.* Appendix F.

[35] Library of Virginia, "Shepherd-Walton Bible record, 1828-1980," Accession No. 33399.

Chapter 8

Eighth Generation

Joseph Harrison Morrow (896)

Joseph Harrison Morrow, son of George P. and Mary Jane (Askew) Morrow, was born on Nov. 16, 1878 at Marble Falls, Burnet County, Texas, and died on April 27, 1947 at Sinton, San Patricio County, Texas. He married Georgia Ann Landrum, daughter of Larkin and Sarah (Umberson) Morrow, on June 23, 1903 in Burnet County. Georgia was born on Feb. 27, 1875 in Gillespie County, Texas and died on Nov. 8, 1958 at Sinton, San Patricio County, Texas.

Children of Joseph H. and Georgia A. (Landrum) Morrow:[1]

1. Lucille Pinkney Morrow was born on July 30, 1904 at Marble Falls and died on Dec. 10, 1965 at Alpine, Brewster County, Texas. She married first Palmer French on July 10, 1928 at Corpus Christi. Lucille married second Zoye Edward Decie, 1904-1975, on May 14, 1932 in El Paso. Lucille taught school after graduating from the University of Texas. Zoye was a rancher. (1018)

2. Joe Harry Morrow was born on April 6, 1908 at Port Lavaca, Calhoun County, Texas and died on April 11, 1966 at Kerrville, Kerr County, Texas. He married first Katie M. Smith on March 3, 1934 at Primera, Texas, and married second Margaret Blount on Jan. 29, 1959 at Alpine, Texas. Joe Harry was a former Texas Ranger and a rancher. (1019)

3. Taft Morrow was born on Sept. 30, 1909 and died on June 2, 2000 in Corpus Christi. He married Alice Mae Pegues on July 14, 1937. (1020)

4. Jack Lankford Morrow was born Jan 29, 1912 at Taft, San Patricio County, Texas, and died Feb. 28, 1999 at Sinton, Texas. He married Frances Nell Dezelle Feb. 20, 1941 in San Marcos, Texas. She was born Jan. 15, 1915 in San Marcos. They had one child, Jack Dezelle Morrow, who married Diane Benson. Jack was a teacher; then began a career with Plymouth Oil, which later became Marathon Oil. Nell was a teacher. Both were members of the Baptist Church. (1021)

---

[1] Information was supplied by Patricia Morrow, 6506 Prairie Dunes, Houston, TX 77069.

James William Walton (900)

James William "Bill" Walton, son of Alfred M. and Barbara A. (Alvis) Walton, was born on Aug. 29, 1953. He married first Jacqulin Ann Meador on Dec. 26, 1970. She was born on Aug. 23, 1954. He married second Alice Hines Coleman[2] on Dec. 30, 1990. She was born on Aug. 6, 1959. Bill is an electrician. Alice works for the Jamestown Foundation. They live in Charles City, Virginia.

Children of James William and Jacqulin A. (Meador) Walton:

> 1. James "Jamie" William Walton Jr. was born on June 6, 1971. He married Chantel Anderson, daughter of Eric and Corleen (Wild) Anderson, on Dec. 8, 1991 in Utah. She was born on Sept. 7, 1970. They have three children: (a) James Erick Walton was born on July 20, 1992. (b) Blake Michael Walton was born on April 24, 1995, and (c) Matthew Thomas Walton was born on Jan. 27, 1997. (1022)
>
> 2. Tracy Lynn Walton was born on Jan. 19, 1976. She married Robert "RJ" Lee Cook on May 24, 1997. (1023)
>
> 3. Jessica Ann Walton was born on Sept. 12, 1980. (1024)

William Anthony Walton (932)

William Anthony Walton, son of Thomas A. and Virginia M. (Purdum) Walton, was born in Appomattox County on May 22, 1894 and died on Nov. 25, 1953.[3] After graduating from from Appomattox High School, he earned a B. A. degree from the University of Richmond, and a M. A. degree from Columbia University. One source says that he married Clara Wilson Atkinson on Dec. 22, 1923 in Dinwiddie County, Virginia. Another source gives his wife's name as Hunter Davis Gwaltney.[4] She was on the 1930 census as his wife. William was an accomplished individual, being a veteran of World War I, a high school teacher and principal, a Master Mason, and he served several terms as a Democrat in the Virginia House of Delegates, from 1950-1953. He died in Office, having won the election to serve in 1954-1955. The William A.

---

[2] Alice has two children from a previous marriage: (1) Jeremy Bradford Coleman, born on May 26, 1977, and (2) Amber Leigh Coleman, born on May 8, 1981.

Walton Elementary School in Prince George County was named for him. Methodist. William's address was Disputanta, Virginia. They had at least one child,

    1. William Anthony Walton Jr. was born in 1925. He grew up in Prince George County, Virginia. (1025)

James Everett Jamerson (937)

James Everett Jamerson,[5] son of Roland F. and Ella (Walton) Jamerson, was born on Oct. 10, 1902 in Appomattox County, Virginia, and died on Jan. 5, 1991 in Appomattox. He married Lula Grey Smith, daughter of Holmes and Annie (Guill) Smith, on Dec. 23, 1928. She was born on Aug. 11, 1908 and died on March 21, 1994. In 1946, he founded the J. E. Jamerson & Sons business, which started as a building supply and home construction company in Appomattox. It expanded later into commercial construction and hardware.

Children of James E. and Lula G. (Smith) Jamerson:

    1. James Robert Jamerson was born on June 12, 1930 and died on Dec. 6, 1986. He married Vicki Ryan. (1026)

    2. William Edward Jamerson was born on Feb. 18, 1934. He married Ellen Paulette. (1027)

    3. Mary Lou Jamerson was born on June 28, 1945. She married John Osborne Harrison. (1028)

---

[3] E. Griffith Dodson, Clerk of the House, *The General Assembly of the Commonwealth of Virginia, 1940-1960*, (Richmond, Virginia: State Publication), 1960, p. 594

[4] *Ibid.* p. 594.

[5] ____, *Appomattox County, Virginia*, (Summersville, West Virginia: Walsworth Publishing Company), 2001, p. 124.

Eighth Generation

Edmund Winston Walker Sr. (943)

Edmund Winston Walker Sr.,[6] son of William Massie Sr. and Mary Etta (Bowles) Walker, was born on Aug. 22, 1899 in Christian County, Kentucky and died Sept. 15, 1968 in Dothan, Alabama. He married Mary Louise Ikerman, daughter of Charles Henry and Rachel Thomas (Alexander) Ikerman, on Sept. 2, 1926 in Selma, Alabama. He attended Western Kentucky State at Bowling Green and received a Master's degree from George Peabody College in Nashville, Tennessee. He taught school for forty-one years, thirty-nine of them at Dothan High School. She graduated from the University of Alabama, and retired from teaching at Young Junior High School in Dothan. Both parents were buried in the Memory Hill Cemetery in Dothan, Alabama.

Children of Edmund W. Sr. and Mary L. (Ikerman) Walker:

1. Mary Elizabeth Walker was born in 1929 in Dothan, Alabama. She married Charles Joseph Fricke on Sept. 2, 1950 in Dothan. (1029)

2. Edmund Winston Walker Jr. was born in 1932. He married Sue Irene Hood on Dec. 15, 1957 in Fairfield, Alabama. (1030)

3. Charles Robert Walker was born in 1933 in Selma, Alabama. He married Monette Strickland on Feb. 24, 1962 at Opp, Alabama. (1031)

William Massie Walker Jr. (944)

William Massie Jr., son of William Massie Sr. and Mary Etta (Bowles) Walker, was born on Sept. 20, 1900 in Christian County, Kentucky, and died on Jan. 23, 1947 in Knoxville, Tennessee. He married Jackie Sue Roberts on Aug. 15, 1935. She died on Aug. 8, 2000.

Child of William Massie Jr. and Jackie S. (Roberts) Walker:

1. William Massie Walker III was born on July 8, 1941 in Nashville, Tennessee and died in 1997 in Florida. (1032)

---

[6] Information on this generation of Walkers was provided by Bettie (Walker) Fricke, 304 North Englewood Ave., Dothan, AL 36303-3012.

Katherine Walker (Walton) Carson (951)

Katherine Walker Walton, daughter of William Jones Sr. and Mildred Frances (Harvey) Walton, was born on July 25, 1918 at Bent Creek, Appomattox County and died on Dec. 5, 2001. Burial was in the Reedy Springs Baptist Church Cemetery. The compiler always admired Katherine for her intelligence and interest in her family heritage. She married George Carson on Sept. 26. 1939. They were farmers, and members of the Baptist Church. Residence: Spout Spring, Appomattox County, Virginia.

Children of George and Katherine W. (Walton) Carson:

1. Frances Adair Carson was born on Sept. 25, 1940 and died Oct. 13, 1996. She married Eugene Watson Carson. (1033)

2. Harriette Walton Carson was born on Aug. 20, 1943. She married Kemper M. Beasley. (1034)

3. William Patterson Carson was born on Dec. 14, 1946 and died in Orangeburg, South Carolina on Aug. 18, 1978. He married Elaine Carter. (1035)

4. Clifton Wayne Carson was born on Sept. 14, 1956. He married Regina Riggby. Clifton graduated from Virginia Tech. He is the Mayor of Wise, Virginia. (1036)

Eugenia Vawter (Walton) Giaretti (952)

Eugenia Vawter Walton, daughter of William Jones Sr. and Mildred Frances (Harvey) Walton, was born on June 23, 1922 at Bent Creek, Appomattox County and died at home on March 30, 2002.[7] She married Remo Anthony Giaretti at the Court Street Catholic Church in Lynchburg on July 28, 1946. He was born on May 6, 1918 in Greenwich Village, New York, and died Aug. 23, 1983 at East Meadow, N.Y.

Children of Remo A. and Eugenia V. (Walton) Giaretti:

---

[7] Death date was taken from a funeral card "In Loving Memory of Eugenia W. Giaretti," in hands of the compiler. Information on this family was provided by Nancy (Potocki) Giaretti of Bellmore, New York.

1. Remo Walton Giaretti was born May 24, 1951 in Manhattan, New York City. He married Nancy Ann Potocki. (1037)

Louise Clifton (Walton) Morris (953)

Louise Clifton Walton, daughter of William Jones Sr. and Mildred Frances (Harvey) Walton, was born on May 13, 1927, in Appomattox County. She graduated from Appomattox High School in 1943, and received a B.A. degree from Lynchburg College, in 1947, majoring in English and Educational Psychology. In 1956, she was the first person to receive a M.A. degree from Longwood College in Farmville, Virginia. Louise taught in elementary schools in Lynchburg, Hampton, and Newport News. She married Edward Welch Morris, who was born on Oct. 8, 1925 and died Dec. 2, 1995. He worked for twenty-five years at the Newport News Shipyard. Residence: Hampton, Virginia.

Children of Edward W. and Louise C. (Walton) Morris:

1. Martha Frances Morris was born April 22, 1959 in Lynchburg, Virginia. She married Dennis Jobe. (1038)

2. Edward Harvey Morris was born on June 29, 1961 in Hampton. He graduated from Kecoughton High School in Hampton. He is employed at the Newport News Shipyard. (1039)

3. Rebecca Lee Morris was born on Feb. 8, 1963 in Hampton. She graduated from Lynchburg College with a degree in Journalism. She is currently the Managing Editor of the News Room of WUSA Channel 9 in Washington, D. C. She married Gary Krimstein on Feb. 16, 1992 in Richmond, Virginia. He was born in Chicago, Illinois on Aug. 17, 1963. Gary works at George Michael's Sports Machine at NBC Channel 4 in Washington, D. C. Residence: North Potomac, Maryland. (1040)

William Jones Walton Jr. (954)

William Jones Walton Jr., son of William Jones Sr. and Mildred F. (Harvey) Walton, was born at Oakville, Appomattox County on May 5, 1930 and died on April 20, 1998 in South Carolina. He graduated from Appomattox High School and attended Lynchburg College for two years. William spent four years in the U.S. Air Force. In November 1956, he married Shirley Wright, who was born in Chesterfield County, South Carolina on Sept. 21, 1934. William retired from INA Bearing Company in Cheraw, South Carolina. Shirley graduated from Cheraw High School (South Carolina) and Mercy School of Hospital Nursing at Charlotte, North Carolina. She retired after working for thirty years. Shirley is active in the First United Methodist Church in Cheraw. In a letter to the compiler written several days before his death, William said, "I have reached the age where all of our past should be left where it is (past). Two hundred years from now we will not know any difference." Included in the letter was a complete account of his family information for the book. Residence: Cheraw, South Carolina.

Children of William J. Jr. and Shirley (Wright) Walton:

1. William Jones Walton III was born on June 24, 1957. He married Penny Ann Ruscue on Sept. 24, 1988. Residence: Kingwood, Texas. (1041)

2. Todd Wright Walton was born on Aug. 8, 1964. He married Dawn Elise Robinson on March 19, 1988 in Tampa, Florida. Residence: Concord, North Carolina. (1042)

3. Shirley Corrieton Walton was born on Dec. 12, 1965. She graduated from Cheraw High School and the Betty Stevens Cosmetology School in Florence, South Carolina. Shirley married David Reginald Roscoe on June 22, 1996. He was born on Dec. 27, 1962. He graduated from Chesterfield High School, and is now employed by INA Bearing in Cheraw. Residence: Chesterfield, South Carolina. (1043)

Harry Walton Bolton (955)

Harry Walton Bolton, son of Carrington A. and Mary Barksdale (Walton) Bolton, was born on Aug. 26, 1923 and died Jan. 22, 1986. He was self-employed and worked as a school bus driver. He married Ruth Naomi Scruggs, daughter of Clarence Douglas and Virginia Estelle (White) Scruggs, June 8, 1956. Ruth was born on Dec. 28, 1936. Residence: Gladstone, Nelson County, Virginia.

Children of Harry W. and Ruth N. (Scruggs) Bolton:

1. Bonnie Kay Bolton was born on May 21, 1957 in Lynchburg. She married Jacob Douglas Bebar on June 5, 1976 in Arlington, Virginia. (1044)

2. Emmett Scott Bolton was born on Feb. 2, 1963 in Lynchburg. He married Linda Diane Tyree. (1045)

Eleanor DuVal (Bolton) Hunter Burge (956)

Eleanor DuVal Bolton, daughter of Carrington A. and Mary Barksdale (Walton) Bolton, was born Sept. 14, 1925. She married first Sherman Benjamin Hunter, son of William Mosley and Myria Hopkins (Martin) Hunter. He was born on Aug. 12, 1912, and died June 9, 1983. Burial was in the Amherst Cemetery. He served in the U.S. Army during World War II, and later served as a deacon in the Maple Grove Baptist Church. Eleanor married second William Fletcher Burge Jr., son of William Fletcher and Elizabeth (Bell) Burge Sr. He worked for the C& O Railroad for thirty-eight years. Fletcher passed away on Oct. 16, 2003.[8] Residence: Gladstone, Virginia.

1. Brenda H. Hunter married Mark Truslow. They have a daughter named Samantha Truslow. Residence: Gladstone, Virginia. (1046)

Winston Davis Walton (958)

Winston Davis Walton, son of Walker S. and Nellie V. (Davis) Walton, was born April 20, 1931. He married Glenice Ann Van Cleef, daughter of Harmon and Alease (House) Van Cleef of Ford, Virginia. Glenice was born on Dec. 17, 1933 at Ford, Dinwiddie County, Virginia. She graduated from Midway High School in Dinwiddie County. Glenice has musical talent, playing the piano and singing. Winston graduated from Appomattox High School in 1948 and Lynchburg College in 1952. He is now retired from teaching at the Lynchburg Training School and devotes his time to farming and raising cattle. He loves horses. Both are active in church. Residence: Spout Spring, Appomattox County, Virginia.

---

[8] *Altavista Journal & Times Virginian*, Altavista, Virginia, October 2003.

Front, left-to-right- Clifton W. Carson, Yolanda Jill Walton, Roger F. Walton, Glenice A. Van Cleef, Winston D. Walton, Rear: Shirley M. Kerns, Nellie V. (Davis) Walton, and Josephine W. Walton. Picture was taken in July 1965 at a Davis reunion at Holiday Lake in Appomattox County, Virginia.

Children of Winston D. and Glenice (Van Cleef) Walton:

1. Yolanda Jill Walton was born on Jan. 12, 1961. She married William Jerry Harris. (1047)

2. Roger Farrel Walton was born Nov. 26, 1962. He married Connie Ruth Sage. (1048)

3. Russel Scott Walton was born on Oct. 30, 1967. He married Jennifer Roach on Oct. 7, 1995 at Pamplin, Virginia. (1049)

4. Amanda Walton was born Dec. 16, 1970 in Appomattox County. She graduated from Appomattox High School and Longwood College. Amanda is a schoolteacher at Granby Elementary School in Granby, Colorado. Amanda received a Master's degree from Adams State College. She married Kurt Edward Stoltz on Aug. 2, 2003. He was born on Feb. 18, 1971 in Brookfield, Wisconsin. Kurt graduated from the University of Wisconsin with a major in microbiology. He owns a construction company, KG Framers, in Fraser, Colorado. (1050)

Shirley Mitchell (Walton) Kerns (960)

Shirley Mitchell Walton, daughter of Walker Scott and Nellie V. (Davis) Walton, was born at Oakville, Appomattox County, on Nov. 10, 1934. She graduated from Appomattox High School in 1952 and James Madison University in 1956, earning a degree in music education. Shirley teaches elementary vocal music in the Arlington County Public School System, presently at Carlin Springs Elementary School. She married Wilmer Lee Kerns, son of Lee Doil and Madeline (Grim) Kerns, at Christ Methodist Church, Arlington, Virginia, on June 19, 1965. He graduated from Dayton High School in Rockingham County, Virginia in 1949. After attending Shenandoah College for one term, he joined the U. S. Navy for three and one-half years. His service was spent as an electronics specialist in the Pacific area and Korea, where he earned an Air Medal for flying twenty-four missions over enemy territory as a combat air crewman aboard a 4-engine PB4Y2 aircraft. In 1957, he earned a B.A. degree from Trevecca Nazarene College in Nashville, Tennessee. After teaching high school mathematics at Norview High School in Norfolk, Virginia in 1957-59, he returned to graduate school at the University of Michigan to earn a M.A. degree in 1960. The next seven years were spent with the Arlington County Public Schools as a guidance counselor and visiting teacher. In 1971, he was awarded a Ph.D. degree by The Ohio State University. His 30-year Federal career in health, education and welfare included positions as branch chief, division chief, senior research analyst, and associate regional commissioner. Some areas that he worked in were: the desegregation of schools during the late 1960s, aid to families with dependent children (AFDC), child support enforcement, medicaid, R & D grant programs, social security and elementary and secondary education. He is listed in numerous biographical references including *Marquis Who's Who in America*. Residence: Arlington, Virginia.

Children of Wilmer L. and Shirley M. (Walton) Kerns:

    1. Robert Todd Kerns was born on April 3, 1969 in Alexandria, Virginia. Rob married Christine R. Albro, daughter of James and Barbara (Bell) Albro, Aug. 3, 1996. (1051)

L-R, Lynelle M. Kerns, Shirley M. Kerns, Jacob S. Kerns, Wilmer L. Kerns, Julia B. Kerns, Christine R. Kerns, Robert T. Kerns, in 2004 at the annual Walton reunion held at Gladstone, Nelson County, Virginia

2. Lynelle Madeline Kerns was born on Nov. 24, 1973 in Evanston, Illinois. She graduated from Yorktown High School in Arlington in 1990, and received a B.S. degree in marketing from Virginia Polytechnic and State University in 1994. After working two years for First Virginia Bank in Northern Virginia, she returned to school to prepare for a career change to the field of education. She earned a Master's Degree in Education from George Mason University in 1998. Lynelle teaches first grade at Bailey's Elementary School in Fairfax County. (1052)

3. Jacob Scott Walton Kerns was born on Feb. 8, 1978 in Alexandria, Virginia. He graduated as a valadictorian from Yorktown High School in 1995 in Arlington, and studied in the School of Engineering at the University of Virginia, where he was initiated into the honor society during his junior year. Also, he is a member of Theta Chi, a social fraternity. He spent the summer of 1999 in an internship program with the Indian Health Service in Bremerton, Washington, and is currently employed by Jenny Craig in Fairfax, Virginia. (1053)

Richard Mosby Harris Sr. (960)

Richard Mosby Harris Sr., son of Daniel M. and Lela M. (Walton) Harris, was born in Appomattox County on June 11, 1916, and died July 5, 2004. He married Mary Lorene Gilliam on Dec. 26, 1941. Residence: Spout Spring, Virginia.

Children of Richard M. Sr. and Mary Lorene (Gilliam) Harris:

1. Richard Mosby Harris Jr. was born on Feb. 22, 1944 at Spout Spring, Virginia. He married Joyce Hartless on March 8, 1969. (1054)

2. Marvin Earl Harris was born on Nov. 26, 1945 in Lynchburg. He married Wanda Linda Jordon on July 26, 1969. (1055)

Front L-R, Jean Carson, Nannie Carson, Lorene Harris, Lela Harris, Back L-R, Richard M. Harris Jr., Elliott O. Carson, Richard M. Harris Sr., Earl Harris, and Mosby Harris

Nannie Franklin (Harris) Carson (961)

Nannie Franklin Harris, daughter of Daniel M. and Lela M. (Walton) Harris, was born on Aug. 7, 1918 in Appomattox County and died on June 28, 1989 at the Virginia Baptist Hospital in Lynchburg. She married Elliott Osborn Carson, son of Walter O.

and Amanda Harriett (Cheatham) Carson, on July 10, 1938. Residence: Spout Spring, Virginia.

Child of Elliott O. and Nannie F. (Harris) Carson:

1. Mildred Jean Carson was born on Sept. 24, 1951. She lives at Spout Spring, Virginia (1056)

Marion Waverly Payne Sr. (962)

Marion Waverly Payne Sr., son of Francis M. and Bessie V. (Walton) Payne, was born on April 30, 1916 at Gladstone, Virginia and died on Aug. 9, 1999 in Richmond. Burial was in the Harris-Payne Cemetery. He was a locomotive engineer for the C&O Railroad (CXX). Marion was a member of Mineral Springs Baptist Church. He married Lucy Ann West, daughter of Thomas Jefferson and Letcher (Powell) West. She was born on April 15, 1913 at Warmister, Nelson County. Residence: Richmond, Virginia.

Children of Marion W. Sr. and Lucy A. (West) Payne:

1. Marion Waverly Payne Jr. was born on Sept. 30, 1934 at Gladstone. He married Betty Huffman on July 12, 1969. Waverly worked as a storeroom clerk and Betty was an office clerk for the C&O Railroad. Residence: Richmond, Virginia. (1057)

2. Frances West Payne was born on June 17, 1942. She married Donald Wills of Spokane, Washington on June 10, 1973. He is retired from the U. S. Air Force, and she retired as a secretary in the Pentagon. Residence: Springfield, Virginia. (1058)

Frederick Eugene Payne Sr. (963)

Frederick Eugene Payne Sr., son of Francis M. and Bessie V. (Walton) Payne, was born at the Walton home at Bent Creek, Appomattox County, on March 2, 1919 and died on April 2, 1971 in Roanoke. Burial was in the Harris-Payne Cemetery. On June 6, 1950, he married first Juanita Cundiff in Lynchburg. She died in 1976, and was buried in Fort Hill Cemetery in Lynchburg. He married second Alma King in 1954 in Bristol, Virginia. One child was born to the first union and none from the second marriage. He served in the U.S. Army during World War II. His occupation was a conductor-brakeman for the Norfolk and Western Railroad. Was a member of Mineral Springs Baptist Church. Residence: Roanoke, Virginia.

Child of Frederick E. Sr. and Juanita (Cundiff) Payne:

1. Frederick Eugene Payne Jr. was born on June 3, 1951. He first married Brenda Ramsey; married second Cheryl Miller; and married third Joan Rebecca Bryant. (1059)

John Gordon Payne Sr. (964)

John Gordon Payne Sr., son of Francis M. and Bessie V. (Walton) Payne, was born Oct. 10, 1920 at Gladstone, Virginia. He served in the U. S. Army in World War II. Memberships included Lodge No. 398 of IOOF Gladstone, Masonic Lodge No. 255 Gladstone, and the Nelson County Men's Club. In addition, he served as a deacon in the Mineral Springs Baptist Church. Gordon did cattle farming and worked as a car inspector for the C&O Railroad. He married Clara Louise Glover, daughter of Robert Leonard and Minnie Lee (Cunningham) Glover, on Sept. 19, 1942. She worked as an assistant postal clerk for the Gladstone post office, and she was active in church and the community. Clara was born on Feb. 3, 1922 in Buckingham County, and died on Dec. 15, 1998 at her home in Gladstone. Burial was in the Harris-Payne Cemetery at *Rose Hill*, Gladstone, Nelson County. Residence: Gladstone, Virginia.

Children of John Gordon and Clara (Glover) Payne:

1. Nancy Louise Payne was born on Dec. 17, 1946. She married George Reine Banton. (1060)

2. Lynn Franklin Payne was born on Dec. 3, 1947 in Lynchburg Hospital. He married Norma Jean Turberville on Aug. 12, 1969. (1061)

3. John Gordon Payne Jr. was born on July 10, 1954. He married first Jeannette Maddox and married second Dianna Sue Creasy. (1062)

Sterling Claiborne Payne (965)

Sterling Claiborne Payne, son of Francis M. and Bessie V. (Walton) Payne, was born on at Gladstone, Nelson County, Virginia on Jan. 31, 1923. He married Annie Barita Wills, daughter of Percy Millard and Laura Barita (Megginson) Wills, on July 8, 1950. He served in the U.S. Navy and worked as a car inspector for the B&O Railroad in Lynchburg. He is a deacon in the Mineral Springs Baptist Church. Annie, born on Feb. 11, 1927, was an elementary school teacher in Amherst County. They live at Gladstone, Nelson County.

Children of Sterling Claiborne and Annie B. (Wills) Payne:

> 1. Ann Sterling Payne was born on June 5, 1951. She married Ray Lewis Cunningham on Oct. 9, 1971. (1063)
>
> 2. Patsy Lyle Payne was born on Sept. 26, 1952. She married first Donald Taylor and married second John William Loukides. (1064)
>
> 3. Millard Claiborn Payne was born on May 31, 1954. He married Doreen Rhode of Minnesota. (1065)
>
> 4. Robert Anthony Payne was born on Sept. 3, 1957. He married Alicia Hill of Madison Heights, Virginia. (1066)

Sallie Ida (Payne) Marks Watts (966)

Sallie Ida Payne, daughter of Francis M. and Bessie V. (Walton) Payne, was born on July 5, 1925 at *Rose Hill*, Gladstone, Virginia. She graduated from Appomattox County High School in 1945. Ida is retired from the C&P Telephone Company. She married first Gene Newton Marks, son of Elmo and Lucy (Christian) Marks, on March 1, 1945, and was divorced in 1947. On Feb. 10, 1950, she married second William Leonidas Watts Jr., son of Dr. W. L. and Lillie (Huff) Watts, in South Carolina. He worked as a yard brakeman for the C&O Railroad at Gladstone. He serves as a deacon in the Gladstone Memorial Baptist Church. Residence: Allen's Creek, Virginia.

Children of Gene N. and Sallie Ida (Payne) Marks:

> 1. Joseph Newton Marks was born on May 8, 1946. He married Nancy Taylor. (1067)

Children of William L. and Sallie Ida (Payne) Watts:

2. William Leonidas Watts III was born on Sept. 27, 1951. He married first Shirley Hanson and married second Brenda Jones. (1068)

3. Hugh Alvin Watts was born on March 21, 1957. He first married Janet Horsley, and was divorced. He married second Margaret Lyons and married third Janice Hudson. (1069)

4. Evelyn Faye Watts was born May 17, 1958. She graduated from Nelson County High School and attended the Community College in Lynchburg. Faye married James Brooks in 2000. Residence: Lynchburg, Virginia. (1070)

5. Bessie Claire Watts was born on March 10, 1961. She married first Delane Fitzgerald Sr. and was divorced. She married second Samuel Angus, and married third William Ragland. She married fourth David W. Angus. (1071)

Walter Jones Payne (967)

Walter Jones Payne was born on Feb. 26, 1928 at *Rose Hill* and died on Sept. 2, 1972 in Lynchburg, after a lengthy illness. Burial was in the Fort Hill Cemetery in Lynchburg. He was a veteran of the U. S. Army, and worked as a detective in the City of Lynchburg. Was a member of Mineral Springs Baptist Church. Walter married Imogene Alpha Robinson in 1948 in South Carolina. She was born in 1932 in Lynchburg. Children:[9] (1072)

Joseph Dudley Payne (968)

Joseph Dudley Payne Sr., son of Francis M. and Bessie V. (Walton) Payne, was born on Nov. 17, 1930, at *Rose Hill* in Nelson County. He married Mary Sue Boaz, daughter of Percy Jennings and Nettie Estelle (Saunders) Boaz, on Nov. 27, 1954 in Amherst. She was born on May 4, 1934 in Amherst County. Sue is retired from the Botetourt County School System. He is a veteran of the U. S. Army and now retired from Wendell Transport Company. He currently serves as a deacon in the Bonsack Baptist Church in

---

[9] According to the format chosen for this book, a family unit consists of not only a head of a household and a spouse, but a child or children. This definition is being waived for this couple at the request of Mary Evelyn (Payne) Strickland.

Roanoke and has membership in the IOOF Lodge in Salem, Virginia. Residence: Blue Ridge, Virginia near Roanoke.

Children of Joseph D. Sr. and Mary Sue (Boaz) Payne:

    1. Carolyn Sue Payne was born on July 25, 1955. She graduated from Virginia Tech in 1977, and owns a small business named Signgraphics in Vinton. Residence: Fincastle, Virginia. (1073)

    2. Wanda Kay Payne was born on Jan. 18, 1957. She graduated from Lord Botetourt High School in 1975, and is employed by Cracker Barrel in Troutville, Virginia. Residence: Blue Ridge, Virginia. (1074)

    3. Joseph Dudley Payne Jr. was born on Aug. 22, 1959. He graduated from Lord Botetourt High School in 1977. He is employed as a terminal manager for Wendell Transport. He married Diane Hodge in 1979. (1075)

Mary Evelyn (Payne) Bailey Strickland (969)

Mary Evelyn Payne, daughter of Francis Marion and Bessie V. (Walton) Payne, was born on July 21, 1933 at historic *Rose Hill* at Gladstone, Nelson County, Virginia. She graduated from Appomattox High School in 1951 and attended Phillips Business College in 1952. Mary Evelyn married first Samuel D. Bailey, son of Ernest and Martha Bailey, June 10, 1956. He was from South Carolina and Richmond, and was employed as a yard conductor for the C&O Railroad. She married second James M. Strickland Sr., son of Edward Ambler and Mary Lucille (Watts) Strickland, on Dec. 10, 1969. He was an Army veteran of World War II, who later worked in the construction field. He was born on Dec. 17, 1924 at Tye River, Virginia and died on May 20, 2001 at his residence. He was buried in Amherst Cemetery. No children were born to either marriage. Mary Evelyn is an active member of Gladstone Memorial Baptist Church, currently serving as an adult Sunday school teacher and "other offices in the church." She is active with the Eugene A. Walton family reunions, and assisted in collecting information for this book. She lives in the ancestral house, *Rose Hill*, at Gladstone, Nelson County, Virginia.[10] (1076)

Mary Evelyn (Payne) Strickland and Lloyd Gray Walton were two of the leaders who planned and organized the annual reunion for the descendants of Eugene A. and Nannie K. (Jones) Walton. They also played enabling roles in collecting information for this book. Shirley M. Kerns is standing in the background.

Marshall Walton Harris (972)

Marshall Walton Harris, son of Willis E. and Nannie E. (Walton) Harris, was born on Oct. 4, 1932 in Buckingham County, Virginia. He graduated from Appomattox High School in 1951 and attended Phillips Business College in 1951-1952. In 1968, he graduated from the University of Virginia Bank Management School and in 1981 from Louisiana State University. He spent a career in the banking business, including bank examiner before his retirement on July 1, 1995. He worked twenty-eight years with the State Corporation

---

[10] The "family unit format" was waived for Mary Evelyn at her request, out of respect for her contribution of information.

Commission, Bureau of Financial Institutions, as the principal financial institutional bank examiner. Marshall married Rachel Alice Goin, daughter of DeWitt Talmadge and Alice (Brown) Goin. They are members of the Assembly of God Church. Marshall's hobby is golf, and he works part time at a golf course. Residence: Manakin, Virginia.

Children of Marshall W. and Rachel (Goin) Harris:

    1. Marshall Talmage Harris was born on Sept. 22, 1958. He is an artist, who is serving as a missionary in Asia. (1077)

    2. Pamela Alice Harris was born on July 19, 1960, and died on April 28, 1963. (1078)

    3. Peyton Alan Harris was born on Aug. 9, 1963. He married Clovia Marie Lee. (1079)

Lloyd Gray Walton (975)

Lloyd Gray Walton, son of Alexander W. and Mary C. (Harris) Walton, was born on Jan. 4, 1936. He married Shirley Elizabeth Williams, daughter of Philip Pierpoint and Bessie Alma (Walters) Williams, on June 10, 1960 at Rock Springs Methodist Church at Ringgold, Virginia. Both have had distinguished careers.

Lloyd received a B.S. Degree in Agricultural Education and a M.S. Degree in Technical Education from Virginia Tech in Blacksburg, and certification for School Superintendence from the University of Virginia in Charlottesville. He had a 35-year career in Public Education, serving for eighteen years as Superintendent of Appomattox County Public Schools. Lloyd taught Vocational Agriculture for four years before being appointed as an Elementary School Principal and Supervisor, Director of Title III programs for Pittsylvania County Public Schools. His last two years were spent in Washington County, Virginia as an Educational Consultant.

Shirley received a B.S. Degree in Home Economics Education from Radford University, Radford, Virginia, and a M.S. Degree in Vocational Technical Education from Virginia Tech in Blacksburg. She taught school for ten years, served as extension agent, Home Economics for ten years, seven of which she served as Appomattox

County Unit Director. Her 21-year career with Virginia Cooperative Extension was completed as she served her last two years as District Director for the Great Southwest and was headquartered in Abingdon, Virginia.

Children of Lloyd G. and Shirley E. (Williams) Walton:

    1. Cheryl Elizabeth Walton was born on July 5, 1963. She married Richard Andrew Gullickson on Aug. 8, 1987. (1080)

    2. Laura Gray Walton was born on Nov. 23, 1964. She married Leonard Nathan Bell on June 20, 1987 (1081)

Alice Rebecca (Davis) Millner (993)

Alice Rebecca Davis, daughter of Ira G. and Alma V. (Walton) Davis, was born on March 1, 1917 at Altavista, Virginia and died on Dec. 21, 1983 in Campbell County, Virginia. She married Beverly Thomas Millner, son of William and Legore (East) Millner, on Oct. 4, 1935. He was born on Feb. 28, 1914 in Halifax County, Virginia, and died on Sept. 28, 1993 in Lynchburg, Virginia.

Children of Beverly T. and Alice R. (Davis) Millner:[11]

    1. Bernard Nelson Millner was born on Dec. 11, 1936 and died on March 25, 1994 in Knoxville, Tennessee. He married first Joyce Burns, who died in 1967 in Charlottesville, Virginia. He married second Lucille Horton Johnson in 1967. She was born on Oct. 30, 1930. He married third Dorothy Cline in Gatlinburg, Tennessee, and married fourth Dorothy Scott on April 15, 1983 in Tennessee. She was born on Sept. 20, 1933. (1095

    2. Beverly Jean Millner was born on Nov. 3, 1938 in Madison Heights, Virginia. She married first Sidney James McCormick on March 14, 1953 in Lynchburg. They had two children: (a) James Robert McCormick was born on Aug. 29, 1954 in Lynchburg. He married first Liza Diane Kyle on March 27, 1976. Their children: Dawn Rena McCormick was born on Sept. 23, 1976 in Lynchburg. James R. married second Susan Karen Spell on March 20, 1982, and their two children: James Dustin McCormick, born on Sept. 30, 1982 in

---

[11] Information on this family unit was provided by Barbara Millner,

Lynchburg, and Caitlin Blaire McCormick was born on May 15, 1989 in Lynchburg. (b) Victoria Virginia McCormick, daughter of Beverly Jean, was born on Dec. 14, 1955 and died on Feb. 20, 1962 in Lynchburg. Beverly Jean (Millner) McCormick married second Richard Franklin Caldwell on April 13, 1962. He was born on Nov. 19, 1930 and died on June 14, 1994 in Lynchburg. They had a child named (c) Paul Lee Caldwell, born on March 28, 1968, who married Angel Lee Johnson on Oct. 11, 1994. Beverly Jean (Millner) Caldwell married third Harold Dean Layne on July 4, 1988. He was born on Nov. 9, 1938 in North Carolina. (1096)

3. Brenda Marie Millner was born on April 30, 1942. She married Burton Eugene Taylor, son of Irvin and Margie (McCormick) Taylor, on Nov. 1, 1958. He was born on Jan 14, 1941. Their children: (a) Cynthia Ann Taylor, born on March 3, 1961, married William "Billy" Ray Carpenter on March 3, 1961. They have one son William Eugene Carpenter, born on Aug. 15, 1982. (b) Burton Eugene Taylor Jr. was born on Dec. 13, 1963. He married Tonya Minnix on March 4, 1988. Their child, Ashley Anne Marie Taylor, was born on Jan. 17, 1990. (1097)

4. Lenard Benson Millner was born on May 12, 1947 in Lynchburg, Virginia. He married first Linda Charlene Smith on Aug. 24, 1964 in Lynchburg. She was born on Oct. 28, 1948 in Carthage, Missouri. They have four children: (a) Darrell Wayne Millner was born on Feb. 9, 1965 in Lynchburg. He married Barbara Ann Wood on Feb. 15, 1985 in Lynchburg. Their child, Elric Shawn Millner, was born on June 5, 1988 in Annandale, Virginia. (b) Victoria Lynn Millner was born on Dec. 16, 1966. She married Tim Rodney Irby, son of Roy and JoAnne (Robertson) Irby. He was born on Dec. 4, 1967. They had four children: Crystal Irby was born on Dec. 10, 1983; Tiffany Irby was born on Nov. 28, 1989; Brittany Nichole Irby was born on March 26, 1992. (c) Heather Marie Millner was born on Feb. 27, 1971. She married Edward Thomas Wilmer, son of Winfred and Helen (Gunter) Wilmer, on Dec. 1, 1990 in Lynchburg. Their two children: Jessica Faye Wilmer was born on Aug. 27, 1993 and Kaitlan Nichole Wilmer was born in 1995. (1098)

Walton Franklin Adams (995)

Walton Franklin Adams, son of William F. and Jessie H. (Walton) Adams, was born on April 17, 1918 in Cumberland

County, Virginia and died on Jan. 12, 1987 at Norton, Wise County, Virginia. He married Earnie Eileen Colley, daughter of Richard and Maud (Thomas) Colley, on July 30, 1938 at Wytheville, Virginia. She was born on Oct. 11, 1923 in Russell County, Virginia and died on Jan. 15, 2000. Both were buried in East Lawn Cemetery in Kingsport, Tennessee.

Children of Walton F. and Earnie E. (Colley) Adams:

    1. Harry Dean Adams was born on Sept. 13, 1939 at Bastian, Bland County, Virginia and died on Aug. 24, 2001 in Radford, Virginia. He was employed with Hercules Powder Company for thirty-two years. He married Sandra Gay Browning on Oct. 15, 1959 in Wise County, Virginia. (1082)

    2. Walton Franklin Adams Jr. was born on Aug. 7, 1944 at Bastian, Bland County. He married Karen "Kay" Lee Crabtree on Aug. 30, 1964. (1083)

    3. Richard Lee Adams was born on Nov. 1, 1946. He married Elizabeth Ann Elkins on Feb. 5, 1968. (1084)

Martha Leich (Adams) Keller (996)

Martha Leich Adams, daughter of William F. and Jessie H. (Walton) Adams, was born on Feb. 9, 1920, and died on May 4, 1996. She married Morris Clifford Keller, son of Washington and Mary (Adcock) Keller, on Dec. 4, 1937. He was born on Feb. 24, 1915, and died March 4, 1977.

Children of Morris C. and Martha L. (Adams) Keller:

    1. Dorothy Marie Keller was born Jan. 30, 1942 and died Sept. 13, 1956. (1085)

    2. Elizabeth Carol "Bettie" Keller was born Dec. 10, 1944. (1086)

    3. Morris Clifford Keller Jr. was born May 5, 1947 (1087)

    4. James Franklin "Jimmie" Keller was born April 13, 1963. (1088)

John Samuel Adams (997)

John Samuel "Sam" Adams, son of William F. and Jessie H. (Walton) Adams, was born on May 26, 1921 in Cumberland County and died on Oct. 23, 1999 in Georgia. He was in the military service in World War II. Sam married Mary LaVerne Jackson on Jan. 9, 1946. She was born on May 15, 1926.

Children of John S. and Mary L. (Jackson) Adams:

   1. Melody Diane Adams was born on April 21, 1947. (1089)

   2. Kela Rebecca Adams, born on Feb. 13, 1963. (1090)

Clyde Ottway Adams (999)

Clyde Ottway Adams, son of William F. and Jessie H. (Walton) Adams, was born on Nov. 16, 1923 in a log cabin near Trent's Mill in Cumberland County. He married Thelma Louise Griffin, daughter of Chilli and Maudie (Atwell) Griffin, on April 9, 1945. She was born on Feb. 7, 1927 in Biloxi, Mississippi. As a young boy, he worked with oxen on his grandfather's farm. He joined the Army just months before Pearl Harbor, and saw a variety of action from Panama to the South Pacific to New Guinea. In 1944, he was reassigned to the Air Force. He served in several capacities, including crew chief of C-47 aircraft. After spending almost twenty-one years in the service, he worked as an automobile salesman in Biloxi, Mississippi. He is a "family man," and interested in history.

Children of Clyde O. and Thelma L. (Griffin) Adams:

   1. Frances Lee Adams was born Aug. 25, 1946 at Keesler Air Force Base, Mississippi. She married Mendum Dees Briscoe (1091)

   2. Peggy Louise Adams was born on Oct. 26, 1948 at Keesler Air Base. She married first O'neil James Nadalich and married second Hugo Moreta. (1092)

George Chambers Adams[12] (1003)

George Chambers "Buster" Adams was born on March 7, 1932 in Cumberland County. He married first Suk Cha Kim on Jan. 11, 1966. Known as "Sue," she was born Jan. 6, 1941 in Seado City, Japan and took her life on Oct. 2, 1984. Buster married second India

---

[12] Information from Dawn Adams, dawn@adamsediting.com on March 23, 2004.

Blanche (Jackson) Simmons on Jan. 2, 1985 and divorced on Nov. 17, 1999.

Children of George C. and Suk C. (Kim) Adams:

    1. William Franklin Adams was born Feb. 23, 1966 in Osan, Korea. He married Jennifer L. Cacchine, whose birthdate is Nov. 16, 1967. Their children: Jessica Diane Adams was born in Virginia on March 19, 1995 and William George Adams was born in Pennsylvania on Jan. 21, 2000. (1093)

    2. Dawn Kim Adams was born Aug. 6, 1967 in Tachikawa AFB, Japan. She married first Michael Todd Vaughan on Oct. 17, 1986 in Farmville, Virginia, and divorced in May 1990. She graduated magna cum laude from Longwood College in Farmville, and earned a M. A. in German from the University of Southern California. She is a freelance writer and editor. Dawn married second Alexander William Vinson on May 23, 1992 in Camden County, Georgia. He was born Oct. 7, 1964. (1094)

Guy Isbell Tutwiler Jr. (1004)

Guy Isbell Tutwiler Jr., son of Guy Isbell Sr. and Edna Mae (Scruggs) Tutwiler, was born on Sept. 24, 1925 in Birmingham, Jefferson Co., Alabama. He married first Jean Ellen Minton on March 12, 1948. She was born Aug. 11, 1929. He married second Elaine G. Greene in Mar 1977.

Children of Guy I. Jr. and Jean E. (Minton) Tutwiler:

    1. Guy Isbell Tutwiler III was born on June 14, 1951 (1095)

    2. Kyle Ann Tutwiler was born on Jan. 20, 1954. (1096)

Chapter 9

Ninth Generation

Taft Morrow (1020)

Taft Morrow, son of Joseph H. and Georgia A. (Landrum) Morrow, was born on Sept. 30, 1909 at Port Lavaca, Calhoun County, Texas and died on June 2, 2000. He married Alice Mae Pegues, daughter of John and Beulah (Flanagan) Pegues, on July 14, 1937 in Crystal City, Zavala County, Texas. She was born on March 27, 1911 in Crystal City and died on Nov. 20, 2000 in Houston, Harris County, Texas. During the Depression, Taft made a living in rodeos and "feeding out cattle." He was an avid outdoorsman and photographer of nature. He retired from farming in 1986. Alice Mae graduated from Texas Woman's University, and taught school. They were members of the Methodist Church.

Children of Taft and Alice M. (Peques) Morrow:[1]

1. Patricia Pegues Morrow was born on Oct. 28, 1939 at Corpus Christi, Nueces County, Texas. She married David Robert Taylor, son of David and Martha (Hatcher) Taylor, on July 29, 1961 at Sinton, Texas. They were divorced in 1986. Patricia graduated from Southwestern University in Georgetown, Texas, and retired from teaching in 2004. They are parents of two children: Lance Wesley Taylor, born in 1967 and Julie Morrow Taylor, born in 1969. Julie married Charles Harter IV in 1998. He works for Harter Machinery, a family business. Julie graduated from the University of Arkansas. Lance married Carolyn Holmes in 2004, and they live in Dallas. Lance graduated from the University of Texas, and works in commercial real estate. Carolyn is a teacher. (1097)

2. Frances Suzanne Morrow was born on Sept. 23, 1943 at Sinton, San Patricio County, Texas. She married Edward Hardin Ellis, son of Edward and Klara (Olsen) Ellis, on Aug. 1, 1963 at Sinton, Texas. They have four children: Christopher Taft Ellis; Jason Hardin Ellis; Laura Patricia Ellis; and Benjamin Morrow Ellis. Suzanne was a teacher; is a community volunteer. Ed is a CPA by profession. Both are affiliated with the United Methodist Church. (1098)

---

[1] Information was provided by Patricia Morrow, 6506 Prairie Dunes, Houston, TX 77069.

James Robert Jamerson (1026)

James Robert Jamerson,[2] son of James E. and Lula G. (Smith) Jamerson, was born on June 12, 1930 in Appomattox County, Virginia, and died on Dec. 6, 1986. He married Vicki Ryan. Robert was very interested in history— collecting and preserving records as well as writing. Both worked together to produce a 150-year history of the Liberty Baptist Church in 1984. The J. Robert Jamerson Memorial Library in Appomattox bears his name. He was a partner in the family firm J. E. Jamerson and Sons, Inc. Children: Kenneth Hawkins and Deborah Hawkins. Residence: Appomattox County, Virginia.

William Edward Jamerson (1027)

William "Bill" Edward Jamerson,[3] son of James E. and Lula G. (Smith) Jamerson, was born on Feb. 18, 1934 in Virginia. Bill graduated from Appomattox High School in 1952[4] and Virginia Polytechnic Institute and State University in Blacksburg in 1956, where he was an outstanding football player. He was an Atlantic Coast Conference Official from the late 1960s to 1991 and for post-season Bowl games. He refereed games such as the Cotton Bowl in 1982, with Texas versus Alabama, and the Orange Bowl on Jan. 1, 1991, with Colorado versus Notre Dame to determine the national championship. Bill is a man for all seasons— a philanthropist, community leader, an athlete, and successful businessman with the firm J. E. Jamerson and Sons, Inc. Bill married Ellen Paulette. Both are deeply interested in historical interpretation and preservation. Residence: Appomattox, Virginia.

Children of William E. and Ellen (Paulette) Jamerson:

---

[2] _____, *Appomattox County, Virginia*, (Summersville, West Virginia: Walsworth Publishing Company), 2001, p. 124, submitted by Ellen (Paulette) Jamerson.

[3] _____, *Appomattox County, Virginia*, (Summersville, West Virginia: Walsworth Publishing Company), 2001, p. 124, submitted by Ellen (Paulette) Jamerson.

[4] The author's wife, Shirley Mitchell Walton, was in Bill's high school graduating class. The 50th anniversary reunion in 2002 was a superb occasion.

1. William Edward Jamerson Jr. was born on April 8, 1957. He is a special education teacher in Connecticut. Ed graduated from Shenandoah College and Conservatory of Music, now Shenandoah University. (1099)

2. Phillip Clifton Jamerson was born on Oct. 30, 1958. He received a degree from Virginia Tech in Blacksburg. He is a partner in the firm founded by his grandfather, J. E. Jamerson and Sons, Inc. in Appomattox. Phillip married Terry Hall. His four children are William Trevor Jamerson, Byron Lee Jamerson, Brittney Diane Jamerson, and Melissa Ann Jamerson. (1100)

Mary Lou (Jamerson) Harrison (1028)

Mary Lou Jamerson, daughter of James E. and Lula G. (Smith) Jamerson was born on June 28, 1945. She graduated from Mary Washington College in Fredericksburg with a degree in Sociology. Mary Lou married John Osborne Harrison, who was born on Nov. 3, 1944 in Virginia Baptist Hospital in Lynchburg. He received a degree in Forestry from Virginia Tech and is presently working as a land and timber investor. Residence: Appomattox, Virginia.

Children of John O. and Mary L. (Jamerson) Harrison:[5]

1. Lisa Michelle Harrison was born Oct. 8, 1968 in Radford, Virginia. She graduated from James Madison University, earning B. S. and M. S. degrees in the field of speech pathology. Lisa married Roy McCall on April 30, 1994. Residence: Durham, North Carolina. (1101)

2. Brenton John Harrison was born March 28, 1971 in Petersburg, Virginia. He graduated from Virginia Tech in the field of building construction. He married Mimi Buchanan on June 3, 1995. Residence: Christiansburg, Virginia. (1102)

3. Joshua Everett Harrison was born Nov. 6, 1978 at Virginia Baptist Hospital in Lynchburg. He has a B. S. in Civil Engineering degree and an M. B. A. degree from Virginia Tech. Josh married Valerie Wilkerson on March 2, 2002. He is a project manager. Residence: Appomattox, Virginia. (1103)

---

[5] Information was given directly by Mary Lou Harrison to the compiler.

Mary Elizabeth "Bettie" (Walker) Fricke (1029)

Mary Elizabeth "Bettie" Walker, daughter of Edmund W. Sr. and Mary L. (Ikerman) Walker, was born in 1929 in Dothan, Alabama. She married Charles Joseph Fricke, son of Roland Macon and Mattie Lou (Jones) Fricke on Sept. 2, 1950. He was born on Nov. 2, 1929 at Guntersville, Alabama and died on Oct. 5, 1988 at Veterans' Hospital in Tuscaloosa, Alabama. He retired as a Lt. Col, after serving in both the Korean and Viet Nam wars. Both parents and their five children and three of their spouses graduated from Auburn University in Alabama. Residence: Dothan, Alabama.

Children of Charles J. and Mary E. "Bettie" (Walker) Fricke[6]1.

1. Carolyn Lorine Fricke was born in Dothan, Alabama. She married Terry Lynn Wallace on Dec. 30, 1971 at Guntersville, Alabama. Carolyn retired from teaching French in the Dothan high schools. Terry has his own Electric Engineering Contracting Company. They have two daughters: Kareth Anne Wallace who married Tommy Mullis; and Jeniffer Michelle Wallace who married Phillip McCullough. (1104)

2. Rachael Susan Fricke was born at Ft. Belvoir, Virginia. She married William Curry Jones III on Aug. 15, 1981 in Guntersville, Alabama. She taught grades K-3 and now works as a Reading Coach. Bill is with the Alabama Forestry Association. Their children: Sarah Nell Jones, William Edmund "Ned" Jones and Margaret Hunter Jones. (1105)

3. Roland Walker Fricke was born at Ft. Benning, Georgia. He married Becky Chance on Jan 27, 1996 at Millbrook, Alabama. He is a tax consultant. Residence: Arab, Alabama (1106)

4. Mary Lou Fricke was born at Ft. McClellan, Alabama. She married William Wilson Griffith on Aug. 7, 1981 at Guntersville, Marshall County, Alabama. She works for the North AL Pipe Manufacturing Company, and her husband is with the Marshall County Schools. Their two children: William Wilson Griffith Jr. and Carolyn Louise Griffith. (1107)

---

[6] Information was provided by Bettie (Walker) Fricke, 304 North Englewood Avenue, Dothan, Alabama 36303-3912. Exact birth dates were not given, per request by Mrs. Fricke in a letter to compiler on July 21, 2004.

5. Charles Joseph Fricke Jr. was born at Ft. McClellan, Alabama. He married Martha Alisa McConnell on Dec. 16, 1989 at Enterprise, Coffee County, Alabama. Alisa is a teacher and he is Comptroller with Standard Demolition in Tampa, and teaches computer courses at a local college. Their two children: Danielle Elizabeth Fricke and Katheryn Alexandria Fricke. Residence: Tampa, Florida. (1108)

Edmund Winston Walker Jr. (1030)

Edmund Winston Walker Jr., son of Edmund W. Sr. and Mary L. (Inkerman) Walker, was born in 1932. He married Sue Irene Hood on Dec. 15, 1957 in Fairfield, Alabama. After graduating from Auburn University, he took a job as a chemical engineer with Monsanto Company in Pensacola and St, Louis. Residence: Ballwin, Missouri.

Children of Edmund W. Jr. and Sue (Hood) Walker:

1. Lisa Sue Walker married George David Smith. Their children: David George Smith and Timothy Winston Smith. (1109)

2. Mark Winston Walker. Was adopted in infancy. Occupation: truck driver. (1110)

Rev. Charles Robert Walker (1031)

Rev. Charles Robert Walker, son of Edmund W. Sr. and Mary L. (Inkerman) Walker was born in 1933 in Selma, Alabama. He married Monette Strickland on Feb. 24, 1962 at Opp, Alabama. He attended Birmingham Southern College and received a Master of Divinity Degree from Candler School of Theology at Emory University in Atlanta. He served in the Alabama—West Florida Methodist Conference. Monette graduated from Montevallo University in Alabama. Residence: Navarre, Florida.

Children of Charles R. and Monette (Strickland) Walker:

1. Charles Robert Walker Jr. married Laura Fessenden. Hr graduated from Huntingdon College in Montgomery. They have two children: Haley Catherine Walker and Winston Thomas Walker. (1112)

2. Merry Monette Walker married Billy Adams (now divorced). She graduated from Huntingdon College. They have two children: Jordan Elizabeth Adams and Madison Nicole Adams. (1113)

Ninth Generation

Frances Adair (Carson) Carson (1033)

Frances Adair Carson, daughter of George P. and Katherine W. (Walton) Carson, was born on Sept. 25, 1940 in Appomattox County, and died Oct. 13, 1996 in Blacksburg, Virginia. Frances attended Radford University and graduated from Virginia Tech. She married Eugene Watson Carson of Appomattox, on Sept. 15, 1960. Frances was a very gifted, intellectually stimulating, and well-informed woman. Gene earned a Ph.D. degree from North Carolina State University, and later held several important posts at Virginia Tech, including a full professorship and the position of Vice Provost for Academic Affairs. He helped shape admission policy and played a leading role in developing automated systems at the University. Residence: Blacksburg, Virginia.

Children of Eugene W. and Frances A. (Carson) Carson:

1. Glenell Louise Carson was born on July 10, 1961. She married Steven R. Peterson in New Mexico. (1114)

2. Mildred Adair Carson was born Nov. 4, 1962. She married Gerry Newman of Portland, Oregon. (1115)

3. Lynn Katherine Carson was born on Nov. 13, 1963. She married Brett Harris of Fairfax County, Virginia. (1116)

Harriette Walton (Carson) Beasley (1034)

Harriette Walton Carson, daughter of George P. and Katherine W. (Walton) Carson, was born on Aug. 20, 1943 in Richmond, Virginia. She graduated from Radford College in 1965, and taught English in high schools in Prince William, Prince Edward, and Appomattox Counties, Virginia. She married Kemper Morton Beasley Jr., son of Kemper Morton Sr. and Ellen (Lowe) Beasley. Residence: Dillwyn, Virginia.

Children of Kemper M. Jr. and Harriette W. (Carson) Beasley:

1. Katherine Ellen Beasley was born on Dec. 28, 1969. She married first Robert Lockwood and married second James M. Garnett. (1117)

2. Kemper Morton Beasley III was born on Oct. 12, 1979 in Farmville. He graduated from Appomattox High School in 1998 and Hampden-

Sydney College in 2002 with a major in History. In 2004, he received a Master of Theological Studies from Duke University. Kemper is employed as assistant manager of the Farmer's Bank in Dillwyn. (1118)

William Patterson Carson (1035)

William Patterson "Pat" Carson, son of George P. and Katherine W. (Walton) Carson, was born on Dec. 14, 1946 in Lynchburg, and died in Orangeburg, South Carolina on Aug. 18, 1978. He was a long-distance truck driver. He married Elaine Carter. Residence: Spout Spring, Virginia.

Children of William P. and Elaine (Carter) Carson:

1. Robin Renee Carson was born on Feb. 4, 1972 in Appomattox County. She married Philip Walton Reynolds. (1119)

2. Patrick Scott Carson was born July 8, 1973. He married Stacy Kolech of New Jersey. (1120)

Clifton Wayne Carson (1036)

Clifton Wayne Carson, son of George P. and Katherine W. (Walton) Carson, was born on Sept. 14, 1956 in Appomattox County, Virginia. He graduated from Virginia Tech. Clifton married Regina Riggsby on Oct. 11, 1980 in Breaks Interstate Park near the Kentucky-Virginia State line. Regina, born on Jan. 28, 1957, in Grundy, Virginia, is a Special Education teacher in the Wise County Public Schools. Clifton works for Maxim Engineering in Coeburn, Virginia. Both are graduates of Virginia Tech, where they met. They live in Wise, Virginia where Clifton is currently (2004) serving as the mayor of the town of Wise.

Children of Clifton W. and Regina (Riggsby) Carson:

1. Rachel Katherine Carson was born on Oct. 24, 1990, who is a student at Addington Middle School in Wise, Virginia. (1121)

Raymond Walton Giaretti (1037)

Remo Walton Giaretti,[7] son of Remo A. and Eugenia V. (Walton) Giarette, was born on May 24, 1951 in Manhattan, New York City. He married Nancy Ann Potocki, April 5, 1970 at St. Raphaels Church, East Meadow, N.Y. Nancy was born on Oct. 15, 1951 at Mercy Hospital, Rockville Centre, N.Y.

Children of Remo W. and Nancy A. (Potocki) Giaretti:

> 1. Jessica Jean Giaretti was born on Sept. 14, 1970. She married James Verdon on June 14, 2002. (1122)
>
> 2. Heather Kathleen Giaretti was born on Oct.23, 1975. (1123)
>
> 3. Raymond Walton Giaretti was born on May 25, 1982. (1124)

Bonnie Kay (Bolton) Bebar (1044)

Bonnie Kay Bolton,[8] daughter of Harry W. and Ruth N. (Scruggs) Bolton, was born in Lynchburg, Virginia on May 21, 1957. She married Mark Ronald Bebar on June 5, 1976 in Arlington, Virginia. He was born in Brooklyn, New York on Jan. 31, 1948. They live in Midlothian, Virginia.

Child of Mark Ronald and Bonnie K. (Bolton) Bebar is:

> 1. Jacob Douglas Bebar was born on Feb. 2, 1980 in Fairfax County. He graduated from James Madison University in 2003 and accepted a teaching position at Spotswood High School in Rockingham County, Virginia. (1125)

Emmett Scott Bolton (1045)

Emmett Scott Bolton, son of Harry W. and Ruth N. (Scruggs) Bolton, was born in Lynchburg on Feb. 2, 1963. He married Linda

---

[7] Also known as Remo Anthony Giaretti., per letter dated Jan. 22, 2004 from Nancy P. Giaretti of Bellmore, NY.

[8] Information on family was provided by Bonnie (Bolton) Bebar. She has been a regular participant in the annual Walton reunions.

Diane Tyree on Jan. 22, 1982 at Riverdale, Virginia. They were divorced in October 1996. Residence: Gladstone, Virginia.

Children of Emmett S. and Linda D. (Tyree) Bolton:

1. Dana Lynn Bolton was born on July 14, 1982 in Lynchburg. (1126)
2. Erika Nicole Bolton was born on July 31, 1990 in Lynchburg. (1127)

Yolanda Jill (Walton) Harris (1047)

Yolanda Jill Walton, daughter of Winston D. and Glenice A. (Van Cleef) Walton, was born on Jan. 12, 1961. She graduated from Appomattox High School in 1979. Jill married William Jerry Harris, son of Tandy Watts and Elna Mae (Freeman) Harris of Evergreen, Appomattox County on June 20, 1981. Jerry was born on May 22, 1960 in Lynchburg Hospital. He graduated from Appomattox High School in 1978, and attended Central Virginia Community College in 1982 with an associate degree in machine technology. Jill also attended the same college for one and a-half years with a concentration in commercial art. Jerry works as a "new products technician" for Founders Fine Furniture. They attend the Evergreen United Methodist Church. Residence: Spout Spring, Virginia.

Children of William Jerry and Yolanda Jill (Walton) Harris:

1. Aaron Paul Harris was born on July 17, 1982 in Lynchburg Baptist Hospital. He graduated from Appomattox High School in 2000, where he played varsity football, baseball and basketball. He attended Ferrum College, and now works as a troubleshooter for Babcock-Wilcox. (1128)

2. Jordan Mark Harris was born on Sept. 17, 1985 in Lynchburg Baptist Hospital. He graduated from Appomattox High School in 2003, where he played varsity basketball. Jordan now lives in Colorado where he is working in the construction business. (1129)

Roger Farrel Walton (1048)

Roger Farrel Walton, son of Winston D. and Glenice A. (Van Cleef) Walton, was born on Nov. 26, 1962 in the Virginia Baptist Hospital in Lynchburg. He graduated from Appomattox High

School and earned an Associate Degree from Central Virginia Community College. He is employed by Framatome Cogema Fuels as a machinist. In addition, he co-owns a beef cattle farm with his father at Spout Spring. Roger married Connie Ruth Sage, daughter of Kermit Herschel and Wonda Ruth (Fannon) Sage, on Oct. 23, 1993 in Rustburg, Virginia. Connie was born on June 27, 1968 in South Boston, Virginia. She graduated from William Campbell High School and graduated with honors from Central Virginia Community College. She expects to receive a bachelor's degree from Bluefield College. Roger and Connie are members of Clearview Baptist Church in Rustburg. Residence: Spout Spring, Virginia.

Children of Roger F. and Connie R. (Sage) Walton:

1. Faith Nicole Walton was born on May 28, 1995 at Virginia Baptist Hospital in Lynchburg. She attends (in 2002) Clearview Christian School in Rustburg, Virginia. (1130)

Russel Scott Walton (1049)

Russel Scott Walton, son of Winston D. and Glenice A. (Van Cleef) Walton, was born on Oct. 30, 1967 at Spout Spring, Virginia. He graduated from Appomattox High School in 1986 and Ferrum College in 1990. Russel was an outstanding athlete in football and baseball at both schools. In January 2005, he was inducted into the Appomattox Scholastic Sports Hall of Fame. Russel is a manufacturing representative with Azdel Inc. in Forest, Virginia. He married Jennifer Marie Roach, daughter of John Aulden and Louise (Ranson) Roach, on Oct. 7, 1995 at Pamplin, Virginia. She was born on Nov. 30, 1972. Jennifer graduated from Appomattox High in 1990 and Radford University in 1994. Jennifer teaches fifth grade at Appomattox Elementary School. Residence: Pamplin, Virginia

Children of Russel and Jennifer (Roach) Walton:

1. Josey Corynn Walton was born in Virginia Baptist Hospital in Lynchburg, on June 14, 2001. (1131)

2. Ethan Walker Walton was born in Virginia Baptist Hospital in Lynchburg, on Dec. 27, 2003. (1132)

Robert Todd Kerns (1051)

Robert Todd Kerns, son of Wilmer L. and Shirley M. (Walton) Kerns, was born on April 3, 1969 in Alexandria, Virginia. He graduated from Yorktown High School in Arlington, Virginia. In 1992, he received a B.S. in Civil Engineering degree from Virginia Polytechnic and State University in Blacksburg. Rob expects to receive his MBA degree from Johns Hopkins University in May of 2005. He was formerly employed as a transportation engineer with Parsons Transportation, Washington, D. C. and now works for Freddie Mac at Tyson's Corner, Virginia. Rob married Christine Renee Albro, daughter of James and Barbara (Bell) Albro, on August 3, 1996 at Truro Episcopal Church in Fairfax, Virginia. Christine graduated with a Bachelor's degree in Psychology from Frostburg State University in Maryland in 1995, and received a Master of Science degree from Johns Hopkins University in Baltimore in 2003. She has held several positions in her career ladder, from an editor at the national headquarters of the American Psychological Association in Washington, D. C. to her present position with Booz, Allen and Hamilton as a senior computer security specialist. Residence: Great Falls, Virginia.

Child of Robert T. and Christine R. (Albro) Kerns:

1. Julia Bell Kerns was born on Aug. 12, 2003 at Reston, Virginia. She was baptized on Nov. 2, 2003 at St. Francis Episcopal Church in Great Falls. Julia is the pride and joy of her parents and grandparents. (1133)

Richard Mosby Harris Jr. (1054)

Richard Mosby Harris Jr., son of Richard M. Sr. and Mary Lorene (Gilliam) Harris, was born at Spout Spring, Virginia on Feb. 22, 1944. He is a dairy farmer. He married Joyce Hartless on March 8, 1969 at Amherst, Virginia. Joyce was born on Dec. 10, 1940. R. M. and Joyce are active in the annual reunion for the descendants of Eugene A. and Nannie K. (Jones) Walton. Residence: Spout Spring, Virginia.

Children of Richard M. Jr. and Joyce (Hartless) Harris:

1. Bryan Keith Harris was born on Oct. 31, 1970. He graduated from Appomattox High School in 1988. He graduated from a 2-year program at Virginia Tech in 1990. He lives at Spout Spring. (1134)

Marvin Earl Harris (1055)

Marvin Earl Harris, son of Richard M. Sr. and Mary Lorene (Gilliam) Harris, was born on Nov. 26, 1945 in Lynchburg, Virginia. He married Wanda Linda Jordon, daughter of James E. and Barbara (Caldwell) Jordon. She was born on May 5, 1950 in Lynchburg. Residence: Spout Spring, Virginia.

Children of Marvin E. and Wanda L. (Jordon) Harris:

1. Angela Lynn Harris was born on Dec. 18, 1972 in Lynchburg. She graduated from Appomattox High School in 1990. She attended Vocational Business College in Lynchburg, and is employed by First Colony Life Insurance in Lynchburg. (1135)

2. Michael Jordon Harris was born on Oct. 11, 1977. In 1996, he graduated from Appomattox High School. He attended Universal Technological Institute in Houston, Texas, and is employed by Valley Fuel Injection in Madison Heights, Virginia. Residence: Spout Spring, Virginia. (1136)

Frederick Eugene Payne Jr. (1059)

Frederick Eugene Payne Jr., son of Frederick E. Sr. and Juanita (Cundiff) Payne, was born on June 3, 1951 in Lynchburg. He first married Brenda Ramsey of Lovingston, Virginia on April 9, 1969 in Gaffney, South Carolina. He married second Cheryl Miller of Roanoke on July 31, 1975. The first two marriages ended in divorce. Freddie works as a supervisor at the Maple Leaf Bakery in Roanoke.[9] On Aug. 12, 2000, he married third Joan Rebecca Bryant of Roanoke. She was born on April 14, 1953 in Botetourt County.

---

[9] Information was provided by Frederick E. Payne Jr. during the Walton reunion at Spout Spring, Appomattox County on July 18, 1999.

Her daughter, Tracy Nicole Bryant, was born on May 18, 1979 in Botetourt County.[10] Residence: Roanoke, Virginia.

Child of Frederick E. Jr. and Brenda (Ramsey) Payne:

1. Bobby Eugene Payne was born on May 9, 1970 in Roanoke. He graduated from William Fleming High School in 1988, and graduated with honors in 2000 from the College of Health Sciences in Roanoke. (1137)

Child of Frederick E. Jr. and Cheryl (Miller) Payne is:

2. Frederick Vaden Payne was born on July 31, 1977 in Roanoke. He works as a quality technician for the Maple Leaf Bakery. (1138)

Nancy Louise (Payne) Banton (1060)

Nancy Louise Payne, daughter of John Gordon and Clara L. (Glover) Payne, was born on Dec. 17, 1946 in Lynchburg. She is employed as sales service coordinator for Crief Brothers Corp. in Gladstone. Nancy married George Reine Banton, son of John Dorman and Elizabeth (Watts) Banton, on June 21, 1969 in the Mineral Springs Baptist Church. He was born on May 21, 1947 at Gladstone. Both are active in the Amherst Baptist Church, and George is involved with Habitat.

Children of George R. and Nancy Louise (Payne) Banton:

1. John Christopher Banton was born on Aug. 26, 1973. He graduated from Radford University and now serves in the U. S. Marine Corps as a pilot. (1139)

2. Allison Payne Banton was born on Aug. 14, 1979. She graduated from Radford University and now works in the Development Office of Sweet Briar College. (1140)

Lynn Franklin Payne (1061)

Lynn Franklin Payne, son of John Gordon and Clara L. (Glover) Payne, was born on Dec. 3, 1947 in the Lynchburg Hospital. He

---

[10] Information was provided by Frederick E. Payne Jr. in July 2001 at the Walton reunion at Gladstone, Virginia.

served in the U. S. Army and is now an owner of a fast food restaurant in Norfolk, Virginia. Lynn married Norma Jean Turberville, daughter of Harold Turberville, on Aug. 12, 1969 at the Chesapeake Baptist Church. Norma teaches school in Chesapeake. Residence: Chesapeake, Virginia.

Children of Lynn F. and Norma Jean (Turberville) Payne:

1. Jennifer Lynn Payne was born on May 17, 1974. She is an audiologist at the Medical College of Virginia in Richmond. She married Kevin Douglas White on Sept. 26, 1998 in Chesapeake. (1141)

2. Michael Lynn Payne was born on April 20, 1976. He is employed by UPS in Chesapeake. (1142)

John Gordon Payne Jr. (1062)

John Gordon Payne Jr., son of John Gordon Sr. and Clara Louise (Glover) Payne, was born on July 10, 1954 in Lynchburg. He married first Jeanette Maddox, daughter of James and Margaret Maddox, of Lynchburg, on Aug. 15, 1974. He married second Dianna Sue Creasy of Bedford on April 30, 2001. He is owner of John Payne Excavating Company at Gladstone. Sue is employed at RR Donnelley & Sons in Lynchburg. Residence: Gladstone, Virginia.

Child of John Gordon Jr. and Jeanette (Maddox) Payne is:

1. Justin Adam Payne was born on Aug. 24, 1977. He married Amanda R. Byrd on July 1, 2000. Residence: West Chester, Ohio. (1143)

Child of John Gordon Jr. and Dianna S. (Creasy) Payne is:

2. Leah Creasy Payne was born on Jan. 24, 1989. (1144)

Ann Sterling (Payne) Cunningham (1063)

Ann Sterling Payne, daughter of S. Claiborne and Annie B. (Wills) Payne, was born on June 5, 1951. She is employed at G. E. Assurance Company in Lynchburg. Ann married Ray Lewis Cunningham, son of Cosby and Evelyn (Banton) Cunningham, on Oct. 9, 1971 at Mineral Springs Baptist Church, Gladstone, Virginia. Residence: Madison Heights, Amherst County, Virginia

Children of Ray L. and Ann S. (Payne) Cunningham: [11]

1. Brian Sterling Cunningham was born on Aug. 11, 1978 in Richmond, Virginia. He married Shannon Nicole Quinn, daughter of John and Denice Quinn, on Oct. 19, 2002. Brian graduated from Amherst County High School in 1996 and is employed by Toys-R-Us. Residence: Madison Heights, Virginia. (1145)

2. Stuart Matthew Cunningham was born on July 4, 1982 in Richmond. He graduated from Amherst High School. (1146)

Patsy Lyle (Payne) Loukides (1064)

Patsy Lyle Payne, daughter of S. Claiborne and Annie B. (Wills) Payne, was born on Sept. 26, 1952 in Lynchburg. She works as a social worker in the Department of Corrections, State of New Jersey. Patti married John W. Loukides, who was born on May 12, 1950 in Maryland. He is employed as an engineer for Metromedia Fiber Network, Inc. Residence: Jackson, New Jersey.

Children of John W. and Patsy L. (Payne) Loukides:[12]

1. Cory Loukides, born on July 7, 1978, and graduated from Virginia Polytechnic Institute in June 2001. (1147)

2. Bret Loukides, born on Dec. 18, 1979, and graduated from Ocean City College in New Jersey in June 2000. (1148)

3. Todd Loukides was born on Feb. 22, 1982. (1149)

4. Neil Loukides was born on Dec. 6, 1984. (1150)

5. Laura Loukides was born on Oct. 23, 1986. (1151)

---

[11] Information was provided by Ann S. (Payne) Cunningham to the compiler in personal interview at the Walton Reunion at Spout Spring, Virginia on July 19, 1998.

[12] Information provided by Mary Evelyn (Payne) Strickland. The family attended the annual Walton reunion in Nelson County, Virginia on July 20, 2003.

Millard Claiborne Payne (1065)

Millard Claiborn Payne, son of S. Claiborne and Annie B. (Wills) Payne, was born on May 31, 1954 in Lynchburg. He served four years in the U. S. Marine Corps and is now employed by Air Logistics of New Iberia, Louisiana. He married Doreen Rhode of Minnesota, the marriage ended in divorce. Residence: New Iberia, Louisiana.

Children of Millard C. and Doreen (Rhode) Payne:

>1. Nicole Elizabeth Payne was born on Oct. 23, 1979. She graduated from The University of Southern California. (1152)

>2. Brandon Travis Payne was born on Dec. 9, 1982. He graduated from New Iberia High School. (1153)

Robert Anthony Payne (1066)

Robert Anthony Payne, son of S. Claiborne and Annie B. (Wills) Payne, was born on Sept. 3, 1957 in Lynchburg. He is employed with Telecon Communications. Robert married Alicia Hill of Madison Heights, Virginia. Residence: Monroe, Virginia.

Children of Robert A. and Alicia (Hill) Payne:

>1. Timothy Craig Payne was born on Dec. 21, 1987. (1154)

>2. Casey Tyler Payne was born on Aug. 12, 1991. (1155)

Joseph Newton Marks (1067)

Joseph Newton Marks, son of Gene Newton and Sallie I. (Payne) Marks, was born on May 8, 1946 in Richmond, Virginia. He married Nancy Taylor of Lovingston on Aug. 1, 1970. Residence: Gladstone, Virginia.

Children of Joseph N. and Nancy (Taylor) Marks:

>1. Jeffrey Lynn Marks was born on July 15, 1971. He married Christine Snell on April 6, 1996. (1156)

>2. Jamie Michelle Marks was born on Sept. 18, 1976. She married John David Madden. She is a medical-surgical nurse at Farmville Hospital. (1157)

William Leonidas Watts III (1068)

William Leonidas Watts III, son of William L. Jr. and Sallie I. (Payne) Watts, was born on Sept. 27, 1951 in Lynchburg. He graduated from Nelson County High School and attended Ferrum College. He first married Shirley Hanson, whom he divorced, and married second Brenda Jones. He and Brenda operate a mercantile business at Gladstone. They are members of the Baptist Church. Residence: Gladstone, Virginia.

Child of William L. and Shirley (Hanson) Watts III:

1. Brian Michael Watts was born on June 18, 1977. (1158)

Child of William L. and Brenda (Jones) Watts III:

2. Courtney Blair Watts was born on Jan. 8, 1990. (1159)

Hugh Alvin Watts (1069)

Hugh Alvin Watts, son of William L. Jr. and Sallie I. (Payne) Watts, was born on March 21, 1957 in Lynchburg. He married first Janet Horsley of Gladstone in June 1974, and married second Margaret Lyons of Appomattox in May 1981, and married third Janice Hudson of Gladstone in April 1988. Hugh and Janice are in the mercantile business at Gladstone, Virginia.

Child of Hugh A. and Janet (Horsley) Watts is:

1. Sylvia Dawn Watts was born on Dec. 19, 1974. (1160)

Child of Hugh A. and Margaret (Lyons) Watts is:

2. Jonathan Watts was born on Dec. 12, 1981. (1161)

Children of Hugh A. and Janice (Hudson) Watts:

3. Jarrett Watts was born on Nov. 11, 1988. (1162)

4. Brittany Watts was born on Oct. 1, 1990. (1163)

Bessie Claire (Watts) Fitzgerald Ragland Angus (1071)

Bessie Claire Watts, daughter of William Jr. and Sallie I. (Payne) Watts, was born on March 9, 1961. She married first Delane

Fitzgerald Sr. on March 5, 1976 and was divorced. She married second Samuel Angus on July 13, 1983, and married third William Ragland on Dec. 12, 1990 and divorced. She married fourth David W. Angus Jr. on Feb. 14, 1999. Residence: Gladstone, Virginia.

Children of Delane and Bessie C. (Watts) Fitzgerald:

1. Delane Fitzgerald Jr. was born on Sept. 21, 1976. (1164)

2. Joseph Fitzgerald was born on Feb. 5, 1980. (1165)

Child of Samuel and Bessie C. (Watts) Angus:

3. Autom Amanda Faye Angus was born on Aug. 15, 1985. (1166)

Joseph Dudley Payne Jr. (1075)

Joseph Dudley Payne Jr., son of Joseph D. Sr. and Mary Sue (Boaz) Payne, was born on Aug. 22, 1959. He graduated from Lord Botetourt High School in 1977. He is employed as a terminal manager for Wendell Transport. He married Diane Hodge in 1979. Residence: Roanoke, Virginia.

Children of Joseph D. Jr. and Dianne (Hodge) Payne:[13]

1. Patricia Ann Payne was born on April 22, 1980. She attended Virginia Western Community College. (1167)

2. Melissa Dawn Payne was born on July 21, 1981. (1168)

3. Christopher Joseph Payne was born on Feb. 10, 1984. (1169)

Peyton Alan Harris (1079)

Peyton Alan Harris, son of Marshall W. and Rachel (Goin) Harris, was born on Aug. 9, 1963 in Richmond. He received a BA in Religious Studies from Virginia Commonwealth University in 1984 and a MDiv from Regent University, School of Divinity, Virginia Beach, Virginia in 1991. He married Clovia Marie Lee on Dec. 18, 1982. Peyton is an ordained minister in the Assemblies of God.

---

[13] Information was provided by Mrs. Joseph D. Payne Sr. during the Walton reunion in Appomattox County on July 18, 1999.

Children of Peyton A. and Clovia M. (Lee) Harris:

1. Emily Marie Harris was born on May 28, 1986. (1170)

2. Grace Lauren Harris was born on Oct. 28, 1989. (1171)

3. Colin Lee Harris was born on July 9, 1991. (1172)

Cheryl Elizabeth (Walton) Gullickson (1080)

Cheryl Elizabeth Walton, daughter of Lloyd G. and Shirley E. (Williams) Walton, was born on July 5, 1963. She married Richard Andrew Gullickson, son of Donald and Betty Gullickson of Huntington, West Virginia, on Aug. 8, 1987 at Memorial United Methodist Church, Appomattox, Virginia. Cheryl received a B.S. Degree in Human Nutrition and Foods at Virginia Tech in Blacksburg. She completed a dietetic internship at Walter Reed Army Hospital, Washington, D. C. Cheryl earned a M.S. Degree in Nutrition at Incarnate Word University, San Antonio, Texas. She is a registered dietician with critical care certification. Richard received B.A. and M.S. Degrees from Marshall University in Huntington, West Virginia in Health, Science and Physical Education. Richard is a career Medical Services Corps officer, Lieutenant Colonel, whose specialty is medical plans and operations.

Children of Richard A. and Cheryl E. (Walton) Gullickson:

1. Hannah Elizabeth Gullickson was born March 12, 1994. (1173)

2. Rebecca Lynn Gullickson was born Dec. 11, 1995. (1174)

Laura Gray (Walton) Bell (1081)

Laura Gray Walton, daughter of Lloyd G. and Shirley E. (Williams) Walton, was born on Nov. 23, 1964. She married Leonard Nathan Bell, son of Howard Morton and Verena (LaFuze) Bell, of Blacksburg, Virginia on June 20, 1987 at Memorial United Methodist Church in Appomattox, Virginia. Laura received a B.S. Degree in Housing, Interior Design, and Resource Management at Virginia Tech in Blacksburg, and a M.S. Degree in Housing and Gerontology at the University of Minnesota in St. Paul. In addition, she received a B.S. Degree in Nursing from Auburn University in Auburn, Alabama. She serves as Director of Quality Management and Research at East Alabama Medical Center, Opelika, Alabama. Leonard received a B.S. Degree in Chemistry at Virginia Tech, Blacksburg, and an M.S. and Ph.D. in Food Science at the University of Minnesota in St. Paul. He teaches and conducts research at Auburn University in Auburn, Alabama, where he is an associate professor.

Children of Leonard N. and Laura G. (Walton) Bell:

1. Matthew Walton Bell was born on June 10, 1991. (1175)

2. Morgan Benjamin Bell was born on Sept. 28, 1992. (1176)

3. Samantha Lauren Bell was born on March 20, 1998. (1177)

Harry Dean Adams (1082)

Harry Dean Adams, son of Walton F. and Earnie E. (Colley) Adams, was born on Sept. 13, 1939 at Bastian, Bland County, Virginia and died on Aug. 24, 2001 in Radford, Virginia. He graduated from high school in Clintwood, Dickenson County, Virginia and attended Clinch Valley College. Harry was employed by the Radford Army Ammunition Plant in Radford, Virginia from 1966 to 1998. Harry married Sandra Gay Browning on Oct. 15, 1959 in Wise County, Virginia. Residence: Radford, Virginia

Children of Harry D. and Sandra G. (Browning) Adams:[14]

1. Harry Dean Adams Jr. was born Sept. 22, 1965 at Norton, Wise County, Virginia. Children from a first marriage: Kristopher Dean Adams was born Nov. 9, 1991, and Jonathon Ray Adams was born Feb. 4, 1993. Jordayn Nicole Halstead is a daughter to his second marriage to Leona Halstead Adams. (1178)

2. Anthony Wayne Adams was born June 2, 1968 at Radford, Virginia. He married Tammy P. Lytton. Their children: Ashley Brooke Adams

---

[14] Information was provided by Anthony W. Adams, in an email <Aadams@kollmorgen> to the compiler on April 1, 2004.

was born Aug. 4, 1997 and Kacie Amber Adams was born Nov. 22, 2000. (1179)

3. Amy Eileen Adams was born Nov. 23, 1972 at Radford, Virginia. She married Jason Greene, whom she divorced in 1977. (1180)

Walton Franklyn Adams Jr. (1083)

Walton Franklin Adams Jr., son of Walton F. and Earnie E. (Colley) Adams Sr., was born on Aug. 7, 1944 at Bastian, Bland County, Virginia. He married Karen "Kay" Lee Crabtree on Aug. 30, 1964 in the Clintwood Baptist church in Dickenson County, Virginia. Kay was born Jan. 14, 1944 at Georges Fork, Dickenson County. Upon graduation from Clintwood High School at age sixteen, he entered Virginia Tech as an Air Force Cadet. After graduation from college, he was given a commission of 1st Lt. and sent to flight school at Craig Air Force Base in Selma, Alabama. He earned his pilot wings at age twenty-two. Frank had a variety of military experiences around the world before retiring in 1985 with the rank of Major. He retired to Dickenson County, where he worked in the field of automotive services.

Children of Walton F. and Karen L. (Crabtree) Adams:[15]

1. Walton Franklyn Adams III was born Feb. 17, 1967 in Tucson, Arizona. He married Corena Kay Rhodes on June 16, 1989 in Columbus, Ohio. He is a musician, and works in a technological field. Their child, Sarah Jane Adams was born Oct. 22, 1989. (1181)

2. Jason Andrew Adams was born April 29, 1969 in Goldsboro, North Carolina. He married Kari Kilgore on May 23, 1992 in Russell County, Virginia. Jason works in the field of computer technology. (1182)

Richard Lee Adams (1084)

Richard Lee Adams, son of Walton F. and Earnie E. (Colley) Adams Sr., was born on Nov. 1, 1946 in Bland County, Virginia. He married Elizabeth "Liz" Ann Elkins, daughter of Troy and Sarah

---

[15] Information on the Adams was provided by Karen (Crabtree) Adams to the compiler over a period of several years.

(Hamilton) Elkins, on Feb. 5, 1968. She was born Sept. 2, 1948 in Clintwood, Dickenson County, Virginia.

Children of Richard L. and Elizabeth A. (Elkins) Walton:

1. Stephania Yvonne Adams was born Dec. 30, 1968 in Kingsport, Tennessee. (1183)

2. Richard Donovan Adams was born July 25, 1970 in Kingsport, Tennessee. He married Kelly Hall on Oct. 30, 1992. She was born Nov. 17, 1972 and died Dec. 27, 1998. Their children: James Richard Lee Adams was born Jan. 11, 1993 and Courtney Danielle Adams was born Nov. 10, 1994. (1184)

Kyle Ann (Tutwiler) Spicer (1096)

Kyle Ann Tutwiler, daughter of Guy I. and Jean E. (Minton) Tutwiler, was born on Jan. 20, 1954 in Okinawa. She married first Daniel E. White on Aug. 24, 1973 in Tulsa, Oklahoma. They divorced in 1993. Kyle married second Thomas O. Spicer on March 18, 1994 in Bella Vista, Arkansas. She received a nursing degree from the University of Arkansas in 1976. She serves as an operating room nurse. Thomas received his B.S., M.S., and Ph.D. degrees in chemical engineering from the University of Arkansas. He is currently serving as Department Head of Chemical Engineering at the University of Arkansas. Residence: Fayetteville, Arkansas.

Child of Daniel E. and Kyle A. (Tutwiler) White

1. Jacob Earl White was born on July 6, 1978 in Springdale, Washington County, Arkansas. (1185)

Child of Thomas O. and Kyle A. (Tutwiler) Spicer

2. Elizabeth Ann Spicer was born on March 19, 1998 in Fayetteville, Washington County, Arkansas. (1186)

Chapter 10

Tenth Generation

Glenell Louise (Carson) Peterson (1114)

Glenell Louise (Carson) Peterson, daughter of Eugene W. and Frances A. (Carson) Carson, was born on July 10, 1961 at Radford, Virginia. She received an undergraduate degree from Virginia Tech in Blacksburg and a Master's degree in Museum Science from Texas Tech in Lubbock, Texas. Glenell married Steven R. Peterson in New Mexico. He was born on July 6, 1959 in Albuquerque. Steve has a degree from Texas Tech, and works for Unichem He is also a volunteer fireman. Residence: Carlsbad, New Mexico.

Children of Steven R. and Glenell L. (Carson) Peterson:

1. Emily Frances Peterson was born on Nov. 25, 1987.

2. Eric Wade Peterson was born on Sept. 7, 1989.

3. Sarah Katherine Peterson was born on April 30, 1994.

Mildred Adair (Carson) Newman (1115)

Mildred Adair Carson, daughter of Eugene W. and Frances A. (Carson) Carson, was born on Nov. 4, 1962 at Radford, Virginia. She received a Bachelors degree in English from Virginia Tech and a degree from the California Culinary Academy. She married Gerry Newman on top of Mount Tamalpais at Mill Valley, California on Sept. 23, 1989. Gerry was born on Dec. 13, 1957 in Portland, Oregon. They own and operate the Albemarle Bakery in Charlottesville, Virginia.

Children of Gerry and Mildred A. (Carson) Newman:

1. Irene Adair Newman was born on Nov. 2, 1991 in Charlottesville.

2. Carson Joseph Newman was born Jan. 3, 1994 in Charlottesville.

3. Frances Ceceilia Newman was born Oct. 5, 2001 in Charlottesville.

Lynn Catherine (Carson) Harris (1116)

Lynn Catherine Carson, daughter of Eugene W. and Frances A. (Carson) Carson, was born on Nov. 13, 1963 in Raleigh, North

Carolina. She married Brett Harris of Fairfax County, Virginia. Both graduated from Virginia Tech with a degree in engineering. Brett earned a Master's degree in engineering from the University of Michigan. He worked for Mechanical Dynamics, Inc. until it was bought by MSC Software in Ann Arbor. Lynn is a substitute teacher in Chelsea and works part time in a knitting shop. Residence: Chelsea, Michigan.

Children of Brett and Lynn C. (Carson) Harris:

1. Duncan Walker Harris, born on Sept. 20, 1991 in Ann Arbor, Michigan. He plays in the Chelsea Fiddle Club.

2. Martin Turner Harris was born on June 19, 1993 in Ann Arbor. He plays in the Chelsea Fiddle Club.

Katherine Ellen (Beasley) Lockwood Garnett (1117)

Katherine Ellen Beasley, daughter of Kemper M. and Harriette W. (Carson) Beasley Jr. was born on Dec. 28, 1969 in Farmville, Virginia. She graduated from Appomattox High School and received a Bachelor's degree from Mary Washington College. In 1998, she received a Master's degree from Lynchburg College. Kathy Ellen taught at Yorktown High School, and is now Librarian at Brentsville High School in Prince William County, Virginia. Her marriage to Robert Lockwood of New Rochelle, New York ended in divorce. Kathy Ellen married second James Mercer Garnett Jr., whose birthday was in August 1970. He is a Farm Bureau Agent in Prince William County. Residence: Manassas, Virginia.

Children of James M. Jr. and Katherine E. (Beasley) Garnett:

1. James M. Garnett III was born Nov. 5, 2001.

2. Carson Beasley Garnett was born Oct. 1, 2003.

3. Jackson Tate Garnett was born Oct. 1, 2003.

Robin Renee (Carson) Reynolds (1119)

Robin Renee Carson, daughter of William P. and Elaine (Carter) Carson, was born on Feb. 4, 1972 in Appomattox County. She married Phillip Walton Reynolds. Residence: Red House, Charlotte County, Virginia.

Children of Philip W. and Robin R. (Carson) Reynolds:

1. Brandon Scott Cash was born on July 19, 1993.

2. Tyler Carson Reynolds was born on June 7, 1998.

Patrick Scott Carson (1120)

Patrick Scott Carson, son of William P. and Elaine (Carter) Carson, was born July 8, 1973. He married Stacy Kolech of New Jersey. Apparently they are separated. Residence: Charlotte Courthouse, Virginia.

Children of Patrick S. and Stacy (Kolech) Carson:

1. Hunter Scott Carson was born on Jan. 8, 1996.

2. Cody Parker Carson.

Jeffrey Lynn Marks (1156)

Jeffrey Lynn Marks, son of Joseph N. and Nancy (Taylor) Marks, was born on July 15, 1971. He married Christine Snell on April 6, 1996 in Lynchburg. He is currently serving with the U.S. Marines in Germany.

Children of Jeffrey L. and Christine (Snell) Marks:

1. Anna S. Marks was born on Jan. 4, 1991 to a previous marriage of Christine's— adopted by Jeffrey.

2. Kaley Samantha Marks was born on Oct. 6, 1999.

3. Magan Sarah Marks was born on May 14, 2002.

Jamie Michelle (Marks) Madden (1157)

Jamie Michelle Marks, daughter of Jeffrey L. and Christine (Snell) Marks, was born on Sept. 18, 1976. She married John David Madden on Dec.18, 2000. She is a medical-surgical nurse at Southside Hospital in Farmville, Virginia.

Child of John D. and Jamie M. (Marks) Madden:
1. Kaleb Alexandria Madden was born on July 7, 2001.

The picture below goes with Numbers (810) and (975)

Front row, L-R, Mary C. (Harris) Walton, Shirley (Williams) Walton, Clarence N. Hancock. Back row, Dallas E. Walton, Ruth (Harris) Walton, Lloyd G. Walton

Chapter 11

Allied Families in Central Virginia Counties

Present-day Appomattox, Amherst, Buckingham, Campbell, Charlotte, Cumberland, Goochland, Nelson, and Powhatan Counties, Virginia were considered to be the western frontier for seventeenth century settlers who lived in the Chesapeake Bay region. Explorers and traders traveled westward through this area in search of Indian villages for commerce and desirable land for settlement. Also, explorers sought to discover the western waters, which they believed to be the Indian Ocean. In 1650, Edward Bland made one such inland journey. In 1670, Capt. William Harris led twenty-one militiamen from Henrico County on a trip west to accompany explorer John Lederer. Governor Sir William Berkeley commissioned the exploration. After crossing what is now Buckingham County, the party stopped just short of the James River, where U.S. 60 passes through the village of Bent Creek in present Appomattox County. Lederer believed that they were in the middle of the Appalachian Mountains. The rolling hills of present Powhatan, Cumberland, Buckingham and Amherst had misled the explorers. They climbed Pruett's Mountain in Western Buckingham—1,000 feet high, and described the next ten miles as barren hills naked of wood and white cliffs (in present-day Amherst and Nelson Counties). Refusing to cross the James River near Bent Creek, the party headed south into North Carolina. This expedition left behind a journal that gave detailed descriptions of the trip. Briceland[1] has proven the exact course of Lederer's expedition by comparing the journal accounts with modern topological maps developed by the U.S. Geological Survey.

By the 1720s, the gentry of Virginia commenced buying western lands for their descendants and for investment purpose. Large tracts of prime land were surveyed in present-day Cumberland, Charlotte, Campbell, Buckingham and Appomattox Counties. Old Virginia names such as Moseley, Randolph, Webb, Mayo—the surveyor, Carrington, and Cary, appeared on the first land patent records. The

---

[1] Alan Vance Briceland, *Westward From Virginia: The Exploration of the Virginia-Carolina Frontier, 1650-1710)*, (Charlottesville, Virginia: University of Virginia Press, 1987), pp. 92-100.

Waltons came West by 1730, which was the beginning of the second decade of expansion.

On Sept. 27, 1729, Henry Cary, 1675-1750, bought 3,942 acres at a place called Buckingham, on the west side and on the branches of Buck River, alias Willis's Creek."[2] We know that Willis Creek originates in Buckingham County, and flows into northern Cumberland County before emptying into the James River near Cartersville. It is believed this land was given to his son Archibald Cary, 1721-1787, who lived, according to eighteenth century maps, along the major road in Buckingham County. This may be misleading, because Archibald developed a tenant farming system—absentee ownership, and maintained his legal residence in Chesterfield County, which County he represented in the Virginia Assembly. The multi-1,000-acre farm was a large agricultural (and possibly mining) operation that employed many slaves and white laborers. In 1763, the overseer for the Cary operation was Joseph Fuqua Sr.

According to the will of Archibald Cary, his house was built at the Fork of Willis River. This farm was willed to daughter Mary, who married Carter Page. Another farm, called "Red Oak," was willed to his daughter Jane Cary, who married Archibald Bolling. Peter Stratton, 1761-1835, later purchased "Red Oak," which is located in the eastern part of present-day Buckingham County.

Aug. 20, 1734, Henry Cary bought[3] "...320 acres on Bent Creek of the Appomattox River adjoining William Moseley and company." This was not the same Bent Creek that flows into the James River where it intersects U.S. Route 60. There was also a Bent Creek that flowed into the Appomattox River. The source of the Appomattox River is at a spring just north of the town of Appomattox, and it flows in the opposite direction to Petersburg,

---

[2] Virginia Land Records, *Goochland County Patents* 13, 1725-30, dated Sept. 27, 1729, p. 423.

[3] Virginia Land Records, *Goochland County Patents* 15, 1732-35, Aug. 20, 1734, p. 272.

Virginia. A third grant for 1,520 acres in Goochland County, adjacent to the second one, was subsequently issued to Henry Cary. A history of ownership of these estates is being studied to determine how they were used to benefit descendants of Henry Cary.

A fourth land patent for 400 acres, also in Goochland County at that time, was issued to Henry Cary on Nov. 25, 1743. This is significant because it has implications for the Harrison and Word families. It was described as being on both sides of Hatcher's Creek, a branch of Willis's River.[4] At first, this appeared to be in Buckingham, but now it is believed that this is the same land that was transferred to his son-in-law and daughter, Benjamin and Priscilla (Cary) Harrison. An additional 200 adjacent acres was granted at Horn's Quarter Creek in Cumberland County. The location of these lands is on the western side of present-day Cumberland County, and north of U.S. Route 60. The land fits the geographical description given in land records, and is registered on U.S. Geological Survey maps.

It should be noted that some of the founding fathers of Cumberland and Buckingham Counties were related. Col. Clement Reed was a vestryman in Cumberland County before he moved to Lunenburg County. The first clerk of the court for Buckingham County was David Bell, who married Judith Cary, daughter of Henry and Anne (Edwards) Cary. Priscilla Harrison and Judith Bell were sisters. David's son, Col. Henry Bell, 1745-1811, married Rebecca Harrison, sister of Lockey Harrison who married Thomas Word, 1740-1815. Henry served as High Sheriff for Buckingham County. Also he was the County Surveyor for many years, including lands for his brother-in-law, Thomas Word. Cary Harrison, son of Benjamin and Priscilla Harrison, married Sarah Bell, sister of Rebecca (Bell) Harrison. He owned a Buckingham estate, according to tax records. All of these families were members of the ruling class.

---

[4] Virginia Land Records, *Goochland County Patents* 23, 1743-45, Nov. 25, 1743, p. 636.

Buckingham County, which today has one of the lowest per capita incomes in the Commonwealth, is rich in minerals. Bernard G. Booker, 1787-1859, started the gold rush in Buckingham County in 1830. The County was a leading Virginia producer of gold for half a century. Willis Mountain has almost been destroyed— leveled— by companies mining valuable minerals, especially kyanite. The kyanite mine is not confined to Willis Mountain, but a vein of the mineral extends bout two miles east of Willis Mountain on land formerly owned by Archibald Cary. This kyanite mine operation is a major supplier of kyanite for the international market. Buckingham slate is also known nationwide.

The genealogy of allied families that follow are the result of many years of research. Although the court records in Buckingham County were destroyed by fire in 1869 and Appomattox County records burned in 1892, these unpublished genealogies were gleaned from a variety of sources such as Federal and State archives, Universitiy libraries and special collections, Bible records and private papers, and on-site research in cemeteries, etc., as well as the surviving court records. For the descendants of Eugene A. Walton, 1850-1921, and his wife Nannie K. Jones of Appomattox County, these chapters contain information on your direct lineage: Christian, Fields, Harris, Harvey, Hunter, Jones, Vawter, Walker, and Williamson.

Chapter 12
Booker Families of Gloucester, Amelia, Cumberland and Buckingham Counties

Booker family researchers believe that Edward Booker, a native of England, was the first Booker to set foot in Virginia.[1] He and his brother-in-law, Richard Glover, were engaged in tobacco trading and shipping between the Colony of Virginia and England. Glover was a London merchant and trader. It is believed that Edward Booker visited the Colony to attend to business, but maintained his residence in England with a brief period in Holland, 1648-1656. Edward Booker appointed his brother-in-law to act as his lawful attorney.[2] There is no direct evidence to prove that this Edward was the originator of Bookers in Colonial Virginia. Indeed, he was probably too old to have been the father of Captain Richard Booker.

Capt. Richard Booker Sr.

Richard Booker Sr. was known as Captain Richard Booker of "ye parish of Abingdon in ye County of Gloucester." At least two land grants were recorded to him in the County: 740 acres in July 1685 (*L Book 7*, p. 540); and 180 acres on April 20, 1694. Also, he bought land in other counties, such as 613 acres in Essex County on Oct. 20, 1704. Booker bought 250 acres from David Coghills on July 20, 1692. The land was situated near the head of Port Tobacco Creek in

---

[1] See *Genealogies of Virginia Families*, (Baltimore, Maryland: Genealogical Publishing Company), Vol. 1, 1981, pp. 174-188. This was a reprint from Vol. VII (1899-1900) of the *Virginia Magazine of History and Biography*, "The Booker Family" by W. G. Stanard. Dr. Jean Marshall von Schilling accomplished the most recent and thorough analysis of the Booker family in her 1996 publication, *Booker Descendants of Captain Richard Booker of Abingdon Parish, Gloucester County, Virginia*. Another comprehensive source is "The Booker Connection" by Don Booker, P. O. Box 210, Dover, AR 72837. He is compiling information on all branches of the Booker family. I also acknowledge a fourteen-page handwritten manuscript in the Alderman Library in the University of Virginia, "Some Booker Genealogy Compiled by Dr. Joseph D. Eggleston of Hampden-Sydney College, George E. Booker, attorney of Richmond, Virginia and the late Capt. John Agee Booker, CSA of Cumberland, Virginia." The citation is "Papers of the Booker, Perkins, and Dabney Families," Accession No. 2317-C, Box Number 2317, Folder Dates 1836-1863, 1935.

[2] York County, Virginia *Record Book 1638-1648*, p. 2.

Rappahannock County. Finally, John and Mary Underhill of York County sold 200 acres to Booker, Sept. 24, 1692. Booker was alluded to as living in the upper side of Fellgate's Creek in Abingdon Parish, Gloucester County.[3]

In 1680, he was listed as a Captain in the Gloucestor County militia.[4] Also, he served as Justice of the Court, and as a member of the Quorum in Gloucester County.

It is believed that Capt. Richard Booker Sr. was twice-married. His first wife was Rebecca Leake whose father, John Leake, was an innkeeper in York County. A record dated in 1672 stated that Richard Booker of Gloucester was his son-in-law. At least six children are known to have been born to the first marriage. Richard Booker married second, in 1694, to Hannah (Hand) Marshall, daughter of Richard and Frances (Purefoy) Hand. Hannah first married William Marshall, formerly of Barbados, who later served as justice of the peace for Elizabeth City County before being murdered in Hampton by sailors in 1692. Capt. Richard and Hannah (Hand) Booker had two children, as shown below.

Children of Capt. Richard Sr. and Rebecca (Leake) Booker:

1. Judith Booker, of whom nothing more is known. Judith was a common name in the Booker family.

2. Ann Booker was born in Abingdon Parish, Gloucester County, Virginia. The will of her half-sister, Frances (Booker) Stokes, suggests that she married Francis Anderson.

3. Edward Booker was baptized June 2, 1680, and died Nov. 2, 1750. he served in the House of Burgesses from 1736 to 1747. He probably married first Mary Goode, and married second Judith (Archer) Worsham, widow of Daniel Worsham, 1690-1727. Edward was one of the first justices in Amelia County, when it was formed from Prince

---

[3] Dr. Jean von Schilling of Richmond, Virginia informed the compiler that Fellgate's Creek is in York County, letter dated April 5, 1996.

[4] William Armstrong Crozier, *Virginia Colonial Militia, 1651-1776*, (Baltimore, Maryland: Genealogical Publishing Company), reprinted 1973, p. 104.

George County in 1736. He also served in the House of Burgesses representing Amelia County during 1736-1747.[5]

Children of Edward and Mary (Goode) Booker:

a. Lucy Booker was born circa 1706 and died circa 1761.[6] She married Richard Clarke on March 10, 1736 in Amelia County. Richard's will was filed in Amelia County on Aug. 29, 1748.

b. Richard Booker[7] was born on July 28, 1707 in Henrico County, Virginia and died on April 13, 1760 in Amelia County. He married Rachel Marot, daughter of Jean and Anne (Pasteur) Marot.

c. Rebecca Booker married Thomas Tabb, son of John Tabb and Martha (Hand) Tabb on April 10, 1736.[8] This was the second marriage for Thomas, his first being to Elizabeth Mayo. Thomas was a wealthy plantation owner, his "Clay Hill" plantation of 6,734 acres being in Amelia County. He was also involved in slave trading. Thomas also served as a justice and sheriff for Amelia County, as well as a representative in the Virginia House of Burgesses. Thomas died on Nov. 23, 1769 at "Clay Hill.".

d. Mary Booker was born circa 1711 and died on Nov. 3, 1769.[9] She married Samuel Tarry. After Mary's death, Samuel married second Mary Crawley.

e. Edward Booker was born on Dec. 30, 1715 and died on his father's plantation "Winterham." His will was filed on Dec. 21, 1759 and was probated on March 27, 1760. Edward married Ann Cobbs, daughter of Samuel and Edith (Marot) Cobbs, on Feb. 21, 1739 in Amelia County.

f. Hannah Booker

Child of Edward and Judith (Archer) Booker:

---

[5] Cynthia Miller Leonard, compiler, *The General Assembly of Virginia, 1619-1978: A Bicentennial Register of Members*, (Richmond, Virginia: The Virginia State Library), 1978, pp. 76-80.

[6] Amelia County, Virginia *Will Book 1*.

[7] http://www.virginians.com/redirect.htm?topics&bk, "The Family History of John W. Pritchett."

[8] *Ibid.*

[9] *Ibid.*

g. Judith Booker married Peter Bland, son of Richard Jr. and Anne (Poythress) Bland, on Nov. 26, 1761 in Amelia County, Virginia.[10]

4. Richard Booker Jr. was baptised Oct. 29, 1688, and died April 25, 1743. He first married Margaret Lowry, daughter of William and Frances (Purefoy) Lowry. His second wife was named Martha Bryan. In 1730, Richard Jr. served as a justice in James City County. He patented 970 acres in Prince George County, now in Amelia County.

5. John Booker was baptised on Aug. 3, 1690, and nothing more is known about him.

6. Edmund Booker was born circa 1692 and died in 1753. His wife was probably Jane Davis.[11] Not much is known about them at this time. No Edmund Booker served in the Virginia House of Burgesses during 1736-1748.[12] This Edmund is not the same person who represented Amelia County in the Virginia House of Burgesses in 1778.

Children of Capt. Richard and Hannah (Hand) Booker:

7. Frances Booker, born circa 1696, married a Mr. Stokes. She filed her will on Nov. 1, 1752 in Amelia County, and it was proven on Dec. 27, 1752 in Amelia, with no issue. A large estate was divided among her relatives, including her brother George and his children.

8. George Booker was born circa 1697 and died about 1760, in Gloucester County. George is said to have first married Grace Richeson and second to Sarah Spann. George is our lineage of interest via his first marriage.

George Booker Sr.

George Booker Sr., son of Capt. Richard and Hannah (Hand) Booker Sr., was born circa 1697 in Gloucester County, and was still

---

[10] http://www.virginians.com/redirect.htm?topics&bk, "The Family History of John W. Pritchett."

[11] See discussion in Jean Marshall von Schilling, Ph. D., *Booker Descendants of Captain Richard Booker of Abingdon Parish, Gloucester County, Virginia*, (Richmond, Virginia: Privately Printed), 1996, p. 35.

[12] See Cynthia Miller Leonard, *The General Assembly of Virginia, 1619-1978: A Bicentennial Register of Members*, (Richmond, Virginia: The Virginia State Library), 1978, pp. 76-81.

living in Gloucester County in 1752 when his sister Frances (Booker) Stokes named him in her will. George married first Grace Richeson, daughter of Peter and Sarah Richeson. She was baptised on March 11, 1700 and died before 1730. George married second Sarah Spann, daughter of Richard Spann, Dec. 11, 1730. Sarah was baptized on Oct. 13, 1706 in Abingdon Parish and died on Nov. 24, 1750. Although no records have been located to document the death date for George Booker, it is believed that he may have died in Amelia County.

Children of George Sr. and Grace (Richeson) Booker:

1. Richard Booker was born about 1720 and died on Jan. 18, 1764. He married Martha Brunskill, of whom more information follows.

2. George Booker Jr. was born March 5, 1721 in Gloucester County, and died in January 1791 in Amelia County.[13] He married Sarah Cobbs, daughter of Col. Samuel and Edith (Marot) Cobbs, of "Huntington," Amelia County, Oct. 12, 1745.

Children of George Jr. and Sarah (Cobbs) Booker:[14]

a. Edith Booker was born circa 1746, and died on Feb. 14, 1822 in Wilkes County, Georgia. Edith married William Booker Jr., son of William Marshall and Mary (Condon) Booker, on May 14, 1768 in Amelia County. William was born on Oct. 10, 1745 in Amelia County, Virginia and died on Sept. 20, 1847 in Wilkes County. He was a soldier in the American Revolution.

b. Judith Booker was born on Nov. 24, 1748 in Amelia County, and died after 1806.[15] She married Blackburn Hughes, son of Anderson, 1747-1818, and Elizabeth (Blackburn) Hughes, on Dec. 22, 1779 in Amelia County. At least four children were born to their union. This family lived in Cumberland County, Virginia.

---

[13] Amelia County, Virginia *Will Book 4*.

[14] The information on the children is a consolidation of information presented by Jean M. von Schilling and Don Booker. Other sources are cited.

[15] http://freepages.genealogy.rootsweb.com/~cobb/

c. Richeson Booker was born circa 1752 and died in 1806 in Amelia County.[16] Richeson served in the Revolutionary War. Apparently he did not marry.

d. Elizabeth Booker was born circa 1754 and died after 1791. She married Burton Hudson, son of Nicholas Hudson, on Oct. 28, 1779 in Amelia County. After Burton's death in 1785, Elizabeth married second Richard Royall of Powhatan County, and married third John Morris.

e. George Booker III was born circa 1756 in Amelia County. He was named in his father's will "if he returns to the States." Dr. Eggleston stated that George went to sea and was not heard from again.[17]

e. Efford Booker was born circa 1758 in Amelia County and died on Oct. 12, 1798 on his plantation "Hog Castle" in Amelia County.[18] He married Mary Hudson, daughter of Nicholas Hudson, on March 2, 1782 in Amelia County.

f. Sarah Booker was born circa 1760 in Amelia County and died before 1797. She married John Childress on Dec. 20, 1780 in Amelia County. John married second Nancy Holly in 1797 in Greenbrier County, Virginia.

g. Grace Booker was born circa 1762 in Amelia County, and died in Prince Edward County, Virginia in 1841. She married Absolom Farmer on May 24, 1787.

3. Sarah Booker was born on Jan. 2, 1722 and was baptized on Jan. 23, 1722, per Parish register in Gloucester County. Sarah married Thomas Mumford, son of Joseph Mumford, on Dec. 22, 1744 in Gloucester County, Virginia. In 1757, they moved to Amelia County, where Thomas later served two terms as sheriff.

4. Edward Booker was born circa 1724 and died in 1761 in Amelia County, Virginia. He married Hannah Clarke, daughter of Richard and Lucy (Booker) Clarke. Their son George Booker settled in Prince Edward County. They had a daughter named Lucy Booker.

---

[16] *Virginia Argus*, Nov. 11, 1806, p. 3, c. 5. Richeson's will was filed in Amelia County *Will Book 6*, pp. 281-282, and *Will Book 7*, p. 201.

[17] "Booker Connections," by Don Booker of Dover, Arkansas.

[18] Amelia County, Virginia *Will Book 2*, p. 77; *Will Book 7*, p. 124; and *Will Book 11*, p. 379.

Children of George and Sarah (Spann) Booker: [19]

    5. John Booker was born on March 8, 1730/1731, and died after 1759. He and his wife Mary had two children who died in 1759 and 1761 respectively.

    6. William Booker was born in 1743 and died in 1748.

    7. Mary Booker was born about 1746 and died in 1786. She married Benjamin Seawell Jr., 1741-1821, of Gloucester and Brunswick Counties. The Seawells moved to North Carolina where Benjamin served in the Revolutionary War.

Richard Booker

Richard Booker, son of George and Grace (Richeson) Booker, was born about 1720, and his will was written and recorded in Amelia County on Jan. 18, 1764. Apparently, he died at age 44. Richard married Martha Brunskill. William Brunskill stated in his will that Richard Booker was his son-in-law.[20]

Children of Richard and Martha (Brunskill) Booker:

    1. George Booker was born about 1750 and allegedly died in 1819 in Buckingham County. If so, there is no record of his being a land owner nor was he assessed for personal property taxes in Buckingham County. von Schilling is correct in her assertion that George Booker never lived in Buckingham County.[21] If George was married, we have no record of his spouse and children. Who was the George Booker who died on Sunday, Nov. 15, 1816 in Elizabeth City in the sixtieth year of his life?[22] Could he have been this George Booker?

    2. Richard Booker Jr. was born about 1751 and died in 1818 in Cumberland County, Virginia. He married Lucy Hobson, daughter of

---

[19] von Schilling, pp. 60-61.

[20] Cumberland County, Virginia *Deed Book 2*, p. 535.

[21] von Schilling devoted Chapter 5 of her book to "The Problem of George," which is a very good analysis. See pp. 84-88.

[22] *Richmond Enquirer*, Dec. 14, 1816 issue, p. 3, c. 5.

Adcock and Joanna (Lawson) Hobson, June 15, 1780, in Cumberland County.

3. Peter Richeson Booker was born circa 1753 and died before 1785. There is disagreement on the identity of this Peter Richeson Booker. The personal property and land tax records do not support the theory that Peter lived in Buckingham County. He is not the same man who died in Amelia County in 1806. Attorney George Booker III wrote to Dr. Joseph D. Eggleston that Peter's wife "Elizabeth Morris was a noted beauty of Buckingham." He added that Peter owned the gold mine in that County.[23] The Peter S. Booker, 1814-1890, who married the beautiful Elizabeth A. Morris in 1837 in Buckingham County was a son of Bernard G. Booker, 1787-1859, and his wife Mary Stratton. The gold mine was not owned by any Peter Booker, but by Peter's father, Bernard G. Booker, as proven by detailed analyses of land tax records for Buckingham County.

4. Samuel Booker Sr. was born circa 1754, and died in 1788.[24] He served as a Captain in the Continental Line of the Revolutionary War.[25] Samuel married Martha Munford, daughter of James Munford, Dec. 25, 1784, in Amelia County.

5. William Booker was born about 1757, and was named in his father's will. He was listed as a minor child in 1771, under the guardianship of Edmund Booker.[26] Nothing further is known about this William.[27]

6. Edward Booker was born circa 1758 in Amelia County, and died intestate in 1800 in Cumberland County. Edward married Edith Cobbs Anderson in 1783 in Amelia County.

---

[23] Jean Marshall von Schilling, Ph. D. *Booker Descendants of Captain Richard Booker of Abingdon Parish, Gloucester County, Virginia*, (Richmond, Virginia: Privately Printed), 1996, p. 79.

[24] von Schilling, p. 81.

[25] William Armstrong Crozier, *Virginia Colonial Militia, 1651-1776*, (Baltimore, Maryland: Genealogical Publishing Company), reprinted 1973, p. 38.

[26] von Schilling, p. 79.

[27] Jean von Schilling believes that this William Booker died relatively young.

7. Marshall Booker was born circa 1759, and died in 1806, in Cumberland County, Virginia. He married Martha "Patsy" Gaines, daughter of Maj. Bernard and Margaret Gaines.

8. Grace Booker, born circa 1761, married John Walthall, an Irishman, on Jan. 8, 1782, in Amelia County. They resettled in Franklin County, Tennessee, where John signed his will in 1817.

Richard Booker Jr.

Richard Booker Jr., son of Richard Sr. and Martha (Brunskill) Booker, was born about 1751 in Amelia County, Virginia and died in 1818[28] in Cumberland County, Virginia. He was living in Cumberland County when the personal property taxes were assessed in 1782. Richard was still living in Cumberland County at Tar Wallet Creek in 1815, four miles southeast of the old courthouse in Cumberland County.[29] He married Lucy Hobson, daughter of Adcock and Joanna (Lawson) Hobson, June 15, 1780, in Cumberland County.

Children of Richard and Lucy (Hobson) Booker:[30]

1. Peter Richeson Booker was born on July 11, 1781 in Cumberland County and died on May 10, 1839 in Maury County, Tennessee.[31] He married first Susan McLemore Gray on April 1, 1806 in Williamson County, Tennessee.[32] Susan died in 1829 and Peter married second

---

[28] *Virginia Patriot and Richmond Daily Mercantile Advertiser*, May 1, 1818 issue, p. 2, c. 5.

[29] Roger G. Ward, compiler, *1815 Directory of Virginia Landowners*, (Athens, Georgia: Iberian Publishing Company), vol 1, 1997, p. 81.

[30] Source of information for the children was von Schilling, p. 80. The information was supplemented by records from Maury County.

[31] Maury County, Tennessee *Will Book of 1838-1839*, p. 447.

[32] From "The Booker Connection," by Don Booker of Dover, Arkansas. See also Jean Marshall von Schilling, Ph. D., *Booker Descendants of Captain Richard Booker of Abingdon Parish, Gloucester County, Virginia*, (Richmond, Virginia: Privately Printed), 1996, p. 80.

Cynthia Holland Rhodes in Giles County, Tennessee.[33] Peter went to Tennessee very early in life where in 1807 he settled near Columbia, Maury County. Peter was an attorney and a wealthy plantation owner at four locations: 640 acres at Cotton Gin, Monroe County, Mississippi; Lauderdale County, Alabama; DeSota County, Mississippi; as well as Maury County. An 1830 deed shows that he owned land in Franklin County, Tennessee.[34] He also owned land in Madison County, Tennessee.[35]

Children of Peter R. and Susan M. (Gray) Booker:[36]

    a. Richard M. Booker was born on July 14, 1808 and died on Nov. 14, 1831. Burial was in the Booker Cemetery in Maury County.

    b. James Gray Booker was born on Nov. 4, 1809 in Williamson County, Tennessee and died on Aug. 19, 1846 in Maury County. He married Eleanor Matheny Smiser on Feb. 24, 1835. James inherited

    c. Lucy Hobson Booker was born in 1813 and died in 1837.

    d. Henry Leonidas Booker was born on Aug. 9, 1814 and died on March 31, 1841. He married Mary Ann Porter on Nov. 10, 1840. She married second William Webster.

    e. Martha Elizabeth Booker was born circa 1816. She married first Adam Dickey and married second Armstead F. Bracken on Aug. 7, 1843 in Alabama.

    f. Albert Booker was born on April 22, 1820 and died on June 25, 1856. He married Ruth Allen Johnson, 1826-1889, daughter of Alexander and Mary (Bellenfant) Johnson, on Oct. 17, 1843 in Maury County. Burial was in

---

[33] Peter named his wife Cynthia in his will dated Oct. 5, 1838 and added a codicil. See Jill K. Garrett and Marise P. Lightfoot, *Maury County, Tennessee Chancery Court Records, 1810-1860*, vol 1, p. 209. Names of Peter's children are listed ordinally.

[34] Franklin County, Tennessee, *Deed Book N*, Jan. 20, 1830, pp. 487-488.

[35] Madison County, Tennessee, *Deed Book 1*, March 29, 1824. He purchased slaves Hardy and Amy and their five youngest children.

[36] Information on the children was obtained from information published by the Maury County, Tennessee Historical Society, especially the research of Nathan Vaught.

Rose Hill Cemetery in Maury County. She married second Judge William Stuart Fleming on Feb. 8, 1860.

g. Susan McLemore Booker was born on July 23, 1823. She married Oliver P. Catron on Oct. 21, 1845.

h. Mary Florida Booker was born on March 12, 1825. She married Lewis M. Scott in March 1847. Lewis was an attorney, born in 1818 in North Carolina. They lived at Gainesville, Sumter County, Alabama.[37]

i. Peter Richeson Booker Jr. was born on Oct. 12, 1827 and died March 11, 1849. Burial was in Rose Hill, Maury County. Peter married Mary Turney Garland. She married second Washington Meredith on Dec. 18, 1850.

j. Cornelia L. Booker was born June 5, 1829. She married Joseph Royall Mosby. They were living in Fayette County, Tennessee in 1850.

2. Martha Brunskill Booker was born on July 13, 1783 and died on Sept. 15, 1815. She married Moses Treadway Jr., son of Moses and Sarah (Hopkins) Treadway, on July 9, 1803. Moses was born in Chesterfield County, Virginia on Sept. 19, 1778 and died in December 1860 in Prince Edward County, Virginia.[38] After Martha's death, Moses married second Elizabeth P. Guerrant of Goochland County on March 26, 1817. They lived in Prince Edward County.

3. Merritt Hobson Booker was born on June 11, 1787 in Cumberland County, Virginia and died on June 11, 1839 in Maury County, Tennessee, from tombstone inscription. He married Martha Finney Mosby, daughter of General Littleberry Mosby Jr., on Tuesday, June 20, 1820, in Powhatan County, Virginia.[39] Martha may have died in 1850, and buried at Culleoka, Maury County, Tennessee. Merritt named his brother Peter R. Booker as his executor, but Peter died first, suddenly. The children of Merritt and Martha Booker were: Rebecca A.

---

[37] U. S. Census for Sumter County, Alabama, Dwelling 493, Family 499, Oct. 24, 1850.

[38] Library of Virginia, Bible Records, "Tredway Family Bible Record," Accession No. 27797.

[39] *Richmond Commercial Compiler*, June 27, 1820, p. 3, c. 1.

Booker, Lucien Booker, Mary Booker, Mahaley Booker, Charlotte P. Booker and Sally Booker.[40]

4. Albert Booker was born on March 6, 1790 and died on Oct. 9, 1816 at the house of Edward Cunningham in Richmond, Virginia.[41] Apparently he did not marry.

5. German Booker was born circa 1794 and died in Cumberland County on Nov. 6, 1854. He married first Martha Ballou, daughter of Thomas and Frances (Hobson) Ballou, on Dec. 28, 1818 in Cumberland County. He married second Anne Fenton Woodson, 1803-1896, daughter of Charles and Judith (Leake) Woodson, on March 27, 1822 in Cumberland County. She died on Jan. 7, 1796 in Cumberland County. German served in the War of 1812.[42]

6. Richard Lawson Booker was born circa 1795 and died on July 29, 1839 in Somerville, Fayette County, Tennessee.[43] He had worked as a cashier in the Bank of Louisiana. At the time of his death, he was a partner in H. & J. Dick and Company in New Orleans. Apparently he did not marry, because his will provided for certain siblings and their children. He is also mentioned by his nephews ("my uncle Richard L. Booker") in a Chancery Court suit in Maury County, Tennessee.[44] Richard was an attorney and banker.

7. Harriett Booker was born in 1801 in Cumberland County and died on Sept. 22, 1848 in Fayette County, Tennessee. She married Dr. Edward Mumford Ford in 1820 in Cumberland County.

---

[40] Jill K. Garrett and Marise P. Lightfoot, *Maury County, Tennessee Chancery Court Records, 1810-1860*, "Frierson vs. Booker, 1845," vol 1, p. 208.

[41] *Virginia Patriot and Richmond Mercantile Advertiser*, Oct. 10, 1816, p. 3. c.

[42] Patrick G. Wardell, *War of 1812: Virginia Bounty Land & Pension Applicants*, (Bowie, Maryland: Heritage Books, Inc.), 1987, p. 42.

[43] "The Booker Connection" by Don Booker. *The Richmond Enquirer*, Aug. 16, 1839 issue, p. 3, c. 4 states that he was a resident of New Orleans, Louisiana. See also *The Lynchburg Virginian*, Aug. 36, 1839, p. 3, c. 3.

[44] Maury County, Tennessee Chancery Court, "Albert Booker vs. James G. Booker, 1846."

8. Grace Booker married Thomas Bedford Crenshaw, 1797-1866, son of Charles and Martha (Bedford) Crenshaw, on March 13, 1824 in Cumberland County. They moved to Shelby County, Tennessee in 1836 where he ran a plantation until his death in 1866.[45]

Captain Samuel Booker Sr.

Captain Samuel Booker Sr., son of Richard and Martha (Brunskill) Booker, was born circa 1754, and died in 1788 in Amelia County.[46] He served as a Captain in the Continental Line of the Revolutionary War.[47] Samuel married Martha Munford, daughter of James Munford, Dec. 25, 1784, in Amelia County. It appears that only two children were born to this couple.[48]

Children Samuel Sr. and Martha (Mumford) Booker:

1. George Booker, son of Capt. Samuel and Martha (Munford) Booker, was born Nov. 14, 1785 in Amelia County, and died March 20, 1848 in Buckingham County. George was buried in a family cemetery at "Montrose."[49] He married Louisa Ann Carrington, 1796-1834, daughter of Benjamin and Betty Ann (Mosby) Carrington, on Dec. 14, 1818 in Cumberland County. George came to Buckingham County in 1812, and soon enlisted as a Captain in the War of 1812. He was an attorney who served in the Virginia State Senate, 1830-1832, representing Buckingham, Campbell and Cumberland Counties. George's will named his "wife," and two sons.

Children of George and Louisa A. (Carrington) Booker:

---

[45] http://www.rootsweb.com/~tnshelby/goodspd-c.htm, which cites Goodspeed, *History of Tennessee*, 1887, Shelby County.

[46] von Schilling, p. 88.

[47] Crozier, p. 38.

[48] Amelia County, Virginia *Will Book 4*, p. 116-118. The will was dated March 13, 1778 and probated on Sept. 25, 1788. He named his son George and stated that his wife was "big" (pregnant).

[49] Janice J.R. Hull, *Buckingham Burials*, (Alexandria, Virginia: Hearthside Press), 1997, pp. 66-67. His death was announced in the *Richmond Whig*, May 16, 1848.

a. Samuel J. Booker Jr., born circa 1824, was mentioned in his father's will, and may have been the Samuel Jones Booker (sic) who was a student at the College of William and Mary during the 1840s.[50] Samuel was an attorney who was living in the household of William H. Word when the 1850 census was taken in Buckingham County. Living in the same household was Millie Booker, presumably his daughter, age two. His wife, Mildred Irving, apparently died before the 1850 U. S. Census was taken. One Samuel Jennings Booker died on Feb. 2, 1856, per Lynchburg, Virginia newspaper. Obviously, this was a different person. More research is needed on this family.

b. Mary Ann Cornelia Booker died in 1844, aged ten years, three months, and twenty-four days.[51]

c. George Willis Booker, 1830-1883, married Sarah Dabney Perkins, 1830-1879.[52] George and Sarah were buried at "Montrose," near Highway 15 in Buckingham County.[53] In 1850, George owned $52,000 in personal property and $30,000 in real estate. That was a tremendous amount of wealth for his time and place.

2. Samuel Booker Jr. was born circa 1788 in Amelia County. He was mentioned in his father's will as "the child my wife is big with." In 1793, a chancery court record in Amelia County listed them as two infant sons of Samuel Booker. Their guardian was Samuel Ford. Possibly Samuel Jr. later went to Kentucky to take up the bounty land that was earned by his father.

Edward Booker

Edward Booker, son of Richard and Martha (Brunskill) Booker, was born circa 1758 in Amelia County, and died intestate in 1800 in Cumberland County. He served as a soldier in the Revolutionary War. Edward married Edith Cobb Anderson, daughter of Francis

---

[50] Jean Marshall von Schilling, Ph. D. *Booker Descendants of Captain Richard Booker of Abingdon Parish, Gloucester County, Virginia*, (Richmond, Virginia: Privately Printed), 1996, p. 81.

[51] *Richmond Whig*, Nov. 15, 1844, p. 4, c. 2.

[52] University of Virginia, Alderman Library, "Papers of the Booker, Perkins, and Dabney Families," Accession No. 2317-C, Box Number 2317, Folder Dates 1836-1863, 1935.

[53] Hull, pp. 66-67.

and Edith (Weldon) Anderson, on Oct. 27, 1783 in Amelia County. Marshall Booker sued the widow and infants of Edward Booker for "a deed of conveyance in fee simple to the plaintiff, for one moiety of the mill and three acres of land."[54] Edward Booker owned the plantation "Woodside" in Cumberland County, where numerous of his family were buried.[55] This was a very prominent branch of the Booker family.

Children of Edward and Edith C. (Anderson) Booker:[56]

1. Mary Marshall Booker was born circa 1784 and died in 1847. She married Stephen Cooke Jr. on Feb. 9, 1805 in Cumberland County, Virginia. Nine children were born to this union.

2. Richard Anderson Booker was born on Dec. 20, 1786 in Cumberland County and died on Dec. 22, 1867 in Buckingham County, Virginia.[57] His obituary said that he had an "unyielding regard for truth and rectitude." He married Elizabeth Davis, who was born on Oct. 22, 1786 in New Kent County, Virginia and died in Buckingham County on Aug. 14, 1869.[58] Richard was a toll keeper in Buckingham County. He was a veteran of the War of 1812.

3. Edward Marshall Booker was born on April 18, 1794 in Cumberland County and died on March 8, 1882 at "Ridgway" in Henry County, Virginia. Edward served in the War of 1812. He married Elizabeth Anglin on Jan. 28, 1820 in Patrick County, Virginia, where he had resettled in 1819. Among their seven children was George W. Booker,

---

[54] Cumberland County, Virginia *Order Book 20*, p. 439.

[55] Cumberland County, Virginia Historical Bulletin, Vol. 6, Aug. 1990, pp. 39-40.

[56] Names and information on children were secured from von Schilling. Probably, there were other unidentified children who were born between 1786 and 1794.

[57] Janice J.R. Hull (compiler), *Buckingham Burials*, (Alexandria, Virginia: Hearthside Press), 1997, p. 92.

[58] *Ibid.*

1824-1883, who served as Attorney General for Virginia in 1868 and Representative in the U. S. Congress in 1870-1871.[59]

4. Martha Brunskill Booker was born June 13, 1796 in Cumberland County and died on Sunday, July 16, 1853. She married John Thompson of Cumberland County.

5. Capt. William Booker was born April 17, 1799[60] in Cumberland County and died April 2, 1855. He served as a Captain in the War of 1812. William married Nancy Dudley Agee, 1799-1869, daughter of John and Cicily Ann (Hall) Agee. The couple was buried at "Woodside" in Cumberland County.

6. James Anderson Booker died in 1847 in Nashville, Tennessee, unmarried.[61]

Marshall Booker

Marshall Booker, son of Richard and Martha (Brunskill) Booker, was born circa 1759 in Amelia County, Virginia and died in 1806 in Cumberland County, Virginia. Marshall was a retail merchant in Cumberland County.[62] Presumably he was also an operator of the Booker Mill on Tar Wallet Creek in Cumberland County, about four miles southeast of the old courthouse. He married Martha "Patsy" Gaines, daughter of Maj. Bernard and Margaret Gaines.[63] She was

---

[59] Alderman Library, University of Virginia, "Papers of the Booker, Perkins, and Dabney Families," Accession No. 2317-C, Box Number 2317, Folder Dates 1836-1863, 1935.

[60] A Cumberland County, Virginia historical bulletin, published in August 1990, on p. 40, gives his birth year as 1789.

[61] Alderman Library, University of Virginia, "Papers of the Booker, Perkins, and Dabney Families," Accession No. 2317-C, Box Number 2317, Folder Dates 1836-1863, 1935.

[62] Cumberland County, Virginia *Order Book 16*, p. 68.

[63] Bernard Gaines was possibly a son of Daniel Gaines who died in Essex County, Virginia in 1757. Bernard died in Buckingham County in 1817. An appraisal of his estate is located in the Archibald Austin Papers at the College of William and Mary.

born in 1762. She continued living in Cumberland County[64] after the death of her husband. Sometime in the 1820s she went to live with her daughter Grace R. (Booker) Austin and her husband Archibald at their "Westfield" plantation Buckingham County, where she died in 1845.[65]

Children of Marshall and Martha "Patsy" (Gaines) Booker:

1. Grace Richardson Booker was born circa 1784 in Cumberland County. She was alive when the 1850 Census was taken in Buckingham County, but was gone before the 1860 census for that County. Grace married Archibald Austin Sr. in 1808.[66] He bought 400 acres from Thomas and Mary Sanders of Davidson County, Tennessee. The Buckingham land was located on both sides of the North Fork of Slate River.[67] The land tax records show that the land transaction took place in 1809. It is believed that his wife Grace inherited land from her grandfather, Bernard Gaines, adjoining this property. The Austin plantation was called "Westfield." According to Archibald's great grandson, John Twyman, the succession of owners was Bernard Gaines, Grace Booker, Archibald Austin, Dr. Iverson S. Twyman and John Twyman.[68] To reach "Westfield," one must go four and eight-tenth miles west of Buckingham Court House on U. S. Route 60, then one and two-tenth miles on State Route 607, then nine-tenths of a mile north (right) on private road leading to the house.[69] Austin served as a U.S. Congressman, 1815-1817, with residence in Buckingham County.

---

[64] Roger G. Ward, compiler, *1815 Directory of Virginia Landowners*, (Athens, Georgia: Iberian Publishing Company).

[65] Letter dated July 26, 1845 from Bernard G. Austin of Westport, Jackson County, Missouri to his brother Thomas Austin in Buckingham County. Bernard said, "I sympathize with you on the death of our beloved grandmother." Austin-Twyman Papers, 69 Au7, Box 1, Folder 3.

[66] *Virginia Argus*, Sept. 23, 1808, p.3, c. 2.

[67] Edythe Rucker Whitley, *Genealogical Records of Buckingham County, Virginia*, (Baltimore, Maryland: Clearfield Company, Inc.), 1996, p. 120. She cites Davidson County, Tennessee, *Deed Book G*, p. 437.

[68] Library of Virginia, "Virginia Historical Inventory," Record No. VHIR/04/0617.

[69] *Ibid*.

He was elected as a Republican to replace John Randolph who planned on moving to Europe for health reasons. Archibald also served several terms in the Virginia Assembly, both in the House and Senate. He was born on Aug. 11, 1772 in Buckingham County and died on Sept. 16, 1837.[70] His obit stated that he was a faithful member of the Anabaptist Church for the past 30-some years prior to his death. Presumably this was the Mulberry Grove Baptist Church that was located near his plantation. Archibald served in the War of 1812, in the 1st Battallion of the 100th Regiment of Buckingham Militia commanded by Capt. Thomas Whitlock.[71] The Austin papers, which contain over 10,000 items, both legal and personal, are housed and maintained in the Manuscripts and Special Accounts Archives of the Swem Library Annex, College of William and Mary at Toano, Virginia.

Children of Archibald Sr. and Grace R. (Booker) Austin:[72]

a. James Marshall Austin was born on Sept. 10, 1809 in Buckingham County, and died in 1865.[73] He married Susanna Eldridge, daughter of Rolfe Eldridge, on May 28, 1833.[74] She was born on May 28, 1812, and died on May 14, 1882. Both were members of the Maysville Presbyterian Church at Buckingham Court House.[75] James was a physician in Buckingham County, where his family lived and died. The Austin-Twyman Papers contain information that a slave accompanied James to his assignments during his service in the Confederacy. In fact, both survived the Battle of Gettysburg.

b. Thomas Austin was born on June 10, 1811 and died in December 1885 in Buckingham County. He was living in his mother's household when the

---

[70] Obituary of Archibald Austin, *The Richmond Enquirer*, Oct. 6, 1837.

[71] College of William and Mary, Austin-Twyman Papers, 69 Au7, "Accounts and Legals, Buckingham County Records, 1811-1812," Folder 388.

[72] Vital dates for the children are taken from the Austin Genealogy in the Austin-Twyman Papers, 69 Au7, in the Manuscript and Special Collections of the College of William and Mary.

[73] Janice J.R. Hull (compiler), *Buckingham Burials*, (Hearthside Press: Alexandria, Virginia), 1997, pp. 372-373.

[74] Carl Coleman Rosen Sr., *History of Maysville Presbyterian Church*, (Book Crafters: Fredericksburg, Virginia), 1997, p. 16.

[75] Hull, p. 373.

1850 census was taken.[76] Apparently he was assisting his mother with the operation of the Westfield plantation that was located west of Buckingham Court House. Thomas was listed as a Master Mason in the Buckingham Union Lodge in 1859.[77] He served in the Confederate army in Company E, 21st Virginia Infantry Regiment, according to a letter he wrote from Randolph County, Virginia (now WV) to his sister Martha on Aug. 21, 1861[78] Known as "Major" to members of his family, he was listed on the 1870 Census as a close neighbor of his sister, Martha E. Twyman, who was living on the "Westfield Plantation."[79] He married Armissie Wade and they had one child.[80]

c. Bernard Gaines Austin was born on Feb. 24, 1813 in Buckingham County, and died in February 1859, probably in Missouri. He first married Mary Eliza Eldridge, daughter of Rolfe Eldridge of Buckingham County, and married second Ellen Pryor.[81] On July 2, 1842, he wrote a letter to his mother stating that he wanted his share of the Austin estate because he was migrating immediately from Virginia.[82] He was an attorney who migrated to Bates County, Missouri in search of a lucrative practice. That didn't go well, so he moved to Westport, Jackson County, Missouri on May 1, 1845, saying that he could not make a living by law practice alone, but needed other work to supplement his income.[83]

d. John Austin was born on Dec. 24, 1819 and died on Dec. 10, 1852 at "Westfield."[84] John studied medicine at the University of Virginia as

---

[76] Benjamin B. Weisiger III (compiler), *Buckingham County, Virginia 1850 United States Census*, (Athens, Georgia: Iberian Publishing Company), p. 111.

[77] Carl Coleman Rosen Sr., *200 Years of Freemasonry in Buckingham County, Virginia*, (Westminster, Maryland: Family Line Publications), 1991, pp. 27.

[78] Austin-Twyman papers, "Letters from Thomas Austin," Folder 20.

[79] Jeanne Stinson (compiler), *Buckingham County, Virginia 1870 U.S. Census*, (Iberian Publishing Company: Athens, Georgia), 1998, p. 108.

[80] College of William and Mary Manuscript and Special Collections, 69 Au7, "Austin-Twyman Papers," Folder 409.

[81] Austin-Twyman Papers, Folder 11, "Letters by Frances A. (Austin) Wright."

[82] Austin-Twyman Papers, Box 1, Folder 3.

[83] Austin-Twyman Papers, Box 1, Folder 3.

[84] *Richmond Whig and Public Advertiser*, Feb. 8, 1853, p.4, c. 5.

evidenced by the letters to and from him as a student.[85] He served as a Constable in Buckingham County during the 1840s.[86] John was a physician and dentist. According to the Gilliam papers, he "extracted two teeth Negro..." for $2.00.[87]

e. Martha Elizabeth Austin was born on Sept. 6, 1822 in Buckingham County[88] and died on Feb. 17, 1904. She married Dr. Iverson Lewis Twyman, son of Samuel and Frances (Rogers) Twyman, on March 29, 1848.[89] He was born on May 2, 1810 in Orange County, Virginia and died on April 18, 1864 at "Westfield Plantation" in Buckingham County. He graduated from the School of Medicine, University of Pennsylvania in 1832. He first married Mary Lavinia Horsley on Nov. 8, 1838, who died in 1844. He practiced medicine while he ran the Westfield plantation, although they lived at Bent Creek and in Nelson County at various times. Their children were well-educated and several entered the teaching profession, after being educated at Peabody College in Nashville.

f. George Booker Austin was born on Oct. 17, 1824 and died in November 1893, probably in West Virginia. He married Rebecca P. Horsley, daughter of Robert Horsley, whom he later divorced.[90] George was a Master Mason in the Buckingham Union Lodge.[91] A letter dated June 11, 1853, addressed to George Booker Austin from Peter V. Fowler of the Bent Creek Masonic Lodge, contained a charge of violating Article 2 of the Constitution.[92] According to Carl C. Rosen of Westminster, Maryland, Article 2 means that he had probably been charged and convicted in a local court for disorderly conduct or as a habitually drunken person. He was enumerated

---

[85] Austin-Twyman Papers, numerous letters to and from John Austin.

[86] Austin-Twyman papers, "Accounts and Legals- Buckingham County Records, 1840-1849," Folder 395.

[87] Carl C. Rosen, *The Papers of Richard H. Gilliam of Buckingham County, Virginia*, (Westminster, Maryland: Family Line Publications), 1992, p. 24.

[88] James Randolph Kidd Jr. (transcriber), *Buckingham County, Virginiq 1860 Federal Census*, (Athens, Georgia: Iberian Publishing Company), p. 3.

[89] *Richmond Whig and Public Advertiser*, April 13, 1848, p. 1, c. 6.

[90] See the Austin-Twyman Papers. Also, Weisiger, p. 97 shows Rebecca in the household.

[91] Carl Coleman Rosen Sr., *200 Years of Freemasonry in Buckingham County, Virginia*, (Westminster, Maryland: Family Line Publications), 1991, pp. 27.

[92] Austin-Twyman papers, Letters, Folder 14.

as a "school master" on the 1850 U.S. Census for Buckingham County.[93] He also taught school in Lincoln, Logan, and Boone Counties, West Virginia.[94] Apparently George was not close to his siblings. One of his letters showed that he was not aware of the death of his brothers Thomas and Archibald until two and three years later, respectively.

    g. Archibald Austin Jr., born in February 1815 and died in February 1886. He was living in the household of Grace R. Austin when the 1850 U.S. Census was taken.[95] He later married his first cousin Agnes Austin. Archibald was the subject of criticism among his siblings.

    h. Grace Booker Austin was born circa 1832 according to the 1850 census.[96] The Austin Bible record stated that she was born in October 1830 and died on Feb. 23, 1869. She was living in her sister's household (Twyman) when the 1860 Census was taken. Apparently she did not marry.

    h. Agnes Frances Austin was born on Dec. 13, 1826, and was still living in 1892 when the "Twyman vs Wright" case came to court.[97] She married James A. Wright. In 1883, he was mentioned in "S. W. Ligon vs Morris Comm." Court case in Buckingham County.[98] He was deceased by 1892 when the "Twyman vs Wright" case came to court.

2. Bernard Gaines Booker was born circa 1787 in Cumberland County, Virginia and died in July 1859 in Calloway County, Kentucky. He married Mary Stratton.

---

[93] Benjamin B. Weisiger III (compiler), *Buckingham County, Virginia 1850 United States Census*, (Athens, Georgia: Iberian Publishing Company), p. 1.

[94] College of William and Mary, Austin-Twyman Papers, Folder 14

[95] Weisiger, p. 3.

[96] Benjamin B. Weisiger III (compiler), *Buckingham County, Virginia 1850 United States Census*, (Athens, Georgia: Iberian Publishing Company), p. 111.

[97] Jeanne Stinson, *Buckingham County, Virginia Undetermined Chancery Files Index*, (Athens, Georgia, Iberian Publishing Company), 1994, p. 65. It cites *Buckingham County Deed Book 6*, p. 514, *Deed Book 9*, p. 366, and *Deed Book 7*, p. 505.

[98] Jeanne Stinson, *Buckingham County, Virginia Undetermined Chancery Files Index*, (Athens, Georgia, Iberian Publishing Company), 1994, p. 40.

Bernard Gaines Booker

Bernard Gaines Booker, son of Marshall and Martha "Patsy" (Gaines) Booker, was born circa 1787 in Cumberland County, Virginia and died in Calloway County, Kentucky in July 1859.[99] His death record stated that he died of palsy; that he was a farmer. His maternal grandfather, Bernard Gaines, gave him a mill, called Booker's Mill, in Cumberland County in 1806.[100] Grandfather Gaines bought a rifle for BGB on Nov. 16, 1805.[101] Bernard moved from Cumberland County to Buckingham County about 1811, where he became interested in gold mining. He served in the War of 1812 with Capt. William Moseley's Company of Cavalry, attached to the First Regiment, Virginia Militia. His rank was Cornet, which was a junior officer who carried the colors (flags).

In 1817, he received 182 acres from the estate of his deceased maternal grandfather, Bernard Gaines.[102] One of the properties that BGB acquired was later known as "The Booker Gold Mine." It was located west of Willis Mountain and on the west side of U. S. Route 15. The mine helped him become a wealthy person, with slaves, servants, and horses and carriages. Oral history says that he had gold buttons made for the vests of his servants, and bridles and harnesses of gold for his team of horses. As often happens when a person is "born with a silver spoon in his mouth," or makes easy money, it is easily lost. He sold part of the gold mine property in

---

[99] 1860 Mortality Schedule for U. S. Census, Calloway County, Kentucky.

[100] Cumberland County, Virginia *Deed Book 11*, pp. 487-488, dated March 11, 1811.

[101] Austin-Twyman Papers, "Accounts of Archibald Austin, 1804-1832," 69 Au7 MsV2, p. 46, Manuscripts and Rare Books Department, Swem Library, College of William and Mary.

[102] Roger G. Ward, compiler, *Buckingham County, Virginia, Land Tax Summaries and Implied Deeds, 1815-1840*, (Athens, Georgia: Iberian Publishing Company), 1994, vol 2, p. 119. The Austin-Twyman Papers, "Accounts and Legals-Buckingham County Records, 1820-1824, Folder 391," shows that Bernard Gaines bought the land from Jesse Garland on June 5, 1802."

1838 to James Garnett[103] and William M. Moseley.[104] It is believed that this signaled the beginning of financial problems for, in 1843-1844, he sold the remainder of his land in Buckingham County, including 694 acres sold to George W. Kyle in 1843 and 721 acres to Obadiah F. Reynolds in 1844.[105] The 1843 personal tax records reveal that he owned forty-six slaves, twelve horses, a coach and a gold watch. In 1844, he paid taxes on ten slaves, twelve horses, and a gold watch (he no longer owned a coach or carriage). Evidently, he sold his gold watch in 1845 for in 1846 he paid taxes on only six slaves and one horse. It appears that he went bankrupt in 1847 after paying taxes on four slaves and one horse.[106]

It appears that his assets were worth less than his debts in 1847, which caused him to search for another location. Being almost penniless, he wrote to his sister Grace R. (Booker) Austin for assistance. She failed to respond and, on Aug. 23, 1847, he made another appeal. "My dear Sister, I have written to you several times to know if you are willing to let me have one of the beds and furniture that Aunt Glover left at your house at the time of her death. I shall start to the West in a few weeks and I wish to take the bed and furniture with me."[107] The 1830 and 1840 censuses for Buckingham County show two females in the household of the

---

[103] See Buckingham County, Virginia *Deed Book 1*, pp 718-723.

[104] William M. Moseley, son of Spotsford Lewis and Mary (Marshall) Moseley, was born on March 15, 1809 in Powhatan County, Virginia and died in 1880 at Danville, Virginia. Mary was a daughter of William and Hannah (Cobbs) Marshall. William M. Moseley married first Emily Frances Osborne and second to Emeline ____ circa 1851. From Warren Forsythe, Box 1299, Ellensburg, WA 98926-1299.

[105] Roger G. Ward, compiler, *Land Tax Summaries and Implied Deeds, 1841-1870*, (Athens, Georgia: Iberian Publishing Company), 1995, p. 35.

[106] Library of Virginia, "Buckingham County, Virginia Personal Property Tax Books, 1842-1852, Reel No. 63."

[107] Austin-Twyman Papers, Manuscripts and Rare Books Department, Swem Library, College of William and Mary, Letters by family to the Archibald Austins, 1840-1853, n.d., Box 1, Folder 3, B.G. Booker (brother of Mrs. Grace R. Booker Austin) concerning his move to the West.

Archibald Austin family who were born between 1760-1770. It appears that one of the ladies was Mrs. Patsy (Gaines) Booker, widow of Marshall Booker, and the other lady may have been Patsy's sister "Aunt Glover."

Bernard had no money to purchase land in Kentucky when he resettled his family during the fall of 1847. He is found on the 1850 U.S. Census for Calloway County, Kentucky, family No. 540, enumerated by the census-taker William Poindexter Guthrey, who was a native of Buckingham County. All of BGB's children moved with him to Kentucky except Martha G. (Booker) Shepherd, Peter Stratton Booker, and Marshall Booker.

Bernard G. Booker married Mary Stratton, daughter of Peter and Mary N. (Steger) Stratton. Mary was born on Dec. 31, 1792 in Powhatan County, Virginia and died in June or July of 1862 at Pleasant Hill, Calloway County, Kentucky.[108] He was not able to recover from his financial losses in Buckingham County. A search of land records in Calloway County shows no evidence that he owned land or taxable personal property before his death in 1859. His wife Mary and her son Samuel Jennings Booker jointly bought a house in 1860 on a 1½-acre lot in Pleasant Hill, on the road that leads from Murray, Kentucky to Paris, Tennessee. They paid $550 to the grantor O. A. and Susan C. Schrader.[109] Apparently the slave labor was used to pay the rent or mortgage payments and living expenses, but this income may have ceased after the Civil War when slaves were declared to be free.

The history of Bernard G. Booker was lost to his descendants who remained in Buckingham County. This compiler has been researching the family since 1966. Not one researcher nor descendant knew or reported that B. G. died pennyless in Kentucky. The ownership of the Buckingham Booker Gold Mine is common knowledge among descendants, a bragging point. The consensus

---

[108] See Calloway County, Kentucky, *Deed Book R*, p. 159 and *Inventory and Appraisal, and Sales Book C*, p. 248.

[109] Calloway County, Kentucky *Deed Book L*, p. 280.

among descendants is that BGB died in Buckingham County and was buried in an unmarked grave. Likewise, his living descendants in Calloway County knew nothing about his coming from Buckingham County, Virginia as a former man of wealth. This fact is highlighted by the research effort of Joseph D. Eggleston, then president of Hampden-Sydney College, who sought an answer to the mystery of Bernard G. Booker. He tried to reach Shepherd families in Buckingham County who were descendants of Martha G. (Booker) Shepherd. They did not respond, even though Eggleston told a member of the Twyman family to "Stir them up!"[110] At last the story is known and is being told in the twenty-first century for the first time.

Children of Bernard G. and Mary (Stratton) Booker:

1. Martha Gaines Booker was born in Buckingham County in 1811 and died on June 24, 1902 at Dillwyn, Buckingham County.[111] She married William Shepherd, May 26, 1830.[112] He was a veteran of the War of 1812. See the chapter on William Shepherd for more detail.

2. Peter Stratton Booker was born on Jan. 13, 1814 in Buckingham County and died on Aug. 17, 1890. He married Elizabeth A. Morris, daughter of Capt. Samuel Morris, Oct. 10, 1837. The Rev. William Moore officiated the wedding.[113] They lived and died at Arcanum, Buckingham County. Both parents are buried in the Morris Cemetery in Buckingham County.

Children of Peter S. and Elizabeth A. (Morris) Booker:[114]

   a. Ann E. Booker was born on June 11, 1846 and died on June 14, 1847.

---

[110] Austin-Twyman Papers, Folder 410, Letters by J. D. Eggleston.

[111] Proof of Martha's vital dates are from the War of 1812 service pension record in National Archives for William Shepherd. Martha received a widow's pension.

[112] *Daily Richmond Whig*, June 5, 1830, p. 3, c. 2.

[113] *Richmond Whig*, March 8, 1838 issue.

[114] Information on this family unit was compiled by William Ruby, 1106 Kingwood Drive, Tacoma Park, MD 20912-6918.

b. Helen Virginia Booker was born on May 4, 1848 and died on March 11, 1931 in Buckingham County. She married Archer Lewis Reynolds, son of Obadia and Lucy (Bell) Reynolds, on Feb. 5, 1868. He was born on Dec. 30, 1842 in Buckingham County and died on April 20, 1919 on the Reynolds' homeplace. He served in "CO A 20 BN HY ARTY CSA."[115]

c. Martha Gaines Booker was born circa 1850 in Buckingham County. She married Edward Stratton Stone. She and her brother Samuel were mentioned in the estate settlement of Nathaniel Morris in March 1869.[116]

d. Samuel Morris Booker was born on Feb. 10, 1851 in Buckingham County and died in 1922. He married Ida Tandy Holman, 1854-1879.

e. Mary Hollay Booker was born on Jan. 15, 1853 and died on Dec. 6, 1859.

f. Elizabeth A. Booker was born on March 5, 1856 and died on Feb. 27, 1858 in Buckingham County.

3. Marshall Booker was born circa 1817 in Buckingham County.

4. Albert Gaines Booker was born about 1819 in Buckingham County. He was taxed in Buckingham County 14 cents on personal property for owning one horse in 1843, and he paid $1.60 in 1844 for having eight slaves. He last appeared on the 1846 tax roll for Buckingham County with no personal property. He married Eliza Jane Moore, who was born in Kentucky in 1830. The 1860 and 1870 U. S. Censuses for Ballard County, Kentucky lists Albert as a farmer. Their children were Amelia C. Booker, born in 1850; George B. Booker, born in 1852; Mary C. Booker, born in 1854; and Willie A. (*female*) Booker, born on March 27, 1859.

5. William H. Booker was born in June 1824[117] in Buckingham County. He was still living in Buckingham County on March 9, 1847 when he sold a slave named Crockett to William M. Moseley of Calloway County, Kentucky, who in turn assigned the slave for $1.00 to "... permit Mary Booker, the wife of Bernard G. Booker of the said

---

[115] Janice J. R. Hull, *Buckingham Burials*, (Alexandria, Virginia: Hearthside Press), 1997, p. 470.

[116] Jeanne Stinson, *Buckingham County, Virginia, Undetermined Chancery Files Index*, (Athens, Georgia: Iberian Publishing Company), 1994, p. 47.

[117] 1900 U. S. Census for Toulumne County, California, Blanket Creek Precinct, Family No. 55.

County and State, the use and benefits of said slave and to take and receive the hires of said slave, for and during her natural life, to her sole and separate use, free from the control, debts or liabilities of her husband, the said Bernard G. Booker, or any other husband she may hereafter have..."[118] William was living in the household of his parents when the 1850 U. S. census was taken for Calloway County, Kentucky. We have not been able to track him further. He was not the William H. Booker of Virginia and Missouri who settled at Sonara, Toulumne County, California during the 1850s.

6. James M. Booker was born about 1826 in Buckingham County and died circa 1892, probably in Carlisle County, Kentucky. He appeared on the personal property tax list in Buckingham County in 1847. James was living in the household of William P. Guthrey, U. S. census taker for Calloway County, Kentucky in 1850. Guthrey was a former neighbor in Buckingham County. In 1870, he was on the census for Ballard County, Kentucky, listed as a small-time farmer. His wife was Mary Jane Lee, born circa 1831 in Virginia or Kentucky. Their only child, Nancy Booker, was born on March 10, 1860, probably in Ballard County, Kentucky and died on Sept. 22, 1899 in Carlisle County. In 1880, James and Mary were enumerated also on the Ballard County census. He is listed as a farmer, age sixty-three. After 1886, they were in Carlisle County, which was formed from Ballard County.

Child of James M. and Mary Jane (Lee) Booker:

   a. Nancy Booker was born on March 10, 1860 in Kentucky, and died on Sept. 22, 1899 in Carlisle County, Kentucky. She married Jacob Collins. See the 1900 Census for Carlisle County for a list of their children.

7. John Bernard Gaines Booker was born about 1827 in Buckingham County and died about 1890 in Calloway County, Kentucky.[119] He appeared on the personal property tax list for Buckingham County in

---

[118] Calloway County, Kentucky *Deed Book F*, p. 152, dated Dec. 20, 1847 in Buckingham County and Jan. 11, 1848 in Calloway County.

[119] Email from Sara Chumbler of Paducah, Kentucky, who said that her grandfather David E. Booker's father died when he (David) was about twelve years old. David E. Booker was born in 1878.

1847.[120] John moved to Calloway County with his parents during the fall of 1847. He married Alice Etheridge, who was born on Nov. 20, 1840 in Tennessee and died on Jan. 26, 1916 in Calloway County.

8. Samuel Jennings Booker was born on March 9, 1830 in Buckingham County and died on Nov. 1, 1906 in Calloway County, Kentucky. He married Nancy Caldona Skaggs, daughter of Simpson Charles and Sarah Ann (Lacey) Skaggs.[121] Nancy was born on Feb. 23, 1854 and died on June 3, 1908. Her obituary said, "Mrs. Sam Booker died of paralysis at her home west of town Tuesday morning. She was about 60 years of age and a well-known citizen. Rev. McPool conducted the funeral services Wednesday, after which the burial took place in the Dale graveyard."[122] Samuel and his mother bought a house in 1860 at Pleasant Hill, Calloway County.

Children of Samuel J. and Nancy C. (Skaggs) Booker:

a. Fannie B. Booker was born circa 1870. She married Eugene Westerfield.

b. Mary Stratton Booker was born in 1873

c. Alice Gaines Booker was born in September 1875

d. Nellie S. Booker was born on April 1, 1880 in Calloway County and died on Oct. 22, 1945 at Murray, Calloway County. She married Willie Dayton Perdue, who was born on July 30, 1877 in Madison County, Tennessee and died on Aug. 31, 1956 in Vero Beach, Florida. They had two children.

e. Mary "Polly" Booker was born in 1882

f. Samuel J. Booker Jr. was born in 1885 and died on March 10, 1943.

g. Juli F. Booker was born in May 1887.

9. Mary Elizabeth Booker was born in 1833 in Buckingham County. She married Amos H. Lacey in Calloway County in Aug. 9, 1855.

---

[120] Buckingham County, Virginia, *Personal Property Tax Books, 1842-1852*, Reel No. 63.

[121] Source of information was Bill Utterback, CGRS, P. O. Box 150, Amarillo, TX 79105-0150, who did record searches for the compiler.

[122] Don Simmons, compiler, *Calloway County, KY, Newspaper Genealogical Abstracts, Volume 7* (Melber, Kentucky: Simmons Historical Publications), 1996, p. 26.

John Bernard Gaines Booker

John Bernard Gaines Booker, son of Bernard G. and Mary (Stratton) Booker, was born about 1827 in Buckingham County, Virginia and died about 1890 in Calloway County, Kentucky.[123] He appeared on the personal property tax list for Buckingham County in 1847.[124] John moved to Calloway County with his parents during the fall of 1847. John was listed as J. G. Booker on the 1880 Census for Calloway County. He married Alice L. Etheridge, who was born on Nov. 20, 1840 in Tennessee and died on Jan. 26, 1916 in Calloway County.

Children of John B. and Alice (Etheridge) Booker:

1. Arcada Booker was born in October 1858 and died on Dec. 29, 1933 in Calloway County. She married William Chesley Scruggs, son of William A. and Mary E. (St. John) Scruggs, in 1874.[125] He was born in June 1856 in Calloway County, and died on Jan. 3, 1941.[126] Both were buried at Martin's Chapel Cemetery in Calloway County.[127] There were several land transactions involving the Scruggs and Bookers in Calloway County.[128]

---

[123] Email from Sara Chumbler who said that her grandfather David E. Booker's father died when he (David) was about twelve years old. David E. Booker was born in 1878.

[124] Buckingham County, Virginia, *Personal Property Tax Books, 1842-1852*, Reel No. 63.

[125] According to Bill Utterback, the parents of William A. Scruggs were Micajah and Celia Scruggs who were enumerated on the 1810 U. S. Census for Buckingham County, Virginia. See the 1900 U. S. Census for Calloway County, Kentucky, Hazel District, Household No. 194.

[126] Kentucky Death Index, 1911- , www.ancestry.com.

[127] Judith Ann Maupin, compiler, *Calloway County Cemeteries*, (Murray, Kentucky: Privately printed), 1981, p. 176.

[128] Calloway County, Kentucky, *Deed Book W*, p. 321, dated March 27, 1882 (signed by W. C. and Arcadia Scruggs), and *Deed Book T*, p. 621, dated May 19, 1877.

Children of William Chesley and Arcada (Booker) Scruggs:[129]

 a. William Bernard Scruggs was born in December 1877 and died on Oct. 23, 1951[130] in Calloway County. He married Effie Harrison on Sept. 30, 1899 in Calloway County. She was born in 1880 and died on Dec. 14, 1942. Burial was in Hazel cemetery in Calloway County.

 b. Elroy Scruggs was born in either April or Sept. 10, 1879 in Calloway County and died on March 7, 1951 in Paris, Tennessee. He married Mary Howard on Dec. 18, 1911 in Paris. She was born on Aug. 7, 1885 and died on June 18, 1958. Burial was in Maplewood Cemetery. They lived on Dunlap Street in Paris, per 1930 U. S. Census for Henry County, Tennessee. His occupation was physician.

 c. Claude M. Scruggs was born in September 1883. He married Leona E. Cathey, daughter of William Cathey, on Oct. 19, 1909, in Calloway County. In 1910, they are shown on the U. S. Census for Owensboro, Davies County, Kentucky. They moved to Hutchinson, Reno County, Kansas,[131] where he established one of the first Coca Cola plants in the United States. Their children (from US Census) Lewis M. Scruggs, born in 1917; Roy Gene Scruggs, born in 1926. .

 d. Cuthbert Scruggs was born in September 1888. He became a dentist with a practice in St. Louis.

 e. Ruby Scruggs was born on March 15, 1893 and died on July 19, 1931.[132] She married Amos L. Wells on July 26, 1911. He was born on March 18, 1888 and died on April 19, 1946.

2. George Bernard Booker was born on March 14, 1862 in Calloway County, and died on March 27, 1930 in Calloway County.[133] He married first Manerva J. Marshall, who was born on Oct. 3, 1871 and

---

[129] Ibid. See also the Calloway County, Kentucky 1850 Census, Household No. 194.

[130] Kentucky Death Index, 1911-Present, www.ancestry.com.

[131] 1920 U. S. Census for Reno County, Kansas, Roll T625_546, E. D. 189, p. 9B.

[132] The 1900 U. S. Census for Calloway County states that she was born in September 1892, but her tombstone in Hazel Cemetery in Calloway County gives a birth date of March 15, 1893.

[133] Maupin, p. 176. See also Calloway County, Kentucky, *U. S. Census for 1870*, Household No. 1092, and *U. S. Census for 1900*, Family No. 216.

died on July 19, 1912. He married second Mackie (King) Finney, widow of James, on March 19, 1919 in Calloway County.

3. William F. Booker was born on Feb. 2, 1865 and died on Aug. 21, 1870.[134]

4. Cora I. Booker was born on April 10, 1874[135] and died of typhoid fever after 1882.[136]

5. David Etheridge Booker[137] was born on April 20, 1878 in Calloway County and died in 1944. He married Clyde Elizabeth Neale, daughter of Richard M. and Sarah Jane (Smith) Neale, on June 8, 1907 in Murray, Kentucky. She was born on Oct. 14, 1884 in Calloway County.[138] They moved to Railroad Street at Hardin, Marshall County, Kentucky, where he founded a bank.

6. Effie Lucinda Booker was born on July 8, 1882 and died on Sept. 11, 1962. She married Everett Adams, son of Isaac W. and Ann Eliza (Wiseman) Alderson Adams, on Aug. 27, 1912 in Henry County, Tennessee. Everett was born on Oct. 22, 1881 in Calloway County and died on July 16, 1940. They were buried at South Pleasant Grove Cemetery in Calloway County.

---

[134] Maupin, p. 176.

[135] Elizabeth Brown, compiler, *Calloway County, Kentucky Vital Statistics- 1874-1878*, (Melber, Kentucky: Simmons Historical Publications), 1995, p. 46.

[136] Verbal information from David E. Booker to his daughter Ruth, who recorded the information in a notebook.

[137] Information was provided by one of his granddaughters, Sara Chumbler, 3239 Jack Gray Drive, Paducah, KY 42001-4273.

[138] MS written by a daughter, Ruth (Booker) Darnall, which was copied and transmitted to the compiler by Sara Chumbler.

Notes on the Ayres Family

Ayres was a very early family in Buckingham County. A 1764 tax list for Buckingham County lists a Matthias Ayres and a Matthias Ayres Jr. A Bible record of a Nathan Ayres has been preserved. This Nathan would have been born during the 1740s, and was possibly a son of one of the Matthias Ayres listed on the 1763 tax list.

Children of Nathan Sr. and Mary (Leake) Ayres:[139]

1. Judith Ayes was born Oct. 1, 1768. She married Moses Spencer, son of Nock and Mary (Leake) Spencer. Moses was born on Jan. 3, 1763.

2. John Ayres, born Jan. 22, 1772, married Elizabeth Bransford.

3. Samuel Ayres was born July 19, 1774.

4. Nathan Ayres Jr. was born Dec. 19, 1776, and married Catherine Cave (Brown) Ford.

5. Walter Ayres was born April 6, 1779 and married Agnes Maxey.

6. Matthias Ayres was born Aug. 31, 1781, and died May 8, 1851. He married Nancy G. Howell, Jan. 19, 1814. Nancy was born Sept. 1, 1797 and died March 4, 1884.

7. Elizabeth Ayres was born Feb. 26, 1784. She married Phillip Maxey.

8. Mary Ayres was born April 8, 1786, and married Aaron Fuqua.

9. Peter Leake Ayres was born Feb. 4, 1789, and married Eleanor Holman on Dec. 23, 1813.[140]

10. Jane Ayres was born May 14, 1791, and married William Holman, on Sept. 23, 1807.

11. Patsy Ayres was born Aug. 2, 1793, and married Jesse Holman, Oct. 19, 1808.

---

[139] Bible was in possession of the Rev. W.P. Hooper of Huntington, West Virginia, and copied by Miss Nellie F. Ayres. Record may now be found at DAR Library, Washington, D. C., in filing cabinet folder *FC Agee*.

[140] Marriage record was recorded in miscellaneous notes scribbled in a *Guthrie's Grammar*, and abstracted and published by Mary Bondurant Warren, *Buckingham County, Virginia: Church and Marriage Records, 1764-1822*, (Heritage Papers: Athens, Georgia), 1993, pp. 69-71.

Chapter 13

Christian Families of Goochland, Albemarle, Amherst and Nelson Counties, Virginia

The Christian surname is associated with the Isle of Mann and Charles City County, Virginia during the early seventeenth century.[1] Numerous of the early Christians moved westward as land opportunities opened along frontiers of the Piedmont belt of Virginia. The relationships between the seventeenth century Christian families have not been completely defined, although it is a reasonable assumption that many, if not all, families were related. A tremendous number of errors have been created and perpetuated on the Christians in Old Virginia. This chapter is an attempt to understand and document one important branch of the larger Christian family, especially one of the several Thomas Christians.

Thomas Christian

Our interest is one Thomas Christian who was born circa 1680 in Charles City County, Virginia and died circa 1737 in Goochland County, Virginia. His will was written in Goochland County on Oct. 16, 1736, and it was probated on May 17, 1737.[2] Thomas married Rebecca New,[3] daughter of Edmund[4] and Mary New. This Thomas has been confused with other Thomas Christian families in Virginia,

---

[1] One source of information on the Christian family is Eunie V. Christian Stacy, *Christian of Charles City*, privately printed in Shreveport, Louisiana, 1982, although her book does not give an account of our ancestor James Christian (ca 1715-1758). Another source for this surname is the *Christian Family Chronicles*, published during the late 1970s and early 1980s by Agnes Branch Pearlman, 2001 North Westwood Avenue, Santa Ana, California 92706. The *Chronicles* do not shed much light on our branch of the Christian family.

[2] Information on the family unit of Thomas and Rebecca (New) Christian was secured from the will of Thomas Christian. Additional information was contributed by Carole Ruff, 40905 Belforest Court, Leesburg, Virginia 20175.

[3] She was not Rebecca Stith, daughter of Drury Stith.

[4] Henrico County, Virginia *Will Book, 1725-1737*, pp. 50, 100, probated on Sept. 5, 1726, (per Carole Ruff).

including his uncle Thomas and his son Thomas Jr. who married Rebecca Price.[5]

Children of Thomas and Rebecca (New) Christian:

    1. Thomas Christian Jr. was born circa 1704 and died circa 1743/44 in Goochland County, Virginia. He married Rebecca Price (ca 1705-1741/42). He was willed 210 acres from his father's estate. He also received a land patent of 392 acres along Bear Garden Creek on the south side of the James River in Goochland County.[6] This was premium land, which now includes the village of New Canton in Buckingham County, near U. S. Route 15 where it crosses the James River. Thomas Jr. owned other lands in Old Goochland County.

    2. Robert Christian was born circa 1708 and died in 1749 in Albemarle County. He married Lucy Bradley. See more information below.

    3. William Christian was born circa 1710 and was living in Albemarle County in 1756.

    4. Ann Mourning Christian was born circa 1712 and died in 1766 in Goochland County, Virginia. She married Samuel Coleman, probable son of John and Ann Coleman, on July 17, 1731 in Goochland County. Samuel was born circa 1707 in Petsworth Parish, Gloucester County, Virginia and died in 1748 in Goochland County.[7] Her father, Thomas Christian, sold 175 acres on Beaverdam Creek to Samuel Coleman on July 17, 1731, which was recorded on their wedding day.[8]

    5. Mary Christian, born circa 1714. She received from her father's will a "featherbed with furniture," "a pleasure horse colt," and five pounds to be paid after she was married.

---

[5] Numerous submissions to Ancestry.com (family trees) have confused Thomas Christian Jr. with his father. Also, some of these submissions mistakenly list the wife of Thomas Jr. as Rebecca Stith.

[6] Denis Hudgins, editor, *Cavaliers and Pioneers, Vol. IV, 1732-1741*, (Richmond, Virginia: Virginia Genealogical Society), 1994, p. 140.

[7] Will was written in Goochland County, Virginia on April 1, 1748 and probated on Sept. 20, 1748, per *Will Book 5*, p. 481.

[8] Goochland County, Virginia *Deed Book 2*, p. 263.

6. James Christian[9] was born circa 1715 and died in 1758 in Albemarle County. He married Susannah, maiden name not proven. This may be the same James Christian who on Dec. 1, 1740 received a patent for 200 acres on the branches of "Beverdam Creek on the North side of James River."[10]

7. Constant Christian was born circa 1717. She received from her father's will a featherbed with furniture, one gelding horse named Edy, and five pounds to be paid from the estate after her marriage.

8. Rebecca Christian was born circa 1718. She received six ewes from her father's estate. Nothing more is known about her.

Robert Christian

Robert Christian, son of Thomas and Rebecca (New) Christian, was born circa 1708 in Virginia and died circa 1749 in Albemarle County.[11] Robert and his partner David Patterson[12] secured a 3,000-acre patent from the Governor and his Council who gave approval in their meeting at the Capitol on Dec. 10, 1735.[13] The land was described as being "on Rockfish River and Goose Creek in Goochland County." His patent was developed into one of the first plantations in what later fell in Albemarle County in 1749, but still later in Amherst County in 1761. He patented 1,000 acres on March 30, 1743, located on the north side of the Fluvanna River, "against

---

[9] Numerous researchers have confused this James with his uncle James Christian who married Ann Macon.

[10] Denis Hudgins, editor, *Cavaliers and Pioneers, Vol. IV, 1732-1741*, (Richmond, Virginia: Virginia Genealogical Society), 1994, p. 233.

[11] Albemarle County, Virginia *Will Book A*, p. 2, will proved in May 1749.

[12] Probably this David Patterson was Robert's uncle, having married Elizabeth Christian who was a sister of Rebecca (New) Christian.

[13] H. R. McIlwaine (editor), *Executive Journals of the Council of Colonial Virginia*, (Richmond, Virginia: The Library of Virginia), Vol IV (October 25, 1721- October 28, 1739), 1978, p. 367.

Rack (sic) Island and Piney Island."[14] On March 4, 1747, two years before his death, he acquired thirteen additional acres "opposite" his plantation, on "Piney Creek in Fluvanna," surveyed by William Cabell.[15] Robert married Lucy Bradley, daughter of William Bradley. Four children were named in his will, with provisions made for a possible unborn child. Residence: Albemarle County, Virginia.

Children of Robert and Lucy (Bradley) Christian:

1. John Christian, born circa 1732 in Virginia, died in Franklin County, Georgia in 1805 after living there for about ten years. He married Mary Bryant, daughter of James and Clara Bryant.

2. Robert Christian Jr. was born circa 1734 and died circa 1791[16] in Amherst County. He married Mary Wynn.

3. Drury Christian was born circa 1726 in Virginia and died circa 1785 in Warren County, North Carolina. His will was written on April 26, 1780 and probated in July 1785. He married Lucretia "Lucy" Williams, daughter of Charles and Ann Williams, on Nov. 23, 1751, according to the St. James Northam Parish record, Goochland County, Virginia. She was born on May 6, 1727 in Prince William County, Virginia and died circa 1790.

4. Lucy Christian, born circa 1746, married Thomas Ridgway, son of Samuel Ridgway.[17] Thomas died in July 1801.[18] Seven children were born to this union according to the Ridgway history.

---

[14] Dennis Ray Hudgins, Editor, *Cavaliers and Pioneers, Vol. 5, 1741-1749*, (Richmond, Virginia: Virginia Genealogical Society), 1994, p. 50.

[15] Eric G. Grundset (abstractor), *Albemarle County, Virginia Surveyors' Plat Books, Volume I, Parts 1 and 2, and Volume 2*, 1744-1853 [and 1892], (Fairfax, Virginia: Privately Printed), 1998, p. 15.

[16] Amherst County, Virginia *Will Book 3*, p. 206, written on June 8, 1785 and probated Oct. 3, 1791.

[17] Gertrude N. Brick and Thurman Ridgway, *Ridgways in the U. S. A.*, (Baltimore, Maryland: Gateway Press, Inc.), 1980, p. 517.

[18] *Ibid.* p. 517.

James Christian Sr.

James Christian Sr., son of Thomas and Rebecca (New) Christian, was born circa 1715 in Virginia and died circa 1758 in Albemarle County. He was an early landowner in Old Albemarle County, Virginia, from which Amherst County was carved.[19] In 1747 and 1753, he made entries for several parcels of ungranted land.[20] One tract was for 390 acres; another for 365 acres, and a third tract for upwards of 2,000 acres. The lands were on both sides of the Fluvanna River, now known as the Upper James River. It is believed that the farms were located in present-day Amherst, Nelson and Appomattox Counties. All of these lands were surveyed during James' lifetime, but he failed to secure a patent for 1,910 of these acres. This omission spawned several court suits over a period of 50 years, with one case reaching the Virginia Supreme Court of Appeals.[21] Fortunately, for genealogists, these court cases offer proof of family compositions and relationships. James Christian filed his will in Albemarle County on May 18, 1752 and proved on June 15, 1759.[22]

The name of James[23] Christian's wife was Susannah, whose maiden name is not proven, although may have been Rogers or

---

[19] William Mumford, *Reports of Cases Argued and Determined In the Supreme Court of Appeals of Virginia*, (Richmond, Virginia: The Franklin Office), 1821, Vol. VI, p. 520.

[20] William Cabell surveyed 400 acres for James Christian on April 22, 1748, "at the head of a branch of Bent Creek, under the Piney Ridge," as reported by Eric G. Grundset in *Albemarle County, Virginia Surveyors' Plat Books Volume I, Parts I and 2, and Volume 3, 1744-1853 [and 1892]*, (Privately Printed: Fairfax, Virginia), 1998, p. 15.

[21] *Reports of Cases Argued and Determined in the Supreme Court of Appeals of Virginia*, (Richmond, Virginia: The Franklin Office), Vol. VI, pp. 534-554.

[22] Edythe Rucker Whitley, *Genealogical Records of Buckingham County, Virginia*, (Baltimore, Maryland: Clearfield Company, Inc.), 1996, p. 79. . Albemarle County, Virginia, *Will Book B*, p. 48.

[23] This James Christian did not marry Ann Macon as erroneously reported.

Harvey.[24] She was born circa 1718 and died in Buckingham County, Virginia on Dec. 12, 1785.[25] She married second Jeremiah Whitney, based on the fact that she was called Mrs. Whitney in a court case.[26] The State Supreme Court case stated that "the lands to which George Christian was entitled by devise from his grandmother Mrs. Whitney,[27] he (George) having died seized of the legal estate thereof, his said widow was entitled to dower in the same..."[28]

> James Christian, James Murphy and Betsy his wife formerly Betsy Christian, William Horsley and Sally his wife formerly Sally Christian and Charles Christian claiming under the will of Susannah Whitney as the heirs of George Christian dec'd. States that Susannah Whitney died on the 12th day of December in the year 1785 leaving an estate not particularly mentioned in her will worth $1,000.00 consisting of horses, cattle, sheep, hogs, household furniture, a crop of corn, tobacco, etc., That at her death John Christian her son named in said will took possession of the whole together with the Negroes named in the will devised to George Christian, which he (John) held during his life about sixteen or seventeen years. Immediately after his (John's) death, John M. Walker who married his daughter-- the only child-- delivered up the Negroes, but did not account for their use or hire, neither has the other property above been accounted for nor the rents nor use of the

---

[24] The name John Harvey Christian (their son) may hint that Susannah was nee Harvey, although there is no direct evidence.

[25] College of William and Mary, Austin-Twyman Papers, 69 au7, Accounts and Legals, Box 42, Folder 391, "Estate of Mrs. Susannah Whitney."

[26] Peachy R. Grattan, *Reports of Cases Decided in the Supreme Court of Appeals of Virginia*. (Richmond, Virginia: Shepherd and Colin), 1847, Vol. III, p. 553.

[27] Susannah, widow of James Christian, married second Jeremiah Whitney circa 1760-1761. See Albemarle County, Virginia Court Papers, Folder 1761, for direct proof. She is not the same Susannah who was married to another Jeremiah Whitney, an older man, during the 1740s. See Albemarle County *Order Book 1744-1748*, p. 255, March 1746.

[28] *Ibid*. p. 553. See, also, Albemarle County, Virginia *Deed Book 3*, pp. 43-45, dated March 4, 1761.

lands devised to be sold in the will, which land is the same mortgaged by Jeremiah Whitney to William Wilson for George Kippers (?) dated 7th January 1772 to secure the payment of lb 214. 7. 5. The land has never been sold nor the debt paid. The land is now worth $4000-5000. It appears that John Christian never qualified to the will of Mrs. Whitney, but that John M. Walker administered with the will annex. In support of this statement, references may be had to Mrs. Whitney's will, a copy of which is marked A and a statement of sundry persons marked B. The children of George Christian claim one-half of the Estate & rents of the land and a reasonable compensation for the hire of three Negroes sixteen or seventeen years." [29]

Children of James and Susannah Christian Sr.:

1. Elizabeth Christian, born circa 1740, married a Mr. Jarrett. She received land and slaves from her father's will.

2. Charles Christian was the eldest son. He was born circa 1741 and died in 1761 without a wife, child, nor will.[30]

3. James Christian Jr. was born circa 1744 in Albemarle County and died in 1781 in Amherst County, without issue.[31] His will was written on Oct. 22, 1772 and probated on June 4, 1781.[32]

4. John Harvey Christian was born circa 1746 and died in 1801 in Buckingham County. He may have married Joyce Patteson.

5. George Christian was born about 1748 and died intestate on Aug. 19, 1784 in Amherst County.[33]

---

[29] College of William and Mary, Austin-Twyman Papers, "Accounts and Legals," Box 42, Folder 391, "Estate of Mrs. Susannah Whitney."

[30] William Mumford, *Reports of Cases Argued and Determined In the Supreme Court of Appeals of Virginia*, (Richmond, Virginia: The Franklin Office), 1821, Vol. VI, p. 520.

[31] Peachy R. Grattan, *Reports of Cases Decided in the Supreme Court of Appeals of Virginia*. (Richmond, Virginia: Shepherd and Colin), 1847, Vol. III, p. 521.

[32] Amherst County, Virginia *Will Book 2*, p. 16.

John Harvey Christian

John Harvey Christian, son of James Sr. and Susannah Christian, was born circa 1746 in Albemarle County, Virginia and died circa 1801 in Buckingham County.[34] It is believed that he married one Joyce Patteson who survived him.

Child of John H. and Joyce (Patteson?) Christian:

1. Susan Christian was born circa 1776[35] in Amherst County and died circa 1845 in Appomattox County. She married John Meriwether Walker, son of Dr. John and Mary Ann (Winston) Walker.[36] John M. was born circa 1772 and died suddenly in Buckingham County on March 6, 1830.[37]

George Christian

George Christian, son of James Sr. and Susannah Christian, of Albemarle County, Virginia, was born circa 1748 and died on Aug. 19, 1784 in Amherst County, Virginia. Based on a will, it appears

---

[33] Peachy R. Grattan, *Reports of Cases Decided in the Supreme Court of Appeals of Virginia.* (Richmond, Virginia: Shepherd and Colin), 1847, Vol. III, p. 528.

[34] Roger G. Ward, compiler, *Buckingham County Land Tax Summaries & Implied Deeds, 1782-1814,* (Athens, Georgia: Iberian Publishing Company), 1993, p. 71.

[35] Her birth year was estimated from the 1810, 1820, 1830, and 1840 censuses for Buckingham County, which show a birth year between 1770 and 1780. It is believed that she was living in the household of her son Samuel J. Walker in 1840, page 397. Her death year was estimated by the same method, in that she was on the 1840 census but gone in 1850.

[36] According to Mrs. Bettie Walker Fricke of Dothan, Alabama, Dr. John Walker, 1726-1777, was a son of Benjamin and Ann (Aylett) Walker. Benjamin, 1698-1738, was the King's Attorney for Caroline County, Virginia.

[37] Library of Virginia, "Walker family Bible record, 1827-1911," Accession No. 26581. The handwriting of Benjamin P. Walker says, "John M. Walker my truly dear Father departed this life on Saturday the 6th day of March 1830 very suddenly..."

that George Christian had brothers named Charles, James and John.[38]

George married Martha Bell, daughter of Henry and Sarah Bell, on Jan. 16, 1775 in Amherst County. Martha was born Aug. 8, 1755, and died in Nelson County, April 19, 1833. George and Martha were married Jan. 16, 1775, and they had only four children as proven in a court of appeals case.[39] After George died, Martha married Capt. Stephen Watts, widower, Jan. 24, 1790. Capt. Watts, who served in the Revolutionary War, first married Elizabeth Farrar who was born on May 16, 1746 and died on Nov. 19, 1789.[40] It is believed that she is the Elizabeth who was named as a daughter of John Farrar, ca 1690-1768, in his will dated Oct. 24, 1764 in Albemarle County, Virginia.[41] John's wife was named Sarah; his parents were Thomas and Katherine (Perrin) Farrar.[42]

Children of George[43] and Martha (Bell) Christian:

1. James Christian was born in 1776 and died on Aug. 3, 1854 in Appomattox County. James married Cordelia Watts, daughter of Capt. Stephen and Elizabeth (Farrar) Watts, Feb. 28, 1795, in Amherst.

2. Elizabeth Christian was born in 1778, and died June 26, 1854, in Buckingham County. She married James Murphy, Sept. 27, 1804, in Amherst County. They had one child: James M. Murphy married Mary Susan Taylor, 1816-1874, in Buckingham County.

---

[38] See Amherst County, Virginia *Will Book I*, p. 408.

[39] Peachy R. Grattan, *Reports of Cases Decided in the Supreme Court of Appeals of Virginia*. (Richmond, Virginia: Shepherd and Colin), 1847, Vol. III, p. 520.

[40] Library of Virginia, "Watts Family Bible," Accession No 26258.

[41] Albemarle County, Virginia *Will Book 2*, p. 244.

[42] John Frederick Dorman, *Adventurers of Purse and Person: VIRGINIA, 1607-1624/5*, (Baltimore Maryland: Genealogical Publishing Company), vol. 1, 2004, p. 931-933, 948.

[43] In his work *The Cabells and Their Kin*, Alexander Brown erroneously stated on page 298 that Martha's husband was James Christian. This error has been perpetuated by other researchers.

3. Charles H. Christian was born circa 1783 in Amherst County and died unmarried on July 4, 1856 in Buckingham County.[44]

4. Sarah "Sally" Christian was born in Amherst County in 1784, and died in Nelson County on March 26, 1865. Sarah married William Horsely III, son of William and Martha (Megginson) Horsley Jr, in 1808. William III was born in 1772 and died on April 21 1865. His occupation was farming, and he served as one of the first magistrates of Nelson County.

Children of William and Sarah (Christian) Horsely Jr.:[45]

    a. Paul J. Murphy Horsley was born on May 15, 1818 in Nelson County, Virginia and died in 1880. He married Martha Elizabeth Abbitt of Buckingham County on Aug. 31, 1842. She was born on Feb. 7, 1821[46] in Appomattox County. Their children were: (1) Lelia Horsely, born in 1844, (2) Benjamin Abbitt Horsley, born in 1848, married Berta Thomas (3) William Horsley IV, born in 1850, married a Miss Cheatham, (4) Paul Murphy Horsley Jr. married Willie Johnson, (5) James Abbitt Horsley, and (6) Mary Horsley.

    b. Martha Elizabeth Horsley was born on Feb. 21, 1821, and died Nov. 29, 1904. She married Willis E. Harris, Aug. 31, 1842. Willis was born on Feb. 1, 1811 and died Feb. 27, 1879. See the section on the Harris family for more information on their descendants.

    c. Mary Cabell Horsely[47] was born ca 1823 in Nelson County. She married Eldridge Gary Jefferson Sr. in 1848. Their children: (1) Sallie Christian Jefferson was born in 1849. (2) Eldridge Gary Jefferson Jr.

---

[44] Library of Virginia, Archives Division, *Buckingham County Death Records, 1853-1890*. His death was reported by his nephew, Charles L. Christian.

[45] One source of information for this family unit is: Alexander Brown, *The Cabells and Their Kin*, (Richmond, Virginia: Garrett and Massie, Incorporated), MCMXXXIX, pp. 298-299.

[46] Vital dates for Paul J. M. and Elizabeth (Abbitt) Horsley were found in their Bible now in possession of Jean Carson of Spout Spring, Virginia. The Bible was printed in 1817.

[47] See James Randolph Kidd Jr., *Buckingham County, Virginia 1860 Federal Census*, (Athens, Georgia: Iberian Press), nd, p. 96.

was born in 1852, and (3) Lindsey Bolling Jefferson was born in 1855. He was a student in Buckingham County when the 1870 U. S. Census was taken. Eldridge Sr. was a Baptist minister and farmer in Buckingham County, Virginia.

James Christian

James Christian, son of George and Martha (Bell) Christian, was born in Amherst County in 1776 and died on Aug. 3, 1854 in Appomattox County.[48] His father, George Christian, died when he was only eight years old, and Reuben Norvell was appointed to be James' guardian. James married Cordelia Watts, daughter of Capt. Stephen and Elizabeth (Farrar) Watts, Feb. 28, 1795, in Amherst County.[49] Cordelia was born about 1775 and died on Jan. 9, 1848.[50] James and Cordelia were stepsiblings, defined by his (James') mother's marriage to Cordelia's father. They lived in a part of Amherst County that later became Nelson County. James also owned properties in Appomattox County. He inherited extensive acres that were tied-up for decades in court cases.[51] James was intelligent, but had "an occasional incapacity to manage his property

---

[48] Library of Virginia, Death records for Appomattox County, 1853-1890.

[49] Capt. Stephen Watts was born on Jan. 12, 1750 in Virginia, and died in Nelson County, Sept. 13, 1832. He served in the Revolutionary War. Stephen first married Elizabeth Farrar, on June 30, 1772, in Amherst County, by whom he had at least six children. After Elizabeth's death in 1789, he married second Martha (Bell) Christian, widow of George Christian, Jan. 24, 1790 in Amherst County. One child by the second marriage, Henry Holloway Watts, was born April 12, 1792, and died in 1832. Henry married first Elizabeth Dillard and married second Catherine Mundy.

[50] The obit of Cordelia (Watts) Christian was published in the *Virginia Conference Sentinel & Richmond Advocate*. It stated that she was survived by eleven children. Obit was provided by Dr. Louis Koenig, 26890 Sherwood Forest, San Antonio, Texas 78258. Dr. Koenig, himself, passed away on May 7, 2003.

[51] Credit is given to Carole Ruff, 40905 Belforest Court, Leesburg, Virginia 20175 for information on the Christian family in general and specifically the family unit of James and Cordelia Christian. She also supplied copies of the court appeals.

judiciously, and (to) properly provide for his family.[52] To complicate matters, his wife's estate was tied up in litigation, too.[53] Stephen Watts, father of Cordelia, died in 1832. He appointed his youngest son, Henry H. Watts, to administer his estate. Henry died within a year of his father, and his second wife, Catherine (Mundy) Watts was appointed as administrex. Silas P. Vawter was appointed Trustee for the estate. The estate settlements of the Christian families are among the most complicated in the history of the Commonwealth of Virginia.

Children of James and Cordelia (Watts) Christian:[54]

1. George H. Christian was born circa 1796 and died about 1849.[55] He married Elvira Mildred Layne, daughter of George W. and Sallie F. (Gilliam) Layne, on Oct. 30, 1830 in Nelson County. She was born in 1808 in Fluvanna County, and died in 1886. She was living in Nelson County in 1850 when the U. S. Census was taken, but she was buried in the Harrison Cemetery in Amherst County.[56]

2. Stephen Watts Christian was born circa 1798 and died Jan. 15, 1879 in Amherst County. He married Lucy Jane Christian, daughter of Drury

---

[52] Peachy R. Grattan, *Report of Cases Decided in the Supreme Court of Appeals and in the General Court of Virginia*, Vol III, (Richmond, Virginia: Shepherd and Colin), 1847, p. 526.

[53] Nelson County, Virginia *Chancery Orders 1851-1860*, Oct. 1, 1851, pp. 45, 47.

[54] The family composition is taken from several sources, primarily the Court references. Ten children are listed in the chancery court suit, Nelson County, Virginia, *Chancery Orders 1851-1860*, Oct. 1, 1851, pp. 45, 47. See also Nelson County, Virginia Deed Book 8, Pt 2, pp. 596-598, and *Deed Book 9*, pp. 4-5. Samuel Hairston Christian was not mentioned, but his name appears later when he bought and sold 360 acres from the estate. See Nelson County, *Virginia Deed Book 18*, Jan. 9, 1874, p. 503. Another source was Charles L. Glover's manuscript *History of the Glover Family With Christian Connections,* which may be found in the Jones Memorial Library in Lynchburg, Virginia.

[55] The 1850 U.S. Mortality Schedule for Nelson County, Virginia shows a George H. Christian who died in June 1849, aged 50 years.

[56] *Gravestone Inscriptions in Amherst County, Virginia*, (Amherst, Virginia: Amherst County Museum and Historical Society), 1999, p. 165.

and Mourning (Christian) Christian, on Aug. 6, 1828, in Amherst County.[57]

3. Elizabeth Farrar Christian was born in 1799 in Amherst County, and died May 26, 1859, in Appomattox County.[58] She married Silas P. Vawter, on Jan. 19, 1824, in Nelson County, Virginia Silas was born in Caroline County in 1797 and died on March 21, 1865[59] at Bent Creek, Appomattox County. Their three children were: a child who died young; Mary Jane Vawter, 1827-1888, who married John W. Walton, and Dr. Benjamin Silas Vawter, 1831-1910, who married Sarah Watts.

4. James B. Christian was born about 1802 in Amherst County. He married Lucy Jane Kyle, daughter of Rowland and Sophia (Christian) Kyle, on June 1, 1837, in Nelson County. He was alive when the U. S. Census for 1850 was taken in Nelson County. He went to court in 1867 regarding the settlement of "Hazel Grove," which was the 348-acre estate of his father.[60]

5. Charles Lawson Christian was born in 1803 and died in Buckingham County on March 27, 1862. He married Cary Ann Lewis, daughter of William and Anna (Glover) Lewis of Buckingham County, on Sept. 9, 1847. He was in public office, including a term as Sheriff of Buckingham County. Cary Ann (Lewis) Christian was born in 1815, and died in Buckingham County on April 26, 1890.[61] Both were buried

---

[57] Library of Virginia, *Amherst County, 1853-1890 Death Records*, provided by Arlene M. Passalacqua, via e-mail on April 3, 1997. Her address is: P.O. Box 652, Sandston Virginia 23150.

[58] Her death certificate in the Library of Virginia states that she died of "lung disease."

[59] Death date was taken from private papers titled "Walton Family Record," in hands of Mary Evelyn (Payne) Strickland of Gladstone, Nelson County, Virginia.

[60] Nelson County, Virginia, "Petition of James B. Christian," May 10, 1867.

[61] Source of information was from Ann Elizabeth (Christian) Glover, who was a daughter of Charles Lawson Christian. Information on the children of James and Cordelia (Watts) Christian was compiled by her husband, Charles L. Glover (1841-1922). The manuscript was titled "History of the Glover Family With Christian Connections," by Charles Lindorf Glover, FF2203, Jones Memorial Library, Lynchburg, Virginia.

in the Christian Graveyard at "Bond 100," near Buckingham Court House, Virginia.[62]

6. William Robert Christian was born about 1804 and died in April 1864 in Amherst County.[63] He married Sarah S. Phillips, daughter of William and Mary Phillips, on Dec. 23, 1851.[64]

7. Martha Ann Christian was born in 1805 and died in 1895. She married Robert Beasley, March 25, 1833. Robert moved his family to Bent Creek, Appomattox County where he ran a mercantile store and an inn. The 1850 census for Appomattox County lists five children: (a) Charles H. Beasley, age fifteen years, (b) Sarah Beasley, age thirteen years, (c) John J. Beasley, age nine years, (d) Stephen H. Beasley, age six years, and (e) Bettie Beasley, age four years. The Aug. 30, 1850 issue of the *Richmond Whig* reported that Lucy Ann Beasley died on Aug. 15, 1850 at the home of her Uncle Silas P. Vawter. The 1850 Census for Appomattox County stated that she was twenty-four years old, or a birth year of circa 1826. An unidentified letter reported that several members of the Beasley family migrated to Montgomery, Alabama. It also mentioned another child, Cordelia Beasley who married Robert Horsley and raised a family in Lynchburg.

8. Sarah Jordon Christian was born about 1806 in Amherst County and died on Dec. 9, 1864 in Missouri. Burial was in the Bellefontaine Cemetery in St. Louis. She married Harrod Brumskill Scott, son of John F. and Martha (Woolfolk) Scott, on Feb. 15, 1823. He was born in 1800 in Caroline County, Virginia and died in 1847[65] in Potosi, Breton Township, Washington County, Missouri. Glover stated that Harrod was a physician who died in St. Louis in 1848.[66] Their children were:

---

[62] Janice J. R. Hull, compiler, Buckingham Burials, (Alexandria, Virginia: Hearthside Press), 1997, vol. 1, p. 219.

[63] Amherst County, Virginia *Will Book 17*, p. 33.

[64] *Richmond Whig and Public Advertiser*, Jan. 15, 1852, p. 4, c.4.

[65] A court record in Caroline County, Virginia, dated Nov. 8, 1847, was filed by the children of Harrod B. Scott (dec'd) and his wife Sarah against the dower of John F. Scott's second wife, Ludy (Todd) Scott, who also died in 1847.

[66] Glover, p. 8,

Martha Elizabeth Scott married Thomas Carter Johnson; Emily Ann Scott; James Murphy Scott; John Scott; Richard Scott; and Charles Scott.

9. Samuel Hairston "Harston" Christian, born circa 1809,[67] lived in Buckingham County but died in Amherst County at about 75 years of age.[68] He was living at Bent Creek on Jan. 9, 1874 when this document was created: "I have bargained, sold and delivered to John W. Walton, trustee for Benjamin S. Vawter, the sum of $500 cash in hand, a tract of land containing 360 acres in Nelson County, the same tract I bought of Benjamin S. Vawter and John W. Walton, executors of , deceased, from S. H. Christian."[69]

10. Rufus C. Christian was born circa 1814. He was listed on the 1850 U.S. census for Nelson County,[70] and enumerated on the 1870 U.S. census for Appomattox County as a mail contractor. He was living with a 50-year old Negro housekeeper who assumed his surname. Apparently, he did not marry. Rufus sold his 8-year-old "Negro boy" named King to Silas P. Vawter.[71] It appears that Rufus created extensive debts that he could not pay and Vawter forced him settle in 1854.[72] George Bagley of Lynchburg wrote the following to Richard H. Gilliam in Buckingham County in December 1851: "Dear Col. [R.H.] Gilliam, Enclosed I take the liberty to hand you Rufus C. Christian's

---

[67] James Randolph Kidd Jr., *Buckingham County, Virginia 1860 Federal Census*, (Athens, Georgia: Iberian Publishing Company), n d, p. 111.

[68] Glover included "Harston" on his list of children, but omitted William Robert Christian. In his place, Glover erroneously listed on page eight a John Christian about "whom nothing is known." It is believed that Samuel Hairston Christian was "Harston."

[69] Nelson County, Virginia *Deed Book 18*, p. 503.

[70] 1850 U. S. Census for Nelson County, Virginia, Census Roll 963, p. 963.

[71] Nelson County, Virginia *Deed Book 13*, dated Oct. 15, 1845, p. 62.

[72] Nelson County, Virginia *Deed Book 15*, June 21, 1854, p. 359. Debts included a bond to Silas P. Vawter for $1,079 with four years of interest due, a bond to Mildred Mosby for $200 carrying interest also, a bond to secure James B. Christian against any loss as his security on several bonds.

bond for $14.95 due Sept. 2, 1850 which you will please do all in your power to collect for me. The man I do not know, the debt was made by one of my young men while he lived in Nelson and...his circumstances are doubtful. Possibly, it may be...& and all full much obliged for your efforts...me in this collection. Very respectfully, George Bagley."[73]

11. Amanda Dudley Christian was born about 1816 and died sometime during the 1860s. She married John A. Scruggs, March 9, 1836 in Nelson County, Virginia.

---

[73] Carl C. Rosen, editor, *The Papers of Col. Richard H. Gilliam of Buckingham County, Virginia*, (Westminster, Maryland: Family Line Publications), 1992, p. 35.

Chapter 14
Julius Coleman of Cumberland and Buckingham

Julius Coleman, 1743-1842, has always been an enigma to Coleman researchers. After combing through the public records in Virginia with no success in determining his roots and origin, a group of researchers[1] hired Debrett Ancestry Research Ltd of Winchester, England to conduct a comprehensive search in the vital records in the British Isles. We provided all that we knew about Julius and his family in this country. The name of Julius Coleman within his time-frame was not found on any register in the United Kingdom. The 64-page report from Debrett contained much of the information that we provided to them. In 1997, James C. Coleman of Pensacola, Florida finished compiling a 99-page paper entitled, "The Descendants of Julius Coleman (1743-1842)," with an index. A copy of this excellent work, which listed and documented 281 descendants, was deposited in the Library of Virginia.

What do we know about Julius Coleman? He left a Bible record that gives a birth year of 1743. The Bible record states that he died on July 10, 1842.[2] He served in the Revolutionary War. He was married in Cumberland County, Virginia to Elizabeth Coleman, daughter of James and Anna (Cocke) Coleman, on Sept. 23, 1789. Elizabeth was born July 15, 1771 and died May 1, 1853 in Buckingham County. Julius settled his family in East Central Buckingham County before 1810, where he was engaged as a farmer. He was not Julius Coleman, 1745-1824, of Caroline County who married Mary Chiles and later moved to Kentucky. Both men served in the War, but both left behind Bible records that set them apart.[3]

---

[1] Names of the researchers who financed the comprehensive research in 1985-1986 were Carl Coleman Rosen, Edward Coleman, Wilmer L. Kerns, J. Cullen Rosen, and James C. Coleman, who was the team leader. This consortium started about 1979, and included Eleanor Coleman Duran.

[2] The Coleman family Bible was in the hands of James M. Anderson Jr. of Enonville, Buckingham County. A copy was deposited in the Library of Virginia,

[3] The compiler wrote and circulated an 11-page research report in 1980 that settled this matter.

Coleman Family

It is now believed that Julius Coleman was a son of one Daniel and Mary Coleman. According to the Bible record of Julius of Buckingham, Daniel Coleman died on Jan. 17, 1821. The second-hand Bible was purchased by Julius Coleman "Anno Domini 1813" from Archibato Morrison of Cumberland County, Virginia. No relationships were stated in that Bible record, but Archibato's marriage to Anne Roper was dated Jan. 31, 1799. Three children were born to the Morrisons: William Stewart Morrison on Oct. 18, 1801; Thomas Roper Morrison on Sept. 16, 1810; and Jane Elizabeth Morrison on Sept. 16, 1813. We have not been able to determine a relationship between the Colemans and Morrisons

Children of Julius and Elizabeth (Coleman) Coleman:[4]

1. Anna Lee Coleman was born on July 20, 1790 in Cumberland County, Virginia and died on July 18, 1871 in Buckingham County. She married Daniel Flood, son of Noah and Sarah (Fuqua) Flood, on June 20, 1812 in Buckingham County. Daniel served in the War of 1812. He was born June 4, 1790 and died Oct. 10, 1850. Daniel was a farmer.

Children of Daniel and Anna L. (Coleman) Flood:[5]

    a. James Monroe Flood was born April 24, 1813 and died Jan. 30, 1898. He married first Jane Ann Spencer Oct. 4, 1837 and married second Ridley Harris.

    b. Elizabeth Ann Flood was born Nov. 6, 1814 and died Dec. 3, 1909.

    c. John H. Flood was born July 4, 1816. He married Mary Ann Druen. He was overseer of the Julius Coleman farm during the 1850s.

    d. Sarah Agnes Flood was born Oct. 2, 1818 and died Oct. 14, 1885. She married James David Anderson Dec. 3, 1840.

    e. William Daniel Flood was born July 1, 1820.

---

[4] From the family Bible of Julius Coleman.

[5] The family Bible lists only six children. H. Edgar Hill lists two more, Aaron Flood and Mary D. Flood. See http://flood.hill-ky.org/pdf/FloodJohn.pdf

f. Martha Daniel Flood was born March 26, 1822 and died Oct. 18, 1907. She married Joseph Fitzgerald on Feb. 18, 1848.

2. Daniel Coleman was born Jan. 22, 1792 and died May 24, 1825. He married Sally M. Coleman, daughter of Henry and Mary Archer (Daniel) Coleman, Oct. 30, 1817.

Children of Daniel and Sally M. (Coleman) Coleman:

a. Virginia Merry Coleman was born April 15, 1819.

b. Mary Daniel Coleman was born Aug. 5, 1820.

3. Martha Coleman was born in Buckingham County in 1793 and died in 1827. She married William Edwards.

4. Eliji E. Coleman was born in 1796 and died in 1829. He married Lillian Edwards in 1819.

5. Sally A. Coleman was born June 17, 1798 and died in March 1855. She married William Palmore Guthrie, Nov. 24, 1800. See the Guthrie family chapter for more information on this family unit.

6. Guliulmus Coleman was born in 1800 and died June 13, 1870. He married Caroline Huddleston, daughter of Thomas and Katherine (Stratton) Huddleston on Aug. 26, 1840. She was born Feb. 28, 1811 and died Jan. 24, 1867.

Children of Guliulmus and Caroline (Huddleston) Coleman:

a. Elizábeth E. Coleman was born Aug. 2, 1841 and died Oct. 29, 1941.

b. Edwin S. Coleman was born Nov. 6, 1842 and died April 23, 1844.

c. Elizabeth Katherine Coleman was born Feb. 26 1844 and died 1936. She married Thomas Henry Dowdy, who was born Dec. 12, 1837 in Cumberland County, Virginia and died in 1908. Thomas served as a quartermaster in the Confederate Service of America.

d. Littleberry I. Coleman was born May 18, 1846 and died May 29, 1849.

e. Luther Dunn Coleman was born Jan. 29, 1849.

f. Mary Caroline Coleman was born Dec. 20, 1850.

g. Ann Levenia Coleman was born June 22, 1854 and died May 10, 1863.

7. Augustus Coleman was born March 8, 1803 and died April 21, 1889 in Buckingham County. He married Lucy C. Edwards, daughter of Flemstead Edwards, Nov. 10, 1830. Lucy was born Nov. 28, 1810 and died July 23, 1899. They were buried at Enonville, Buckingham County.

Children of Augustus and Lucy C. (Edwards) Coleman:

a. James Frederick Coleman was born in 1831 and died in 1914. He married Catherine Fitzgerald. James served as a Pvt. In Co C, 25th Bn. VA Infantry, and received a pension for partial disability. The family lived in Buckingham County all their lives, as farmers. The Colemans were Methodists.

b. Elizabeth G. Coleman was born in 1833 and died in 1836.

c. Patsey J. Coleman was born in 1834 and died in 1852.

d. Edward Francis Coleman was born in 1838 and died May 28, 1864 in Richmond, Virginia of wounds received in the Civil War.

e. Mary A. D. Coleman was born in 1842 and died in 1843.

f. Julius Henry Lee Coleman was born Jan. 20, 1845 and died Feb. 22, 1920 at Enonville, Buckingham County. He married Pattie Ann Ranson, daughter of the Rev. Henry Trent and Carolyn Virginia (Anderson) Ranson, on Nov. 6, 1878. Pattie was born Oct. 8, 1858 in Buckingham County and died Feb. 19, 1944 at Enonville. Augustus served in the Civil War in Co. C, 25th Batt'n Virginia Infantry.

g. Augustus Early Coleman was born April 29, 1850 and died May 20, 1928. He married first Mollie A. Dunnevant Dec. 23, 1877. After her death in 1892, Augustus married second Josephine Anderson Ranson Sept. 20, 1896. Josephine was born April 29, 1876 and died May 13, 1957 in Lynchburg. He was a farmer and salesman, father of fourteen.

8. Mary Ann Coleman was born in 1807 and died in 1864. She married a Mr. Runn.

9. Julius C. Coleman was born in 1811. He married Mary A. Woodson in 1839.

Chapter 15

Davies or Davis Family of Cornwall County, England to Buckingham County, Virginia

Davies is a common surname that originated in Wales; came to Cornwall County, England in the eighteenth century; and to Buckingham County, Virginia in 1850.[1] The name was changed from Davies to Davis when Joshua and John Davies immigrated to this country. The source of the Welsh surname Davies was from the forename—first name—David. The Welsh used a patronymic second name system. This was a simple idea whereby the father's first name was given to a son as his surname. For example, a father who was named David would name his son Robert of David (or Robert ap David). If a father was named John, and named his son William, the son's name would be William ap John. As the population grew in the eighteenth century and names became more scarce, the Welsh were forced to adopt a two-name system that followed the English pattern. The name David became the surname Davies. The name John became the surname Jones and so forth.

The name Davies was not known in England before the Norman Conquest. It was introduced when the Welsh people emigrated to England after coal from Wales was shipped to Cornwall County for smelting iron, tin, copper, and other metals. During the early 1800s, the surname Davies represented eighteen percent of the population in Wales. Therefore, surnames during the eighteenth century and earlier in Wales were very difficult to track.

The first known ancestors in this direct Davis lineage were George and Mary Davies, who christened their son, Jacob Davies, in Crowan Parish, Cornwell County, England, on June 4, 1775.[2] We

---

[1] This genealogical interest commenced in 1965 when the compiler participated in a Davis family reunion at Holiday Lake in Appomattox County. A paper was prepared for a later Davis reunion that was held in Buckingham County on May 13, 1989. It was revised in 1994 after a research trip to the LDS Library in Salt Lake City, Utah. Numerous descendants have contributed genealogical information, especially Mrs. Ruby F. (Davis) Walton of Dillwyn, Virginia.

[2] Microfilm No. 246797, LDS Library in Salt Lake City, Utah.

have not been able to locate George and Mary in Cornwall County Parish registers, except for the christening of Jacob. It is hypothesized that George and Mary Davies emigrated from Wales to Cornwall County because they were attracted to ventures in mining.

Not much has been found on Jacob Davies, except that his wife was named Elizabeth, and that six of their children were also baptized in Crowan Parish. It is believed that Jacob moved his family to another parish sometime after the year 1811, possibly as late as 1830. Records of the family in a nearby parish have not yet been located. A photograph of the Davies mansion house in Cornwall County was brought to America by grandson Joshua Davies, 1828-1898. Tradition says that the house was located in the vicinity of Penzance. The name Jacob was not passed along to the Davies who came to Virginia.

Cornwall County was a good mining area, and Cornish people were known for their love for mining. As raw materials diminished in their homeland during the 1840s, many immigrated to the USA to work in a land with abundant copper, lead, zinc, coal, tin, or gold mines. Also, Cornwall was known for its cornish hens.

According to a roadside marker along US Route 15 on the south side of Dillwyn, Buckingham County, a gold mine was opened in 1835 by members of the Morrow family. Could this have been a spelling variation of the surname Moyle? The Moyles were well-known for their mining exploits in Cornwall County. We should mention that another Englishman named Walter Staples and his family also came to mine gold near New Canton, Buckingham County. We have not been able to establish kinship with the Staples family, but there was a connection to Cornwall County.

Children of Jacob Sr. and Elizabeth Davies:[3]

> 1. Jacob Davies Jr. was born April 20, 1800 and baptized on May 25. Nothing more is known about him at this time.

---

[3] Information on members of this family unit were obtained from the Crowan Parish records in Cornwall County, England.

2. John Davies was born on Nov. 1, 1801 and baptized on Nov. 15. He died Jan. 17, 1861, probably in Cornwall County. John married Margaret Moyle. This John Davies was father of at least four children: Joshua, John Jr., Carrie, and Eliza.

3. George Davies was born Feb. 12, 1803 and christened on March 12. It is believed that he married Elizabeth Williams, Oct. 22, 1828.

4. Elizabeth Davies was born July 30, 1804.

5. Francis Davies was born Jan. 26, 1806.

6. James Davies was born June 9, 1811.

We know nothing more about five of the children named above, but are making efforts to locate descendants in Cornwall County, England. John Davies is recognized because his birth date in church records coincides with family records brought to Virginia. On March 26, 1826, John Davies married Margaret Moyle, daughter of John and Mary (Walters) Moyle.[4] John Davies was listed on the marriage license as as a bachelor and Margaret as a spinster. John could read but Margaret could not, according to the Rev. John Peter, the curator who performed the marriage ceremony in Crowan Parish. This was in the Church of England or the Anglican Church. Margaret Moyle was born on April 25, 1804 and was christened on May 13. She died on July 26, 1869, probably in Cornwall County.[5]

---

[4] John Moyle, born circa 1777, married Mary Walters, July 20, 1801 in Crowan Parish, Cornwall County. John Moyle's occupation was registered as a miner. Their children were listed as John Jr., Margaret, Henry, Jennifer, and Matthew Moyle, all of whom are recorded in the Crowan Parish Register. Matthew Moyle, son of John and Mary, immigrated to Rowan County, North Carolina to mine gold. Mary Walters was christened Dec. 16, 1781. Mary's parents, John and Charity (Williams) Walters were married in Crowan Parish on Feb. 2, 1781.

[5] Source for the birth dates of John and Margaret Davies were the Crowan Parish records, and the death dates for both were furnished from private records by Mrs. Joseph (Elva) Jones of Lynchburg, Virginia.

Margaret had both a brother and an uncle named Matthew Moyle. Two grandsons in Virginia were named Matthew Moyle Davis.[6]

At least four children of John and Margaret (Moyle) Davies immigrated to the United States. Tradition says that a fifth sibling came, but went west to follow mining opportunities. It is believed that John and Margaret remained in Cornwall County where they presumably died.

Known children of John and Margaret (Moyle) Davies:

> 1. Joshua Davies was born on June 6, 1828, and died in Buckingham County, Virginia on May 18, 1898. He married Mary E. Guthrie.
>
> 2. John Davies Jr. was born in 1830 and died in Buckingham County in 1900. He married Margaret Price.
>
> 3. Carrie B. Davies was born in Cornwall County, England circa 1845.[7] She crossed the Atlantic Ocean twice before she died in Fluvanna County, Virginia. On the second trip, she sailed from Liverpool, England on the ship "City of Paris," on Nov. 1, 1869. The record stated she was twenty-four years old, single and a citizen of the United States. Carrie later married and outlived two medical doctors. She visited relatives and kept them informed about other members of the family. She married first in Buckingham County Dr. Abraham Walter Fontaine, 1832-1878, whose first wife was Mildred Spencer, daughter of Nathan and Martha Spencer. Mildred was born on April 30, 1835 and died on Dec. 18, 1861.[8] Abraham and Carrie Davis were married on Oct. 28, 1873 in Buckingham County. Abraham was a son of Clement Rush and Elizabeth W. Fontaine.[9] Carrie had one child, Clement Overton Fontaine, born on Dec. 11, 1875 in Buckingham County, and died in

---

[6] Matthew M. Davis, son of Joshua, misspelled his name as Morrell. It is not known whether this was a phonetic spelling error or an attempt to change the name to create a distance between two related families in Buckingham County.

[7] Carrie gave her age as thirty-three years old the 1880 U.S. Census for Buckingham County, Virginia

[8] Posted on Genforum.com by Fred Fontaine, who since died on April 1, 2001. fredfontaine@att.net

[9] Buckingham County, Virginia Marriage Records, 1853-1890, Library of Virginia.

1911 in Campbell County, Virginia. He married Louise M. Poindexter, daughter of Joseph P. Poindexter of Maryville, Campbell County. Clement was a physician with the Norfolk and Western Railroad. They had no children. After Clement's death, Louise married a Mr. Ware.[10]

After the death of Dr. Fontaine, Carrie married second Dr. William Beverly Pettit, who was born on July 22, 1853, and died in New Canton, Virginia on April 27, 1918 from a self-inflicted gunshot wound.[11] They were married on Oct. 20, 1887. Dr. Pettit was a graduate of the University of Maryland School of Medicine. Both are buried at the Glen Burnie family farm located about one mile north of Palmyra, Fluvanna County, on US Route 15. Dates were not placed on Carrie's tombstone, so we are still searching for her vital records. She had no biological children by this marriage. On her marriage application filed in Buckingham County, Carrie claimed her hometown as Penzance, Cornwall County, England.

4. Eliza Davies, was born at Redruth, Cornwall County, Sept. 19, 1837. Possibly Redruth is the location of the house that was photographed and brought to Virginia by her brother Joshua. Eliza married John Buckett about 1860. She died Jan. 11, 1928, and was buried on Bird Island, Renville, Minnesota.[12] John went to Michigan to mine copper.

Joshua Davis

Joshua Davis, son of John and Margaret (Moyle) Davies, was born in Cornwall County, England on June 6, 1828, and died in Buckingham County, Virginia on May 18, 1898. He married Mary Elizabeth Guthrie, daughter of William Palmore and Sarah "Sallie"

---

[10] Charles J. Ragland, *Ancestors and Descendants of the Reverend Peter Fontaine (1691-1759) of Westover Parish, Charles City County, Virginia*. Part 1. (Winston-Salem, NC: The Author). pp. 155-157. Source was provided to the compiler by stemmatis@aol.com.

[11] *Vital Records: Directory of Deceased American Physicians, 1804-1929*, found on http://www.genealogy.com

[12] Information given by email, June 17, 1996, by Paula Frighetti of Arizona, address= willow@AZStarNet.com

A. (Coleman) Guthrie.[13] They were married in Buckingham County, Nov. 13, 1851. Mary Elizabeth was born Nov. 24, 1832 and died Dec. 26, 1912. She served as a midwife, meaning that she delivered babies in her neighborhood.

Joshua Davis 1828-1898

---

[13] William P. Guthrie, father-in-law of Joshua Davis, was born Nov. 24, 1800, in Cumberland County, Va., and died March 3, 1861. His first wife was Sarah "Sallie" A. Coleman, daughter of Julius and Elizabeth (Coleman) Coleman. Sallie (Coleman) Guthrie was born Jan. 17, 1798 and died in March 1885, in Buckingham County.

Both Joshua and Mary Elizabeth were buried in a family graveyard, located about one-fourth mile behind a log-processing company along the northern outskirts of Dillwyn, Buckingham County.

Joshua Davis and his brother John Davis Jr. immigrated to Rowan County, North Carolina circa 1848 and to Buckingham County, Virginia during the gold rush era, in 1850. The gold rush fever struck not only in western territories such as Colorado, Nevada, and California, but also in Virginia. Joshua and John Davis first went to Gold Hill, Rowan County, where their cousin, Matthew Moyle, supervised a large mining operation. They are found on the 1850 census for both Rowan and Buckingham Counties. The 1850 census for Buckingham County shows that Joshua and John Davis were boarding with Charles G. Hesse, a German emigrant who apparently came here for gold. Occupation of the Davis brothers was listed as (gold) miner. The 1870 census stated that Joshua Davis was employed as a "gold washer."

By 1860, Joshua Davis had purchased a store in the Dillwyn area of Buckingham County, where he later served as the second postmaster. Although he did numerous kinds of work, he was generally considered in public records to have been a merchant. He was the first Sunday school superintendent at Rocky Mount Methodist Church in Dillwyn.

Joshua was unable to serve in the military during the Civil War because of a crippling disability. He accidentally shot himself in the leg while killing a blacksnake.

Children of Joshua and Mary Elizabeth (Guthrie) Davis:[14]

1. John James Davis was born June 1, 1853 in Buckingham County, and died March 3, 1926 at Evington, Virginia. He married Rebecca Oliver, who died May 13, 1925. Two children: (a) Elva Davis was born July 24, 1888 and died in February 1978. She married Joseph Jones of Lynchburg, Virginia. He was born on July 15, 1886 and died in May

---

[14] Information provided from Bible record of Joshua Davis by one of his granddaughters, Mrs. Elva (Davis) Jones of Lynchburg, Virginia.

1970 in Lynchburg. She had the Davis family Bible. (b) Vernie Davis was born on Sept. 10, 1896 and died in November 1985 in Richmond. She married Frank Brockman who was born on Sept. 21, 1895 and died in February 1977 in Amherst, Virginia.

2. Joshua Lee Davis was born July 13, 1855 and died Oct. 28, 1936. He married first Mary D. Apperson, daughter of Sterling and Eliza Apperson, on July 28, 1881, and married second Octavia Gough, a widow. She was born in May 1871. Joshua Lee was buried in the Davis family graveyard at Dillwyn, Virginia. Buried adjacent to him was a son named Andrew B. Davis, who was killed in a train wreck. His vital dates were Aug. 18, 1882 to Oct. 22, 1923. Three mysterious letters (KKK) were engraved on his stone, presumably the Ku Klux Klan. A second son, Clarence Davis, went to West Virginia. A third son, John Wesley Davis was born in 1884; went to New Orleans, Louisiana and married Lucy___. The fourth son, Robert Lee Davis, was born Oct. 1, 1888. He married Jemima Moss and moved to Mercer County, West Virginia.

3. Sarah Jane Davis[15] was born Aug. 8, 1857 in Buckingham County, and died Feb. 20, 1926.[16] She married John "Jack" LeSueur, Jan. 14, 1880, in Buckingham County, and they raised a large family. Jack LeSueur was born on Nov. 20, 1848 and died on March 9, 1928. Children of Jack and Sarah J. (Davis) LeSueur were: (a) Mary Elizabeth LeSueur was born June 30, 1881 and died July 28, 1939. She was buried in the Dunkum family cemetery in Buckingham County. She married James Garland Dunkum, son of James Burley and Mary Elizabeth (Ayres) Dunkum. James G. was born April 6, 1878 and died Aug. 10, 1948. (b) Rosa B. LeSueur was born Feb. 20, 1883 and died Feb. 26, 1969. Burial was in Brown's Chapel, Buckingham County. She married William Elijah Dunkum, son of James B. and Mary E. (Ayres) Dunkum, on Dec. 27, 1904. He was born June 17, 1884 and died June 16, 1971. (c) John Cleveland LeSueur was born on Nov. 20, 1884 and died on April 15, 1966.[17] (d) Margaret Elmonia LeSueur was born Aug. 8, 1886 and died Nov. 18, 1978. Burial was in the Rocky Mount Methodist Church Cemetery in Buckingham County. She married James Nathan Ayres, son

---

[15] Much of the information on Sarah Jane Davis and family came from Ruby Talley Smith of Wheaton, Maryland.

[16] Another source gives a death date of Jan. 30, 1926.

[17] Social Security Death Index.

of John Stanley and Melissa Catherine (Duncan) Ayres, in 1901. (e) Joshua Lee LeSueur was born on Aug. 20, 1887 and died on June 2, 1989. He married Alice Blanche Dunsford. (f) Robert Moses LeSueur was born about 1891 and died in 1960. He first married Willie Danford, and married second Willie Ethel Allen, Jan. 3, 1934. (g) Edgar Overton LeSueur was born June 26, 1892 and died July 24, 1984 at Blackstone, Virginia. Burial was in the Cedar Baptist Church Cemetery in Buckingham County. He married Martha Bryant. (h) Travis Conrad LeSueur was born on April 7, 1896 and died July 12, 1985 at Farmville Hospital. Burial was in the Cedar Baptist Church Cemetery. He married Mattie Sue Thomas on March 9, 1916. (i) Carrie E. LeSueur was born in 1901, and lives in Weynoake Retirement Home in Farmville, Virginia. She married Duree S. Jamison.

4. Margaret Ann Davis was born May 18, 1860 in Buckingham County, and died June 1, 1940. She was buried in the Joshua Davis family graveyard at Dillwyn, Buckingham County. Margaret married Moses LeSueur, son of Peyton and Mary LeSueur, Nov. 17, 1880. The officiating minister was the Rev. John Spencer. Moses LeSueur was born May 18, 1853 and died Feb. 13, 1922. Their only child was Etta LeSueur who married James J. Phaup[18].

5. Travis Henry Davis was born Feb. 3, 1863 and died June 19, 1907. He married Rosa L. Harris, who was a daughter of A.B. and Willie A. Harris, Dec. 30, 1896. The Rev. W.E. Grant was officiating minister for the wedding. Travis was working as a miner in Alleghney County, Virginia, at the time of his marriage. Travis was buried in the Davis family graveyard at Dillwyn. Buried nearby was his son, Bernard L. Davis, who went swimming after dinner; developed cramps; and was drowned. His vital dates were April 30, 1904 to July 19, 1928. A daughter of Travis named Mamie A. Davis was also buried nearby. Her tombstone inscription says that she was born July 23, 1902 and died July 11, 1903.

6. Mary Eliza Davis was born March 20, 1865 and died Jan. 30, 1936. She married first Robert Madison Baird, son of Robert Bonepart and Sarah (Price) Baird,[19] Aug. 30, 1886. Robert M. Baird was born March 6,

---

[18] Mattie Davis, daughter of Matthew M. and Josephine Davis, was raised by this family.

[19] Robert B. Baird Sr .was born on Jan. 31, 1832 and died on June 17, 1869. Sarah Price, his spouse, was born on June 2, 1834. Information was given to Wilmer L.

1860 and died Nov. 27, 1906. Mary Eliza married second Edgar C. Kellinger, born in 1875 in Pennsylvania. Relatives did not like E. C. because he would not tell anyone where he was from, nor anything about his family. E.C. and Mary Eliza were murdered during the course of a robbery by a tenant laborer on Jan. 30, 1936. They were beaten to death. The murderer was given a life sentence in the Virginia State Prison System. Carrie E. Davis, sister of Eliza, was living in the house and ran upstairs when the robbery was underway. A strong lock on the door saved her life. The robber then went to the yard and told Carrie to throw money down on the ground from her second-floor room. Known as a very stingy old maid, she threw only about a dollar in coins. Someone saw the robber running from the scene and summoned the sheriff, who caught the man immediately.

Children of Robert M. and Mary Eliza (Davis) Baird:[20]

(a) Nanny E. Baird married first Bernard M. Wooten Sr., Sept. 21, 1910, and married second George Fitzgerald. Nanny's children were:

[1] Bernard Maynard Wooten Jr. was born Sept. 5, 1911 and died after 1965. He retired as a Brig. General from the Armed Services. Maynard married Lillian Harris of Roanoke and they had Robert Lee Wooten, born Dec. 5, 1946; and James Mayfield Wooten, born March 16, 1949.

[2] Dorothy Marie Wooten was born June 3, 1913. She married William Ralph Britton. Their children: Barbara Lee Britton was born Jan. 1, 1946; and William Ralph Britton Jr. was born Aug. 13, 1947.

[3] Robert Haskin Wooten was born on April 16, 1916. He married Audrey Green of Richmond. Their children: Jacqueline Elizabeth Wooten was born May 29, 1950; Robert Stanley Wooten was born Feb. 22, 1952; and Sharon Leigh Wooten was born April 3, 1954.

[4] George Patterson Fitzgerald was born Nov. 26, 1926.

(b) Minnie Baird married Artemas Rhodes, Sept. 21, 1910, and lived in Afton, Virginia.

Kerns by Nannie (Davis) Fitzgerald of Farmville, Virginia during a visit to her house in 1975.

[20] From Bible record given to compiler by Nannie (Davis) Fitzgerald to compiler in 1975.

7. Matthew Morrell Davis was born June 13, 1867 and died Jan. 14, 1957. He married Josephine Shepherd, daughter of Benjamin Franklin and Malissa Frances (Word) Shepherd, Dec. 31, 1891, in Buckingham County. She was born July 28, 1868 and died Sept. 15, 1952. Both were buried in the Salem Methodist Church cemetery in eastern Buckingham County.

8. Robert Nicholas Davis was born Oct. 3, 1869 and died Oct. 31, 1935. He married Rosa Shepherd, who was a daughter of Benjamin Franklin Sr. and Malissa Frances (Word) Shepherd. They lived in Buckingham County.[21] Children of Robert N. and Rosa (Shepherd) Davis:

  a. Mrs. A. Robertson of Dillwyn.

  b. Annie Davis was born in 1906. She married Clifford A. Jones, son of Edward W. and Nettie Jones of New Canton. He was born on Sept. 23, 1901 and died on Dec. 19, 1992 in Buckingham County.

  c. Joshua B. Davis was born on July 20, 1907 in Buckingham County and died in August 1972 at Kimball, McDoewll County, West Virginia.[22]

  d. Henry M. Davis of Ivy Depot, Virginia, born on Feb. 6, 1910.

  e. Roy Matthew Davis was born Oct. 29, 1911 and died Sept. 3, 1988.[23]

  f. John Davis was twenty years old when his father died.

  g. Gladys Mae Davis was twelve years old when her father died.

9. Carrie Elizabeth Davis was born July 21, 1872 and died unmarried, March 8, 1957. She was buried in the Davis family graveyard at Dillwyn.

10. Nannie Beadles Davis was born Sept. 28, 1875 and died unmarried, Sept. 27, 1960. She was buried in the Smyrna Methodist Church cemetery. Nannie taught school at Saratoga School in Buckingham County. She lived with her niece, Etta (LeSeuer) Phaup.

11. Samuel William Davis was born Sept. 14, 1879 and died unmarried, in 1935. He suffered from a disease that affected the central nervous

---

[21] Buckingham County *Will Book 4*, dated Nov. 18, 1935, pp. 81-82.

[22] Social Security Death Index.

[23] Social Security Death Index.

system, and died in Western State Hospital in Staunton, Virginia. No one seems to know much about him.

Matthew Morrell Davis

Matthew Morrell[24] Davis, son of Joshua and Mary Elizabeth (Guthrie) Davis, was born in Buckingham County, Virginia on June 13, 1867 and died in the same county, Jan. 14, 1957. Matthew misspelled his name as Morrell, instead of Moyle. He was a farmer in the eastern part of Buckingham County.

He married Josephine Shepherd, who was a daughter of Benjamin Franklin Sr. and Malissa Frances (Word) Shepherd, on Dec. 31, 1891, at the home of her parents, in Buckingham County. Officiating minister was the Rev. John J. Spencer, Baptist minister.

Josephine (Shepherd) Davis was born July 28, 1868 and died Sept. 13, 1952 near Dillwyn. She and her husband were buried at Salem Methodist cemetery in the eastern section of Buckingham County.

Five of their children died of childhood diseases, which was a terrifying experience for the family. Both parents were stricken with typhoid fever, but recovered. When diphtheria struck into the family unit, diphtheria serum was brought from a Richmond hospital to New Canton, via a James River packet boat. Dr. Garland, the family physician, rode horseback from Dillwyn to pick up the serum at New Canton. One characteristic of descendants of Matthew and Josephine is a preoccupation with germs and cleanliness. Also, perfectionism is one of the traits associated with the family.

Children of Matthew M. and Josephine (Shepherd) Davis:[25]

---

[24] The correct spelling for this name is Moyle. Apparently, the name was changed to Morrell to distinguish from his first cousin, Matthew Moyle Davis of New Canton.

[25] Joshua Davis Family Bible, court records, and personal interviews with descendants.

1. Frank Morrell (*sic*) Davis was born Sept. 29, 1892 and he died Feb. 21, 1963. He served in the U.S. Navy during World War I. On April 4, 1925, he married Annie Lee Paul. They had no children, but she had two children: Willie Paul and Albert Paul.

2. John Rolfe Davis was born Nov. 25, 1895 and died Oct. 24, 1903, of typhoid fever.

3. Mattie Ruth Davis was born May 13, 1899 and died Sept. 2, 1987. When she was an infant, the parents sent her to live with her aunt Margaret (Davis) LeSeur. The move was successful in preventing Mattie from contracting diphtheria. She married first John Robert Baird, son of Robert M. and Mary E. (Davis) Baird, on Aug. 13, 1921. He was born May 25, 1889 and died Nov. 4, 1946. Two children were born to this union: Ruth Baird and Marietta Baird. Mattie married second Lloyd Daniel Hammonds, Dec. 27, 1948.

Wilmer L. Kerns, Nellie V. (Davis) Walton, and Shirley M. (Walton) Kerns at the Davis reunion in July 1965 at Holiday Lake in Appomattox County.

4. Arthur James Davis was born Aug. 9, 1901 and died Jan. 14, 1903, of a childhood disease. He was a twin brother of Etta Pearl.

5. Etta Pearl Davis was born on Aug. 9, 1901 and died July 4, 1902, of diphtheria. She was a twin sister of Arthur J.

6. Joshua Hazel Davis was born July 6, 1903 and died Jan. 10, 1906 of diphtheria.

7. Henry Howard Davis was born May 28, 1905 and died Jan. 9, 1906, of diphtheria.

8. Nellie Virginia Davis was born Sept. 7, 1907 and died Jan. 20, 1973. She married Walker Scott Walton, son of Eugene A. and Nannie K. (Jones) Walton. They were married Aug. 2, 1930.

9. Ruby Frances Davis was born June 27, 1909. She married John Christian Walton, Dec. 22, 1939. John was born Jan. 7, 1902 and died Jan. 3, 1986. He was a brother of Walker Scott Walton, and both were sons of Eugene A. and Nannie (Jones) Walton of Bent Creek. One child: John Christian Walton Jr. was born March 29, 1950. He is exactly 100 years younger than his grandfather Walton.

10. Wilbur Clyde Davis was born on Sept. 17, 1911. He married: first Audrey Lee Smith, on Aug. 16, 1937, in Cumberland County, Virginia. Their daughter Barbara Ann Davis married Johnny Marr. Both are missionaries. Clyde married second Elnora Belle (Williams) Green of Wheeling, West Virginia. She was born on Feb. 18, 1912 and took her life on April 25, 1999 at her home in Dillwyn. Clyde and Elnora were farmers in Buckingham County. They are members of the Salem Methodist Church.

John Davies Jr.

John Davies Jr., 1832-1900, son of John Sr. and Margaret (Moyle) Davies, settled at New Canton, Buckingham County in 1850 where he married Margaret Price and raised a family. John and his brother Joshua Davis migrated from Cornwall County, England to Gold Hill, Rowan County, North Carolina circa 1848 before settling in Buckingham County. John Jr. was commissioned a Lieutenant in C 44 Virginia Regiment, of the Confederate States of America. In 1870, he was listed as a farmer. By 1880 he was a farmer, merchant, and postmaster at New Canton, which is a waterport town along the James River. More information is being sought on his son John Davis III and his family. The U.S. Censuses for 1870 and 1880 provided a list of their children, and further information was garnered from gravestone inscriptions at the Trinity Presbyterian Church in New Canton.

Children of John Sr. and Margaret (Price) Davis:

1. Henry Davis was born in 1852, and was listed as a salesman on the census. Henry married Nettie (Thomas) Coleman, daughter of James M. Thomas, Dec. 7, 1876, at Red Bank, Fluvanna County, Virginia.[26]

2. John Davis III, born in 1854, married Margaret Mitchell. He ran a ferry across the James River.

3. Matthew Moyle Davis was born Nov. 1, 1857 and died Feb. 11, 1914. In 1880, Matthew was assistant postmaster at New Canton. He was buried in the Trinity Presbyterian Church Cemetery, New Canton.

4. Margaret "Maggie" Davis, born circa 1860, was a school teacher.

5. Harrison Davis was born circa 1863.

6. Virginia Davis was born in 1865, and nothing more is known.

7. Carrie Davis was born in 1868 and died in 1922. She did not marry. Carrie and Matthew M. are buried near their father, John Davis Jr., in the Trinity Presbyterian Cemetery Cemetery at New Canton, Buckingham County. The church was established in 1840 to serve the riverport town.

8. Minnie Davis was born in 1871.

9. Nettie Davis, born circa 1876, married Peter B. Patteson. They were buried in the Trinity Presbyterian Church Cemetery at New Canton. Nettie's unmarried sister, Carrie Davis, lived with them.

Eliza (Davies) Buckett

Eliza Davies, daughter of John and Margaret (Moyle) Davies, was born at Redruth, Cornwall County, England, on Sept. 19, 1837, and died June 25, 1923 in Minneapolis, Minnesota. She married John Buckett, son of John and Sarah Buckett, circa 1860 in England. John was born Nov. 1, 1835 at Nancegollan, Cornwall County, England, and died Jan. 11, 1892 at Bird Island, Renville, Minnesota. They came to the USA during the 1880s, when John brought his family to Michigan. According to Paula Frighetti, the Buckett family emigrated from England to Ishpeming, Marquette County, Michigan to work the copper mines.

Children of John and Eliza (Davies) Buckett:

---

[26] *The Richmond Whig*, Saturday, Dec 23, 1876, p. 2, c. 3

1. Caroline Buckett was born at Nancegollan, Cornwall County, England, July 3, 1863, and died Dec. 23, 1899 at Ishpeming, Michigan. She came to the USA with her parents. Caroline married William Behenna.

2. Eliza Jane Buckett was born Nov. 10, 1864 at Nancegollan, and died in Minneapolis, Minnesota, Nov. 4, 1950. She married George Davies, son of Capt. Henry and Jane (Sampson) Davies, Sept. 15, 1892, at Bird Island, Renville, Minnesota. George was born Oct. 23, 1866 at Rockland, Michigan, and died July 30, 1946, in Minneapolis, Minnesota. It is probable that George Davies is related to Eliza's family, in that both came from Cornwall County, England.

3. John Buckett was born Dec. 30, 1866 at Nancegollan, and died March 28, 1940. He married Eugenia Bowlen.

4. William Tremayne Buckett was born in Nancegollan on Feb. 25, 1868, and died March 8, 1934 at Bisbee, Cochise County, Arizona. Burial was in Evergreen Cemetery. William married Mary Charlotte Ask (changed her name to Johnson), Feb. 17, 1892, in Ohio Grove, DeKalb County, Illinois. Cary C. was born in November 1881 in Ostergotland, Sweden, and died July 10, 1926 at Bisbee, Arizona. They had six children, all daughters.

5. Ernest Buckett was born Feb. 11, 1874 in Nancegollan, and died Sept. 11, 1951. He married Laura Robinson, who was born circa 1879 in Missouri.

6. Frederick Buckett was born Sept. 8, 1880 in Nancegollan, Crowan Parish, Cornwall County, England, and died Nov. 10, 1905 in Minneapolis, Minnesota.

Information is still being sought on other possible children of John and Margaret (Moyle) Davies and their descendants.

Chapter 16

Fields Family of Campbell County, Virginia

The earliest known and proven ancestor with this surname was Andrew Fields, 1753-1794. Chilton[1] and Evans[2] stated that Andrew Fields was a son of John and Sarah (Milbert) Fields. Their source was based on research concluded in 1898 by Chapman Hunter Chilton, 1832-1917, who was a former Superintendant of the Appomattox County Schools. Gilliland[3] believes that someone has made an error in identifying John Fields and his wife Sarah Milbert. He cites a Bible record of a John and Jane (Millen) Field that lists a son, Andrew Field, born in July 1, 1785, who married Franky Holland on March 28, 1808, in Bedford County, Virginia. This John Field, 1753-1825, was born in Loudoun County and died in Bedford County.[4] Gilliland suggests that the two Johns are erroneously identified as being two different persons with the same name, when in reality they are the same person. It appears that Mr. Gilliland has confused the names of parents of our Andrew Fields, 1753-1794, with names of the parents of the other Andrew Field—born in 1785. These two Andrews were not from the same generation, and their surnames were spelled differently, one with an s on the end of Field and the other without. We believe that our conclusions are correct on this matter. Chilton conducted his research more than 100 years ago, and has been proven to be reliable. Secondly, the two Johns do

---

[1] Harriett A. Chilton of Falls Church, Virginia was the compiler of *Hundred Hunter Cousins,* published in 1976.

[2] Dr. Joseph W. Evans of Boulder, Colorado was a compiler of Campbell County families, including the Fields family. His massive records and files have been computerized and deposited with interested persons. Lack of documentation may be a shortcoming of some parts of these files.

[3] Another view is held by Porter M. Gilliland, of Ft. Payne, Alabama, in *The Red Tower,* the quarterly publication for the Clan Galbraith Association. It states this Andrew was a son of Dr. Richard and Nancy (Meade) Fields of Brunswick County, Virginia, but no proof is offered.

[4] Letter from Porter M. Gilliland to Wilmer L. Kerns, dated Nov. 16, 1996. John Field, veteran of the Revolutionary War, and Jane Millen had ten children, ranging birth years from 1764 to 1788. Gilliland said, "I got this information at Jones Memorial Library in Lynchburg, Virginia."

not belong to the same generation of time, which makes it more difficult to confuse two people. Thirdly, Sarah Milbert and Jane Millen are sufficiently different spousal names.

Andrew Fields was born circa 1753 in Virginia, and died in 1794 in Campbell County, Virginia. The year of his death is proven by a letter from James Galbreath to John R. Gaston, dated March 15, 1802. It says, "Sister Fields has been a widow for eight years, her husband was killed at the raising of his own barn."[5] Sister Fields was nee Margaret Galbreath, who was born in Northampton County, Pennsylvania in 1754, and died in 1835 in Campbell County. Margaret was a daughter of Alexander and Agnes (Miller) Galbraith. After 1794, Margaret Fields was listed, and not Andrew, as the living parent named on the marriage records of their children. The Fields lived in Campbell County.

Children of Andrew and Margaret (Galbraith) Fields:[6]

1. Mary (Mercy) Fields married Samuel Caldwell on Jan. 3, 1793 in Campbell County. The parent was listed on the marriage bond as Andrew Fields.

2. Rachel Fields married James Shannon on Dec. 9, 1794 in Campbell County. The parent listed was Andrew Fields.

3. Isabella Fields was born circa 1780 and died June 27, 1847 in St. Clair County, Alabama. She married Robert Means Jr., son of Robert Sr. and Elizabeth (Robertson) Means, Oct. 15, 1800, in Campbell

---

[5] *East Tennessee Roots*, Vol. VII, No. 4, pp. 190-193. The article reports on some early letters written by members of the Galbreath and Gaston families. Article was supplied by Glenn Smith of Muskogee, Oklahoma.

[6] Information on the family unit of Andrew and Margaret Fields is a synthesis of three sources: (1) Zelphia Lee Koon and Mrs. James Paul Galbreath, *Galbreath Clan and Their Descendants*, (The Clan Galbreath Association), no date, p. 147. It includes information that was sent to Ms. Koon by Porter M. Gilliland, Ft. Payne, Alabama. (2) Computer file on the Galbreath-Fields families that was researched and created by the late Dr. Joseph W. Evans, 5103 Williams Fork Trail, #109, Boulder, Colorado 80301. (3) Information provided to the compiler in 1980 by Ms. Harriett A. Chilton of Falls Church, Virginia, including the research of her grandfather Chapman Hunter Chilton.

County. Robert Jr. was born in 1777 in North Carolina and died in 1817 in Greenville, Tennessee.[7]

4. Martha "Patsy" Fields married John Caldwell, 1768-1813, Oct. 17, 1802, in Campbell County.[8]

5. Elizabeth Fields was born in 1780 in Buckingham County, Virginia, and died April 18, 1855, in Campbell County. She married Benjamin Hunter, who was born in 1770 and died June 23, 1845. They were married on Feb. 17, 1804. The compiler copied their tombstone inscriptions from the Hunter-Marshall Cemetery in Appomattox County, Virginia.

6. Margaret G. "Peggy" Fields was born circa 1786 and died March 9, 1868. She married Richard Harvey on Sept. 12, 1803, in Campbell County.

7. Nancy (Agness) Fields married John Jones on Nov. 7, 1803, in Campbell County.

8. Daniel Fields married Rachel Hunter, daughter of John Hunter, April 11, 1808, in Campbell County. They moved to Green County, Tennessee, and later to Blount County, Alabama, when Robert and Isabella Means Jr. moved their family to Alabama.

9. Sarah Fields, of whom nothing further is known.

10. Jemima Harker Fields married Thomas Hunter on Oct. 11, 1810, in Campbell County.

---

[7] Gilliland provided this information.

[8] From tombstone inscriptions in the Marshall-Hunter Cemetery in Appomattox County.

Walker Scott Walton and his wife Nellie V. (Davis) Walton

A Walton-Davis reunion in Buckingham County in 1985 that was a forerunner to the Eugene A. Walton reunion in Appomattox.. Seated: Josephine W. Walton, Mattie R. Baird Hammonds, Shirley M. Kerns, Jacob S. Kerns, Wilmer L. Kerns. Row two: Elnora Davis, Wilbur C. Davis, Amanda Walton, Aaron Harris, Yolanda J. (Walton) Harris, Jerry Harris. Third row: Glenice Walton, Ruby F. (Davis) Walton, Russel S Walton's friend. Fourth row: Winston D. Walton, John C. Walton, Robert T. Kerns and Russel S. Walton, descendants of the Fields family.

Chapter 17

The Guthrey or Guthrie Family of Cumberland and Buckingham Counties, Virginia

The Guthrey surname is believed to have its origin in Scotland. The name has been spelled many ways, including, Guttery, Guthery, Guttrey, Guthrey, Guthree, and Guthrie, of which the latter is preferred by our branch.[1] The earliest-known ancestor of this family branch was Thomas Guthrey of St. John Parish, King William County, Virginia. Born circa 1716, he later settled in Cumberland County where his will was filed on Oct. 6, 1790, and where his will was proven on Sept. 22, 1800. Executors for his estate were Robert Anderson, Samuel Anderson, and Alexander Guthrey Sr. The name of Thomas' spouse was Sarah, but her maiden name has not been proven. Some researchers believe she was nee Sarah Oakes, this based on a statement in the will of her son Alexander K. Guthrey. It is possible that Sarah was his second wife. Lawrence R. Guthrie[2] believed that Thomas Guthrey married Patsy Baskerville, but no evidence has been presented.

Children of Thomas and Sarah Guthrey:

1. Susanna Guthrey was born circa 1736 in Virginia, and died June 3, 1824 in Green County, Kentucky. She married Robert Moore. Susanna received her father's "large Bible" that was mentioned in his Cumberland County will. Also, she received two Negro women whose names were Violet and Bruce (*sic*). The Moore family immigrated to Green County, Kentucky about 1800, where Robert died in 1808.[3]

Children of Robert and Susannah (Guthrie) Moore:

a. Richard Moore died about October 1825 in Washington County, Kentucky. He married a woman named Margaret.

---

[1] Those who settled in Buckingham County, Virginia most often spelled the name as Guthrie.

[2] One source of information is *American Guthries and Allied Families*, published by Lawrence R. Guthrie in 1933. The work is basic, but lacks detail on some of the Guthries in Buckingham County. This chapter was written to fill in gaps of information.

[3] Information submitted on June 22, 1998 from RobertR150@aol.com

b. Elizabeth Moore, born circa 1756, married Richard Walker on Nov. 7, 1792.

c. William Moore was born Nov. 3, 1757 in Buckingham County, Virginia and died Feb. 23, 1843 in Prairie Township, Jackson County, Missouri. He married Drusilla Weatherford on Feb. 24, 1785 in Buckingham County.

d. Thomas Guthrie Moore was born on Jan. 24, 1760 in Buckingham County, and died Nov. 2, 1843 in McCoupin County, Illinois.

e. Sarah Moore was born circa 1761 in Virginia and died Jan. 25, 1852 in Summersville, Green County, Kentucky. She married Andrew Chaudoin on Dec. 20, 1786.

f. Lucy Moore, born circa 1762, married Robert Clark.

g. John G. Moore died in 1832 in Pike County, Missouri. He married Nancy Carlile on Dec. 1, 1803 in Green County, Kentucky.

h. Travis S. Moore was born on Aug. 31, 1780 in Buckingham County, Virginia and died July 19, 1852 in Monroe County, Missouri. He married Sally Mitchell on July 23, 1803 in Green County, Kentucky.

2. Alexander King Guthrey Sr.[4] was born in 1738 in St. David's Parish, King William County, and died in 1817 in Littleton Parish, Cumberland County. He owned land in various jurisdictions, including St. Thomas Parish in Orange County, Virginia; Cumberland County, Virginia; and in Kentucky. Alex was a Captain in the Revolutionary War. He first married Sarah, possibly nee Coleman, and married second a widow, Mary Anderson Pearce.

Children of Alexander K. Guthrey Sr.:

a. Benjamin Guthrey received, in 1802, one-half of the land in Kentucky that was secured by James Harrod, Esq. Also, he received a small bore gun and a Negro slave named Tobis and a bay mare with her increase. In 1819, Benjamin was living in Woodford County, Kentucky, when he and his brother Alexander Jr. sold their share of land to Thomas Maddox.

---

[4] See Cumberland County, Virginia *Will Book 5*, p. 308, and *Deed Book 16*, p. 1.

b. Alexander Guthrey Jr. received the other half of his father's land in Kentucky, and a Negro boy named Tobie (son of Jenny). He married Martitia Wilhoit in Woodford, Kentucky on June 16, 1797. In 1819, Alexander Jr. was living in Owen County, Kentucky.

c. Hannah Guthrey married Thomas Maddox. In 1819, they purchased her father's land in Cumberland County for $377. They reserved a dower right of 200 acres for widow Mary Guthrey. Hannah received two Negro girls named Dinah and Milly. One of Hannah's sons, Anderson Maddox, received his grandfather's "library of books."

d. Elizabeth Guthrey married Jesse Davis, who died in Lynchburg in 1832. Their eldest son was named Alexander Davis. Elizabeth received from the will of her father a sorrell mare, a red cow, a Negro man named Jack "who was given to me by my grandmother Elizabeth Oakes." Children of Jesse and Elizabeth were: (1) Alexander King Davis married Frances Hendrick, (2) Elizabeth Davis married Jacob Anderson, (3) Sarah Davis married Wilson Carter, (4) Hannah Davis married Livingston S. Guthrie, (5) Shelton Davis married Mary H. Meador, and John C. Davis married Mary Pennick.[5]

e. Sarah Guthrey married Jesse Parker, 1763-1839, son of David and Elizabeth (Brown) Parker.

3. Francis Guthrey received a Negro man named Bob. One source said that he married Nancy Hill.[6]

4. Elizabeth Guthrey married David Morris, ca 1752-1831, of Louisa County, Virginia on Jan. 20, 1782. Her father's will gave her a Negro woman named Amy. According to Ann Avery Hunter,[7] these were the children of David and Elizabeth (Guthrey) Morris:

a. George Morris died about 1824 in Louisa County. He married Martha Lea on Nov. 10, 1808, in Louisa County.

---

[5] Information on the Davis family was provided by Ann and Wyatt Davis, 3914 West Franklin Street, Richmond, Virginia 23221.

[6] Sent to the compiler by Dan Hendricks of Colorado on Feb. 24, 2001, who said it was "downloaded from a CD."

[7] Ann Avery Hunter, 9 Malvern Ave., #1, Richmond, Virginia 23221-2126, states that David Morris lived in neither Cumberland nor Buckingham Counties.

b. Samuel Morris, born about 1771, married Martha Biggers, Aug. 27, 1791, in Louisa County.

c. Sally Morris, born about 1774, married Gideon Floyd on May 2, 1793, in Louisa County.

d. Mary Morris was born Nov. 7, 1778 in Louisa County and died Aug. 7, 1866 in the same County. She married William Hunter on Feb. 9, 1796. He was born on Oct. 18, 1768, and died in 1835 in Louisa County. Eight children were born to their union.

e. Guthrie Morris was born about 1779 and died before November 1842 in Henry County, Kentucky. He married Dolley Holland on Oct. 1, 1799, in Louisa County.

f. Joshua Morris was born about 1780 and died circa 1824 in Louisa County. He married Ann Lea on Dec. 21, 1801.

g. David Morris was born on Jan. 20, 1784 in Louisa County.

h. Elizabeth Morris was born about 1785 and died after 1860. She married George Hunter on Dec. 22, 1803, in Louisa County.

i. Caroline Matilda Morris was born after 1789. She married Jacob Fackler on Oct. 19, 1810 in Louisa County.

5. Henry Guthrey died in Cumberland County about 1808.[8] He had at least one proven son, Bernard Guthrey, who was living in Prince Edward County, Virginia in 1815.[9] Another possible son was named Peyton Guthrey.[10]

---

[8] The inventory of Henry Guthrey's estate is found in Cumberland County *Will Book 3*, p. 427. Among other items, Henry left eighteen gallons of brandy and 309 acres in his estate.

[9] Library of Virginia, Land Tax Records for Cumberland County, 1815.

[10] Cumberland County *Will Book 3*, p. 272, shows that a Peyton Guthrey died in 1800. On Nov. 25, 1799, one Peyton Guthrey and one Bernard Guthrey took a mortgage to William Guthrey for 5 shillings. It involved 100 acres and a Negro named Joeffry. Money was owed to Gulielius Coleman. These two men may have been from an earlier generation of Guthreys, and may not have been the sons of Henry Guthrey.

6. William Guthrey was born Aug. 16, 1751 and died in 1826 in Cumberland County. William married Rebecca Noel. More information is provided on his descendants.

7. Sarah Guthrey was born on May 10, 1752 in Cumberland County, Virginia, and died on June 27, 1825 in Trimble County, Kentucky. Sarah married the Rev. Benjamin Coleman, a Baptist minister, on Feb. 18, 1771 in Amherst County, Virginia.[11] Benjamin was born on Sep. 3, 1751 in Cumberland County, Virginia and died on Sep. 13, 1834 in Trimble County, Kentucky. Although not proven, it is believed that this Benjamin was a son of Daniel, 1704-1772, and Patience (Thompson) Coleman of Cumberland County. There were several Daniel Colemans, but this Daniel's will was probated in 1773 in Goochland County.[12]

8. John Guthrey was born circa 1759, and may have been the same John who died in Halifax County on July 25, 1836. He married Betty Ann Allen, May 25, 1785, in Cumberland County. John allegedly served in the Revolutionary War. In 1815, John bought 132 acres from the estate of Archibald Cary, situated next to his brother William Guthrey.[13] His wife was deceased by 1834 as proven by chancery court records in Cumberland County.[14] Researchers should be aware that another John Guthrie lived in Halifax County, whose relationship with the Cumberland County Guthries has not been determined. Information on this family unit is very tentative; more research is necessary for a more accurate and complete account.

Children of John and Betty A. (Allen) Guthrey:[15]

---

[11] From website http://sheppardpioneers.terrashare.com/105/ cldg17.htm

[12] Letter from Ann Aden of Indianola, Mississippi to Wilmer L. Kerns dated June 26, 1981.

[13] Cumberland County, Virginia *Deed Book 13*, pp. 192-193.

[14] Cumberland County, Virginia *Chancery Book I*, September 1834, p. 55, and 1836, pp. 95-96.

[15] Names of children given below were copied from the chancery court records in Cumberland County. Not listed here is Allen Guthrey, born circa 1788, who married Mary M. Bostick, according to Carol Klein.

Guthrie Family

1. John Guthrey Jr. may have married Edna Adams.[16]

2. William Guthrey may have married Sarah Street[17]

3. Richard A. Guthrey married Martha (Yeates) Toombs on Jan. 5, 1828 in Halifax County.[18]

4. Martha "Patsy" Guthrey married Leonard Kesling on July 21, 1810 in Halifax County.

5. Elizabeth Guthrey married James McCraw

6. Sarah Guthrey married Mr. Crews

7. Nancy Guthrey married Thomas Walton on Nov. 18, 1823.

8. Rebecca Guthrey, 1801-1854,[19] married Archibald Rowlett on Nov. 22, 1824 in Halifax County.

9. Susan Guthrey

10. Francis (or Frances) W. Guthrey was born on Jan. 11, 1802.[20]

11. Jonathan Guthrey

William Guthrey Sr.

William Guthrey Sr., son of Thomas Guthrey and Sarah his wife, was born Aug. 16, 1751, probably in King William County. William received the land and plantation of his father, Thomas Guthrey. In 1826, in Cumberland County, William's personal property was inventoried and appraised for an estate sale. Nov. 25, 1778. William

---

[16] E-mail from Carol Klein to Wilmer L. Kerns on April 22, 2000 (cdklein@earthlink.net).

[17] *Ibid.*

[18] Martha Yeates was first married to Thomas Toombs on July 22, 1822. Martha died at Weakley, Tennessee. Source: e-mail from Carol Klein to Wilmer L. Kerns, dated April 22, 2000, (cdklein@earthlink.net).

[19] *Ibid.*

[20] *Ibid.*

married Rebecca Noel, daughter of John and Ann (Garnett) Noel.[21] Rebecca was born on March 25, 1761 and died Jan. 5, 1836[22] in Cumberland County. Her son, William Guthrie Jr., was administrator for her estate.

Children of William Sr. and Rebecca (Noel) Guthrie:

1. John Guthrie was born Sept. 22, 1779, and died Nov. 30, 1856. He was married four times: (a) Nancy Jane Palmore (b) Martha "Patsy" Ayers (c) Mary "Polly" Ayers, and (d) Elizabeth "Betsy" Ayers. More information is given later in this section.

2. William "Buck" Guthrey Jr. was born Sept. 24, 1781 and died April 14, 1857 in Buckingham County. William Jr. married Elizabeth T. Coleman, daughter of Gulielmus Sr. and Eleanor (Turner) Coleman.[23] Elizabeth was born Aug. 25, 1783, and died in 1859 in Buckingham County. Seven children were born to them, according to a family Bible in possession of Mr. and Mrs. Royce Charlton, Dillwyn, Virginia, who deposited a copy in the Library of Virginia.

Children of William Jr. and Elizabeth T. (Coleman) Guthrie:

a. Louzanie Garnett Guthrie was born April 14, 1804. She married William E. Shepard of Buckingham County.

b. Nancy Turner Guthrie was born on March 30, 1806, and nothing more is known about her at this time.

c. Edward Turner Guthrie was born Feb. 9, 1808, at "Flint Hill," and died April 6, 1853. He married Louisa Cook Garnett, Sept. 14, 1830.

d. William Poindexter Guthrie was born Sept. 9, 1810 and died Aug. 11, 1893. He married Eliza Jane England in 1835. William owned land and lived

---

[21] John Noel's will was probated on Nov. 19, 1776 in Cumberland County, Virginia.

[22] Rebecca's death date is in a Bible record of her daughter Sarah Noel (Guthrie) Apperson, found in the Jones Memorial Library, Lynchburg, Virginia, "Harris-Apperson-Kern Bible Record, FF3318."

[23] According to Mrs. Aubrey A. Aden of Indianola, Mississippi, Gulielmus Coleman Sr. was born circa 1756 and died about 1825 in Cumberland County.

in Buckingham County until 1843 when he moved to Calloway County, Kentucky. He was a U.S. Census taker in 1850.[24]

e. Elizabeth Eleanor Guthrie was born on June 9, 1813 in Buckingham County. She married Burwell Shepard.

f. John James Guthrie was born Nov. 4, 1817, and died March 4, 1892. He married Martha Agnes Goodman, daughter of Thomas Goodman of Amelia County, Virginia, on April 3, 1839. Martha died in December 1892.

g. Ireland Guthrie was born Dec. 30, 1824.

3. Nancy Ann Garnett Guthrie was born Feb. 1, 1783 and died before 1826. Nancy Ann married first James White, Dec. 8, 1803, and married second Gulielmus Coleman Jr, son of Gulielmus Sr. and Eleanor (Turner) Coleman, in 1812. Gulielmus Jr. was born Jan. 29, 1789 and died Oct. 22, 1856 in Buckingham County.

Child of James and Nancy (Guthrie) White:

a. Sarah Howard White was born on Sept. 5, 1804 in Buckingham County, and died May 16, 1888. She married John Stanback Coleman, son of Gulielmus and Eleanor (Turner) Coleman, on Oct. 31, 1822 in Buckingham County. Seven children were born to their union.

Children of Gulielmus Jr. and Nancy (Guthrie) Coleman:

a. John Baptiste Coleman was born on March 2, 1813 and died Jan. 19, 1892. He married Arabella Catherine Smith on Dec. 22, 1841.

b. Virgil Coleman was born on March 4, 1815. He graduated from Hampton-Sidney College and became an attorney. Virgil married Valerie Cobb.

c. Ann Rebecca Coleman was born on Aug. 10, 1820, and died later in 1820.

d. James W. Coleman was born on March 4th (year torn from Bible page).

e. Alexander Elmus Coleman was born in September (day and year torn from Bible page).

4. Sarah "Sallie" Noel Guthrie, daughter of William and Rebecca (Noel) Guthrie, was born Jan 28, 1786. She married James Apperson, probably a son

---

[24] U.S. Census for Calloway County, Kentucky, Family No. 540. His children were Mary E. Guthrey, and John J. Guthrey, born in Virginia and William P. Guthrey Jr., born in Kentucky. James Booker, age 24, was living in the household. It is believed that he was a son of Bernard G. and Mary (Stratton) Booker, who also moved to Calloway County in 1843.

of Jacob and Elizabeth (Beverly) Apperson,[25] on Aug. 29, 1805, in Buckingham County. James was born on July 19, 1783.[26]

Children of James Sr. and Sarah N. (Guthrie) Apperson:[27]

a. William N. Apperson was born on Oct. 9, 1806 in Buckingham County. He married Elizabeth ____ on Dec. 21, 1831. They were enumerated on the 1860-1870 U. S. Censuses for Nelson County, Virginia, where Elizabeth was born in 1810. William's occupation was farm overseer.

b. Nancy W. Apperson was born on June 6, 1809. She married Samuel W. Harris on Dec. 30, 1824. He was born on Nov. 7, 1795 and died on April 22, 1864.

c. Sterling Guthrie Apperson was born Feb. 18, 1812. He married Eliza Newton on Feb. 17, 1836. In 1853, he bought land from the Julius Coleman estate, located near Salem Methodist Church in east-central Buckingham County.[28]

d. Rebecca J. Apperson, who was born Sept. 24, 1815, married Edmund L. England, son of Robert and Elizabeth England, on Dec. 21, 1831.[29] Edmund was born circa 1807 and died on July 20, 1853. He was a wheelright in Cumberland County.

---

[25] One John R. Apperson, son of Jacob and Elizabeth Apperson, died in Cumberland County, Virginia on Dec. 28, 1865, aged seventy-six years.

[26] The Bible record states that Jacob Apperson died in Buckingham County on Feb. 22, 1836, but does not say that Jacob is the father of James Apperson. Jacob may have had a daughter named Lucy, who died in 1832. The Bible also shows a William Apperson, son of Jacob Apperson, who died in September 1842. Certain information on the Appersons was contributed by Marsha Moses, 22 Greenspring Circle, Huntington, West Virginia 25705. Marsha discovered this information among family papers while researching her husband's ancestors. The compiler later found a copy of the same Bible record in the Jones Memorial Library in Lynchburg, Virginia, under Harris-Apperson-Kern Bible Record FF3318.

[27] Names and dates for the children are from the James Apperson family Bible. Credit is given to Greg Bonner of Ann Arbor, Michigan and Ruby Talley Smith of Wheaton, Maryland for their comments.

[28] Roger G. Ward, compiler, *Land Tax Summaries & Implied Deeds, Vol. 3*, (Athens, Georgia: Iberian Publishing Company), 1995, p.122.

[29] Cumberland County, Virginia: *Circuit Court Chancery Orders, 1831-1851*, September 1834 Term, p. 63.

e. Malinda L. Apperson was born on June 25, 1817. She married a Mr. Hill on Feb. 17, 1836.

f. James Apperson Jr. was born on Dec. 18, 1819, and married Susan Newton, daughter of William and Edna (Taylor) Newton, in February 1842. James' household was included in the 1850 and 1860 censuses for Buckingham County.

g. John G. Apperson was born on Oct. 16, 1824. He was still alive on June 1, 1900 when the Census for Campbell County, Virginia gave his address as 1309 Grace Street in Lynchburg. Living in the household was his wife, Sarah E. born in April 1825, and two grandsons. John G. and Sarah were married in 1855. The census stated that Sarah had given birth to one child who was deceased. That child was a male, based on the surname of two grandchildren.

h. Thomas Guthrie Apperson was born on July 9, 1826 in Cumberland County, Virginia, and died June 14, 1887 in Graves County, Kentucky. He married Mary B. Hawkins in 1860 in Montgomery County, Tennessee. Mary was born in Montgomery County in 1836 and died on Jan. 29, 1887 in Graves County.

i. Emmanuel H. Apperson was born on July 9, 1826.

We are reasonably certain that only four children belonged to William Guthrey's family unit, based on the Bible record that is on file in the Library of Virginia in Richmond.

John Guthrie

John Guthrie, son of William Sr. and Rebecca (Noel) Guthrey, was born in Cumberland County on Sept. 22, 1779, and died in Buckingham County, Virginia on Nov. 30, 1856. He was a farmer. Married four times, John was father of sixteen children born between 1800 and 1855. Yes, his first child was fifty-five years older than the last child! John's first wife was Nancy Jane Palmore, 1778-1819, daughter of William and Elizabeth (Boatright) Palmore. Nancy Jane died about 1819, and John married second Martha "Patsy" Ayers, who was born Aug. 11, 1798, and died in the 1820s. Her parents were John and Jane (Salle) Ayers. Apparently, John and Patsy had no children, and she died after a brief marriage. John then married third Mary "Polly" Ayers, name of parents not proven.[30]

---

[30] Nellie F. Ayres, in her book *Ayres Kin* (Memphis, Tennessee: Accurate Duplicating Service), 1961, p. 95, speculated that this Mary Ayres was a daughter

Polly died of childbirth on April 24, 1831. Finally, John Guthrie married Elizabeth "Betsy" Ayers, daughter of William and Mildred (Claiborne) Ayres. Descendants say that Betsy was a first cousin of Polly Ayers. Betsy always called her husband "Mr. Guthrie" because of the thirty-five years of age differential.[31] She was born in 1814 and died Jan. 13, 1902. She gave birth to nine children. Elizabeth's mother, "Milly" or Mildred Ayers, born circa 1782, was living in the household of William Williams when the 1860 census was taken for Buckingham County. William Ayres died before 1850.

Children of John and Nancy Jane (Palmore) Guthrie:

1. William Palmore Guthrie was born Nov. 24, 1800 and died of pneumonia on March 3, 1861 in Buckingham County.[32] He married Sarah "Sallie" Ann Coleman, daughter of Julius and Elizabeth (Coleman) Coleman, Nov. 14, 1819. William P. was a farmer. Sallie Coleman was born June 17, 1798 and died in March 1885 in Buckingham County. They raised a large family, but names of only six children are known:

    a. William H. Guthrie was born circa __. He married Sarah A. Harris on Jan. 9, 1852 by Elder John Spencer in Buckingham County.[33]

    b. James A. Guthrie was born in 1828 and died in Petersburg, Virginia "of Camp fever," on Oct. 15, 1862.[34] He married Susan Rebecca Apperson, daughter of Sterling and Eliza Apperson, on May 16, 1856, in Buckingham County.[35]

---

of Matthias and Mary (Howell) Ayres. This cannot be, because a Bible record shows that Mary Ayres was born on Feb. 15, 1827.

[31] Story was given to me by Ruby Talley Smith of Baltimore, Maryland.

[32] Library of Virginia, *Death Records, Buckingham County, Virginia, 1853-1890*.

[33] *Religious Herald*, Feb. 12, 1852, source furnished by Kathy Brown on June 3, 2001.

[34] Library of Virginia, *Death Records, Buckingham County, Virginia, 1853-1890*.

[35] Library of Virginia, *Marriage Records, Buckingham County, Virginia, 1853-1890*.

Guthrie Family

c. Mary Elizabeth Guthrie was born Nov. 24, 1832 and died Dec. 26, 1912, in Buckingham County. She married Joshua Davis, son of John and Margaret (Moyle) Davis, Nov. 13, 1851. They were parents of eleven children. See the chapter on the Davis family.

d. Nancy Palmore Guthrie was born July 24, 1833, and died July 12, 1918, at Dillwyn, Buckingham County. Nancy married first John Sharpe,[36] with whom she had three children, and married second to Poindexter Jamerson and married third to M. L. Creasey, son of Edward and Julia Creasey, Sept. 14, 1915, by Rev. J.J. Spencer, Baptist minister. Nancy was a midwife, according to her death certificate.[37]

e. Sarah L. Guthrie, born circa 1839, married Henry B. Jimmerson, Jan. 17, 1861, in Buckingham County.

f. Travis L. Guthrie was born in 1841, according to the 1850 and 1860 Censuses[38]

2. Rebecca Noel Guthrie was born in 1804. She married William James Ferguson, on Feb. 18, 1824, in Cumberland County.[39]

3. Elizabeth Catherine Boatwright Guthrie was born in 1807, and married a Mr. Shepard after 1827.[40]

4. John Garnett Guthrie was born on May 22, 1810 and died June 13, 1886 in Missouri. John G. worked for his mother's brother (Uncle Palmore) in Petersburg, Virginia., who sent him with a shipment of tobacco to New York City. He remained there and became a tobacco broker in partnership with Joseph Sexton Hawkins. John G. married his partner's daughter, Elizabeth Seymour Hawkins, Nov. 5, 1862, in Yonkers, New York. While living in New York City, John G. served on the vestry of Trinity Church. During the Civil War, he was arrested and imprisoned, accused of being a Southern sympathizer and a spy for the

---

[36] Information was furnished by Nell C. Hailey of Fredericksburg, Virginia

[37] *Ibid.*

[38] Benjamin B. Weisinger III, *Buckingham County, Virginia 1850 United States Census*, (Privately Published: Richmond, Virginia), p. 42

[39] A chancery court record in Cumberland County (1827 *Order Book*, pp. 98-99) gives her name and the name of her husband.

[40] *Ibid.* Name was given as Eliza Catherine in the court record, and she was not married in 1827.

Confederate States. He later migrated with his wife and three children to Saline County, Missouri. Four more children were born in Missouri.[41]

5. James Smith Guthrie was born Sept. 22, 1813 at Petersburg, Virginia, and died Jan. 4, 1900 at Excelsor Springs, Missouri. James married Helen Temple Brown, Aug. 5, 1837, in Albemarle County, Virginia. They first migrated to Kentucky, and then went to Saline County, Missouri in 1841.

6. Daniel Travis Guthrie was born June 17, 1817 in Buckingham County, and died in Saline County, Missouri on Feb. 23, 1880. He married Harriett Maria Brown, daughter of John Brown.

Only child of John and Mary "Polly" (Ayers) Guthrie:

7. Martha Ann Guthrie was born April 24, 1831, and died in 1881. She married Samuel Leake Anderson on April 28, 1857, and moved to Saline County, Missouri. Samuel was born on Nov. 29, 1817 in Buckingham County. Martha's mother died of childbirth, this being her only child.

Children of John and Elizabeth (Ayers) Guthrie:[42]

8. Joseph Lee Guthrie was born Aug. 28, 1834 and died "of chronic disease," in June 1865, unmarried.[43]

9. Mary Susan Guthrie was born Dec. 8, 1836 and died of "chronic disease," on Sept. 30, 1865, unmarried.[44]

10. Poindexter Watkins Guthrie was born May 1, 1838 in Buckingham County. He served in the Civil War.

---

[41] John G. Guthrie III, of Maquoketa, Iowa, shared information on John G. Guthrie, in letter to Wilmer L. Kerns, dated Feb. 1, 1984.

[42] Information on the children named below was provided by Ruby Talley Smith, formerly of Fluvanna County, Virginia, but later of Baltimore and Wheaton, Maryland. Ruby furnished a record, which may have been copied from a family Bible that was maintained by Joseph Lee Guthrie. Ruby descends from Nancy Catherine Guthrie who married Willis W. Newton.

[43] Library of Virginia, Death Records, Buckingham County, Virginia, 1853-1890.

[44] Library of Virginia, Death Records, Buckingham County, Virginia, 1853-1890.

11. Emily Jane Guthrie was born Aug. 2, 1839. She married William Williams on May 16, 1860.[45] He was sheriff of Buckingham County.

12. Nathaniel Dunn Guthrie was born Oct. 7, 1841 and died April 15, 1861, unmarried.

13. Nancy Catherine Guthrie was born Oct. 2, 1847 and died Dec. 31, 1901. She married Willis Wade Newton, son of John Edwin and Mary Anna (Duncan) Newton, June 15, 1870.[46] Willis was born Oct. 8, 1848 and died Aug. 24, 1903.

14. Kizzie Geneva Guthrie was born July 9, 1849 and died in 1936. She married Willis W. Newton, who was her brother-in-law. Both were buried, along with first wife Nancy C., in the Newton Family Cemetery at Wealthia, Buckingham County, Virginia.[47]

15. Mildred M. Guthrie was born on April 20, 1852.

16. Matthew Leake Guthrie was born Dec. 25, 1855. He died at Western State Hospital in Staunton, and is buried there.

Mary Elizabeth Guthrie, wife of Joshua Davis

---

[45] *Lynchburg Daily Virginian*, June 14, 1860, p. 3, c. 1, and The Library of Virginia, Marriage Records of Buckingham County, Virginia, 1853-1890.

[46] Library of Virginia, Marriage Records of Buckingham County, Virginia, 1853-1890.

[47] Information by Ruby Talley Smith of Wheaton, Maryland.

Chapter 18

Harris Family of Nelson County, Virginia

The Harris,[1] Horsley, Christian, Walton, and Payne familes were intermarried in Central Virginia. The Harris surname is found so frequently that it is almost impossible to untangle the various branches. The earliest proven name that we have is Nathan Harris who married Sarah Mosby.[2] Allegedly, Nathan's parents were Lee and Winnie (Phillips) Harris. Nathan's son, Willis E. Harris,[3] and his descendants is the subject of this chapter. Willis was born on Feb. 1, 1811 and died Feb. 27, 1879 in Nelson County. Willis married Martha Elizabeth Horsley, daughter of William and Sarah (Christian) Horsley Jr., on Aug. 31, 1842. Martha was born on Feb. 21, 1821, and died Nov. 29, 1904. They lived at *Rose Hill*, the ancestral home at Gladstone, Nelson County. A Harris-Payne family cemetery was established on the estate.

Children of Willis E. and Martha E. (Horsley) Harris:

1. William Horsley Harris was born Dec. 25, 1847 at *Rose Hill*, Gladstone, Nelson County, and died in 1937. On Oct. 13, 1875, he married Laura George Payne, daughter of William Armistead and Martha Jane (Tindall) Payne, at "Woodlawn," Gladstone. She was born on Oct. 17, 1851 and died Sept. 7, 1925. William died on Aug. 27, 1937. They were members of the Baptist Church.

Children of William H. and Laura G. (Payne) Harris:

    a. Mabel Clare Harris was born Feb. 16, 1878 at "Woodlawn," and died Oct. 24, 1973. She served as postmistress of the Gladstone Post Office.

    b. Martha Payne Harris was born Feb. 19, 1880 at "Woodlawn," and died on Dec. 29, 1958. Martha was a teacher. She married Allen Davis Jordan, a farmer at Allen's Creek. They had no children.

    c. Laura Florine Harris was born on Aug. 14, 1882 at "Greenway" and died in Nelson County in 1976.

---

[1] Mary Evelyn (Payne) Strickland graciously assisted me in collecting information for this chapter.

[2] See *Deed Book 10*, p. 287; *Deed Book 13*, p. 211; *Deed Book 16*, p. 242; *Deed Book 26*, p. 113; and *Deed Book 28*, p. 210.

[3] Willis E. Harris had a brother named Daniel Mosby Harris, who died on Dec. 17, 1878.

d. Armistead Axtell Harris was born on Dec. 14, 1883. He married Audrey Nelson of Parson, Kansas and they had William Armistead Harris, Jimmy Harris, and Paul Harris.

Rose Hill, *the historic estate of Willis E. and Martha (Horsley) Harris in Nelson County. Mary Evelyn (Payne) Strickland is the current owner and resident.*

2. Sallie Ida Harris was born Jan. 3, 1850, at *Rose Hill*, Nelson County and died Aug. 2, 1922. She married Sterling Claiborne Payne, son of William A. and Martha J. (Tindall) Payne, on Nov. 3, 1869. He was born on Sept. 22, 1846 and died on Sept. 10, 1916. Sterling C. served in the Civil War where he was taken as a prisoner of war. He received a war pension in 1911, and Sallie received a widow's pension in 1920. He later entered the merchantile business with his father at Greenway, Nelson County. Also, he became involved in the lumber business at Gladstone. Burial was in the Harris Cemetery in Nelson County.

Children of Sterling C. and Sallie Ida (Harris) Payne:

a. Maude Eleanor Payne was born Sept. 18, 1870 and died July 4, 1932. She married Emmett Dudley Major on May 25, 1897. He was born on Oct. 24, 1864 and died April 23, 1925. Emmett was engaged in merchantile business at Allen Creek.

b. Mary Horsley Payne was born on Aug. 9, 1872 and died Jan. 7, 1937. She married Samuel Terrell Atkinson, who was born in 1871 and died in 1932. He worked as a telegraph operator for the C&O Railroad at Greenway, Nelson County.

c. Ida Florence Payne was born on Aug. 16, 1875 and died Oct. 19, 1881.

d. Pearl Lelia Payne was born on June 6, 1878 and died July 3, 1967. She married Joseph Lee Terry on June 4, 1902. He ran a motel at Gladstone, and later moved to Bedford, where he operated a news stand on Main Street.

e. William Armistead Payne was born on July 30, 1880, and died Jan. 29, 1966. He was a locomotive engineer for the C&O Railroad. William married Edna Moon, who was born on Jan. 9, 1881, and died on Jan. 26, 1961.

f. John Howard Payne was born on April 1, 1883 at *Rose Hill*, and died in 1953. He married Irene Spickard of Lynchburg. John served as a yard master for the Southern Railroad in Lynchburg. They had no children.

g. Francis Marion Payne was born on Aug. 25, 1885 at *Rose Hill* and died March 24, 1958. He served as clerk of the Mineral Springs Baptist Church. On May 10, 1915, he married Bessie Vawter Walton, daughter of Eugene A. and Nannie K. (Jones) Walton, of Bent Creek, Appomattox County.

h. Claude Melville Payne was born on June 14, 1888 and died March 11, 1947. He married Eubelia Bradshaw, who was born on Feb. 3, 1891 and died Nov. 15, 1980.

3. Frederick Joseph Harris Sr. was born on June 26, 1851 and died on Dec. 12, 1932. He married Roberta Drummond at Sandidge, Virginia on Dec. 23, 1879. Roberta was born on March 29, 1857 and died June 1, 1937. Both are buried in the Westview Cemetery in Radford, Virginia.

Children of Frederick J. Sr. and Roberta (Drummond) Harris:

a. Percy Harris was born on March 18, 1881 at Greenway, Virginia, and died Feb. 4, 1955. He graduated from the Medical College of Virginia and practiced medicine in Scottsville, Albemarle County. Percy married Innes Randolph, daughter of Peyton and Mary E.

(Fisher) Randolph, on Sept. 20, 1904, in Pelham, N.C. Innes died on Oct. 22, 1966.

b. Montague Harris was born on July 21, 1883 and died on Nov. 11, 1884, in infancy.

c. Mattie Belle Harris was born on June 11, 1885, and died on Jan. 14, 1886.

d. Mary Elizabeth Harris was born on June 11, 1885 and died July 13, 1972 in Radford, Virginia. She married Orville Bradley Bynum, son of John Gray and Nannie Bradley (Phipps) Bynum, on Aug. 18, 1920. They had one child: (1) John Gray Bynum was born on Jan. 9, 1922, and died Oct. 30, 1953, unmarried.

e. Sallie Richardson Harris was born in Amherst County. She married William Ingles on June 10, 1908.

f. Joseph Harris was born on May 23, 1889 and died in June 1889.

g. Frederick Joseph Harris Jr. was born on June 22, 1890 and died July 23, 1891.

h. Elberta Harris was born on Nov. 23, 1892 and died in Radford on May 18, 1975. She married Amos Miller on July 6, 1927 in Roanoke. They had no children.

4. Walter Mosley Harris was born on Aug. 20, 1852, and died July 16, 1925. He married Mary Franklin Cunningham, daughter of William and Sallie (Jordan) Cunningham, on Feb. 8, 1893. Mary F. was born on Jan. 28, 1868 in Nelson County and died on Oct. 22, 1943 at Gladstone, Nelson County, Virginia.

Children of Walter M. and Mary F. (Cunningham) Harris:

a. Daniel Mosby Harris was born on June 9, 1894 at Greenway, and died Aug. 28, 1976 at Spout Spring, Appomattox County. He was a dairy farmer. Mosby married Lela Mitchell Walton, daughter of Eugene A. and Nannie Katherine (Jones) Walton.

b. Ruth Stringfellow Harris was born on June 11, 1896, and died June 9, 1991. Married on Feb. 13, 1929, she was the second wife of Dallas Eugene Walton, son of Eugene A. and Nannie Katherine (Jones) Walton. No children were born to this union.

c. Willis Ewart Harris was born on Dec. 29, 1898, and died April 17, 1979 at Spout Spring. He married Nannie Evelyn Walton, daughter of

Eugene A. and Nannie Katherine (Jones) Walton. She was born on July 15, 1899, and died on June 22, 1941, at Bent Creek, Appomattox County. Their three children were: Willis Lyle Harris, Calvin Walker Harris, and Marshall Walton Harris.

d. Thomas Montague Harris was born on March 4, 1901, and died on May 4, 1994 at Southside Community Hospital in Farmville. He married Mary Elizabeth Jamerson, daughter of Roland F. and Ella (Walton) Jamerson, on Oct. 3, 1942. She was born on March 10, 1911 and died on April 26, 1996, in Richmond. Burial was in Liberty Baptist Cemetery in Appomattox.

Children of Thomas M and Mary E. (Jamerson) Harris:

(1) Anne Elizabeth Harris married Herbert Bromhall. They live in Rosewell, Georgia.

(2) Betty Franklin Harris married Steve Macko. They live in Richmond, Virginia.

(3) Sandra Ella Harris married Dr. Rodney Wood. They live in Las Cruces, New Mexico.

e. Holmes Fleming Harris was born on Dec. 21, 1903, and died May 1, 1981 in Richmond. Burial was in Washington Memorial Park in Richmond. He was a locomotive engineer for the C&O Railroad. Holmes first married Eva Campbell of Lovingston, and married second Fannie D. Harris. No children were born to either union, but he adopted Catherine Gowen of Gladstone, who married a Mr. Clark.

f. Mary Cabell Harris was born on Nov. 7, 1906, and died in Alta Vista on Dec. 23, 1996. She married Alexander Wilson Walton, son of Eugene A. and Nannie Katherine (Jones) Walton. Their two children: Mary Elizabeth Walton married Clarence N. Hancock; and Lloyd Gray Walton married Shirley Williams. See the main section on the Walton family for more information.

g. Joseph Horsley Harris was born on June 19, 1911, in Buckingham County, and died on March 1, 1955, at Clifton Forge. He was employed by the C & O Railroad. Joseph did not marry. During his later years, he lived with his sister Ruth S. (Harris) Walton.[4]

---

[4] Appomattox County, Virginia *Will Book 3*, p. 53, Jan. 22, 1955.

On the left, Marion Waverly Payne (962) of Gladstone, Nelson County, Virginia, is a descendant of Willis Harris. He was born at Rose Hill, the Harris estate. He attended the Walton reunions prior to his passing in 1999. On the right is Bessie Vawter (Walton) Payne (814), the mother of Marion.

Chapter 19
Benjamin Harrison of Horn Quarter, Cumberland County, Virginia

Benjamin Harrison, ca 1715-1761, of Horn Quarter, Cumberland County, has been an enigma to genealogical researchers.[1] To complicate the problem, two different Benjamin Harrisons were living in Cumberland County in 1761, and a third Benjamin Harrison was an absentee land owner. The latter bought 1,500 acres of land on Oct. 3, 1737 "on both sides of a South Branch of Willis River...(adjoining) a corner of other land of the said Harrison."[2] Carter Harrison, son of Benjamin and Anne (Carter) Harrison IV was "Author of the Resolutions of Cumberland County, April 22, 1776—The First Positive Instructions for the American Independence." This branch of Harrisons lived in the northernmost part of the county, where Willis River empties into the James River. Cartersville, Virginia, a river port on the James River, was named for this family.

They were not the only Harrison families in Old Cumberland County during the Colonial period. The second Benjamin Harrison and his wife Elinor signed a deed in Cumberland County in 1762 that suggested ties to Richmond County. If Benjamin and Elinor left descendants in Cumberland County, we have found no evidence.

It is believed that the third Benjamin Harrison married Priscilla Cary, daughter of Henry and Anne (Edwards) Cary, circa 1738. This Benjamin is identified with Horn Quarter Creek, which is also in the Willis Creek watershed at a location north of U. S. Route 60 near the Buckingham County line. It is less than a mile from a community center known as Trent's Mill. While no direct proof has

---

[1] A good analysis of the various Benjamin Harrisons was achieved by Malcom N. Gardner of Arlington, Virginia, in 1972 and published in *Harrison Heritage*, Ruth Harrison Jones, editor, December 1986, pp. 747-751. Gardner identified and studied early land records for various Benjamin Harrisons, not only to discriminate between the several Benjamins, but to find evidence that Benjamin's wife Priscilla was nee Cary.

[2] *Land Patent Book 17*, p. 420, Library of Virginia and Archives, Richmond, Virginia.

been found, we believe that circumstantial evidence strongly suggests the relationship. A study of land records and naming patterns of descendants enable us to infer that this is probably the case. First, the land records: Henry Cary made two crucially significant gifts of land to (his son-in-law) Benjamin Harrison of Horn Quarter. On July 6, 1742, Henry Cary conveyed 400 acres on both sides of Willis River at Horn Quarter Creek, which was then in Goochland County, but later in Cumberland County.[3] Benjamin Harrison was called a Planter, and records show that his plantation was a major producer of tobacco and grain. Harrison paid only 10 shillings, current money, for the plantation farm, which was a giveaway. On May 30, 1746, Henry Cary of Henrico County deeded an additional 200 acres to Benjamin Harrison, adjacent to the 400 acres. Again, only 10 shillings was paid for this land, which was essentially a gift.[4] The land was carved from a large land patent that Henry Cary secured from the Governor of Virginia in 1729.

In the 1761-will of Benjamin Harrison Sr., he stated that Archibald Cary, his brother-in-law, and Clement Read had verbally promised to give Benjamin's two sons 1,000 acres each. Gardner cited two deeds from Archibald Cary to Cary and Benjamin Harrison Jr. for 500 acres each in Bedford County.[5] Also, Uncle Archibald conveyed 200 acres of land in Cumberland County to Cary Harrison, on Feb. 20, 1781.[6] The land adjoined the estate of Benjamin Harrison Sr., deceased. Apparently, these transfers of land were in partial fulfillment of a promise made to Benjamin Harrison Sr., prior to his death in 1761.

The surname Cary was given as a Christian name to Benjamin and Priscilla's children (e.g. Cary Harrison), grandchildren, and

---

[3] Goochland County, Virginia *Deed Book 4*, p.29.

[4] Goochland County, Virginia *Deed Book 5*, pp. 122-126.

[5] Bedford County, Virginia *Deed Book 4*, pp. 347 and 349; and *Deed Book 6*, p. 272. The two deeds were dated Aug. 24, 1772. The land was sold at a nominal price for 500 acres.

[6] Cumberland County, Virginia *Deed Book 6*, p. 93.

their great-grandchildren. The name Benjamin was also popular with descendants. One would expect the Cary and Lockey surnames to be passed down through the Bell family, due to direct descendancy from David and Judith (Cary) Bell, but not in the other families. For example, in the Word family, Benjamin's granddaughter Lockey (Word) Noel named three of her children William Cary Noel, Benjamin Noel, and Lockey Harrison Noel. Her brother George Washington Word, 1785-1853, named a son William Cary Word, Lockie Word, and Benjamin Harrison Word. Their sister, Mary Harrison (Word) McCraw, named two of her children Lockie Harrison McCraw and Cary Harrison McCraw. Although these naming practices do not prove that Priscilla was a Cary, it certainly suggests it, not to mention of the numerous times that Harrison descendants were named for Judith (Cary) Bell, sister of Priscilla (Cary) Harrison.

Fairfax Harrison failed to discover Priscilla during the research process for his book *The Virginia Carys*. His excellent work did not claim to be the final word on the Cary family, but lamented over gaps of knowledge. Perhaps a distraction to researchers is the presence of at least one prominent Benjamin Harrison branch whose relatives intermarried with the children of Archibald Cary, 1721-1787, presumed brother of Priscilla (Cary) Harrison. This Benjamin is sometimes referred to as "the presidential branch," and one that many Harrison researchers seek to connect a direct lineage.

The following list of children is presented in the order that they were named in the 1761-will of Benjamin Harrison, with an exception of Benjamin Harrison Jr. All of the children were given female slaves "and their increase."

Children of Benjamin and Priscilla (Cary) Harrison:[7]

> 1. Ann Harrison, born circa 1739, allegedly married Joseph Allen.[8] Ann was not alive in 1805, when her sister, Elizabeth, wrote her will in Charlotte County.

---

[7] See the will of Benjamin Harrison, Cumberland County, Virginia *Will Book I*, pp. 215-217.

2. Priscilla Harrison, born circa 1741, was promised in her father's will a Negro named Agge. Nothing more is known about Priscilla, except that she was alive in 1805.

3. Elizabeth Harrison was born circa 1743 in Cumberland County and died in 1810 in Charlotte County. She first married Thomas Booth[9] and married second Philip King.[10] Apparently, Elizabeth was childless, because her 1805 will named only her brothers and sisters (except for Ann and Cary, who were deceased).

4. Lockey Harrison was born circa 1745 and died circa 1835 in Buckingham County. She received a Negro named Rachel from her father's will. Lockey married Thomas Word, and raised a family of six children.

5. Mary Harrison was born circa 1747. Her father, Benjamin, willed her "one Negro girl named Amy." Nothing more is known about Mary at this time.

6. Martha Harrison, born circa 1749, and was to receive "one Negro girl named Darkeys (Dorcas?)," per Benjamin Harrison's will.

7. Cary Harrison was born circa 1750, and died in 1797, in Buckingham County. The fact that Cary served as surety for the marriage bond for his sister Rebecca, in 1773, is proof that he was born no later than 1751. Cary married Sarah (Bell) Langhorn,[11] daughter of David and Judith (Cary) Bell, Jan. 29, 1789. Sarah first married John

---

[8] Gardner, *Harrison Heritage*. If this Ann Harrison married Joseph Allen, then Ann would have been about twelve years old when she gave birth to her second child.

[9] Letter from Harland to Kerns, Jan. 24, 1984, stated that, upon the death of Thomas Booth, Elizabeth relinquished all rights of property except her own personal belongings to her brother-in-law, John Booth of Amelia County.

[10] The marriage bond for Elizabeth Booth to Philip King was signed by her brothers, Benjamin and Cary Harrison.

[11] When Sarah and daughter Judith moved to Kentucky in 1798, Maurice Langhorn was appointed as her attorney in Cumberland and Buckingham Counties. See Cumberland County, Virginia *Deed Book 8*, p. 280.

Langhorne.[12] One child was born to Cary and Sarah Harrison: Judith Cary Harrison, born circa 1791, went to Bourboun County, Kentucky in 1798 with her mother.[13] Cary was a Deputy Surveyor for Buckingham County.[14]

8. Rebecca Harrison was born June 9, 1752[15] in Cumberland County, and died in 1793 in Buckingham County. She married Henry Bell, son of David and Judith (Cary) Bell, on June 12, 1773. Henry was born June 17, 1745 in Chesterfield County, and died in 1811 in Kentucky.[16] Henry was a surveyor, sheriff, and vestryman for Buckingham County, where his father David was Clerk of the Court. Henry was mentioned in the will of his uncle, Archibald Cary. He also served in the Revolutionary War, rising to the rank of Colonel.

Children of Henry and Rebecca (Harrison) Bell: [17]

a. Elizabeth Bell, born in 1774, married Henry Rawlings.

b. Rebecca Harrison Bell was born Jan. 18, 1777, and died Dec. 31, 1858, in Buckingham County. She married Matthew Branch, 1776-1828, who first married Martha Cox.

c. Henry Cary Bell was born April 7, 1779. He married Susan P. Moseley.

---

[12] Harland stated to Kerns, in 1984, that these children were born to John and Sarah (Bell) Langhorne: Maurice Langhorn, David Bell Langhorne, and John Trotter Langhorne.

[13] Cary Harrison's sister Ann Booth wrote her will in 1805 in Charlotte County. Cary's share of her estate was given to daughter Judith Cary Harrison of Kentucky.

[14] Library of Virginia, *Buckingham County Records, 1768-1786*, Accession No. 21435. Cary Harrison surveyed 200 acres of land that was being sold to his uncle, Archibald Cary.

[15] The date for Rebecca conflicts with the date given for her brother Benjamin Jr. Someone has made a copying error, or misinterpreted the calendar. I believe that Benjamin Jr. was born in 1758, not in 1752.

[16] Edith Rucker Whitley, "British Mercantile Claims," *Genealogical Records of Buckingham County, Virginia*, (Baltimore, Maryland: Clearfield Company, Inc.), 1996, p. 123.

[17] Source of information on the family unit of Henry Bell was the "Grandparent Papers," DAR Library, Washington, D.C.

d. Mary Bell, born Sept. 22, 1781, married Bolling Branch.

e. David Bell was born on Jan. 17, 1784 and died unmarried.

f. Benjamin Harrison Bell was born March 18, 1786 and died unmarried.

g. Virginia Bell was born Sept. 13, 1791 and died unmarried.

9. Benjamin Harrison Jr. was born March 15, 1758 in Cumberland County, and died in Buckingham County on Aug. 25, 1811. In 1773, Benjamin was named as a tithable in the household of his aunt, Judith (Cary) Bell. He married Elizabeth Wilborne, daughter of William and Jane (Alsom) Wilbourne.[18] Elizabeth was born Dec. 15, 1775 and died June 5, 1811.[19] Benjamin Jr. died suddenly without a will. He had intended to emancipate a slave named Nick Scott, but waited too long to act. Names of only two children are known: Nancy Harrison married William Shelton Lewis of Pittsylvania County, and Benjamin Harrison III, Esq., was probably an attorney. He was able to emancipate his father's slave, named Nick Scott, through a petition to the Virginia Governor and the General Assembly of Virginia, dated Oct. 18, 1814.

Postscript: Some researchers believe that the parents of Benjamin Harrison of Horn Quarter were James and Elizabeth (Read) Harrison. Becky Bonner and Josephine L. Bass show on their website how this is possible, by studying the relationships based on land transactions.

http://freepages.genealogy.rootsweb.com/~harrisonrep/Harrison/d0035/g0000074.html

---

[18] Josephine Lindsay Bass and Becky Bonner bbbonner@yahoo.com have done extensive research on Benjamin Harrison. I suggest that you run a search on Google or other internet search engine for "Benjamin Harrison" to find their website, which has changed residences several times.

[19] From Estelle Ranson Phillip's *Notebook,* who received information from Mrs. Dexter Otey with this notation: "see chart in Allen Book." Notebook was in possession of Mrs. Conrad P. Harland of Richmond.

Chapter 20

Thomas Harvey of Charlotte County

There were two contemporary Thomas Harveys in Charlotte County, Virginia. One was designated "Thomas of Butterwood Creek" and the other "Thomas the blacksmith." Thomas Harvey, 1760-1844, of Butterwood Creek married first Barbara Walton, daughter of the Rev. Simeon and Agnes (Hester) Walton, 1741-1798. He married second Mary "Polly" Vawter, who was born in 1770 in Cumberland County,[1] and was still alive in 1853. Thomas Harvey, who died on Sept. 19, 1844 in Charlotte County,[2] was a soldier in the American Revolution.

This chapter is concerned with Thomas the blacksmith, and will hereafter be referred to as Thomas.[3] Thomas Harvey, ca 1747-1812, the blacksmith, married Macca Barksdale. If she was a daughter of Collier and Sarah (Randolph) Barksdale, as sometimes claimed, she was not mentioned in the will of Collier Barksdale.[4] Thomas Harvey was born circa 1747, and may have been a son of Thomas and Elizabeth Harvey of Charlotte County. Thomas, the younger, wrote his will on April 9, 1812[5] and it was probated on July 6, 1812. His wife, Macca, was born circa 1748 and died before 1812. The Harvey estate was located on State Highway 615 between Madisonville and Red House in Charlotte County. The property was located on lower Cub Creek near Rolling Hill.

Children of Thomas and Macca (Barksdale) Harvey:

---

[1] 1850 U. S. Census for Charlotte County, Virginia, Family No. 728.

[2] Alycon Trubey-Pierce (abstractor), *Selected Final Pension Payment Vouchers, 1818-1864*, (Athens, Georgia: Iberian Publishing Company), Vol. 1, p. 256.

[3] Certain vital dates and genealogical data on the Harvey family were furnished to this compiler by Dr. Joseph W. Evans, 5103 Williams Fork Trail, #109, Boulder, CO 80301-3417. I have since learned that Dr. Evans died in October 1997. Further documentation for these records is being pursued by several researchers, including the compiler, Harry O. Alvis, 20 Luster Drive, Batesville, Arkansas 72501, and Dr. Ward H. Oliver, 9025 Nolen Drive, Baton Rouge, LA 70810-1710.

[4] Charlotte County, Virginia *Will Book 1*, pp. 117, 118.

[5] Charlotte County, Virginia *Will Book 3*, p. 197.

1. Molly Harvey was born circa 1769 and died before 1812, when her father died. Molly, sometimes called "Polly," married Douglas Hancock on Nov. 5, 1787, in Charlotte County. They migrated to Jefferson County, Georgia, where he became a county tax collector.

2. Sarah "Sally" Harvey was born circa 1771 and died June 6, 1846. She married Martin Hancock on Sept. 1, 1790. Martin was born March 9, 1767, probably in Chesterfield County, and died Sept. 21, 1838. Both were buried in the Hancock-Marshall cemetery located about one mile from their Red House home. Martin was a large landowner, tobacco farmer, merchant, tavern owner and veteran of the War of 1812.[6] Nine sons and two daughters were born to Martin and Sarah.

3. Elizabeth "Betsy" Harvey was born circa 1772. She married Pleasant Jennings, son of Dickerson and Frances (Bagley) Jennings, Jan. 3, 1791, in Charlotte County.

4. Nathan Harvey was born circa 1773 and died before March 2, 1840, when his will was offered in a chancery court suit. Nathan's will[7] was dated Aug. 11, 1836. He first married Mary Ann Williamson, daughter of Cuthbert Jr. and Susannah (White) Williamson, on Sept. 3, 1792, in Charlotte County. The 1810 census for Charlotte County showed that Nathan owned ten slaves. He lived on land adjoining his brother Thomas, who owned six slaves.

Children of Nathan and Mary Ann (Williamson) Harvey:

a. Thomas Williamson Harvey was born on Dec. 1, 1795 and died Dec. 28, 1841. He married Elizabeth May Hunter, daughter of Benjamin and Elizabeth (Fields) Hunter, Jan. 27, 1821, in Campbell County, Virginia. She was born Dec. 14, 1804 and died May 14, 1880 at Hunter's Tavern in Appomattox County. Both were buried in the Harvey Graveyard at Rolling Hill, Charlotte County. Thomas W. was a farmer and grist mill owner and operator on the Falling River at Springs Mills. Elizabeth was listed on the 1850 census for Appomattox County. On Feb. 28, 1854, she married second Thomas Elliott, son of Robert and Mary (Wilson) Elliott.

b. Sarah "Sally" Barksdale Harvey was born circa 1798 in Charlotte County, and died Nov. 8, 1867, in Franklin County, Alabama. She married Theodore Henderson Reed, son of John Orr and Martha (Frazer) Reed, May 23, 1814,

---

[6] See Charlotte County, Virginia *Will Book 8*, p. 102 and *Will Book 9*, p. 17.

[7] See Charlotte County, Virginia *Will Book 8*, pp. 163-164, 235; *Deed Book 14*, pp. 7-8; and *Order Book 30*, pp 239-240, and 244.

in Charlotte County. Theodore farmed in Campbell County until 1832, when his family moved to Franklin County, Alabama. Eleven children were born to this family unit.

c. Charles Collier Harvey was born on July 2, 1802 in Charlotte County, and died intestate on Nov. 2, 1875.[8] He married Nancy Miller Hunter, daughter of Benjamin and Elizabeth (Fields) Hunter, Dec. 6, 1823, in Campbell County. She was born Feb 22, 1806 and died Aug. 17, 1887. Both were buried in the Harvey Ccmetery located about 3.2 miles east of Red House, Charlotte County. Charles was a farmer, merchant, deputy sheriff, and tavern operator in Charlotte County. This family was united with the Little Concord Presbyterian Church in Charlotte County, where Charles served as an elder.

d. Susan Catherine Harvey was born on Sept. 13, 1807, in Charlotte County, and died Oct. 9, 1895, in Appomattox County. She married Washington Hunter, son of Benjamin and Elizabeth (Fields) Hunter, Nov. 17, 1825, in Lynchburg, Virginia. Washington was born on Aug. 24, 1802, and died April 2, 1864. He was a prosperous farmer at Spout Spring, Appomattox County.

e. Mary Ann Harvey was born in 1810. Her death date is not known. She married John Thornhill on Nov. 21, 1828, in Charlotte County. He was a wheelright. After Mary Ann's death, John married second a Miss Brent.

f. Macca[9] Barksdale Harvey was born March 26, 1813 and died July 3, 1892. She married Nathaniel Daniel Price on Oct. 5, 1829. He was born July 28, 1808 and died May 8, 1859. Nathaniel D. was a merchant, farmer, deputy sheriff and a member of the Masonic Order. This family lived at Madisonville, Charlotte County, where they raised ten children.

g. Martha Ann M. Harvey was born on Oct. 16, 1818 and died Oct. 15, 1905. She was buried in Liberty Baptist Church Cemetery in Appomattox. On Nov. 11, 1831, Martha married Clement Harvey Hancock in Lynchburg, Virginia. He was born on July 26, 1810, and died July 30, 1858. Clement was a farmer, merchant, and tavern owner in Charlotte County. Also, he served as a representative in the Virginia House of Delegates.

5. Drucilla Harvey, daughter of Thomas and Macca (Barksdale) Harvey, was born circa 1778 and died May 3, 1860. She married Isham Harvey, son of John and Ann (Richardson) Harvey, Jan. 6, 1796 in Charlotte County.

6. Susannah Harvey was born circa 1783 and died Feb. 1, 1851. She married William Lacy Thornton, son of Francis Thornton, Dec. 5, 1796 in Charlotte County.

---

[8] See Charlotte County, Virginia *Order Book 38*, p. 453, and *Will Book 16*, p. 83.

[9] Dr. Joseph W. Evans of Boulder, Colorado believed that Macca is an abbreviation or nickname for Andromache.

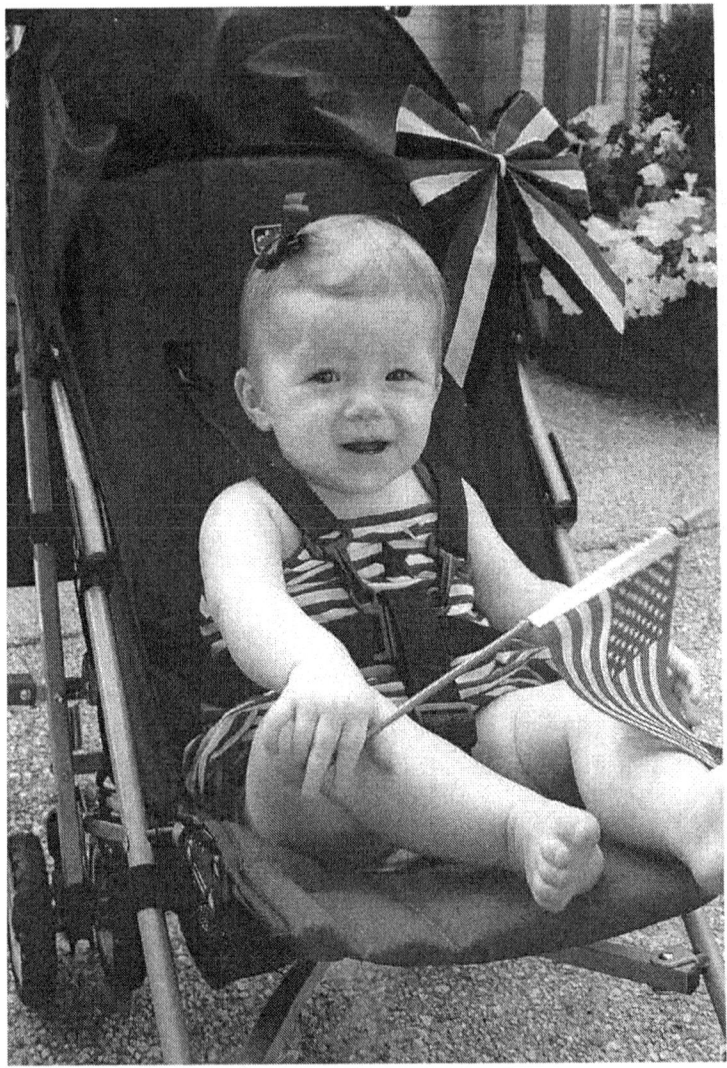

Julia Bell Kerns, daughter of Robert T. and Christine R. (Albro) Kerns of Great Falls, Virginia. Julia is a great-great-great-great-great-great granddaughter of Thomas Harvey the blacksmith. Above, Julia is celebrating July 4, 2004.

Chapter 21

The Hunters of Campbell and Appomattox

The progenitor of the Hunter family in Central Virginia is said to have been John Hunter Sr. and his wife Henrietta Davidson of Scots-Irish descent.[1] In 1898, Chapman Hunter Chilton, retired Superintendent of Appomattox County, Virginia Public Schools, compiled a sketch of his Hunter family roots. He stated that his ancestor Benjamin Hunter, 1770-1845, had exactly one-hundred grandchildren, of whom he was one. Chilton's granddaughter, Harriett A. Chilton of Falls Church, Virginia, researched and found the names of the one-hundred grandchildren. In July 1976, she produced a booklet *Hundred Hunter Cousins: In Honor of Our Nation's Bicentennial*. There is much interest in the Hunter family today because they intermarried with some of the leading families in Central Virginia and left many descendants.

From another source,[2] John Hunter Sr., the alleged immigrant, was born in 1683 and died in 1761. His wife Rachel, whom he married in 1704, was born in 1686 and died in 1769. The couple settled in 1730 in the Dumfries area of present Prince William County, Virginia. In both Chilton accounts, one generation is missing. If the senior Hunters were married in 1704 and their son John was not born until the mid-1730s, it is unrealistic for a child to be born thirty-some years after the parents were married.

The person whom Chilton called "John Hunter II" would be a grandson rather than a son of John and Henrietta Hunter Sr. Andrews also believed that the son was named John Hunter Jr., but

---

[1] Ruth Hairston Early, *Campbell Chronicles and Family Sketches*, (Baltimore, Maryland: Genealogical Publishing Co., Inc.), reprinted in 1978 from original version in 1927, pp. 430-432.

[2] Mrs. Andrew J. Andrews, *Kelso and Harding Families*, (nd), p. 74. This is a limited circulation publication, not copyrighted, maintained in the DAR Library in Washington, D. C.

offered no vital information.[3] A possible answer to this problem of a missing generation is offered in the McFarland genealogy.[4]

John McFarland, 1706-1784, and his wife Mary Montgomery, 1712-1782, of Ireland and Scotland respectively, immigrated to Pennsylvania where they met and married. Both died in Bedford County, Virginia. Their daughter Rachael McFarland was born on March 27, 1737 in Lancaster, Pennsylvania and died in 1784 in Campbell County, Virginia. She is the one in Chilton's genealogy who married "John Hunter II." Rachel had a sister, Mary McFarland, 1743-1821, who married James Hunter, Sept. 13, 1762. Parents of this James Hunter were Alexander Hunter, 1706-1768, and his wife Elizabeth Steele, ca 1720-1770.[5] He bought 1,060 acres on Wreck Island Creek, which I believe is presently in both Campbell and Appomattox Counties. Alexander died in Bedford County, Virginia.[6] There is good circumstantial evidence to build a case for this Alexander Hunter being the missing generation. They were both in the same geographic area of Virginia. The name Alexander is passed down in the Virginia Hunters. It is a good assumption that John and James Hunter, sons of Alexander Hunter, were brothers, although not proven. More research needs to be done in primary sources.

John Hunter Jr.

John Hunter Jr.,[7] son of Alexander and Elizabeth (Steele) Hunter, was born circa 1737 and died in 1795.[8] He married first

---

[3] These issues and sources were discussed in a letter from Wilmer L. Kerns to Harriett A. Chilton of Annandale Road, Falls Church, Virginia, Aug. 18, 1980.

[4] http://www.geneajourney.com/mcfar.html

[5] http://www.geneajourney.com/mcfar.html

[6] Bedford County, Virginia *Will Book I*, pp. 50-52, dates Dec. 21, 1767 and probated March 22, 1768.

[7] John is not a proven son of Alexander Hunter. The Jr. is given because that is how he is often recognized. It does not mean that his father was named John Hunter Sr.

[8] Campbell County, Virginia *Will Book 1*, pp. 323-325.

Rachel McFarland, 1737-1784, daughter of John and Mary (Montgomery) McFarland. John Jr. and Rachel are buried in the Old Concord Presbyterian Cemetery in Appomattox County. John married second Mary (Stith) Early, widow of Jeremiah Early, Feb. 5, 1790 in Campbell County. In 1751, John Jr. bought 400 acres of land in Lunenburg County, Virginia. In 1756, he patented 800 acres in Bedford County, now in present Appomattox County. In 1768, he bought ninety acres along the Falling River. He called his farm *Clover Green.* John Jr. built a tavern along the "Great Road to Richmond."[9] He served in the Colonia militia. John's professions were surveyor and planter.

Children of John Jr. and Rachel (McFarland) Hunter:

1. John Hunter III was born July 10, 1760 in Virginia. He served in the Revolutionary War.[10] In 1833, he applied for a pension through a deposition given in the Campbell County Court. The application was successful, earning him a pension of $60.40 per month. He stated that he was seventy-three years old; that he had lived in North Carolina, Tennessee and Kentucky., and had returned to Campbell County in 1830. John III married Susanna Preston April 16, 1785 in Bedford County, Virginia. They spent much of their life in Kentucky.

2. Elizabeth Hunter was born Nov. 12, 1762 in Bedford County and died July 17, 1848[11] in Rockingham County, North Carolina. Elizabeth married John May on April 19, 1779. John was born in May 1756 and died March 20, 1844.[12]

3. Alexander Hunter was born circa 1763 and died circa 1836 in Campbell County. He married Nancy Jones, daughter of Thomas Sr.

---

[9] Early, p. 430.

[10] Bedford County, Virginia Militia, *Order Book 1774-1782.*

[11] From the records of Dr. Joseph W. Evans that he transmitted to the compiler. He shared with me computer diskettes of his data base. An earlier version of his work, in hardcopy, was deposited in the Jones Memorial Library in Lynchburg, Virginia. One drawback of Dr. Evans' research is that he rarely documented his sources.

[12] Guilford County, North Carolina *Deed Book 3*, p. 105, per Dr. Joseph W. Evans.

and Sarah Jones, Nov. 24, 1784 in Campbell County. Alexander served as sheriff for Campbell County in 1787-1798.

4. Robert Hunter was born in 1766 and died circa 1828.[13] He married Nancy Ellis. Robert was a prominent man in County affairs. He ran the Hunter Tavern that was inherited from his father. Robert served as sheriff in 1823-1824. Both parents are buried in Concord Cemetery No. 2 near the Campbell/Appomattox County boundary.

5. James Hunter was born Jan. 19, 1769 and died Jan. 24, 1815.[14] He married Elizabeth Howlett who was born March 29, 1773 and died July 29, 1835. They moved to Kentucky in 1804, where they settled near Russelville.

6. Benjamin Hunter was born in 1770 and died June 23, 1845. He married Elizabeth Fields. See information below.

Benjamin Hunter

Bemjamin Hunter, son of John Jr. and Rachel (McFarland) Hunter, was born in Campbell County in 1770 and died June 23, 1845. He married Elizabeth Fields, daughter of Andrew and Margaret (Galbreath) Fields, in 1801. Benjamin settled on land that was purchased by his father-in-law, Andrew Fields, in 1779.[15] The land included the fork of Falling River and Reedy Creek that was then in Bedford County and later Campbell County, and presently in Appomattox County. Benjamin became one of the most prominent men of his day. In 1807, he was listed as a Major in the 117th Campbell County Militia. He served as a ruling elder in the Old Concord Presbyterian Church. He was elected to and served four terms as a Delegate to the Virginia Assembly, 1824-1829.[16] He and

---

[13] Campbell County, Virginia *Will Book 6*, p. 25, dated Dec. 12, 1827. See also Early, pp. 431.

[14] Logan County, Kentucky *Will Book A*, p. 393, dated Feb. 20, 1818, the estate of James Hunter. William Curd was one of the administrators.

[15] Bedford County, Virginia *Deed Book 6*, dated May 11, 1779, p. 320.

[16] Cynthia Miller Leonard, compiler, *The General Assembly of Virginia: a Bicentennial Register of Members, 1619-1978*, (Library of Virginia: Richmond, Virginia, 1978), pp. 328, 333, 338, and 343.

his wife Elizabeth are buried in the Hunter Cemetery that is located on their former estate. Situated on Route 679 near the Falling River in Appomattox County, a sign in 2004 states the name of the burial ground as Hunter-Marshall Cemetery.

Children of Benjamin and Elizabeth (Fields) Hunter:

1. Washington Hunter was born Aug. 24, 1802 and died April 2, 1864. He married Susan Catherine Harvey. See additional information and a picture below.

2. Elizabeth May Hunter was born Dec. 14, 1804 and died May 14, 1880 at Hunter's Tavern. She married Thomas Williamson Harvey, son of Nathan and Mary A. (Williamson) Harvey, on Jan. 27, 1821. He was born Dec. 1, 1795 and died Dec. 28, 1841. Thomas owned and operated a grist mill. Elizabeth married second Thomas Elliott on Feb. 28, 1854.

3. Nancy Miller Hunter was born Feb. 22, 1806 and died Aug. 17, 1877. She married Charles Collier Harvey, son of Nathan and Mary A. (Williamson) Harvey, on Dec. 6, 1823. Charles was born July 2, 1802 in Charlotte County.

4. Edward Hunter was born Oct. 14, 1807 in Campbell County and died Dec. 31, 1843 in St. Charles, Missouri. He married Eliza Ann Gwatkin, daughter of Charles and Mary (Callaway) Gwatkin, on April 25, 1836 in Beford County, Virginia. She married second George Steptoe Johnson on March 1, 1848.[17]

5. Caroline Matilda Hunter was born May 9, 1809 and died June 2, 1857. She married Archibald Alexander LeGrand Nov. 1, 1826. He was born April 26, 1803 and died Feb. 28, 1879.

6. Adeline Virginia Hunter was born March 29, 1812 and died Sept. 29, 1834. She married John Poindexter Chilton on June 7, 1831. He was born July 15, 1809 and died July 15, 1868.

7. Margaret Harvey Hunter was born Sept. 22, 1813 and died Sept. 5, 1880. She married William Alexander Elliott April 23, 1839. He was born Dec. 27, 1813 and died Aug 8, 1865. Farmer in Appomattox.

---

[17] Mary Denham Ackerly and Lula Eastman Jeter Parker, *Our Kin*, (Harrisonburg, Virginia: C. J. Carrier Company), 1976, p. 276.

8. Benjamin Hunter Jr. was born Sept. 15, 1815 and died Nov. 28, 1889. He married Sarah Moseley Williams on July 27, 1846. Sarah died in February 1869 and he married second Mache E. Plunkett. Benjamin Jr. was a well-to-do farmer in Appomattox County.

9. Rachel McFarland Hunter was born June 7, 1817 and died in February 1882. She married William Franklin Wood.

10. Mary Evelyn Hunter was born June 11, 1819 and died Dec. 15, 1870. She married Douglas Hancock Marshall,[18] May 9, 1839. He was born Nov. 29, 1815 and died Dec. 19, 1895.

11. Henrietta Louisa Hunter was born Sept. 11, 1820 and died May 5, 1900. She married John Bartholomew Dupuy on Dec. 22, 1844. He was born June 18, 1812 in Prince Edward County and died June 13, 1890.

12. Elvira Fields Hunter was born Aug. 12, 1822 and died in April 1883. She married John Martin Marshall on Nov. 15, 1843. He was born March 15, 1814.

Washington Hunter

Washington Hunter, son of Benjamin and Elizabeth (Fields) Hunter, was born Aug. 24, 1802 in Campbell County, and died April 2, 1864 in Appomattox County. He married Susan Catherine Harvey, daughter of Nathan and Mary Ann (Williamson) Harvey, on Nov. 17, 1825 in Lynchburg. She was born on Sept. 13, 1807 in Charlotte County, and died Oct. 9, 1895, in Appomattox County. He was a prosperous farmer and owner of the Hunter Tavern at Spout Spring, Appomattox County. Washington was prominent in political and community affairs, including a Deacon in the Concord Presbyterian Church. He served as one of the first Justices for Appomattox County when it was formed in 1845. The tavern was burned down circa 1988. The roadbed of the Lynchburg-to-Richmond Stage Road is visible across his former estate, now owned in part by Winston D. and Glenice Walton of Spout Spring, Virginia.

Children of Washington and Susan C. (Harvey) Hunter:[19]

---

[18] He was listed as a farmer on the 1850 U. S. Census for Appomattox County, adjoining the farm of Benjamin Hunter Jr. See Census Roll M432_933, p. 188.

1. Charles Williamson Hunter was born on Sept. 20, 1827 in Appomattox County, and died Feb. 13, 1895. He married Susan Harris, 1833-1903, in 1853. Charles served in the Civil War, in Company A of the 44th Virginia Regiment.

2. Mary Ann Hunter, born on Aug. 13, 1830, and died in 1923. She married the Rev. William G. Miller, Methodist minister, and they lived for awhile in Peoria, Illinois. Mary A. was buried at the Old Concord Presbyterian Church Cemetery in Appomattox County.

3. Sarah E. Hunter was born on March 3, 1832, and died May 23, 1913. She married Dr. Daniel Septimus Evans, on Feb. 22, 1853. He was born on July 10, 1824, and died May 2, 1895.

4. Macca Barksdale Hunter was born on June 6, 1835, and died in April 1885 in Appomattox County. She married Lameck Jones on June 20, 1853. He was born on Jan. 14, 1831 and died in 1906.

5. Adeline Virginia Hunter[20] was born on July 7, 1837, and died in Fort Worth, Texas Aug. 29, 1916. She was buried at Stephenville, Texas. Adeline married first Thomas A. Williams, Oct. 13, 1856. He was born Feb. 25, 1835, and died April 29, 1871, in Virginia. She married second the Rev. Lawrence Ferdinand Way, son of Ferdinand Gephart and Rebecca Hinkle (Wartman) Way. He was born July 28, 1833 at Harrisonburg, Virginia, and died Dec. 6, 1921, in Lubbock, Texas. In 1882 they moved to Oklahoma and later settled in Texas.

6. Nathan Harvey Hunter was born in 1839 and died on April 15, 1874 in Hempstead, Texas. He married Emma Plunkett, daughter of John and Cynthia Ann M. (Staples) Plunkett of Appomattox County and they moved to Texas. He was a dentist.

7. Martha Susan Hunter was born March 10, 1842 in Appomattox, Virginia, and died Oct. 17, 1922, in Shreveport, Louisiana. She married William Arthur Jones, son of Peter R. and Letitia V. (Moseley) Jones,

---

[19] Unless otherwise noted, information on this family unit was derived from a family Bible that gives vital information on the family unit of Washington and Susan C. Hunter, in possession of Mrs. W. Conway Thetford, 3725 Mockingbird Lane, Dallas Texas 75205. Information was supplemented with the late Harriett A. Chilton's *Hundred Hunter Cousins*, (Falls Church, Virginia), 1976.

[20] Information on Adeline and her family was provided by Harry O. Alvis of Batesville, Arkansas.

on Nov. 5, 1862 in Campbell County. He was born on Oct. 27, 1836 in Campbell County,, and died on Dec. 28, 1885, in Brownwood, Texas.

7. Washington B. Hunter was born Jan. 14, 1851, and died Feb. 18, 1853, "of fever."[21]

Washington Hunter, 1802-1864[22]

---

[21] Library of Virginia, *Appomattox County, Virginia Death Records, 1853-1896.*

[22] The photograph was supplied by Lloyd G. Walton of Appomattox, Virginia. Lloyd's source was Lena (Caldwell) Eversole. Tom Almquest has the same picture on his website, but believes that it is Maj. William Jones. His picture was copied from Betty K. Ford of Appomattox who told the copier, a Mr. Marshall, that her late husband descended from this man. The compiler believes the person in the picture above is probably Washington Hunter. The issue is discussed at this website: http://stithvalley.com/ancestry/jones/jones.htm.

Chapter 22

Three Thomas Jones of Campbell County

The Jones surname has the third highest frequency of all surnames in the United States.[1] Anyone with a Jones ancestor in his or her family tree knows that the research task is formidable. Descendants of Eugene A. and Nannie Katherine (Jones) Walton of Appomattox County have three Thomas Jones in their family tree, each living during the 1700s in the same geographic area of Central Virginia. Below is a sketch of each of the three ancestral family units: Thomas Jones Sr., 1698-1768; Thomas Jones Sr, 1730-1818; and Major Thomas Jones, 1754-1826. This research is tentative and ongoing rather than final.[2] Although the compiler took copious notes during the 1970s at the Campbell County courthouse in Rustburg, some of the source material is not retrievable before this manuscript goes to the press.

More than likely, the origin of the Joneses was Wales. At one time, the name was Johns.

Thomas Jones (1)

The first Thomas Jones was born circa 1698 and died intestate, without a will, in 1768 in Buckingham County, Virginia, which is based on a District Court case in Prince Edward County, Virginia.. He purchased 400 acres along the south branches of the Slate River in Goochland County, Virginia on June 10, 1740,[3] which is now in Buckingham County. On July 20, 1742, Thomas Jones Sr. bought 323 acres on the north side of the Falling River in Brunswick County. On the same day, his son, Thomas Jones Jr. bought 400

---

[1] This is based on a 1976 study prepared for the bi-centennial celebration (200 years) by the Office of Research and Statistics, Social Security Administration, Washington, D. C. The compiler was an employee in that Office and has a copy of the unpublished research paper.

[2] Thanks to Tammy Jones of Columbia, Missouri and Tom Almquest, Talqt@aol.com, for generously sharing information. Tom credits John Jones of Houston, Texas for his unrelenting effort to construct a Jones genealogy. In addition, the compiler appreciates the data shared by the late Dr. Joseph W. Evans of Boulder, Colorado.

[3] Library of Virginia, Archives and Manuscripts, "Land Office Grants."

acres on the south side of the Falling River. Both properties are now in Campbell County. These men were wealthy, pioneer settlers along the frontier of the Piedmont belt in the Colony of Virginia.[4]

Known children of Thomas Jones Sr.:

1. John Jones was born circa 1722 and died about 1798 in Buckingham County. His wife was Elizabeth Walker. (2)

2. William Jones was born about 1725 and died about 1804. Speculation is that he married Lucy Anthony, based on the clue of a son named John Anthony Jones. William was one of the early landowners on the east side of the Falling River. (3)

3. Josias Jones was born circa 1727 and died in Buckingham County in 1815.[5] (4)

4. Thomas Jones Jr. was born circa 1730 and died circa 1818 in Campbell County, Virginia. His wife was named Sarah. (5)

John Jones (2)

John Jones, son of Thomas Jones Sr., was born circa 1722, probably in Old Goochland or Brunswick Counties, Virginia and died about 1798 in Buckingham County, Virginia. He married Elizabeth Walker, daughter of Joel and Sarah Walker. John held major tracts of land in Buckingham County. Patrick Henry was the attorney for John Jones regarding a land dispute that was heard in the District Court in Prince Edward County.

Children of John and Elizabeth (Walker) Jones:

1. John Jones Jr. was born circa 1750, married Elizabeth Easley, daughter of Thomas and Mary Easley.[6] (6)

---

[4] See Ruth Early, *Campbell Chronicles and Family Sketches of Campbell County, Virginia,*" pp. 443-445.

[5] Roger G. Ward, compiler, *Land Tax Summaries & Implied Deeds, 1815-1840*, (Athens, Georgia: Iberian Publishing Co.), 1994, p. 193. His land was on the North Fork of the Slate River in Buckingham County. His estate had not been settled when the land taxes were assessed in 1840.

[6] Charlotte County, Virginia *Order Book I*, Sept. 7, 1778.

2. Capt. William Jones was born circa 1753 in Buckingham County and died in the Revolutionary War on March 15, 1781 at Guilford, North Carolina. He married Agnes Walker, 1749-1826.[7] After his death, she married second Thomas Lewis. (7)

3. Maj. Thomas Jones was born on Nov. 6, 1754 and died in 1826 in Campbell County. (8)

4. Keziah Jones was born Feb. 10, 1760 in Buckingham County and died in October 1826.[8] She married Anthony Winston in Prince Edward County on March 11, 1776. Anthony was born Nov. 25, 1750 in Hanover County, Virginia and died at Tuscumbia, Alabama Nov. 8, 1827. He was a veteran of the Revolutionary War, rising to the rank of Captain. Anthony served as High Sheriff of Buckingham County before moving to Davidson County, Tennessee in 1789. About 1810 he moved his family to Alabama, where in 1818 he was a member of the first Legislature of Alabama.[9] (9)

5. Joel W. Jones was born in 1761 in Buckingham County and died in 1792. He married Sarah Patrick on March 18, 1782 in Campbell County. (10)

6. Capt. Arthur Jones was born Oct. 21, 1769 in Buckingham County and died Oct. 24, 1836 at Tuscumbia, Alabama. He married first Sarah Baker, 1779-1828, daughter of Caleb Baker, on Jan. 8, 1795 in Prince Edward County, Virginia.[10] They and other Jones families went to Alabama in 1817. Capt. Arthur married second Mrs. Eliza Jones, 1780-1837. They were Baptists and Democrats. (11)

7. Charles Jones, circa 1770-1815, married Elizabeth Walker circa 1795 in Buckingham County. (12)

---

[7] See Campbell County, Virginia *Will Book 1, 1782-1800*, pp. 52, 62, 147 and 158.

[8] Alfred Sumner Winston III, *The Winstons of Hanover County, Virginia and Related Families, 1666-1992*, (Baltimore, Maryland: Gateway Press, Inc.), 1992, pp. 520 and 577.

[9] Capt. Arthur Henley Keller, *History of Tuscumbia, Alabama*, (Sheffield, Alabama: Tennessee Valley Historical Society), 1981 reprint from the 1888 edition, p. 39.

[10] Catherine L. Knorr, *Marriages of Prince Edward County, Virginia*, (Privately Published), 1950, p. 43.

8. Maj. Samuel Jones was born May 20, 1777 and died Dec. 17, 1837 in Alabama. It is believed that he married and had children who went to Kentucky. (13)

Thomas Jones Jr. (5)

Thomas Jones Jr., son of Thomas Jones Sr., was born circa 1730 in Goochland County, Virginia and died circa 1818 in Campbell County.[11] His wife was named Sarah.[12] Information on his family is skimpy, but this section on the Jones family is intended to provide an impetus for further research.

Children of Thomas Jr. and Sarah Jones:

1. Elizabeth Jones was born circa 1758 and died before 1817. She married John Cock, 1758-1822, who died in Wilson County, Tennessee. (14)

2. Thomas Jones Jr. was born circa 1760 and died before 1799. He married Mrs. Judith Jones. Judith married second Pleasant Rosser on March 27, 1805 in Campbell County. (15)

3. Jesse Jones was born circa 1764 and died circa 1826 in Campbell County. He married Sally Johns on Nov. 24, 1784 in Campbell County.

4. Nancy Jones was born circa 1768 in Bedford County and died circa 1835 in Campbell County. She married Alexander Hunter, 1763-1836, on Nov. 17, 1784 in Campbell County. (16)

5. John Jones was born circa 1771 and died in 1816 in Campbell County. He married first Jenny Hightower, 1775-1800, on March 15, 1794 in Campbell County. John married second Nancy Fields on Nov. 7, 1803 in Campbell County. She was born in 1770 in Pennsylvania and died after 1850 in Appomattox County. (17)

6. A daughter Jones married Robert Saunders. (18)

7. William Jones was born circa 1780 and died circa 1834 in Campbell County. He married Elizabeth Jones in 1803 in Buckingham County.

---

[11] Campbell County, Virginia *Will Book 4*, p. 151.

[12] Campbell County, Virginia *Deed Book 5*, p. 173.

Elizabeth was born in 1784 in Buckingham County and died in December 1849 in Buckingham. (19)

8. Dorothea Broomhead Jones was born circa 1784 and died after 1837. She married James Glass on Nov. 25, 1803 in Campbell County.[13] (20)

Maj. Thomas Jones (8)

Thomas Jones, son of John and Elizabeth (Walker) Jones, was born on Nov. 6, 1754, probably in Buckingham County, Virginia.[14] His will was written in Campbell County on Feb. 18, 1826,[15] and probated on July 10, 1826. Thomas married Elizabeth "Betsy" Johns, daughter of William and Ann Johns, circa 1776. She was born on Nov. 7, 1757 and died on Nov. 13, 1837 in Campbell County.[16] Thomas Jones was commissioned an ensign on April 23, 1781.[17] Apparently, he was promoted to major during his militia service in the Revolutionary War. Therefore, we are referring to him as Maj. Thomas Jones.

Major Jones murdered his son-in-law, John F. Wood in April 1825.[18] It is said that Wood was abusive to his wife Martha Jane, and he threatened her father, who drew his pistol for the fatal shot. Apparently, Jones was acquitted for shooting in self-defense. Here is the newspaper account:

> It is with regret that we relate an occurrence which took place in this County a few days past. Major Thomas Jones, an old and respectable citizen, being assaulted by his son-in-law, by the name of Wood, whose grievances he had borne with for a number of years, drew his pistol and

---

[13] See Campbell County, Virginia *Will Book 8, 1836-1841*, p. 100.

[14] Some researchers believe that he was born in Bedford County, Virginia.

[15] Campbell County, Virginia *Will Book 5*, p. 319.

[16] Campbell County, Virginia *Will Book 8*, p. 158. Vital dates were secured from "The Grandfather Papers" in the DAR Library in Washington, D. C.

[17] Campbell County, Virginia *Order Book, 1774-1782.*

[18] *Richmond Commercial Appeal*, May 2, 1825, p. 2, c. 1

shot him dead on the spot. He immediately sent for a neighboring Magistrate and surrendered himself into custody.[19]

It has been told that one trait of this branch of the Jones family was obesity. Major Thomas was a heavy-set man and two of his daughters weighed more than 200 pounds.[20] The Joneses were also noted for their beautiful eyes. Mrs. Andrews cited Mrs. C. R. Morton of Spout Spring, Virginia as a typical Jones in appearance and personality. Mrs. Morton was nee Nellie W. Bates—born July 29, 1898 and died in November 1983. Nellie was a granddaughter of Lamech Jones and great granddaughter of Maj. William Jones.

Maj. Thomas Jones was a large landowner and planter in the Falling River area of Campbell County. Many slaves were required to run the tobacco farms. His very detailed will indicates that he was one of the wealthiest men of his time.

Children of Maj. Thomas and Elizabeth (Johns) Jones:[21]

1. Rhoda Jones was born on Jan. 11, 1777 in Bedford County, Virginia and died in February 1851 in Meade County, Kentucky. She married first Thomas Jefferson Stith, 1768-1821, son of Richard and Lucy (Hall) Stith, on March 12, 1793 in Campbell County. Rhoda married second Matthew Partridge on Oct. 21, 1828 in Meade County. On May 1, 1845, she married third John H. Gibbs in Meade County. Finally, she married fourth Henry S. Bell on Sept. 19, 1847 in Meade County.[22] (21)

---

[19] From a message by Tammy Jones that was posted on the Virginia History discussion group, March 5, 1999.

[20] Letter to the compiler dated Aug. 19, 1980 from Mrs. A. J. (Karolyn) Andrews, 5722 Alvarade, Houston, TX 77035.

[21] Names and vital dates were secured from "The Grandfather Papers" in the DAR Library in Washington, D. C. Tammy Jones of Columbia, Missouri deserves credit for information in several emails. The compiler did extensive research in the Campbell County courthouse during the 1960s and 1970s, but failed to cite all the references.

[22] 1850 U. S. Census for Meade County, Kentucky, Family No. 329. Henry and Rhoda constitute that household as free inhabitants within the Kentucky District.

2. Elizabeth Jones was born on Jan. 5, 1779 in Bedford County and died on Aug. 24, 1843, probably in Meade County, Kentucky. Elizabeth married Richard Stith Jr., son of Richard and Lucy (Hall) Stith, on Dec. 27, 1798 in Campbell County. (22)

3. Nancy Jones was born on Dec. 9, 1781 and died on Jan. 2, 1849 in Hardin County, Kentucky. Burial was in the Jesse Stith Cemetery. Nancy married William B. Stith, son of Richard and Lucy (Hall) Stith, on Dec. 28, 1796 in Campbell County. (23)

4. William Jones, known as "Major Billy," was born July 4, 1783 and died July 3, 1858. He married Nancy Hunter. See additional information on his family unit below. (24)

5. Thomas Jones Jr. was born circa 1784 and died before 1817. He married Elizabeth Wood, daughter of Edmund and Jane (Franklin) Wood, on Dec. 25, 1804 in Campbell County. After his death, Elizabeth married second Lewis Franklin on Oct. 24, 1817. (25)

6. John Jones was born circa 1785 in Campbell County and died circa 1826. He married first Edna Martin, daughter of Charles and Lockey (Johns) Martin, on Feb. 15, 1817 in Campbell County. Edna was born Nov. 6, 1795 and died Nov. 8, 1822. John married second Jane B. Talbot, February 27, 1823 in Campbell County. If this is the correct John, he was deceased when his father wrote his will in 1826, and left these children: John Martin Jones, Charles Thomas Jones, and Amanda Jones. (26)

7. Buckner Jones was born circa 1786 in Campbell County. He was a student at Hampden Sydney College in 1809. Buckner inherited from his father 245 acres of land on Meadow Creek that was bought from Robert Hawkins. Buckner did not marry. Apparently, he was ruled incompetent during his last years because William Jones was assigned to be his Committee by the Circuit Court.[23] (27)

8. Joel Jones was born circa 1787 in Campbell County and died Oct. 26, 1842. He married Dolly Cobbs, daughter of Edmund Johns, on May 22, 1823 in Campbell County.[24] He received 700 acres and slaves from his father's will. (28)

---

[23] Campbell County, Virginia *Circuit Court Will Book 9*, pp. 125, 248-249.

[24] *Ibid.* pp. 249.

9. Dr. James Jones was born in 1789 in Campbell County and died May 29, 1869 in Buckingham County. He married first Nancy Jones, daughter of Charles and Elizabeth Jones, circa 1815. Nancy was born in 1797 and died Feb. 7, 1839. Dr. Jones married second Martha W. Jones Jan. 18, 1840. She was born in 1795 and died from measles on June 2, 1847.[25] Dr. Jones married third Leanna Mary Glover Oct. 7, 1847. (29)

10. Martha Jane Jones was born in 1801 and died in 1869 in Campbell County. She married first John Franklin Wood on Feb. 26, 1814 in Campbell County and died in April 1825 from a pistol shot by his father-in-law. Apparently, he was abusive to his wife and belligerent toward his father-in-law. Martha married second Patterson Jennings on April 17, 1826. (30)

William Jones (24)

William Jones, son of Thomas and Elizabeth (Johns) Jones, was born on July 4, 1783 in Campbell County, Virginia and died on July 3, 1858 in Campbell County.[26] Known as "Major Billy," he married Nancy Hunter, daughter of Alexander and Nancy (Jones) Hunter, on Dec. 19, 1804 in Campbell County. Nancy was born on Oct. 17, 1790 in Campbell County and died on Feb. 5, 1863 in Lynchburg.

The house that he built on his land during the 1820s, known today as *Blenheim*, still stands and is excellently preserved. The house is near the confluence of the Big Falling River and the South Fork of the Falling River, which is about ten miles from the County courthouse in Rustburg. The plantation slaves made the bricks for the house. His father, who was a rich man for his time, owning about 3200 acres, gave the plantation to Major Billy.

Major Billy and Nancy were both buried on the plantation between the house and the river, but no grave markers remain. Tenant farmers, who farmed the land, dug up the gravestones. After

---

[25] Library of Virginia, Glover Family Bible Record (image 4), 1785-1962, Archives and Manuscript Room, Call No. 31066.

[26] Campbell County, Virginia *Will Book 12*, pp. 86-89.

Major Billy died, his wife Nancy lived in Lynchburg in 1860 with two of her grand children, Charles W. Jones and Mary F. Harvey.[27]

Children of Maj. William and Nancy (Hunter) Jones:[28]

1. Jesse Jones was born in 1805 in Campbell County and died on Jan. 29, 1876. He allegedly went to Kentucky in early life where he married Lucy Catherine Stith, his cousin, on Oct. 7, 1830 in Meade County, Kentucky. They later returned to Campbell County.[29] (31)

2. Peter Rhodes Jones was born circa 1807 in Campbell County and died in 1865 in Hempstead, Austin County, Texas. He married Letitia Victoria Moseley. (32)

3. Lynch Jones was born on March 17, 1810 in Campbell County and died on May 5, 1864 in the same County.[30] He married Mary Magdalene Moseley, daughter of Francis and Mary (Saunders) Moseley of Buckingham County, Virginia. She was born on Feb. 28, 1814 and died on Oct. 22, 1865 in Campbell County. Lynch was a farmer. (33)

4. Thomas Hunter Jones was born in 1815 in Campbell County and died after 1870. He married first Nancy Hunter, daughter of Thomas Edward and Jemima (Fields) Hunter, on Sept. 10, 1832 in Campbell County. Nancy was born March 31, 1813 and died March 1, 1836.[31]

---

[27] From the research of Dr. Joseph W. Evans to the compiler.

[28] Lena (Caldwell) Eversole of Appomattox County provided information on this family unit. Additional information was gleaned from the compiler's research in the Campbell County, Virginia courthouse at Rustburg. Unfortunately, the compiler did not record all of the sources when the information was copied during the 1960s.

[29] Information on Jesse and his family was secured from Ancestry.com, Family Trees. Descendants claim that she was born in Kentucky, but the 1850 and 1870 U. S. Censuses for Campbell County, Virginia state that Lucy was born in Virginia. Dr. Joseph W. Evans believed that this Jesse Jones married Paula A. Jennings, daughter of Powhatan Jennings, on Sept. 15, 1832 in Campbell County, Virginia. More research is necessary on this Jesse Jones.

[30] See Campbell County, Virginia *Will Book 13*, p. 191.

[31] From obituary by images.ancestry.com. She left one child, Charles Jones.

Pauline Martha Talbot, daughter of Williston and Nancy (Keese) Talbot, on Wednesday, Jan. 18, 1837 in Campbell County.[32] (34)

5. Evalina Jones was born in 1816 and died on Jan. 18, 1878 in Meade County, Kentucky. She married William Stith, son of Thomas and Rhoda (Jones) Stith, on Jan. 14, 1832 in Campbell County. She married second Henry Hardaway on Feb. 17, 1842 in Meade County, Kentucky. (35)

6. William Windham Jones was born about 1818 and died after 1870. He married Margaret Fields (Hunter) Jones, widow of his first cousin, George Washington Jones, on Feb. 19, 1852 in Campbell County. She was born in 1830 and died Aug. 5, 1886. Margaret was a daughter of Thomas Edward and Jemima H. (Fields) Hunter. (36)

7. Elizabeth W. Jones was born in 1821 in Campbell County and died after 1860. She married Daniel Price on May 18, 1842 in Campbell County. (37)

8. Nancy M. Jones was born on Nov. 10, 1825 and died in 1890 in Campbell County. She married first Nathan Harvey on Jan. 19, 1846, and married second Alexander P. Watson, on Oct. 10, 1860 in Campbell County. Nathan Harvey was born on Dec. 27, 1822 and died on Sept. 8, 1847. (38)

9. Alexander W. Jones was born on Nov. 27, 1827 in Campbell County, and died on Aug. 12, 1865 in Breckinridge County, Kentucky. He married Catherine Board on Oct. 6, 1853 in Breckinridge County, Kentucky. Catherine was born on Nov. 15, 1835 and died on Oct. 18, 1902. Alexander was a hotel owner. (39)

10. Lamech Jones was born on Jan. 13, 1831 in Campbell County and died in 1902. He married Macca Barksdale Hunter. (40)

Lamech Jones (40)

Lamech Jones, son of Maj. William and Nancy (Hunter) Jones, was born in Campbell County, Virginia on Jan. 13, 1831, and died

---

[32] *The Lynchburg Virginian*, issue of Feb. 2, 1837. The paper gives her middle initial as A., which may have been an error.

in Appomattox County in 1902.[33] The name Lamech comes from the Holy Bible in Genesis 4: 19-24, where Lamech was the first recorded polygamist in the Bible. We learn in Luke 3:36 that Lamech was a son of Methuselah and grandson of Enoch, all of whom were ancestors of Jesus.

Lamech Jones married Macca Barksdale Hunter,[34] daughter of Washington and Susan Catherine (Harvey) Hunter, on June 20, 1853. Macca was born on June 6, 1835, in Campbell County, and died in April 1885, probably in Appomattox County. The Jones were Presbyterians. Lamech possessed the farm that was previously owned by his father-in-law, Washington Hunter, at Spout Spring in present Appomattox County, but formerly in Campbell County prior to 1845. The 366-acre farm was purchased at a sale in 1864. The farm included the Hunter Tavern, which was a stopping point for travelers along the Richmond-to-Lynchburg Turnpike. The roadbed is still visible where it crossed the farm. William Campbell, the present owner, caused the Tavern to be burned down several years ago. Winston D. Walton, who is a great grandson of Lamech Jones, owns a chip of the land that was originally the Hunter-Jones farm. Lamech's will of 1902 directed his sons Walter S. and William Hunter Jones to manage the farm and to take care of Ella, who had a disability. If these three children died without offspring, the farm would be divided equally among the living heirs. The two sons died unexpectedly in 1918 and 1921, after which Alexander "Zan" W. Jones continued the farming and caring for his sister Ella until his death in 1956. Walker Scott Walton assisted them in their later years. Ella, who outlived all ten of her siblings, died in 1962 at the age of eighty-two years. Residence: Spout Spring, Appomattox County, Virginia.

---

[33] Appomattox County, Virginia *Will Book 1*, p. 126. Family historians have recorded a death date of 1906, but this is an error, in that his will was written on May 1, 1901 and probated on Oct. 12, 1902.

[34] Information on the Hunter family came from a Bible record.

Children of Lamech and Macca Barksdale (Hunter) Jones:[35]

1. Mary Elizabeth Jones was born on July 20, 1854 and died on July 23, 1867. (41)

2. Walter S. Jones, born on Aug. 31, 1856, and died on Jan. 8, 1918. He was unmarried. Walter was buried in the Old Concord Presbyterian Cemetery in the Spout Spring District, Appomattox County. (42)

3. William Hunter Jones was born Jan. 21, 1859 and died on Sept. 24, 1921, unmarried. He was buried in the Old Concord Presbyterian Cemetery. (43)

4. Nannie Katherine Jones was born Jan. 26, 1862 and died Dec. 28, 1931 in Appomattox County. She married Eugene Adolphus Walton, son of John William and Mary Jane (Vawter) Walton, on Oct. 24, 1884. Eugene was born on Aug. 16, 1850 and died Dec. 19, 1921. Both were buried on their farm near Bent Creek, Appomattox County. He was a farmer, storekeeper and deputy sheriff for Appomattox County. (44)

Alexander W. Jones, son of Lamech Jones at Spout Spring

5. Lena Livert Jones was born July 6, 1864 in Appomattox County and died on March 20, 1901 in Lynchburg. She married Leonard Ellis

---

[35] Information on this family unit came from a copy of the family Bible record in the hands of Lena (Caldwell) Eversole of Appomattox County, Virginia.

Smith, son of Thomas A. and Nancy J. (LaGrand) Smith, on Oct. 27, 1891. Leonard was born on June 6, 1865 and died Oct. 8, 1947. (45)

6. Edmonia Hunter Jones was born Oct. 12, 1866 and died July 12, 1962. "Eddie" was engaged to be married, but on the night before the wedding, she climbed through her bedroom window to elope with Rufus Hill Bates. He was employed by the Norfolk and Western Railroad. They had eleven children: Norman H. Bates, Macca V. Bates, Robert Hunter Bates, Eva Fleming Bates married Frank L. Turner, Arthur Daniel Bates, Nellie Walker Bates married Clement Reade Morton, Rufus William Bates, Edmund Lamech Bates, Lena Liverta Bates married L. W. Adams, Susie "Monk" Ellen Bates married Ernest Thornhill Sours, and Mary Lucille "Cassie" Bates, who was born in 1910. See photograph of the eleven children, below. Both parents were buried in the Spring Hill Presbyterian Cemetery in Lynchburg. (46)

Rufus H. and Edmonia H. (Jones) Bates are seated. Their children are standing.

7. Susan "Susie" Daniel Jones was born March 17, 1869 and died Dec. 22, 1938 (not 1968 as wrongly reported). She married Madison Clark Caldwell on Jan. 23, 1895. He was born Nov. 25, 1864 and died Feb. 23, 1938. This family interested me on the Jones genealogy. The compiler used to visit their daughter Lena (Caldwell) Eversole, 1902-

1988, who shared information with me during the 1960s. We later attended a fiftieth wedding anniversary for her sister, Ruby (Caldwell) Lewis, in Appomattox County on Aug. 31, 1976. Lena and Ruby had a brother named Clark Caldwell who was killed. We have photos. There were other siblings, although the compiler never met them. A cemetery is located in the Lewis yard, but Susan is buried in the Old Concord Presbyterian Church Cemetery in Appomattox County. (47)

8. Evie Virginia Jones was born Jan. 1, 1872 at Spout Spring, and died of childbirth on Jan. 31, 1899. She married Richard Walker Smith on July 7. 1898. They had no children. (48)

9. Alexander Wirt Jones was born on Nov. 10, 1875 and died Aug. 4, 1956,[36] unmarried. He lived on the Washington Hunter estate at Spout Spring, Virginia. My wife's brother, Winston D. Walton, owns and farms a piece of Washington Hunter's former estate. The roadbed of the Richmond-to-Lynchburg Turnpike is still visible on his land. (49)

10. Richard McIlwaine Jones was born on Nov. 7, 1877 and died in 1881. (50)

11. Ella Olivia Jones was born on May 1, 1880 at Spout Spring, and died on Aug. 17, 1962, unmarried.[37] Ella, who was disabled, outlived all of her siblings. (51)

Finale: Although Lamech and Macca B. (Hunter) Jones had eleven children, including four sons, there is no living descendant to carry the Jones name forward.

---

[36] The death date was recorded in a funeral book that listed "Relatives Attending," "Friends who Called," etc. This book is in possession of the compiler. A death year of 1954 has been circulated among genealogists, which is incorrect.

[37] Tombstone inscriptions in the Old Concord Presbyterian Church Cemetery in Appomattox County, Virginia.

Chapter 23

William Shepherd of Buckingham County

There were two contemporary William Shepherds in Buckingham County, relationship not determined. According to military records in the National Archives, our William Shepherd saw service in the War of 1812. He served as a private in Capt. William J. Freeland's Company of the 9th Virginia Troops under General Cocke, and was discharged for "indisposition." His service period was for six months, from Aug. 29, 1814 to Feb. 3, 1815. According to his war pension papers, William was born in 1791 and died Jan. 28, 1868. This distinguishes him from the other William Shepherd in Buckingham County, whose relationship, if any, is not known. Our William was probably a son of Samuel Shepherd. The name Shepard or Sheppard was also common in Buckingham County, but was not related to the Shepherds.

May 26, 1830, William Shepherd married Martha Gaines Booker, daughter of Bernard Gaines and Mary (Stratton) Booker.[1] The officiating minister was the Rev. John Ayres. Martha was born in 1811 in Buckingham County, per census records, and died on June 24, 1902 in the same county. She received a widow's pension, which records gave her date of death. Bernard G. Booker's parents were Marshall and Patsy (Gaines) Booker of Cumberland County.

William and Martha G. Shepherd lived just west of Sprouse's Corner and east of Buckingham Court House along U. S. Route 60. He converted their large house into a tavern or inn that was strategically located on the Richmond-to-Lynchburg Stage Road. The roadbed is still visible. General Robert E. Lee and his troops spent the night at Shepherd's Tavern on the day following the surrender at Appomattox. The Buckingham Chapter of the Daughter's of the Confederacy declared the Tavern as an historic house. An undated issue of the *Farmville Herald* ran a picture of the house before it was restored. It described the "quaint old house" as having wooden pegs for nails, hand-sown lumber and heart pine floors. A fire consumed the dwelling in June 1985, and only two

---

[1] *Daily Richmond Whig*, June 5, 1830, p. 3, c. 2.

chimneys remain on the site. Across the road from the former tavern is the Shepherd family cemetery.

Martha G. Shepherd received a widow's pension from her late husband's service in the War of 1812. In 1871, Martha sold 100 acres to her son Benjamin F. Shepherd, adjoining the lands of B.R. Eldridge and William H. Word.[2] Benjamin F. later built a house on this land. The previous year, in 1870, Martha G. Shepherd conveyed land to George Shepherd, a Negro (presumably a former free servant).[3] Three acres of this land were later sold to the Commonwealth of Virginia to create the Wayside Park on U.S. Route 60, between Dillwyn and Buckingham Court House. The deed stated that old William Shepherd had purchased this land from Samuel Jennings Booker, which was formerly owned by Jordon Shoemaker. In 1878, a survey of 95 acres was made for Martha G. Shepherd to satisfy debts of her late husband.[4]

Children of William and Martha G. (Booker) Shepherd:

1. Bernard Gaines Shepherd was born in 1831, and probably died in Buckingham County. He married Mary P., maiden name not known. Bernard inherited thirty acres from his father along New Canton Road. They had these children:

   a. John A. Shepherd was born in 1857.

   b. Bettie Shepherd was born in 1860.

   c. Georgia A. Shepherd was born in 1863 and died on Feb. 1, 1889 in Bedford County, Virginia. She married E. H. Myler.[5]

   d. Peter Jennings Shepherd was born Aug. 22, 1867, and died June 5, 1953. He married Allie R. Turner, who was born Dec. 2, 1869 and died

---

[2] Buckingham County, Virginia Deed *Book I*, p. 474.

[3] *Ibid*, p. 466.

[4] Buckingham County, Virginia Deed *Book 3*, pp. 62-63.

[5] Roger G. Ward, *Buckingham County, Virginia Natives Who Died Elsewhere, 1853-1896*, (Athens, Georgia: Iberian Publishing Company), 1994, p. 77.

May 30, 1940. They were farmers. Both were buried at Buckingham Courthouse.

e. Gertrude V. Shepherd was born in August 1869.

f. Nora (or Rosa) Lee Shepherd was born in 1871 and died Dec. 18, 1875, of croup.

g. Unnamed male was born in July 1871, and died in his sixth day.

2. Samuel Jennings Shepherd was born in 1833, and died May 7, 1889, of pneumonia. Burial was in the Shepherd family graveyard near Buckingham Court House. Samuel J. served in Company B, 25 Virginia Infantry during the Civil War. He first married Frances "Fannie" E. Harvey, and married second Mary "Mollie" L. Pendleton, July 19, 1865.[6] The couple lived in Buckingham County and had these children:

a. John M. Shepherd was born in 1855. He married Courtney Virginia Taylor, daughter of Anderson and Lucy Taylor, Dec. 6, 1882. Apparently, John M. was from his father's first marriage.

b. James A. Shepherd was born in 1865, and died Nov. 22, 1882, aged sixteen years, of diphtheria.

c. Emma L. Shepherd was born in 1868.

d. Mary F. Shepherd was born in December 1869 and died Feb. 10, 1871.

e. Ella Shepherd was born in 1870.

f. Martha A. Shepherd was born in 1872, and died Nov. 25, 1882, of diphtheria.

g. Maggie M. Shepherd was born in 1874, and died Dec. 2, 1882 of diphtheria.

h. William L. Shepherd was born in 1876.

i. Hattie Shepherd, born in 1878, married Snoddy Bowles, per 1910 census for Buckingham County.

---

[6] Marriage Records for Buckingham County, Virginia, 1853-1890, Library of Virginia.

3. Benjamin Franklin Shepherd was born Oct. 20, 1840 and died Jan. 23, 1927. He served in Company B, 25 Virginia Infantry during the Civil War. Benjamin married Malissa Frances Word, daughter of Thomas Harrison and Caroline (Word) Word. Both were buried in the Shepherd family graveyard at Dillwyn, Virginia.

Children of Benjamin F. and Malissa F. (Word) Shepherd:

    a. Josephine Shepherd was born July 28, 1868 and died Sept. 13, 1952. She married Matthew Morrell Davis, son of Joshua and Mary Elizabeth (Guthrie) Davis. They had ten children (see Davis report). They were members of the Salem Methodist Church in Buckingham County.

    b. Benjamin Franklin Shepherd was born Feb. 23, 1870, and died Aug. 7, 1938. He married Willie S. Polly Newton, daughter of Manes E. and Jane Ann (Apperson) Newton, Dec. 27, 1893.. She was born June 9, 1875 and died Jan 7, 1926.

    c. Henry Mosby Shepherd was born March 14, 1872 and died June 6, 1909. He was buried in the Shepherd family cemetery. Henry did not marry.

    d. Nora Frances Shepherd was born in 1872 and May 7, 1955. She did not marry.

    e. Lelia Jane Shepherd was born in 1876 and died Feb. 6, 1951, unmarried. Lelia and Nora were buried in the Shepherd family graveyard.

    f. Ada Virginia Shepherd was born Jan. 2, 1878, and died Sept. 6, 1906. Ada married James T. Turnes, son of Aaron and Mary L. Turnes, Sept. 16, 1901. James was born in Prince Edward County in 1857.

    g. Rosa Ethel Shepherd was born in March 1879. She married Robert Nichols Davis, son of Joshua and Mary Elizabeth (Guthrie) Davis. They lived near Dillwyn, Buckingham County.

    h. Mattie Mae Shepherd was born March 19, 1880 and died Nov. 23, 1970. She married John W. Rosen, son of W.T. and L.M. Rosen, Nov. 19, 1905. John was born on July 9, 1873 and died July 11, 1954. Burial was in the Buckingham C.H. Presbyterian Church Cemetery.

4. Peter Shepherd, born in 1842, was killed in the Civil War.

5. Willie P. Shepherd, born in 1844, married Clifford J. Taylor, son of Anderson and Lucy Taylor, July 13, 1881, in Buckingham County.

6. Nannie P. Shepherd, born circa 1845, married Samuel Moss on March 3, 1869 by the Rev. John Spencer. [7]

7. Margaret Shepherd was born in 1849. She married Robert Word, son of Thomas Harrison and Caroline (Word) Word, Dec. 23, 1879.

8. Virginia "Jennie" M. Shepherd, born in 1852, married John Piele, who came from Cumberland County, England. Their marriage date in Buckingham County was April 13, 1881.

9. Mary "Polly" B. Shepherd was born in February 1854. She married William Piele, Nov. 3, 1880. He was a civil engineer and surveyor who was born Sept. 1842 in Cumberland County, England. William came to Virginia in 1878. His parents were named John and Mary Piele.

---

[7] Library of Virginia, *Buckingham County, Virginia, Marriage Records 1853-1890*.

Postscript: African American Descendants

George Shepherd Sr., 1830-1891, was a servant of William and Martha G. (Booker) Shepherd. He may have been fathered by William Shepherd because George not only bore the Shepherd surname but he received an inheritance. There was a very close personal relationship between the families. After William died, George was given land from the estate. George's wife was Mary, maiden name not known. Names of children from the 1870 and 1880 censuses for Buckingham County were: George Shepherd Jr., 1856-1927; Frank Shepherd; Louis Shepherd;[8] Thomas Shepherd; James Shepherd; Doctor Shepherd; and Hales Shepherd. George Jr. came into ownership of the Shepherd land. A little known historical tidbit of Buckingham County is that George Jr. donated three acres to the Commonwealth of Virginia for Robert E. Lee Wayside Park on U. S. 50, just east of Buckingham Court House. George Jr. died Dec. 22, 1927.[9] Court records show these heirs of George Shepherd Jr.: (1) Lilly Shepherd, age thirty-eight in 1928, married Walter Davis. (2) Maggie Shepherd, age thirty-five, in 1928, married Wesley Agee. Maggie left these children when she died in 1942: Harmon, Margaret, James, Leon, Samuel, George and Maude Agee. (3) Mary Shepherd, age forty, married a Johnson, and moved to Richmond. (4) Benjamin Shepherd, age thirty, moved to Cleveland, Ohio and lost contact with his family. (5) William A. Shepherd, age thirty-two, moved to Raleigh County, West Virginia.[10] Descendants of George Shepherd are engaged in research of their ancestor, but were not prepared to submit information before this book went to the printer.

---

[8] This may be the Lewis Shepherd who married Mildred Hicks in West Virginia.

[9] Buckingham County, Virginia *Will Book 3*, p. 109.

[10] Another George Shepherd died on Dec. 30, 1891, in Buckingham County. George was a Negro, and his wife was named Mary. Could this have been the slave or servant of William Shepherd? The George Shepherd who donated land for the Robert E. Lee Wayside Park was born in 1857 according to the 1920 U. S. Census for Buckingham County.

Chapter 24
Peter Baugh Stratton

Stratton was one of the earliest names in the Colony of Virginia, being related to the Shippy and Baugh families in the early 1600s. Due to space limitations and the fact that the Stratton family is fairly well researched, only the most important family unit is included here to interface with the Booker family.[1]

Peter Baugh Stratton, son of Peter and Nancy (Baugh) Stratton, was born July 11, 1761 in Cumberland County, Virginia, in present Powhatan, and died in Buckingham County, June 18, 1835. His father was a well-to-do planter in Powhatan County. Peter married Mary Netherland Steger, daughter of Hans and Catherine (Harris) Steger, Dec. 4, 1787. Mary was born on Sept. 2, 1764, and died sometime in the 1830s in Buckingham County. The family belonged to the Baptist Church.

Peter had one brother, Capt. William Stratton, who married Frances Steger. William lived near the Peterville Baptist Church in Cumberland County. They had five children, including a daughter Frances Stratton, who married the well-known Creed Taylor.

Family tradition says that Peter B. Stratton served in the War of the Revolution, and was known as "Fighting Peter." Allegedly, he was at Yorktown during the surrender of Cornwallis. According to County real estate tax records, in 1807, Peter B. Stratton moved his family from Powhatan County to Buckingham County, purchasing a 960-acre farm from G. Flournoy. However, family tradition says that Peter came to "Red Oak" in 1787 when he purchased the farm from Archibald Bolling, who was a son-in-law of first settler and landowner, Archibald Cary. Tradition says that house was built of lumber hewed and sawed by hand and hand-made shingles. The house was owned by a grandson, David Molloy Gannaway, 1863-1932, into the 20th century. Tax records identify the property as being on the drains of the Willis River. The Stratton family graveyard is on the property, but few of the graves are marked.

Children of Peter B. and Mary N. (Steger) Stratton:

---

[1] See Harriett Russell Stratton, *A Book of Strattons*, (New York, NY: The Grafton Press), vol II.

1. Hans Stratton was born in Powhatan County on Sept. 2, 1788 and died unmarried in 1866, in Buckingham County. He owned land.[2]

2. Mary "Polly" Stratton was born Dec. 31, 1792 in Powhatan County, and died in June 1862 in Calloway County, Kentucky. She married Bernard Gaines Booker, son of Marshall and Martha (Gaines) Booker.

3. Jane Baugh Stratton was born June 15, 1795, and died April 29, 1826 or Aug. 29, 1830. She married David Malloy, son of Daniel T. and Nancy (Knight) Malloy of Buckingham County. David served in Capt. William Jackson's Militia during the War of 1812, and later served as a deputy sheriff in Cumberland County. Two children: (a) Mary C. Malloy married Richard Woodson, who lived at Red Oak, and (b) Sarah Knight Malloy married the Rev. Archibald Clark.[3]

4. James Harvey Stratton was born on Sept. 17, 1801, and died young.

5. Peter Baugh Stratton Jr.[4] was born Jan. 1, 1807 in Powhatan and died in Sedalia, Missouri in March 1892. He married Jane E. Swan, daughter of Thomas and Annie (Taylor) Swan of Cumberland. In 1843, they moved to Missouri where Peter B. became a prominent lawyer.

6. John H. Stratton was born Jan. 2, 1808 in Buckingham County, and was killed in his own yard by Union soldiers in Missouri. They also burned down his house because of his sympathy for the Confederacy. John married Julia Holman on March 24, 1841. Six children.

7. William Harvey Stratton was born on Aug. 7, 1811, and died in Missouri on Sept. 19, 1846. William did not marry.

8. Richard Baugh Stratton was born Sept. 14, 1815 in Buckingham. He married Eliza Michaux McLaurine on Feb. 10, 1836. Richard B. moved to Missouri in 1843, where he was a Baptist clergyman.

---

[2] Roger G. Ward, compiler, *Land Tax Summaries & Implied Deeds, 1841-1870*, (Athens, Georgia: Iberian Publishing Co.), 1995, p. 286.

[3] See Cumberland County, Virginia *Chancery Court, 1831-1851*, pp. 223-224.

[4] *Ibid.* Aug. 29, 1848, p.44. The chancery court record gives a list of heirs of Thomas T. Swan. It states that Jane (Swan) Stratton's mother was Sally Macon.

Chapter 25

The Vawters of Lynchburg[1]

Benjamin Vawter Sr., son of Richard Vawter of Essex County, Virginia,[2] was the progenitor of the Vawters who settled in Lynchburg, Virginia. Benjamin was born circa 1758 in Essex County and died in 1815 in Caroline County, Virginia.[3] According to personal property tax records in Caroline County, he paid taxes in that County from 1787-1799.[4] He was there when the 1810 U. S. Census was taken for Caroline County.[5] There is no evidence that this Benjamin Vawter Sr. lived in Lynchburg, but it was his sons John and Benjamin Jr. There were two Benjamin Vawters who served in the Revolutionary War, one of whom may have been our Benjamin. Our Benjamin Sr. married Susannah Parker,[6] who was born about 1761 and died on March 14, 1837 at the home of her son, Silas Vawter, at Bent Creek, Buckingham County. She was a member of the Baptist Church.[7] Burial was in Lynchburg with the Vawter burial plots.

Children of Benjamin Sr. and Susannah (Parker) Vawter:

---

[1] The compiler appreciates the assistance by Ms. Georgene Jurgensen, 2142 Crowsnest Drive, Palm Harbor, FL 34685-1503, who has a national database on the Vawters of America, including the monumental research of William Snyder Vawter.

[2] Benjamin Vawter was appointed Executor of his father's will that was dated Oct. 24, 1798 and proven on Jan. 24, 1799 in Essex County.

[3] Caroline County, Virginia *Will Book 19*, pp. 216-217. This document provides an account of the sale of Vawter's personal property by Sheriff John Scott, July 8, 1816.

[4] Library of Virginia, Personal Property Tax Records for Caroline County, Virginia, 1787-1799. A study of the taxes from 1800-1815 has not been completed.

[5] 1810 U. S. Census for Caroline County, Virginia, p. 48.

[6] A letter written on Dec. 13, 1928 by William Snyder Vawter, 359 Front Street, New York City to George H. Vawter, (son of Benjamin Silas Vawter, M.D.), 221 West Cumberland Street, Philadelphia, Pennsylvania stated that Benjamin's wife was Mary "Polly" Parker. The public records show her name as Susannah

[7] *The Lynchburg Virginian*, p. 3, c. 3, March 16, 1837.

1. Benjamin Vawter Jr. was born circa 1787 in Caroline County, Virginia and died on April 25, 1830. He married Mildred Gentry on Jan. 7, 1811 in Lynchburg. A Richmond newspaper gave this report on the death of Benjamin Vawter Jr. of Lynchburg: "On Sunday morning the 25th inst. Mr. Benjamin Vawter, of this place, terminated his mortal existence by cutting his throat! He was, it seems, at the time of committing the fatal deed in a high state of intoxication."[8] Mildred married second the Rev. Obadiah Echols of Pittsylvania County on Aug. 4, 1831.[9] Robert B. Semple, Baptist historian, said this about his ministry regarding the Lower Falls Baptist Church: "The downfall of Obadiah Echols was very affecting to all churches to which he had ever ministered. This church participated in the distress."[10]

Children of Benjamin Jr. and Mildred (Gentry) Vawter:

    a. Silas Vawter was born circa 1811 and died on July 31, 1833 in Lynchburg.[11] He married Sarah Fear (Farrar?) on Dec. 28, 1830 in Lynchburg by the Rev. Robert Ryland.[12] Sarah married second Daniel B. Hurley in 1839 in Lynchburg. They moved to and lived in Pittsylvaina County where Daniel worked as a tailor.

    b. Benjamin Vawter III was born circa 1813 and was buried on Oct. 23, 1827.[13]

    c. Bransford Vawter was born circa 1815 and died on Nov. 15, 1838.[14] He was a poet, and a member of the Patrick Henry Society.[15] Bransford attended the University of Virginia.

---

[8] *The Richmond Whig*, May 3, 1830, p. 2.

[9] A prenuptial agreement and marriage contract may be found in Lynchburg City Courthouse, *Deed Book K*, p. 329, dated July 7, 1831.

[10] Robert Baylor Semple, *History of the Baptists in Virginia*, (New Orleans, Louisiana: Polyanthos, Inc.) reprinted in 1972, p. 275.

[11] *The Lynchburg Virginian*, Aug. 8, 1833, p. 3.

[12] *The Lynchburg Virginian*, Jan. 3, 1831, p. 1.

[13] Lucy Harrison Miller Baber *Behind the Old Brick Wall, A Cemetery Story*, (Richmond, Virginia: Whittet and Shepperson), 1968, p. 173.

2. Aaron Vawter, born circa 1790, received a plot of land in Caroline County from his father. Researchers who claim him as an ancestor are in error, in that this Aaron "died without descendants."[16] The court record stated that this Aaron died intestate and unmarried. Evidently, the Aaron Vawter who lived in Goochland County and received Revolutionary War land in Kentucky was not the same person.

3. Moses Vawter received land in Caroline County from his father. He died intestate, unmarried and without descendants. A study of the land records in Caroline County will shed more light on the dates and circumstances.[17]

4. John Vawter was born circa 1793 and was deceased by 1839. John married Mary ____. He served in the War of 1812; was living in Lynchburg during that period, and was on the 1830 Census for Campbell County.[18]

5. Phoebe Vawter, born circa 1794 in Caroline County, married first Charles Hay Beasley, son of Cornelius Beasely, of Bowling Green, Virginia. After his death about 1832, she married John Lumpkin.[19] According to the 1870 U. S. Census for Caroline County, Phebe was born circa 1783. The 1850 census shows her birth year circa 1798 and her husband John Lumpkin with a birth year of circa 1788. Louisa Lumpkin, presumably their daughter, was born circa 1834. My guess is that Phoebe was born somewhere between those dates, circa 1794.

---

[14] Lucy Harrison Miller Baber, *Behind the Old Brick Wall, A Cemetery Story*, (Richmond, Virginia: Whittet and Shepperson), 1968, p. 173.

[15] *The Lynchburg Virginian*, Nov. 22, 1838, p. 3, c. 5.

[16] Caroline County, Virginia *Deed Book 45*, p. 137, Feb. 22, 1846.

[17] *Ibid.*

[18] Ruth Hairston Early, *Campbell Chronicles and Family Sketches*, (Baltimore, Maryland: Regional Publishing Company), 1978, p. 279-280.

[19] The 1850 U. S. Census for Caroline County, Virginia, p. 286, Family No. 992 gives Phoebe's age as fifty years, and John Lumpkin as sixty-two years.

6. Silas Parker Vawter was born in 1797 in Caroline County, and died on March 21, 1865 at Bent Creek, Appomattox County. He married first Martha Phelps and married second Elizabeth Farrar Christian.

Silas Parker Vawter

Silas Parker Vawter, son of Benjamin and Susanna (Parker) Vawter, was born in 1797 in Caroline County, and died on March 21, 1865 at Bent Creek, Appomattox County. Silas may have gone to live with his brothers in Lynchburg after their father's death in 1815. He was buried on a hill overlooking the Walton Cove Farm in Appomattox County. He was scheduled to be buried beside his wife in a Christian family graveyard in Nelson County, but the James River was at a flood-level and could not be crossed. Silas married first Martha Phelps on Dec. 25, 1820 in Campbell County. Martha died circa 1822, without any record of children being born to their union. Silas P. married second Elizabeth Farrar Christian, daughter of James and Cordelia (Watts) Christian, on Jan. 19, 1824, in Nelson County, Virginia. Elizabeth was born in 1799 in Nelson County and died May 26, 1859 in Appomattox County. She was buried in a Christian family cemetery in Nelson County. When a young person, Silas P. Vawter was bound to Ambrose Page of Lynchburg to do an apprenticeship as a tailor. Silas P. accumulated a large estate through his ability as a businessman. He was a partner in several companies in the Bent Creek area, and served as an attorney and justice for Appomattox County. His primary residence was at Bent Creek in Appomattox County. The medical society stated that his medical practice was "allopath."

Children of Silas P. and Elizabeth F. (Christian) Vawter:

1. Martha Susan Vawter was born on Jan. 11, 1825 at Bent Creek and died young.

2. Mary Jane Vawter was born on Oct. 9, 1827 at Bent Creek and died June 24, 1888 in Nelson County.[20] She married John William Walton,

---

[20] A death certificate in the Library of Virginia states that she died of "heart disease."

son of William and Elizabeth W. (Chick) Walton, April 2, 1844, in Nelson County. Mary Jane was educated at Hollins College.

3. Benjamin Silas Vawter was born at Bent Creek on Aug. 28, 1831, and died Jan. 5, 1910 in Washington, D.C. He married Sarah Watts.

Dr. Benjamin Silas Vawter

Dr. Benjamin Silas Vawter, son of Silas P. and Elizabeth F. (Christian) Vawter, was born on Aug. 28, 1831 at Bent Creek in Buckingham County, Virginia and died in Washington, D. C. on Jan. 5, 1910.[21] He graduated from the University of Virginia and the Medical College of the University of Pennsylvania. He was listed as a physician and dentist in the *Chataigne's Virginia Gazetteer and Business Directory for Appomattox County, Virginia, 1888-1889*, with practices in Bent Creek.

Unknown to most people in his county, Dr. Vawter had a clandestine romantic relationship with and eventually married Sarah "Sally" Watts, daughter of Edmond and Lucy (Davis) Watts.[22] Sarah, who was born in May 1857 in Appomattox County, was a Negro who was twenty-six years younger than Benjamin. Sarah's parents lived next door to Dr. Vawter at Bent Creek, and may have had slave status prior to emancipation in 1866. Sarah gave birth to their first child when she was only seventeen years old. The child was named Edmund Silas Watts, for both of his male grandparents. Sarah worked for a family on the other side of the James River, in Nelson County, when the first children were born.

Benjamin was enumerated as a single man when the 1880 census was taken for Appomattox County.[23] Sally Watts was enumerated

---

[21] *Vital Records: Directory of Deceased American Physicians, 1804-1929*, per Genealogy. com

[22] The 1870 U. S. Census for Appomattox County, Virginia, Stonewall District, p. 81, Family No. 8, states that Edmund Watts, a "cripple," was born circa 1804. Lucy, his wife, was born circa 1824. Sarah was listed as "Sally," age thirteen, occupation "cook."

[23] The 1880 U. S. Census for Appomattox County, Virginia, Stonewall District, p. 404A.

with her two children, Edmund and Annie Watts, on the 1880 Nelson County census.[24] Sally stated that she was a widow, which was a cover for her *de facto* husband.

Evidently, Dr. Vawter loved her deeply or he would not have fathered eight of her children. In 1890, Dr. Vawter decided to move to Washington, D. C. where they could have privacy. Rumors about Dr. Vawter had been circulating for sometime in the Bent Creek community. After the move to Washington, D. C., the children's' names were then changed from Watts to Vawter, as proven by the censuses, to reflect their true biological surname. Sarah's name changed, too, from Watts to Vawter.[25] Their children were listed as mulattos on the 1900 census.

In 1900, she stated to the census taker in Washington, D. C. that she had been married twenty-seven years and that five of her eight children were still living. This is consistent with the Bible record that was maintained by one of their children. When the 1920 U. S. Census was taken in Washington, D. C., she was listed as Sarah Vawter. They lived at a good address in the North West section of Washington, D. C.

Children of Benjamin S. and Sarah (Watts) Vawter:[26]

1. Edmund Silas Vawter was born on Aug. 1, 1874 in Nelson County, Virginia when his mother was seventeen years old. Edmund was named for his two grandfathers. He was listed in the census household of his mother in 1900 in Washington, D. C. where his surname had been changed from Watts to Vawter. He was living on Elsworth Street in

---

[24] 1880 U. S. Census for Nelson County, Virginia, Livingston District, p. 21, family No. 204.

[25] 1900 U. S. Census for District of Columbia, E. D. 50, Sheet No. 17, p. 68A.

[26] Information on the children was provided by Edmund S. Vawter, 1410 North 18th Street, Philadelphia, Pennsylvania to William Snyder Vawter, GPO Box 361, and New York City, undated. The birthplaces are from the same source. The document was forwarded to the compiler by Georgene Jurgensen, 2142 Crowsnest Drive, Palm Harbor, FL 34685-1503, who is the authority on the Vawter family of America.

Philadelphia when the 1910 Census was taken.[27] He and his wife Mamie were classified as Black. The 1920 census lists Mayme Vawter as a widow, forty years old, employed by the War Department. Edmund and Mamie were married in 1906 and had no children when the census was taken. Edmund was employed as a waiter in a restaurant.

2. Lucy Elizabeth Vawter was born on Sept. 14, 1875 and died in Nelson County in 1876. She was named for her two grandmothers.

3. Alice Louise Vawter was born on Nov. 17, 1876 and died in July 1878 in Nelson County.

4. Annie Mitchell Vawter[28] was born on March 15, 1878 at Bent Creek, Appomattox County. She was living in her mother's household in Washington, D. C. when the U. S. Census was taken in June 1900. She was named for her father's niece, Annie (Walton) Mitchell of Appomattox County.

5. George Henderson Vawter was born on July 16, 1880, in Nelson County. He moved with his parents to Washington, D. C. about 1890. On Oct. 1, 1903, he married Annie H. Harley in Alexandria, Virginia.[29] George married second Amelia H. Green, who was born in 1899 in Mississippi. George visited his Walton relatives about 1928 in Appomattox County, after which he wrote a letter containing information on the Negro (mulatto) Vawters and their Walton relatives. He visited Dallas Walton, John C. Walton and Lizzie Abbitt. George's address at that time was 311 Cumberland Street, Philadelphia, Pennsylvania. The 1930 U. S. Census for Philadelphia lists his occupation as a "clothes dyer," and his race as a Negro. No children were listed in their household.

6. David Doggett Vawter was born on March 19, 1882 in Nelson County He was listed as a jeweler on the 1910 U. S. Census for

---

[27] 1910 U. S. Census for the 36th Ward of Philadelphia, Pennsylvania, p. 25A, Sheet 11A, Family No. 232.

[28] The 1880 U. S. Census for Nelson County, Virginia, Lovingston District, p. 21, Family No. 204, gives her name as Ann Marie Watts.

[29] Wesley E. Pippenger, *Alexandria, Virginia Marriage Index, 1893-1905*, (Westminster, Maryland: Willow Bend Books), 1999, p. 103.

Washington, D. C., E. D. 147, Sheet 5B, Line 66 His wife was named Sarah Louisa, who was born in the West Indies. They were married in 1905, but were still childless in 1910. Both were classified as mulattos.

7. Abraham Benjamin Vawter was born on June 27, 1884 in Appomattox County and died on June 25, 1893 in Washington, D. C.

8. Enoch Marvin Vawter was born on April 5, 1888 in Lynchburg. When the 1900 Census was taken, he was listed as a student in school. On Jan. 8, 1905, he married Lularetta Ricks in Alexandria, Virginia.[30]

---

[30] *Ibid.* p. 163.

Chapter 26
John Meriwether Walker of Buckingham County

John Meriwether Walker, son of John[1] and Mary Ann (Winston) Walker, was born circa 1772 and died suddenly on March 6, 1830 in Buckingham County, Virginia.[2] He married Susan Christian, daughter of John Harvey and Joyce P. Christian. Susan was born circa 1776[3] in Amherst County and died circa 1845 in Appomattox County. This is not the same John Walker of Buckingham County whose death was reported in the Aug. 7, 1828 issue of *The Lynchburg Virginian*.

Tax records reveal that John M. Walker lived on the estate of his father-in-law, John H. Christian. Farrar[4] stated that Samuel J. Walker lived at "Oakland," a house now in Appomattox County that was built in 1800 by his father, John Meriwether Walker.

Children of John M. and Susan (Christian) Walker:

1. Benjamin Philip Walker, son of John M. and Susan (Christian) Walker, was born in 1806 in Buckingham County, and died on Nov. 10, 1888 in Bedford County, Virginia. He married first Mary Jane

---

[1] Dr. John Walker, 1726-1777, was a son of Benjamin and Ann (Aylett) Walker. Benjamin, 1698-1738, was the King's Attorney for Caroline County, Virginia. Information on the Walker ancestry was provided by Bettie (Walker) Fricke of Dothan, Alabama.

[2] Library of Virginia, "Walker family Bible record, 1827-1911," Accession No. 26581. The handwriting of Benjamin P. Walker says, "John M. Walker my truly dear Father departed this life on Saturday the 6th day of March 1830 very suddenly..."

[3] Her birth year was estimated from the 1810, 1820, 1830, and 1840 censuses for Buckingham County, which show a birth year between 1770 and 1780. It is believed that she was living in the household of her son Samuel J. Walker in 1840, page 397. Her death year was estimated by the same method, in that she was on the 1840 census but gone in 1850.

[4] Stuart McDearmon Farrar, *Historical Notes of Appomattox County, Virginia*, (Pamplin, Virginia: Privately Published), p. 204.

Branch, daughter of Samuel Branch,[5] on Nov. 14, 1827. Benjamin married second Sallie B. Tompkins.

2. Isaac W. Walker was born on Aug. 7, 1810[6] in Buckingham County and died on Oct. 1, 1839 at the home of his brother in Buckingham County.[7] His residence was in Amherst County where he was an official of the Court. "Amherst County October Court 1839, It being announced to the Court that since the last term, Isaac W. Walker, one of its members, has departed this life. And impressed with a deep sense of distinguished merit and integrity..."[8] Samuel M. Garland, Clerk of the Court was directed to send condolences to Walker's widow. Isaac W. Walker married Sarah Elizabeth Branch, daughter of Samuel and Winifred Jones (Guerrant) Branch. Sarah was born in Charlotte County, Virginia on April 29, 1811.

3. Samuel Jennings Walker was born on Jan. 23, 1809 in Buckingham County, and died on Aug. 21, 1866 in Appomattox County, Virginia. He married Martha Ann Walton, daughter of William and Elizabeth White (Chick) Walton. He is said to have been a Godly man of sterling character. Additional information on Samuel J. Walker may be found in the Walton section.

Isaac W. Walker

Isaac W. Walker, son of John M. and Susan (Christian) Walker, was born on Aug. 7, 1810[9] in Buckingham County and died on Oct. 1, 1839 at the home of his brother in Buckingham County.[10] His residence was in Amherst County where he was an official of the

---

[5] *Southern Religious Telegraph*, Oct. 2, 1830, p. 3, c. 2.

[6] From tombstone inscription at "Oakland estate" in Appomattox County, now owned by Danny Cash.

[7] *Richmond Whig and Public Advertiser*, Oct. 11, 1839, p. 1, c. 7.

[8] *The Lynchburg Virginian*, Aug. 19, 1839, p. 3, c.3.

[9] From tombstone inscription at "Oakland estate" in Appomattox County, now owned by Danny Cash.

[10] *Richmond Whig and Public Advertiser*, Oct. 11, 1839, p. 1, c. 7. This would be near Bent Creek in present Appomattox County.

Court. "Amherst County October Court 1839, It being announced to the Court that since the last term, Isaac W. Walker, one of its members, has departed this life. And impressed with a deep sense of distinguished merit and integrity..."[11] Samuel M. Garland, Clerk of the Court was directed to send condolences to Walker's widow. Isaac W. Walker married Sarah Elizabeth Branch, daughter of Samuel and Winifred Jones (Guerrant) Branch. Sarah was born in Charlotte County, Virginia on April 29, 1811.

Child of Isaac W. and Sarah E. (Branch) Walker:

1. Samuel Branch Walker was born in 1834 and died in 1906.[12] He married Mollie R. Venable, 1837-1913, daughter of James E. Venable of Petersburg, on June 1, 1859.[13]

Sarah E. married second Dr. Reuben Dejarnett Palmer, son of Elias and Hannah (LeGrand) Palmer of Halifax County, Virginia, in 1843. They had no children. Reuben was first married to Martha Frances P. Christian, 1796-1829,[14] daughter of Henry and Martha (Patteson) Christian of Amherst County, on May 21, 1818. Reuben was one of the first justices from Campbell County when Appomattox County was formed in 1845. Dr. Palmer graduated from the University of Pennsylvania College of Medicine. He was born in 1789 and died on March 20, 1861[15] in Appomattox County. From the Sept. 12, 1861 issue of *The Lynchburg Virginian*, "The

---

[11] *The Lynchburg Virginian*, Aug. 19, 1839, p. 3, c.3.

[12] N. R. Featherston, *History of Appomattox*, (Marceline, Missouri: Walsworth Brothers, Printers), 1948, p. 277.

[13] His birth year was found on the 1850 Census for Appomattox County (Family No. 195). His marriage record was reported by Stuart McDearmon Farrar, *Historical Notes of Appomattox County, Virginia*, (Pamplin, Virginia: Privately published), page 141. He cited the source as a Lynchburg newspaper dated July 15, 1859.

[14] *Lynchburg Virginian*, Thursday, Jan. 29, 1829, p. 3, c. 4. "Died at her residence in Campbell County on Sunday, Jan. 20, 1829..."

[15] These dates do not match. Could it be that the funeral sermon was a belated memorial service?

funeral sermon of Dr. Reuben D. Palmer, dec'd, will be preached by the Rev. John E. Edwards at Mount Comfort (Methodist) Church, in Appomattox County, on Sunday the 22nd of September."[16] His former plantation of 2,000 acres, located on the drains of Wreck Island Creek in Appomattox County, is now a Bed and Breakfast called Spring Grove.

Benjamin Philip Walker

Benjamin Philip[17] Walker, son of John M. and Susan (Christian) Walker, was born in 1806 in Buckingham County, and died on Nov. 10, 1888 at the home of his daughter, Mrs. Henry F. Bocock, in Bedford County, Virginia.[18] According to the Bible record of Benjamin P. Walker, he married Mary Jane Branch, daughter of Samuel Branch,[19] on Nov. 14, 1827. She was born on Oct. 3, 1809 in Charlotte County, Virginia and died on Sept. 23, 1830 in Buckingham County.[20] The Bible record stated that she was ill for six weeks. Benjamin P. served as one of the first justices of the peace when Appomattox County was formed in 1845. He was a member of the Whig Party.

Children of Benjamin P. and Mary J. (Branch) Walker:

    a. Susan Winifred Walker was born on Monday, Oct. 13, 1828 at the home of Mrs. Jane Whitworth in Buckingham County, according to the

---

[16] Stuart McDearmon Farrar, *Historical Notes of Appomattox County, Virginia*, (Pamplin, Virginia: Privately published), p. 167.

[17] Morrison, Alfred James. *College of Hampden-Sidney, Dictionary of Biography*.: Hampden-Sydney, Virginia). 1921, p. 277. His middle name was Philip, not Patteson, according to Hampden-Sydney college records.

[18] The Library of Virginia, "Walker family Bible record, 1827-1911," Accession No. 26581.

[19] *Southern Religious Telegraph*, Oct. 2, 1830, p. 3, c. 2.

[20] *Daily Richmond Whig*, Oct. 1, 1830, p. 3, c. 2.

family Bible. Susan died on Nov. 26, 1901 in Houston, Texas.[21] She married Henry Flood Bocock, 1817-1894, son of John T. and Mary (Flood) Bocock, on May 12, 1847. He served as Clerk of the Appomattox County Court.

b. Sarah Heath Walker was born on Saturday, June 5, 1830 in Buckingham County and died on April 25, 1894 in Roanoke. Burial was in Lynchburg.[22] She married Joseph Abbitt, son of Benjamin Jr. and Mary (Patterson) Abbitt, on Jan. 8, 1856.[23] Joseph was born in 1831 and died on April 7, 1917 in Cabell County, West Virginia.[24]

Featherston[25] stated that Benjamin P. Walker married second Maria Boyd and had Maria, Kate, and Daniel Walker. This appears to be an error, in that Benjamin P. Walker's family Bible states that he married Sallie Byrd Tompkins, daughter of Alexander Tompkins, Esq, in Lynchburg at 10:00 a. m. on Feb. 12, 1845.[26] Sallie died at her home in Lynchburg on May 30, 1888.[27]

Children of Benjamin P. and Sallie B. (Tompkins) Walker:

1. Lelia Lee Walker was born in Lynchburg on Dec. 21, 1845 and died on Oct. 21, 1887. She married James A. Scudday.

2. Nanny Anna Byrd Walker was born on July 12, 1847 and died on Oct. 7, 1848.

---

[21] H. Edgar Hill, 5411 Navajo Road, Louisville, Kentucky 40207, compiler of a paper titled "Descendants of John Flood," February 2002, p. 36.

[22] *The Richmond Dispatch*, April 27, 1894 issue.

[23] *The Lynchburg Virginian*, Jan. 14, 1856.

[24] *The Huntington Herald-Dispatch,* April 8, 1917.

[25] N. R. Featherston, *History of Appomattox*, (Marceline, Missouri: Walworth Brothers, Printers), 1948, p. 277.

[26] *The Lynchburg Virginian* says they were married on Feb. 13, 1845; that her surname was Thompson.

[27] Library of Virginia, "Walker family Bible record, 1827-1911, Accession No. 26581.

3. Maria Eveline Walker was born in Lynchburg on March 2, 1849 and was living on 5th Street in Lynchburg with her brother Daniel when the 1920 Census was accomplished. She did not marry.

4. Ellen Conway Walker was born on Oct. 5, 1850 and died on June 19, 1852.

5. Daniel Trigg Walker was born on Jan. 10, 1854 and died on March 11, 1924, per cemetery inscription. He did not marry.

6. Catherine Tompkins Walker was born on Oct. 16, 1856 and died on Aug. 3, 1911 at her house in Lynchburg.

7. John Meriwether Walker was born on Sunday morning on March 28, 1858 and died on July 1, 1864.

Chapter 27

Cuthbert Williamson of Charlotte County

Cuthbert Williamson Sr., said to have been a son of John[1] and Elizabeth (Chamberlyne) Williamson, was born circa 1710 and died circa 1743 in Henrico County, Virginia. Bell[2] erroneously stated that he married Elizabeth Allen. Actually, Cuthbert Sr. married Elizabeth Curd, daughter of Edward Curd. The confusion entered when, after Cuthbert's death, Elizabeth married second Samuel Allen. *The Curd Family in America,* published in 1915 by Benjamin F. Curd, did not discover the Williamson connection. After a series of updates in 1927 and 1938 by three different people, Thomas H. S. Curd Jr.[3] published a supplement in 1981, which corrected a name from Williams to Williamson.[4] In a letter written by Col. John C. Bell of Nashville, Tennessee to Mr. Curd on Oct. 12, 1988, a convincing case was made for Elizabeth (Curd) Williamson Allen being a daughter of Edward Curd. Mr. Curd accepted the evidence, but stated that he has no plans to publish another revision.[5]

Elizabeth, wife of Cuthbert Sr., stated on her deathbed in Cuthbert Jr.'s home on April 20, 1786, "Cuthbirt, I want what little I have divided between you three," specifying Cuthbert Williamson Jr., Mary Price, and Susannah Williamson.[6]

---

[1] The will of John Williamson was written on Jan. 30, 1731 and probated May 17, 1732 in Surry County, Virginia.

[2] Landon C. Bell, *The Old Free State*, (Richmond, Virginia: The William Byrd Press, Inc.), vol II, p. 377.

[3] Thomas H. S. Curd Jr., 1325 Lakewood Drive, S. W., Roanoke, VA 24015

[4] Curd Supplement, Section V (Additions, Corrections, and Modifications), S-10, p. 1.

[5] Copies of these letters were forwarded to the compiler by Dr. Ward O. Oliver, 9025 Nolen Drive, Baton Rough, LA 70810-2710. Dr. Oliver is the foremost authority on the Curd/Allen/Williamson issue.

[6] Charlotte County, Virginia *Will Book 1*, p. 386.

Cuthbert Williamson Jr.

Cuthbert Williamson Jr., son of Cuthbert Sr. and Elizabeth (Curd) Williamson, was born circa 1742 in Henrico County, Virginia, and died in Charlotte County, Virginia in 1811.[7] He married first Obedience Price in 1761, in Lunenburg County, Virginia and married second Susanna White, daughter of John White,[8] on Sept. 7, 1772, in Charlotte County. She was not a daughter of William and Ann (Brunfield) Johnston as erroneously assumed by descendants. Oliver has proven that William Johnston's daughter Mary was a wife to James White, not John White.[9] Oliver estimates that Susanna White was born in 1754 and died in 1848. Cuthbert Jr. served in the Revolutionary War, first as a Private in Capt. John Harvey's Company. On May 7, 1781, he was commissioned as an Ensign in Capt. John Barksdale's Company. He saw action at Camden, New Jersey in August 1780; Guilford Court House in March 1781; and the siege of Yorktown in the Fall of 1781.[10] Susanna (White) Williamson was granted a widow's pension of $40 per month on Nov. 30, 1838, which she drew until her death in 1848.[11] Names of fifteen children are given below, but tradition says that one more child was born and died young, allegedly named Sally Williamson.

Children of Cuthbert and Obedience (Price) Williamson Jr.:

---

[7] Charlotte County, Virginia *Will Book III*, pp. 184-185, Aug. 9, 1811.

[8] Charlotte County, *Virginia Will Book I*, pp. 141-142, written March 2, 1782 and proved Nov. 4, 1782.

[9] "Mary, Wife of John White of Charlotte County: A Correction," The Southsider, Vol XV, No. 4, 1996.

[10] See Application No. 309925, Genealogical Records Committee, Daughters of the American Revolution, Washington, D.C.

[11] The late Dr. Joseph W. Evans of Boulder, Colorado was a prominent genealogical record compiler on families in Central Virginia Counties. His data on the Williamson and Harvey families were shared by computer diskette, June 6, 1996. His work was more often raw data than finished product.

1. John Williamson was born in 1763 and died in 1820 in Botetourt County, Virginia. He married Martha Davis Nov. 5, 1786 in Lunenburg County, Virginia and married second Elizabeth Jackson in 1800.

2. Rebecca Williamson was born circa 1764, and died in 1842 in Franklin County, Missouri. She married Ezekiel Rogers on July 2, 1787 in Charlotte County.

3. Elizabeth Williamson, born June 6, 1768, married Samuel L. Bland, 1752-1820, son of Samuel and Martha (Merritt) Bland, June 2, 1781 in Charlotte County.

Children of Cuthbert and Susanna (White) Williamson Jr.:

4. Mary Ann Williamson was born in 1773 and died Feb. 25, 1831,[12] in Charlotte County. She married Nathan Harvey, son of Thomas and Macca (Barksdale) Harvey, on Sept. 8, 1792 in Charlotte County. Nathan was born in 1773 and died March 3, 1840. He was a merchant, tavern owner and farmer. The family lived four miles from Red House, near Rolling Hill, in Charlotte County. The Harvey's were members of the New Salem Baptist Church. Seven children were born to Nathan and Mary.

5. Catherine Williamson was born circa 1775 and died circa 1811.

6. Martha "Patsy" Williamson was born in 1779 and died in 1842. She married John R. Roach on Dec. 7, 1796 in Charlotte County.

7. Charles Williamson was born March 5, 1781 and died in 1824 in Franklin County, Missouri. He married Elizabeth Smith Brown Oct. 15, 1806 in Charlotte County. They moved to Franklin County, Missouri in 1819, along with two of Charles' siblings.

8. Susanna Price Williamson was born Jan. 14, 1783, and died in Oct. 1, 1870 at Gray's Summit. Franklin County, Missouri, where they immigrated in 1819. She married Achilles Jeffries, 1783-1859, on March 27, 1804.[13]

---

[12] Death record published in the *Religious Herald*, a Baptist publication.

[13] DAR Library, Washington, D. C. *Grandparent Papers*, lineage of Dr. Charles Williamson Jeffries states that Susanna Price (Williamson) Jeffries was born Jan. 14, 1783 and died in 1870.

9. Nancy Williamson was born circa 1785 in Charlotte County and died Sept. 9, 1855 in Lauderdale County, Alabama. Nancy married Samuel Haraway, 1772-1840, son of Charles Harroway. They moved to Giles County, Tennessee during the War of 1812 and thence to Alabama circa 1821.[14]

10. Samuel Williamson was born in 1786 in Charlotte County and died in 1860 in Giles County, Tennessee. He married Judith Ann Woodfin on Feb. 10, 1811 in Charlotte County.

11. Cuthbert Williamson III was born Oct. 7, 1791 and died in Franklin County, Missouri in 1872.[15] He married Obedience Green Bailey, daughter of Andrew and Mary Ann (Green) Bailey. She was born July 28, 1803 and died Aug. 29, 1844. He was a farmer.

12. Capt. Daniel White Williamson, born circa 1798, married Martha Armistead, daughter of the Rev. Samuel Armistead, Feb. 15, 1831 in Campbell County, Virginia.

13. Frances White Williamson was born in 1799 in Charlotte County. She married Jordon Taylor in Charlotte County on Dec. 13, 1822, by the Rev. Samuel Armistead. They moved to his home County of Buckingham, where they raised a family on Jordon's income as a small-time farmer.

14. William Barrett Williamson[16] was born in 1794 and died in 1872 in Petersburg. He married Permilia Forte Jackson on Dec. 19, 1822, by the Rev. Samuel Armistead.

15. Matthew Williamson was born in 1800 in Charlotte County and died in 1824 in Floyd County, Virginia.

---

[14] A family group sheet was sent on June 30, 1997 to the compier by Dr. Ward H. Oliver, 9025 Nolen Drive, Baton Rouge, LA 70810-2710. He stated that Ronnie B. Haraway of Rogersville, Alabama has published on the Haraway family.

[15] 1850 U. S. Census for Franklin County, Missouri, District 1, Family No. 1889.

[16] See Landon Bell, *The Old Free State: History of Lunenburg County and Southside Virginia*, (Richmond, Virginia: The William Byrd Press, Inc.), Vol. II, p. 378, for more detailed information on descendants.

Chapter 28

Word Family of Buckingham County

Several hypotheses have been made regarding the origin and immigration to America of the Word family. Roberts[1] suggested that John Word Sr. was a seventeenth century immigrant to New Kent County, Virginia, originating from the town of Landaff in the Province of Glamorganshire, Wales. Possibly, he was the same John Wor (*sic*) who was transported to the Virginia Colony in 1652 by William Gaulett.[2] New Kent County is one of the "burnt counties" in Virginia, meaning that most of the early records have been destroyed.

From John Word Sr., allegedly, came a son named John Word Jr. He was living in New Kent County, Virginia in 1710, when his son, Charles Word was baptized on May 14. Some researchers list these children for John Word Jr.: Charles Word, 1710-1792, married Sarah; John Word III married Elizabeth. He allegedly died in Halifax County in 1790;[3] William Word and James Word.

John Word III, who married Elizabeth, allegedly settled in Buckingham County. However, no records have been found in the predecessor counties—Goochland, Cumberland, and Albemarle— to support this claim. Their son, Thomas Word, did migrate to Cumberland County before 1761, and resettled several years later near present-day Buckingham Court House. Thomas married Lockie Harrison, daughter of Benjamin and Priscilla (Cary) Harrison. Following is an account of what is known about Thomas Word's family unit, plus several generations of genealogical information.

Thomas Word

Thomas Word, son of John and Elizabeth Word III, was born circa 1740 in New Kent County, Virginia, and died in Buckingham County

---

[1] Lesbia Word Roberts, *Word Family Tree,* (Fort Worth, Texas), 1962. Unpublished manuscript, *Mississippi. AC. 76-131,* Tennessee State Library and Archives, Nashville, Tennessee.

[2] George Cabell Greer, *Early Virginia Immigrants, 1623-1666.*

[3] Roberts, p. 3

in 1816.[4] Thomas Word appeared in the Cumberland County records on March 23, 1761, when he received a license to keep an ordinary at Maurice Langhorne's house.[5] About 1763, son Thomas Word married Lockey Harrison, ca. 1746-1835, daughter of Benjamin and Priscilla (Cary) Harrison of Cumberland County, Virginia. It is believed that Thomas met his wife-to-be through his association with the Langhorne family. Priscilla was probably a daughter of Henry Cary, as discussed in the previous section.[6] Thomas and Lockey raised a large family, although names of only seven children are known.[7] Thomas settled briefly along Buffalo Creek, but later moved his family to the Hatcher's Creek area of Buckingham County, just 2-3 miles southwest of the courthouse.[8] Descendants still live in the same community. It is believed that Thomas Word built Mohawk as early as 1770. Benjamin Eldridge, clerk of court, owned this house from 1850-1885. Its present owners are Mr. and Mrs. Harold F. Swartz.[9] The names Cary,

---

[4] One source says that John Word III and his wife Elizabeth settled in Buckingham County; that John III built "Mohawk" on a large estate. Also, he allegedly served as one of the first sheriffs of the new County that was formed in 1761. The writer has found no public records in Goochland, Cumberland, or Buckingham Counties to substantiate these claims. It is more probable that Thomas Word built Mohawk.

[5] Cumberland County, Virginia, *Order Book*, March 23, 1761, p. 311.

[6] The complete genealogical record of Henry Cary's family unit has not been preserved. We are making a case that Priscilla Harrison was his daughter, based on analyses of land records, and of naming patterns in which Lockey and Cary are passed down in all branches of the Harrison family descendants. Becky Bonner of Oklahoma City is developing a Harrison database on the World Wide Web at this address: (http://www.uokhsc.edu/~rbonner).

[7] Names of four children were found in Bible record established by Noah and Sallie (Word) Flood. Filed in the Library of Virginia, the Bible includes certain selected names of grandchildren of Thomas and Lockey Word, but not a complete account. The writer possesses a copy of the records cited.

[8] Proven by the real estate tax records for Buckingham County, Virginia State Archives.

[9] Margaret A. Pennington and Lorna S. Scott, *"The Courthouse Burned—"* (Waynesboro, Virginia: McClure Printing, Inc.), 1986, p. 25.

Benjamin, Lockey and Harrison were passed along as Christian names in the Word family.

Children of Thomas and Lockey (Harrison) Word were:

1. Sallie Word was born on June 2, 1764, and died circa 1785, possibly of childbirth. She married Noah Flood, son of John and Agnes (Payne) Flood, Oct. 30, 1784. Noah was born on Nov. 2, 1763, and died in Buckingham County, on Oct. 2, 1818.[10] According to real estate tax records, they had at least one child, "John Flood of Noah." The Flood family Bible has this notation, "Lavinia Martha Flood, daughter to John and Frances his wife, born July the 31st, 1816, Monday morning." After Sallie's death, Noah married second Sarah Fuqua, daughter of William and Mary (Ford) Fuqua, Nov. 30, 1785.[11] In 1841, Sarah (Fuqua) Flood applied for a pension based on the service of Noah Flood in the Revolutionary War. It is believed that Noah and Sarah Flood had one son named Daniel Flood who married Ann L. Coleman, daughter of Julius and Elizabeth (Coleman) Coleman.

2. Elizabeth Word was born circa 1766. She married Publius Jones Sr., 1765-1817, son of Michael and Anne Jones. Michael's will was filed in 1780 and probated in 1791 in Bedford County, Virginia.[12] Publius served in the Revolutionary War in in a militia from Campbell County, Virginia.

---

[10] Noah Flood's birth date is taken from his family Bible, and his death date was obtained from his widow's application for a pension. The real estate tax records for Buckingham County suggest that Noah died in 1818. His widow, Sarah, stated that the year of death was 1819. His brother, Moses Flood, stated that the year of death was 1815, obviously from a faulty memory. See, also, The Charltons of Buckingham County, Virginia, by Elizabeth Jane (Dunkum) Charlton, 1990, page 257.

[11] This marriage date was given by Sarah (Fuqua) Flood when she applied for a Revolutionary War widow's pension. It is believed that the date is optimistic, i.e., occurred at a later time, such as 1786 or thereafter. On one affidavit, Sarah stated that she married Noah on Jan. 1, 1784. When questioned about the battles and the military commanders, Sarah stated that she married Noah after the War, and was not familiar with his service record. If that is true, the marriage probably occurred after 1785.

[12] Bedford County, Virginia *Will Book 1*, p. 385.

Children of Publius Sr. and Elizabeth (Word) Jones were:

    a. Publius Jones Jr., 1781-1811, married Rebecca Moore on Dec. 4, 1799. They lived in Charlotte County.

    b. Frances Jones, born circa 1783, married William Clarke Oct. 7, 1803 in Campbell County, Virginia.

    c. Elizabeth Jones, born circa 1784, married William Micajah Clark.

    d. Cary Jones, 1792-1852, married Nancy Omohundro. They left descendants in Fluvanna County, Virginia.

3. Mary Harrison Word was born on May 30, 1768 and died after 1850, presumably in Buckingham County. She married Francis McGraw Jr., son of Francis Sr. and Mary (Woodson) McCraw, Feb. 7, 1795. Francis was born May 9, 1760 in Powhatan County, Virginia and died Sept. 28, 1834, in Buckingham County. Francis was sent to England to study for the Anglican priesthood, but he returned to Buckingham County and became a lawyer instead. He enlisted in the Revolutionary War from Powhatan County, and applied for a pension on June 8, 1833 in Buckingham County. His widow Mary applied for a widow's pension on Nov. 21, 1848, when she was living in Prince Edward County. McCraw was an early and influential name in Cumberland County. According to a Bible record, these were the children of Francis Jr. and Mary H. (Word) McCraw.[13]

    a. Lockey Harrison McCraw was born Nov. 15, 1795, and died Sept. 19, 1861, in Prince Edward County. She married her cousin, James B. Woodson, Oct. 30, 1818. The Flood Bible record says they had a son, "Booker Woodson, son to Lockey H. and James B. Woodson, born 29th Aug. 1819." After Lockey's first husband died, she married second John Wesley Redd (1794-1874), son of John and Mary (Truman) Redd.

---

[13] Information on the McCraw family came from three sources: The Noah Flood Bible Record in the DAR Library, Wash., D.C.; Frank McCraw of Manassas, Virginia; and Mary (McCraw) Harland of Richmond, Virginia. After this manuscript was developed, on June 24, 1996, the writer received manuscript pages from Mrs. Gene McCraw, 546 McKinley Ave., Woodland, California 95695-3858. She has either published or is about to to publish the third edition of a book titled *It is McCraw not McGraw*. Mrs. McCraw states that her coauthor is the late Mary McCraw (Nelson) Harland. This is to acknowledge the excellent research conducted by these ladies.

Three children were born to this union. They were members of the Briery Branch Church and were buried there in Prince Edward County.

b. Thomas Word McCraw was born May 18, 1797, and died in Buckingham County in December 1859. He married Martha Ann Agee Bondurant, daughter of John and Sarah (Garrett) Bondurant, June 5, 1822. They had 12 children in Buckingham County.

c. Mary Alice McCraw was born on Dec. 26, 1798, and died in 1888. She married Joseph Berry Sharp in 1831.

d. Cary Harrison McCraw was born on Oct. 6, 1800, and died in 1875 in Buckingham County. He married Susanna Hix, daughter of Stephen and Sarah (McCraw) Hix, on Dec. 14, 1823. After her death, he married second Mary Woolridge Gilliam, daughter of Richard Curd and Mary (Robertson) Gilliam. Five children were born to the first union and two to the second marriage. Cary H. lived near Andersonsville, Buckingham County.

e. Nancy Ann Word McCraw born June 30, 1802, and died May 19, 1891 in Buckingham County. She married William H. Ranson on May 19, 1825.

f. Francis Dancy McCraw III was born July 16, 1804, and died circa 1881 in Virginia. He married Lavinia Walthal Flood, daughter of John and Frances Flood, and granddaughter of Noah and Sallie (Word) Flood. Lavinia was born on July 31, 1816 in Buckingham County, according to Noah Flood's Bible record. Francis and Lavinia had 12 children.

g. Miller Woodson McCraw was born Sept. 5, 1807, and died in 1866 in Dallas County, Arkansas. He studied medicine under Dr. Willis R. Crute in Mecklenburg County, and later married Crute's daughter, Mary Ellen Crute. They moved to Arkansas about 1841 to accumulate a large acreage of land and to practice medicine where there was a high demand for his services.

4. Judith Word was born July 22, 1770 in Buckingham County, and died on Jan. 10, 1844, in Hopkins County, Kentucky. She married Joseph Fuqua Jr.[14] son of Joseph Sr. and Judith (Daniel) Fuqua. He was

---

[14] Judith's name was not recorded in the Flood Bible record

born Aug. 18, 1766 in Cumberland County, and died May 8, 1829 in Hopkins County. They had seven children.

5. Benjamin Harrison Word was born circa 1778, and died circa 1816. He married Sally Jones, daughter of Robert Jones[15] of Buckingham County on March 14, 1803,[16] in Buckingham County. Sally Jones was born in 1779 and died in December 1853, near Maysville, Buckingham County.

6. A male Word was born circa 1781, possibly John F. Word.

7. Lockey Ann Word was born circa 1783, in Buckingham County, and died in Hopkins County, Kentucky. She married William Noel.[17] William and Lockey Noel moved to Kentucky with the Joseph Fuqua Jr. family, about 1807 and settled in Madisonville. William was a shoemaker, but he also ran a tavern and held the office of Jailor. Children of William and Lockey (Word) Noel were: (a) Dr. George Washington Noel was born on June 25, 1810 in Madisonville, Kentucky. He married Emma M. Summers of Christian County. George was a physician, who also served a term as sheriff. (b) Thomas Jefferson Noel married Elizabeth Laird on Feb. 12, 1833,[18] (c) William Cary Noel, (d) Benjamin Noel, (e) Virginia Noel, (f) Marcissa Allen Noel, and (g) Lockey Harrison Woodefolk Noel.

8. George Washington Word, son of Thomas and Lockey (Harrison) Word, was born on Feb. 22, 1785, in Buckingham County, and died in 1853 in Buckingham County.[19] George W. married Frances "Fannie"

---

[15] Her father is proven by Sally (Jones) Word's death record in Library of Virginia. Robert Jones bought 550 acres of land from John Glover in 1784. He was related to Josiah Jones and Samuel Jones. Residence was within the drains of Slate River. Robert Jones died in 1831, and William H. Word bought six acres in 1836 from the Jones estate.

[16] Marriage date is from the family Bible of Noah Flood cited earlier.

[17] See Maj. Maurice K. Gordon, *History of Hopkins County, Kentucky*, which provides extensive information on William Noel and his family.

[18] Information sent to the compiler on April 30, 1985 by Pamela Fox, 56 Crystal Circle, Carbondale, CO 81623.

[19] Roger G. Ward, compiler, *Buckingham County Land Tax Summaries & Implied Deeds, 1841-1870*, (Athens, Georgia: Iberian Publishing Company), 1995.

Gregory, daughter of Thomas and Mary (Sample) Gregory, May 6, 1813, in Buckingham County.

9. Thomas H. Word,[20] son of Thomas and Lockey (Harrison) Word, was born circa 1788 in Buckingham County and died circa 1818, possibly in Cumberland County. He married Elizabeth C., maiden name not known. She was born in 1790 according to the various U.S. Census years for Buckingham County; was alive in 1860, and gone in 1870. It appears that they lived near Buckingham Court House. Elizabeth and her family unit were enumerated on the 1820, 1830, 1840, 1850, 1860, and 1870 censuses for Buckingham County. Elizabeth did not remarry after the death of her husband.

Children of ____ and Elizabeth C. Word were:[21]

1. Robert Word[22] was born in Buckingham County on Sept. 9, 1806, and died in Christian County, Kentucky on June 3, 1875, where he had settled in 1835.[23] He married Martha E. Gary, daughter of William B. Gary (1785-1844), who also migrated from Buckingham County to Kentucky. Robert and Martha Word had ten children.

---

[20] Not a proven son. Whomever Elizabeth married, he may have died during or as a result of injuries received in the War of 1812. More research is needed. One hypothesis is that the family lived during that era temporarily in Pennsylvania.

[21] Proof of the family composition of Elizabeth C. Word is found in Buckingham County, Virginia *Deed Book 2*, March 1, 1872, p. 714. It was also confirmed by the U.S. Census records for Buckingham County, 1810-1870.

[22] It is probable but not proven that Robert Word was a son of John and Elizabeth C. Word. We considered Robert as a possible son of Benjamin Harrison Word, but the birth date for Robert is in conflict with Frederick D. Word, two months apart. Also, the 1810 Census shows three males under 10 years for Benjamin H.'s family unit, and they have been accounted for. We wanted to believe that Robert was named for his grandfather, Robert Jones, but that does not appear to be the case, unless Thomas H. Word married a daughter of Robert Jones. The fact that Benjamin H. and his alleged brother, Thomas H. Word, died between 1815 and 1820, leaves some uncertainty regarding their family compositions.

[23] *Family Histories• Christian County, Kentucky• 1797-1986*, (Christian County Genealogical Society: Hopkinsville, Kentucky), 1986, pp.440-441. Source was contributed by Mrs. Pauline P. Word.

2. Jane Word was born in 1808. She was living with her mother when the 1860 Census was taken and living in her own household in 1870. Listed in the same house was Melville Word, white male aged 20 years.[24] The 1880 census lists Melvin C. Word, aged 29 years, a son of Jane or June Word.

3. Eliza Word was born in 1810. She was listed on the 1850 Census for Buckingham County in the household of Sophia Gregory. Apparently, Eliza did not marry.

4. Albert W. Word was born circa 1814, implied on the U.S. Census for Buckingham County in 1820, and listed on the personal property tax roll for Buckingham County in 1841. It is believed that he either died before 1850 or possibly migrated to Kentucky. There is an Albert V (or W) Word, age 28, born in Virginia, dwelling # 862, family # 862, in District 1, Christian County, Kentucky on the 1850 U. S. Census. He was in the same household with Robert J. Dupey, age 20, born in Virginia.

5. (male) Word was born circa 1815, on U. S. Census for 1820.

6. Caroline Word, born circa 1817 and died after 1880, married Thomas Harrison Word, son of George W. and Frances (Gregory) Word, on Feb. 10, 1846 in Buckingham County.[25]

7. Benjamin Franklin Word Sr. was born on Aug. 10, 1817 and died on July 25, 1858 in Buckingham County. He married Catherine Ann Housewright on Sept. 14, 1848. She was listed on the 1860 U. S. Census for Buckingham County. According to Bible[26] and census records, their children were: Thomas Fletcher Word, born on June 19, 1849 and died on Oct. 2, 1857. John Robert Word was born on Feb. 6, 1851; Benjamin Heath Word was born on Dec. 29, 1852 and died on Oct. 5, 1856;[27] Amelia Ann Word was born and died on June 1, 1855;

---

[24] Jeanne Stinson, compiler, *Buckingham County, Virginia: 1870 U. S. Census*, (Iberian Publishing Company: Athens, Georgia), 1998, p. 183

[25] *Richmond Whig*, Feb. 27, 1846, p. 4, c. 5.

[26] "Word and Saunders Bible Records," *Virginia Genealogical Society Quarterly*, v 16, 1978, pp. 5-6.

[27] Library of Virginia, *Death Records for Appomattox County, Virginia, 1853-1880*.

James Henry Word was born on Aug. 22, 1856; and Franklin Lafayette Word was born on March 8, 1859 and died on Aug. 18, 1859. In 1850, Ben Word purchased a lot in Maysville from Dr. James Jones and sold it to his mother in 1855.[28] Catherine married second to Nathaniel Saunders on May 13, 1862. They lived near Buckingham Court House.

Benjamin Harrison Word

Benjamin Harrison Word, son of Thomas and Lockey (Harrison) Word, was born circa 1778, and died circa 1816.[29] He married Sally Jones, daughter of Robert Jones[30] of Buckingham County on March 14, 1803,[31] in Buckingham County. Sally Jones was born in 1779 and died in December 1853, near Maysville, Buckingham County.

Children of Benjamin H. and Sally (Jones) Word were:[32]

1. William Harrison Word was born Dec. 25, 1804, and died Nov. 25, 1885.[33] He was a merchant— a well-respected man in the county. William's place of business was on Lot No. 17 (Davidson House) in Buckingham Court House. He married Joanna Branch Garnett, daughter of William and Mary "Polly" Branch (Cook) Garnett. Joanna was born on Aug. 3, 1813 and died June 17, 1896.[34]

---

[28] Roger G. Ward, *Land Tax Summaries & Implied Deeds, 1841-1870*, (Athens, Georgia: Iberian Publishing Company), 1995, p. 328

[29] Date of death is estimated from the personal property tax lists for Buckingham County. The death rate in 1816 was very high because of volcanic ash that covered the earth.

[30] Her father is proven by Sally (Jones) Word's death record in Buckingham County Death Records, 1853-1890, Library of Virginia. Robert Jones bought 550 acres of land from John Glover in 1784. He was related to Josiah Jones and Samuel Jones. Residence was within the drains of the Slate River. Robert Jones died in 1831, and William H. Word bought six acres in 1836 from the Jones estate.

[31] Marriage date from family Bible of Noah Flood.

[32] Names and dates of their children were found in the Bible record of Noah Flood.

[33] Burial was in the family graveyard near Buckingham Court House.

[34] Vital dates are from tombstone inscriptions in Tall Oaks Cemetery near Buckingham Courthouse.

His home was called Tall Oaks, which was owned earlier by his father, Benjamin H. Word. After William's death, the property fell into the hands of his son John W. Word in 1868 and to Mrs. Benjamin Gilliam in 1917. Joseph Love is the current owner, according to Pauline P. Word, who cites the history of ownership on the authority of the WPA books that are maintained in the County Library. The precise family composition is not known for certain, but miscellaneous evidence is reported from public records and the family group sheets of Aden.[35]

Children of William H. and Joanna B. (Garnett) Word were:

> a. William R. Word was born on Nov. 13, 1841 and died Nov. 12, 1862, "of fever." Allegedly, he served in the Civil War.
>
> b. Quinn Irvin Word was born in 1843, and was killed in the Battle of Rich Mountain, July 11, 1861. Killed in battle on the same day, among more than 300 other soldiers, were his comrades William S. Smith and William A. Gillespie of Buckingham County.[36] The Battle was fought in what is now Randolph County, West Virginia.
>
> c. John W. Word was born in Aug. 1847, and died on June 27, 1913.[37] He served in the Civil War. John W. married Eliza Hooper, who was born in December 1853, and died March 23, 1916. They had no children. Burial was in the family cemetery at Tall Oaks. He remained on the ancestral Word home place, and served as a constable and later as sheriff for Buckingham County.
>
> d. Wilber Word allegedly was born in 1847, and died in 1850 at age 3 years.[38]

---

[35] Letter dated June 7, 1981 from Mrs. Aubrey A. Aden, 404 Alexander, Indianola, MS 38751 to the compiler that contained family group sheets of the Garnett and William H. Word families.

[36] Death records for Buckingham County, Library of Virginia.

[37] *Minister's Book*, Buckingham Court House Presbyterian Church.

[38] Pauline P. Word believes that a Wilber Word died in 1850 at age 3, but he has the same birth year as John W. Word's. It appears that John's middle name was Wilber, unless twins were born. Also, Pauline believes that a daughter named Louise Word died in 1860. No documentation was cited.

2. Frederick Dashwood Word was born Nov. 6, 1806. He married Mary Isabella Jones, daughter of William and Lucy (Dobyns) Mott Jones, on March 20, 1834 in Hopkins County, Kentucky. She was born on Jan. 2, 1816 in Hopkins County. Frederick was a medical doctor. Their residence was in Madisonville, Kentucky.[39]

3. Benjamin Harrison Word was born Aug. 31, 1808, and nothing more is known about him at this time. There was a Benjamin Word on the 1850 Census for Casey County, Kentucky, who is not accounted to any branch.

4. Sarah Word was born May 10, 1810. She married William H. Burton, probably a native of Buckingham County, but later a bricklayer in Portsmouth, Virginia. He was born circa 1790 and died in September 1849, per Mortality Schedule for the 1850 U. S. Census. His widow Sarah was listed as "Keeper of the Poor House" in Portsmouth when the 1850 Census was taken. Their son, Harrison W. "Harry Scratch" Burton Jr., wrote and published a *History of Norfolk, Virginia* in 1877 while serving as a reporter for the *Norfolk Virginian* newspaper. The 1850 census indicates that he was born in 1830. Other children of Sarah (Word) Burton were Sarah Burton, born in 1833; Jane Burton, born in 1836; and Robert Burton, born in 1840. William Burton was listed on the 1830 U. S. Census for Buckingham County and living in Portsmouth when the 1840 U. S. Census was taken for Norfolk County, Virginia.

5. Quinn Morton Word was born Aug. 22, 1812, and died in 1894. He married Mary Scott McClanahan, daughter of Col. James and Elizabeth (Walton) McClanahan, on Jan. 4, 1856, in Roanoke County, Virginia. He was a member of the Buckingham Baptist Church before moving to Roanoke.

Children of Quinn M. and Mary S. (McClanahan) Word:

---

[39] Information was provided by Mrs. Gloria Ann (Word) Burns of Grand Rapids, Michigan. She descends from Frederick's son Quinn Word of Madisonville, Kentucky.

a. Betty Blanche Word, born circa 1857, married William Dabney Stewart, June 18, 1884, in Roanoke, Virginia.[40]

b. Sallie B. Word, born circa 1858, married P. W. Reynolds, Nov. 24, 1885, at St. John's Episcopal Church, Roanoke.

George Washington Word

George Washington Word, son of Thomas and Lockey (Harrison) Word, was born on Feb. 22, 1785, in Buckingham County, and died in 1853 in Buckingham County.[41] The 1850 census suggests that he was born in 1779. George W. served in the War of 1812, with Holcomb's 1st Regiment (Cavalry), Virginia Militia. His military rifle went to Alabama with descendants, and has recently been returned to a new home in the Buckingham County Museum, courtesy of Mrs. Pauline P. Word. George W. married Frances "Fannie" Gregory, daughter of Thomas and Mary (Sample) Gregory,[42] May 6, 1813, in Buckingham County. The 1850 census for Buckingham County showed that Fannie was born in 1795, and that her husband was a farmer. An 1853 land survey shows that George W. Word, deceased, left an estate of 197 acres. Six neighbors had adjoining lands when the survey was made: William Wilson, Sarah (Jones) Word, Eli Tutwiler, William Shepherd, Mr. Rees, and Susan Williams. The 200-acre farm was located about 2-3 miles SE of Buckingham Court House.

Children of George W. and Frances (Gregory) Word were:

1. Thomas Harrison Word was born in 1814, and died before 1870. He married his first cousin, Miss Caroline Word, daughter of

---

[40] Roanoke, Virginia *Marriage Book 1*, Page 1, line 18.

[41] Roger G. Ward, compiler, *Buckingham County Land Tax Summaries & Implied Deeds, 1841-1870,* (Athens, Georgia: Iberian Publishing Company), 1995.

[42] Thomas and Mary (Sample) Gregory had these known children: (a) William Gregory immigrated to Missouri. (b) Mary "Polly" Gregory married a Rev. Mr. Moore. (c) Fannie Gregory married George W. Word. One Thomas Gregory was a land owner in Buckingham County from 1782 (or earlier) through 1811. Thomas Gregory was on the Buckingham County U. S. Census for 1820 and 1830. Two William Gegrorys are on the 1820 Census for the same County.

Thomas H. and Elizabeth C. Word, on Feb. 10, 1846 in Buckingham County.[43]

2. Lockey Word was born in 1815, and died Feb. 15, 1891. She married Albert D. Chockley, a saddler, who was born in Lunenburg County in 1820. It is believed they were married in Charlotte County, but later lived near Farmville, Prince Edward County, Virginia. They were listed on the 1850 census for Buckingham County, living next to Lockey's parents.

3. Benjamin Harrison Word was born Dec. 15, 1819, and died April 15, 1893.[44] Ben served in the Civil War. He married Louisa Mason, daughter of Henry and Martha (Malloy) Mason, Nov. 20, 1844. Louisa was born on Dec. 15, 1819, and died in 1883.

4. William Cary Word was born March 20, 1819, and died Jan. 8, 1892. William married Frances A. Snoddy, born June 19, 1829 and died Oct. 3, 1912. Their wedding year was about 1850. He was a merchant and farmer near Gold Hill, Buckingham County.

Children of William C. and Frances A. (Snoddy) Word were:

a. Quinn Morton Word Sr., born in 1852, and died Jan. 10, 1919. He married and had children named Vernie Word, Mable Word, and Quinn Morton Word Jr.

b. Susan M. Word, born in 1856, married George Guthrie and moved to Big Stone Gap, Virginia.

c. Mary Willie Word, born in 1858, married C.H. Clark.

d. William Word married Anna Wenzel.

e. Albert Chalkley Word married Laura Koch.

f. John W. Word was born Aug. 8, 1862, married Lois Lane.

---

[43] *Richmond Whig*, Feb. 27, 1846, p. 4, c. 5.

[44] Information on Benjamin H, Word was provided by Pauline (Peters) Word of Buckingham County. We compared notes on Word family research for two decades.

g. Edgar B. Word was born Dec. 5, 1871, and died April 4, 1894. He was buried in front of Buckingham Baptist Church, adjacent to his parents.

Thomas Harrison Word

Thomas Harrison Word, son of George W. and Frances (Gregory) Word, was born in 1814 in Buckingham County, Virginia, and died before 1870. He married his first cousin, Miss Caroline Word, possible daughter of Thomas H. and Elizabeth Word, on Feb. 10, 1846 in Buckingham County.[45] The Rev. J. H. Fitzgerald was the officiating minister. Caroline was born circa 1817, and was alive when the census was taken in 1880. Thomas and his family were members of Mt. Tabor (Enon) Baptist Church in Buckingham County. He was an active churchman, serving as a delegate to the James River Baptist Association in 1836. The U.S. Census listed Thomas was a carpenter. They lived on the south side of Buckingham Court House.

Children of Thomas H. and Caroline (Word) Word:

1. Robert Alonza Word Sr. was born Oct. 1846 and was alive when the 1910 census was taken. He married Margaret A. Shepherd, daughter of William and Martha G. (Booker) Shepherd, on Dec. 23, 1879. Robert owned and operated a farm at Sugar Hill, along State Route 633, in Buckingham County.

Children of Robert A. Sr. and Margaret A. (Shepherd) Word were:

a. Willie E. Word was born in November 1880, and died in 1903.

b. Carrie Virginia Word was born in April 1883. She married Granderson Witt Crews. In 1930, they were still living, with three sons enumerated on the U. S. Census for Buckingham County.

c. Robert Alonza Word Jr. was born in June 1885. He married Carrie (Crews) Gilliam. Carrie was born June 21, 1889, and died June 12, 1981. Burial was in the Shepherd Cemetery at Lee Wayside, near Buckingham Court House. They had a son Thomas A. Word who was born about 1918.

---

[45] *Richmond Whig*, Feb. 27, 1846, p. 4, c. 5.

d. Thomas Harrison Word was born in June 15, 1888, and died Oct. 13, 1955. He did not marry. Burial was in the Shepherd Family Cemetery near Lee Wayside between Sprouses Corner and Buckingham Court House.

2. Malissa Frances Word was born Aug. 1, 1849, and died Jan. 6, 1927. She married Benjamin Franklin Shepherd Sr.,[46] son of William and Martha Gaines (Booker) Shepherd, Dec. 20, 1866.[47] He was born Oct. 20, 1840 and died Jan. 23, 1927. Both were buried in the Shepherd family Cemetery at "Rose Hill" near Sprouse's Corner. Benjamin F. served as a Sgt. in Co. B 25 VA Inf. Confederate States of America. See the chapter on William Shepherd for more information.

3. Mary Elizabeth "Betty" Word was born in 1856. She married Willis W. Hackett, daughter of John and Sally E. Hackett, Sept. 17, 1873. When the 1900 census was taken for Francisco District, Buckingham County, Willis W. had married second Nancy J. Carter in 1899, and her four children had adopted the Hackett surname.[48]

Benjamin Harrison Word

Benjamin Harrison Word was born Dec. 15, 1819, and died April 15, 1893.[49] Ben served in the Civil War. He married Louisa Mason, daughter of Henry and Martha (Malloy) Mason, Nov. 20, 1844. Louisa was born on Dec. 15, 1819, and died in 1883.

Children of Benjamin H. and Louisa (Mason) Word were:

---

[46] Buckingham County, Virginia, *Will Book 2*, July 21, 1924, p. 543. His will was probated on Feb. 8, 1927.

[47] Marriage Records for Buckingham County, Virginia, 1853-1890, Library of Virginia.

[48] 1900 Census, Buckingham County, Virginia, Volume 9, E.D. 56, Sheet 17, Line 63.

[49] Information on this family unit was provided by Pauline (Peters) Word of Buckingham County. Pauline hesitated to share more information on Benjamin H. Word's descendants because of her plans to publish a booklet on the Word family.

1. Lavina Harrison Word was born on Sept. 18, 1845, and died on Nov. 30, 1889. She married George Ferneyhough on Oct. 24, 1867 at Oak Hill, Buckingham County.[50]

2. Henry Clay Word was born on Jan. 10, 1848.

3. George Washington Word was born on Aug. 23, 1849.

4. William Cary Word was born on Oct. 13, 1851.

5. David Malloy Word was born June 16, 1853, and died Jan. 10, 1924. He married Minnie H. Morgan (1859-1934) on Jan. 13, 1879. Burial was in Enon Baptist Church Cemetery.

6. Benjamin Harrison Word was born in 1856.

7. Andrew Broadus Word, born in 1858, married Birdie Jones and moved to Alabama.

8. Martha "Patty" Louise Word was born on July 28, 1860 and died in 1904.

9. James Walker Word was born circa 1864.

---

[50] Library of Virginia, Archives and Manuscripts, "Garnett Family Bible Record, 1788-1872," Accession No. 21268.

Appendix A

Samuel L. Walton (426)

Samuel L. Walton, son of Joseph M. and Lucy T. (Gills) Walton, was born on Jan. 5, 1854 in Alabama, and died on March 10, 1913 in Hale County, Alabama. He married Sallie E. Melton on Jan. 20, 1875. She was born on Sept. 27, 1853 and died Nov. 6, 1936. Burial was in the Greensboro City Cemetery in Hale County, Alabama. The 1900 U. S. Census for Greensboro Precinct, Hale County gave names of ten children. In 1900, he was listed as the Clerk of the Circuit Court. In 1910, the census for Hale County listed him as a fertilizer salesman.

We were unable to locate a private source of information on the children of Samuel and Sallie. From the 1900 and 1910 census records of Hale County and cemetery records of Greensboro City, here is a tentative list of names and dates: Hubert Walton, 1879; Ellen Walton, 1880; Samuel W. Walton, 1880-1885; Wilma Josephine Walton, born April 3, 1883 and died Dec. 19, 1939, married Walter Lee Ellis; Torbert C. Walton was born Feb. 3, 1885 and died Aug. 16, 1925; Gay Walton, 1887; Lucille or Lucinda, 1890; Annie, 1890; Robert Walton, 1892; Joshua Walton, July 1894; and Pickett Walton, Sept. 1896. (750)

Samuel L. Walton had a daughter, Wilma Josephine who married Walter Lee Ellis. She was born April 3, 1883 in Hale County and died December 19, 1939. She married Walter Lee Ellis on December 20, 1910. He was born April 27, 1868 and died April 23, 1935. They are both buried in Providence Cemetery in Dallas County. He was a farmer. They had four daughters: (a) Elizabeth Attilla Ellis was born December 24, 1911. She married Franklin Comer Sewell on November 26, 1943. She died November 20, 2002 and he died November 1, 2002, without children. (b) Wilma Leon Ellis was born November 11, 1913 and died November 21, 1973, unmarried; (c) Annie Lee Ellis was born June 25, 1917 and died June 4, 2001. She married James Ervin "Bebo" Jones on June 7, 1936. He was born November 1, 1915. They had three children: James Ervin Jones, Jr., Joanne Ellis (Jones) Givhan, and Walter Lee Jones; and Martha Amanda Ellis was born November 9, 1922 and died February 7, 2004., unmarried.

Source: Mrs. Eleanor C. Drake of Alabama in an email to the compiler on Jan. 11, 2005, edrake@judson.edu.

John T. and Sarah F. (Gills) Walton of Hale County, Alabama

Antebellum home of John T. Walton

Appendix B

Edward Walton of Hanover County, Virginia

Edward Walton (ca 1720-1791) of Hanover County, Virginia is classified as miscellaneous, although there is a strong possibility that he belongs to the Waltons of New Kent County from which Hanover was formed. One hypothesis is that he was a son of Edward Jr. and Elizabeth Walton. There is a parallel between Edward of Hanover and John Walton, 1709-1772, of the same County. Both were associated with the Baker and Sims families.[1] Edward was a witness to the will of John Walton who married Mary Sims, which indicates a possible relationship. However, the naming pattern does not lend support of the hypothesis, because there were no Edward, Robert, nor George Waltons in the early generations. The name of Edward's wife is not known but her maiden name may have been Thompson. Edward's branch is often referred to as "The Albemarle Waltons."

Children of Edward Walton: [2]

1. Elizabeth Walton was born Sept. 17, 1743 in Hanover County.

2. Agnes Walton was born Jan. 7, 1745. She married Lewis Davis Sr. in Albemarle County.

3. Thompson Walton was born on Jan. 4, 1747 in Hanover County, and died before Sept. 3, 1827 in Albemarle County. He married a woman named Sarah and these children were born to them:

   a. David Rice Walton was born on Oct. 10, 1776. He married Rebecca Fraley on Dec. 10, 1797 in Albemarle County.

   b. Sarah Walton was born on Aug. 15, 1778 in Albemarle County. She married Ephraim Spears on Nov. 24, 1802 in Albemarle County.

   c. Lurane Walton was born on Sept. 8, 1780, and married a Mr. Spears.

---

[1] ____ Davis, *Hanover County Deeds, 1783-1792*, ( ), p. 396. This citation is from Julia Crosswell's website (see following footnote).

[2] Julia Crosswell and George W. Walton, contributed information for this branch of Waltons. Julia lives at 9008 Mahan Drive, Fort Worth, TX 76116. She has done extensive research on Edward Walton of Hanover County. Julia asked for the following statement to be included for credit purposes: "Many researchers have contributed information to the Edward Walton Web Page: http://www.geocities.com/~jcrosswell/Walton which is hosted by Julia Crosswell <jcross@metronet.com>" George W. Walton is an employee of the U.S. Department of State. His former website contained extensive information on Waltons: *http://www.familytreemaker.com/users/w/a/l/George W. Walton/*. His regular address is: Col. George W. Walton, P.O. Box 46091, Washington, D.C. 20050-6091.

d. Elizabeth Walton was born on Dec. 5, 1782. She married Henry Marshall on Jan. 22, 1810 in Orange County, Virginia.

e. Judah Walton, born on July 17, 1782, married Charles Hicks on Jan. 7, 1809 in Albemarle County.

f. John Walton was born in May, probably in 1785.

g. Olley Walton was born in December, probably 1789.

h. Jesse Rice Walton, born on July 9, 1790, married Nancy Gentry on May 6, 1816 in Albemarle County.

i. Emely Walton was born in February 1793 in Albemarle County. She married John Dowell on Nov. 9, 1814, in Albemarle County.

4. Ison Walton Sr. was born March 15, 1749-1750 in Hanover County and died in Albemarle County on March 5, 1832. He first married Elizabeth Sims, and married second Patsy Bruce.

Children of Ison Sr. and Elizabeth (Sims) Walton Sr.:

a. Martha "Patsy" Walton was born in 1773 in Hanover County. She married her first cousin, Lewis Davis Jr.

b. Jane Walton was born circa 1775. She married Solomon Stanley.

c. Ann Walton was born circa 1778. She married Richard Golding on April 27, 1798 in Albemarle County.

d. Matthew Pate Walton was born circa 1780 in Hanover County and died on Aug. 15, 1856 in Albemarle County. He married Susanna Naylor, daughter of Thomas and Rosanna (Spencer) Naylor, on Aug. 27, 1826 in Albemarle County.

e. Mary Walton was born circa 1782 in Albemarle County.

f. John Walton was born circa 1784 in Albemarle County. He married Agnes Snow on Jan. 28, 1808 in Albemarle County.

g. Artemissy Walton, born circa 1786 in Albemarle County, married John Wood on Jan. 4, 1818 in Albemarle County.

Children of Ison and Patsy (Bruce) Walton:

h. Alamond Walton was born circa 1808 in Albemarle County. He married Charlotte F. Dowel on Dec. 12, 1833 in Albemarle County.

i. Caroline Walton was born circa 1810 in Albemarle County.

j. Emily Walton was born circa 1812 in Albemarle County. She married Willis Wood on Feb. 18, 1831.

k. Ison Walton Jr. was born circa 1814. He married Ann Dickenson on Aug. 3, 1835 in Albemarle County.

l. Melissy Walton was born circa 1816 in Albemarle County.

m. Hilary G. Walton was born in Albemarle County circa 1818.

5. Richmond Walton was born June 27, 1753 in Hanover County, Virginia and died in either 1831 or 1832, in Albemarle County, Virginia. His first wife died before Jan. 12, 1786. He married second Elizabeth ___ who died sometime between 1839 and 1846.

Children of Richmond and Elizabeth Walton:[3]

a. Ison Walton was born circa 1773 and died before May 6, 1850 in Albemarle County. He married Franky Watson on Jan. 4, 1796 in Albemarle County.

b. Elizabeth Thompson Walton was born about 1775 and died Dec. 15, 1846. She married Isham Dalton on Jan. 20, 1794.

c. Mary Carlton Walton was born about 1776 in Albemarle County.

d. Francis Hart Walton was born about 1778 in Albemarle County and died after Dec. 15, 1846. He married Nancy Spears on Dec. 24, 1799, in Albemarle County.

e. Edward Byerus Walton was born about 1780 and died in 1851. He married Susannah Jones on Feb. 13, 1803 in Madison County, Kentucky.

f. Dyce Boalis Walton was born about 1782 and died Aug. 26, 1840 in Albemarle County. She married Russell Jones on Nov. 30, 1802, in Albemarle County.

g. Edmund Pendleton Walton was born in 1782 and died in 1843, in Bath County, Virginia. He married Elizabeth Maupin on Nov. 19, 1803, in Albemarle County.

h. Richmond Terrill Walton was born about 1784 in Albemarle County. He married first Sarah Alexander on Jan. 27, 1807. His second marriage was to Ann Anderson in 1809.

---

[3] Information for the family unit of Richmond and Elizabeth Walton was provided by Julia Crosswell, 9008 Mahan Drive, Fort Worth, Texas 76116.

i. John Thompson Walton was born on Jan. 12, 1786, and died in October 1859 in Rockbridge County, Virginia. He married Rhody Davis on Nov. 25, 1812 in Albemarle County.

j. Joel Walton was born about 1789 in Albemarle County, and died before May 31, 1832. He married Elizabeth Coleman on Nov. 5, 1810, in Albemarle County.

k. Jane P. Walton was born in 1790 and died before Aug. 7, 1857 in Albemarle County. She married Thomas Chapman Naylor on Jan. 4, 1814, in Albemarle County.

l. Kerenhappuch Walton was born in 1799 in Albemarle County, and died before Dec. 15, 1846. She married Edmund Davis on Jan. 17, 1818, in Albemarle County.

6. Sally Walton was born on April 21, 1756, and died before Oct. 9, 1767 in Hanover County.

7. Lucrecy Walton was born on Dec. 4, 1764.

8. Betty Walton was born on Aug. 3, 1765.

9. Salley Walton was born on Oct. 9, 1767.

10. Milley Walton was born June 6, 1770.

11. John Walton was born June 22, 1774, in Hanover County.

Appendix C

George Walton (1680-1766)

One George Walton, 1680-1766, settled in Brunswick County, Virginia to become the progenitor of "The Brunswick Waltons.". This George may have come to Virginia via Barbados. He was not the same George Walton who married Sarah Roper in New Kent County, Virginia about 1710. According to the Ledbetter family history, George settled in Brunswick County, Virginia, where he had a distinguished record.[1] He was elected High Sheriff on May 7, 1734, and was elected Judge of Chancery Court on June 5, 1746. George died on Oct. 31, 1766 in St. Andrews Parish in Brunswick County. His will was dated July 7, 1764 and it was probated on Jan. 26, 1767.[2] Elizabeth, widow of George Walton, filed her will in Brunswick County on Feb. 12, 1771. She named the same children as her husband in his will. A Harris history says that Elizabeth's maiden name was Scott.[3] Others say that her maiden name was Rowe. It is interesting to note that George Walton's immediate descendants lived in Brunswick County, and we find no evidence of intermarriage with other branches of the Waltons in Virginia. The most authoritative research on George Walton of Brunswick was published in 1983 by Tinney.[4] Residence Brunswick County, Virginia.

Children of George and Elizabeth Walton:

1. John Walton was born in 1706 in Surry County, Virginia and died Jan. 21, 1796 in Meherin Parish, Brunswick County.[5] John received from his father the "upper Tract of land whereon I now live, that belongs to me, that lies on both sides of Quarrel Swamp." John married Rebecca Person in 1734.

Children of John and Rebecca (Person) Walton:

a. George Walton was born in 1734 and died in Brunswick County in 1804. He married a woman named Angelica and they had six children: (1) Littleton Walton, 1765-1825, married Sally Phillips. (2) Joshua Walton married Susan Hicks in 1806 (3) Anabelle Walton (4) Lucretia Walton married John Watson

---

[1] Roy C. Ledbetter, William R. Ledbetter, Justus R. Moll, and James D. Tillman Jr., *Ledbetters From Virginia*, (Dallas, Texas: Wilkinson Printing Company), 1964, pp. 45-50.

[2] Brunswick County Virginia *Will Book 3, 1751-1769*, pp. 462-463.

[3] *Ledbetters From Virginia*, p. 45.

[4] Joe C. Tinney, *The Walltons of Brunswick County, Virginia: Descendants of George and Elizabeth (Rowe) Walton*, Privately Printed, 1983.

[5] Brunswick County, Virginia Will *Book 6, 1795-1804*, pp. 11-12.

(5) Patsy Walton married Edward Lanier on Aug. 29, 1793, and (6) Frances Walton.

    b. Rebecca Walton married the Rev. Edward Dromgoole on March 5, 1777 in Brunswick County. Edward, 1751-1835, was an Irish immigrant from Sligo, Ireland, who settled in Maryland in 1770. In 1772, he converted from Roman Catholicism to the Methodism, and became a minister by 1776. A letter from John Wesley in 1783 to Dromgoole may be seen in the Dromgoole Papers.[6]

    c. William Walton died in 1789.

    d. Thomas Walton was born in 1736 and died in 1789 in Brunswick County. He fathered four males by his first marriage to Rebecca Morris and no children by his second wife Mary Skinner.

2. Mary Walton was born on Oct. 23, 1711 in Prince George County, Virginia, and died July 17, 1779 in Brunswick County. She married Richard Ledbetter, a surveyor.

3. Catherine Walton was born in 1717 in Surry County and died in 1812 in Greenville County. She married Nathan Harris.[7]

4. Isaac Rowe Walton was born in 1719 in Surry County and died on Oct. 22, 1770 in Meherin Parish, Brunswick County.[8] He married Elizabeth Ledbetter in Brunswick County. Isaac inherited the home plantation of his father.

Children of Isaac Rowe and Elizabeth (Ledbetter) Walton:

    a. Mary Walton was born circa 1750 and died before 1801. She married a Mr. Marby.

    b. Henry Walton was born in 1753 in Brunswick County and died in 1813 in Greensville County, Virginia. He married Rebecca Brewer on Aug. 18, 1775 in Brunswick County. Henry served as a Captain in the Revolutionary War. As the eldest son, Henry received his father's plantation, which was the plantation of his grandfather George Walton.[9]

---

[6] Library of the University of North Carolina, "Southern Historical Collection No. 230, Edward Dromgoole Papers."

[7] Greensville County, Virginia Will *Book 2*, p. 297.

[8] Brunswick County Virginia *Will Book 4, 1761-1777*, pp. 29-31.

[9] *Ibid.* p. 29.

c. Elizabeth Walton was born in 1754 and died Nov. 20, 1801. She married George Ledbetter on June 27, 1772. George was born in 1734 in Brunswick County and died in 1803 in Rutherford, North Carolina.

d. Daniel Walton, 1755-1797, married Sally Webb on Sept. 7, 1793, in Greenville County.

e. David Walton was born in 1760 in Brunswick County and died on May 9, 1848 in Huntsville, Alabama. He married Rebecca Wyche on March 6, 1788.

f. Drury Walton was born in 1762 in Brunswick County and died in 1810 in Sumner County, Tennessee. He married Gracy Ingram on Sept. 27, 1785.

g. Isaac Rowe Walton Jr. was born in 1759 in Brunswick County and died in 1833 in Greenville County. He married Elizabeth Allen on Nov. 22, 1787 in Brunswick County.

h. Frances Walton, 1768-1794, married Braxton Robinson on Nov. 20, 1789.

i. Nancy Walton reportedly died in late 1804 or early 1805. She married Nathaniel Peebles on Feb. 7, 1804.

5. Elizabeth Walton was born in 1723 and died July 7, 1764. She married Adam Sims.

Russel S. and Jennifer (Roach) Walton and Ethan and Josey Walton
(See Family No. 1049)

Index

Females are indexed under their maiden names, which are enclosed in parentheses in the text. If her maiden name is not known, she is indexed by married name. The index includes names in footnotes, except for authors of literature. Prefix titles and nicknames are not indexed. This index was created by Jane Ailes of White Post, Virginia.

A

Abbitt: Benjamin, Jr. 140, 193, 433; Dallas 193; George P. 140, 193; Joseph 433; Lizzie 427; Martha E. 330; Mary E. 193; Mary L. 140;
Abraham: Jacob L. 38;
Adams: Amy E. 279; Anthony W. 278; Ashley B. 278; Billy 264; Clyde O. 231, 257; Courtney D. 280; Dawn K. 258; Edna 366; Everett 319; Frances L. 257; George C. 232, 257, 258; Harry D. 256, 278; Harry D., Jr. 278; Isaac W. 319; James R. 280; Jason A. 279; Jessica D. 258; Jessie J. 232; John S. 231, 256, 257; Jonathan R. 278; Jordon E. 264; Kacie A. 279; Kela R. 257; Kristopher D. 278; Leona H. 278; L. W. 411; Madison N. 264; Mark 231; Martha L. 231, 256; Melody D. 257; Peggy L. 257; Randy 231; Richard D. 280; Richard L. 256, 279; Sarah J. 279; Stephania Y. 280; Thomas M. 232; Walton F. 231, 255, 256, 278; Walton F., III 279; Walton F., Jr. 256, 279; Walton F., Sr. 279; Wendy 231; William F. 207, 231, 255, 256, 257, 258; William G. 258; William H. 231; William T. 231;
Adcock: Mary 231, 256;
Aden: Ann 365; Aubrey A. 367, 448;
Agee: Elizabeth 93, 158, 207; George 418; Harmon 418; James 418; John 304; Leon 418; Margaret 418; Mary 46; Maude 418; Nancy D. 304; Samuel 418; Wesley 418; William 46;

Albro: Christine R. 244, 269, 390; James 244, 269;
Alexander: John 17; Rachel T. 219, 238; Sarah 460;
Allen: Amanda S. 143; Betty A. 365; Drusilla 129; Eliza A. 179, 213; Elizabeth 435, 463; Frances 129; Isaac A. 157, 204; James B. 129; Joseph 383, 384; Judith 44; Lavinia 157, 204, 227, 229; Samuel 435; Sarah J. 157; Willie E. 349;
Alley: Jacob 112;
Almquest: Tom 398, 399;
Alsom: Jane 386;
Alvis: Barbara A. 178, 213, 236; Harry O. 387, 397; James B. 178, 213;
Amer: Michael 120;
Amonet: Judith 76;
Anderson: Ann 460; Carolyn V. 340; Chantel 236; Charles 102; Edith C. 296, 302, 303; Elizabeth 110; Ella 143; Eric 236; Frances 34, 35, 38, 40, 68, 134; Francis 290, 302; Hannah 41, 73; Jacob 363; James D. 338; James M., Jr. 337; Katherine 151; Katherine S. 86, 88, 147, 150; Lillie 143; Lucy M. 102; Madge E. 203; Martha A. 190; Patrick J. 102; Robert 361; Samuel 361; Samuel L. 373; Susan 110; Susanna 49, 51, 102;
Andrews: A. J. 404; Karolyn 404;
Anglin: Elizabeth 303;
Angus: Autom A. 276; David W. 250; David W., Jr. 276; Samuel 250, 276;
Anthony: Lucy 400;
Apperson: Eliza 348, 371; Elizabeth 369; Emmanuel H. 370; Jacob 369; James 368; James, Jr. 370; James, Sr. 369; Jane A. 416; John G. 370; John R. 369; Lucy 369; Malinda L. 370; Martha A. 231; Mary D. 348; Nancy W. 369; Rebecca J. 369; Sarah E. 370; Sterling 348, 371; Sterling G. 369; Susan R. 371; Thomas G. 370; William 369; William N. 369;
Archer: Judith 290, 291; Marjorie 203;
Argo: Margaret J. 215;
Armistead: Agnes 109; Elizabeth 38; Elizabeth P. 110; Fannie 109; Frances 38; George E. 110; Hannah 35, 38, 109; James 35; James A. 38, 124; Jesse 97; Jesse S. 134; Joanna

34; John 38; Lockey J. 109;
Martha 438; Mary B. 109; Mildred
38, 68, 69, 121, 123, 124; Mildred A.
40; Nancy 18, 38, 39, 40, 41, 68, 76,
78, 82, 194; Nancy A. 37, 38, 109,
194; Phebe W. 109; Robert B. 109;
Samuel 438; Theodosia 38; Thomas
J. 109; William 34, 35, 38, 39, 40, 42,
68, 69, 122, 194; William A. 68;
William H. 61, 108, 109; William T.
110;
Ashby: Benjamin F. 120;
Ashworth: Robert C. 174;
Ask: Mary C. 356;
Askew: Americus L. 173; Charles M.
173; E. 172; Eliza 106; George A.
172; George C. 106, 171, 172, 211;
James B. 172; James T. 105, 106,
171; Joseph W. 172; Josiah 106;
Judith 106; Judith E. 172; Laura
172; Lithia 172; Margaret L. 173;
Mary J. 173, 211, 235; Nancy E. 173;
Sarah A. 173; Thomas P. 173;
Thomas W. 106; William A. 172;
Willie L. 173;
Atkins: William 8;
Atkinson: Clara W. 236; Elizabeth A.
57; Joshua 29, 30, 56; Samuel T.
376; Sherwood W. 56; Thomas 30,
56; Thomas W. 56;
Atwell: Maudie 231, 257;
Atwood: Judith 136;
Austin: Agnes 309; Agnes F. 309;
Archibald 305, 309, 311, 312;
Archibald, Jr. 309; Archibald, Sr.
305, 306; Bernard G. 305, 307;
George B. 308; Grace B. 309; Grace
R. 309; James M. 306; John 307;
Martha 75, 126; Martha E. 308;
Mary 70, 123; Mildred 70; Mildred
A. 203; Robert 70; Thomas 305,
306; Virginia 70; William C. 70;
William D. 70; Willie A. 70;
Avery: Anna B. 182; Clark M. 61;
Edward W. 182; Ella G. 182; Jerry
Y. 182; Joseph W. 182; Lucy A.
182; Reba W. 214; Virginia E. 182;
William 182; William A. 116, 182;
Wilma J. 182;
Ayers: Elizabeth 367, 371, 373; John
370; Martha 367, 370; Mary 367,
370, 373;

Aylett: Ann 328, 429;
Ayres: Elizabeth 320; James N. 348;
Jane 320; John 320, 413; John S.
349; Judith 320; Mary 320; Mary
E. 348; Matthias 320, 371; Matthias,
Jr. 320; Mildred 371; Nathan 320;
Nathan, Jr. 320; Nathan, Sr. 320;
Nellie F. 320; Patsy 320; Peter L.
320; Samuel 320; Walter 320;
William 371;

B

Babcock: Bradley W. 134;
Bagby: Bennett M. 198; Bennett W.
141, 198, 226; Carrie E. 198;
Elizabeth 63, 117; Mollie 198;
Mollie S. 199, 226; Molly S. 227;
Richard 198;
Bagley: Frances 388; George 335, 336;
Bagnois: Nancy 25;
Bailey: Andrew 438; Ann 48; Ann L.
19; Ernest 251; Martha 33, 251;
Martha W. 106; Obedience G. 438;
Samuel D. 225, 251;
Baird: John R. 353; Marietta 353;
Minnie 350; Nanny E. 350; Robert
B. 349; Robert B., Sr. 349; Robert
M. 349, 350, 353; Ruth 353;
Baker 6, 457: Caleb 401; Idelle 183;
Mary 20, 48; Sarah 401; William
20;
Ball: Anna 152; Nancie O. 97, 161;
Ballenger: Joseph 16;
Ballou: Martha 300; Thomas 300;
Ballow: Leonard 13; Thomas 13;
Bandy: George W. 110;
Banton: Allison P. 271; Evelyn 272;
George R. 248, 271; John C. 271;
John D. 271;
Barfield: Frances M. 227;
Barford: Nellie 177;
Barksdale: Collier 387; John 436;
Macca 387, 389, 437;
Barren: Cynthia A. 161;
Barrow: John T. 201;
Basham: Dorothy W. 234; Floyd M.
209, 234; William M. 234;
Baskerville: Patsy 361;
Bass: John S. 128; Josephine L. 386;
Bates: Arthur D. 411; Edmund L. 411;
Edward 95; Emily C. 97, 161; Eva

F. 411; Frederick 95, 97, 161; James 95; Lena L. 411; Macca 411; Macca V. 191; Margaret M. 72; Mary L. 411; Nellie W. 411; Nicholas 2; Norman H. 411; Robert H. 411; Rufus H. 411; Rufus W. 411; Susannah 97; Susannah W. 47, 95, 161; Susie E. 411; Thomas F. 47, 95;
Baugh 419: Nancy 419;
Baygents: J. V. 216;
Bays: Mary V. 212;
Beard: William 2;
Beasely: Kemper M. 239;
Beasley: Bettie 334; Charles H. 334, 423; Cordelia 334; John J. 334; Katherin E. 282; Katherine E. 265; Kemper M., III 265; Kemper M., Jr. 264, 265, 282; Kemper M., Sr. 265; Lucy A. 334; Robert 104, 334; Sarah 334; Stephen H. 334;
Beauman: Carl 217;
Bebar: Jacob D. 242, 266; Mark R. 266;
Beck: John R. 117;
Bedford: Martha 301;
Behenna: William 356;
Bell: Barbara 244, 269; Benjamin H. 386; Charles 141; David 287, 383, 384, 385, 386; Elizabeth 242, 385; George 104; Henry 287, 329, 385; Henry C. 385; Henry S. 404; Henry T. 165; Howard M. 277; John C. 435; Judith 287; Lelia L. 141; Leonard N. 254, 277, 278; Lucy 314; Martha 329, 331; Mary 386; Matthew W. 278; Morgan B. 278; Rebecca 287; Rebecca H. 385; Robert M. 210; Samantha L. 278; Sarah 287, 329, 384, 385; Virginia 386;
Bellenfant: Mary 298;
Bennett: Milner 51;
Benson: Diane 235;
Berkeley: William 285;
Berry 197:
Betts: Elisha 25;
Beverley: William 104;
Beverly: Elizabeth 369;
Biars: Kate L. 77;
Bickerstaff: Johnson 152;
Bigger: Ellsworth 204; Martha L. 206, 229; Walter S. 204, 229;

Biggers: Martha 364;
Billingsley: Anne H. 165;
Bingham: Margaret 219;
Binnion: Francis 62; Martin 62;
Birch: Elizabeth 90;
Black: Elizabeth 52; William H. 102;
Blackburn: Elizabeth 293;
Blackwell: Kate 107; William 109;
Bland: Edward 285; Peter 292; Richard, Jr. 292; Robert E. 162; Samuel 437; Samuel L. 437;
Blanton: Robert I. 206;
Blevins: Louisa 198; Sallie E. 141, 197; William M. 197, 198;
Blick: Nathaniel 146;
Blount: Margaret 235;
Board: Catherine 408;
Boatright: Elizabeth 370;
Boaz: Mary S. 224, 250, 251, 276; Perce J. 250;
Bocock: Henry F. 432, 433; John T. 104, 433;
Boggan: Sally S. 163;
Bolling: Archibald 286, 419;
Bolton: Bonnie 266; Bonnie K. 222, 242, 266; Carrington A. 196, 222, 241, 242; Dana L. 267; Eleanor D. 222, 242; Emmett S. 242, 267; Erika N. 267; Floyd 222; Harry W. 222, 241, 266, 267;
Bonds: Hillard 216;
Bondurant: John 443; John P. 18; Martha A. 443;
Bonner: Becky 386, 440; Greg 369;
Booker: Albert 298, 300; Albert G. 314; Alice G. 316; Amelia C. 314; Ann 290; Ann E. 313; Arcada 317, 318; Bernard G. 288, 309, 310, 312, 313, 314, 315, 317, 368, 413, 420; B. G. 311; Charlotte P. 300; Cora I. 319; Cornelia L. 299; David E. 315, 317, 319; Don 293; Edith 293; Edmund 292, 296; Edward 56, 289, 290, 291, 294, 296, 302, 303; Edward M. 303; Effie L. 319; Efford 294; Elizabeth 294; Elizabeth A. 314; Fannie B. 316; Frances 290, 292, 293; George 292, 294, 295, 301; George, III 294, 296; George, Jr. 293; George, Sr. 292, 293; George B. 314, 318; George W. 302, 303; German 300; Grace 294, 297, 301, 305; Grace R.

305, 306, 311; Hannah 291; Harriett 300; Helen V. 314; Henry L. 298; James 368; James A. 304; James G. 298, 300; James M. 315; J. G. 317; John 292, 295; John B. 315, 317; Judith 290, 292, 293; Juli F. 316; Louisa 91; Lucien 300; Lucy 291, 294; Lucy H. 298; Mahaley 300; Marshall 297, 303, 304, 305, 310, 312, 314, 413, 420; Martha B. 299, 304; Martha E. 298; Martha G. 312, 313, 314, 413, 414, 418, 452, 453; Mary 291, 295, 300, 314, 316; Mary A. 302; Mary C. 314; Mary E. 316; Mary F. 299; Mary H. 314; Mary M. 303; Mary S. 316; Merritt H. 299; Millie 302; Nancy 315; Nellie S. 316; Peter R. 296, 297, 298, 299; Peter R., Jr. 299; Peter S. 296, 312, 313; Rebecca 291; Rebecca A. 299; Richard 289, 291, 292, 293, 295, 301, 302, 304; Richard, Jr. 292, 295, 297; Richard, Sr. 289, 290, 292, 297; Richard A. 303; Richard L. 300; Richard M. 298; Richeson 294; Ruth 319; Sally 300; Sameul M. 314; Samuel, Jr. 302; Samuel, Sr. 296, 301; Samuel J. 302, 312, 316, 414; Samuel J., Jr. 302, 316; Sarah 294; Susan M. 299; Thomas 91; William 295, 296, 304; William, Jr. 293; William F. 319; William H. 314, 315; William M. 293; Willie A. 314;

Boone: Daniel 26; Louisa M. 98, 166;

Booth: Ann 385; Elizabeth 384; John 384; John W. 200; Thomas 384;

Bostick: Mary M. 365;

Boston: Elizabeth 94; Fontaine C. 159; Margaret E. 94, 159, 160, 207;

Bowlen: Eugenia 356;

Bowler: R. L. 68;

Bowles: Goerge W. 219; Mary E. 192, 219, 238;

Boyce: Jean 118, 119; Jean L. 184;

Boyd: Maria 433;

Bracken: Armstead F. 298;

Brackett: Anne 47, 95, 97, 100; Anne H. 162, 164, 166; Ludwell 95; Nancy 87;

Bradley: Edward 62; John B. 18; Lucy 322, 324; William 324;

Bradshaw: Eubelia 377;

Branch: Archibald 73, 74; Bolling 386; Harriet 74; John A. 74; Martha 73; Mary J. 429, 430, 432; Matthew 385; Samuel 430, 431, 432; Sarah E. 430, 431;

Brand: Bryan B. 183; Mollie 116; Sarah 74; Susan 116, 183;

Brandenburg: Emily 186, 217;

Bransford 195: Elizabeth 320; Jane G. 100; John 76; John W. 77; Judith W. 77; Phoebe A. 77; Samuel 41, 76, 77; Samuel J. 77; Thomas A. 77;

Breedlove: William 64;

Breeze: Hamilton 74; Nancy W. 74; Sarah E. 74; William 74; William T. 74;

Brent 389: Nancy N. 34;

Brewer: Rebecca 462; Thomas 2;

Briscoe: Mendum D. 257;

Britton: Barbara L. 350; William R. 350; William R., Jr. 350;

Broche: John 2;

Brockman: Frank 348;

Bromhall: Herbert;

Brooks: James 250; John 20;

Brown: Alice 253; Bently R. 168; Betty R. 204, 227, 228; Catherine C. 320; Daniel 48; Edmonia T. 168; Edward S. 46, 47, 75, 95; Elizabeth 363; Elizabeth S. 437; Emnella 168; Harriett M. 373; Helen T. 373; James 48; John 373; Kathy 371; Martha J. 168; Thomas C. 101, 168; Walter C. 168; Walter E. 163; William A. 163;

Browning: Sandra G. 256, 278;

Bruce: Patsy 458;

Brunfield: Ann 436;

Brunskill: Martha 293, 295, 297, 301, 302, 304; William 295;

Bryan: Martha 292;

Bryant: Clara 324; James 324; Joan R. 248, 270; Martha 349; Mary 324; Tracy N. 271;

Buchanan: Isabella 150; James 201; Mimi 261;

Buckett: Caroline 356; Eliza J. 356; Ernest 356; Frederick 356; John 345, 355, 356; Sarah 355; William T. 356;

Burge: William F., Jr. 222, 242; William

F., Sr. 242;
Burke 175:
Burnett: Thomas 106;
Burns: Joyce 254;
Burr: Aaron 165;
Burton: Harrison W., Jr. 449; Jane 449; Robert 449; Sarah 449; Seth 62; William H. 449;
Busser: Carrie 176;
Bynum: John G. 378; Orville B. 378;
Byrd: Amanda R. 272; Lydia 182;

C

Cabell 59: William 324, 325;
Cabera: Rocky 217;
Cacchine: Jennifer L. 258;
Caldwell: Barbara 270; Clark 412; John 359; Lena 398, 407, 410, 411; Madison C. 411; Paul L. 255; Richard F. 255; Ruby 412; Samuel 358;
Callahan: Lillian M. 188;
Callaway: Amelia 27; Anna 27; Caleb 27; Elizabeth 27; Frances 27; George 27; Isham 27; John 27, 28; Joseph, Jr. 26; Lydia 28; Mary 27, 395; Mildred 27; Richard 12, 26; Sarah 27; Theodosia 28; William 27, 28; Zachariah 27;
Camber: Dorothy 22, 55, 105;
Campbell: Eva 379; Jennie 112, 175; William 175, 409;
Candler: C. 143;
Carlile: Nancy 362;
Carlyle: Betsy 56;
Carpenter: William E. 255; William R. 255;
Carrington 285: Benjamin 301; Codrington 157; Cornelia 157; Frances A. 45, 89, 90, 155; Louisa A. 301; Martha A. 157; Nathaniel 45, 89; Peyton 90; Robert C. 157, 158;
Carson: Alma B. 227; Clifton W. 239, 243, 265, 266; Cody P. 283; Elliott O. 223, 246, 247; Eugene W. 239, 264, 281; Frances A. 239, 264, 281; George 221, 239; George P. 264, 265; Glenell L. 264, 281; Harriette W. 239, 264, 265, 282; Hunter S. 283; Jean 246, 330; Lynn C. 281, 282; Lynn K. 264; Mildred A. 264,
281; Mildred J. 247; Nannie 246; Patrick S. 265, 283; Rachel K. 266; Robin R. 265, 282, 283; Walter O. 246, 247; William P. 239, 265, 282, 283;
Carter 195: Aileen 177; Anne 381; Archibald W. 74, 75, 126, 189; A. W. 126; Cannon M. 154, 201; David 43; Elaine 239, 265, 282, 283; Frances 22, 53; Henry C. 127; James M. 152; Janie 189; John 22, 53; John B. 18; John W. 126, 189; Martha A. 127; Mary S. 126; Nancy J. 453; Patty A. 189; Rawley W. 50; Samuel A. 127; Sherwood 126; Susan 189, 195; Susan G. 127, 189, 190; Susie K. 201; Theodorick 75, 126; Wilson 363;
Cary 285: Archibald 286, 288, 365, 382, 383, 385, 419; Henry 286, 287, 381, 382, 440; Jane 286; Judith 287, 383, 384, 385, 386; Mary 286; Priscilla 287, 381, 382, 383, 439, 440;
Case: James M. 106;
Cash: Brandon S. 283; Danny 430;
Cates: Catherine M. 56;
Cathey: Leona E. 318; William 318;
Catron: Oliver P. 299;
Chamberlyne: Elizabeth 435;
Chance: Becky 262;
Charlton: Royce 367;
Chatlin: Elizabeth D. 176;
Chaudoin: Andrew 362;
Cheatham 330: Amanda H. 247; Elizabeth E. 63, 110, 111; Isham 63, 110;
Chick 81, 104: Elizabeth 42, 78, 79, 82, 138; Elizabeth W. 42, 78, 81, 82, 127, 130, 134, 136, 425, 430; James A. 104; Richard 79, 104; William 42, 78, 79, 104;
Childress: John 294;
Chiles: Mary 337;
Chilton: Chapman H. 357, 358, 391; Harriett A. 357, 358, 391, 392; John P. 395;
Chockley: Albert D. 451;
Christian 288, 375, iii: Amanda D. 83, 141, 142, 199, 336; Ann E. 333; Ann M. 322; Betsy 326; Charles 40, 64, 326, 327, 329; Charles H. 330; Charles L. 104, 330, 333; Constant

323; Drury 324, 332; Elijah L. 65; Elizabeth 39, 323, 327, 329; Elizabeth A. 65, 127, 189; Elizabeth F. 82, 138, 333, 424, 425; Emily M. 65; Evelina 64, 65; George 44, 326, 327, 328, 329, 331; George H. 332; Henry 39, 431; James 83, 130, 141, 321, 323, 326, 329, 331, 332, 333, 424; James, Jr. 327; James, Sr. 325, 327, 328; James B. 333, 335; James G. 65; John 64, 65, 324, 326, 327, 329; John H. 130, 326, 327, 328, 429; Joyce 130; Joyce P. 429; Lucy 249, 324; Lucy J. 332; Martha 39, 64; Martha A. 334; Martha F. 431; Mary 322; Mourning 333; Rebecca 323; Robert 322, 323, 324; Robert, Jr. 324; Robert W. 64; Rufus C. 335; Sally 326; Samuel H. 332, 335; Samuel P. 104; Sarah 65, 330, 375; Sarah J. 334; S. H. 335; Sophia 333; Stephen W. 332; Susan 81, 130, 328, 429, 430, 432; Susannah 130, 323, 325, 327, 328; Thomas 321, 322, 323, 325; Thomas, Jr. 322; Thomas C. 65; Walter 37, 40, 68; Walter, Sr. 64; Walter L., Jr. 65; Wesley E. 64; William 322; William L. 65; William R. 334;
Chumbler: Sara 315, 317, 319;
Claiborne: Elizabeth 22; Leonard, Jr. 22; Mildred 371;
Clapham: William 2;
Clark 379: A. H. 124; Archibald 420; C. H. 451; Frank 217; James A. 202; Robert 362; William M. 442;
Clarke: Hannah 294; Richard 294; William 442;
Clay: Henry 169, 170, 211; Mary B. 142;
Clements: Floyd 175; Joyce 175;
Cline: Dorothy 254;
Cobb: Anne 33; Caleb 33; Charles 14, 33; Charles R. 33; E. C. 212; Frances C. 34; Jesse 33; John 13, 33; Mary 34; Samuel D. 34; Susannah 10, 13, 31, 33; Thomas 34; Valerie 368; William W. 34;
Cobbs: Ann 291; Charles 33; Dolly 405; Hannah 311; Samuel 291, 293; Sarah 293; Thomas 33; Thomas, Jr. 33; Thomas, Sr. 33;

Cock: John 402;
Cocke 413: Anna 337;
Cocker: Samuel 21;
Coffman: Elizabeth 205;
Coghills: David 289;
Cole: Dorothy 2;
Coleman: Alexander E. 368; Alice H. 213, 236; Amber L. 236; Ann 322; Anna L. 338; Ann L. 340, 441; Ann R. 368; Augustus 340; Augustus E. 340; Benjamin 365; Catherine 70; Daniel 338, 339, 365; Edward 337; Edward F. 340; Edwin S. 339; Eliji E. 339; Elizabeth 337, 338, 346, 371, 441, 460; Elizabeth E. 339; Elizabeth G. 340; Elizabeth K. 339; Elizabeth T. 367; Gulielius 364; Gulielmus, Jr. 368; Gulielmus, Sr. 367, 368; Guliulmus 339; Henry 339; James 337; James C. 337; James F. 340; James W. 368; Jeremy B. 236; John 322; John B. 368; John S. 368; Julius 337, 338, 346, 371, 441; Julius C. 340; Julius H. 340; Littleberry I. 339; Lucy F. 100; Luther D. 339; Martha 339; Mary 338; Mary A. 340; Mary C. 339; Mary D. 339; Patsey J. 340; Sally A. 339; Sally M. 339; Samuel 104, 322; Sarah 362; Sarah A. 345, 346, 371; Virgil 368; Virginia M. 339;
Colley: Earnie E. 231, 256, 278, 279; Richard 256;
Collins: Jacob 315;
Condon: Mary 293;
Conti: Emma B. 177;
Conway: Elizabeth 161; Joseph 161; Louise 161; Withers 52;
Cook: Armistead B. 154; Ellen 154; John H. 154; Kate W. 154; Mary 20; Mary B. 447; Mary G. 154, 201; Robert L. 236; Susan W. 154; Thomas H. 233; William H. 154; William O. 153;
Cooke: Jane 2; John 2; Stephen, Jr. 303; William O. 88;
Cornwallis 57:
Cottrell: June 53;
Covington: Milly 50; William 50;
Cowherd: Alice D. 233; Anne T. 233; Marion L. 233; Mary J. 233;

Roderick G., Jr. 233; Roderick G., Sr. 209, 233; Walton R. 233;
Cox: Ann E. 95; Bartholomew 15; George 10, 15, 16; Henry 16; Martha 11, 15, 16, 17, 34, 35, 36, 37, 42, 44, 46, 48, 385; Rebecca 15; William R. 215;
Crabtree: Karen L. 205, 230, 231, 256, 279;
Cragwall: Linda S. 205;
Crank: Ann 69, 187; Ann M. 122; Lipscomb 69, 122; Richard 122;
Cravens: Adeline 122, 187, 188;
Crawford: Annie P. 214; Elizabeth 27; Nancy 128; Sarah E. 163;
Crawley: Mary 291;
Creasey: Edward 372; Julia 372; M. L. 372;
Creasley: John 17;
Creasy: Dianna S. 248, 272;
Crenshaw: Charles 301; Thomas B. 301;
Crews 366: Carrie 452; Granderson W. 452; Joseph 104;
Crosswell: Amanda 124; Julia 6, 457, 459;
Crowder: Herbert 50; Laura 172;
Crute: Mary E. 443; Willis R. 443;
Cummings: Charles 177;
Cundiff: Juanita 224, 247, 248, 270;
Cunningham: Brian S. 273; Cosby 272; Edward 300; Louis M. 200; Mary F. 197, 226, 378; Minnie L. 248; Ray L. 249, 272, 273; Stuart M. 273; William 378;
Curb: Chellie 216; Clarence W. 216; Edward P. 216; Florence A. 216; Mabel S. 216; Margaret I. 217; Mary V. 217; Mattie G. 216; Ruby 216; Sarah A. 217; Walter A. 216; Walter T. 181, 216;
Curd: Edward 435; Elizabeth 435, 436; Thomas H., Jr. 435;

D

Daggett: Charles W. 153; Grace A. 152; Harriett H. 152; Henry 152; Julia D. 153; Mary G. 153; Napthali 152; Pete 88, 152; Stephen 88, 152;
Dale: Nicholas 2; Thomas 2;
Dalton: Isham 459;
Dandridge: Martha 4;

Danford: Willie 349;
Daniel: Abraham 70, 123; Henry 121; Judith 121, 443; Margaret 186; Martha A. 68, 121; Mary 81, 134; Mary A. 339;
Danrig: Wilmuth 70;
Darn: Mary 200;
Dauro: Susan 100;
Davenport: Jesse 99; Mary E. 97, 98, 162, 163; William B. 97, 99, 100, 162;
Davidson: Henrietta 391;
Davies: Carrie 343; Carrie B. 344, 345; Eliza 343, 345, 355; Elizabeth 342, 343; Francis 343; George 341, 342, 343, 356; Henry 356; Jacob 341, 342; Jacob, Jr. 342; Jacob, Sr. 342; James 343; John 341, 343, 344, 345, 355, 356; John, Jr. 343, 344, 354; John, Sr. 354; Joshua 341, 343, 344, 345; Mary 341, 342;
Davis: Alexander 363; Alexander K. 363; Alice R. 230, 254; Alma V. 230; Amos 33; Andrew B. 348; Ann 363; Annie 351; Arthur J. 353; Barbara A. 354; Bernard L. 349; Carrie 355; Carrie E. 350, 351; Clarence 348; Edmund 460; Elizabeth 303, 363; Elnora 360; Elva 347; Etta P. 353; Frank M. 353; Gladys M. 351; Hannah 363; Harrison 355; Henry 355; Henry H. 354; Henry M. 351; Ira G. 206, 230, 254; Jane 292; Jeduthan H. 72; Jesse 363; John 206, 230, 351, 372; John, III 354, 355; John, Jr. 347, 355; John C. 363; John J. 347; John R. 353; John W. 348; Josephine 349; Joshua 345, 346, 347, 352, 354, 372, 374, 416; Joshua B. 351; Joshua H. 354; Joshua L. 348; Lewis, Jr. 458; Lewis, Sr. 457; Lucy 425; Mamie A. 349; Margaret 353, 355; Margaret A. 349; Martha 437; Mary E. 349, 350, 353; Matthew M. 196, 197, 222, 225, 344, 349, 351, 352, 355, 416; Mattie 349; Mattie R. 353; Minnie 355; Nannie 350; Nannie B. 351; Nellie V. 196, 222, 242, 243, 244, 353, 354, 360; Rhody 460; Robert L. 348; Robert N. 351, 416; Roy M. 351; Ruby F. 197, 225, 341,

354, 360, iii; Samuel W. 351; Sarah 363; Sarah J. 348; Shelton 363; Travis H. 349; Vernie 348; Virginia 355; Walter 418; Wilbur C. 354, 360; Wyatt 363;
Deacon: William 137;
Deane: Elizabeth H. 73;
Decie: Zoye E. 235;
DeGraffendreidt: Francis 24;
deLoney: Laura V. 165;
Dempsey: William 64;
Denton: Mary E. 112; Thomas J. 154;
DePriest: John W. 205; Rebecca 158, 229, 230; Rebecca J. 205;
Dezelle: Frances N. 235;
Dickenson: Ann 459;
Dickerson: Sally 191;
Dickey: Adam 298;
Dighton: Samuel R. 210;
Dillard: Elizabeth 331; William 104;
Dixon: Jane 33;
Dobbs: Lady A. 137;
Dobyns: Lucy 449;
Doggett: Sarah 211;
Doswell: Sarah C. 133; Thomas 133;
Douglas: David 22;
Dowdy: Ernest 178; Thomas H. 339;
Dowel: Charlotte F. 459;
Dowell: John 458;
Downey: William T. 116;
Doyle: R. E. 159;
Drake: Alpheus 213; Alpheus B. 113, 178, 179, 213, 214; Betsy iii; Bryant W. 214; Clarence W., Sr. 177; Edith 213; Eleanor C. 114, 115, 179, 182, 455; Elizabeth W. 111, 112; Joseph P. 214; Lucy C. 214; William W. 179, 213, 214;
Draper: Charles L. 161;
Drayton: John 2;
Drinkard 137:
Dromgoole: Edward 462;
Druen: Mary A. 338;
Drummond: Roberta 377;
Drumwright: Eliza C. 176;
Duckett: Joseph N. 172;
Duiguid: Mary 42;
Duncan: Marvin 174; Mary A. 374; Melissa C. 349; Roland 58;
Dunkum: Frances W. 100; James B. 348; James G. 348; John 104; William E. 348;

Dunlap: Ernest B. 179;
Dunnevant: Mollie A. 340;
Dunsford: Alice B. 349;
Dupey: Robert J. 446;
Dupuy: Ann 31; Henry R. 164; Joel W. 164; John B. 396;
Duran: Eleanore C. 337;
Dyche: Arvazena S. 86, 147;

E

Eagle: Roseanna C. 167;
Early: Bishop 46; Jeremiah 393;
Easley: Elizabeth 400; Mary 400; Thomas 400;
East: Legore 254;
Echols: Obadiah F. 422;
Edmondson: Andrew J. 88, 150; Mozelle 182; Robert 150; Robert W. 150;
Edwards: Anne 287, 381; Elizabeth 66, 67, 119; Flemstead 340; Hannah 65; Irene 229; John E. 137, 432; Lillian 339; Lucy C. 340; William 48, 339;
Eggleston 294: Joseph D. 296, 313;
Elam: Ann M. 74;
Eldridge: Benjamin 440; B. R. 414; Mary E. 307; Paulina P. 164; Rolfe 307; Susanna 306;
Elgin: John 37;
Elkins: Elizabeth A. 256, 279, 280; Troy 279, 280;
Ellington: Branch H. 85, 145; Charles E. 146; Cornelia F. 146; Josephine 146; Maria L. 146; Martha T. 146; Mary J. 146; Nathan H. 146; Rosalind C. 146; Roseanne C. 146; Sarah E. 145; William, Jr. 145; William H. 146; Winfield S. 146;
Elliott: Nancy A. 129, 191; Robert 388; Thomas 388, 395; William 17; William A. 191, 395; William R. 134;
Ellis: Annie L. 455; Benjamin M. 259; Benjamin R. 152; Christopher T. 259; Edward 259; Edward H. 259; Elizabeth 184; Elizabeth A. 455; Jason H. 259; Laura P. 259; Martha A. 455; Nancy 394; Walter L. 455; Wilma L. 455;
Elva: Joseph 343;
Emett: Martha J. 142, 199; Thomas T. 142, 199;

England: Edmund L. 369; Elizabeth 369; Eliza J. 367; Robert 369;
Erwin: William C. 60;
Etheridge: Alice 316; Alice L. 317;
Evans: Daniel S. 397; Joseph 137, 357; Joseph W. 358, 387, 389, 393, 399, 407, 436;

F

Fackler: Jacob 364;
Falls: Neilson 108;
Fannon: Wonda R. 268;
Farmer: Absolom 294;
Farrar: Elizabeth 329, 331; John 329; Sarah 329, 422; Stuart M. 81, 130, 132; Thomas 329;
Farrell: Beulah L. 219;
Farris: Sarah I. 167;
Faulkner: William 203;
Fear: Sarah 422;
Ferguson: David H. 104; Margaret 78, 81, 136; Mary J. 218; Richard F. 219; Tommy W. 219; William J. 372;
Fernandez: Flora 202;
Ferneyhough: George 454;
Ferrell 175:
Fessenden: Laura 264;
Field: Charles A. 165; John 357;
Fields 288, 360: Andrew 357, 358, 394; Charles A. 165; Daniel 359; Elizabeth 359, 388, 389, 394, 395, 396; Isabella 358; Jemima 407; Jemima H. 359, 408; John 357; Margaret G. 359; Martha 359; Mary 358; Nancy 359, 402; Rachel 358; Richard 357; Sarah 359;
Finch: Elizabeth V. 133, 192;
Fines: Beatrice 178;
Finney: Eliza E. 147; James 319;
Fisher: Mary E. 377, 378;
Fitzgerald: Catherine 340; Delane, Jr. 276; Delane, Sr. 250, 275, 276; George 350; George P. 350; J. H. 452; Joseph 276, 339; William A. 220;
Fitzsimmons: Gayle M. 14, 33;
Flanagan: Beulah 259;
Fleming: Callie 173; William S. 299;
Flippen: Daniel B. 100; Elizabeth 43; Francis 47; Jane 18, 43, 84, 87; Philip 47, 48; Ralph 18, 43; Robert A. 47; Thomas 43; William 47, 48;
Flood: Aaron 338; Daniel 338, 441; Elizabeth A. 338; Frances 441, 443; James M. 338; Joel W. 104; John 121, 441, 443; John H. 338; Lavinia M. 441; Lavinia W. 443; Martha D. 339; Mary 433; Mary D. 338; Moses 441; Noah 338, 440, 441, 443, 444, 447; Sarah A. 338; William D. 338;
Flournoy: G. 419;
Floyd 133: Gideon 364;
Fogg: Anne 27;
Fone: Rhoda 30, 56;
Fontaine: Abraham W. 344, 345; Clement O. 344; Clement R. 344; Elizabeth W. 344; Fred 344;
Ford: Betty K. 398; Christopher 55; Edward M. 300; Mary 441; Samuel 302;
Forsythe: Warren 311;
Fowler: Lavender O. 104; Owans C. 79; Owen C. 104; Peter V. 308; William 149;
Fowlkes: Nancy 63, 113, 114, 115;
Fox: Pamela 444;
Fraley: Rebecca 457;
Franklin: Jane 405; Lewis 405; Mary A. 42; Mary L. 31;
Frayser: Albert R. 72; Benjamin F. 73; Elizabeth W. 72; John R. 72; Julia A. 72; Melissa M. 72; Nancy M. 72; Robert 41, 71, 72; Robert B. 72; William J. 72;
Frazer: Martha 388;
Freeland: William J. 413;
Freeman: Elna M. 267; Hattie T. 178, 213;
French: Marie A. 99, 167; Palmer 235;
Fricke: Bettie W. 131, 132, 192, 328, 429; Carolyn L. 262; Charles J. 238, 262; Charles J., Jr. 263; Danielle E. 263; Katheryn A. 263; Mary L. 262; Rachael S. 262; Roland M. 262; Roland W. 262;
Frighetti: Paula 345, 355;
Fuqua: Aaron 320; George 128; Joseph, Jr. 443, 444; Joseph, Sr. 286, 443; Sarah 338, 441; William 441;
Furbush: Eunise E. 191;

G

Gaines: Bernard 297, 304, 305, 310; Daniel 305; Margaret 297, 304; Martha 297, 304, 305, 310, 420; Patsy 312, 413;
Galbraith: Alexander 358;
Galbreath: James 358; Margaret 358, 394;
Gannaway: Cordelia 143; David M. 419; Warren 143;
Gardner: Malcom N. 381;
Garland 352: James J. 119; Jesse 310; Lora 222; Martha H. 193; Mary T. 299; Samuel M. 430, 431;
Garnett 454: Ann 367; Carson B. 282; Jackson T. 282; James 311; James M. 265; James M., III 282; James M., Jr. 282; Joanna B. 447, 448; Louisa C. 367; William 447;
Garrett: David B. 227; Magdaline 171; Sarah 443;
Garrette: Alfra J. 227; Alice E. 227; Cary A. 198, 227; Frances C. 227; Garland B. 227; Joseph H. 199, 226; Joseph M. 227; Lyle N. 227; Marshall J. 227; Monroe L. 199, 226, 227;
Gary: Martha E. 445; William B. 445;
Gaston: John R. 358;
Gates 59: Benjamin G. 146; Charles R. 148; Horatio 31; Joseph N. 148;
Gaulett: William 439;
Gentry: Mildred 422; Nancy 458;
George: Elizabeth 35;
Getto: Lottie 199;
Giaretti: Heather K. 266; Jessica J. 266; Raymond W. 266; Remo A. 239, 266; Remo A., Sr. 221; Remo W. 240, 266;
Gibbs: John H. 404;
Gibson: Mahala 65; Mary 165; William B. 65;
Giesler: W. J. 117;
Gilbert: Frances C. 199, 226;
Gilcrease: William E. 110;
Gillespie: James H. 106; William A. 448;
Gilliam: Benjamin 448; John B. 125; Mary L. 223, 246, 269, 270; Mary W. 443; Richard C. 443; Richard H. 335; Sallie F. 332;

Gilliland: Porter M. 357;
Gills: Lucy 63; Lucy T. 115, 181, 183, 455; Margaret A. 63, 111; Mary J. 63, 114; Pleasant 63, 113, 114, 115; Sarah F. 63, 113, 179, 180;
Gilman: Lucille 177;
Gist: Nathaniel 57;
Glass: Cora L. 209, 234; E. C. 190; Edward C. 127, 189, 190, 195; Edward C., Jr. 190; Elizabeth C. 190; Henry B. 190; James 403; Mary C. 190; Nancy D. 190; Robert 190; Robert H. 127, 189; Susan S. 190;
Glasscock: Blanche 24;
Glaze: Annie Z. 208; Haidee L. 208; Harriet T. 208; Luther D. 208;
Glover 312: Anna 333; Charles L. 333; Clara L. 224, 248, 271, 272; Edward 61; John 444, 447; Leanna M. 406; Richard 289; Robert L. 248; Wiliamson A. 59;
Goen: Samuel 104;
Goin: Alice 225; DeWitt T. 225, 253; Rachel 225, 276; Rachel A. 253;
Golding: Richard 458;
Gooch: Charles I. 103;
Goode: Mary 290, 291;
Goodman: Annie P. 100; David 91, 98, 99, 100, 162, 167; Elizabeth H. 99; Hugh F. 167; Indiana 167; Jane F. 100; John H. 168; Laura 167; Louise A. 91; Martha A. 368; Martha J. 101; Mary A. 100; Mary E. 100; Meriwether 99, 167; Nancy 99; Noton 47, 99, 100, 167, 168; Robert J. 100; Sally J. 99, 100; Sarah J. 97, 162; Thomas 91, 368; Thomas A. 100; William R. 167;
Goodrich: James 32; Samuel E. 32;
Gordon: Annie 201; Elaine W. 16; James 201; James R. 153, 200, 201; Joanna H. 153; Obadiah 104; Robert 88, 153, 200; Robert J. 201;
Gough: Octavia 348;
Gowen: Catherine 379;
Grant: W. E. 349;
Gray: Susan M. 297, 298;
Grayson: Linton 98, 164;
Green 217: Amelia F. 427; Audrey 350; Joseph G. 143; Mary A. 438; Richard A. 143;
Greene: Elaine G. 232, 258; James M.

151; Jason 279;
Greenlee: David S. 136; Samuel 107; Virginia C. 81, 136, 137;
Greenstreet: Rebecca 110; William 110;
Greer: Stephen, Jr. 97;
Gregory: Fannie 450; Frances 444, 445, 446, 450, 452; Kent 39, 75, 76, 77, 126, 195; Mary 450; Robert A. 76; Sophia 446; Thomas 445, 450; William 450;
Griffin: Chilli 231, 257; Thelma L. 231, 257;
Griffith: Carolyn L. 263; Robert P. 145; William W. 262; William W., Jr. 263;
Grigg: Jesse 50;
Grigsby: Hannah I. 136;
Grim: Madeline 223, 244;
Grinage: Sara 12, 23;
Grooms: Emily A. 109;
Guerrant: Elizabeth P. 299; Winifred J. 430, 431;
Guill: Annie 219, 237;
Gullickson: Betty 277; Donald 277; Hannah E. 277; Rebecca L. 277; Richard A. 254, 277;
Gunter: Helen 255;
Guthrey: Alexander, Jr. 362, 363; Alexander, Sr. 361; Alexander K. 361; Alexander K., Sr. 362; Allen 365; Benjamin 362; Bernard 364; Elizabeth 363, 366; Frances W. 366; Francis 363; Francis W. 366; Hannah 363; Henry 364; John 365; John, Jr. 366; John J. 368; Jonathan 366; Martha 366; Mary 363; Mary E. 368; Nancy 366; Peyton 364; Rebecca 366; Richard A. 366; Sarah 63, 114, 361, 362, 363, 365, 366; Susan 366; Susanna 361; Thomas 361, 366; William 364, 365, 366, 370; William, Jr. 367; William, Sr. 366, 370; William P. 312, 315; William P., Jr. 368;
Guthrie: Daniel T. 373; Edward T. 367; Elizabeth C. 372; Elizabeth E. 368; Eliza C. 372; Emily J. 374; George 451; Ireland 368; James A. 371; James S. 373; John 367, 370, 371, 373; John G. 372; John G., III 373; John J. 368; Joseph L. 373; Kizzie G. 374; Lawrence R. 361;

Livingston S. 363; Louzanie G. 367; Martha A. 373; Mary E. 344, 345, 346, 347, 352, 372, 374, 416; Mary S. 373; Matthew L. 374; Mildred M. 374; Nancy A. 368; Nancy C. 373, 374; Nancy P. 372; Nancy T. 367; Nathaniel D. 374; Poindexter W. 373; Rebecca N. 372; Sarah L. 372; Sarah N. 367, 368, 369; Theresa 225; Travis L. 372; William 368; William, Jr. 367; William, Sr. 367; William H. 371; William P. 339, 345, 346, 367, 371;
Gwaltney: Hunter D. 218, 236;
Gwatkin: Charles 27, 395; Eliza A. 395;

H

Hackett: John 453; Sally E. 453; Willis W. 453;
Hailey: Nell C. 372;
Hale: John 135; Minnie M. 202;
Hall: Cicily A. 304; Kelly 280; Lucy 404, 405; Mary 14; Richard G. 86; Terry 261;
Halstead: Jordayn N. 278;
Hamersly: Adaline 84;
Hamilton: Sarah 279, 280;
Hammer: W. 164;
Hammersley: James H. 141;
Hammonds: Lloyd D. 353; Mattie R. 360;
Hamner: Earl, Jr. 7;
Hancock: Carter 226; Clarence N. 226, 284, 379; Clement H. 389; Douglas 388; Martin 388;
Hand: Hannah 290, 292; Martha 291; Richard 290;
Handy: Wesley K. 233;
Hansford: Nancy 67;
Hanson: George E. 227; Shirley 250, 275;
Haraway: Ronnie B. 438; Samuel 438;
Hardaway: Henry 408;
Harland 384, 385: Conrad P. 386;
Harley: Annie H. 427;
Harper: Melvin C. 215;
Harris 195, 288, 375: Aaron 360; Aaron P. 267; A. B. 349; Alma 183; Angela L. 270; Anne E. 379; Armistead A. 376; Betty F. 379; Brett 264, 282; Bryan K. 270;

Calvin 193; Calvin W. 37, 225, 379; Catherine 419; Colin L. 277; Daniel M. 196, 223, 246, 375, 378; Duncan W. 282; Earl 246; Elberta 378; Emily M. 277; Fannie D. 379; Frederick J., Jr. 378; Frederick J., Sr. 377; Grace L. 277; Holmes F. 379; Jerry 360; Jimmy 376; John 98; John, Jr. 42; John, Sr. 42; John A. 42; John M. 104; John W. 153; Jordan M. 267; Joseph 378; Joseph H. 379; Laura F. 375; Lee 375; Lela 246; Lillian 350; Lorene 246; Lucy H. 209; Mabel C. 375; Marshall T. 253; Marshall W. 225, 252, 253, 276, 379; Martha P. 375; Martin T. 282; Marvin E. 246, 270; Mary C. 197, 226, 253, 284, 379; Mary E. 378; Mattie B. 378; Michael J. 270; Montague 378; Mosby 246; Nannie F. 223, 246, 247; Nathan 375, 462; Pamela A. 253; Paul 376; Percy 377; Peyton A. 253, 276, 277; Phoebe 45, 89; Richard M. 223; Richard M., Jr. 246, 269; Richard M., Sr. 246, 269, 270; Ridley 338; Robert 20, 104; Rosa L. 349; Ruth 196, 284; Ruth S. 378, 379; Sallie I. 224, 376; Sallie R. 378; Sally I. 197; Samuel W. 369; Sandra E. 379; Sarah A. 371; Sarah E. 45, 91; Susan 397; Tandy W. 267; Thomas M. 219, 379; Walter M. 197, 226, 378; William 80, 285; William A. 104, 376; William H. 375; William J. 243, 267; Willie A. 349; Willis 380; Willis E. 197, 225, 252, 330, 375, 376, 378; Willis L. 225, 379;
Harrison 287: Ann 383, 384; Benjamin 287, 381, 382, 383, 384, 386, 439, 440; Benjamin, III 386; Benjamin, IV 381; Benjamin, Jr. 382, 383, 385, 386; Benjamin, Sr. 382; Brenton J. 261; Carter 381; Cary 287, 382, 384, 385; Effie 318; Elinor 381; Elizabeth 38, 383, 384; Fairfax 383; Hannah 38; James 386; John M. 184; John O. 237, 261; Joshua E. 261; Judith C. 385; Lisa M. 261; Lockey 287, 384, 440, 441, 444, 445, 447, 450; Lockie 439; Martha 384; Mary 384; Mary L. 261; Nancy 386; Priscilla 287, 384; Rebecca 287, 384, 385; William 38; Zadoc 184;
Harrod: James 362;
Harter: Charles, IV 259;
Hartless: Joyce 246, 269;
Harvey 288: Charles C. 389, 395; Drucilla 389; Elizabeth 387, 388; Frances E. 415; Isham 389; John 389, 436; Macca B. 389; Martha A. 389; Mary A. 389; Mary F. 407; Mildred F. 195, 220, 221, 239, 240; Molly 388; Nathan 388, 395, 396, 408, 437; Richard 359; Sarah 388; Sarah B. 388; Susan C. 389, 395, 396, 409; Susannah 326, 389; Thomas 51, 387, 388, 389, 390, 437; Thomas W. 388, 395; William 51, 195; William C. 220;
Haskins: Frances 56;
Hatcher: Alice 178; Elizabeth 47, 95, 96; Martha 259; Sallie W. 72; Samuel 93;
Hawkins: Elizabeth S. 372; Joseph S. 372; Mary B. 370; Robert 405;
Hay: Patrick 205;
Hayden: Middy 127, 128, 192; Rollin 127, 128, 192;
Haynes: Elijah 124;
Hearst: Joseph 109;
Henderson: Mary 173; Robert 93; Samuel 27;
Hendley: Vergie 212;
Hendrick: Frances 363; Louisa 186; William W. 77;
Hendricks: Dan 363;
Hendrix: William W. 109;
Henry: Patrick 21, 55, 400;
Hesse: Charles G. 347;
Hester: Agnes 20, 51, 102, 387; Barbara 20; Robert 20, 51;
Hewlitt: Thomas H. 93;
Hickman: Richard 28;
Hicks: Charles 458; Mary 66; Mildred 418; Susan 461;
Higgens: James 110;
Higgins: Sarah 58;
Hightower: Jenny 402;
Hill 370: Alicia 249, 274; Cornelius P. 135; H. E. 338; Isaac 23; Mary A. 142; Nancy 363;
Hilton: George 14; Hester 14; James 14;

Hix: Lucy 31, 44; Stephen 443;
  Susanna 443;
Hobson: Adcock 296, 297; Benjamin
  72; Elizabeth 99; Frances 300;
  Joanna L. 44, 87, 147, 149, 150, 151,
  152, 153, 154; Lucy 295, 297;
  Martha M. 72; Mary 19, 36, 46, 95,
  99; William 46, 87;
Hocutt: Oscarlene 214;
Hodge: Diane 251, 276;
Hodges: Katie 163;
Hogan: David 109;
Holder: John 27;
Holland: Dolley 364; Franky 357;
  Martha D. 66;
Holly: Nancy 294;
Holman: Eleanor 320; Jesse 320; Julia
  420; William 320;
Holmes: Carolyn 259;
Holton: Elizabeth 52; John C. 103;
  Mary B. 103;
Hood: Jesse 104; Sue I. 238;
Hooper: Eliza 448; W. P. 320;
Hopkins: Sarah 299;
Horn: Harry R. 214;
Horsley 104, 375: Benjamin A. 330;
  James A. 330; Janet 250, 275; Lelia
  330; Martha 376; Martha E. 375;
  Marth E. 330; Mary 330; Mary C.
  330; Mary L. 308; Paul J. 330;
  Paul M. 330; Rebecca P. 308;
  Robert 308, 334; William 326;
  William, III 330; William, IV 330;
  William, Jr. 330, 375;
House: Alease 242;
Houser: Teresa J. 188;
Housewright: Catherine A. 446, 447;
Howard: Mary 318; Maude M. 164;
Howell: Mary 371; Nancy G. 320;
Howlett: Elizabeth 394;
Huddleston: Caroline 339; Mary J. 205,
  229; Thomas 339;
Hudgens: Mary 47;
Hudgins: Jane D. 63, 113, 178;
Hudson: Burton 294; Charles C. 77;
  Janice 250, 275; Mary 294;
  Nicholas 294;
Huff: Lillie 249;
Huffman: Betty 247;
Hughes: Anderson 293; Anthony 21;
  Ashford 16; Blackburn 293; Eliza
  21; Isaac 16, 35; John 54; Martha
  12, 14, 16, 24, 30; Mary 11, 21, 53,
  54; Rebecca 101; Robert 11, 21, 22,
  24; Susannah 13;
Hulett: Edwin 93;
Hull: John 3;
Humlong: Susan 52;
Hundley: Anthony 31; Anthony, Jr. 31;
  Elizabeth 56; Susannah M. 31;
Hunt: Mary 219;
Hunter 288: Adeline V. 395, 397;
  Alexander 392, 393, 402, 406; Ann A.
  363; Benjamin 359, 388, 389, 391,
  394, 395, 396; Benjamin, Jr. 396;
  Brenda H. 242; Caroline M. 395;
  Charles W. 397; Edward 395;
  Elizabeth 393; Elizabeth M. 388,
  395; Elvira F. 396; George 364;
  Henrietta L. 396; James 392, 394;
  Jessie 87; John 359, 392; John, III
  393; John, Jr. 391, 392, 393, 394;
  John, Sr. 391; Macca B. 194, 397,
  408, 409, 410, 412; Margaret F. 408;
  Margaret H. 191, 395; Martha S. 397;
  Mary A. 397; Mary E. 396; Nancy
  405, 406, 407, 408; Nancy M. 389,
  395; Nathan H. 397; Rachel 359,
  391; Rachel M. 396; Robert 394;
  Sarah E. 397; Sherman B. 222, 242;
  Susan C. 397; Thomas 359; Thomas
  E. 407, 408; Washington 389, 395,
  396, 397, 398, 409, 412; Washington
  B. 398; William 364; William M.
  242;
Hurley: Daniel B. 422;
Hurt: Gus W. 163;
Hutchings: Mary 50; Moses 50;
Hutchison: Elvira R. 86;

I

Ikerman: Charles H. 219, 238; Mary L.
  219, 238, 262;
Ingles: William 378;
Ingraham: Marguerite L. 183;
Ingram: Gracy 463;
Inkerman: Mary L. 263;
Irby: Brittany N. 255; Crystal 255; Roy
  255; Tiffany 255; Tim R. 255;
Irvine: Bettie 75; Hugh 75; James 75;
  Jennie 75; Samuel 75; Samuel R.
  75;
Irving: Elizabeth D. 73; Mildred 302;

Robert 73; Washington 169;
Isbell 195: Amanda M. 76; Caroline M. 75; Daniel 75; Eliza A. 74; James D. 94; James T. 74, 157; Lewis 41, 73; Lewis D. 75; Mariah E. 75; Martha 45, 92, 93, 158, 159; Martha J. 74; Mary S. 74, 126, 189; Matthew 126, 189; Phoebe A. 73, 92, 125; Polly 34; Thomas W. 73, 74; Virginia 76; William 41, 73, 125, 126; William P. 74, 92;
Ivy: Emma W. 75, 95;

J

Jackson: Andrew 105, 150; Elizabeth 437; India B. 257, 258; Mary L. 231, 257; Nathaniel 26; Permilia F. 438; Thomas J. 129; William 420;
Jamerson: Brittney D. 261; Byron L. 261; Carrie V. 219; Daniel 218; Deborah H. 260; Ella J. 219; Henry 219; James E. 219, 237, 260, 261; James R. 237, 260; Kenneth H. 260; Louise H. 218; Mary E. 219, 379; Mary L. 237, 261; Melissa A. 261; Nancy S. 219; Paul W. 218; Phillip C. 261; Poindexter 372; Raymond F. 219; Roland F. 187, 218, 237, 379; Roland W., Jr. 219; Roland W., Sr. 218; William E. 237, 260, 261; William E., Jr. 261; William R. 219; William T. 261;
James 183: Mary 18, 37;
Jamison: Duree S. 349;
Janney: Roby B. 233;
Jarrett 327:
Jeems: Pious 201;
Jefferson: Eldridge G. 330; Eldridge G., Jr. 330; Lindsey B. 331; Sallie C. 330;
Jeffries: Achilles 437;
Jenkins: James 30; Maria A. 211; Mary 30;
Jennings: Dickerson 388; Elizabeth 19; Patterson 406; Paula A. 407; Pleasant 388; Powhatan 407;
Jimmerson: Henry B. 372;
Johns 399: Ann 403; Edmund 405; Elizabeth 403, 404, 406; Lockey 405; Sally 402; William 403;
Johnson 67, 418: Alexander 298; Angel L. 255; Daniel 40, 65; David 45; Elizabeth 48; George S. 395; Harry L., Jr. 216; J. R. 163; Lucille H. 254; Mary C. 356; Rebecca 40, 65, 118, 119, 121; Reins 104; Ruth A. 298; Susan 45; Thomas C. 335; Willie 330;
Johnston: John 176; Mary 436; N. J. 181; T. P. 179; William 436;
Jones 288: Alexander E. 212; Alexander W. 408, 409, 410, 412; Amanda 405; Ann E. 128; Anne 441; Annie E. 191; Arthur 401; Birdie 454; Brenda 250, 275; Buckner 405; Cary 442; Charles 401, 406, 407; Charles T. 405; Charles W. 407; Charles Y. 129; Clifford A. 351; Cornelia C. 130; David C. 39, 78, 81, 82, 103, 127, 128, 129, 190, 191, 192; Dorothea B. 403; Edmonia H. 411; Edward W. 351; Eliza 401; Elizabeth 26, 402, 405, 406, 442; Elizabeth W. 408; Ella 409; Ella O. 412; Ellen V. 129; Elliott R. 191; Evalina 408; Evie 153; Evie V. 412; Fonue 231; Frances 177, 442; Frank B. 129, 190, 191; Frank O. 191; George W. 408; Herbert S. 191; Howard M. 130; Ida W. 129, 191; Isabel B. 130, 191, 192; James 76, 406, 447; James E. 455; James E., Jr. 455; James L. 175; James S. 182; Jesse 402, 407; Joanne E. 455; Joel 405; Joel W. 401; Johh, Jr. 400; John 359, 399, 400, 402, 403, 405; John A. 400; John M. 405; Joseph 347; Josiah 444, 447; Josias 400; Judith 402; Judith E. 167; Keziah 401; Lamech 194, 408, 409, 410, 412; Lameck 397; Lena L. 410; Lester E. 175; Lynch 407; Margaret H. 262; Margaret R. 191; Martha J. 403, 406; Martha S. 128; Martha W. 406; Marvin H. 191; Mary A. 128; Mary E. 410; Mary I. 449; Mattie L. 262; Michael 441; Nancy 76, 393, 402, 405, 406; Nancy M. 408; Nannie K. 140, 194, 195, 196, 220, 222, 223, 224, 225, 252, 270, 288, 354, 377, 378, 379, 399, 410; Nettie 351; Palatia E. 12, 23; Peter R. 397, 398, 407; Philadelphia 49; Publius, Jr.

442; Publius, Sr. 441, 442; Rhoda 404, 408; Richard 2; Richard M. 412; Robert 444, 445, 447; Rowland 127; Russell 459; Sally 444, 447; Sally P. 129; Samuel 402, 444, 447; Sarah 393, 394, 400, 402, 450; Sarah N. 262; Susan D. 411; Susannah 459; Tammy 399, 404; Tazewell 75; Thomas 393, 394, 399, 401, 403, 404, 406; Thomas, Jr. 400, 402, 405; Thomas, Sr. 399, 400, 402; Thomas H. 407; Walter L. 455; Walter S. 409, 410; William 398, 400, 401, 402, 405, 406, 407, 408, 449; William A. 397; William C., III 262; William E. 262; William H. 133, 215, 409, 410; William R. 129; William S. 191; William W. 408;
Jordan: Allen D. 375; Ann M. 42; Sallie 378; Samuel 17; William C. 42;
Jordon: Absalom 14; James E. 270; Mary A. 14; Wanda L. 246, 270;
Jouett: Charlotte 28; Frances 28; Henretta 28; John 28; Mary 28, 29; Mary S. 29; Matthew 28; Susanna 28, 29, 56; Susannah 12, 25;
Jurgensen: Georgene 421, 426;

K

Kayser: Janet W. 209; William F. 209;
Kearney: James W. 165, 210; Mary 165, 210;
Keese: Nancy 408;
Kelbough: Edward, Sr. 232;
Keller: Dorothy M. 256; Elizabeth C. 256; James F. 256; Morris C. 231, 256; Morris C., Jr. 256; Washington 231, 256;
Kellinger: Edgar C. 350;
Kerns 384, 385: Christine R. 245; Jacob S. 245, 360; Julia B. 245, 269, 390; Lee D. 223, 244; Lynelle M. 245; Robert T. 244, 245, 269, 360, 390; Shirley M. 243, 245, 252, 360; Wilmer L. 223, 244, 245, 269, 337, 349, 353, 357, 360, 365, 366, 373, 392;
Kesee: Christopher 94;
Kesling: Leonard 366;
Kilgore: Kari 279;
Kim: Suk C. 232, 257, 258;

King: Alma 224, 247; Mackie 319; Philip 384;
Kingston: Ellen 191;
Kinney: Martha E. 188;
Kinser: Andrew 173; Mary C. 173;
Kippers?: George 327;
Kirk: Leo E. 216;
Kirkland: Lola 108;
Klein: Carol 365, 366;
Klingenpeel: Karen 234;
Knight: Hughes W. 29; John 25, 29; John W. 29; Matthew J. 29; Nancy 420; Sherwood W. 29; Woodson 25;
Koch: Laura 451;
Koenig: Louis 84, 85, 331;
Koger: Henry H. 173, 174; Tillman 174;
Kolech: Stacy 265, 283;
Krimstein: Gary 240;
Kyle: George W. 104, 311; Liza D. 254; Lucy J. 333; Rowland 333;

L

Lacey: Amos H. 316; Sarah A. 316;
Lafayette 169:
LaFuze: Verena 277;
LaGrand: Nancy J. 411;
Laird: Elizabeth 444;
Lambeth: Elizabeth F. 142; Lafayette W. 142;
Landman: John 2;
Landrum: Courtney 64; Georgia A. 212, 235, 259;
Lane: Lois 451; William 79;
Langhorn: John 385; Maurice 384, 385;
Langhorne: David B. 385; John 385; John T. 385; Lockey 35, 61; Maurice 440;
Lanier: Edward 462; Eliza J. 101; John 101; Mary 50, 101;
Latta: Johnny 178;
Lavender: Mildred 14, 31;
Lawhorn: Minnie 160;
Lawrence: Nancy L. 8;
Lawson: Joanna 296, 297;
Laydon: John 2;
Layne: Eliza 63, 111; Elvira M. 332; Geoge W. 332; Harold D. 255; Laura M. 199; William 79;
Lea: Ann 364; Martha 363;
Leach: James 123, 124;
Leake: John 290; Judith 300; Mary 40,

64, 320; Rebecca 290;
Leber: Effie W. 176;
Ledbetter 461: Elizabeth 462; George 463; Richard 462;
Lederer: John 285;
Lee 133: Clovia M. 253, 276, 277; Henry 2; Henry B. 190; Mary J. 315; Priscilla 106; Richard H. 190; Robert E. 413, 418;
LeGrand: Archibald A. 395; Hannah 431; Henry D. 134;
LeGrande: Henry D. 131;
Lester E.: Nora L. 212;
LeSueur: Carrie E. 349; Edgar O. 349; Etta 349, 351; John 348; John C. 348; Joshua L. 349; Margaret E. 348; Mary 349; Mary E. 348; Moses 349; Peyton 349; Robert M. 349; Rosa B. 348; Travis C. 349;
LeVert: Cara N. 170, 171, 211; Caroline H. 171, 211; Claudia A. 171; Henrietta C. 170; Henry C. 171; Henry S. 105, 169, 170, 211; Octavia W. 171; Sally W. 171;
Lewis: Cary A. 333; Lydia 159; Merewether 104; Thomas 401; William 333; William M. 104; William S. 386;
Ligon: S. W. 309;
Lincoln 200: Abraham 95;
Linthicum: Henry 104; William G. 121;
Lipscomb: Henry 49;
Lockwood: Robert 265, 282;
Long: Burnette 175;
Longfellow: Henry W. 169, 170;
Loukides: Bret 273; Cory 273; John W. 249, 273; Laura 273; Neil 273; Todd 273;
Love: Joseph 448;
Lovell: Wesley M. 113; William M. 113;
Loving 133:
Lowe: Ellen 265;
Lowery: Cornelius 180;
Lowry: Margaret 292; William 292;
Lumpkin: John 423; Louisa 423;
Lusk: Sarah 211; Sarah H. 106, 171, 172; William 171;
Lyon: Joel 64;
Lyons: Margaret 250, 275;
Lytton: Tammy P. 278;

M

McCall: Roy 261;
McClanahan: James 449; Mary S. 449;
McConnell: Martha A. 263;
McCormick: Caitlin B. 255; Dawn R. 254; James D. 254; James R. 254; Margie 255; Sidney 230; Sidney J. 254; Victoria V. 255; William J. 234;
McCoy: Anthony 104; Elizabeth 33; James 52; Stephen 80;
McCrae: Eleanore H. 42;
McCraw: Cary H. 383, 443; Francis, Sr. 442; Francis D., III 443; Frank 442; Gene 442; James 366; Kenneth 200; Lockey H. 442; Lockie H. 383; Mary 442; Mary A. 443; Miller W. 443; Nancy A. 443; Sarah 443; Thomas W. 443;
McCullough: Phillip 262;
McDaniel: Sarah J. 123; Sarrah J. 70;
McDearmon: James 81, 134; John H. 136; Margaret J. 136; Mary E. 135; Samuel D. 81, 83, 134, 135, 138; Samuel W. 136; Victoria 136; William J. 136;
McEntire: James 32, 60; Jennie 32, 59; Martha M. 32, 60, 106; Nancy 32;
McFarland: John 392, 393; Mary 392; Rachael 392; Rachel 393, 394;
McGee: Nancy 150;
McGehee: Anna 84; Martha L. 93;
McGhee: Mary E. 126, 189;
McGraw: Francis, Jr. 442;
McGuire: John 27;
Machen: Richard A. 146;
McIlwaine: Francis A. 215, 216;
McKeen: C. 142;
MacKenzie: James F. 227;
McKesson: Charles F. 108;
McKinney: Daniel W. 137; John H. 82; Nannie E. 137; William R. 137;
McLaurin: Anselm J. 200;
McLaurine: Eliza M. 420; Janette C. 45, 92, 93; John L. 90; Nancy 93; William 92;
Macon: Ann 323, 325; Sally 420;
Macko: Steve;
McPool 316:
McQueen: Ann D. 208; Florence T. 208; Joseph P. 208; Margaret 208;

McRae: Nancy R. 165;
Madden: John D. 274, 283, 284; Kaleb A. 284;
Maddox: Anderson 363; James 272; Jeanette 272; Jeannette 248; Margaret 272; Snowden 121; Thomas 362, 363;
Magri: Joseph 221;
Major: Emmett D. 376;
Malloy: Daniel T. 420; David 420; Martha 451, 453; Mary C. 420; Sarah K. 420;
Malone: William W. 208;
Mann: Sally 111, 174; Sally F. 36, 62, 63, 110, 112, 114, 115, 117; William F. 36, 62;
Marby 462:
Marks: Anna S. 283; E. A. 140; Elmo 249; Gene 224; Gene N. 249, 274; Jamie M. 274, 283, 284; Jeffrey L. 274, 283; Joseph N. 249, 274, 283; Kaley S. 283; Magan S. 283;
Marot: Edith 291, 293; Jean 291; Rachel 291;
Marr: Johnny 354;
Marsden: Madge I. 232;
Marshall: Douglas H. 396; Henry 458; John M. 396; Lucy J. 190; Manerva J. 318; Mary 311; William 290, 311;
Martin 54, 181: Charles 405; Edna 405; Ella V. 215; Ethel A. 214; Fitz H. 219; Henry E. 215; Henry R. 180, 214; John 137; John T. 181; Mary 215; Myria H. 242; O. L. 137; Paul F. 215; Rebecca E. 219; Robert A. 214; Sally H. 65; Samuel R. 137;
Marvel: William 135;
Mason: Elizabeth 9; Henry 451, 453; James 99; John 20; Lemuel 9; Louisa 451, 453;
Massey 129:
Massie: Jane R. 133, 192, 219; Lucy 134; William G. 133, 192;
Maupin: Elizabeth 459;
Maxey: Agnes 320; Phillip 320;
May: John 393;
Mayfield: Edward H. 190; Katherine S. 212;
Mayo 285: Elizabeth 291;
Mays: James 142; Lavender E. 199; Marcellus H. 142; Rosanna 142;

Meade: Nancy 357;
Meador: Jacqulin A. 213, 236; Mary H. 363;
Meanly: Edmund S. 218;
Means: Isabella 359; Robert, Jr. 358, 359; Robert, Sr. 358;
Megginson: Laura B. 249; Martha 330;
Melton: Sallie E. 116, 455;
Meredith: Washington 299;
Meriwether: Lizzie D. 142;
Merritt: Martha 437;
Merryman: Elizabeth 46; John T. 36;
Milbert: Sarah 357, 358;
Millen: Jane 357, 358;
Miller: Agnes 358; Amos 378; Cheryl 248, 270, 271; Donald C. 203; Ebenezer 154; Ebenezer E. 89; Edwin H. 155; Eliza 90, 155, 203; Frances 174; George 155, 201, 202; George, Jr. 202; Herbert A. 203; Hugh R. 89, 154, 201, 202; Jesse 18, 34; Jesse, Jr. 34; John 35, 38; Josiah W. 149; Judith 35; Kate 202; Lucy 202; Martha 35; Nannie 35, 38; Robert W. 202; Russell 202; Sally 34; Stephen 149; Susanna 27; Thomas 34, 88, 147, 148; Virginia 202; William 34; William G. 397; Yancey W. 202;
Millner: Barbara 205, 230, 254; Bernard N. 254; Beverly J. 254, 255; Beverly T. 230, 254; Brenda M. 255; Darrell W. 255; Elric S. 255; Heather M. 255; Lenard B. 255; Victoria L. 255; William 254;
Minnix: Tonya 255;
Minton: Fred 232; Jean E. 232, 258, 280;
Mitchell: George W. 140, 194; Judith 140; Margaret 355; Sally 362;
Monroe 166:
Montgomery: Mary 392, 393;
Moody: Helen C. 146;
Moon: Edna 377;
Moore 450: Amanda M. 76; Bernard G. 296; Clement C. 148; Daniel R. 173; Elizabeth 362; Eliza J. 314; Jane 148; John 29; John G. 362; John T. 88, 147, 148, 227; John T., Jr. 148; Lucy 362; Margaret 361; Mary 148; Mattie 148; Myrtle 105; Nancy 150; Rebecca 442; Richard

361; Robert 104, 361; Sarah 362; Susan 148; Susanna 28; Susan W. 198; Thomas 25; Thomas G. 362; Travis S. 362; William 313, 362;
Morano: Mary 176;
Moreta: Hugo 257;
Morgan: Minnie H. 454;
Morris: Anna M. 188; Caroline M. 364; David 363, 364; Edward 221; Edward H. 240; Edward W. 240; Elizabeth 296, 364; Elizabeth A. 296, 313; George 363; Guthrie 364; H. A. 148; John 294; Joshua 22, 364; Martha F. 240; Mary 364; Nathaniel 314; Rebecca 462; Rebecca L. 240; Richard G. 104; Sally 364; Samuel 313, 364; W. W. 106;
Morrison: Archibato 338; Elizabeth 338; Thomas R. 338; William L. 193; William S. 338;
Morrow 342: Alden G. 212; Alice M. 105; Clarence T. 212; Frances S. 259; George P. 173, 211, 235; Georgia L. 212; Ida E. 212; Jack D. 235; Jack L. 235; Joe H. 235; John T. 212; Joseph H. 212, 235, 259; Larkin 235; Lucille P. 235; Patricia 32, 105, 106, 171, 172, 211, 235, 259; Patricia P. 60, 259; Taft 235, 259; William 211;
Morton: Clement R. 411; Martha 11, 21, 24; William 25;
Mosby: Agnes 18, 36, 61, 108; Betty A. 301; Edward 18, 36, 61; Elizabeth 18; Hezekiah 13, 18; Joseph R. 299; Littleberry, Jr. 299; Martha 18; Martha F. 299; Mildred 335; Sarah 375; Susan 157, 204; Thomas 18, 43;
Moseley 285: Alexander 104; Elizabeth 73, 74; Emeline 311; Francis 407; Letitia V. 397, 398, 407; Mary M. 407; Spotsford L. 311; Susan P. 385; William 3, 286, 310; William M. 311, 314;
Moses: Charles T. 187; James D. 187; Marsha 369;
Moss: Jamie F. 195; Jemima 348; Richard T. 143; Samuel 417;
Mountney: Alexander 1;
Moyle 342: Henry 343; Jennifer 343; John 343; John, Jr. 343; Margaret 343, 344, 345, 354, 355, 356, 372; Matthew 343, 344, 347;
Mueller: John 63;
Mullins: Henry 14; John 14;
Mullis: Tommy 262;
Mumford: Joseph 294; Thomas 294;
Mundy: Catherine 331, 332; Richard 76;
Munford: James 296, 301; Martha 296, 301;
Murff: Jacob, Jr. 113;
Murfree: John H. 151;
Murphy: Elizabeth T. 220; Harriet L. 61; James 326, 329; James M. 329; Margaret E. 61, 107;
Murray: Ann 20; Anthony 18, 37, 38; Mary 38; Nancy 19, 32, 44, 46, 57, 73, 89, 91, 92; Nancy A. 92, 125; Phoebe 18, 37, 40, 64, 65, 68, 71; Rebecca E. 47; Richard 44;
Musgrove: Bessie 232;
Myers: Mary V. 155;
Myler: E. H. 414;

N

Nadalich: O'neil J. 257;
Naylor: Susanna 458; Thomas 458; Thomas C. 460;
Neale: Clyde E. 319; Richard M., Sr. 319;
Neely: Sarah 159, 207;
Negroes: Absolem 69; Agge 384; Alexander 122; Amanda 86; Amy 298, 363, 384; Bob 363; Bruce 361; Crockett 314; Darkeys 384; Dinah 363; Dorcas? 384; Fanny 46; Gabriel 46; George 86; Hardy 298; Jack 363; Jenny 363; Joeffry 364; King 335; Mariah 93; Milly 363; Nancy 86; Peter 46; Rachel 384; Randolph 69; Thornton 46; Tobie 363; Tobis 362; Violet 361; Wilson 46;
Nehls 201:
Neilson: Ella 153, 200;
Nelson: Audrey 376; Eli E. 208; John J. 208; Mary 43; Mary M. 442; William E. 209;
Nemes: Beverly D. 225, 226;
New: Edmund 321; Mary 321; Rebecca 321, 322, 323, 325;
Newman: Carson J. 281; Frances C.

281; Gerry 264, 281; Irene A. 281;
Newton: Eliza 369; John E. 374;
Manes E. 416; Susan 370; William 370; Willie S. 416; Willis W. 373, 374;
Nichols: William N. 62;
Nickles: Lillian P. 151;
Nixon: Chellie L. 114, 181, 215, 216; George W. 70, 123; Margaret 70, 123; Stuart 70, 123; William 70, 123; Wilmuth 70, 123;
Noel: Benjamin 383, 444; Cornelius 27, 34; George W. 444; John 367; Lockey H. 383, 444; Marcissa A. 444; Rebecca 365, 367, 368, 370; Thomas A. 27; Thomas J. 444; Virginia 444; William 444; William C. 383, 444;
Noell: Ann 34;
Nolan: McEdward M. 216;
North: Elizabeth P. 83, 140, 141, 197, 198;
Norvell: Reuben 331;
Nowlin: James 82; Thomas 104;
Nuckols: Charles 49; Richard 49; William A. 229;

O

Oakes: Elizabeth 363; Sarah 361;
Oliver: Rebecca 347; Ward H. 387, 438; Ward O. 435;
Olsen: Klara 259;
Omohundro: Nancy 442;
Osborne: Charles 103; Emily F. 311; Martha A. 103; Mary 2;
Otey: Dexter 386;
Overton: Keziah 20;

P

Pace: F. K. 234;
Page: Ambrose 424; Carter 286;
Palmer: Elias 431; Reuben D. 431, 432; William 17;
Palmore 372: Ann 124; Fleming, Jr. 70, 124; Judith 63; Judith C. 117; Nancy J. 367, 370, 371; Newton N. 125; Pubilus C. 125; Robert 63, 117; Sarah F. 124; Sarah L. 124; William 124, 370; William F. 124;
Pangle: Martha L. 212;

Pankey: Elizabeth 26;
Parish: Polly 69, 122;
Parker: David 363; Ella 115; Ida 115; Isham T. 115; Jesse 62, 63, 114, 363; Jesse D. 63, 113, 114; John J. 115; Louisa 115; Mary 421; Mary A. 115; Sarah F. 115; Susanna 424; Susannah 421; Willa 115;
Parkes: Ethelrod H. 120;
Parks: Ebenezer 109; Elizabeth 109; Lucy 50; Rebecca 120; William 109;
Parr: James C. 183; Jane 8; John W. 182;
Partridge: Matthew 404;
Pasteur: Anne 291;
Patrick: Sarah 401;
Patterson: David 323; Mary 433; Mary S. 140, 193;
Patteson: John 104; Jonathan 39; Joyce 327, 328; Martha 39, 431; Peter B. 355;
Patton: James W. 60; Thomas T. 60;
Paul: Albert 353; Annie L. 353; Willie P. 353;
Paulette: Ellen 237, 260, 261;
Payne 375: Agnes 441; Ann S. 249, 272, 273; Bobby E. 271; Brandon T. 274; Carolyn S. 251; Casey T. 274; Christopher J. 276; Claude M. 377; Cornelius 101; Evelyn B. 90, 155, 157, 204, 205; Frances W. 247; Francis M. 197, 224, 247, 248, 249, 250, 251, 377; Frederick E. 224; Frederick E., Jr. 248, 270, 271; Frederick E., Sr. 247, 248, 270; Frederick V. 271; Ida F. 377; Jennifer L. 272; John G. 224, 271, 272; John G., Jr. 248, 272; John G., Sr. 248, 272; John H. 377; Joseph D. 224; Joseph D., Jr. 251, 276; Joseph D., Sr. 250, 251, 276; Justin A. 272; Laura G. 375; Leah C. 272; Lynn F. 248, 272; Marion W. 380; Marion W., Jr. 247; Marion W., Sr. 224, 247; Mary E. 140, 225, 250, 251, 252, 273, 333, 375, 376, iii; Mary H. 376; Maude E. 376; Melissa D. 276; Michael L. 272; Millard C. 249, 274; Mosby H. 192; Nancy L. 248, 271; Nicole E. 274; Patricia A. 276; Patsy L. 249, 273; Pearl L. 377;

484   *Index*

Robert A. 249, 274; Sallie I. 224, 249, 274, 275; Samuel 192; Samuel G. 130; S. C. 272, 273, 274; Sterling C. 197, 224, 248, 249, 376; Timothy C. 274; Walter J. 224, 250; Wanda K. 251; William A. 375, 376, 377;
Peacock: Mary 149;
Pearce: Mary A. 362;
Pearson: Charles 12; John H. 108;
Peebles: Nathaniel 463;
Pegues: Alice M. 235, 259; John 259;
Pendleton: Lucy 64; Mary E. 142, 199; Mary L. 415; Richard 64;
Penick: William 52;
Penn: Gabriel 27; Martha S. 129; William 6, 54;
Pennick: Mary 363;
Pepper: Samuel G. 103; William H. 103;
Perdue: Willie D. 316;
Perkins: Samuel 79; Sarah D. 302;
Perrin: Katherine 329; William K. 104;
Perris: Francis 2;
Perrow: Charles 38;
Person: Rebecca 16, 461;
Peter: John 343;
Peterman: Helen L. 212;
Peters: Pauline 451, 453;
Peterson: Emily F. 281; Eric W. 281; Sarah K. 281; Steven R. 264, 281;
Pettit: William B. 345;
Peyton: Carrington 204;
Phaup: James J. 349;
Phelps: Alexander 104; Charles 79, 104; James 104; Jonathan B. 79; Jonathan P. 103; Martha 424;
Phillip: Estelle R. 386;
Phillips: Almedia 165, 210; Mary 334; Sally 461; Sarah S. 334; William 334; Winnie 375;
Phipps: Nannie B. 378;
Piele: John 417; Mary 417; William 417;
Pleasant: Ann 20, 50, 101;
Pleasants: Julia 112, 213;
Plunkett: Ambrose 104; Arthur 188; Arthur H. 188; David A. 135; Emma 397; James C. 188; John 397; Lewis E. 188; Mache E. 396;
Poe: Edgar A. 169;
Poindexter: Joseph P. 345; Louise M. 345;

Pollard: Julia 43, 84, 176;
Pond: Raymond A. 175;
Pool: Chloe 48;
Pope: Virginia R. 215;
Porter: Ellen 149; Ellen W. 88; Mary A. 298;
Potocki: Nancy 239; Nancy A. 240, 266;
Potterwith: James 65;
Powell: Baxter B. 230; Letcher 247;
Poythress: Anne 292;
Preston: Susanna 393;
Prewitt: Abner 150; Mary J. 88, 150, 151;
Price: Daniel 408; John W. 120; Louise 120, 185; Margaret 344, 354; Mary 435; Maude 151; Nathaniel D. 389; Obedience 436; Rebecca 322; Sarah 349;
Proctor 175: John 175;
Proffitt: Annie V. 176; Bessie W. 177; Chastain D. 112, 176; Chastain D., Jr. 176; Eliza M. 177; George R. 176; Hugh M. 177; Johnathan A. 177; Shem W. 176;
Proter: Robert G. 152;
Pryor: Ellen 307;
Purdum: Edward E. 187; Emily 187; Rufus K. 186, 217; Virginia 186, 217; Virginia M. 236;
Purefoy: Frances 290, 292;

Q

Quinn: Denice 273; James 66; John 273; Shannon N. 273;

R

Ragland: Cynthia B. 159; Jean 79; William 250, 276;
Ragsdale: Amarilla M. 150; William H. 150;
Ramsey 129: Brenda 248, 270, 271;
Randolph 285: Innes 377; John 306; Peyton 377, 378; Sarah 387;
Ranson: Henry T. 340; Josephine A. 340; Louise 268; Pattie A. 340; William H. 443;
Rawlings: Henry 385;
Ray: Stephen 31;
Reab: George W. 55, 211; Lawrence A.

171, 211; Regail L. 211;
Read: Clement 382; Elizabeth 386;
Redd: John 442; John W. 442;
Reed: Clement 24, 287; John O. 388;
   Theodore H. 388;
Rees 450: Sarah 20;
Reid: Margery 89, 154; Rose 148;
Renn: Betty L. 229; Edwin E. 229;
Reynolds: Archer L. 314; Martha A. 98, 166; Obadia 314; Obadiah F. 311; Philip W. 265; Phillip W. 283; P. W. 450; Tyler C. 283;
Rhode: Doreen 249, 274;
Rhodes: Artemas 350; Corena K. 279; Cynthia H. 298;
Rhyne: Mary A. 188;
Ricard: James R. 113, 178;
Rice: Clayborn 13; Clayborn, Jr. 13; Edward 13;
Richardson 35: Agnes 51; Ann 389;
Richart: Laura B. 165;
Richeson: Grace 292, 293, 295; Peter 293; Sarah 293;
Richmond: Lena P. 202;
Ricks: Lularetta 428;
Riddle: Watkins 157;
Ridgway: Samuel 324; Thomas 324;
Riggby: Regina 239;
Riggsby: Regina 265, 266;
Rison: Peter 56;
Roach: Jennifer 243; Jennifer M. 268; John A. 268; John R. 437;
Roberts: Jackie S. 238; James, Jr. 28; Mary A. 114, 179;
Robertson 75, 133: A. 351; Edward 52; Elizabeth 358; Jackie S. 220; JoAnne 255; Martha A. 102; Mary 101, 443; Virgina A. 115; William D. 191;
Robinson: Braxton 463; Dawn E. 241; Imogene A. 224, 250; Laura 356;
Rock: Pauline J. 85, 144, 145;
Rodgers: Floyd 197; Roy E. 197;
Rogers: Ezekiel 437; Frances 308; James P. 104; Nathaniel 34; Susannah 325;
Roper: Anne 338; Sarah 5, 461;
Roscoe: David R. 241;
Rose: Anne F. 75;
Rosen: Carl C. 308, 337; J. C. 337; John W. 416; L. M. 416; W. T. 416;

Rosser: Pleasant 402;
Rowan: Mary V. 230;
Rowe: Elizabeth 6, 461;
Rowlett: Archibald 366; Peter 10; William 10;
Royall: Richard 294;
Ruby: William 313;
Ruff: Carole 39, 83, 98, 142, 199, 321, 331, iii;
Ruffin: H. C. 87; John D. 146; Reuben 146; Rubin 146;
Runn 340:
Ruscue: Penny A. 241;
Rushing: Alexander 207;
Russell: Thomas 104;
Rutledge: Priscilla A. 88, 152;
Ryan: Vicki 237, 260;
Ryland: Robert 422;

S

Sage: Connie R. 243, 268; Kermit H. 268;
St. Clair: Aubrey L. 174; Aubrey L., Jr. 174; Dorothy B. 174; Eva 175; Eva N. 174;
St. John: Mary E. 317;
Salle: Jane 370;
Sample: Mary 445, 450;
Sampson: Jane 356;
Sanders: Mary 305; Thomas 305;
Sanderson: William P. 228;
Sandy: Ellen M. 210;
Sanford: Margaret F. 125;
Santos: Isabel M. 210;
Sarrels: Joseph J. 173;
Sauer: John 110;
Saul: Wilhelmina 214;
Saunders 446: Mary 407; Nathaniel 447; Nettie E. 250; Robert 402;
Savary: William 2;
Sawyer: Alice 145;
Schrader: O. A. 312; Susan C. 312;
Sclater: Richard O. 158;
Scott 24, 133: Alice D. 168; Charles 335; Dorothy 254; Elizabeth 6, 461; Emily A. 335; George E. 117, 118; Harrod B. 334; James 48; James M. 335; John 43, 335, 421; John F. 334; Judith 17, 43; Lewis M. 299; Martha 18, 43, 69, 122; Martha E. 335; Nick 386; Richard 335; Sarah

486 *Index*

334;
Scruggs iii: Amanda E. 142; Amine J. 141, 198, 226; Andrew 141; Andrew B. 141; Ann E. 143; Anthony T. 96, 99; Betty L. 197; Celia 317; Clarence D. 222, 241; Claude M. 318; Cuthbert 318; Edmund P. 199; Edna M. 208, 232, 258; Elroy 318; Finch 99; Frances C. 142; Frederick C. 142, 199; George D. 232; Henry 125; Isaac B. 84; James A. 198; James L. 83, 142, 143; John 42, 83, 140, 141, 142; John A. 83, 141, 142, 199, 336; John C. 200; John J. 142, 143; Laura 199; Leila 141; Lewis M. 318; Lucy C. 142; Lucy F. 143; Martha 84; Martha A. 142; Martha H. 200; Mary 200; Mary E. 142; Mary J. 84; Mary V. 143; Mason A. 198; Micajah 317; Nancy 83, 84; Nancy F. 141; Nannie L. 197; Palmer R. 143; Roy G. 318; Ruby 318; Ruth N. 222, 241, 266, 267; Samuel A. 84; Samuel T. 199; Sterling A. 143; Terisha D. 142; Thomas B. 143; Thomas E. 199; Thomas E., Jr. 141, 197; Thomas W. 83, 104, 140, 141, 142, 197, 198; Walter L. 141; William A. 84, 317; William B. 318; William C. 317, 318; William E. 142; William M. 143; William W. 198;
Scudday: James A. 433;
Sears: Edward 104;
Seawell: Ann 9; Benjamin, Jr. 295;
Seay: Isham 85, 86; Margaret A. 63, 111, 112, 175, 176, 177; Matthew 63, 111;
Semple: Robert B. 422;
Sewell: Franklin C. 455; Thomas 2;
Shackleford: Raymond 198;
Shannon: James 358;
Sharp: Ann 49; Joseph B. 443; Nancy O. 49;
Sharpe: John 372;
Sheffield: Melissa 141;
Shelton: Nancy W. 101;
Shepard 372: Burwell 368; William E. 367;
Shepherd: Ada V. 416; Benjamin 418; Benjamin F. 351, 414, 416; Benjamin F., Sr. 351, 352, 453; Bernard G. 414;
Bettie 414; Doctor 418; Ella 415; Emma L. 415; Frank 418; George 414; George, Jr. 418; George, Sr. 418; Georgia A. 414; Gertrude V. 415; Hales 418; Hattie 415; Henry M. 416; James 418; James A. 415; John A. 414; John F. 209; John M. 415; Josephine 196, 197, 222, 225, 351, 352, 416; Lewis 418; Lelia J. 416, 417; Lilly 418; Louis 418; Madeline 105; Maggie 418; Maggie M. 415; Margaret 417; Margaret A. 452; Martha A. 415; Martha G. 414; Mary 418; Mary B. 417; Mary F. 415; Mary P. 414; Mattie M. 416; Millie E. 209; Mollie E. 161, 232, 233, 234; Nannie P. 417; Nora F. 416; Nora L. 415; Peter 416; Peter J. 414; Rosa 351; Rosa E. 416; Rosa L. 415; Samuel 413; Samuel J. 415; Thomas 418; Virginia M. 417; William 313, 413, 414, 418, 450, 452, 453; William A. 418; William L. 415; Willie P. 417;
Sherman: Sara 233;
Sherwood: Baylor R., Jr. 146; Frances 10, 11, 21, 23, 26, 28;
Shippy 419:
Shoemaker: Jordon 414;
Shores: Chastain 92; Nancy 45, 91; Thomas 45;
Shrader: John 69;
Sims 6: Adam 463; Agnes 20; Arianne S. 132; Bernard 72; Elizabeth 458; Mary 6, 10, 19, 20, 48, 50, 51, 457; Reuben F. 72; Reuben T. 124; Sarah 48;
Sinclair: William 111;
Skaggs: Nancy C. 316; Simpson C. 316;
Skinner: Mary 462;
Smart: Daniel 173; Mary P. 106; Nancy F. 172; Sarah 173;
Smiser: Eleanor M. 298;
Smith: Arabella C. 368; Audrey L. 354; Charles S. 108; David 49; David G. 263; Floyd 43; Frances 218; George, Jr. 90; George D. 263; Glenn 358; Holmes 219, 237; Justine L. 59; Katie M. 235; Leonard E. 410; Linda C. 255; Lula G. 219, 237, 260, 261; Mary A. 90, 155, 203, 204; Maxie 216; Myrtle

206; Nancy 49; Richard W. 412; Robert 90, 203; Ruby T. 72, 205, 228, 348, 369, 371, 373, 374; Sarah J. 319; Thomas A. 411; Timothy W. 263; William 203; William S. 448;
Snead: Charles H. 175;
Snell: Christine 274, 283;
Snoddy: Frances A. 451;
Snow: Agnes 458;
Soanes: Henry 2;
Sours: Ernest T. 411;
Spann: Richard 293; Sarah 292, 293, 295;
Spearman: Mary 48;
Spears 458: Ephraim 458; Hannah 63, 110; John 72; Maria V. 72; Nancy 459;
Spell: Susan K. 254;
Spencer: Edward 2; Elmina H. 58; Jane A. 338; J. J. 372; John 349, 371, 417; John J. 352; Martha 344; Mary A. 38; Mildred 344; Moses 320; Nathan 344; Nock 320; Rosanna 458; Thomas 104;
Spicer: Elizabeth A. 280; Kyle T. 159, 160, 208, 232; Thomas O. 280;
Spickard: Irene 377;
Spradlin: Blanche 226;
Stacy: Eunie V. 47, 64;
Stanley: Solomon 458;
Staples: Cynthia A. 397; Robert E. 187; Walter 342;
Starkes: Thomas 104;
Steele: Elizabeth 219, 392;
Steger: Albert G. 73, 92, 125; Albert G., Jr. 125; Anna W. 125; Benjamin 45; Edward W. 91; Elizabeth E. 92; Elmina A. 94, 160, 209; Elmina H. 74, 92; Frances 419; Francis E. 92, 94, 160; Hans 419; Jeanette 67; John P. 45, 91; John R. 125; Kyle T. 160; Marietta V. 71, 73, 125; Mary F. 92; Mary N. 312, 419; Phoebe A. 92; Thomas H. 45, 74, 91, 125; William 67, 189; William D. 125; William E. 46, 91, 126, 127, 189; William F. 45;
Stephenson: Joseph A. 182;
Stevens: Elizabeth 67; Emma 188;
Stewart: John 53; Johnnie T. 216; Mary J. 125; Temperance A. 207; William D. 450;
Stickland: Monette 238;
Stickley: Mary F. 136; William W. 136;
Stites: Mary 109;
Stith: Drury 321; Jesse 405; Lucy C. 407; Mary 393; Rebecca 321, 322; Richard 404, 405; Richard, Jr. 405; Thomas 408; Thomas J. 404; William 408; William B. 405;
Stockard: Eudora E. 159, 207; James 159, 207;
Stokely: John H. 172; Sarah 173; Sarah J. 172;
Stokes 292: Lucy 102;
Stoltz: Kurt E. 243;
Stonar: Alexander 2;
Stone: Edward S. 314; Elizabeth R. 143; Samuel 314;
Strange: Harriet M. 160, 208;
Stratton: Frances 419; Hans 420; James H. 420; Jane B. 420; John H. 420; Katherine 339; Martha 16; Mary 296, 309, 312, 313, 317, 368, 413, 420; Peter 286, 312, 419; Peter B. 419; Peter B., Jr. 420; Richard B. 420; William 419; William H. 420;
Street: Elizabeth 91; Martha 34; Sarah 366;
Strickland: Edward 180; Edward A. 251; James, Sr. 225; James M., Sr. 251; Martha A. 180; Monette 263; Solomon 180;
Stroup: James B. 188;
Sturdevant: M. O. 124;
Stutz: William P. 205;
Sullens: Richard 109;
Summers: Emma M. 444;
Swafford: Johnnie 216;
Swan: Jane E. 420; Thomas 420; Thomas T. 420;
Swann: George T. 92; Sally 93;
Swartz: Harold F. 440;
Swicegood: Bessie I. 216; Gladwin 213;

T

Tabb: John T. 291; Margaret 18, 35, 61, 62; Thomas 35, 291;
Talbot: Eliza 105; Jane B. 405; Pauline M. 408; Williston 408;
Talley: Gene 69, 121; Joshua 69, 122;
Tanner 50: Sally 50, 101;
Tarry: Samuel 291;

Tate: Tabitha 27;
Tatum: Emma L. 205, 229; William E. 205, 229;
Taylor: Anderson 415, 417; Annie 420; Ashley A. 255; Burton E. 255; Burton E., Jr. 255; Clifford J. 417; Courtney V. 415; Creed 419; Cynthia A. 255; David 259; David R. 259; Donald 249; Edna 370; Irvin 255; Jordon 438; Julie M. 259; Lance W. 259; Linda 86, 144; Lucy 415, 417; Mary S. 329; Nancy 249, 274, 283; Nancy E. 119, 184; Narcissa W. 92, 160; Nicholas P. 65;
Terrill: Jeremiah 14;
Terry: Joseph L. 377; Mary 109; Mary A. 62;
Thaxton: Mary A. 65;
Thetford: W. C. 397;
Thomas: Annie E. 181, 215; Della 183; Elliott R. 66; James M. 355; Mattie S. 349; Maud 256; Nancy 99; Nettie 355;
Thompson 6, 457: Bob F. 11, 87, 88, 89, 147, 148, 151, 152, 154, 200, 201, 203; Eliza A. 200, 201; Jacob 201; John 304; Patience 365;
Thornhill: Jesse 67; John 389; Lucy 118; William 66, 67, 104, 129; William A., Jr. 129;
Thornton: Francis 389; William L. 389;
Thorpe 176:
Thurman: Pleasant 67;
Tiernan: James 85, 144; Sarah S. 85, 144;
Tilman: Elizabeth 14, 31, 32, 44, 57, 59, 60; Thomas 31, 44;
Tindall: John L. 148, 149; Martha J. 375, 376;
Tittle: Louisa 197;
Todd: Ludy 334; William R. 151;
Tompkins: Alexander 433; Sallie B. 430, 433;
Toombs: Thomas 366;
Treadway: Moses 299; Moses, Jr. 299;
Trent: Alexander 66; Elizabeth 66; Henry 66; Mary E. 66; Nancy P. 66, 67, 119, 120, 185; Thomas 66, 67, 119; Thomas, Jr. 66; William 66;
Trice: Ernest S. 230;
Truman: Mary 442;
Truslow: Mark 242; Samantha 242;

Tucker: Debra 41, 73; Nell 180; Pertice 220; Pleasant 38; Thomas E., Jr. 181;
Turberville: Harold 272; Norma J. 248, 272;
Turner: Agnes 61; Allie 414; Eleanor 367, 368; Frank L. 411;
Turnes: Aaron 416; James T. 416; Mary L. 416;
Turnipseed: W. O. 179;
Tutwiler: Ann D. 208; Eli 450; Eli E. 160, 208, 232; Erskine W. 208; Guy I. 208, 280; Guy I., III 258; Guy I., Jr. 232, 258; Guy I., Sr. 232, 258; Haidee 208; Harriett S. 208; Kyle A. 94, 258, 280; Margaret C. 208; Mary B. 208; Pickens M. 232; Thomas H. 160, 208;
Twyman 313: Iverson L. 308; Iverson S. 305; John 305; Martha E. 307; Samuel 308;
Tyler: John 69; John W. 68;
Tyree: John H. 77; Linda D. 242, 267; Nicholas 104; Walter P. 190; Walter P., Jr. 190;

U

Umberson: Sarah 235;
Underhill: John 290; Mary 290;
Utley: Isabella 172;
Utterback: Bill 316, 317;

V

Valentine: John B. 148; Mary 149;
Van Cleef: Glenice A. 223, 242, 243, 267, 268; Harmon 242;
Vaughan: Ann E. 157; Anne E. 85, 144; Henrietta 85, 144; Joseph 85, 144; Michael T. 258;
Vaught: Nathan 298;
Vawter 288: Aaron 423; Abraham B. 428; Alice L. 427; Annie M. 427; Benjamin 424; Benjamin, III 422; Benjamin, Jr. 421, 422; Benjamin, Sr. 421; Benjamin S. 140, 333, 335, 421, 425, 426; Bransford 422; David D. 427; Edmund S. 426; Enoch M. 428; George H. 421, 427; John 421, 423; Lucy E. 427; Mamie 427; Martha S. 424; Mary 51, 387, 423;

Mary J. 82, 138, 193, 194, 333, 410, 424, 425; Mayme 427; Moses 423; Phoebe 423; Richard 421; Samuel 51; Sarah 426; Sarah L. 428; Silas 421, 422; Silas P. 37, 82, 104, 138, 332, 333, 334, 335, 424, 425; William S. 421, 426;
Venable: James E. 431; Mollie R. 431;
Verdon: James 266;
Vinson: Alexander W. 258;
von Schilling: Jean 290, 296; Jean M. 293;

W

Wade: Armissie 307; Calvin 213; Margaret 213; Patricia 213;
Walchup: Gus 181;
Walker 288: Agnes 401; Alice 206, 230; Anna L. 220; Ann E. 134; Benjamin 328, 429; Benjamin P. 104, 328, 429, 430, 432, 433; Benjamin W. 132; Bessie 180; Bettie 238, 262; Carrie L. 180; Catherine T. 434; Charles R. 238, 263; Charles R., Jr. 264; Charlie M. 134; Daniel 433; Daniel T. 434; David J. 181; Edmund W. 133, 192, 219; Edmund W., Jr. 238, 263; Edmund W., Sr. 238, 262, 263; Edna M. 180; Eleanor 180; Elizabeth 220, 400, 401, 403; Elizabeth F. 193; Ellen C. 434; Fannie G. 180, 214; Florrie 180; George B. 220; Haley C. 264; Harvey C. 131, 133; Isaac W. 133, 430, 431; James A. 129; James E. 220; Joel 400; John 129, 328, 429; John A. 233; John M. 81, 130, 326, 327, 328, 429, 430, 432, 434; John W. 132; Joseph A. 114, 179, 180, 214; Karen 109; Kate 433; Lelia L. 433; Lisa S. 263; Maria 433; Maria E. 133, 434; Mark W. 263; Martha W. 193; Mary 15, 132; Mary E. 238, 262; Mary V. 134, 193, 220; Merry M. 264; Mildred 195, 220; Nannie L. 193; Nanny A. 433; Nell H. 227; Richard 362; Robert W. 180; Samuel B. 431; Samuel J. 81, 130, 131, 192, 328, 429, 430; Samuel J., Jr. 134; Samuel J., Sr. 132; Sarah 400; Sarah F. 134; Sarah H. 433; Sarah

M. 55, 105, 169; Susan C. 134; Susan W. 432; Walton H. 132; William H. 133; William M. 192; William M., III 220, 238; William M., Jr. 220, 238; William M., Sr. 219, 238; Winston T. 264;
Wallace: Dan B. 124; Jeniffer M. 262; Kareth A. 262; Matthew 2; Terry L. 262;
Walters: Bessie A. 253; John 343; Mary 343;
Walthall: John 297;
Walton 104, 286, 375: Ada B. 174, 228; Agnes 51, 457; Agnes E. 47; Agnes M. 109; Alamond 459; Alexander W. 197, 226, 253, 379; Alfred 111, 174; Alfred, Jr. 162; Alfred F. 58; Alfred M. 177, 178, 213, 236; Alice 114, 166, 179, 180, 214; Alice N. 210; Allen L. 230; Alma V. 206, 230, 254; Almedia 210; Amanda 185, 243, 360; Amanda C. 119; Amelia T. 59; Anabelle 461; Angelica 461; Ann 48, 458; Anna 103; Anna B. 185; Anna M. 117; Ann C. 234; Anne 14, 33; Anne H. 95; Annette 152; Ann G. 164; Ann H. 51, 97; Annie 187, 204, 205, 207, 427, 455; Annie E. 138, 140, 194; Ann P; 30; Anthony 66, 67, 120; Anthony, Jr. 66, 68, 121, 186; Anthony, Sr. 40, 65, 66, 67, 118, 119, 121; Anthony A. 70, 123; Anthony A., Jr. 123, 124; Anthony A., Sr. 123; Arkansas A. 188; Artemissy 458; Arthur 161; Arthur, Jr. 209, 234; Arthur, Sr. 209, 232, 233, 234; Augustus T. 96, 97, 100, 162, 163; Augustus W. 163; Barbara 49, 51, 102, 387; Benjamin H. 91; Bessie L. 175; Bessie V. 197, 224, 247, 248, 249, 250, 251, 377, 380; Bettie B. 184; Bettie C. 140, 193; Bettie M. 216; Betty 460; Betty M. 181; Blake M. 236; Blanche 111; Blanche C. 117; Britain W. 26; Caroline 165, 459; Caroline F. 210; Caroline M. 96, 98, 99; Carolyn A. 213; Carrie 187; Carrie M. 205, 229; Carrington 228; Carrington N. 204, 227; Catherine 462; Catherine J. 138; Charles 111; Charles A. 147; Charles C. 165, 210; Charles

C., Jr. 210; Charles H. 164; Charles S. 145; Charles W. 84, 86, 147, 150, 162; Charles W., Jr. 147; Charles Y. 82; Charley 185; Charlotte 29, 31; Cheryl E. 254, 277; Clarence 228; Cora L. 209; Cornelia B. 137; Cornelia J. 94; Daisy 185; Dallas 427; Dallas E. 37, 195, 284, 378; Dan A. 86; Daniel 6, 7, 463; David 463; David R. 457; Dorothy M. 215; Doshia 25, 30; Drury 463; Drury E. 186; Dyce B. 459; E. A. 194, 195; Edmund P. 459; Edward 6, 19, 20, 32, 33, 44, 45, 52, 57, 66, 67, 89, 91, 104, 111, 158, 205, 229, 230, 457; Edward, Jr. 3, 6, 9, 10, 11, 12, 15, 19, 45, 92, 93, 94, 158, 159, 457; Edward, Sr. 9, 10, 92; Edward B. 459; Edward C. 90, 206; Edward C., Jr. 229; Edward C., Sr. 229; Edward F. 160; Edward G. 93, 158, 207; Edward J. 159, 207; Edward M. 58, 61; Edward S. 107; Edwin D. 86; Edwin T. 86; Elaine 215; Elenora 82; Eliza A. 81, 112, 127, 128, 176, 190, 191; Elizabeth 6, 9, 10, 11, 12, 15, 18, 19, 20, 32, 34, 36, 37, 40, 41, 47, 52, 53, 63, 67, 71, 72, 113, 114, 449, 457, 458, 459, 461, 463; Elizabeth A. 49, 86, 102; Elizabeth C. 98; Elizabeth F. 122, 157; Elizabeth H. 36; Elizabeth M. 112; Elizabeth T. 58, 61, 120, 459; Ella 107, 237, 379; Ella A. 187, 218; Ellen 116, 455; Ellen H. 158; Ellen S. 90; Elmina 58; Elmina A. 209, 232, 233; Emaline L. 137; Emely 458; Emily 459; Emma 46, 117; Emma B. 162; Emma J. 118; Emma V. 187; Emmett A. 183; Ernest 207; Ethan W. 269; Eugene A. 37, 140, 194, 195, 196, 220, 222, 223, 224, 225, 251, 252, 270, 288, 354, 360, 377, 378, 379, 399, 410, iii; Eugenia 181, 221; Eugenia V. 221, 239, 266; Eva L. 215; Eva N. 174; Evelyn W. 158; Everett 162; Faith N. 268; Fannie 47, 160; Fannie E. 113; F. G. 152; Florence 210; Florence L. 108; Floyd A. 205, 229; Frances 12, 14, 20, 24, 26, 29, 42, 45, 49, 56, 70, 82, 83, 101, 119, 124, 140, 141, 142, 147, 462, 463;

Frances J. 30; Francis 161; Francis H. 459; Frank A. 161; Frankie 221; Freda L. 185; Frederick 49; Frederick B. 161; Garland 49; Gay 455; Gay F. 144; George 1, 2, 5, 6, 7, 10, 11, 12, 14, 18, 19, 21, 22, 23, 24, 30, 32, 35, 36, 54, 55, 61, 62, 90, 105, 108, 109, 211, 457, 461, 462; George, Jr. 11, 25, 55, 105, 169; George, Sr. 105; George A. 187; George C. 89, 90, 117; George C., Jr. 155, 203, 204; George C., Sr. 90, 155, 203; George H. 62, 122; George S. 58; George T. 151; George W. 457; Georgie, Jr. 187; Glenice 360, 396; Haidee Z. 160, 207, 232; Harris H. 159; Harvey S. 205; Hattie W. 185; H. D. 205; Helen C. 157; Helen J. 152; Henry 58, 67, 68, 90, 462; Henry C. 157, 204, 227, 229; Henry D. 204; Henry W. 210; Herbert L. 177; Herman L., Jr. 230; Herman L., Sr. 230; H. H. 159; Hilary G. 459; Howard 183; Hubert 455; Hubert H. 108; Hugh A. 275; Hugh C. 108; Ida 117, 151; Ida E. 163, 204, 229; Ida M. 174; Irene 175; Isaac 43; Isaac R. 462; Isaac R., Jr. 463; Isabel P. 185; Isham C. 111; Isibia 117; Ison 459; Ison, Jr. 459; Ison, Sr. 458; Ivey 36; Jack P. 161; Jack T. 179; James 8, 118, 228; James A. 188; James C. 81, 93, 136, 137, 138; James E. 236; James L. 215; James M. 58; James S. 30; James T. 144, 181, 215; James W. 60, 119, 213, 236; James W., Jr. 236; Jane 458; Jane C. 58, 60; Jane P. 460; Jane S. 88, 149, 150; Jane W. 93; Jasper 116; Jesse 14, 15, 20, 23, 30, 32, 36, 44, 50, 87, 101, 102, 147, 149, 150, 151, 152, 153, 154; Jesse, Jr. 50; Jesse E. 177; Jesse H. 24; Jesse L. 88; Jesse R. 458; Jesse S. 12, 23, 101; Jesse T., Jr. 58; Jesse T., Sr. 58; Jesse W. 62, 63, 110, 111, 112, 177, 213; Jessica A. 236; Jessie E. 181; Jessie H. 207, 230, 231, 255, 256, 257; Jessie V. 183; Joanna J. 149; Joel 48, 460; John 1, 2, 3, 6, 16, 19, 20, 22, 29, 30, 32, 49, 50, 51, 54, 102, 429, 457, 458, 460, 461; John, III 49; John, Jr. 20,

48; John, Sr. 10, 48; John A. 60, 69, 121, 122, 187; John B. 25, 51, 147; John C. 53, 193, 194, 197, 225, 354, 360, 427; John C., Jr. 225; John H. 103; John J. 114, 179; John L. 122, 187, 188; John L., Jr. 188; John M. 107, 165, 210; John T. 63, 112, 113, 174, 178, 179, 180, 185, 213, 460; John W. 30, 37, 82, 137, 138, 193, 194, 333, 335, 410, 424; Joseph 12, 23; Joseph, M. 13; Joseph C. 188; Josephine 93, 116; Josephine W. 204, 223, 243, 360; Joseph L. 178; Joseph M. 60, 63, 112, 115, 118, 181, 183, 455; Joseph M., Jr. 117; Joseph P. 113, 114, 180, 181, 215, 216; Joseph W. 183; Josey C. 269; Joshua 455, 461; Josiah 30, 43, 51, 52, 84, 87; Josiah, Sr. 18, 42, 43; Josiah N. 11, 88, 150, 151; Josiah S., Jr. 44; Josias W. 58; Judah 458; Judith 32, 44, 57, 105; Judith C. 58; Julia A. 114, 178, 179; Julia W. 145; Katherine 221; Katherine W. 221, 239, 264, 265; Kearney P. 210; Kerenhappuch 460; Langhorn T. 35; Laura G. 254, 277, 278; Laura H. 8; Laurine E. 207; Lavinia 165; Lavinia A. 96, 98, 166; Lela M. 196, 223, 246, 378; Lena 179; Lewis, III 161; Lewis, Jr. 160; Lewis I. 94, 159, 160, 207, 209; Linda L. 234; Littleton 461; Lloyd G. 37, 129, 191, 226, 252, 253, 254, 277, 284, 379, 398, iii; Lockey 36, 61, 62; Lonie 217; Lottie 183; Louisa A. 60, 101; Louisa E. 98, 165; Louisa H. 158; Louisa J. 8, 14; Louisa W. 60; Louise 221; Louise C. 221, 240; Louise E. 96; Louise M. 217; Louise P. 185; Lucille 455; Lucinda 455; Lucius A. 161; Lucrecy 460; Lucretia 461; Lucy 32, 67, 103, 108, 114, 129; Lucy C. 88, 153, 178, 179, 213; Lucy E. 183; Lurane 458; Luther L. 206; Mabel R. 215; Malvina A. 103; Margaret 2; Margaret T. 107; Margaret W. 82, 137; Mariah A. 157; Mariah L. 82; Maria M. 90; Marie E. 187; Marion E. 209; Marion J. 175; Martha 17, 18, 36, 37, 38, 39, 40, 44, 47, 50, 61, 64, 83, 104, 119, 187, 458; Martha A.

Waltons of Old Virginia 491

81, 121, 130, 132, 192, 430; Martha B. 187; Martha J. 145; Martha M. 60, 62, 108; Martha S. 94, 140; Martha V. 158; Martha W. 91, 163; Martin 48; Martina V. 120; Mary 10, 12, 20, 23, 42, 43, 49, 50, 52, 53, 61, 168, 184, 210, 458, 462; Mary A. 14, 116, 163, 181; Mary B. 196, 222, 241, 242; Mary C. 459; Mary E. 88, 111, 122, 153, 165, 200, 215, 226, 379; Mary F. 81, 134, 135; Mary H. 96, 185; Mary J. 152; Mary L. 58; Mary M. 178; Mary P. 161; Mary S. 85, 145; Mary V. 183; Mary W. 94; Mary Z. 209; Matilda 184; Matthew 29, 30, 103; Matthew P. 458; Matthew T. 236; Mattie 184; Maude W. 209, 233, 234; Maurice H. 36; Melissy 459; Meredith 49; Meriwether L. 120, 185; Mildred 221; Mildred A. 70, 122; Mildred F. 221; Mildred I. 216; Milley 36, 460; Minjum H. 36, 62, 63, 110, 111, 112, 114, 115, 175; Minjum H., Jr. 63, 117; Minjum H., Sr. 112, 117; Minnie A. 179; Minta H. 151; Mizapina 20; Molly 24; Moses 6; Murry T. 119, 184; Nancy 33, 38, 44, 52, 72, 463; Nancy A. 41, 73, 126; Nancy B. 88, 147, 148; Nancy F. 62, 162; Nancy H. 25, 46; Nancy L. 48, 234; Nancy M. 50, 58, 105, 106, 171; Nancy T. 185; Nannie 195; Nannie E. 197, 225, 252, 378; Narcissus 62; Nathan, Jr. 144; Nathaniel 6, 90, 155, 157, 204, 205; Nathaniel W. 157; Nathan W. 11, 85, 87, 144, 145; Nelson 49; Newell 20; Octavia C. 105, 169, 170, 211; Ola 228; Olivia 151, 174; Olley 458; Ophelia H. 151; Orah 179; Oscar O. 206; Patsy 462; Patty 25, 35; Pauline 32; Pearl E. 188; Peggy 36; Phebe 111; Philip L. 97; Phoebe 41, 66, 69, 74, 76, 77; Phoebe A. 45, 90, 91, 125; Phoebe C. 61, 108, 109; Pickett 455; Pleasant 50; Pleasant W. 102; Pocahontas 205; Polly 47, 99, 167; Polly L. 88; Raymond H. 177; Rebecca 12, 30, 462; Rebecca A. 119; Rebecca E. 230; Rebecca 3; Richard A. 163; Richard L. 165, 280; Richard P. 96, 98, 164, 210; Richard

T. 137, 138; Richard W. 71; Richmond 459; Richmond T. 460; Robert 1, 2, 3, 10, 16, 19, 20, 24, 32, 36, 38, 40, 46, 47, 52, 55, 64, 66, 67, 68, 69, 70, 95, 99, 116, 118, 121, 123, 124, 184, 455, 457; Robert, III 22, 53; Robert, IV 53; Robert, Jr. 11, 21, 26, 28, 53, 54; Robert, Sr. 11, 21, 23; Robert A. 97, 161, 165, 215; Robert B. 68, 71; Robert III 24; Robert J. 67, 118, 119, 122; Robert L. 163; Robert M. 137; Robert N. 101; Robert P. 187; Robert W. 70, 105; Roger F. 243, 268; Romulus F. 183; Rosa B. 175; Roy K. 206; Ruby 175, 178, 187; Ruby T. 229; Russel S. 243, 268, 360; Ruth E. 206; Salley 460; Sallie F. 112, 174; Sally 22, 24, 53, 54, 460; Sally C. 206; Samuel L. 116, 455; Samuel M. 8; Samuel W. 455; Sam W. 8; Sarah 25, 45, 85, 87, 113, 122, 181, 457, 458; Sarah D. 86, 151; Sarah E. 111, 116, 117, 137, 149, 181, 182; Sarah G. 90; Sarah H. 88, 152, 181; Sarah R. 163; Scottie L. 137; Shelton 205, 229; Sherwood 12, 21, 25, 26, 28, 29, 30, 56; Shirley 5, 175, iii; Shirley C. 241; Shirley M. 223, 244, 260, 269, 353; Simeon 20, 49, 51, 102, 387; Simeon, Jr. 51; Singleton A. 185; Stuart B. 213; Susan A. 111; Susan C. 131; Susan E. 205; Susan G. 89, 154, 201; Susanna 29, 30, 52, 103; Susannah 14, 25, 46; Susan W. 162; Tabitha 52, 103; Temperance 25, 49; Thesius 18; Thomas 4, 6, 11, 13, 16, 17, 26, 32, 36, 37, 39, 40, 41, 42, 60, 67, 68, 69, 106, 195, 226, 366, 462; Thomas, C. 55; Thomas, Jr. 5, 17, 18, 37, 38, 39, 40, 41, 64, 65, 68, 71, 73, 76, 78, 82, 83, 103, 194; Thomas, Sr. 5, 10, 15, 16, 17, 18, 34, 35, 37, 41, 42, 44, 46; Thomas A. 186, 217, 236; Thomas B. 157; Thomas C. 66, 67, 119, 120, 185; Thomas D. 94; Thomas E. 121, 186, 217, 218; Thomas G. 8, 18, 36, 61, 106, 107, 108; Thomas H. 47, 95, 96, 97, 98, 100, 116, 120, 161, 162, 163, 164, 166, 183, 185; Thomas H., Jr. 185; Thomas L. 102; Thomas M. 45, 58, 88, 89, 90, 117, 151, 152, 155; Thomas M., Jr. 90; Thomas P. 165; Thomas W. 101, 162; Thompson 457; Tilman 31, 32, 44, 57, 105; Tisdale 58; Todd W. 241; Tommy 184; Torbert C. 455; Tracy L. 236; Una G. 215; Victoria V. 159; Virginia 175; Virginia A. 188; Virginia C. 82, 137; Virginia E. 175; Walker S. 80, 196, 222, 242, 244, 354, 360, 409; Watkins 103; William 4, 6, 10, 11, 12, 13, 14, 16, 20, 23, 36, 37, 38, 39, 40, 41, 42, 44, 47, 49, 50, 53, 66, 67, 69, 71, 78, 79, 80, 81, 82, 83, 86, 92, 101, 102, 103, 118, 119, 127, 130, 134, 136, 138, 149, 195, 217, 425, 430, 462; William, III 32, 57, 59, 60; William, Jr. 14, 31, 32, 57, 59, 60; William, Sr. 12, 31, 33; William A. 120, 122, 185, 236; William A., Jr. 237; William A., Sr. 218; William B. 163; William D. 147; William F. 206; William H. 88, 114, 149, 151; William J. 80; William J., III 241; William J., Jr. 221, 240, 241; William J., Sr. 195, 220, 221, 239, 240; William M. 61, 63, 111, 112, 174, 175, 176, 177; William O. 58; William P. 8, 116, 210; William R. 124; William S. 43, 84, 85, 144, 145, 147; William T. 81, 188; William W. 215; Willis R. 149; Wilma J. 455; Winfrey A. 178; Winnie D. 175; Winnie E. 188; Winston D. 80, 223, 242, 243, 267, 268, 360, 396, 409, 412; W. Lindsey 23; Wyllie A. 179; Yolanda J. 243, 267, 360;
Ward: Agatha 28;
Ware 345: Judith 17;
Wartman: Rebecca H. 397;
Washington: George 4, 169; John 3;
Waters: Edward J. 229;
Watkins: Ann E. 96; Frances 29; Isham 20; Joseph 57; Mary W. 96; Mollie 97; Nannie 97; Robert 53; Robert R. 96; Thomas 53; Thomas, Jr. 22;
Watson: Alexander P. 408; Franky 459; John 461;
Watts: Annie 426; Bessie C. 250, 275, 276; Brian M. 275; Brittany 275; Cordelia 83, 141, 329, 331, 332, 333, 424; Courtney B. 275; Edmond 425;

Edmund 426; Edmund S. 425;
Elizabeth 271; Evelyn F. 250;
Henry H. 331, 332; Hugh A. 250;
Jarrett 275; Jonathan 275; Mary L.
251; Sarah 333, 425, 426; Stephen
329, 331, 332; Sylvia D. 275;
William L., III 250, 275; William L.,
Jr. 224, 249, 275; W. L. 249;
Way: Ferdinand G. 397; Lawrence F.
397;
Weatherford: Drusilla 362;
Webb 66, 285: Elizabeth 66; Sally 463;
Webber: Elizabeth 145;
Webster: Alfred 145; Daniel 169;
William 298;
Weiland: Nancy J. 186;
Weldon: Edith 303;
Wells: Amos L. 318;
Wenzel: Anna 451;
Wesley: John 462;
West: Lucy A. 224, 247; Thomas J. 247;
Westbrook: William N. 152;
Westerfield: Eugene 316;
Wheat: Annie C. 167; David G. 167;
James E. 167; Lavinia A. 95;
Patrick H. 98, 166; Patrick H., Jr.
167; Pauline 215; Richard H. 167;
Robert S. 167; Thomas I. 166;
Wheelhouse: Jemima 146;
White: Andrew 78, 81, 136; Catharine T.
125; Daniel E. 280; Elizabeth 78,
79; Jacob E. 280; James 368, 436;
John 436; Kevin D. 272; Mary E.
81, 136, 137; Sarah H. 368; Susanna
436, 437; Susannah 388; Virginia E.
222, 241;
Whitehead: Irving P. 193; Thomas 193;
Whitney: Jeremiah 326, 327; Susannah
326, 327;
Whitworth: Jane 432;
Wilborne: Elizabeth 386;
Wilbourne: William 386;
Wilburn: Mary E. 177;
Wild: Corleen 236;
Wiley: Carolina V. 153, 200, 201;
Elizabeth C. 155, 201, 202; Yancey
200, 201, 202;
Wilhoit: Martitia 363;
Wiliamson: Cuthbert, Sr. 435, 436;
Wilkerson: Mary L. 179, 213; Presley H.
179, 213; Valerie 261, 262;
Wilkinson: John 90;

Willborne 47:
Willett 146:
Williams: Ann 324; Catherine 104;
Charity 343; Charles 324; Elizabeth
343; Elnora B. 354; Frances H. 29;
George 104; Joseph T. 178; Lucretia
324; Maria L. 56; Philip P. 253;
Samuel L. 56; Sarah M. 396;
Shirley 284, 379; Shirley E. 226, 253,
254, 277; Susan 450; Thomas A.
397; William 371, 374;
Williamson 288: Catherine 437; Charles
437; Cuthbert, III 438; Cuthbert, Jr.
388, 435, 436, 437; Daniel W. 438;
Elizabeth 437; Frances W. 438;
John 435, 437; Martha 437; Mary
A. 388, 395, 396, 437; Matthew 438;
Nancy 438; Rebecca 437; Sally
436; Samuel 438; Susannah 435;
Susanna P. 437; Thomas 150;
William B. 438;
Wills: Annie B. 224, 249, 272, 273, 274;
Betty 34; Donald 247; Euclid 33;
Mina A. 33; Percy M. 249;
Wilmer: Edward T. 255; Jessica F. 255;
Kaitlan N. 255; Winfred 255;
Wilsher: George W. 199; Nannie G.
199;
Wilson: Catherine 68; Elizabeth 40, 64,
68, 69, 70, 118, 119, 184, 208; James
P. 182; John P. 68; Margaret 208;
Martha A. 72; Mary 388; Reuben
W. 68, 71; Robert 68; Samuel 89;
Walter S., Jr. 208; Walter S., Sr. 208;
William 327, 450;
Winfrey: John 21;
Winn: James 120; Mary E. 120;
Sharlee 36, 61;
Winston: Anthony 401; Mary A. 328,
429;
Winter: Virginia 192;
Winters: Elzora 203;
Wise 133:
Wiseman: Ann E. 319;
Withers: Robert W. 134; Sterling 99;
Witt: Peter 89; Peter M. 18, iii;
Womack: Charles 86; Nathan 84; Sally
43, 84, 85, 144, 145, 147; Thomas F.
72;
Wood: Arthur L. 207; Barbara A. 255;
Buford A. 234; Edmund 405;
Elizabeth 405; Henry D. 100; Henry

W. 92; James, Jr. 57; John 458; John F. 403, 406; John T. 92; Karen 51; Kenny 207; Lathana 103; Robert M. 207; Rodney; William F. 396; William P. 159; Willis 459; Woodfin: Judith A. 438; Nancy 44; Woodson: Anna S. 96; Anne F. 300; Anthony W. 80; Booker 442; Carolyn M. 47, 95; Charles 300; Charles L. 98, 164; Drury 121; Drury W. 186; Elizabeth 25, 111; Elizabeth B. 36, 62; James B. 442; John M. 96, 98; John P. 110; Leander 111; Martha 217; Martha E. 121, 186, 218; Mary 187, 442; Mary A. 340; Mary F. 83, 143; Mary J. 98, 164, 210; Richard 420; Sarah 111; Tucker 22; Woolfolk: Agnes 20; Martha 334; Woolridge: Kate 57; Wooten: Bernard M., Jr. 350; Bernard M., Sr. 350; Dorothy M. 350; Jacqueline E. 350; James M. 350; Jemima 51; Robert H. 350; Robert L. 350; Robert S. 350; Samuel 52; Sharon L. 350; Wor: John 439; Word 287: Albert C. 451; Albert V. 446; Albert W. 446; Amelia A. 446; Andrew B. 454; Ben 447; Benjamin F., Sr. 446; Benjamin H. 383, 444, 445, 446, 447, 448, 449, 451, 453, 454; Betty B. 450; Caroline 416, 417, 446, 450, 452; Carrie V. 452; Charles 439; David M. 454; Edgar B. 452; Eliza 446; Elizabeth 439, 440, 441, 442, 452; Elizabeth C. 445, 451; Franklin L. 447; Frederick D. 445, 449; George W. 383, 444, 446, 450, 452, 454; Gloria A. 449; Henry C. 454; James 439; James H. 447; James W. 454; Jane 446; Johh, III 440; John 445; John, III 439; John, Jr. 439; John, Sr. 439; John F. 444, 452; John R. 446; John W. 448, 451; Judith 443; June 446; Lavina H. 454; Lockey 383, 451; Lockey A. 444; Lockie 383; Louise 448; Mable 451; Malissa F. 351, 352, 416, 453; Martha L. 454; Mary E. 453; Mary H. 383, 442; Mary W. 451; Melville 446; Melvin C. 446;

Pauline P. 445, 448, 450; Quinn 449; Quinn I. 448; Quinn M. 449; Quinn M., Jr. 451; Quinn M., Sr. 451; Robert 417, 445; Robert A., Jr. 452; Robert A., Sr. 452; Sallie 440, 441, 443; Sallie B. 450; Sarah 439, 449; Susan M. 451; Thomas 287, 384, 439, 440, 441, 444, 445, 447, 450; Thomas A. 452; Thomas F. 446; Thomas H. 416, 417, 445, 446, 450, 451, 452, 453; Vernie 451; Wilber 448; William 439, 451; William C. 383, 451, 454; William H. 302, 414, 444, 447, 448; William R. 448; Willie E. 452;
Worsham: Daniel 290; Frances 10;
Wright: Archibald D. 93; James 104; James A. 309; John 104; Lucinda 136; Pryor 136; Robert 104; Sarah J. 136; Shirley 221, 240, 241;
Wyche: Rebecca 463;
Wynn: Mary 324;

Y

Yancey: Keziah 49; Richard 49; Robert 49; Thomas J. 116;
Yarbrough: Joseph 25;
Yates: Sarah E. 49;
Yeates: Martha 366;
Young: Nancy 32, 60;
Younger: Ida B. 76, 195;

Wilmer L. Kerns
4715 North 38th Place
Arlington, VA 22207-2914